The Pocket
English/French
Dictionary

Published in this edition 1996 by Grandreams Limited,
Jadwin House, 205/211 Kentish Town Road, London NW5

© 1996 Geddes & Grosset Ltd,
David Dale House, New Lanark, Scotland

ISBN 1 85830 426 1

Printed and bound in the UK

Abbreviations/Abréviations

abrev	abbreviation	abréviation
adj	adjective	adjectif
adv	adverb	adverbe
art	article	article
auto	automobile	automobile
aux	auxiliary	auxiliaire
bot	botany	botanique
chem, chim	chemistry	chimie
col	colloquial term	expression familière
com	commerce	commerce
compd	compound	mot composé
comput	computers	informatique
conj	conjunction	conjonction
excl	exclamation	exclamation
f	feminine noun	substantif féminin
fam	colloquial term	expression familière
fig	figurative	figuré
geol	geology	géologie
gr	grammar	grammaire
imp	impersonal	impersonnel
inform	computers	informatique
interj	interjection	interjection
invar	invariable	invariable
irr	irregular	irrégulier
jur	law term	juridique
law	law term	droit
ling	linguistics	linguistique
m	masculine noun	substantif masculin
mar	marine term	vocabulaire marin
mat, math	mathematics	mathématiques
med	medicine	médecine
mil	military term	vocabulaire militaire
mus	music	musique
n	noun	substantif
orn	ornithology	ornithologie

pej	pejorative	péjoratif
pl	plural	pluriel
pn	pronoun	pronom
poet	poetical term	vocabulaire poétique
prep	preposition	préposition
rad	radio	radio
rail	railway	chemin de fer
sl	slang	argot
thea	theatre	théâtre
tec	technology	technologie
TV	television	télévision
vi	intransitive verb	verbe intransitif
vr	reflexive verb	verbe réfléchi
vt	transitive verb	verbe transitif
zool	zoology	zoologie

A

à *prép* (in) to; at; on; by, per; **c'est ~ toi**
it's yours; it's your turn.

abaissement *m* fall, drop.

abaisser *vt* to lower; **s'~ à faire qch**
to stoop to doing sth.

abandon *m* abandonment, desertion.

abandonné *adj* deserted.

abandonner *vt to* abandon, leave.

abasourdir *vt* to stun.

abat-jour *m* lampshade.

abattement *m* despondency; exhaustion.

abattre *vt* to shoot; slaughter.

abattu *adj* despondent; exhausted.

abbaye *f* abbey.

abcès *m* abscess.

abdiquer *vt vi* to abdicate.

abeille *f* bee.

aberrant *adj* aberrant; absurd.

aberration *f* aberration.

abêtissant *adj* mindless.

abîme *m* chasm.

abîmer *vt* spoil, damage; *** s'~** *vr* to get
spoiled *ou* damaged.

abjurer *vt* to abjure.

ablatif *m* ablative.

ablation *f* (*med*) removal.

aboiement *m* bark.

abolir *vt* to abolish.

abolition *f* abolition.

abominable *adj* abominable.

abondance *f* abundance.

abondant *adj* abundant, plentiful.

abonder *vi* to be abundant *ou* plentiful.

abonné *m* -ée *f* subscriber.

abonnement *m* subscription.

abonner *vt* ~ qn to subscribe, take out
a subscription (*à* to); *** s'~** *vr* to subscribe, take out a subscription (*à* to).

abord *m*: **d'~** first (of all).

abordable *adj* affordable.

aborder *vt* to approach.

aboutir *vi* to succeed.

aboutissement *m* outcome; success.

abrasif *adj* abrasive.

abrégé *m* summary; **en ~** briefly.

abréger *vt* to shorten; abridge.

abreuver *vt* to water.

abréviation *f* abbreviation.

abri *m* shelter.

abricot *m* apricot.

abriter *vt* to shelter; *** s'~** *vr* to shelter.

abroger *vt* to repeal.

abrupt *adj* abrupt.

abruti *m* -e *f* idiot; ***** *adj* idiotic.

abrutissant *adj* stunning; mind-numbing.

absence *f* absence.

absent *adj* absent.

absenter (s') *vr* to leave, go out.

abside *f* apse.

absolu *adj* absolute; ~ment *adv* absolutely; ***** *m* absolute.

absorber *vt* to absorb.

absoudre *vt* to absolve.

abstenir (s') *vr* to abstain (from).

abstinence *f* abstinence.

abstraction *f* abstraction.

abstrait *adj* abstract; ***** *m* abstract; abstract art.

absurde *adj* absurd.

absurdité *f* absurdity.

abus *m* abuse.

abuser *vt* ~ **de** to exploit; abuse.

abusif *adj* improper.

académie *f* academy; learned society.

académique *adj* academic.

acajou *m* mahogany.

acariâtre *adj* cantankerous.

accabler *vt* to overwhelm.

accalmie *f* lull, calm.

accéder *vi*: ~ **à** to reach.

accélérateur *m* accelerator.

accélération *f* acceleration.

accélérer *vi* to speed up, accelerate.

accent *m* accent.

accentué *adj* pronounced.

accentuer *vt* to accentuate.

accepter *vt* to accept.

accès *m* access.

accessoire *adj* secondary;* *m* accessory.

accident *m* accident.

accidentel *adj* accidental.

acclamations *fpl* cheers; acclamation.

accolade *f* embrace.

accommoder *vt* to prepare; adapt.

accompagnateur *m* **-trice** *f (mus)* accompanist; guide.

accompagnement *m* accompaniment.

accompagner *vt* to accompany.

accomplir *vt* to achieve, accomplish.

accomplissement *m* accomplishment.

accord *m* agreement; **d'~!** okay!, all right!; **être d'~** to agree.

accordéon *m* accordion.

accorder *vt* to grant; **s'~** *vr* to agree.

accoster *vt* to accost.

accouchement *m (med)* delivery.

accoucher *vi* to give birth.

accoudoir *m* armrest.

accouplement *m* coupling; joining.

accourir *vi* to run up (*à, vers* to).

accoutrement *m (peg)* outfit, dress.

accréditer *vt* to accredit.

accroc *m* tear.

accrocher *vt* to hang up *(à* on).

accroissement *m* increase.

accroître *vt* to increase.

accroupir (s') *vr* to crouch.

accueil *m* welcome, reception.

accueillir *vt* to welcome.

accumulateur *m* battery.

accumuler *vt* to accumulate.

accusatif *m* accusative (case).

accusation *f* accusation.

accusé *m* **-e** *f (jur)* accused, defendant.

accuser *vt* to accuse.

acerbe *adj* harsh; acrid.

acharné *adj* bitter, fierce; unrelenting.

acharnement *m* relentlessness; determination.

achat *m* purchase.

acheminer *vt* to convey.

acheter *vt* to buy.

achèvement *m* completion.

achever *vt* to finish; complete.

acide *adj* acid, sour; * *m* acid.

acier *m* steel.

aciérie *f* steelworks.

acné *f* acne.

acompte *m* deposit; downpayment.

à-côté *m* side issue.

à-coup *m* jolt.

acoustique *adj* acoustic; * *f* acoustics.

acquérir *vt* to buy, purchase.

acquiescer *vi* to agree; acquiesce.

acquis *adj* acquired; * *m* experience.

acquisition *f* acquisition; purchase.

acquittement *m* payment; *(jur)* acquittal.

acquitter *vt* to acquit; pay.

acre *f* acre.

âcre *adj* acrid.

acrylique *m, adj* acrylic.

acte *m* act; deed.

acteur *m*, **actrice** *f* actor.

actif *adj* active; * *m (ling)* active (voice).

action *f* act, action; share.

actionner *vt* to activate; drive.

activer *vt* to speed up; **s'~** *vr* to bustle about.

activité *f* activity; hustle and bustle.

actualité *f*: **l'actualité** current events.

actuel *adj* current, present.

acuité *f* acuteness; shrillness.

adaptateur *m* adaptor.

adapter *vt* to adapt (*à* to); **s'~** *vr* to adapt o.s. (*à* to).

additif *m* additive.

addition *f* addition; bill.

additionnel *adj* additional.

additionner *vt* to add up.

adepte *mf* follower; enthusiast.

adéquat *adj* suitable, appropriate.

adhésif *adj* adhesive.

adjectif *m* adjective.

adjoint *m* **-e** *f* assistant, deputy.

adjudication *f* sale by auction.

adjuger *vt* to auction.

admettre *vt* to admit; accept; assume.

administrateur *m* **-trice** *f* administrator.

administratif *adj* administra-tive.

administration *f* management; administration.

administrer *vt* to run; administer.

admiration *f* admiration.

admirer *vt* to admire.

admissible *adj* allowable.

admission *f* admission.

adolescence *f* adolescence.

adolescent *m* **-e** *f* adolescent.

adopter *vt* to adopt; pass.

adoption *f* adoption; passing.

adorable *adj* adorable.

adorer *vt* to adore, worship.

adoucir *vt* to soften.

adresse *f* address; skill.

adresser *vt* to address; send; **s'~** *vr* **s'~ à** to apply to; to speak to.

adroit *adj* deft, skilful.

aduler *vt* to flatter.

adulte *mf* adult, grown-up; *adj* adult, full-grown.

adultère *m* adultery.

adverbe *m* adverb.

adversaire *mf* adversary, opponent.

adversité *f* adversity.

aération *f* ventilation.

aérer *vt* to air.

aérien *adj, f* **-ne** air, airy; aerial.

aérodrome *m* aerodrome, airfield.

aérodynamique *adj* aerodynamic; * *f* aerodynamics.

aérogare *f* (air) terminal.

aéroglisseur *m* hovercraft.

aéroport *m* airport.

aérospatial *adj* aerospace.

affable *adj* affable.

affaiblir *vt* to weaken; **s'~** *vr* to weaken, grow weaker.

affaiblissement *m* weakening.

affaire *f* matter.

affaissement *m* subsidence.

affaisser *vt* to cause to subside *ou* cave in; **s'~** *vr* to subside; to cave in.

affamer *vt* to starve.

affectation *f* allocation *(à to);* affectation.

affecter *vt* to affect.

affection *f* affection.

affermir *vt* to strengthen; to make firm.

affermissement *m* strengthening.

affichage *m* bill posting.

affiche *f* poster.

afficher *vt* to post *ou* put up.

affiner *vt* to refine.

affirmatif *adj* affirmative.

affirmation *f* assertion.

affirmer *vt* to assert.

affluent *m* tributary.

affluer *vi* to rush *(à* to).

afflux *m* influx, rush.

affolant *adj* alarming.

affolement *m* panic.

affoler *vt* to throw into a panic; **s'~** *vr* to get into a panic.

affranchir *vt* to frank, stamp; free.

affranchissement *m* stamping, franking; freeing.

affréter *vt* to charter.

affreux *adj* horrible; awful.

affrontement *m* confrontation.

affronter *vt* to confront; **s'~** *vr* to confront one another.

afin *prép:* **~ de** (in order) to; **~ que** in order that, so that.

africain *adj, mf* African.

agacer *vt* to annoy, irritate.

âge *m* age; **quel ~ as-tu?** how old are you?

âgé *adj* old; **~ de 10 ans** 10 years old.

agence *f* agency; branch; offices.

agencer *vt* to arrange; equip.

agenda *m* diary.

agenouiller (s') *vr* to kneel (down).

agent *m* agent; policeman.

agglomération *f* town, urban area.

aggravation *f* worsening, aggravation; increase.

aggraver *vt* to make worse; increase; **s'~** *vr* to get worse, worsen; increase.

agile *adj* agile, nimble.

agilité *f* agility.

agir *vi* to act.

agitateur *m* **-trice** *f* agitator.

agitation *f* agitation.

agiter *vt* to shake; wave; **s'~** *vr* to move about; fidget.

agneau *m* lamb.

agrafe *f* staple; hook.

agrafeuse *f* stapler.

agraire *adj* agrarian; land.

agrandir *vt* to make bigger; widen; expand; **s'~** *vr* to get bigger; widen; expand.

agrandissement *m* enlargement.

agréable *adj* agreeable, pleasant.

agresser *vt* to attack.

agresseur *m* attacker.

agressif *adj* aggressive.

agression *f* attack.

agricole *adj* agricultural.

agriculteur *m* farmer.

agriculture *f* agriculture, farming.

agripper *vt* to grab (hold of); **s'~ à** *vr* to grab on to.

agrumes *mpl* citrus fruits.

ahuri *adj* stunned; stupefied.

aide *f* help; aid.

aider *vt* to help.

aigle *m* eagle.

aigre *adj* sour, bitter.

aigreur *f* sourness; acidity.

aigri *adj* bitter, embittered.

aigu *adj, f* **aiguë** shrill; acute; sharp.

aiguille *f* needle.

aiguiller *vt* to direct; shunt.

aiguiser *vt* to sharpen.

ail *m* garlic.

aile *f* wing.

ailleurs *adv* elsewhere; **partout ~** everywhere else; **nulle part ~** nowhere else; **d'~** moreover; by the way.

aimable *adj* kind.

aimant *m* magnet.

aimanter *vt* to magnetise.

aimer *vt* to love.

aîné *m*, **aînée** *f* eldest *ou* oldest child; * *adj* elder, older; eldest, oldest.

ainsi *adv* so, thus.

air *m* air.

aire *f* area.

aise *f* ease, comfort.

aisé *adj* easy; well-off.

aisselle *f* armpit.

ajournement *m* adjournment; postponement.

ajourner *vt* to adjourn; defer, postpone.

ajout *m* addition.

ajouter *vt* to add.

ajuster *vt* to adjust.

alarme *f* alarm.

alarmer *vt* to alarm; **s'~** *vr* to get alarmed *(de* at, about*)*.

albâtre *m* alabaster.

album *m* album.

alcalin *adj* alkaline.

alcool *m* alcohol.

alcoolique *adj* alcoholic; * *mf* drunkard.

alcoolisme *m* alcoholism.

aléatoire *adj* uncertain; risky.

alentours *mpl* surroundings, neighbourhood.

alerte *adj* alert; agile; * *f* alarm, alert.

alerter *vt* to alert; notify; warn.

algèbre *f* algebra.

algue *f* seaweed.

alibi *m* alibi.

aliénation *f* alienation.

aliéner *vt* to alienate.

alignement *m* alignment; aligning.

aligner *vt* to align, line up.

aliment *m* food.

alimenter *vt* to feed; **s'~** *vr* to eat.

alinéa *m* paragraph.

allée *f* avenue; path.

alléger *vt* to make lighter; alleviate.

alléguer *vt* to allege, put forward.

aller *vi* to go; **comment allez-vous?** how are you?; **allons-y** let's go; **s'en aller** to go away, leave.

allergie *f* allergy.

allergique *adj* allergic *(à* to).

alliance *f* alliance; marriage; wedding ring.

allié *m* **-e** *f* ally; * *adj* allied.

allô *excl* hello!

allocation *f* allocation; allowance.

allongé *adj* **être allongé** to be lying (down).

allonger *vt* to lengthen; **s'~** *vr* to lengthen; lie down.

allouer *vt* to allocate.

allumage *m* ignition.

allumer *vt* to light; turn *ou* switch on.

allumette *f* match.

allure *f* speed; look.

alors *adv* then; **~ que** while; whereas.

alouette *f* lark.

alourdir *vt* to make heavy; increase.

alphabet *m* alphabet.

alphabétique *adj* alphabetical.

alpinisme *m* mountaineering.

altération f alteration, change.

altérer vt to change, alter.

alternatif adj alternate.

alternative f alternative.

alterner vt vi to alternate. *(avec with)*.

altitude f altitude, height.

aluminium m aluminium.

amabilité f kindness.

amaigrir vt to make thin(ner).

amaigrissant adj slimming.

amalgamer vt to combine.

amande f almond.

amant m lover.

amarrer vt to moor.

amas m pile, heap.

amasser vt to amass, pile up.

amateur m amateur; connoisseur.

ambassade f embassy.

ambassadeur m **-drice** f ambassador.

ambiance f atmosphere.

ambigu adj, f **ambiguë** ambiguous.

ambiguïté f ambiguity.

ambitieux adj ambitious.

ambition f ambition.

ambre m amber.

ambulance f ambulance.

ambulant adj travelling, mobile.

âme f soul.

amélioration f improvement.

améliorer vt to improve; **s'~** vr to improve.

aménager vt to fit out; adjust; develop.

amende f fine.

amendement m amendment.

amener vt to bring.

amer adj bitter.

Américain m **-e** f American.

américain adj American.

amertume f bitterness.

ameublement m furniture.

ami m **-e** f friend.

amiante m asbestos.

amical adj friendly.

amincir vt to thin (down).

amiral m admiral.

amitié f friendship.

amnésie f amnesia.

amnistie f amnesty.

amoindrir vt to weaken; reduce.

amoindrissement m weakening; reduction.

amoncellement m pile; accumulation.

amorcer vt to bait; begin.

amortir vt to soften; deaden.

amour m love.

amoureux adj in love *(de with)*.

ampère m ampere, amp.

amphibie adj amphibious.

amphithéâtre m amphitheatre.

ample adj roomy; wide.

ampleur f fullness; range.

ampoule f bulb; phial; blister.

amputation f amputation.

amputer vt to amputate.

amuser vt to amuse.

an m year; **avoir vingt ~s** to be 20 (years old).

anabolisant m anabolic steroid.

anachronisme m anachronism.

analgésique adj analgesic.

analogie f analogy.

analogique adj analogical.

analogue adj analogous *(à to)*.

analyse f analysis; test.

analyser vt to analyse.

analyste mf analyst; psychoanalyst.

analytique adj analytical.

ananas m pineapple.

anarchie *f* anarchy.

anarchiste *mf* anarchist.

anatomie *f* anatomy.

ancestral *adj* ancestral.

ancêtre *m* ancestor.

anchois *m* anchovy.

ancien *adj* old; former.

ancienneté *f* (years of) service; seniority; age.

ancre *f* anchor.

ancrer *vt* to anchor.

âne *m* ass, donkey.

anéantir *vt* to annihilate.

anéantissement *m* annihilation.

anémie *f* anemia.

anesthésie *f* anaesthetic; anaesthesia.

anesthésique *m* anaesthetic.

ange *m* angel.

angélique *adj* angelic.

angine *f* tonsillitis.

Anglais *m* -e *f* Englishman; Englishwoman.

anglais *adj* English; * *m (ling)* English.

angle *m* angle; corner.

angoisse *f* anguish.

angoisser *vt* to cause anguish.

animal *m* animal.

animateur *m* -trice *f* host, compère; leader.

animation *f* animation; hustle and bustle.

animé *adj* busy; lively.

animer *vt* to lead; host; liven up; **s'~** *vr* to liven up.

animosité *f* animosity.

anneau *m* ring.

année *f* year.

annexe *f* annexe; * *adj* subsidiary.

annihiler *vt* to annihilate.

anniversaire *m* birthday; **joy-eux ~!** happy birthday!

annonce *f* advertisement; announcement.

annoncer *vt* to announce *(à to)*.

annoter *vt* to annotate.

annuaire *m* telephone directory, phone book.

annuel *adj* annual **annuler** *vt* to cancel; nullify.

anodin *adj* insignificant.

anomalie *f* anomaly.

anonyme *adj* anonymous; impersonal.

anorexie *f* anorexia.

anorexique *adj, mf* anorexic.

anormal *adj* abnormal.

anse *f* handle.

antagonisme *m* antagonism.

antagoniste *adj* antagonistic.

antenne *f (rad, TV)* aerial; (zool) feeler.

antérieur *adj* earlier, previous.

anthologie *f* anthology.

anthropologie *f* anthropology.

antiaérien *adj* antiaircraft.

anticipation *f* anticipation.

anticonceptionnel *adj* contraceptive.

anticonformiste *adj, mf* nonconformist.

anticorps *m* antibody.

anticyclone *m* anticyclone.

antidépresseur *adj, m* antidepressant.

antidote *m* antidote.

antigel *m* antifreeze.

antipathie *f* antipathy.

antipathique *adj* unpleasant.

antique *adj* ancient.

antirouille *adj invar* rustproof.

antisémite *mf* anti-semite; *adj* anti-semitic.

antiseptique *adj* antiseptic.

antisocial *adj* antisocial.

antitétanique *adj* (anti-)tetanus.

antivol *m invar* anti-theft*ou* security device; lock; * *adj invar* anti-theft.

antre *m* den.

anus *m* anus.

anxiété *f* anxiety.

anxieux *adj* anxious.

août *m* August.

apaisant *adj* soothing.

apaisement *m* calm(ing down); relief.

apaiser *vt* to calm (down); relieve.

apathie *f* apathy.

apathique *adj* apathetic.

apercevoir *vt* to see; catch a glimpse of.

aperçu *m* (overall *ou* general) idea.

apéritif *m* aperitif.

apeuré *adj* frightened.

aphrodisiaque *adj*, *m* aphrodisiac.

apiculteur *m* beekeeper.

apitoyer *vt* to move to pity; **s'~** *vr* to feel pity (*sur* for*)*.

aplanir *vt* to level (out); smooth away.

aplatir *vt* to flatten (out).

apolitique *adj* apolitical; non-political.

apologie *f* apology.

apostrophe *f* apostrophe.

apôtre *m* apostle.

apparaître *vi* to appear.

appareil *m* device; appliance; (tele)phone;**~-photo** camera.

appareiller *vi* (*mar*) to cast off.

apparemment *adv* apparently.

apparence *f* appearance.

apparent *adj* apparent.

apparition *f* appearance; apparition.

appartement *m* flat, appart-ment.

appartenance *f* membership.

appât *m* bait.

appâter *vt* to lure; bait.

appauvrir *vt* to impoverish; **s'~** *vr* to grow poorer.

appauvrissement *m* impoverishment.

appel *m* call; appeal.

appeler *vt* to call; call out; **s'~** *vr* **je m'appelle Léon** my name is Leon.

appellation *f* appelation; name.

appendicite *f* appendicitis.

appesantir *vt* to weigh down; strengthen; **s'~** *vr* to grow heavier; grow stronger.

appétissant *adj* appetizing.

appétit *m* appetite (*de* for*)*.

applaudir *vt vi* to applaud.

applaudissements *mpl* applause.

applicable *adj* applicable (*à* to*)*.

application *f* application; use.

appliquer *vt* to apply (*à* to*)*.

apport *m* supply.

apporter *vt* to bring.

apposer *vt* to append; affix.

appréciable *adj* appreciable.

appréciatif *adj* evaluative; appreciative.

appréciation *f* estimation, assessment

apprécier *vt* to appreciate; to assess

appréhender *vt* to apprehend; dread.

appréhension *f* apprehension.

apprendre *vt* to learn.

apprenti *m* -**e** *f* apprentice.

apprêter *vt* to dress; to size; **s'~** *vr* to get ready.

apprivoiser *vt* to tame.

approbateur *adj*, *f* -**trice** approving.

approbation *f* approval.

approche *f* approach.

approcher *vt* to move near; approach; **s'~** *vr* to approach.

approfondir *vt* to deepen.

approprier (s') *vr* to appropriate.

approuver *vt* to approve of.

approvisionnement *m* supplying.

approvisionner *vt* to supply; **s'~** *vr* to stock up *(de, en* with*)*.

approximatif *adj* approximate.

approximation *f* approximation.

appui *m* support.

appuie-tête *m invar* headrest.

appuyer *vt* to press; lean; support *vi* to press; *vr* **s'~** to lean against.

âpre *adj* bitter, harsh.

après *prép* after; **d'~ elle** according to her;* *adv* after(wards); **tout de suite ~** immediately after *ou* afterwards.

après-demain *adv* the day after tomorrow.

après-midi *m/f invar* afternoon.

âpreté *f* bitterness.

apte *adj* capable *(à* of*)*.

aptitude *f* aptitude; ability.

aquarium *m* aquarium.

aquatique *adj* aquatic.

arachide *f* peanut, groundnut.

araignée *f* spider.

arbitrage *m* arbitration.

arbitraire *adj* arbitrary.

arborer *vt* to wear; bear.

arbre *m* tree.

arbrisseau *m* shrub.

arbuste *m* bush.

arc *m* bow; arc; arch.

arcade *f* arcade.

arc-bouter (s') *vr* to lean.

arc-en-ciel *m, pl* **arcs-en-ciel** rainbow.

archaïque *adj* archaic.

arche *f* arch.

archéologie *f* archaeology.

archéologue *mf* archaeologist.

archevêque *m* archbishop.

architecte *mf* architect.

architectural *adj* architectural.

architecture *f* architecture.

archives *fpl* archives, records.

ardent *adj* ardent, burning.

ardeur *f* ardour.

ardoise *f* slate.

ardu *adj* difficult.

arène *f* arena.

arête *f* (fish)bone.

argent *m* silver; money.

argenté *adj* silver; silver-plated.

argenterie *f* silverware.

argile *f* clay.

argot *m* slang.

argumenter *vi* to argue *(sur* about*)*.

aride *adj* arid.

aridité *f* aridity.

aristocrate *mf* aristocrat.

aristocratie *f* aristocracy.

aristocratique *adj* aristocratic.

arithmétique *f* arithmetic.

armature *f* (frame)work.

arme *f* arm, weapon.

armée *f* army.

armement *m* 'arms, weapons; armaments.

armer *vt* to arm; **s'~** *vr* to arm o.s.

armistice *m* armistice.

armoire *f* cupboard; wardrobe.

armure *f* armour.

aromatique *adj* aromatic.

aromatiser *vt* to flavour.

arôme *m* aroma; flavour.

arpenteur *m* (land) surveyor.

arqué *adj* curved, arched.

arrachement *m* wrench; pulling *ou* tearing off.

arracher *vt* to pull (out); tear off.

arrangeant *adj* obliging.

arranger *vt* to arrange; fix; **s'~** *vr* to come to an arrangement; manage; get better.

arrestation *f* arrest.

arrêt *m* stopping; stop (button).

arrêté *m* order.

arrêter *vt* to stop; **s'~** *vr* to stop.

arrhes *fpl* deposit.

arrière *m invar* back; **en ~** back(wards);* *adj invar* back, rear.

arriéré *adj* backward.

arrière-goût *m* aftertaste.

arrière-pensée *f* ulterior motive.

arrière-plan *m* background.

arrimer *vt* to stow.

arrivage *m* delivery.

arrivant *m* **-e** *f* newcomer.

arrivée *f* arrival, coming.

arriver *vi* to arrive, come.

arriviste *mf* careerist; social climber.

arrogance *f* arrogance.

arrogant *adj* arrogant.

arrondi *adj* round(ed).

arrondir *vt* to make round; round off.

arrondissement *m* district.

arrosage *m* watering.

arroser *vt* to water.

arsenal *m* arsenal.

arsenic *m* arsenic.

art *m* art.

artère *f* artery; road.

artichaut *m* artichoke.

article *m* article.

artifice *m* trick.

artificiel *adj* artificial.

artillerie *f* artillery.

artisan *m* artisan, craftsman.

artisanat *m* craft industry.

artiste *mf* artist.

artistique *adj* artistic.

as *m* ace.

ascendance *f* ancestry.

ascendant *adj* upward, rising; * *m* (strong) influence, ascendancy *(sur over)*.

ascenseur *m* lift.

ascension *f* ascent.

aseptiser *vt* to sterilise; disinfect.

asexué *adj* asexual.

asiatique *adj* Asian.

asile *m* refuge; asylum.

aspect *m* appearance, look.

asperge *f* asparagus.

asperger *vt* to splash *(de with)*.

aspérité *f* bump.

asphalte *m* asphalt.

aspirateur *m* vacuum cleaner.

aspirine *f* aspirin.

assagir *vt* to quieten (down); **s'~** *vr* to quieten (down).

assaillant *m* assailant.

assainir *vt* to clean up; purify.

assainissement *m* cleaning up.

assaisonnement *m* seasoning.

assaisonner *vt* to season.

assassin *m* murderer; assassin.

assassinat *m* murder; assassination.

assassiner *vt* to assassinate.

assaut *m* assault, attack *(de on)*.

assécher *vt* to drain; **s'~** *vr* to dry (up *ou* out).

assemblée *f* meeting.

assembler *vt* to assemble; **s'~** *vr* to assemble.

assentiment *m* assent.

asseoir (s') *vr* to sit down.

assermenté *adj* on oath.

assertion *f* assertion.

asservissement *m* enslavement; slavery.

assez *adv* enough; quite, rather; **avoir ~ d'argent** to have enough money; **~ bien** quite well; **j'en ai ~!** I've had enough!; I'm fed up.

assidu *adj* assiduous; regular.

assiduité *f* assiduity; regularity.

assiéger *vt* to besiege.

assiette *f* plate.

assigner *vt* to assign.

assis *adj* seated, sitting (down).

assistance *f* audience; assistance.

assistant *m* **-e** *f* assistant.

assister *vt* to attend; assist.

association *f* association.

associé *m* **-e** *f* associate, partner.

associer *vt* to associate (*à* with); **s'~** *vr* to join together.

assombrir *vt* to darken; **s'~** to darken.

assommer *vt* to stun.

assortiment *m* assortment.

assortir *vt* to match; **s'~** *vr* to go well together.

assoupir (s') *vr* to doze off.

assoupissement *m* doze.

assouplir *vt* to make supple; relax.

assourdir *vt* to deafen; muffle.

assouvir *vt* to satisfy.

assujettir *vt* to subjugate.

assumer *vt* to assume.

assurance *f* (self-)assurance; assurance; insurance (policy).

assurer *vt* to assure; **s'~** *vr* to insure o.s.

astérisque *m* asterisk.

asthmatique *adj*, *mf* asthmatic.

asthme *m* asthma.

asticot *m* maggot.

astiquer *vt* to polish.

astre *m* star.

astreindre *vt* to force, compel; **s'~** *vr* **s'~ à faire** to force *ou* compel o.s. to do.

astrologie *f* astrology.

astrologique *adj* astrological.

astrologue *m* astrologer.

astronaute *m* astronaut.

astronome *m* astronomer.

astronomie *f* astronomy.

astronomique *adj* astronomical.

astucieux *adj* astute.

atelier *m* workshop; studio.

atermoyer *vi* to procrastinate.

athée *mf* atheist; *adj* atheistic.

athlète *mf* athlete.

athlétique *adj* athletic.

athlétisme *m* athletics.

atlas *m* atlas.

atmosphère *f* atmosphere.

atmosphérique *adj* atmospheric.

atome *m* atom.

atomique *adj* atomic.

atomiseur *m* spray; atomiser.

atout *m* trump; advantage, asset.

âtre *m* hearth.

atroce *adj* atrocious; dreadful.

atrocité *f* atrocity.

attachant *adj* endearing.

attache *f* fastener.

attaché *m* **-e** *f* attaché; assistant.

attachement *m* attachment (*à* to).

attacher *vt* to tie together; tie up; fasten; attach (*à* to).

attaque *f* attack.

attaquer *vt* to attack; tackle.

attarder (s') *vr* to linger.

atteinte *f* attack (*à* on); **hors d'~** beyond *ou* out of reach.

attendre *vt* to wait; **en attendant** meanwhile, in the meantime; **s'~** *vr* : **s'~ à qch** to expect sth.

attendrir *vt* to fill with pity; move; tenderise; **s'~** *vr* to be moved (*sur* by).

attendrissant *adj* touching, moving.

attendrissement *m* emotion.

attendu *adj* expected; long-awaited.

attentat *m* attack (*contre* on); murder attempt.

attente *f* wait; expectation.

attentif *adj* attentive; careful.

attention *f* attention; care.

attentionné *adj* considerate, thoughtful (*pour* towards).

atténuation *f* alleviation; easing.

atterrir *vi* to land, touch down.

atterrissage *m* landing, touch down.

attirail *m* gear.

attirant *adj* attractive.

attirer *vt* to attract.

attitude *f* attitude; bearing.

attraction *f* attraction.

attrait *m* attraction, appeal.

attraper *vt* to catch.

attrayant *adj* attractive.

attribuer *vt* to attribute; award.

attribut *m* attribute.

attrister *vt* to sadden.

attroupement *m* crowd, gathering.

au = à le.

aube *f* dawn, daybreak.

auberge *f* inn; **~ de jeunesse** youth hostel.

aucun *adj* no; not any; any; **~ement** *adv* in no way; not in the least; * *pn* none; not any; any (one).

audace *f* audacity; daring.

audacieux *adj* audacious, bold; daring.

audience *f* audience; hearing.

audiovisuel *adj* audio-visual.

auditeur *m* -**trice** *f* listener; auditor.

auditoire *m* audience.

augmentation *f* increase, rise (*de* in); increasing, raising (*de* of).

augmenter *vt* to increase, raise.

aujourd'hui *adv* today.

auparavant *adv* before, previously; before, first.

auprès *prép* : **~ de** next to; (compared) with.

auquel = à lequel.

auréole *f* halo, aureole; ring (mark).

aurore *f* dawn, first light.

aussi *adv* too, also; so; **nous ~** us too; **une ~ belle journée** such a beautiful day; **il est ~ petit qu'elle** he is as small as she is.

aussitôt *adv* immediately; **~ dit, ~ fait** no sooner said than done; **~ que** as soon as.

austère *adj* austere.

austérité *f* austerity.

autant *adv* as much; as many; so much; such; so many; such a lot of; the same; **~ que je sache** as far as I know.

autel *m* altar.

auteur *m* author.

authenticité *f* authenticity.

authentifier *vt* to authenticate.

authentique *adj* authentic.

autobiographie *f* autobiography.

autocuiseur *m* pressure cooker.

autodéfense *f* self-defence.

automate *m* automaton.

automatique *adj* automatic.

automatiser *vt* to automate.

automne *m* autumn.

automobile *f* (motor) car.

automobiliste *mf* motorist.

autopsie *f* autopsy, post-mortem (examination).

autorisation *f* authorisation, permission; permit.

autoriser *vt* to authorise, give permission for; allow.

autoritaire *adj* authoritarian.

autorité *f* authority.

autoroute *f* motorway.

auto-stop *m* hitch-hiking; **faire de l'~** to hitch-hike.

auto-stoppeur *m* **-euse** *f* hitch-hiker.

autour *prép* **~ de** (a)round; * *adv* (a)round; **il y en a tout ~** there is/are some all around.

autre *adj* other; **~ chose** something else *ou* different; **~ part** somewhere else; **d'~ part** on the other hand; moreover; * *pn* another (one); **j'en veux un ~** I'd like another (one).

autrefois *adv* in the past, in days gone by.

autrement *adv* differently; otherwise.

autruche *f* ostrich.

autrui *pn* others.

aux = **à les**.

auxiliaire *adj* auxiliary; * *m* auxiliary; * *mf* assistant.

avalanche *f* avalanche.

avaler *vt* to swallow.

avance *f* advance; lead; **arriver en ~** to arrive early; **payer d'~** to pay in advance; **réserver à l'~** to book in advance; **avoir de l'~ sur** to have the lead over.

avancement *m* promotion; progress; forward movement.

avancer *vt* to move forward; bring forward; put forward; **s'~** *vr* to advance, move forward; * *vi* to move forward, advance; make progress; project, stick out.

avant *prép* before; **~ peu** shortly; **~ tout** above all; * *adv* before; **en ~** in front, ahead; * *m* front; (*mar*) bow; forward.

avantage *m* advantage.

avantager *vt* to favour; flatter.

avantageux *adj* profitable, worthwhile; attractive; flattering.

avant-bras *m invar* forearm.

avant-dernier *m* **-ière** *f*, *adj* next to last, second last, last but one.

avant-garde *f* avant-garde; vanguard.

avant-hier *adv* the day before yesterday.

avant-première *f* preview.

avare *mf* miser; *adj* miserly.

avarice *f* avarice, miserliness.

avec *prép* with; to.

avenir *m* future.

aventure *f* adventure; venture; experience; affair.

aventurer (s') *vr* to venture.

avenue *f* avenue.

avérer (s') *vr* to turn out, prove to be.

averse *f* shower (of rain).

avertir *vt* to warn; inform (*de* of).

avertissement *m* warning.

aveu *m* admission, confession.

aveugle *adj* blind; * *mf* blind person.

aveuglement *m* blindness.

aviateur *m* **-trice** *f* pilot, aviator.

aviation *f* flying; aviation.

avide *adj* greedy; eager.

avidité *f* greed; eagerness.

avilissant *adj* degrading.

avion *m* (air)plane, aircraft.

avis *m* opinion.

avisé *adj* wise, sensible.

aviser *vt* to advise, inform; notice; **s'~** *vr* **s'aviser de** to realise suddenly.

avocat *m* **-e** *f* lawyer, advocate; * *m* avocado (pear).

avoine *f* oats.

avoir *vt* to have; **il y a** there is/are; **il y a deux mois** two months ago; **qu'as-tu?** what's wrong (with you)?; **il n'avait qu'à le dire** he only had to say (the word).

avortement *m* abortion.

avorter *vi* to abort; fail.

avoué *m* solicitor.

avouer *vt* to admit (to); confess (to).

avril *m* April.

axe *m* axis; axle; main road.

B

babines *fpl* chops.

babiole *f* trinket, trifle.

bâbord *m (mar)* port.

babouin *m* baboon.

bac *m* ferry.

bâche *f* tarpaulin, cover.

bafouer *vt* to scorn.

bafouiller *vi* to stammer; babble.

bagage *m* luggage.

bagarre *f* fight, brawl.

bagarrer (se) *vr* to fight; riot.

bagatelle *f* trinket; trifling sum.

bague *f* ring.

baguette *f* stick; loaf of French bread.

baie *f (geog)* bay.

baigner *vt vi* to bathe; * **se ~** *vr* to have a bath, swim.

bâiller *vi* to yawn.

bâillon *m* gag.

bâillonner *vt* to gag.

bain *m* bath; bathe; swim.

baiser *m* kiss; * *vt* to kiss.

baisse *f* fall, drop.

baisser *vi* to fall, drop; * *vt* to lower.

bal *m* dance.

balade *f (fam)* walk; drive.

balader (se) *vr (fam)* to go for a walk; to go for a drive.

balai *m* broom, brush.

balance *f* scales; balance.

balancer *vt* to swing; to balance.

balançoire *f* swing; seesaw.

balayer *vt* to sweep, brush.

balbutier *vt* to stammer, babble.

balcon *m* balcony.

baleine *f* whale.

balistique *f* ballistics.

ballast *m* ballast.

balle *f* bullet; ball.

ballon *m* ball; balloon.

balourd *adj* stupid; clumsy.

bambou *m* bamboo.

banal *adj* banal, trite.

banalité *f* banality, triteness.

banane *f* banana.
bancaire *adj* banking, bank.
bancal, *pl* **bancals** *adj* lame.
bandage *m* bandage.
bande *f* band; tape.
bandeau *m* headband; blindfold.
bander *vt* to bandage; stretch.
bandit *m* bandit.
banlieue *f* suburbs.
bannière *f* banner.
bannir *vt* to banish; prohibit.
banque *f* bank; banking.
banquette *f* seat, stool.
banquier *m* banker.
baptême *m* baptism.
baptiser *vt* to baptise.
bar *m* bar; (*zool*) bass.
barbare *adj* barbarian; barbaric.
barbe *f* beard.
barbelé *adj* barbed.
barboter *vi* to dabble; splash.
barbouiller *vt* to smear; scrawl.
barème *m* list, schedule.
baril *m* barrel, cask.
bariolé *adj* multicoloured, motley.
baromètre *m* barometer.
baron *m* baron **-ne** *f* baroness.
barque *f* small boat.
barrage *m* barrage, barrier, dam.
barre *f* bar, rod.
barreau *m* rung; bar (cage).
barrer *vt* to bar, block.
barrette *f* (hair) slide, brooch.
barricader *vt* to barricade.
barrière *f* barrier; fence.
baryton *m* baritone.
bas *adj* low, base; * *n* stocking; sock.
bas-côté *m* verge; aisle.
bascule *f* weighing machine, scales.

base *f* base; basis.
baser *vt* to base; **se ~ sur** *vr* to depend on, rely on.
basket *m* basketball.
basse *f* (*mus*) bass.
bassin *m* pond, pool; dock.
bassine *f* bowl.
basson *m* bassoon.
bas-ventre *m* lower abdomen.
bataille *f* battle.
batailler *vi* (*fig*) to fight, battle.
batailleur *adj* combative, aggressive.
bataillon *m* (*mil*) battalion.
bâtard *adj* bastard, illegitimate.
bateau *m* boat, ship.
batelier *m* boatman.
bâtiment *m* building; ship.
bâtir *vt* to build.
bâtisse *f* building, house.
bâton *m* stick, staff.
battant *m* clapper (bell); shutter.
batte *f* bat.
battement *m* banging; beating.
batterie *f* battery.
batteur *m* drummer; batsman.
battre *vt* to beat, defeat.
battu *adj* beaten.
baudet *m* donkey.
baume *m* balm, balsam.
bavard *m* **-e** *f* chatterbox; * *adj* talkative, loquacious.
bavardage *m* chatting, gossiping.
bavarder *vi* to chat, gossip.
bave *f* dribble, slobber.
baver *vi* to dribble, drool.
bavure *f* smudge, blunder.
bazar *m* bazaar; general store.
béant *adj* gaping, wide open.
beau *adj,* *f* **belle** beautiful, lovely.

beaucoup *adv* a lot, a great deal; **~ de monde** a lot of people.

beau-fils *m* son-in-law; stepson.

beau-frère *m* brother-in-law.

beau-père *m* father-in-law; stepfather.

beauté *f* beauty, loveliness.

beaux-arts *mpl* fine arts.

beaux-parents *mpl* in-laws.

bébé m baby.

bec *m* beak, bill.

bée *adj* open-mouthed, flabbergasted.

bégaiement *m* stammering, faltering.

bégayer *vi* to stammer, stutter.

beignet *m* fritter; doughnut.

bêlement *m* bleating.

bêler *vi* to bleat.

Belge *mf* Belgian.

belge *adj* Belgian.

belle-fille *f* daughter-in-law, step-daugher.

belle-mère *f* mother-in-law, stepmother.

belle-sœur *f* sister-in-law.

belligérant *m* **-e** *f* belligerent; * *adj* belligerent.

bémol *m (mus)* flat.

bénéficiaire *mf* beneficiary.

bénéficier *vi* to benefit; enjoy.

bénévole *adj* voluntary; unpaid.

bénin, f bénigne *adj* benign; minor; harmless.

bénir *vt* to bless.

bénit *adj* consecrated, holy.

benne *f* skip; tipper.

béquille *f* crutch; prop.

berceau *m* cradle.

bercement *m* rocking.

bercer *vt* to rock, cradle.

berceuse *f* lullaby; rocking chair.

béret *m* beret.

berge *f* riverbank.

berger *m* shepherd.

bergerie *f* sheepbarn.

berner *vt* to fool, hoax.

besogne *f* work; job.

besoin *m* need; want; **avoir ~ de** to need.

bestial *adj* bestial.

bétail *m* livestock; cattle.

bête *adj* stupid, silly * *f* animal.

bêtifier *vt* to play the fool; prattle stupidly.

bêtise *f* stupidity, foolishness.

béton *m* concrete.

betterave *f* beetroot.

beurre *m* butter.

beurrer *vt* to butter.

bévue *f* blunder.

biais *m* slant angle; bias.

bibelot *m* curio.

biberon *m* baby's bottle.

bible *f* bible.

bibliographie *f* bibliography.

bibliothécaire *mf* librarian.

bibliothèque *f* library; bookcase.

biceps *m* biceps.

biche *f* doe; darling, pet.

bicyclette *f* bicycle.

bidon *m* tin, can; flask.

bien *adv* well; properly; very; **c'est ~ cela** that's right; * *n* property, estate.

bien-être *m* well-being.

bienfaiteur *m* benefactor, **-trice** *f* benefactress.

bienheureux *adj* blessed; lucky; happy.

bientôt *adv* soon.

bienveillant *adj* benevolent, kindly.

bienvenu *adj* welcome.

bienvenue *f* welcome.

bière *f* beer; coffin.

bifteck *m* steak.

bifurcation *f* bifurcation, fork.

bifurquer *vi* to fork, branch off.

bigot *adj* bigoted.

bijou *m* jewel.

bijouterie *f* jewellery.

bilan *m* balance sheet; assessment.

bile *f* bile.

billard *m* billiards.

bille *f* marble; billiard ball.

billet *m* ticket; note.

billetterie *f* cash dispenser.

billion *m* billion.

binaire *adj* binary.

biochimie *f* biochemistry.

biographie *f* biography.

biologie *f* biology.

biologique *adj* biological.

biscornu *adj* crooked, misshapen; odd, outlandish.

biscuit *m* cake; biscuit.

bisexuel *adj* bisexual.

bizarre *adj* bizarre, strange.

bizarrerie *f* strangeness, singularity.

blafard *adj* pale, pallid.

blague *f* joke, trick.

blaguer *vi* to joke.

blagueur *m* -**euse** *f* joker, wag; * *adj* jokey, teasing.

blaireau *m* badger.

blâme *m* blame, rebuke.

blâmer *vt* to blame, rebuke.

blanc *adj*, *f* **blanche** white; * *m* white; blank; * *mf* white person; * *f* (*mus*) minim.

blancheur *f* whiteness.

blanchir *vi* to turn white; to become lighter.

blanchissage *m* laundering; refining.

blanchisserie *f* laundry.

blason *m* blazon, coat of arms.

blasphème *m* blasphemy.

blé *m* wheat.

blême *adj* pale, wan.

blêmir *vi* to turn pale.

blessant *adj* cutting, hurtful.

blesser *vt* to injure, wound.

blessure *f* injury, wound.

bleu *adj* blue; * *m* blue; bruise.

bleuet *m* cornflower.

bleuir *vt vi* to turn blue.

blindage *m* armour plating.

bloc *m* block, group, unit.

blocage *m* blocking, freezing.

blocus *m* blockade.

blond *adj* blond, fair.

blondir *vi* to turn blond, turn golden; * *vt* to bleach.

bloquer *vt* to block, blockade.

blottir (se) *vr* to curl up, snuggle up.

blouse *f* blouse; overall.

blouson *m* windcheater, bomber jacket.

bobine *f* reel, bobbin.

bocal *m* jar; bowl.

bœuf *m* ox, bullock.

bohémien *m* -**ne** *f* Bohemian.

boire *vt* to drink; * *vi* to drink, tipple.

bois *m* wood.

boisson *f* drink.

boîte *f* box.

boiter *vi* to limp.

boiteux *adj* lame.

boîtier *m* case, body.

boitiller *vi* to hobble slightly.

bol *m* bowl.

bolet *m* boletus.

bombarder *vt* to bombard, bomb.

bombe *f* bomb.

bombé *adj* rounded, domed.

bon *adj*, *f* **bonne** good; * *m* slip, coupon.

bonbon m sweet, candy.

bond m leap; bounce.

bonde f stopper, plug.

bondé adj packed.

bondir vi to jump, leap; to bounce.

bonheur m happiness; luck.

bonhomme m, pl **bonshommes** chap, fellow.

bonification f improvement; bonus.

bonifier vt to improve; * **se ~** vr to improve.

bonjour m hello, good morning.

bonnet m bonnet, hat.

bonsoir m good evening.

bonté f goodness, kindness.

bord m side, edge.

bordée f broadside, volley.

border vt to edge, border.

bordereau m note; invoice.

bordure f frame, border.

borgne adj one-eyed.

borne f boundary; milestone.

borné adj narrow-minded.

borner vt to restrict, limit.

bosse f hump, knob.

bosseler vt to dent, emboss.

bossu m -e f hunchback; * adj hunchbacked.

botanique f botany; * adj botanical.

botaniste f botanist.

botte f boot.

bottine f ankle boot, bootee.

bouche f mouth.

bouché adj cloudy, overcast.

bouchée f mouthful.

bouche-à-bouche m kiss of life.

boucher vt to block, clog up; * **se ~** vr to become cloudy; m, **-ère** f (woman) butcher.

bouchon m cork.

boucle f curl; buckle.

boucler vt to buckle; to surround.

bouclier m shield.

bouddhisme m Buddhism.

boudeur adj sullen, sulky.

boue f mud.

bouée f buoy.

boueur m dustman.

bouffée f whiff, puff.

bouffi adj swollen, puffed up.

bougeoir m candlestick.

bouger vi to move; * vt to move, shift.

bougie f candle.

bouillant adj boiling.

bouillir vi to boil.

bouilloire f kettle.

bouillon m broth.

bouillonner vi to bubble, foam.

bouillotte f hot-water bottle.

boulanger m **-ère** f baker.

boule f ball, bowl.

bouleversement m confusion, disruption.

bouleverser vt to confuse, disrupt.

boulon m bolt.

bouquin m (fam) book.

bouquiniste mf second-hand bookseller.

bourbeux adj muddy.

bourbier m quagmire.

bourdonnement m buzz, buzzing.

bourdonner vi to buzz, hum.

bourgeon m bud.

bourgeonner vi to bud.

bourreau m torturer, executioner.

bourrelet m pad, cushion.

bourrer vt to stuff, cram.

bourse f purse; **la Bourse** stock exchange.

boursier *m* **-ière** *f* broker; speculator.

boursouflé *adj* bloated, swollen.

bousculade *f* hustle, scramble.

bousculer *vt* to jostle, hustle.

boussole *f* compass.

bout *m* end; piece, scrap.

bouteille *f* bottle.

boutique *f* shop, store.

bouton *m* button.

boutonner *vt* to button.

boutonnière *f* buttonhole.

bouture *f* cutting.

boxe *f* boxing.

boxeur *m* boxer.

boyau *m* guts, insides.

bracelet *m* bracelet.

braconnier *m* poacher.

brader *vt* to sell at a discount.

braderie *f* discount sale.

braguette *f* fly (trousers).

braise *f* embers.

brancard *m* shaft, stretcher.

branche *f* branch.

branchement *m* branching; connection.

brancher *vt* to connect, link.

branchies *fpl* gills.

brandir *vt* to brandish, flourish.

branlant *adj* loose; shaky.

bras *m* arm.

brasier *m* brazier, furnace.

brasse *f* breaststroke.

brassée *f* armful.

brasser *vt* to brew; to mix.

brasserie *f* bar; brewery.

bravade *f* bravado.

brave *adj* brave, courageous.

braver *vt* to brave, defy.

bravoure *f* bravery, courage.

brebis *f* ewe.

brèche *f* breach, gap.

bredouillant *adj* mumbling.

bredouiller *vi* to mumble.

bref *adj*, *f* **brève** brief, concise; **en ~** *adv* in short.

bretelle *f* strap, sling.

brevet *m* licence, patent.

breveté *adj* patented.

bribe *f* bit, scrap.

bricoleur *m* handyman.

bride *f* bridle.

brider *vt* to restrain, restrict.

brièveté *f* brevity.

brigade *f* brigade.

brigadier *m* corporal, sergeant (police).

brillant *adj* brilliant, shining.

briller *vi* to shine.

brin *m* stalk, strand.

brindille *f* twig.

brique *f* brick, slab.

briquet *m* lighter.

brise *f* breeze.

briser *vt* to smash, shatter.

brocante *f* second-hand dealing.

brocanteur *m* **-euse** *f* second-hand dealer.

broche *f* brooch.

brochure *f* brochure, booklet.

broder *vt* to embroider, *vi* to embellish, elaborate.

broderie *f* embroidery.

bronchite *f* bronchitis.

bronzage *m* tan.

bronze *m* bronze.

bronzer *vi* to get a tan.

brosse *f* brush.

brosser *vt* to brush.

brouette *f* wheelbarrow.

brouillard *m* fog, mist.

brouiller *vt* to blur, confuse.
brouillon *m* rough copy, draft.
broussailleux *adj* bushy, overgrown.
brousse *f* undergrowth, bush.
brouter *vt vi* to graze.
broyer *vt* to grind, pulverise.
broyeur *adj* crushing, grinding.
bruine *f* drizzle.
bruissement *m* rustle.
bruit *m* noise, sound.
bruitage *m* sound-effects.
brûler *vt vi* to burn.
brûlure *f* burn.
brume *f* haze, mist.
brumeux *adj* hazy, misty.
brun *m* dark-haired man, **brune** *f* brunette; * *adj* brown.
brusquer *vt* to offend; hasten.
brut *adj* crude, raw.
brutal *adj* brutal, rough.
brutalité *f* brutality.
brute *f* brute; beast.

bruyant *adj* noisy.
bruyère *f* heather.
bûche *f* log.
budget *m* budget.
buée *f* condensation; steam.
buffet *m* sideboard, buffet.
buisson *m* bush.
bulbe *m* bulb.
bulle *f* bubble; blister.
bulletin *m* bulletin.
buraliste *mf* tobacconist.
bureau *m* office; desk.
bureaucrate *mf* bureaucrat.
bureaucratie *f* bureaucracy.
burin *m* chisel.
bus *m* bus.
buste *m* bust, chest.
but *m* objective, goal.
buté *adj* stubborn.
butin *m* booty, loot.
buvette *f* refreshment-room.

C

ça *pm* that; it; ~ **va?** How goes it?; ~ **y est** that's it; **qui ~?** who (do you mean)?; **comment ~?** how (do you mean)?; ~ **alors!** you don't say!
cabane *f* cabin, shed.
cabanon *m* cottage; chalet.
cabaret *m* cabaret; tavern.
cabine *f* cabin, cab; cockpit.
cabinet *m* surgery; office, study.
câble *m* cable.
câbler *vt* to cable.
cabosser *vt* to dent.

cabotage *m* coastal navigation.
cabriolet *m* convertible.
cacahuète *f* peanut.
cacao *m* cocoa.
cache *m* cache; mask; hiding place.
cacher *vt* to hide, conceal.
cacheter *vt* to seal.
cachette *f* hideout, hiding place.
cachot *m* dungeon, prison cell.
cachottier *m* **-ière** *f* secretive.
cadavre *m* corpse.
cadeau *m* present.

cadenas *m* padlock.

cadet *m* **-te** *f* youngest child.

cadran *m* dial, face.

cadre *m* frame; context; scope.

caduc *adj*, *f* **caduque** null and void; obsolete.

cafard *m* hypocrite; cockroach.

café *m* coffee.

cafétéria *f* cafeteria.

cafetière *f* coffeepot.

cage *f* cage.

cageot *m* crate.

cagoule *f* cowl; balaclava.

cahier *m* notebook.

cahot *m* jerk, jolt.

caillot *m* clot.

caillou *m* stone; pebble.

caisse *f* box; till; fund.

caissier *m* **-ière** *f* cashier.

cajoler *vt* to cajole, coax; to pet.

cajou *m* cashew.

calamité *f* calamity.

calcium *m* calcium.

calcul *m* sum, calculation.

calculateur *adj*, *f* **-trice** calculating.

calculatrice, calculette *f* calculator.

calculer *vt* to calculate, reckon; *vi* to budget carefully.

cale *f* (*mar*) wedge, hold.

caleçon *m* shorts, pants.

calendrier *m* calendar.

caler *vi* to stall; to give up; to wedge.

calibre *m* calibre, bore.

calice *m* chalice.

câlin *m* cuddle; * *adj* cuddly.

câliner *vt* to cuddle.

calmant *m* tranquilliser, sedative; * *adj* tranquillising.

calmar *m* squid.

calme *m* calm, stillness; * *adj* calm, still.

calmer *vt* calm, soothe, pacify.

calorie *f* calorie.

calque *m* tracing; copy.

calquer *vt* to trace; to copy.

calvitie *f* baldness.

camarade *mf* companion, friend.

camaraderie *f* camaraderie, friendship.

cambouis *m* dirty grease.

cambré *adj* arched.

cambriolage *m* burglary.

cambrioler *vt* to burgle.

cambrioleur *m* **-euse** *f* burglar.

caméléon *m* chameleon.

camélia *m* camellia.

caméra *f* camera.

camion *m* lorry.

camionneur *m* lorry driver, trucker.

camomille *f* camomile.

camoufler *vt* to camouflage.

camp *m* camp.

campagnard *m* countryman, **-e** *f* countrywoman; * *adj* country, rustic.

campagne *f* country, countryside.

campement *m* camp, encampment.

camper *vi* to camp.

campeur *m* **-euse** *f* camper.

canal *m* canal, channel.

canaliser *vt* to channel, funnel.

canapé *m* sofa, settee.

canard *m* duck.

cancer *m* cancer.

candeur *f* ingeniousness.

candidat *m* **-e** *f* candidate.

candidature *f* candidature, candidacy.

candide *adj* guileless, ingenuous.

canevas *m* canvas; framework.

canicule *m* heatwave.

canif *m* penknife.

canine *f* eye tooth.

caniveau *m* gutter.

canne *f* cane, rod.

cannelle *f* cinnamon.

canoë *m* canoe.

canon *m* cannon, gun.

canot *m* boat, dinghy.

cantatrice *f* opera singer.

cantine *f* canteen.

cantonner (se) *vr* to take up position in.

caoutchouc *m* rubber.

cap *f* cape; course.

capable *adj* capable, competent.

capacité *f* capacity.

cape *f* cloak.

capitaine *m* captain.

capital *adj* capital, cardinal, major; * *m* capital, stock.

capitale *f* capital (letter, city).

capitaliste *mf* capitalist.

capiteux *adj* heady, strong.

capitonner *vt* to pad.

capituler *vt* to capitulate.

caporal *m* corporal.

capot *m* bonnet, hood.

capoter *vt* to capsize, overturn.

câpre *m* caper.

caprice *m* caprice, whim.

capricieux *adj* capricious.

capsule *f* capsule.

capter *vt* to catch; to pick up.

capteur *m* captor; pick-up.

captif *m* **-ive** *f* captive; * *adj* captive.

captiver *vt* to captivate, en-thrall.

captivité *f* captivity.

capuche *f* hood.

car *conj* for; because; * *m* bus; van.

carabine *f* carbine, rifle.

caractère *m* character, disposition.

caractérisé *adj* marked, blatant.

caractériser *vt* to characterise.

caractéristique *f* characteristic, fea-ture; * *adj* characteristic.

carambolage *m* pile-up (car).

caramel *m* caramel.

caraméliser *vt* to caramelise.

carapace *f* carapace, shell.

carat *m* carat.

caravane *f* caravan.

carbone *m* carbon.

carburant *m* motor-fuel.

carburateur *m* carburettor.

carcasse *f* carcass.

carcéral *adj* prison.

cardiaque *adj* cardiac.

cardinal *m* cardinal; * *adj* cardinal.

carême *m* fast, fasting.

carence *f* deficiency; insolvency.

caressant *adj* affectionate.

caresse *f* caress.

caresser *vt* to caress, fondle.

cargaison *f* cargo, freight.

cargo *m* cargo-boat.

caricature *f* caricature.

carié *adj* decayed.

caritatif *adj* charitable.

carnassier *m* carnivore, **-ière** *f* gamebag; *adj* carnivorous.

carnaval *m* carnival.

carnet *m* notebook.

carnivore *mf* carnivore; *adj* carnivorous.

carotte *f* carrot.

carpe *f* carp.

carpette *f* rug, doormat.

carré *m* square; * *adj* square; straight-forward.

carreau *m* tile; pane.

carrefour *m* crossroads.

carrelage *m* tiling.

carrément *adv* bluntly, directly.

carrière *f* career.

carrosse *m* coach.

carrosserie *f* bodywork.

carrure f build, stature.

cartable *m* satchel.

carte *f* card; map.

cartilagineux *adj* cartila-ginous.

cartomancien *m* **-ne** *f* fortune-teller.

carton *m* cardboard.

cartonner *vt* to bind (book).

cartouche *f* cartridge.

cas *m* case; circumstance.

cascade *f* waterfall; stunt.

cascadeur *m* **-euse** *f* acrobat, stuntman.

case *f* square; box.

caser *vt* (*fam*) to set up (job, marriage).

caserne *f* barracks.

casier *m* compartment; filing cabinet.

casino *m* casino.

casque *m* helmet.

casquette *f* peaked cap.

cassant *adj* brittle.

casse-croûte *m invar* snack.

casser *vt* to break; **se ~** *vr* to break.

casserole *f* saucepan.

casse-tête *m invar* puzzle, conundrum.

cassette *f* cassette; cash-box.

cassis *m* blackcurrant.

cassure *f* break, crack.

castor *m* beaver.

castration *f* castration.

castrer *vt* to castrate.

catalogue *m* catalogue.

cataloguer *vt* to catalogue.

catalyseur *m* catalyst.

catapulte *f* catapult.

catastrophe *f* catastrophe.

catastrophique *adj* catastroph-ic.

catéchisme *m* catechism.

catégorie *f* category.

catégorique *adj* categorical.

cathédrale *f* cathedral.

cathode *f* cathode.

catholicisme *m* Catholicism.

catholique *adj* Catholic.

cauchemar *m* nightmare.

cause *f* cause, reason.

causer *vt* to cause; to chat; ***** *vi* to talk, chat.

caution *f* deposit; guarantee.

cautionner *vt* to guarantee.

cavalerie *f* cavalry.

cavalier *m* **-ière** *f* rider.

cave *f* cellar.

caveau *m* tomb; small cellar.

caverne *f* cave, cavern.

caverneux *adj* cavernous.

cavité *f* cavity.

ce *adj* **cet** (*before vowel and mute h*), *f* **cette**, *pl* **ces** this, these; **cet homme-là** that man; ***** *pn*; **c'est le facteur** it's the postman; **~ sont mes lunettes** these are my glasses; **~ que tu veux** what you want.

ceci *pn* this.

cécité *f* blindness.

céder *vi* to give in; ***** *vt* to give up, transfer.

ceindre *vt* to put round, encircle.

ceinture *f* belt, girdle.

ceinturer *vt* to surround.

cela *pn* that; *emphasis* **qui ~?** who? (do you mean)?; **comment ~?** how? (do you mean?).

célèbre *adj* famous.

célébrer *vt* to celebrate.

célébrité *f* fame, celebrity.

célérité f celerity, speed.

célibat m celibacy.

célibataire mf single person; * adj single, unmarried.

cellulaire adj cellular.

cellule f cell, unit.

cellulite f cellulite.

celui pm, f **celle** this one, pl **ceux** these ones.

cendre f ash.

cendrier m ashtray.

censé adj supposed; deemed.

censure f censorship.

censurer vt to censor.

cent adj a hundred.

centaine f about a hundred, a hundred or so.

centième mf hundredth; * adj hundredth.

centigrade m centigrade.

centimètre m centimetre.

central adj central.

centre m centre.

centrer vt to centre, focus.

centrifuge adj centrifugal.

cependant conj however.

céramique f ceramic.

cerceau m hoop.

cercle m circle, ring.

cercueil m coffin.

cérébral adj cerebral.

cérémonial adj ceremonial.

cérémonie f ceremony.

cérémonieux adj ceremonious.

cerf-volant m kite.

cerise f cherry.

cerne f ring.

cerner vt to circle, encompass.

certain adj certain, sure; ~s pn some, certain people.

certificat m certificate.

certifier vt to certify; to guarantee.

certitude f certainty, certitude.

cerveau m brain.

cervelle f brains.

césarienne f Caesarean.

cesser f to cease, stop.

cessez-le-feu m cease-fire.

cet adj, f **cette** see **ce**.

ceux se e **ce**.

chacun pn each one.

chagrin m sorrow, grief.

chahut m row, uproar.

chahuter vi to make a row.

chaîne f chain.

chaînon m link.

chair f flesh.

chaise f chair.

châle m shawl.

chaleur f heat.

chaleureux adj warm, cordial.

chalumeau m blowlamp.

chambre f room.

chameau m camel.

champ m field.

champêtre adj rural, country.

champignon m mushroom.

champion m **-ne** f champion.

championnat m championship.

chance f luck.

chanceler vi to stagger, totter.

chanceux adj lucky, fortunate.

chandelier m candlestick.

chandelle f candle.

changeant adj changeable, variable.

changement m change, changing.

changer vi to change; * vt to change.

chanson f song.

chant m song; singing.

chantage m blackmail.

chanter *vt vi* to sing.

chanteur *m* **-euse** *f* singer.

chantier *m* building site.

chantonner *vt vi* to hum.

chapeau *m* hat.

chapelet *m* rosary; string.

chapelle *f* chapel.

chapitre *m* chapter.

chaque *adj* each.

char *m (mil)* tank; chariot.

charbon *m* coal.

charcutier *m* **-ière** *f* pork butcher.

charge *f* load; responsibility.

chargé *adj* loaded.

chargement *m* loading; freight.

charger *vt* to load; **se ~ de** to take responsibility for, attend to.

chariot *m* waggon; freight car.

charisme *m* charisma.

charitable *adj* charitable, kind.

charité *f* charity.

charmant *adj* charming, delightful.

charme *m* charm.

charmer *vt* to charm, beguile.

charmeur *m* **-euse** *f* charmer; * *adj* winning, enchanting.

charnel *adj* carnal.

charnière *f* hinge, pivot.

charnu *adj* fleshy.

charpente *f* structure, framework.

charpentier *m* carpenter.

charrette *f* cart.

charrier *vt* to cart, carry.

charrue *f* plough.

chasse *f* hunting; chase.

chasse-neige *m invar* snowplough.

chasser *vt* to hunt, chase.

chasseur *m* **-euse** *f* hunter.

chaste *adj* chaste.

chasteté *f* chastity.

chat *m*, **chatte** *f* cat.

châtaigne *f* chestnut.

châtain *adj* chestnut brown.

château *m* castle.

chaton *m* kitten.

chatouiller *vt* to tickle.

chatoyant *adj* shimmering.

châtrer *vt* to castrate.

chaud *adj* warm, hot.

chaudière *f* boiler.

chaudron *m* cauldron.

chauffage *m* heating.

chauffard *m* road-hog.

chauffer *vi* to heat; * *vt* to heat up.

chauffeur *m* driver.

chaumière *f* cottage.

chaussée *f* road, street.

chaussette *f* sock.

chausson *m* slipper.

chaussure *f* shoe.

chauve *adj* bald.

chauve-souris *f* bat.

chauvin *adj*, *f* **chauvine** chauvinistic.

chaux *f* lime.

chavirer *vi* to capsize, overturn.

chef *m* head, boss; chef.

chef-d'œuvre *m* masterpiece.

chemin *m* way, road; **~ de fer** railway.

cheminée *f* chimney.

chemise *f* shirt.

chêne *m* oak.

chenille *f* caterpillar.

chèque *m* cheque.

chéquier *m* chequebook.

cher *adj*, *f* **chère** dear; expensive.

chercher *vt* to look for.

chercheur *m* **-euse** *f* researcher; seeker.

chéri m **-ie** f darling, dearest; * adj beloved, cherished.

cheval m horse.

chevalet m easel.

chevelure f hair, head of hair.

cheveu m hair.

cheville f ankle.

chèvre f goat.

chèvrefeuille m honeysuckle.

chez prép at home: **je rentre ~ moi** I'm going home; **~ ta tante** at your aunt's.

chic m style, stylishness.

chien m, **chienne** f dog.

chiffon m rag, cloth.

chiffonné adj crumpled, rumpled.

chiffre m figure.

chimie f chemistry.

chimique adj chemical.

chimiste mf chemist.

chimpanzé m chimpanzee.

chiot m puppy.

chipoteur m **-euse** f haggler.

chirurgical adj surgical.

chirurgie f surgery.

chirurgien m surgeon.

chlore m chlorine.

chloroforme m chloroform.

choc m shock, crash.

chocolat m chocolate.

chœur m choir, chorus.

choir vi to fall.

choisir vt to choose.

choix m choice.

chômage m unemployment.

chômeur m **-euse** f unemployed person.

choquant adj shocking, appalling.

choquer vt to shock.

chose f thing, matter, object.

chou m cabbage.

chouette f owl.

chou-fleur m cauliflower.

choyer vt to cherish.

chrétien m **-ne** f Christian, adj christian.

christianisme m Christianity.

chrome m chromium.

chromosome m chromosome.

chronique adj chronic; * f chronicle, column, page.

chronologique adj chronological; **~ment** adv chronologically.

chuchotement m whisper, rustling.

chuchoter vi to whisper.

chuintement m hissing.

chuinter vi to hiss.

chute f fall, drop.

chuter vi to fall.

ci adv: **ces fleurs-ci** these flowers; **ci-joint** enclosed; **ci-dessous** below; **ci-contre** opposite; in the margin; annexed.

cible f target.

cibler vt to target.

cicatrice f scar.

cidre m cider.

ciel m, pl **cieux, ciels** sky.

cierge m candle.

cigale f cicada.

cigare m cigar.

cigarette f cigarette.

cil m eyelash.

ciller vi to blink.

cime f summit.

ciment m cement.

cimetière m cemetery.

cinéma m cinema.

cinglant adj bitter, lashing, cutting.

cingler vt to lash, sting.

cinq m five.

cinquantaine f about fifty.

cinquante *m* fifty.

cinquantenaire *m* fiftieth anniversary.

cinquantième *mf* fiftieth, *adj* fiftieth.

cinquième *mf* fifth, *adj* fifth.

cintre *m* arch.

cirage *m* polish.

circonférence *f* circumference.

circonscription *f* division, constituency.

circonstance *f* circumstance.

circuit *m* circuit, tour.

circulaire *adj* circular.

circulation *f* circulation; traffic.

circuler *vi* to circulate, move.

cire *f* wax.

cirer *vt* to polish.

cirque *m* circus.

ciseau *m* chisel; **~x** *pl* scissors.

cité *f* city.

citer *vt* to quote, cite.

citerne *f* water tank.

citoyen *m* **-ne** *f* citizen.

citron *m* lemon.

citrouille *f* pumpkin.

civière *f* stretcher.

civil *adj* civil.

civilisation *f* civilisation.

civiliser *vt* to civilise.

civique *adj* civic.

clair *adj* clear, bright.

clairière *f* clearing, glade.

clairsemé *adj* scattered.

clairvoyance *f* perspicacity; clairvoyance.

clameur *f* clamour.

clan *m* clan.

clandestin *adj* clandestine.

clapoter *vi* to lap (water).

claque *f* slap, smack.

claquement *m* clapping, slamming.

claquer *vi* to bang, slam.

clarifier *vt* to clarify; **se ~** *vr* to become clear.

clarinette *f* clarinet.

clarté *f* light, brightness.

classe *f* class, standing.

classement *m* filing; grading.

classer *vt* to file, classify.

classeur *m* filing cabinet.

classique *adj* classical, standard.

claustrer *vt* to confine.

claustrophobie *f* claustrophobia.

clavicule *f* collarbone.

clavier *m* keyboard.

clé, clef *f* key.

clémence *f* clemency, mildness.

clergé *m* clergy.

cliché *m* cliché; negative.

client *m* **-e** *f* client.

cligner *vi* to blink.

clignotant *m* indicator.

clignoter *vi* to blink, flicker.

climat *m* climate.

climatisation *f* air conditioning.

climatiser *vt* to air condition.

clin d'œil *m* wink.

clinique *f* clinic.

cliqueter *vi* to jingle, clink.

clochard *m* **-e** *f* tramp.

cloche *f* bell.

clocher *m* steeple, bell tower.

cloison *f* partition.

cloîtrer (se) *vr* to enter the monastic life.

clore *vt* to close, conclude.

clos *adj* closed, enclosed.

clôture *f* fence, hedge.

clou *m* nail.

clouer *vt* to nail.

coaguler *vi* to coagulate.

coaliser *vt vi* to form a coalition.

cobaye *m* guinea-pig.

cocaïne f cocaine.

coccinelle f ladybird.

cocher vt to notch, tick off.

cochon m -ne f pig.

code m code.

coder vt to code.

codifier vt to codify.

cœur m heart.

coffre m chest; ~-fort safe.

coffret m casket.

cogner vi to hammer, bang.

cohabiter vi to cohabit.

cohérent adj coherent.

cohésion f cohesion.

cohue f crowd.

coiffer vt to arrange so's hair; se ~ vr to do one's hair.

coiffeur m -euse f hairdresser.

coiffure f hairstyle.

coin m corner.

coincer vt to wedge, jam.

coïncidence f coincidence.

col m collar; neck.

colère f anger.

colérique adj quick-tempered, irascible.

colique f diarrhoea.

colis m parcel.

collaborateur m -trice f collaborator, colleague.

collaborer vi to collaborate.

collant adj clinging, sticky; * m leotard.

collectif adj collective.

collection f collection.

collectionner vt to collect.

collectionneur m -euse f collector.

collectivité f community; collective ownership.

collège m secondary school.

collègue mf colleague.

coller vt to stick, glue; * vi to stick, be sticky.

collier m necklace.

colline f hill.

colombe f dove.

colonel m colonel.

colonie f colony.

coloniser vt to colonise.

colonne f column.

colorant m colouring.

coloration f colouring, staining.

coloré adj coloured.

colorier vt to colour in.

coloris m colouring, shade.

colossal adj colossal.

colporter vt to peddle.

comateux adj comatose.

combat m combat, fight.

combativité f combativeness.

combattant adj fighting, combatant.

combattre vt to fight, combat; * vi to fight.

combien adv how much, how many; ~ de temps? how much time?; ~ sont-ils? how many are they?

combinaison f combination.

combiner vt to combine.

comble m height, peak.

combler vt to fill; to fulfil.

combustible m fuel.

comédie f comedy.

comédien m -ne f actor.

comète f comet.

comique adj comic.

comité m committee.

commandant m commander.

commande f command, order.

commandement m command, commandment.

commander *vt vi* to order, command.

commanditer *vt* to finance, sponsor.

comme *conj* as, like; **~ ci ~ ça** so-so; **~ il faut** properly; *adv* how.

commémorer *vt* to commemorate.

commencer *vt vi* to begin, start.

comment *adv* how; **~ dire?** how shall we say?; **~ cela?** what do you mean?

commentaire *m* comment; commentary.

commentateur *m* **-trice** *f* commentator.

commenter *vt* to comment.

commerçant *m* **-e** *f* merchant, trader.

commerce *m* business, commerce.

commercial *adj* commercial.

commercialiser *vt* to market.

commère *f* gossip.

commettre *vt* to commit.

commissaire *m* representative; commissioner.

commission *f* commission, committee.

commissionnaire *m* messenger; agent.

commode *adj* convenient, comfortable.

commodité *f* convenience.

commun *adj* common, joint.

communal *adj* council; common, communal.

communautaire *adj* community.

communauté *f* community; joint estate.

commune *f* town, district.

communication *f* communication.

communier *vi* to receive communion.

communion *f* communion.

communiquer *vt* to communicate, transmit; * *vi* to communicate.

communisme *m* communism.

communiste *mf* communist.

compact *adj* compact, dense.

comparaison *f* comparison.

comparaître *vi* to appear.

comparer *vt* to compare.

compartiment *m* compartment.

compas *m* compass.

compassion *f* compassion.

compatir *vi* to sympathise.

compatissant *adj* compassionate.

compenser *vt* to compensate; offset; **se ~** *vr* to balance each other, make up for.

compétence *f* competence.

compétent *adj* competent, capable.

compétitif *adj* competitive.

compétition *f* competition.

complaisance *f* kindness; complacency.

complaisant *adj* kind; complacent.

complément *m* complement; extension.

complet *adj* complete, full.

compléter *vt* to complete; **se ~** *vr* to complement one another.

complexe *adj* complex, complicated.

complexé *adj* mixed up.

complication *f* complication.

complice *mf* accomplice.

compliment *m* compliment.

complimenter *vt* to compliment, congratulate.

compliqué *adj* complicated, intricate.

compliquer *vt* to complicate.

complot *m* plot.

comportement *m* behaviour; performance.

comporter *vt* to consist of, comprise; **se ~** *vr* to behave.

composant *m* component, constituent.

composante *f* component.

composer *vt* to compose, make up; **se ~** *vr.* **se ~ de** to be made up of.

composition *f* composition, formation.

compréhensif *adj* comprehensive, understanding.

comprendre *vt* to understand; consist of.

compression *f* compression; reduction.

comprimé *adj* compressed; restrained; * *m* tablet.

comprimer *vt* to compress; to restrain.

compromettre *vt* to compromise.

compromis *m* compromise.

comptabilité *f* accountancy.

comptable *adj* accounting; * *mf* accountant.

compte *m* account.

compter *vt vi* to count.

compteur *m* meter.

comptoir *m* counter, bar.

comte *m* count, **comtesse** *f* countess.

concéder *vt* to grant, concede.

concentration *f* concentration.

concentrer *vt* to concentrate; **se ~** *vr* to concentrate.

conception *f* conception, design.

concerner *vt* to concern, regard.

concert *m* concert.

concertation *f* dialogue, consultation.

concession *f* concession; privilege.

concevoir *vt* to imagine, conceive.

concierge *mf* caretaker, concierge.

conciliant *adj* conciliatory.

concis *adj* concise.

concision *f* conciseness, brevity.

concluant *adj* conclusive, decisive.

conclure *vt* to conclude; to decide; **se ~** *vr* to conclude, come to an end.

concombre *m* cucumber.

concordance *f* agreement, accord.

concorder *vi* to agree, coincide.

concours *m* competition; conjuncture.

concret *adj* concrete, solid.

concrétiser *vt* to put in concrete form.

concurrence *f* competition.

concurrent *m* **-e** *f* concurrent; competitor.

condamnation *f* condemnation; sentencing.

condamné *m* **-e** *f* convict; sentenced person.

condamner *vt* to condemn; to sentence.

condenser *vt* to condense, compress.

condescendant *adj* condescending.

condition *f* condition, term.

conditionnement *m* conditioning; packaging.

conditionner *vt* to condition; to package.

condoléances *fpl* condolences.

conducteur *m* **-trice** *f* driver; operator.

conduire *vt vi* to lead; to drive.

conduite *f* conduct; driving; behaviour.

cône *m* cone.

conférence *f* conference.

conférencier *m* **-ière** *f* speaker; lecturer.

confesser *vt* to confess; **se ~** *vr* to go to confession.

confiance *f* confidence, trust.

confiant *adj* confident; confiding.

confidence *f* confidence; disclosure.

confident *m* **-e** *f* confidant.

confidentiel *adj* confidential.

confier *vt* to confide, entrust; **se ~** *vr* to confide in.

confiner *vt* to confine; **se ~** to be confined; *vr:* **se ~ à** to confine o.s. to.

confirmation *f* confirmation.

confirmer *vt* to confirm; **se ~** *vr* to be confirmed.

confisquer *vt* to confiscate, impound.

confiture *f* jam.

conflit *m* conflict, contention.

confondre *vt* to confuse, mingle.

conforme *adj* consistent; true.

conformer *vt* to model; **se ~** *vr* to conform.

conformiste *mf* conformist.

confort *m* comfort.

confortable *adj* comfortable, cosy.

confrère *m* colleague.

confrontation *f* confrontation; comparison.

confronter *vt* to confront.

confus *adj* confused, indistinct.

confusion *f* confusion, disorder.

congé *m* leave; holiday.

congédier *vt* to dismiss.

congélateur *m* freezer.

congeler *vt* to freeze.

congestion *f* congestion; stroke.

congratuler *vt* to congratulate.

congrégation *f* congregation.

congrès *m* congress, conference.

conifère *m* conifer.

conjoint *m* **-e** *f* spouse; * *adj* joint; linked.

conjuration *f* conspiracy, plot.

conjurer *vt* to conspire; to implore; to ward off.

connaissance *f* knowledge; consciousness.

connaisseur *m* **-euse** *f* connoisseur; expert.

connaître *vt* to know, be acquainted with.

connecter *vt* to connect.

connexion *f* connection, link.

connivence *f* connivance.

connotation *f* connotation.

connu *adj* known; famous.

conquérant *m* **-e** *f* conqueror; * *adj* conquering.

conquérir *vt* to conquer.

conquête *f* conquest.

conquis *adj* conquered, vanquished.

consacrer *vt* to devote, dedicate; **se ~** *vr* to dedicate o.s. to.

consciencieux *adv* conscientious.

conscient *adj* conscious, aware.

conseil *m* advice, counsel.

conseiller *m* **-ère** *f* counsellor, adviser; * *vt* to advise, counsel.

consentant *adj* consenting, willing.

consentement *m* consent.

consentir *vi* to consent, acquiesce.

conséquence *f* consequence, result.

conséquent *adj* consequent; substantial.

conservateur *m* **-trice** *f* conservative; curator.

conservation *f* conservation.

conservatoire *m* conservatory; academy.

conserve *f* canned food.

conserver *vt* to keep, preserve; **se ~** *vr* to keep.

considérable *adj* considerable; notable.

considération *f* consideration, respect.

considérer vt to consider, regard.

consigne f orders, instructions.

consistance f consistency; strength.

consister vi: ~ **en** to consist of.

consolation f consolation, solace.

console f console.

consoler vt to console, comfort.

consommateur m **-trice** f consumer.

consommation f consumption; accomplishment.

consommé adj consummate, accomplished; * m consommé.

consommer vt to consume, use.

consonne f consonant.

conspiration f conspiracy, plot.

constant adj constant, continuous.

constante f constancy.

constat m report; acknowledgement.

constater vt to record; to verify.

constellation f constellation, galaxy.

consterner vt to dismay.

constituer vt to constitute, form.

constitution f constitution, formation.

constitutionnel adj constitutional.

constructeur m **-trice** f builder, maker.

constructif adj constructive.

construction f building, construction.

construire vt to construct, build.

consultant m **-e** f consultant; * adj consulting.

consultation f consultation, advice.

consulter vt to consult, take advice from.

consumer vt to consume, spend; se ~ vr to be burning, waste away.

contact m contact, touch.

contacter vt to contact, approach.

contagieux adj contagious, infectious.

contaminer vt to contaminate, pollute.

conte m story, tale.

contempler vt to contemplate, meditate.

contemporain adj contemporary.

contenance f capacity, volume.

contenir vt to contain.

contentement m contentment, satisfaction.

contenter vt to please, satisfy; **se** ~ vr: **se** ~ **de** to content o.s. with.

contenu m contents, enclosure.

contestation f dispute, controversy.

contester vt to contest, dispute.

continental adj continental.

contingent m quota; draft (mil).

continu adj continuous, incessant.

continuel adj continual, continuous.

continuer vt to continue, proceed with; * vi to continue, go on.

contour m contour, outline.

contourner vt to bypass, skirt.

contraceptif adj contraceptive.

contraception f contraception.

contracter vt to contract, acquire; se ~ vr to contract, shrink.

contradiction f contradiction, discrepancy.

contradictoire adj contradictory, conflicting.

contraindre vt to constrain, compel.

contrainte f constraint, compulsion.

contraire m opposite, contrary; * adj opposite, contrary.

contrariant adj contrary; perverse.

contrarier vt to annoy; to oppose.

contrariété f annoyance, disappointment.

contraste m contrast.

contrat m contract, agreement.

contre *prép* against; **parier à 10 ~ 1** to bet at 10 to 1; **~ toute attente** contrary to all expectations; **par ~** on the other hand.

contre-attaque *f* counter-attack.

contrebande *f* contraband, smuggling.

contrebandier *m* **-ière** *f* smuggler.

contrecarrer *vt* to thwart, oppose.

contrecœur: à ~ reluctantly.

contrecoup *m* rebound, repercussion.

contredire *vt* to contradict, refute.

contrefaçon *f* counterfeit, forgery.

contrefaire *vt* to counterfeit, forge.

contremaître *m* foreman.

contrepartie *f* compensation; consideration.

contre-plaqué *m* plywood.

contresens *m* nonsense; misunderstanding; mistranslation.

contretemps *m* mishap; contretemps; (*mus*) syncopation.

contribuable *mf* taxpayer.

contribuer *vt vi* to contribute.

contribution *f* contribution; tax.

contrôle *m* control, check.

contrôler *vt* to control, check.

contrôleur *m* **-euse** *f* inspector; auditor.

controverse *f* controversy.

controversé *adj* disputed.

convaincre *vt* to convince, persuade.

convenable *adj* fitting, suitable.

convenir *vi* to agree, accord.

convention *f* convention, agreement.

conventionnel *adj* conventional; contractual.

converger *vi* to converge.

conversation *f* conversation, talk.

conversion *f* conversion.

convertir *vt* to convert; **se ~** *vr* to be converted.

convexe *adj* convex.

conviction *f* conviction.

convier *vt* to invite; to urge.

convivial *adj* convivial; user-friendly.

convoi *m* convoy; train.

convoiter *vt* to covet.

convulsion *f* convulsion.

coopératif *adj* cooperative.

coopération *f* cooperation.

coopérative *f* cooperative.

coopérer *vi* to cooperate, collaborate.

coordinateur *m* **-trice** *f* coordinator.

coordination *f* coordination; committee.

coordonner *vt* to coordinate.

copain *m* friend, pal.

copeau *m* shaving, chip.

copie *f* copy, reproduction.

copier *vt* to copy, reproduce.

copieux *adj* copious, abundant.

copine *f* friend, mate.

copropriété *f* co-ownership, joint ownership.

coq *m* cock, rooster.

coque *f* (*mar*) hull; shell.

coquelicot *m* poppy.

coquet *adj* stylish, smart.

coquetterie *f* smartness, stylishness.

coquillage *m* shellfish.

coquille *f* shell, scallop.

coquin *m* **-e** *f* naughty, mischievous.

cor *m* (*mus*) horn; corn.

corail *m* coral.

coran *m* Koran.

corbeau *m* crow.

corbeille *f* basket.

corbillard *m* hearse.

cordage *m* rope; rigging.

corde *f* rope; string.

cordée *f* roped mountaineering party.

cordial *adj* cordial, warm.

cordialité *f* cordiality, warmth.

cordon *m* cord, string; cordon.

cordonnier *m* **-ière** *f* shoemender, cobbler.

coriace *adj* tough; tight.

coriandre *m* coriander.

corne *f* horn, antler.

corneille *f* crow.

cornemuse *f* bagpipes.

cornet *m* cone, cornet.

corniche *f* cornice; ledge.

corporatif *adj* corporative, corporate.

corporation *f* corporation, guild.

corps *m* body, corpse.

corpus *m* corpus.

correct *adj* correct, accurate.

correcteur *m* **-trice** *f* examiner; proof-reader.

corrélation *f* correlation.

correspondance *f* correspondence, communication.

correspondant *m* **-e** *f* correspondent; * *adj* corresponding.

correspondre *vi* to correspond, communicate.

corridor *m* corridor, passage.

corriger *vt* to correct.

corroborer *vt* to corroborate.

corroder *vt* to corrode.

corrompre *vt* to corrupt, debase.

corrosif *adj* corrosive.

corrosion *f* corrosion.

corruption *f* corruption, debasement.

corsage *m* blouse, bodice.

corsé *adj* rich, full-bodied.

corset *m* corset.

cortège *m* cortège, procession.

cosmétique *m* cosmetic.

cosmique *adj* cosmic.

cosmonaute *mf* cosmonaut.

cosmopolite *adj* cosmopolitan.

costume *m* costume, dress.

côte *f* coast; rib; slope.

côté *m* side; point.

coteau *m* hill.

côtelé *adj* ribbed.

coter *vt* to quote; to classify.

côtier *adj* coastal, inshore.

coton *m* cotton.

côtoyer *vt* to mix with, skirt.

cou *m* neck.

couchant *adj* setting.

couche *f* layer, coat.

coucher *vt* to put to bed; **se ~** *vr* to go to bed.

coucou *m* cuckoo.

coude *m* elbow.

coudé *adj* angled, bent.

coudoyer *vt* mix with, rub shoulders with.

coudre *vt* *vi* to sew.

couette *f* duvet.

couler *vi* to flow, run.

couleur *f* colour, shade.

couleuvre *f* grass snake.

coulis *m* sauce, purée.

coulisse *f* groove; (*thea*) wings.

coulisser *vi* to slide, run.

couloir *m* corridor, passage.

coup *m* blow; shot; **~ sur ~** one after another, incessantly; **tout à ~** suddenly; **~ de feu** shot; **jeter un ~ d'œil** to glance; **~ de coude** nudge; **~ de**

téléphone phone call; **~ de soleil** sun-stroke.

coupable *mf* culprit; * *adj* guilty.

coupe *f* cut; cutting.

coupe-papier *m invar* paper knife.

couper *vt* to cut, slice.

coupole *f* dome.

coupon *m* coupon, voucher, ticket.

coupure *f* cut; break.

cour *f* court, yard, courtyard.

courage *m* courage, daring.

courageux *adj* courageous.

courant *adj* current; present; * *m* stream, current.

courbature *f* stiffness; ache.

courbe *f* curve; contour.

courber *vt* to curve, bend.

coureur *m* **-euse** *f* runner.

courgette *f* courgette.

courir *vi* to run, race.

couronne *f* crown, wreath.

couronnement *m* coronation.

couronner *vt* to crown.

courrier *m* mail, post.

courroie *f* strap, belt.

cours *m* course; flow; path.

course *f* running; race; flight; journey.

coursier *m* **-ière** *f* courier, messenger.

court *adj* short, brief.

court-circuit *m* short-circuit.

courtier *m* **-ière** *f* broker, agent.

courtois *adj* courteous.

courtoisie *f* courtesy, courteousness.

cousin *m* **-e** *f* cousin.

coussin *m* cushion, pillow.

coût *m* cost, charge.

couteau *m* knife.

coûter *vt vi* to cost.

coûteux *adj* costly, expensive.

coutume *f* custom, habit.

coutumier *adj* customary, usual.

couture *f* sewing, needlework.

couturier *m* couturier, fashion designer.

couturière *f* dressmaker.

couvent *m* convent.

couver *vt* to hatch, incubate; * *vi* to smoulder, lurk.

couvercle *m* lid, cap.

couvert *m* shelter; cover; pretext; * *adj* covered; secret; obscure.

couverture *f* blanket; cover; roofing.

couvre-feu *m* curfew.

couvrir *vt* to cover; **se ~** *vr* to cover up; to become overcast.

cracher *vt* to spit.

crachin *m* drizzle.

craie *f* chalk.

craindre *vt* to fear.

crainte *f* fear, dread.

craintif *adj* timid, cowardly.

crampe *f* cramp.

cramponner *vt* to cramp, clamp; **se ~** *vr* to cling, hang on.

cran *m* notch, cog.

crâne *m* cranium, skull.

crapaud *m* toad.

crapule *f* villain.

crapuleux *adj* villainous, vicious.

craquement *m* crack, creaking, snap.

craquer *vi* to creak, squeak, crack.

crasseux *adj* grimy, filthy.

cratère *m* crater.

cravate *f* tie.

créateur *m* **-trice** *f* creator, author.

créatif *adj* creative.

création *f* creation.

créativité *f* creativity.

créature *f* creature.

crèche *f* crèche; crib.

crédibilité *f* credibility.

crédit *m* credit, trust.

crédule *adj* credulous, gullible.

créer *vt* to create, produce.

crémaillère *f* rack, chimney hook.

crème *f* cream.

crémerie *f* dairy.

crémeux *adj* creamy.

crêpe *f* pancake; * *m* crepe, crape.

crépiter *vi* to crackle; to rattle.

crépuscule *m* twilight, dusk.

cresson *m* watercress.

crête *f* crest, comb.

crétin *m* **-e** *f* cretin, idiot.

creuser *vi* to dig, burrow; * *vt* to dig, hollow.

creux *adj* hollow, empty.

crevaison *f* puncture, flat.

crever *vt* to burst; to gouge; *vi* to burst; to split.

crevette *f* prawn.

cri *m* cry, howl, yell.

criard *adj* yelling; scolding.

crible *m* riddle, sieve.

cric *m* (*auto*) jack.

crier *vi* to cry, shout.

crime *m* crime, offence.

criminel *m* **-le** *f* criminal; * *adj* criminal.

crinière *f* mane.

criquet *m* locust.

crise *f* crisis, attack.

crisper *vt* to shrivel; to clench.

cristal *m* crystal, glassware.

cristallisation *f* crystallisation.

cristalliser *vt* to crystallise.

critère *m* criterion, standard.

critiquable *adj* censurable, open to criticism.

critique *adj* critical, censorious; * *f* criticism; critique.

critiquer *vt* to criticise, censure.

croc *m* fang; hook.

croche *f* quaver.

crochet *m* hook, clasp.

crocodile *m* crocodile.

croire *vt* to believe, think.

croisade *f* crusade.

croisement *m* crossing, junction.

croiser *vt* to cross; to fold; **se ~** *vr* to cross, intersect.

croisière *f* cruise.

croissance *f* growth, increase.

croissant *adj* growing, increasing; * *m* croissant; crescent.

croître *vi* to grow, rise.

croix *f* cross.

croquer *vt* to crunch.

croquis *m* sketch, outline.

crosse *f* (*rel*) crozier; butt, grip.

crotte *f* manure, dung.

croupir *vi* to stagnate, wallow.

croûte *f* crust.

croûton *m* crust, crouton.

croyance *f* belief.

croyant *adj* believing.

cru *adj* raw, uncooked; * *m* vineyard; wine.

cruauté *f* cruelty, inhumanity.

cruche *f* pitcher.

crucial *adj* crucial, decisive.

crudité *f* crudity, coarseness.

crue *f* flood.

cruel *adj* cruel.

crustacé *m* crustacean, shellfish.

crypter *vt* to encode, scramble.

cube *m* cube, block.

cubique *adj* cubic.

cubisme *m* cubism.

cueillir *vt* to pick, gather.

cuiller, cuillère *f* spoon, spoonful.

cuir *m* leather, hide.

cuire *vi* to cook.

cuisine *f* kitchen; cookery.

cuisinier *m* **-ière** *f* cook.

cuisinière *f* cooker, stove.

cuisse *f* thigh.

cuisson *f* cooking, baking.

cuivre *m* copper.

cul *m* (*col*) bottom, ass.

cul-de-sac *m* blind alley, cul-de-sac.

culinaire *adj* culinary.

culminer *vi* to culminate, tower.

culot *m* cheek, nerve.

culotte *f* knickers; underpants; shorts.

culte *m* cult, veneration.

cultivateur *m* **-trice** *f* farmer.

cultiver *vt* to cultivate; **se ~** *vr* to improve o.s.

culture *f* culture; cultivation.

culturel *adj* cultural.

culturisme *m* body-building.

cumuler *vt* to accumulate; to hold concurrently.

cupide *adj* greedy; **~ment** *adv* greedily.

cupidité *f* greed, cupidity.

cure *f* cure; treatment.

curé *m* parish priest, parson.

cure-dents *m* toothpick.

curieux *m* **-euse** *f* inquisitive person; onlooker; * *adj* curious, inquisitive.

curiosité *f* curiosity, inquisitiveness.

cuve *f* vat, tank.

cuvette *f* basin, bowl.

cycle *m* cycle; stage.

cyclisme *m* cycling.

cycliste *mf* cyclist; * *adj* cycle.

cyclomoteur *m* moped.

cyclone *m* cyclone.

cygne *m* swan.

cylindre *m* cylinder.

cylindrée *f* capacity (engine).

cylindrique *adj* cylindrical.

cymbale *f* cymbal.

cynique *adj* cynical.

cynisme *m* cynicism.

D

daigner *vt* to deign, condescend.

daim *m* deer.

dalle *f* flagstone, slab.

dalmatien *m* Dalmatian.

daltonien *adj* colour-blind.

dame *f* lady; dame.

damier *m* draughtboard.

damnation *f* damnation.

damner *vt* to damn.

danger *m* danger, risk.

dangereux *adj* dangerous, risky.

dans *prép* in; into; **il a ~ les trente ans** he's thirty or so.

danse *f* dance; dancing.

danser *vi* to dance.

danseur *m* **-euse** *f* dancer.

dard *m* sting.

date *f* date.

dater *vt* to date.

datte *f (bot)* date.

dattier *m* date palm.

dauphin *m* dolphin.

davantage *adv* more.

de *prép* of; from; **~ bonne heure** early; **deux ~ plus** two more; * *art* some, any.

dé *m* dice; thimble.

déambuler *vi* to stroll.

débâcle *f* disaster; collapse.

déballage *m* unpacking; display.

déballer *vt* to unpack; to display.

débandade *f* rout, stampede.

débarbouiller *vt* to wash; **se ~** *vr* to wash o.s.

débarcadère *m* landing; wharf.

débarquement *m* landing, disembarkment.

débarquer *vt* to land, unship; * *vi* to disembark, land.

débarrasser *vt* to clear, rid; **se ~** *vr*: **se ~ de** to rid o.s. of.

débat *m* debate; dispute, contest.

débattre *vi* to debate, discuss.

débauche *f* debauchery, dissoluteness.

débaucher *vt* to debauch, corrupt.

débile *adj* weak, feeble.

débilitant *adj* debilitating, weakening.

débit *m* debit; turnover; flow.

débiter *vt* to debit; to produce.

débiteur *m* **-trice** *f* debtor.

déblayer *vt* to clear away, remove.

déblocage *m* unblocking; freeing, releasing.

débloquer *vt* to release, unlock.

déboîtement *m* dislocation.

débordant *adj* exuberant, overflowing.

débordé *adj* overwhelmed.

débordement *m* overflowing; outflanking.

déborder *vi* to overflow; to outflank.

débouché *m* outlet; issue.

déboucher *vt* to open, uncork; * *vi* to pass out, emerge.

debout *adv* upright, standing; **être ~** to stand.

déboutonner *vt* to unbutton.

débraillé *adj* untidy, disordered.

débrancher *vt* to disconnect.

débrouiller *vt* to disentangle, unravel; **se ~** *vr* to cope, manage.

début *m* beginning, outset.

débuter *vi* to start, begin; * *vt* to lead, start.

décaféiné *adj* decaffeinated.

décalage *m* gap, interval; discrepancy.

décaler *vt* to shift; to stagger.

décaper *vt* to clean, scour.

décapotable *adj* convertible; * *f* convertible.

décapsuler *vt* to take the lid off.

décapsuleur *m* bottle-opener.

décathlon *m* decathlon.

décéder *vi* to die.

décelable *adj* detectable.

déceler *vt* to detect; to disclose.

décembre *m* December.

décence *f* decency.

décennie *f* decade.

décent *adj* decent, proper.

décentralisation *f* decentralisation.

décentraliser *vt* to decentralise.

déception *f* disappointment; deceit.

décerner *vt* to award, confer.

décès *m* death, decease.

décevant *adj* disappointing; deceptive.

décevoir *vt* to disappoint; to deceive.

déchaîner *vt* to unleash; **se ~** *vr* to break loose, run wild.

décharge *f* discharge; receipt.

décharger *vt* to unload, discharge.

déchéance *f* decay, decline.

déchet *m* loss, waste.

déchiffrer *vt* to decipher, decode.

déchiqueter *vt* to tear; to slash; to shred.

déchirant *adj* harrowing, excruciating.

déchirer *vt* to tear, rip.

déchirure *f* tear, rip.

déchoir *vi* to decline; to sink.

décimal *adj* decimal.

décisif *adj* decisive, conclusive.

décision *f* decision.

déclarer *vt* to declare, announce; **se ~** *vr* to speak one's mind.

déclenchement *m* release, setting off.

déclencher *vt* to release, set off; **se ~** *vr* to release itself, go off.

déclic *m* click; trigger.

déclin *m* decline, deterioration.

décliner *vi* to decline, refuse.

déclivité *f* declivity, slope.

décloisonner *vt* to decompart-mentalise.

décoder *vt* to decode, decipher.

décodeur *m* decoder, decipherer.

décoincer *vt* to loose, release.

décollage *m* take-off, lift-off.

décoller *vi* to unpaste, steam off; to take off; * *vt*; **se ~** *vr* to come unstuck, become detached.

décolleté *adj* low-necked, low-cut; *m* decolletage, low neckline.

décolorant *adj* bleaching, decolorising; * *m* bleaching substance.

décolorer *vt* to decolour, bleach.

décombres *mpl* rubble, debris.

décomposer *vt* to decompose; to break up; to dissect; **se ~** *vr* to decompose, decay.

décomposition *f* decomposition, breaking up.

décompression *f* decompression.

décomprimer *vt* to decompress.

décompte *m* discount; deduction.

déconcentrer *vt* to devolve; to disperse; **se ~** *vr* to lose concentration.

déconcerter *vt* to disconcert.

décongeler *vt* to thaw, defrost.

déconnecter *vt* to disconnect.

déconnexion *f* disconnection.

décontenancé *adj* embarrassed; disconcerted.

décontracter *vt* to relax; **se ~** *vr* to relax.

décontraction *f* relaxation.

décor *m* scenery; setting.

décorateur *m* **-trice** *f* decorator; set designer.

décoratif *adj* decorative, ornamental.

décoration *f* decoration, embellishment.

décorer *vt* to decorate, adorn.

décortiquer *vt* to husk, shell.

découler *vi* to flow; to ensue.

découper *vt* to carve, cut up.

décourageant *adj* discouraging, disheartening.

décourager *vt* to discourage, dishearten; **se ~** *vr* to become discouraged.

décousu *adj* unsewn; loose; disconnected.

découvert *adj* uncovered; open; * *m* overdraft.

découverte *f* discovery.

découvrir *vt* to discover.

décret *m* decree, enactment.

décréter *vt* to decree, enact.

décrire *vt* to describe.

décrocher *vt* to take down; to unhook.

décroissant *adj* decreasing, lessening.

décroître *vi* to decrease, diminish.

déçu *adj* disappointed.

dédaigner *vt* to disdain, scorn.

dédaigneux *adj* disdainful, scornful.

dédain *m* disdain, scorn.

dedans *adv* inside, indoors; * *m* inside; **au ~** inside.

dédicace *f* dedication.

dédommagement *m* compensation, damages.

dédouanement *m* customs clearance.

déduction *f* deduction.

déduire *vt* to deduct; to deduce.

déesse *f* goddess.

défaillance *f* faintness; exhaustion; blackout.

défaillir *vi* to faint; to weaken.

défaire *vt* to undo, dismantle.

défaite *m* defeat, overthrow.

défaitiste *adj, mf* defeatist.

défaut *m* defect, fault.

défavorable *adj* unfavourable.

défection *f* defection.

défectueux *adj* defective, faulty.

défendeur *m* **-eresse** *f* defendant.

défendre *vt* to defend, protect; to prohibit; **se ~** *vr* to defend o.s.

défense *f* defence; prohibition.

défenseur *m* defender.

défensif *adj* defensive.

défi *m* defiance; challenge.

défiant *adj* mistrustful, distrustful.

déficience *f* deficiency.

déficient *adj* deficient; weak.

déficit *m* deficit, shortfall.

déficitaire *adj* deficient, in deficit.

défier *vt* to challenge, defy.

défilé *m* procession, parade.

défiler *vi* to parade, march.

définir *vt* to define, specify.

définitif *adj* definitive, final.

définition *f* definition.

déflation *f* deflation.

défoncer *vt* to smash in; to dig deeply.

déformation *f* deformation, distortion.

déformer *vt* to deform, distort; **se ~** *vr* to bend; to lose its shape.

défoulement *m* outlet; release.

défunt *m* **-e** *f* deceased; * *adj* late, deceased.

dégagé *adj* clear; open.

dégager *vt* to free, clear; **se ~** *vr* to free o.s., extricate o.s.

dégarnir *vt* to empty; to clear.

dégât *m* havoc, damage.

dégel *m* thaw.

dégeler *vt vi* to thaw, melt.

dégénérer *vi* to degenerate, decline.

dégivrer *vt* to de-ice, defrost.

dégonfler *vt* to deflate, empty.

dégourdir *vt* to warm up, revive.

dégoût *m* disgust, distaste.

dégoûter *vt* to disgust.

dégradation *f* degradation, debasement.

dégrader *vt* to degrade, debase; **se ~** *vr* to become degraded, debased.

dégrafer *vt* to unfasten, unhook.

degré *m* degree; grade.

dégrèvement *m* reduction; redemption.

déguisement *m* disguise.

déguiser *vt* to disguise; **se ~** *vr* to disguise o.s.

dehors *adv* outside, outdoors; **au ~** outwardly; **en ~ de** outside; apart from; * *m* outside, exterior.

déjà *adv* already.

déjeuner *vi* to lunch; * *m* lunch.

delà *adv*: **au ~ de** beyond; **par ~** beyond.

délabré *adj* dilapidated, ramshackle.

délai *m* delay; respite; time limit.

délaisser *vt* to abandon, quit.

délassant *adj* relaxing, refreshing.

délasser *vt* to refresh, relax; **se ~** *vr* to rest, relax.

délateur *m* **-trice** *f* informer.

délavé *adj* diluted; faded.

délayer *vt* to thin; to drag out.

délectation *f* delectation, delight.

délecter (se) *vr* to delight, revel.

délégation *f* delegation.

délégué *m* **-e** *f* delegate, representative.

déléguer *vt* to delegate.

délibération *f* deliberation; resolution.

délibéré *adj* deliberate; resolute.

délicat *adj* delicate, dainty.

délicatesse *f* delicacy, daintiness.

délice *m* delight, pleasure.

délicieux *adj* delicious, delightful.

délinquance *f* delinquency.

délinquant *m* **-e** *f* delinquent, offender; * *adj* delinquent.

délirant *adj* delirious, frenzied.

délirer *vi* to be delirious.

délit *m* offence, misdemeanour.

délivrance *f* deliverance; release; delivery.

délivrer *vt* to deliver; to release; **se ~** *vr* to free o.s.

déloger *vt* to evict, dislodge.

déloyal *adj* disloyal, unfaithful.

déloyauté *f* disloyalty, treachery.

deltaplane *m* hang-glider.

demain *adv* tomorrow.

demande *f* request, petition; question.

demander *vt* to ask, request; **se ~** *vr* to wonder.

démangeaison *f* itch; longing.

démarche *f* gait, walk, step.

démarrer *vi* to start up, move off; * *vt* to start, get started.

démarreur *m* starter.

démasquer *vt* to unmask, uncover.

démêlage *m* disentangling; combing.

démêler *vt* to disentangle, unravel; comb.

déménagement *m* removal; moving (house).

déménager *vi* to move house.

déménageur *m* removal man.

démener (se) *vr* to struggle, strive.

dément *adj* mad, insane, crazy.

démenti *m* denial, refutation.

démentir *vt* to deny, refute.

démesuré *adj* excessive, inordinate.

démettre *vt* to dislocate; to dismiss.

demeure *f* residence, dwelling place.

demeurer *vi* to live at, reside, stay.

demi *adj* half; **à ~** halfway; * *m* half.

demi-cercle *m* semicircle.

demi-douzaine *f* half-dozen.

demi-droite *f* half-line.

demi-finale *f* semi-final.

demi-heure *f* half-hour.
démilitariser *vt* to demilitarise.
demi-lune *f* half-moon.
demi-pension *f* half-board.
démission *f* resignation.
démissionner *vi* to resign.
démocrate *mf* democrat.
démocratie *f* democracy.
démocratique *adj* democratic.
démocratiser *vt* to democratise.
démodé *adj* old-fashioned, out-of-date.
demoiselle *f* young lady; spinster; damsel.
démolir *vt* to demolish, knock down.
démolition *f* demolition.
démon *m* demon, fiend.
démonstrateur *m* **-trice** *f* demonstrator.
démonstratif *adj* demonstrative.
démonstration *f* demonstration; proof.
démonter *vt* to dismantle, take down, dismount; **se ~** *vr* to come apart, be nonplussed.
démontrer *vt* demonstrate; to prove.
démoraliser *vt* to demoralise; **se ~** *vr* to become demoralised.
démunir *vt* to deprive; to divest.
démystifier *vt* to demystify, disabuse.
dénégation *f* denial.
déneiger *vt* to clear snow from.
déni *m* denial, refusal.
dénicher *vt* to dislodge; to unearth.
dénier *vt* to deny, disclaim.
dénigrer *vt* to denigrate, disparage.
dénombrer *vt* to number, enumerate.
dénomination *f* denomination, designation.

dénoncer *vt* to denounce; to inform against.
dénonciation *f* denunciation.
dénouement *m* dénouement; unravelling; outcome.
dénouer *vt* to unravel, untie, undo.
dénoyauter *vt* to stone (fruit).
denrée *f* commodity, provisions, foodstuff.
dense *adj* dense, thick.
densité *f* density, denseness.
dent *f* tooth.
dentaire *adj* dental.
dentelé *adj* jagged, perforated.
dentelle *f* lace.
dentier *m* denture, dental plate.
dentifrice *m* toothpaste.
dentiste *mf* dentist.
dénuder *vt* to bare, denude; **se ~** *vr* to strip off.
dénué *adj* devoid, bereft.
dénuement *m* destitution; deprivation.
déodorant *m* deodorant.
dépannage *m* repairing, fixing.
dépanner *vt* to repair, fix.
dépanneuse *f* breakdown lorry.
dépareillé *adj* unmatched; odd.
déparer *vt* to spoil; to disfigure.
départ *m* departure; start.
département *m* department.
dépasser *vt* to exceed; to go past.
dépaysé *adj* disoriented, out of one's element.
dépêcher *vt* to dispatch, send; **se ~** *vr* to hurry, rush.
dépendre *vi* to depend on, be dependent on.
dépens *mpl*: **aux ~ de** at the expense of.

dépense *f* expenditure, outlay.

dépenser *vt* to expend, spend; **se ~** *vr* to exert o.s.

dépérir *vi* to decline, waste away.

dépistage *m* tracking; detection.

dépister *vt* to track.

dépit *m* spite; grudge; **en ~ de** in spite of.

dépité *adj* vexed; frustrated.

déplacé *adj* misplaced; ill-timed.

déplacement *m* displacement; removal.

déplacer *vt* to displace; to move; **se ~** *vr* to change residence.

déplaire *vi* to displease; to offend.

déplaisant *adj* disagreeable, unpleasant.

dépliant *m* prospectus, leaflet; * *adj* extendible; folding.

déplier *vt* to unfold; to open out.

déploiement *m* (*mil*) deployment; display.

déplorable *adj* deplorable, disgraceful.

déplorer *vt* to deplore, bewail.

déportation *f* deportation, transportation.

déporté *m* -e *f* deportee.

déposer *vt* to lodge, deposit.

dépositaire *mf* depository; trustee.

dépôt *m* deposit; warehouse.

dépourvu *adj* lacking, wanting; **au ~** off guard.

dépoussiérer *vt* to dust.

dépravation *f* depravity, corruption.

dépravé *adj* depraved, corrupt.

dépréciation *f* depreciation.

dépressif *adj* depressive.

dépression *f* depression, slump; dejection.

déprimant *adj* depressing.

déprimer *vt* to depress; to discourage.

depuis *prép* since, from; after.

député *m* deputy, delegate.

déraisonner *vi* to talk irrationally, rave.

dérangement *m* derangement; inconvenience.

déranger *vt* to upset, unsettle; **se ~** *vr* to move; to put o.s. out.

dérapage *m* skid.

déraper *vi* to skid, slip.

déréglé *adj* out of order; irregular; unruly.

dérèglement *m* disturbance; irregularity; dissoluteness.

dérégler *vt* to disturb; to put out of order; to upset.

dérision *f* derision, mockery.

dérisoire *adj* derisory; pathetic.

dérivation *f* derivation; diversion.

dérive *f* drift; **aller à la ~** to drift away.

dériver *vi* to drift.

dernier *adj* last; latest; back; * *m* -ière *f* last one; latter.

dernièrement *adv* recently; lately.

dérobade *f* sidestepping; evasion.

dérober *vt* to steal; to hide; **se ~** *vr* to steal away, escape.

dérogation *f* derogation; dispensation.

déroger *vi* to derogate; to detract.

déroulement *m* unfolding; progress, development.

dérouler *vt* to unwind, uncoil; **se ~** *vr* to develop; to unfold.

déroutant *adj* disconcerting.

déroute *f* rout, overthrow.

dérouter *vt* to rout, overthrow.

derrière *prép* behind; * *adv*; **par ~** at

the back; * *m* bottom; back; **de ~** back, rear.

des *art* = **de les**; *see* **un, une**.

dès *prép* from, since; **~ que** when; as soon as.

désaccord *m* disagreement, discord.

désaffecté *adj* disused.

désagréable *adj* disagreeable, unpleasant.

désagréger *vt* to break up, disintegrate; **se ~** *vr* to break up, disintegrate

désagrément *m* displeasure, annoyance.

désapprobateur *adj* disapproving.

désapprobation *f* disapproval.

désarmement *m* disarmament.

désarmer *vt* to disarm; to unload.

désarroi *m* disarray, confusion.

désarticuler *vt* to dislocate; to upset.

désastre *m* disaster.

désastreux *adj* disastrous, unfortunate.

désavantage *m* disadvantage; prejudice.

désavantager *vt* to disadvantage, handicap.

désaveu *m* disavowal, retraction.

descendre *vi* to descend, go down; * *vt* to take down, bring down.

descente *f* descent, way down.

descriptif *adj* descriptive, explanatory.

description *f* description.

désemparé *adj* helpless; distraught.

désenchantement *m* disenchantment; disillusion.

désenfler *vi* to become less swollen.

déséquilibre *m* imbalance, unbalance.

déséquilibré *adj* unbalanced, unhinged.

déséquilibrer *vt* to unbalance, throw off balance.

désert *m* desert, wilderness; * *adj* deserted.

déserter *vt* to desert.

déserteur *m* deserter.

désertion *f* desertion.

désespérant *adj* desperate, hopeless; discouraging.

désespéré *adj* desperate, hopeless.

désespérer *vi* to despair, give up hope.

désespoir *m* despair, despondency.

déshabiller *vt* to undress; **se ~** *vr* to undress.

désherbant *m* weed killer.

déshériter *vt* to disinherit.

déshonorant *adj* dishonourable, disgraceful.

déshonorer *vt* to dishonour, disgrace.

déshydrater *vt* to dehydrate; **se ~** *vr* to become dehydrated.

désigner *vt* to designate, indicate.

désillusion *f* disillusion; disappointment.

désillusionner *vt* to disillusion; to disappoint.

désinfectant *m* disinfectant; * *adj* disinfectant.

désinfecter *vt* to disinfect.

désinfection *f* disinfection.

désintégration *f* disintegration.

désintégrer *vt* to split, break up; **se ~** *vr* to disintegrate.

désintéressé *adj* disinterested, unselfish.

désintéresser (se) *vr* to lose interest in.

désinvolte *adj* easy, offhand, casual.

désir *m* desire, wish, longing.

désirer *vt* to desire, wish, long.

désobéir *vi* to disobey.

désobéissance *f* disobedience.

désobéissant *adj* disobedient.

désobligeant *adj* disobliging; uncivil.

désodorisant *m* deodorant; * *adj* deodorising, deodorant.

désodoriser *vt* to deodorise.

désœuvré *adj* unoccupied, idle.

désœuvrement *m* idleness.

désolation *f* desolation; ruin; grief.

désolé *adj* desolate; disconsolate, grieved.

désordonné *adj* untidy; inordinate; reckless.

désordre *m* disorder, confusion, disturbance.

désorganisation *f* disorganisation.

désorienté *adj* disorientated.

désormais *adv* from now on, henceforth.

despotique *adj* despotic.

dessèchement *m* dryness, drying up, withering.

dessécher *vt* to dry, parch, wither; **se ~** *vr* to dry out, become parched.

dessein *m* design, plan, scheme; **à ~** intentionally.

desserrer *vt* to loosen; to unscrew; to slacken; **se ~** *vr* to work loose, come undone.

dessert *m* dessert, sweet.

dessin *m* drawing, sketch; draft.

dessinateur *m* **-trice** *f* drawer, draughtsman.

dessiner *vt* to draw, sketch; to design.

dessous *adv* under, beneath; * *m* underside, bottom.

dessus *adv* over, above.

destabiliser *vt* to destabilise.

destin *m* destiny, fate, doom.

destination *f* destination; purpose.

destinée *f* destiny, fate.

destiner *vt* to determine; to intend, destine, aim.

destituer *vt* to dismiss, depose.

destructeur *adj* destructive, ruinous.

destruction *f* destruction.

désuétude *f* disuse **tomber en ~** to fall into disuse.

détaché *m* (*mus*) detached.

détachement *m* detachment, indifference.

détacher *vt* (*mus*) to detach; to unfasten; **se ~** *vr* to become detached.

détail *m* detail, particular.

détaillant *m* **-e** *f* retailer.

détailler *vt* to detail; to sell retail.

détecter *vt* to detect.

détection *f* detection.

détective *m* detective.

déteindre *vi* to lose colour, fade.

détendre *vt* to release, loosen; **se ~** *vr* relax, calm down.

détendu *adj* slack; relaxed.

détenir *vt* to detain; to hold.

détente *f* relaxation, easing.

détériorer *vt* to damage, impair; **se ~** *vr* to deteriorate, worsen.

détermination *f* determination; resolution.

déterminé *adj* determined, resolute.

déterminer *vt* to determine, decide.

détestable *adj* detestable, odious.

détester *vt* to detest, hate.

détonateur *m* detonator.

détonation *f* detonation, explosion.

détonner *vi* to clash (colour); to go out of tune.

détour *m* detour; curve; evasion.

détourné *adj* indirect, oblique.

détournement *m* diversion, rerouting.

détourner *vt* to divert, reroute.

détraquer *vt* to upset; to disorder; **se ~** *vr* to become upset; to go wrong.

détresse *f* distress, trouble.

détriment *m*: **au ~ de** to the detriment of.

détritus *m* refuse, rubbish.

détroit *m* strait.

détrôner *vt* to dethrone, depose.

detruire *vt* to destroy, demolish.

dette *f* debt.

deuil *m* mourning, bereavement, grief.

deux *adj* two; * *m* two; **entre les ~** soso, fair to middling; **en moins de ~** in a jiffy.

deuxième *adj* second * *mf* second.

dévaler *vt vi* to hurry down, tear down.

dévaliser *vt* to burgle; to rifle.

dévalorisation *f* depreciation.

dévaloriser *vt* to depreciate, reduce the value of.

devancer *vt* to outstrip, outrun; to precede.

devant *prép* in front of, before; * *adv* in front; * *m* front; **prendre les ~s** to make the first move, pre-empt; **aller au-~ de** to anticipate.

développement *m* development; growth; progress.

développer *vt* to develop, expand; **se ~** *vr* to develop, grow.

devenir *vi* to become, grow.

déverser *vt* to pour; to dump.

dévêtir *vt* to undress; **se ~** *vr* to get undressed.

déviation *f* deviation; diversion.

dévier *vi* to deviate; to turn aside; to swerve.

devin *m* **-eresse** *f* seer, soothsayer.

deviner *vt* to guess; to solve; to foretell.

devis *m* estimate, quotation.

dévisager *vt* to stare at.

devise *f* currency.

dévisser *vt* to unscrew, undo.

dévoiler *vt* to unveil, disclose.

devoir *m* duty; homework; *vt* to owe; to have to.

dévorer *vt* to devour, consume.

dévotion *f* devotion, piety.

dévoué *adj* devoted, dedicated.

dévouement *m* devotion, dedication.

dévouer (se) *vr* to devote o.s., sacrifice o.s.

dextérité *f* dexterity, adroitness.

diabète *m* diabetes.

diabétique *adj* diabetic.

diable *m* devil.

diagnostic *m* diagnosis.

diagnostiquer *vt* to diagnose.

diagonale *f* diagonal.

diagramme *m* diagram; graph.

dialecte *m* dialect.

dialogue *m* dialogue, conversation.

diamant *m* diamond.

diamètre *m* diameter.

diarrhée *f* diarrhoea.

dictateur *m* **-trice** *f* dictator.

dictée *f* dictating; dictation.

dicter *vt* to dictate, impose.

dictionnaire *m* dictionary.

dièse *f* sharp *(mus)*.

diète *f* light diet.

diététicien *m* **-ne** *f* dietician.

dieu *m* god.

diffamation *f* defamation, slandering.

diffamer *vt* to defame, slander.

différé *adj* postponed; (*rad*, *TV*) pre-recorded.

différence *f* difference.

différenciation *f* differentiation.

différencier *vt* to differentiate.

différend *m* disagreement, difference of opinion.

différent *adj* different; various.

différer *vt* to differ; to vary.

difficile *adj* difficult; awkward, tricky.

difficulté *f* difficulty; problem.

difforme *adj* deformed, misshapen.

difformité *f* deformity.

diffuser *vt* to diffuse, circulate, broadcast.

diffusion *f* diffusion, circulation, broadcasting.

digérer *vt* to digest.

digestif *adj* digestive.

digestion *f* digestion.

digital *adj* digital.

digne *adj* worthy; dignified.

dignité *f* dignity.

dilapider *vt* to squander; to embezzle.

dilatation *f* dilation, distension.

dilater *vt* to dilate, distend; **se ~** *vr* to dilate, distend.

dilemme *m* dilemma.

dilettante *mf* dilettante.

diluer *vt* to dilute.

dilution *f* dilution.

dimanche *m* Sunday.

dimension *f* dimension, size.

diminuer *vt* to diminish, reduce; ** vi* to diminish, lessen.

diminutif *m* diminutive.

diminution *f* reduction, lessening.

dinde *f* turkey hen.

dindon *m* turkey cock.

dîner *vi* to dine; ** m* dinner.

dinosaure *m* dinosaur.

diplomate *mf* diplomat.

diplomatie *f* diplomacy.

diplomatique *adj* diplomatic.

diplôme *m* diploma, certificate.

dire *vt* to say; to tell.

direct *adj* direct.

directeur *m* **-trice** *f* director.

direction *f* direction, management.

directive *f* directive, order.

dirigeant *m* **-e** *f* leader, ruler; ** adj* ruling, executive.

diriger *vt* to run, direct; **se ~** *vr*: **se ~ vers** to head for, make for.

discernement *m* discernment, judgment.

discerner *vt* to discern, distinguish.

disciple *m* disciple.

disciplinaire *adj* disciplinary.

discipline *f* discipline.

discontinu *adj* discontinuous.

discordant *adj* discordant, conflicting.

discorde *f* discord, dissension.

discothèque *f* discotheque.

discourtois *adj* discourteous.

discréditer *vt* to discredit.

discret *adj* discreet.

discrétion *f* discretion, prudence.

discriminer *vt* to distinguish; to discriminate.

disculper *vt* to excuse, exonerate.

discussion *f* discussion, debate.

discutable *adj* debatable, questionable.

discuter *vt vi* to discuss, debate.

disgrâce *f* disgrace.

disgracieux *adj* awkward, ungraceful.

disjoncter *vi* to cut off, disconnect.

disparaître *vi* to disappear, vanish.

disparate *adj* disparate, incongruous.

disparité *f* disparity, incongruity.

disparition *f* disappearance; death; extinction.

dispense *f* dispensation, exemption.

dispenser *vt* to dispense, exempt; **se ~** *vr.* **se ~ de** to dispense with; to avoid.

disperser *vt* to spread, scatter; **se ~** *vr* to disperse, scatter.

dispersion *f* dispersal, scattering.

disponible *adj* available.

dispos *adj* **ref**reshed; alert; in form.

disposer *vt* to arrange, dispose; **se ~** *vr.* **se ~ à** to prepare to do; * *vi* to leave.

disposition *f* arrangement, layout.

dispute *f* dispute, argument.

disputer *vt* to dispute, rival; **se ~** *vr* to quarrel, argue.

disqualifier *vt* to disqualify.

disque *m* disk; record.

disquette *f* diskette.

dissection *f* dissection.

dissemblable *adj* dissimilar; different.

dissentiment *m* disagreement, dissent.

disséquer *vt* to dissect.

dissertation *f* dissertation.

dissidence *f* dissidence, dissent.

dissident *adj* dissident.

dissimuler *vt* to dissemble, conceal; **se ~** *vr* to conceal o.s.

dissipation *f* dissipation, waste.

dissiper *vt* to dispel; to dissipate; **se ~** *vr* to disperse, become undisciplined.

dissociation *f* dissociation.

dissoudre *vt* to dissolve.

dissuader *vt* to dissuade.

distance *f* distance, interval.

distancier (se) *vr* to distance o.s. from.

distant *adj* distant.

distiller *vt* to distil.

distillerie *f* distillery.

distinct *adj* distinct, different.

distinctif *adj* distinctive.

distinction *f* distinction.

distinguer *vt* to distinguish; to discern; **se ~** *vr* to distinguish o.s.

distorsion *f* distortion.

distraction *f* inattention; absentmindedness; abstraction.

distraire *vt* to distract; to amuse; **se ~** *vr* to enjoy o.s.

distrait *adj* inattentive, absent-minded.

distrayant *adj* entertaining, diverting.

distribuer *vt* to distribute.

distribution *f* distribution.

divagation *f* wandering, rambling.

divaguer *vi* to ramble, rave.

divergence *f* divergence.

divergent *adj* divergent.

divers *adj* diverse, varied.

diversification *f* diversification.

diversifier *vt* to vary, diversify; **se ~** *vr* to diversify.

diversion *f* diversion.

diversité *f* diversity, variety.

divertir *vt* to amuse, entertain.

divertissant *adj* amusing, entertaining.

divertissement *m* entertainment, recreation.

dividende *m* dividend.

divin *adj* divine, exquisite.

divination *f* divination.

divinité *f* divinity.

diviser *vt* to divide, split; **se ~** *vr* to split up, divide into.

division *f* division.

divorce *m* divorce.

divorcé *m* **-e** *f* divorcee; * *adj* divorced.

divorcer *vi* to divorce.

divulgation *f* disclosure, divulgence.

divulguer *vt* to divulge, disclose.

dix *adj, m* ten. .

dix-huit *adj, m* eighteen.

dix-huitième *adj, mf* eighteenth.

dixième *adj* tenth * *mf* tenth.

dix-neuf *adj, m* nineteen.

dix-neuvième *adj, mf* nineteenth.

dix-sept *adj, m* seventeen.

dix-septième *adj, mf* seventeenth.

dizaine *f* ten, ten or so.

docile *adj* docile, submissive.

docilité *f* docility, submissiveness.

dock *m* dock, dockyard.

docteur *m* doctor.

doctorat *m* doctorate.

doctrine *f* doctrine.

document *m* document.

documentaliste *mf* researcher.

documentation *f* documentation; information.

documenter *vt* to document; **se ~** *vr* to gather information on.

dogmatique *adj* dogmatic.

dogme *m* dogma.

doigt *m* finger.

domaine *m* domain, estate; to sphere.

dôme *m* dome, vault.

domestique *adj* domestic, household.

domestiquer *vt* to domesticate, tame.

domicile *m* domicile, address.

domicilié *adj* domiciled.

dominant *adj* dominant, prevailing.

dominante *f* dominant characteristic.

dominateur *adj* governing; domineering.

dommage *m* damage; harm; **c'est ~** it's a pity.

dompter *vt* to tame, train.

dompteur *m* **-euse** *f* trainer, tamer.

don *m* gift; talent.

donateur *m* **-trice** *f* donor.

donation *f* donation.

donc *conj* so, therefore, thus; **pourquoi ~?** why was that?

donné *adj* given; fixed; **étant ~** seeing that, in view of.

donner *vt* to give; * *vi* to yield (crop).

donneur *m* **-euse** *f* giver, donor; dealer.

dont *pn* whose, of which.

dopage *m* doping.

doper *vt* to dope; **se ~** *vr* to take drugs, dope o.s.

dorénavant *adv* from now on, henceforth.

dorer *vt* to gild; to tan.

dorloter *vt* to pamper, pet.

dormir *vi* to sleep, be asleep; to be still.

dortoir *m* dormitory.

dos *m* back; top; ridge.

doser *vt* to measure out, proportion; to strike a balance.

dossier *m* dossier, file; case.

dot *f* dowry.

doter *vt* to provide with a dowry; to endow.

douane *f* customs.

douanier *m* customs officer.

double *adj* double, duplicate, dual; * *m* copy, double, replica; twice as much.

doubler *vt vi* to double, duplicate.

doublure *f* lining; (*thea*) understudy.

doucereux *adj* sugary; mawkish; suave.

douceur *f* softness, gentleness.

douche *f* shower.

doucher *vt* to give a shower to; **se ~** *vr* to take a shower.

doué *adj* gifted, endowed with.

douille *f* case; cartridge.

douillet *adj* delicate, tender; soft.

douleur *f* pain, ache; anguish.

douloureux *adj* painful, grievous.

doute *m* doubt; **sans ~** without doubt.

douter *vi* to doubt, question; **se ~** *vr* **se ~ de** to suspect someone; **se ~ que** to suspect that, expect that.

douteux *adj* doubtful, dubious.

doux *adj*, *f* **douce** soft; sweet; mild.

douzaine *f* dozen.

douze *adj*, *m* twelve.

douzième *adj* twelfth; * *mf* twelfth.

doyen *m* **-ne** *f* dean; doyen.

dragon *m* dragon.

dramatique *adj* dramatic, tragic.

dramatiser *vt* to dramatise.

dramaturge *mf* playwright.

drame *m* drama.

drap *m* sheet; **--housse** fitted sheet; **être dans de beaux ~s** to be in a fine mess.

drapeau *m* flag.

draper *vt* to drape.

dressage *m* taming; pitching.

dresser *vt* to draw up; to put up; **se ~** *vr* to stand up; to rear up.

dresseur *m* **-euse** *f* trainer, tamer.

dribbler *vi* to dribble.

drogue *f* drug.

drogué *m* **-e** *f* drug addict.

droguer *vt* to drug, administer drugs;

se ~ *vr* to dose up; to take drugs.

droit *adj* right; straight; sound; honest; * *adv* straight, straight ahead; * *m* right; law; tax.

droite *f* right side; right (wing); straight line.

droitier *adj* right-handed.

droiture *f* uprightness, honesty.

drôle *adj* funny, amusing; peculiar.

dru *adj* thick, dense; sturdy.

du *art* of the.

dû *adj* owed; due.

dualité *f* duality.

dubitatif *adj* doubtful, dubious.

duc *m* duke, **duchesse** *f* duchess.

duché *m* duchy.

duel *m* duel; dual.

dune *f* dune.

duo *m* duo; duet.

dupe *adj* easily duped; * *f* dupe.

duper *vt* to dupe, take in.

dupliquer *vt* to duplicate.

dur *adj* hard, tough; difficult.

durable *adj* durable, lasting.

durant *prép* during, for.

durcir *vt vi* to harden; **se ~** *vr* to become hardened.

durcissement *m* hardening.

durée *f* duration, length.

durer *vi* to last.

dureté *f* hardness; austerity, harshness.

duvet *m* down.

dynamique *f* dynamic; dynamics; * *adj* dynamic.

dynamisme *m* dynamism.

dynamite *f* dynamite.

dynamiter *vt* to dynamite.

dynastie *f* dynasty.

E

eau *f* water; rain.

eau-de-vie *f* brandy.

ébahir *vt* to astonish, stupefy, dumbfound.

ébahissement *m* astonishment, amazement.

ébauche *f* rough draft, rough outline.

ébaucher *vt* to sketch; to roughcast.

ébène *f* ebony.

ébéniste *m* cabinetmaker.

éblouir *vt* to dazzle; to fascinate.

éblouissant *adj* dazzling; amazing.

ébouillanter *vt* to scald; to blanch; **s'~** *vr* to scald oneself.

éboulement *m* collapse, caving in; fall.

ébouriffé *adj* tousled, ruffled.

ébranler *vt* to shake; to unsettle, disturb.

ébrécher *vt* to chip, indent; to break into (fortune).

ébrouer (s') *vr* to shake oneself.

ébruiter *vt* to disclose, divulge; **s'~** *vr* to spread, be noised abroad.

ébullition *f* boiling; effervescence; turmoil.

écaille *f* scale; shell.

écailler *vt* to scale; to chip; **s'~** *vr* to flake off, peel off.

écarlate *adj* scarlet.

écart *m* distance; interval; discrepancy; **rester à l'~** to steer clear of.

écarteler *vt* to tear apart; to quarter.

écarter *vt* to separate; to avert; to dismiss; **s'~** *vr* to make way; to swerve.

échafaud *m* scaffold.

échafaudage *m* scaffolding.

échange *m* exchange, barter, trade.

échanger *vt* to exchange.

échantillon *m* sample.

échappée *f* breakaway; glimpse.

échappement *m* exhaust; release.

échapper *vi* to escape, avoid, elude; **s'~** *vr* to escape from; to leak.

échauffement *m* heating; warm-up; constipation.

échauffer *vt* to heat, overheat; to excite; **s'~** *vr* to warm up; to get worked up.

échéance *f* expiry; maturity date.

échec *m* failure, defeat; chess.

échelle *f* ladder; scale.

échelon *m* rung; grade.

échelonner *vt* to grade; to stagger, set at intervals; **s'~** *vr* to be graduated, staggered.

échine *f* backbone, spine.

échiquier *m* chessboard.

écho *m* echo; rumour.

échographie *f* ultrasound scan.

échouer *vi* to fail; to end up; to run aground.

éclair *m* flash; lightning flash; spark.

éclairage *m* lighting, light.

éclairagiste *m* electrician; lighting engineer.

éclaircir *vt* to lighten; to thin down; to brighten up; **s'~** *vr* to clear (up).

éclaircissement *m* clearing up, explanation, elucidation.

éclairer *vt* to light, illuminate; clarify, explain.

éclat *m* brightness, glare; splinter; splendour.

éclatant *adj* bright, blazing; resounding; blatant.

éclatement *m* explosion, bursting, rupture.

éclater *vi* to explode; to break out; to exclaim.

éclipser *vt* to eclipse, overshadow; **s'~** *vr* to disappear, vanish.

éclore *vi* to hatch out; to blossom.

éclosion *f* hatching; blooming; birth.

écluse *f* lock.

écœurement *m* nausea, disgust; discouragement.

écœurer *vt* to nauseate, disgust.

école *f* school, schooling; sect, doctrine.

écolier *m* schoolgirl, **-ière** *f* schoolgirl.

écologie *f* ecology.

écologique *adj* ecological.

écologiste *mf* ecologist.

économe *adj* thrifty; * *mf* steward, treasurer; (*mar*) bursar.

économie *f* economy, thrift; economics.

économique *adj* economic.

économiser *vt* to economise, save.

écorce *f* bark, peel, skin.

écorchure *f* scratch; graze.

Écossais *m* Scotsman, **-e** *f* Scotswoman.

écossais *adj* Scottish.

écoulement *m* flow, discharge, outlet; disposal, selling.

écouler *vt* to flow, discharge; to sell; **s'~** *vr* to leak, flow out; to pass by; to sell.

écoute *f* listening, audience.

écouter *vt* to listen to.

écran *m* screen.

écraser *vt* to crush; to overwhelm; to run over; **s'~** *vr* to crash; to get crushed.

écrin *m* box, casket.

écrire *vt* to write; to spell.

écriteau *m* notice, sign.

écriture *f* writing; handwriting; script.

écrivain *m* writer.

écrou *m* nut.

écrouler (s') *vr* to collapse, crumble.

écru *adj* raw; unbleached; untreated.

écueil *m* reef, shelf; peril.

écume *f* foam, froth; scum.

écureuil *m* squirrel.

écurie *f* stable.

écusson *m* badge, shield.

édification *f* erection, construction.

édifice *m* edifice, building.

éditer *vt* to publish, produce; to edit.

éditeur *m* **-trice** *f* publisher; editor.

édition *f* publishing; edition; editing.

éducation *f* education; upbringing.

édulcorant *m* sweetener.

éduquer *vt* to educate; to bring up, raise.

effaré *adj* alarmed, bewildered.

effaroucher *vt* to frighten off; to alarm.

effectif *m* staff; size, complement; * *adj* effective, positive.

effectuer *vt* to effect, execute, carry out.

effervescent *adj* effervescent; excited.

effet *m* effect, impression; spin; bill, note.

effleurer *vt* to touch lightly, skim across.

effondrer (s') *vr* to collapse, cave in.

efforcer (s') *vr* to endeavour, do one's best.

effort *m* effort, exertion; stress, strain.

affrayer *vt* to frighten, scare.

effriter *vt* to crumble; **s'~** *vr* to crumble away, disintegrate.

effroi *m* terror, dismay.

effronté *adj* shameless, impudent, cheeky.

effroyable *adj* horrifying, appalling.

égal *adj* equal; even, level; equable.

égaler *vt* to equal, match.

égalisation *f* equalisation; levelling.

égaliser *vt* to equalise; to level out.

égalitaire *adj* egalitarian.

égalité *f* equality; equableness; evenness.

égard *m* consideration, respect; **à l'~ de** concerning, regarding; **à tous ~s** in all respects.

égarer *vt* to mislead, lead astray; **s'~** *vr* to get lost; to wander from the point.

égayer *vt* to enliven, cheer up.

église *f* church.

égocentrique *adj* egocentric, self-centred.

égout *m* sewer.

égoutter *vt* to strain; to wring out.

égratignure *f* scratch, scrape.

éjecter *vt* to eject, throw out.

élaboration *f* elaboration, development.

élaborer *vt* to elaborate, develop.

élan *m* surge, momentum, speed; spirit, elan.

élancer (s') *vr* to rush, spring, hurl oneself.

élargir *vt* to widen, stretch; **s'~** *vr* to get wider.

élargissement *m* widening, stretching, enlarging.

élastique *adj* elastic; flexible; * *m* elastic, elastic band.

élection *f* election; choice.

électorat *m* electorate; constituency; franchise.

électricien *m* electrician.

électricité *f* electricity.

électrique *adj* electric.

électronique *f* electronics; * *adj* electronic.

élégance *f* elegance, stylishness.

élégant *adj* smart, elegant, stylish.

élément *m* element, component; cell; fact.

élémentaire *adj* elementary; basic.

éléphant *m* elephant.

élevage *m* rearing, breeding.

élève *mf* pupil, student.

élevé *adj* high; heavy; lofty, exalted.

élever *vt* to bring up, raise; to put up, lift up; **s'~** *vr* to rise, go up.

éleveur *m* **-euse** *f* stockbreeder.

élimination *f* elimination.

éliminatoire *adj* eliminatory; * *f* preliminary heat.

éliminer *vt* to eliminate, discard.

élire *vt* to elect.

élite *f* elite.

élitisme *m* elitism.

elle *pn* she; it; her; **c'est à ~** it's up to her; it's hers; **~-même** herself.

elliptique *adj* elliptic.

élocution *f* elocution, diction.

éloge *m* praise; eulogy.

éloigné *adj* distant, remote.

éloigner *vt* to move away, take away; **s'~** *vr* to go away; to grow distant.

éloquence *f* eloquence.

éloquent *adj* eloquent.

émacié *adj* emaciated, wasted.

émail *m* enamel.

émailler *vt* to enamel.

émancipation *f* emancipation, liberation.

émaner *vi* to emanate, issue.

emballage *m* packing paper, wrapping paper.

emballer *vt* to pack up, wrap up.

embarcadère *m* landing stage, pier.

embargo *m* embargo.

embarquement *m* loading; embarkation.

embarquer *vt* to embark; to load; * *vi* to embark, go aboard.

embarras *m* embarrassment, confusion; trouble.

embarrasser *vt* to embarrass; to hinder, hamper; **s'~** *vr* to burden oneself with; to be troubled by.

embaucher *vt* to take on, hire.

embêter *vt* (*fam*) to bore; to get on one's nerves; **s'~** *vr* to be bored, fed up.

emblème *m* symbol, emblem.

emboîter *vt* to fit together; **s'~** *vr* to fit together; to fit into each other.

embouchure *f* mouth (river); mouthpiece.

embouteillage *m* traffic jam; bottling.

embranchement *m* junction; side road.

embrasser *vt* to kiss, embrace.

embrayage *m* clutch.

embrouiller *vt* to tangle up, mix up; **s'~** *vr* to become muddled, confused.

embuscade *f* ambush.

émeraude *f* emerald.

émerger *vi* to emerge; to stand out.

émerveiller *vt* to astonish, amaze; **s'~** *vr* to marvel at.

émetteur *adj*, *f* **-trice** transmitting.

émettre *vt* to send out, emit, transmit.

émeute *f* riot.

émietter *vt* to crumble; to disperse, break up; **s'~** *vr* to crumble; to disperse, break up.

émigrer *vi* to emigrate.

éminence *f* hill, elevation; eminence, distinction.

éminent *adj* eminent, distinguished.

émission *f* sending out; transmission; broadcast; emission.

emmêler *vt* to entangle; confuse; **s'~** *vr* to tangle.

emménager *vi* to move in.

emmener *vt* to take away; to lead.

émoi *m* agitation, emotion.

émotion *f* emotion; commotion.

émouvant *adj* moving, touching.

émouvoir *vt* to move, disturb, upset; **s'~** *vr* to be moved; to get worried, upset.

empailler *vt* to stuff.

emparer (s') *vr* to seize, grab; to take possession of.

empêchement *m* obstacle, hitch; impediment.

empêcher *vt* to prevent, stop; **s'~** *vr*: **s'~ de** to refrain from doing something.

empereur *m* emperor.

empêtrer *vt* to entangle;; **s'~** *vr* to get involved in, get mixed up in.

emphase *f* pomposity; emphasis, stress.

empiler *vt* to pile up, stack.

empire *m* empire; influence, ascendancy.

empirer *vi* to get worse, deteriorate.

empirique *adj* empirical.

emplacement *m* site, location.

emploi *m* use; job, employment.

employé *m* **-e** *f* employee.

employer *vt* to use, spend; to employ.

employeur *m*, **euse** *f* employer.

emporter *vt* to take; to carry off; to involve; **s'~** *vr* to lose one's temper.

empreinte *f* imprint, impression, stamp.

emprisonner *vt* to imprison, trap.

emprunt *m* borrowing, loan.

emprunter *vt* to borrow; to assume; to derive.

ému *adj* moved, touched, excited.

émulsion *f* emulsion.

en *prép* in; to; by; on; **~ tant que** as; *pn* from there; of it, of them; **je n'~ veux plus** I don't want any more of them; **s'~ faire** to worry; **il ~ va de même pour** the same goes for.

encadrement *m* framing; training; managerial staff.

encadrer *vt* to frame; to train; to surround.

encaissement *m* collection; receipt; cashing.

encaisser *vt* to collect, receive; to cash.

enceinte *adj f* pregnant.

encens *m* incense.

encercler *vt* to encircle, surround.

enchaînement *m* linking; link; sequence.

enchaîner *vt* to chain.

enchantement *m* enchantment, delight.

enchanter *vt* to enchant, delight.

enchère *f* bid, offer.

enclencher *vt* to engage; to set in motion.

enclin *adj* inclined, prone.

enclore *vt* to enclose, shut in.

encolure *f* neck; collar size.

encombrant *adj* unwieldy, cumbersome.

encombrer *vt* to clutter, obstruct; **s'~** *vr* to burden oneself.

encore *adv* still; only; again; more; **~ que** even though.

encouragement *m* encouragement.

encourager *vt* to encourage; to incite.

encre *f* ink.

encyclopédie *f* encyclopaedia.

endettement *m* indebtedness; debt.

endetter *vt* to get so into debt; **s'~** *vr* to get into debt.

endoctrinement *m* indoctrination.

endoctriner *vt* to indoctrinate.

endommager *vt* to damage.

endormir *vt* to put to sleep; **s'~** *vr* to fall asleep.

endossement *m* endorsement.

endroit *m* place; side part; **à l'~** regarding.

enduire *vt* to coat, smear.

enduit *m* coating.

endurance *f* endurance, stamina.

endurci *adj* hardened; hard-hearted.

endurcir *vt* to harden; **s'~** *vr* to become hardened.

endurer *vt* to endure, bear.

énergétique *adj* energy; energising.

énergie *f* energy; spirit, vigour.

énergique *adj* energetic, vigorous.

énervement *m* irritation; nervousness.

énerver *vt* to irritate, annoy; to get on one's nerves; **s'~** *vr* to get excited, worked up.

enfance *f* childhood; infancy.

enfant *mf* child; native.

enfantin *adj* childish, infantile.

enfer *m* hell.

enfermer *vt* to lock up; to confine; to box in.

enfiévrer *vt* to stir up, inflame.

enfiler *vt* to string, thread; to put on.

enfin *adv* at last; in short; after all.

enflammer *vt* to set on fire; to inflame, kindle; **s'~** *vr* to catch fire, ignite.

enfler *vi* to swell up, inflate.

enfoncer *vt* to stick in, thrust; to break open; **s'~** *vr* to sink into, disappear into.

enfouir *vt* to bury.

enfuir (s') *vr* to run away, flee.

engagement *m* agreement, commitment, undertaking; engaging; opening.

engager *vt* to bind; to involve; to insert; to open; **s'~** *vr* to undertake to; to take a job.

engelure *f* chilblain.

engin *m* machine; instrument; contraption.

engorgement *m* obstruction, clogging; glut.

engouffrer *vt* to devour, swallow up, engulf; **s'~** *vr* to rush into, sweep, surge.

engourdir *vt* to numb; to dull, blunt; **s'~** *vr* to become numb, to grow sluggish.

engraisser *vi* to get fatter; * *vt* to fatten; to fertilise.

énigmatique *adj* enigmatic.

énigme *f* enigma, riddle.

enivrer *vt* to intoxicate, make drunk; **s'~** *vr* to get drunk.

enjeu *m* stake.

enjoliver *vt* to ornament; to embroider (truth).

enlacer *vt* to embrace, intertwine.

enlaidir *vt* to make ugly; **s'~** *vr* to become ugly.

enlèvement *m* abduction, kidnapping; removal.

enlever *vt* to remove; to take off; to deprive; to abduct.

ennemi *m* -e *f* enemy.

ennui *m* boredom, tedium, weariness.

ennuyer *vt* to bore, bother; **s'~** *vr* to get bored.

ennuyeux *adj* boring, tedious.

énorme *adj* enormous, huge.

énormité *f* enormity, hugeness; howler.

enquête *f* inquiry, investigation; survey.

enquêter *vi* to hold an inquiry; to investigate.

enragé *adj* furious; keen.

enregistrement *m* recording; registration.

enregistrer *vt* to record; to register.

enrichir *vt* to enrich, expand; **s'~** *vr* to get rich.

enrober *vt* to wrap, cover, coat.

enrôler *vt* to enlist, enrol.

enrouement *m* hoarseness.

enrouer *vt* to make hoarse.

enrouler *vt* to roll up, wind up.

enseignant *m* -e *f* teacher.

enseigne *f* sign; (*mil*) ensign.

enseignement *m* education, training, instruction.

enseigner *vt* to teach.

ensemble *adv* together, at the same time; * *m* unity; whole.

ensoleillé *adj* sunny.

ensorceler *vt* to bewitch, enchant.

ensuite *adv* then, next, afterwards.

entaille *f* cut, gash.

entamer *vt* to start, open, make a hole in.

entassement *m* piling up, heaping up.

entasser *vt* to pile up, heap up.

entendre *vt* to hear; to intend, mean; to understand; **s'~** *vr* to agree; to know how to.

entendu *adj* agreed; **bien ~** of course.

entente *f* harmony, understanding; accord.

enterrement *m* burial; funeral.

enterrer *vt* to bury, inter.

en-tête *m* heading, header.

entêté *adj* stubborn, obstinate.

entêtement *m* stubbornness, obstinacy.

enthousiasme *m* enthusiasm.

enthousiaste *adj* enthusiastic; * *mf* enthusiast.

entier *adj* entire, whole; intact.

entièrement *adv* entirely, wholly, completely.

entorse *f* sprain.

entortiller *vt* to twist, twine; to hoodwink, wheedle.

entourer *vt* to surround, frame, encircle; **s'~** *vr*: **s'~ de** to surround oneself with.

entracte *m* interval, intermission.

entraider (s') *vr* to help one another.

entrailles *fpl* entrails, guts; womb.

entraînement *m* training, coaching; force, impetus.

entraîner *vt* to drag; to lead; to train; **s'~** *vr* to train oneself.

entraîneur *m* trainer, coach.

entre *prép* between, among, into.

entrecouper *vt* to intersperse, interrupt with.

entrée *f* entry, entrance; admission; insertion.

entrejambes *m* crotch.

entrelacer *vt* to intertwine, interlace.

entremets *m* sweet, dessert.

entreposer *vt* to store, put into storage.

entrepôt *m* warehouse, bonded warehouse.

entreprenant *adj* enterprising.

entreprendre *vt* to embark upon, undertake.

entreprise *f* company; venture, business.

entrer *vi* to enter, go in.

entretenir *vt* to maintain, look after; to speak with.

entretien *m* upkeep, maintenance; conversation.

entrevoir *vt* to make out; to glimpse; to anticipate.

entrevue *f* meeting, interview.

entrouvert *adj* half-open.

énumération *f* enumeration, listing.

énumérer *vt* to enumerate, list.

envahir *vt* to invade, overrun.

envahissant *adj* invasive; intrusive; pervasive.

enveloppe *f* envelope; covering; exterior.

envelopper *vt* to envelop; to wrap up; to veil.

envergure *f* breadth, scope, scale.

envers *prép* towards, to; * *m*; **à l'~** inside out, upside down.

envie *f* desire, longing, inclination; envy.

envier *vt* to envy.

envieux *adj* envious.

environ *adv* about, around.

environnement *m* environment.

environner *vt* to surround, encircle.

envisager *vt* to view, envisage.

envoi *m* dispatch, remittance; kick-off.

envol *m* takeoff, flight.

envoler (s') *vr* to fly away; to disappear.

envoûter *vt* to bewitch.

envoyé *m* **-e** *f* messenger, envoy.

envoyer *vt* to send, dispatch; hurl. fire.

épais *adj* thick; deep.

épaisseur *f* thickness; depth.

épaissir *vi* to thicken; to deepen; * *vt*; **s'~** *vr* to thicken, get thicker.

épanoui *adj* radiant, beaming.

épanouir *vt* to brighten, light up; open out; **s'~** *vr* to bloom.

épargne *f* saving, savings.

épargner *vt* to save; to spare.

éparpiller *vt* to scatter, distribute; **s'~** *vr* to scatter.

épaule *f* shoulder.

épauler *vt* to support, back up.

épave *f* wreck; derelict; ruin.

épée *f* sword.

épeler *vt* to spell.

éperdu *adj* distraught, overcome.

éphémère *adj* ephemeral, fleeting.

épi *m* ear; tuft.

épice *m* spice.

épicé *adj* spicy; juicy.

épidémie *f* epidemic.

épier *vt* to spy on.

épilation *f* removal of hair.

épilepsie *f* epilepsy.

épileptique *adj* epileptic.

épiler *vt* to remove hair, pluck.

épilogue *m* epilogue; conclusion.

épinard *m* spinach.

épine *f* spine; thorn.

épineux *adj* thorny, prickly; tricky.

épingle *f* pin.

épique *adj* epic.

épisode *m* episode.

épisodique *adj* occasional; transitory.

épitaphe *f* epitaph.

éplucher *vt* to clean; to peel; to sift.

épluchure *f* peeling, paring.

éponge *f* sponge.

éponger *vt* to sponge, mop.

épopée *f* epic.

époque *f* time, epoch, age, period.

épousseter *vt* to dust.

épouvantail *m* scarecrow.

épouvante *f* terror, dread.

épouvanter *vt* to terrify, appal.

époux *m* **épouse** *f* spouse.

éprendre *vr*: **s'~ de** to fall in love with.

épreuve *f* test; ordeal, trial; proof.

éprouvant *adj* trying, testing.

éprouver *vt* to feel, experience.

éprouvette *f* test tube.

épuisement *m* exhaustion.

épuiser *vt* to exhaust, wear out; **s'~** *vr* to run out; to exhaust oneself.

épurer *vt* to purify, refine.

équateur *m* equator.

équation *f* equation.

équatorial *adj* equatorial.

équerre *f* square; bracket.

équestre *adj* equestrian.

équilibre *m* balance, equilibrium; harmony.

équilibrer *vt* to balance; **s'~** *vr* to balance each other.

équipage *m* crew; gear, equipment.

équipe *f* team, crew, gang, staff.

équiper *vt* to equip, fit out.

équivalence *f* equivalence.

équivalent *adj* equivalent, same; ** m* equivalent.

équivoque *adj* equivocal, questionable.

érable *m* maple.

érafler *vt* to scratch, scrape.

ère *f* era.

érection *f* erection; establishment.

éreintant *adj* exhausting, backbreaking.

ériger *vt* to erect; to establish.

ermite *m* hermit.

éroder *vt* to erode.

érotique *adj* erotic.

érotisme *m* eroticism.

errant *adj* wandering, stray.

errer *vi* to wander, roam.

erreur *f* error, mistake, fault.

érudit *adj* erudite, learned; ** m* scholar.

escabeau *m* stool; stepladder.

escadron *m* squadron, platoon.

escalade *f* climbing; escalation.

escalader *vt* to climb, scale.

escale *f* port of call, touchdown.

escalier *m* stairs, steps.

escamoter *vt* to dodge, evade; to pilfer.

escapade *f* escapade; prank, jaunt.

escargot *m* snail.

esclavage *m* slavery, bondage.

esclave *mf* slave.

escompte *m* discount.

escompter *vt* to discount.

escorte *f* escort; retinue.

escorter *vt* to escort.

escrime *f* fencing.

escrimeur *m* **-euse** *f* fencer.

escroc *m* crook, con man.

escroquer *vt* to swindle, con.

espace *m* space, interval.

espacement *m* spacing, interval.

espacer *vt* to space out.

espèce *f* sort, kind; species.

espérance *f* hope, expectation.

espérer *vt* to hope.

espion *m* **-ne** *f* spy.

espionnage *m* espionage, spying.

espionner *vt* to spy.

espoir *m* hope.

esprit *m* mind, intellect; spirit; wit.

esquimau *m* **-de** *f* Eskimo.

esquisse *f* sketch, outline.

esquisser *vt* to sketch, outline.

esquiver *vt* to dodge; to shirk.

essai *m* test, trial; attempt; essay.

essayer *vt* to test, try, try on.

essence *f* petrol; essential oil.

essentiel *adj* essential, basic.

essieu *m* axle.

essorer *vt* to wring, mangle.

essouffler *vt* to wind; **s'~** *vr* to get out of breath.

essuyer *vt* to wipe, mop; **s'~** *vr* to wipe oneself.

est *m* east.

esthéticien *m* **-ne** *f* beautician.

estimation *f* valuation; estimation, reckoning.

estime *f* esteem, respect, regard.

estimer *vt* to value, assess, estimate.

estival *adj* summer; summery.

estivant *m* **-e** *f* holidaymaker, summer visitor.

estomac *m* stomach.

estomper *vt* to blur, dim; **s'~** *vr* to become blurred.

estrade *f* platform, rostrum.

et *conj* and.

étable *f* cowshed.

établi *adj* established; * *m* workbench.

établir *vt* to establish, set up; **s'~** *vr* to settle; to set oneself up as; to become established.

établissement *m* building; establishment.

étage *m* floor, storey; stage, level.

étagère *f* shelf.

étalage *m* display, display window; stall.

étalagiste *mf* window dresser.

étaler *vt* to spread, strew; to stagger; to display.

étalon *m* stallion.

étanche *adj* waterproof.

étang *m* pond.

étape *f* stage, leg; staging point.

état *m* state, condition; statement.

étau *m* vice.

étayer *vt* to prop up, support.

été *m* summer.

éteindre *vt* to put out, extinguish; **s'~** *vr* to go out; to die; to evaporate.

éteint *adj* faded; extinct.

étendard *m* standard, flag.

étendre *vt* to spread, extend; to floor; **s'~** *vr* to spread; to stretch out; to increase.

étendu *adj* extensive, sprawling, wide.

étendue *f* expanse, area; duration.

éternel *adj* eternal, everlasting.

éterniser *vt* to draw out; to immortalise; **s'~** *vr* to drag on, linger on.

éternité *f* eternity; ages.

éternuer *vi* to sneeze.

ethnique *adj* ethnic.

étincelant *adj* sparkling; gleaming.

étinceler *vi* to sparkle, gleam.

étincelle *f* spark; gleam, glimmer.

étiqueter *vt* to label, mark.

étiquette *f* label, tag; etiquette.

étirer *vt* to stretch, draw out; **s'~** *vr* to stretch out.

étoffe *f* material, fabric; stuff.

étoile *f* star.

étonnement *m* surprise, astonishment.

étonner *vt* to astonish, surprise; **s'~** *vr* to be astonished.

étouffer *vt* to suffocate; to muffle; **s'~** *vr* to be suffocated, to swelter.

étourdi *adj* absentminded.

étourdir *vt* to stun, daze; to deafen.

étourdissement *m* blackout, dizzy spell; surprise.

étourneau *m* starling.

étrange *adj* strange, funny.

étranger *m* -**ère** *f* foreigner, stranger, alien; * *adj* foreign, strange, unknown.

étrangeté *f* strangeness, oddness.

étrangler *vt* to strangle, stifle; **s'~** *vr* to strangle oneself, choke.

être *vi* to be; **c'est-à-dire** namely, that is to say; * *m* being, person, soul.

étreindre *vt* to embrace, hug; to seize.

étreinte *f* embrace; stranglehold.

étrier *m* stirrup.

étroit *adj* narrow; strict.

étude *f* study; survey; office.

étudier *vt* to study, examine.

étui *m* case; holster.

eu = *p.p.* **avoir** had.

eucalyptus *m* eucalyptus.

euphorique *adj* euphoric.

européen *m* **-ne** *f* European; * *adj* European.

eux *pn* they, them; **c'est à ~** it's up to them; it's theirs; **~-mêmes** themselves.

évacuation *f* evacuation; emptying.

évacuer *vt* to evacuate, clear.

évader (s') *vr* to escape.

évaluation *f* evaluation, appraisal.

évaluer *vt* to evaluate, appraise.

évangile *m* gospel.

évanouir (s') *vr* to faint, pass out.

évanouissement *m* faint, blackout.

évaporation *f* evaporation.

évaporer (s') *vr* to evaporate.

évasif *adj* evasive.

évasion *f* escape; escapism.

éveil *m* awakening; dawning.

éveiller *vt* to waken, arouse; **s'~** *vr* to wake up.

événement *m* event, incident.

éventail *m* fan; range.

éventualité *f* eventuality, possibility.

éventuel *adj* possible.

évêque *m* bishop.

évidence *f* evidence, proof.

évident *adj* obvious, evident.

évier *m* sink.

évincer *vt* to oust; to evict.

éviter *vt* to avoid; to spare.

évocation *f* evocation, recall.

évolué *adj* developed, advanced; enlightened.

évolution *f* evolution, development.

exact *adj* exact, accurate.

exagération *f* exaggeration.

exagérer *vt* to exaggerate.

examen *m* examination, survey, investigation.

examinateur *m* **-trice** *f* examiner.

examiner *vt* to examine, survey.

exaspération *f* exasperation.

exaspérer *vt* to exasperate.

exaucer *vt* to fulfil, grant.

excédent *m* surplus, excess.

excellent *adj* excellent.

exceller *vi* to excel.

excentricité *f* eccentricity.

excentrique *adj* eccentric.

excepté *adj* apart, aside; * *prép* except, but for.

exception *f* exception.

exceptionnel *adj* exceptional.

excès *m* excess, surplus.

excitant *m* stimulant; * *adj* exciting, stimulating.

excitation *f* excitation, stimulation; incitement.

exciter *vt* to excite, stimulate; **s'~** *vr* to get excited.

exclamation *f* exclamation.

exclamer (s') *vr* to exclaim.

exclure *vt* to exclude, oust, expel.

exclusif *adj* exclusive.

exclusion *f* exclusion, suspension.

exclusivité *f* exclusive rights.

excrément *m* excrement.

excursion *f* excursion, trip.

excursionniste *mf* tripper; walker.

excuse *f* excuse, pretext.

excuser *vt* to excuse, forgive; **s'~** *vr* to apologise for.

exécuter *vt* to execute, carry out, perform; to produce.

exécution *f* execution, carrying out, performance.

exemplaire *m* copy, archetype; * *adj* model, exemplary.

exemple *m* example, model, instance.

exempt *adj* exempt, free from.

exercer *vt* to exercise, perform, fulfil; **s'~** *vr* to practise.

exercice *m* exercise, practice, use; financial year.

exhiber *vt* to exhibit, show; to produce; **s'~** *vr* to show off; to expose oneself.

exhibition *f* exhibition, show; display.

exhibitionniste *mf* exhibitionist.

exigeant *adj* demanding, exacting.

exigence *f* demand, requirement; exigency.

exiger *vt* to demand, require.

exil *m* exile.

exilé *m* -e *f* exile;* *adj* exiled.

exiler *vt* to exile, banish; **s'~** *vr* to go into exile.

existence *f* existence, life.

exister *vi* to exist; to be.

exode *m* exodus; drift, loss.

exonération *f* exemption.

exonérer *vt* to exempt.

exorbitant *adj* exorbitant, outrageous.

exorciser *vt* to exorcise.

exotique *adj* exotic.

exotisme *m* exoticism.

expansif *adj* expansive, outgoing.

expansion *f* expansion, development.

expatrié *m* -e *f* expatriate; * *adj* expatriate.

expectative *f* expectation, hope; **être dans l'~** to be waiting (to see, to hear).

expédier *vt* to send, dispatch; to dispose of.

expéditeur *m* -trice *f* sender; shipper, consignor.

expédition *f* dispatch; consignment.

expérience *f* experience; experiment.

expérimental *adj* experimental.

expérimentateur *m* -trice *f* experimenter.

expérimentation *f* experimentation.

expérimenter *vt* to test; to experiment with.

expert *adj* expert, skilled in; * *m* expert; connoisseur; assessor.

expertise *f* expertise; expert appraisal.

expirer *vi* to breathe out, expire.

explicatif *adj* explanatory.

explication *f* explanation, analysis.

explicite *adj* explicit .

expliquer *vt* to explain, account for; to analyse.

exploitant *m* -e *f* farmer, smallholder.

exploitation *f* working; exploitation; operating; concern; smallholding.

exploiter *vt* to work, exploit; run, operate.

explorateur *m* -trice *f* explorer.

exploration *f* exploration.

explorer *vt* to explore.

exploser *vi* to explode.

explosif *adj* explosive; * *m* explosive.

explosion *f* explosion.

exportateur *m* -trice *f* exporter.

exportation *f* export, exportation.

exporter *vt* to export.

exposé *m* exposition, overview, statement.

exposer *vt* to display; to explain, state; to expose; **s'~** *vr* to expose oneself to, run the risk of.

exposition *f* display; exposition; exposure.

exprès *adj* express.

express *adj* fast; * *m* fast train.

expressif *adj* expressive.

expression *f* expression.

exprimer *vt* to express, voice; **s'~** *vr* to express oneself.

expulser *vt* to expel; to evict.

expulsion *f* expulsion; eviction.

exquis *adj* exquisite.

extase *f* ecstasy; rapture.

extasier (s') *vr* to go into ecstasies.

extension *f* extension; stretching; expansion.

exténuant *adj* exhausting.

exténuer *vt* to exhaust; **s'~** *vr* to exhaust oneself.

extérieur *m* exterior, outside; * *adj* outer, external, exterior.

extérioriser *vt* to show, express; to exteriorise.

extermination *f* extermination.

exterminer *vt* exterminate.

externe *adj* external, outer.

extincteur *m* extinguisher.

extinction *f* extinction, extinguishing.

extraction *f* extraction; mining.

extradition *f* extradition.

extraire *vt* to extract; to mine.

extrait *m* extract; (*jur*) abstract.

extraordinaire *adj* extraordinary.

extraterrestre *mf* extraterrestrial; * *adj* extraterrestrial.

extravagant *adj* extravagant, wild.

extraverti *m* **-e** *f* extrovert; * *adj* extrovert.

extrême *adj* extreme.

extrémiste *mf*, *adj* extremist.

extrémité *f* end, extremity, limit.

exubérance *f* exuberance.

exubérant *adj* exuberant.

F

fable *f* fable, story, tale.

fabricant *m* **-e** *f* manufacturer, maker.

fabrication *f* manufacture, production.

fabrique *f* factory.

fabriquer *vt* to manufacture; to forge; to fabricate.

fabuleux *adj* fabulous, mythical, legendary.

face *f* face, side, surface, aspect; **en ~** opposite, over the road; **~ à** facing; **faire ~ à** to confront, face up to.

facette *f* facet.

fâché *adj* angry; sorry.

fâcher *vt* to anger, make angry; to grieve; **se ~** *vr* to get angry.

fâcheux *adj* deplorable, regrettable.

facile *adj* easy; facile.

facilité *f* easiness, ease; ability; facility.

façon *f* way, fashion; make; imitation; **de toute ~** at any rate; **non merci, sans ~** no thanks, honestly.

façonner *vt* to shape, fashion, model; to till.

facteur *m* postman.

factice *adj* artificial, imitation.

facture *f* bill, invoice; construction, technique.

facturer *vt* to invoice, charge for.

facultatif *adj* optional.

faculté *f* faculty; power, ability; right.

fade *adj* insipid, bland, dull.

fagot *m* faggot, bundle of firewood.

faible *adj* weak, feeble; slight, poor.

faille *f* fault; flaw; weakness.

faillir *vi*: to come close to; to fail.

faillite *f* bankruptcy; collapse.

faim *f* hunger; appetite; famine.

fainéant *m* **-e** *f* idler, loafer.

faire *vt* to do; to make; **rien à ~!** nothing doing!; **se ~ à** to get used to; **s'en ~** to worry.

faisable *adj* feasible.

faisan *m* pheasant.

faisceau *m* bundle, stack; beam.

fait *m* event; fact; act.

faîte *m* summit; rooftop.

falaise *f* cliff.

falloir *vi*: to be necessary; **il faut, que tu partes** you must leave.

falsifier *vt* to falsify, alter.

fameux *adj* famous; excellent.

familial *adj* family, domestic.

familiariser *vt* to familiarise; **se ~** *vr* to familiarise o.s.

familiarité *f* familiarity.

familier *adj* familiar; colloquial; informal.

famille *f* family.

famine *f* famine.

fanatique *adj* fanatic; * *mf* fanatic; zealot.

fanatisme *m* fanaticism.

fané *adj* faded, withered.

faner *vt* to turn (hay); to fade; **se ~** *vr* to wither, fade.

fanfare *f* fanfare, flourish; brass band.

fantaisie *f* whim, extravagance; imagination.

fantasme *m* fantasy.

fantasmer *vi* to fantasise.

fantastique *adj* fantastic.

fantôme *m* ghost, phantom.

faon *m* fawn.

farce *f* joke, prank; farce.

farceur *m* **-euse** *f* joker; clown.

farcir *vt* to stuff, cram.

fard *m* make-up.

fardeau *m* load, burden.

farder *vt* to make up; to disguise; **se ~** *vr* to make o.s. up.

farine *f* flour.

farineux *adj* floury, powdery.

farouche *adj* shy, timid; unsociable; fierce.

fascination *f* fascination.

fasciner *vt* to fascinate, bewitch.

fascisme *m* fascism.

fasciste *mf, adj* fascist.

fastidieux *adj* tedious, boring.

fatal *adj* fatal, deadly; fateful.

fatalité *f* fatality; inevitability.

fatigant *adj* tiring, fatiguing.

fatigue *f* fatigue, tiredness.

fatigué *adj* tired, weary; overworked, strained.

fatiguer *vt* to tire; to overwork, strain; **se ~** *vr* to get tired.

faubourg *m* suburb.

faucher *vt* to reap; to flatten, knock down.

faucon *m* falcon, hawk.

faufiler *vt* to tack; to insinuate, introduce; **se ~** *vr* to worm one's way in.

faune *f* wildlife, fauna.

faussaire *mf* forger.

fausser vt to distort, alter; to warp.

faute f mistake, foul, fault; **~ de mieux** for lack of anything better.

fauteuil m armchair.

fautif m -**ive** f culprit, guilty party; * adj at fault, guilty; faulty, incorrect.

faux adj false, forged, fake; wrong; bogus.

faux-fuyant m evasion, equivocation.

faux-semblant m sham, pretence.

faveur f favour.

favorable adj favourable, sympathetic.

favori m -**te** f favourite; * adj favourite.

fébrile adj feverish, febrile.

fécond adj fertile; prolific, fruitful; creative.

féconder vt to impregnate; to fertilise, pollinate.

fécule f starch.

féculent adj starchy; * m starchy food.

fédéral adj federal.

fée f fairy.

feindre vt to feign, pretend.

feinte f dummy, feint.

fêlé adj cracked, hare-brained.

félicitation f congratulation.

féliciter vt to congratulate.

femelle f female.

féminin adj feminine, female.

féminisme m feminism.

féministe mf feminist; * adj feminist.

féminité f femininity.

femme f woman; wife; **~ de ménage** cleaning woman; **~ de chambre** chambermaid.

fendiller vt to chink, crack, craze; **se ~** vr to be covered in small cracks.

fendre vt to split, cleave, crack; **se ~** vr to crack.

fenêtre f window.

fente f crack, fissure; slot.

fer m iron, point, blade; **~ à cheval** horseshoe.

ferme adj firm, steady; * f farm.

fermé adj closed; exclusive; inscrutable.

fermentation f fermentation, fermenting.

fermenter vi to ferment, work.

fermer vt to close; block; turn off; **se ~** vr to close, shut up; to close one's mind to.

fermeté f firmness, steadiness.

fermeture f closing, shutting; latch; fastener.

fermier m -**ière** f farmer.

féroce adj ferocious, savage.

ferraille f scrap iron.

ferronnerie f ironworks; ironwork.

fertile adj fertile, productive.

fertilisation f fertilisation.

fertiliser vt to fertilise.

fertilité f fertility.

fervent adj fervent, ardent.

ferveur f fervour, ardour.

fesse f buttock.

festin m feast.

festival m festival.

fêter vt to celebrate, fête.

feu m fire; light; hearth; **en ~** on fire.

feuillage m foliage, greenery.

feuille f leaf.

feuilleter vt to leaf through.

feuilleton m serial, series.

feutre m felt; felt hat.

fève f broad bean.

fiabilité f accuracy; dependability.

fiable adj reliable; dependable.

fiançailles fpl engagement, betrothal.

fiancer (se) vr to become engaged.

fibreux *adj* fibrous, stringy.

ficeler *vt* to tie up.

ficelle *f* string; stick (bread).

fiche *f* card; sheet; certificate.

ficher *vt* to file, put on file.

fichier *m* catalogue; file.

fictif *adj* fictitious; imaginary.

fiction *f* imagination, fiction.

fidèle *adj* faithful, loyal.

fidélité *f* fidelity, loyalty.

fier (se) *vr* to trust, rely on.

fier *adj* proud, haughty; noble.

fierté *f* pride; arrogance.

fièvre *f* fever, temperature; excitement.

fiévreux *adj* feverish.

figer *vt* to congeal, freeze; to clot; **se ~** *vr* to congeal, freeze; to clot.

figue *f* fig.

figurant *m* **-e** *f* extra, walk-on; stooge.

figuratif *adj* figurative, representational.

figure *f* face; figure; illustration, diagram.

figurer *vt* to represent; * *vi* to appear, feature; **se ~** *vr* to imagine.

fil *m* thread; wire; cord; **~ de fer** wire; **~ à plomb** plumb line.

filature *f* spinning; mill; tailing.

file *f* line, queue; **à la ~** in line, in succession; **stationner en double ~** to double-park.

filer *vt* to spin; to tail; to draw out; * *vi* to run, trickle; to fly by; to make off.

filet *m* dribble, trickle; fillet; net.

filière *f* path; procedures; network.

fille *f* daughter, girl.

fillette *f* (small) girl.

filleul *m* **-e** *f* godson, godchild.

film *m* film, picture.

filmer *vt* to film.

filon *m* vein, seam.

fils *m* son.

filtre *m* filter.

filtrer *vt* to filter; to screen.

fin *f* end, finish; **prendre ~** to terminate, come to an end; * *adj* thin, fine; delicate.

final *adj* final.

financer *vt* to finance.

finesse *f* fineness; sharpness; neatness; delicacy.

finir *vt* to finish, complete; * *vi* to finish, end; to die.

finition *f* finish, finishing.

fissure *f* crack, fissure.

fixation *f* fixation; fixing, fastening.

fixer *vt* to fix, fasten; to arrange; **se ~** *vr* to settle.

flacon *m* bottle, flask.

flageolant *adj* shaky.

flair *m* sense of smell, nose; intuition.

flairer *vt* to smell, sniff; to scent.

flambeau *m* torch; candlestick.

flamboyant *adj* blazing; flamboyant.

flamboyer *vi* to blaze, flash, gleam.

flamme *f* flame; fervour; ardour.

flanc *m* flank, side.

flanelle *f* flannel.

flâner *vi* to stroll; to lounge about.

flatterie *f* flattery.

flatteur *m* **-euse** *f* flatterer.

flèche *f* arrow.

fléchir *vi* to bend, yield, weaken; * *vt* to bend, sway.

flegmatique *adj* phlegmatic.

flegme *m* composure, phlegm.

flétrir *vt* to wither, fade; to stigmatise; **se ~** *vr* to wither, wilt.

fleur *f* flower.

fleuri *adj* in bloom; flowery.

fleurir *vi* to blossom, flower; * *vt* to decorate with flowers.

fleuriste *mf* florist.

fleuve *m* river.

flexible *adj* flexible, pliant.

flic *m* (*fam*) cop, policeman.

flocon *m* fleck, flake.

flore *f* flora.

flot *m* stream, flood; floodtide; wave.

flotte *f* fleet; (*col*) rain.

flottement *m* wavering; vagueness, imprecision.

flotter *vi* to float; to drift; to wander; to waver.

flotteur *m* float.

flou *adj* blurred, hazy.

fluctuation *f* fluctuation.

fluide *adj* fluid, flowing.

fluorescent *adj* fluorescent.

fluorure *m* fluoride.

flûte *f* flute; French stick (bread).

flux *m* flood; flow; flux.

focaliser *vt* to focus; **se ~** *vr* to be focused on.

foetus *m* foetus.

foi *f* faith, trust.

foie *m* liver.

foin *m* hay.

foire *f* fair, trade fair.

fois *f* time, occasion.

folie *f* madness, insanity; extravagance.

foncé *adj* dark, deep (colours).

foncer *vi* to hammer along, rush at; * *vt* to make darker; (*tec*) to sink, bore.

foncièrement *adv* fundamentally, basically.

fonction *f* post, duty; function.

fonctionnaire *mf* civil servant.

fonctionnement *m* working, functioning, operation.

fonctionner *vi* to work, function, operate.

fond *m* bottom, back; **au ~** basically, in fact; **à ~** thoroughly, in depth; **dans le ~** in reality, basically; **~ de teint** foundation.

fondamental *adj* fundamental, basic.

fondamentalisme *m* fundamentalism.

fondamentaliste *mf*; * *adj* fundamentalist.

fondant *adj* thawing, melting.

fondateur *m* **-trice** *f* founder.

fondation *f* foundation.

fondement *m* foundation; ground.

fonder *vt* to found; to base.

fondre *vi* to melt; to vanish; to slim; * *vt* to melt; to cast; to merge.

fonds *m* business; fund; money; stock.

fondu *adj* melted; molten; cast.

fontaine *f* fountain, spring.

forage *m* drilling, boring.

force *f* strength, force, violence, energy; **à ~ de** by dint of.

forcené *adj* deranged, frenzied.

forcer *vt* to force, compel; track down; * *vi* to overdo, strain; **se ~** *vr* to force o.s. to.

forestier *adj* forest; forestry.

forêt *f* forest.

forfait *m* set price, package; (*sport*) withdrawal.

forfaitaire *adj* fixed, set, inclusive.

forge *f* forge, smithy.

forger *vt* to forge, form, mould.

forgeron *m* blacksmith, smith.

formaliser (se) *vr* to take offence at.

formalité *f* formality.

format *m* format, size.

formation *f* formation; training.

forme *f* form, shape; mould, fitness; **être en ~** to be on form.

formel *adj* definite, positive; formal.

former *vt* to form, make up; to train; **se ~** *vr* to form, gather; to train o.s.

formidable *adj* tremendous; fantastic.

formulaire *m* form.

formule *f* formula; phrase; system.

formuler *vt* to formulate; express.

fort *adj* strong; high; loud; pronounced * *adv* loudly; greatly; most; * *m* fort; strong point; (*mus*) forte.

forteresse *f* fortress.

fortifiant *m* tonic.

fortifier *vt* to fortify, strengthen.

fortune *f* fortune, luck.

fortuné *adj* wealthy; fortunate.

fosse *f* pit; grave.

fossé *m* ditch; gulf.

fossette *f* dimple.

fossile *m* fossil.

fou *adj*, *f* **folle** mad, wild; tremendous; erratic.

foudre *f* lightning.

foudroyer *vt* to strike (lightning).

fouet *m* whip; whisk.

fouetter *vt* to whip, flog.

fougère *f* fern.

fougue *f* ardour, spirit.

fouiller *vt* to search, scour.

foulard *m* scarf.

foule *f* crowd; masses, heaps.

four *m* oven; furnace; fiasco.

fourche *f* pitchfork; crotch.

fourchette *f* fork.

fourchu *adj* forked; cloven.

fourgon *m* coach, wagon, van.

fourmi *f* ant.

fourmiller *vi* to swarm, teem.

fourneau *m* stove.

fournir *vt* to supply, provide.

fourniture *f* supplying, provision.

fourré *adj* filled; fur-lined; * *m* thicket.

fourrer *vt* to stuff; to line.

fourrure *f* coat, fur.

foutu *adj* bloody, damned; lousy.

foyer *m* home; fireplace; club; focus.

fracas *m* crash; roar, din.

fraction *f* fraction, part.

fractionnement *m* splitting up, division.

fracture *f* fracture.

fracturer *vt* to fracture, break open.

fragile *adj* fragile, delicate.

fragilité *f* fragility, flimsiness.

fragment *m* fragment.

fragmentation *f* fragmentation; splitting up.

fragmenter *vt* to break up, fragment; **se ~** *vr* to fragment, break up.

fraîcheur *f* freshness, coolness.

frais *mpl* expenses; * *adj*, *f* **fraîche** fresh, cool.

fraise *f* strawberry.

framboise *f* raspberry.

franc *adj*, *f* **franche** frank, open; clear; absolute.

Français *m* Frenchman, **-e** *f* Frenchwoman.

français *adj* French; * *m* French.

franchir *vt* to clear, get over, cross.

frange *f* fringe; threshold.

frappant *adj* striking.

frapper *vt* to hit; to strike down; to infringe; * *vi* to strike, knock.

fraterniser *vi* to fraternise.

fraude *f* fraud, cheating.

frauduleux *adj* fraudulent.

frayeur *f* fright.

frein *m* brake; check.

freinage *m* braking; slowing down.

freiner *vi* to brake, slow down; * *vt* to slow down; to curb, check.

frêle *adj* flimsy, fragile.

frémir *vi* to quiver, tremble.

frémissement *m* shudder, quiver.

frénétique *adj* frenetic.

fréquence *f* frequency.

fréquent *adj* frequent.

frère *m* brother.

fric *m* (*fam*) cash, lolly.

friction *f* friction.

frigidaire *m* refrigerator.

frigide *adj* frigid.

frileux *adj* susceptible to cold; chilly.

frire *vt* to fry.

frisé *adj* curly, curly-haired.

friser *vi* to curl, be curly; * *vt* to curl; to graze, skim.

frisson *m* shiver, shudder.

frissonnement *m* shuddering, shivering.

frissonner *vi* to shudder, tremble, shiver.

frite *f* chip.

friteuse *f* chip pan.

frivole *adj* frivolous, shallow.

frivolité *f* frivolity.

froid *adj* cold, cool;* *m* cold; coolness; refrigeration.

froideur *f* coldness, chilliness.

froissement *m* creasing; rustling, rustle.

froisser *vt* to crease; to offend; **se ~** *vr* to crease; to take offence.

frôler *vt* to brush against; to verge on.

fromage *m* cheese.

front *m* forehead; face; front.

frontal *adj* frontal.

frontière *f* border, frontier.

frottement *m* rubbing, scraping.

frotter *vt* to rub, scrape.

fructifier *vi* to bear fruit.

frugal *adj* frugal.

fruit *m* fruit, result.

frustrer *vt* to frustrate, deprive.

fugace *adj* fleeting, transient.

fugitif *m* **-ive** *f* fugitive; * *adj* fugitive, runaway.

fuir *vi* to avoid; to flee; to leak.

fuite *f* flight, escape; leak.

fumée *f* smoke; vapour.

fumer *vi* to smoke, steam, give off smoke; * *vt* to smoke.

fumet *m* aroma.

fumeur *m* **-euse** *f* smoker.

fumier *m* dung, manure.

funérailles *fpl* funeral.

funeste *adj* disastrous; harmful.

fureur *f* fury; violence.

furie *f* fury, rage.

furieux *adj* furious, violent.

furtif *adj* furtive; stealthy.

fusée *f* rocket, missile.

fusible *m* fuse.

fusil *m* rifle, gun.

fusillade *f* fusillade; gunfire; shoot-out.

fusiller *vt* to shoot.

fusion *f* fusion; melting; merger; blending.

fusionner *vt* to merge, combine.

fût *m* trunk; shaft; barrel.

futé *adj* crafty, cunning.

futile *adj* futile.

futilité *f* futility.

futur *adj* future; * *m* intended, fiancé; future.

fuyant *adj* fleeting; evasive.

G

gabarit *m* size, build; calibre.

gâcher *vt* to mix; to waste.

gachette *f* trigger.

gâchis *m* mess.

gadget *m* gadget; gimmick.

gage *m* security; pledge; proof.

gagnant *m* -e *f* winner; * *adj* winning.

gagner *vt* to earn, to win, beat; to gain; * *vi* to win; to spread.

gaieté *f* cheerfulness, gaiety.

gain *m* earnings; gain, profit, benefit; saving.

gaine *f* girdle; sheath.

galant *adj* gallant, courteous.

galanterie *f* gallantry.

galaxie *f* galaxy.

galerie *f* gallery; tunnel.

galet *m* pebble.

Gallois *m* Welshman, -e *f* Welshwoman.

gallois *adj* Welsh; * *m* Welsh (language).

galon *m* braid; stripe.

galop *m* gallop; canter.

galoper *vi* to gallop; to run wild.

galvaniser *vt* to galvanise.

gamba *f* large prawn.

gamin *m* -e *f* kid, street urchin.

gamme *f* range; scale.

gangrène *f* gangrene.

gant *m* glove.

garage *m* garage.

garantie *f* guarantee, surety.

garantir *vt* to guarantee, secure.

garçon *m* boy; assistant; waiter.

garde *f* custody; guard; surveillance; * *m* guard, warder.

garde-boue *m* mudguard.

garde-chasse *m* gamekeeper.

garde-fou *m* railing, parapet; safeguard.

garder *vt* to look after; to stay in; to keep on.

garderie *f* day nursery.

garde-robe *f* wardrobe.

gardien *m* -ne *f* guard, guardian, warden; protector.

gare *f* rail station; (*mar*) basin; depot.

garer *vt* to park; to dock; **se ~** *vr* to avoid, steer clear of.

gargarisme *m* gargle.

gargouillement *m* gurgling; rumbling.

gargouiller *vi* to gurgle; to rumble.

garnir *vt* to fit with; to trim, decorate.

garnison *f* (*mil*) garrison.

garniture *f* trimming, lining; garnish.

gars *m* (*fam*) lad; bloke.

gaspillage *m* waste; squandering.

gaspiller *vt* to waste, squander.

gastrique *adj* gastric.

gâteau *m* cake.

gâter *vt* to ruin; to spoil; **se ~** *vr* to go bad, go off.

gâteux *adj* senile; (*fam*) doddering.

gauche *adj* left; awkward, clumsy: * *f* left; left wing.

gaucher *adj* left-handed.

gaufre *f* waffle.

gaz *m invar* gas; fizz; wind.

gaze *f* gauze.

gazelle *f* gazelle.

gazon *m* lawn; turf.

gazouiller *vi* to chirp, warble.

géant *m* giant, **-e** *f* giantess.

geindre *vi* to groan; to whine.

gel *m* frost; gel.

gélatine *f* gelatine.

gelé *adj* frozen; cold, unresponsive.

gelée *f* frost; jelly.

geler *vi* to freeze, be frozen; * *vt* to freeze, turn to ice; to suspend.

gélule *f* capsule.

gémir *vi* to groan, moan.

gémissement *m* groan, moan; groaning.

gênant *adj* annoying; awkward.

gencive *f* gum.

gendarme *m* policeman; gendarme.

gendarmerie *f* police force, constabulary.

gendre *m* son-in-law.

gêne *f* discomfort; trouble; embarrassment.

généalogie *f* genealogy.

généalogique *adj* genealogical.

gêner *vt* to bother; to hinder; to make uneasy; **se ~** *vr* to get in each other's way.

général *adj* general, broad; common; * *m* general, (*thea*) dress rehearsal.

généralisation *f* generalisation.

généraliser *vt* to generalise; **se ~** *vr* to become widespread.

généraliste *m* general practitioner.

généralité *f* majority; general points.

générateur *m* generator.

génération *f* generation.

générer *vt* to generate

généreux *adj*, *f* **-euse** generous; noble; magnanimous.

générosité *f* generosity; nobility; magnanimity.

génétique *adj* genetic.

génial *adj* inspired, of genius.

génie *m* genius; spirit; genie.

génital *adj* genital.

genou *m* knee.

genre *m* kind, type; gender; genre.

gens *mpl* people, folk.

gentil *adj*, *f* **-le** kind; good; pleasant.

gentillesse *f* kindness; favour.

géographie *f* geography.

géologie *f* geology.

géologue *mf* geologist.

géométrie *f* geometry.

géranium *m* geranium.

gérant *m* **-e** *f* manager.

gerbe *f* sheaf, bundle; collection.

gercer *vt* to chap, crack; **se ~** *vr* to chap, crack.

gerçure *f* (small) crack.

gérer *vt* to manage, administer.

germe *m* germ; seed.

gestation *f* gestation.

geste *m* gesture; act, deed.

gesticuler *vi* to gesticulate.

gestion *f* management, administration.

ghetto *m* ghetto.

gibier *m* game; prey.

gicler *vi* to spurt, squirt.

gicleur *m* jet.

gifle *f* slap, smack.

gifler *vt* to slap, smack.

gigantesque *adj* gigantic, immense.

gilet *m* waistcoat.

gingembre *m* ginger.

girafe *f* giraffe.

girouette *f* weather vane.

gisement *m* deposit; mine; pool.

gitan *m* **-e** *f* gipsy.

gîte *m* shelter; home.

givre *m* frost, rime.

givré *adj* covered in frost.

glace *f* ice; ice cream; mirror.

glacé *adj* icy; frozen; glazed; chilly.

glacer *vt* to freeze; to chill; to glaze.

glacier *m* glacier; ice cream maker.

glacière *f* icebox.

glaçon *m* icicle; ice cube.

glaise *f* clay.

gland *m* acorn.

glande *f* gland.

glauque *adj* murky; shabby, run-down.

glissade *f* slide, skid.

glissant *adj* slippery.

glissement *m* sliding; gliding; downturn, downswing.

glisser *vi* to slide, slip, skid.

glissière *f* slide; runner.

global *adj* global, overall.

globe *m* globe, sphere; earth.

globule *m* globule; corpuscle.

gloire *f* glory; distinction; celebrity.

glorieux *adj* glorious.

glorifier *vt* to glory, honour; **se ~** *vr* to glory in; to boast.

glouton *m* **-ne** *f* glutton; * *adj* gluttonous, ravenous.

glucose *m* glucose.

glycérine *f* glycerine.

gobelet *m* beaker, tumbler.

gober *vt* to swallow; to fall for.

goéland *m* gull.

goinfre *m* pig; * *adj* piggish.

golf *m* golf.

golfeur *m* **-euse** *f* golfer.

gomme *f* gum; rubber, eraser.

gommer *vt* to rub out; to gum.

gond *m* hinge.

gondoler *vi* to crinkle, warp, buckle; **se ~** *vr* to crinkle; to split one's sides laughing.

gonflement *m* inflation, swelling.

gonfler *vt* to pump up, inflate; **se ~** *vr* to swell; to be puffed up.

gorge *f* throat.

gorgée *f* sip, gulp.

gorille *m* gorilla.

gosier *m* throat, gullet.

gosse *mf* (*fam*) kid.

goudron *m* tar.

gouffre *m* gulf, chasm, abyss.

goulu *adj* greedy, gluttonous.

goupille *f* pin.

gourd *adj* numb (with cold).

gourde *f* gourd; flask.

gourmand *adj* greedy.

gourmandise *f* greed, greediness.

gourmet *m* gourmet.

gousse *f* pod.

goût *m* taste; liking; style.

goûter *vt* to taste; to appreciate; * *vi* to have a snack; to taste good; * *m* snack.

goutte *f* drop; dram; gout.

gouttière *f* gutter; drainpipe.

gouvernail *m* rudder; helm.

gouvernement *m* government.

gouverner *vt* to govern, rule; to control; to steer.

gouverneur *m* governor.

grâce *f* grace; favour; mercy; pardon; **~ à** thanks to.

gracier *vt* to pardon.

gracieux *adj* gracious.

grade *m* rank; grade; degree.

gradé *m* officer; * *adj* promoted.

gradin *m* tier; step; terrace.

graduel *adj* gradual; progressive;.

graduer *vt* to step up; to graduate.

grain *m* grain, seed; bead.

graine *f* seed.

graisse *f* grease, fat.

graisser *vt* to grease, lubricate.

grammaire *f* grammar.

grammatical *adj* grammatical.

gramme *m* gram.

grand *adj* big; tall; great; leading; **pas ~-chose** not a lot, not up to much.

grandeur *f* size; greatness; magnitude.

grandiose *adj* imposing, grandiose.

grandir *vi* to grow bigger, increase; * *vt* to magnify; exaggerate.

grand-mère *f* grandmother.

grand-père *m* grandfather.

grand-parents *mpl* grandparents

granit(e) *m* granite.

granuleux *adj* granular; grainy.

graphique *m* graph; * *adj* graphic.

graphite *m* graphite.

grappe *f* cluster, bunch.

gras *adj*, *f* **-se** fatty; fat; greasy; crude.

gratin *m* cheese dish, gratin.

gratis *adv* free, gratis.

gratter *vt* to scratch, scrape.

gratuit *adj* free, gratuitous; disinterested.

grave *adj* grave, solemn.

graver *vt* to engrave, imprint.

graveur *m* engraver, woodcutter.

gravier *m* gravel.

gravir *vt* to climb.

gravité *f* gravity.

gravure *f* engraving, carving.

gré *m*: liking, taste; **au ~ de** depending on, at the mercy of; **bon ~ mal ~** like it or not, willy-nilly; **savoir ~** to be grateful.

greffe *f* transplant, graft.

greffer *vt* to transplant, graft.

grégaire *adj* gregarious.

grêle *f* hail.

grêlon *m* hailstone.

grenade *f* pomegranate; grenade.

grenouille *f* frog.

grésiller *vi* to sizzle; splutter.

grève *f* strike; shore.

gribouillage *m* scrawl, scribble.

gribouiller *vi* to doodle; * *vt* to scribble, scrawl.

griffe *f* claw.

griffer *vt* to scratch.

griffonner *vt* to scribble, jot down.

grignoter *vi* to nibble at, pick at; * *vt* to nibble at; to eat away.

gril *m* grill pan; rack.

grillade *f* grilled meat.

grille-pain *m invar* toaster.

griller *vt* to toast, scorch; to put bars on; * *vi* to toast, grill.

grillon *m* cricket.

grimper *vi* to climb up.

grincer *vi* to grate, creak.

grincheux *adj* grumpy.

grippe *f* flu, influenza.

grippé *adj* suffering from flu.

gris *adj* grey.

griser *vt* to intoxicate; **se ~** *vr* to get drunk.

grive *f* thrush.

grognement *m* grunt, grunting.

grogner *vi* to grumble, moan.

grognon *m* grumbler, moaner, *adj* grumpy, surly.

grommeler *vi* to mutter; to grumble; * *vt* to mutter.

grondement *m* rumbling, growling.

gronder *vt* to scold; * *vi* to rumble, growl.

gros *adj*, *f* **-se** big; fat; thick; serious; heavy; coarse; **en ~** in bulk; * *m* bulk; wholesale; fat man.

groseille *f* currant.

grossesse *f* pregnancy.

grosseur *f* thickness; lump; fatness.

grossier *adj* coarse; unrefined; base.

grossièreté *f* rudeness; coarseness.

grossir *vi* to get fatter; to swell, grow; * *vt* to magnify; to exaggerate.

grossiste *mf* wholesaler.

grotte *f* cave; grotto.

grouiller *vi* to mill about; to swarm; **se ~** *vr* (*fam*) to get a move on.

groupe *m* group; party; cluster.

grouper *vt* to group together; to bulk; **se ~** *vr* to gather.

grue *f* crane.

grumeau *m* lump.

gruyère *m* gruyère (cheese).

guêpe *f* wasp.

guère *adv* hardly, scarcely.

guéridon *m* pedestal table.

guérir *vi* to get better; to heal; * *vt* to cure, heal; **se ~** *vr* to get better; to recover srom.

guérison *f* recovery; curing.

guerre *f* war; warfare.

guerrier *m* **-ière** *f* warrior.

guet *m* watch; **faire le ~** to be on the watch.

guetter *vt* to watch; to lie in wait for.

gueule *f* (*fam*) mouth; face; muzzle.

gueuler *vi* (*fam*) to bawl; bellow.

guichet *m* counter; ticket office, booking office.

guichetier *m* **-ière** *f* counter clerk.

guidage *m* guides; guidance.

guide *m* guide.

guider *vt* to guide; **se ~** *vr* to be guided by.

guidon *m* handlebars.

guignol *m* puppet; puppet show.

guindé *adj* stiff, uptight.

guirlande *f* garland.

guise *f* manner, way; **en ~ de** by way of; **à ta ~** as you please.

guitare *f* guitar.

gymnase *m* gymnasium.

gymnastique *f* gymnastics.

H

habile *adj* skilful, skilled; clever.

habileté *f* skill, skilfulness; clever move.

habiliter *vt* to qualify; to authorise.

habillement *m* clothing, dress, outfit.

habiller *vt* to dress, clothe; **s'~** *vr* to get dressed.

habit *m* clothes; apparel; dresscoat; outfit.

habitant *m* **-e** *f* inhabitant; occupant; dweller.

habitat *m* habitat; housing conditions.

habitation *f* dwelling; residence; house.

habité *adj* manned.

habiter *vi* to live; * *vt* to live in; occupy.

habitude *f* habit, custom, routine.

habituel *adj* usual, customary.

habituer *vt* to accustom; to teach; **s'~** *vr* to get used to.

hache *f* axe, hatchet.

hacher *vt* to chop, mince.

hagard *adj* wild; haggard; distraught.

haie *f* hedge.

haine *f* hatred.

haineux *adj* full of hatred; malevolent.

haïr *vt* to hate, detest.

hâle *m* tan, sunburn.

hâlé *adj* tanned, sunburnt.

haleine *f* breath, breathing.

haleter *vi* to pant, gasp for breath.

halte *f* stop, break; stopping place.

haltère *f* dumbbell.

hameçon *m* fish-hook.

handicap *m* handicap.

handicaper *vt* to handicap

hangar *m* shed, barn; hangar.

hanter *vt* to haunt.

harassant *adj* exhausting, wearing.

harcèlement *m* harassment; pestering.

harceler *vt* to harass; to pester; to plague.

hardi *adj* bold, daring; brazen.

hareng *m* herring.

hargne *f* spite.

hargneux *adj* aggressive, belligerent.

haricot *m* bean.

harmonie *f* harmony; wind section.

harmonieux *adj* harmonious; well-matched.

harmoniser *vt* to harmonise; **s'~** *vr* to be in harmony.

harnais *m* harness; equipment.

harpe *f* harp.

hasard *m* chance; accident; hazard; risk.

hasardeux *adj* hazardous, risky.

hâte *f* haste; impatience.

hâtif *adj* precocious; early; hasty.

hausse *f* rise, increase.

hausser *vt* to raise; to heighten.

haut *adj* high, tall; upper; superior.

hautain *adj* haughty, lofty.

hautbois *m* oboe.

hauteur *f* height; elevation; haughtiness; bearing.

haut-parleur *m* loudspeaker.

hebdomadaire *adj*; * *m* weekly.

hébergement *m* accommodation; lodging.

héberger *vt* to accommodate, lodge.

hélice *f* propeller; helix.

hélicoptère *m* helicopter.

hélium *m* helium.

hémisphère *m* hemisphere.

hémoglobine *f* haemoglobin.

hémophile *adj* haemophiliac.

hémophilie *f* haemophilia.

hémorragie *f* bleeding, haemorrhage.

hémorroïde *f* haemorrhoid, pile.

henné *m* henna.

hépatite *f* hepatitis.

herbe *f* grass; **en ~** in the blade.

héréditaire *adj* hereditary.

hérédité *f* heredity; heritage; right of inheritance.

hérésie *f* heresy.

hérétique *adj* heretical.

hérissé *adj* bristling; spiked.

hérisser *vt* to bristle; to spike; *** se ~** *vr* to stand on end; to bristle.

hérisson *m* hedgehog.

héritage *m* inheritance; heritage, legacy.

hériter *vi* to inherit.

héritier *m* heir **-ière** *f* heiress.

hermaphrodite *m* hermaphrodite; ***** *adj* hermaphrodite.

hermine *f* ermine; stoat.

hernie *f* hernia, rupture.

héroïne *f* heroine; heroin.

héroïque *adj* heroic.

héroïsme *m* heroism.

héron *m* heron.

héros *m* hero.

herpès *m* herpes; cold sore.

hésitant *adj* hesitant.

hésitation *f* hesitation.

hésiter *vi* to hesitate.

hétérosexuel *adj* heterosexual.

hêtre *m* beech.

heure *f* hour; time of day; **de bonne ~** early; **tout à l'~** a short time ago, just now.

heureux *adj* lucky; happy.

heurter *vt* to strike, hit; to jostle.

hibernation *f* hibernation.

hibou *m* owl.

hideux *adj* hideous.

hier *adv* yesterday.

hiérarchie *f* hierarchy.

hiérarchique *adj* hierarchical.

hilarant *adj* hilarious, side-splitting.

hilarité *f* hilarity, laughter.

hindouisme *m* Hinduism.

hippocampe *m* sea horse.

hippodrome *m* racecourse.

hippopotame *m* hippopotamus.

hirondelle *f* swallow.

hirsute *adj* dishevelled, tousled

hisser *vt* to hoist, haul up.

histoire *f* history; story; business; **~ de dire** just to say.

historique *adj* historic; historical.

hiver *m* winter.

hivernal *adj* winter; wintry.

hocher *vt* to nod; to shake one's head.

hochet *m* rattle; toy.

holocauste *m* holocaust.

homard *m* lobster.

homéopathie *f* homeopathy.

homicide *m* homicide.

hommage *m* homage, tribute; **rendre ~ à** to pay homage to.

homme *m* man.

homme-grenouille *m* frogman.

homosexuel *m* **-le** *f* homosexual.

honnête *adj* honest; decent; honourable.

honnêteté *f* honesty, decency.

honneur *m* honour; integrity; credit; **en l'~ de** in honour of.

honorable *adj* honourable; reputable.

honoraire *adj* honorary.

honoraires *mpl* fees.

honorer *vt* to honour; to esteem; to do credit to; **s'~** *vr*: **s'~ de** to pride oneself on.

honte *f* shame, disgrace.

honteux *adj* shameful; disgraceful.

hôpital *m* hospital.

horaire *m* timetable; ***** *adj* hourly.

horizon *m* horizon.

horizontal *adj* horizontal.

horloge *f* clock.

hormone *f* hormone.
horoscope *m* horoscope.
horreur *f* horror.
horrible *adj* horrible; dreadful.
horrifier *vt* to horrify.
hors *prép* outside; beyond; save; except;
~ **série** incomparable, outstanding;
special issue.
hors-bord *m invar* speedboat.
hors-jeu *m invar* offside.
horticulteur *m* horticulturist.
horticulture *f* horticulture.
hospice *m* home, asylum; hospice.
hospitalier *adj* hospital; hospitable.
hospitalisation *f* hospitalisation.
hospitaliser *vt* to hospitalise.
hospitalité *f* hospitality.
hostie *f* host.
hostile *adj* hostile.
hostilité *f* hostility.
hôte *m* **hôtesse** *f* host; landlord.
hôtel *m* hotel.
hôtellerie *f* inn; hotel business.
hotte *f* basket.
houblon *m* hop.
houille *f* coal.
houleux *adj* stormy; turbulent.
houppe *f* tuft; tassel.
houx *m* holly.
hublot *m* porthole.
huer *vt* to boo.
huile *f* oil; petroleum.
huit *adj*, *m* eight.
huitaine *f* eight or so.
huitième *adj* eighth; * *mf* eighth.
huître *f* oyster.
humain *adj* human; humane; hu-
manely; * *m* human.
humanisme *m* humanism.

humanitaire *adj* humanitarian.
humanité *f* humanity.
humble *adj* humble; modest.
humecter *vt* to dampen, moisten.
humeur *f* mood, humour; temper.
humide *adj* humid.
humidité *f* humidity.
humiliation *f* humiliation.
humilier *vt* to humiliate.
humoristique *adj* humorous.
humour *m* humour.
hurlement *m* roar, yell; howl.
hurler *vi*; * *vt* to roar, yell.
hutte *f* hut.
hybride *adj* hybrid; * *m* hybrid.
hydratant *adj* moisturising.
hydraulique *adj* hydraulic.
hydravion *m* seaplane.
hydrogène *m* hydrogen.
hyène *f* hyena.
hygiène *f* hygienics; hygiene.
hygiénique *adj* hygienic.
hymne *m* hymn.
hypermétrope *adj* long-sighted; * *mf*
long-sighted person.
hypnose *f* hypnosis.
hypnotique *adj* hypnotic.
hypnotiser *vt* to hypnotise.
hypocondriaque *mf* hypochondriac;
* *adj* hypochondriac.
hypocrisie *f* hypocrisy.
hypocrite *mf* hypocrite; * *adj* hypocritical.
hypothèque *f* mortgage.
hypothéquer *vt* to mortgage.
hypothétique *adj* hypothetical.
hystérie *f* hysteria.
hystérique *mf* hysterical; * *adj* hysteric.

I

iceberg *m* iceberg.

idéal *adj;* * *m* ideal.

idéaliser *vt* to idealise.

idéaliste *adj* idealistic; * *mf* idealist.

idée *f* idea.

identifier *vt* to identify; **s'~** *vr* to identify with.

identique *adj* identical.

identité *f* identity; similarity.

idiot *m* -e *f* idiot, fool; * *adj* idiotic, stupid.

idole *f* idol.

igloo *m* igloo.

ignorance *f* ignorance.

ignorant *adj* ignorant; unacquainted; uninformed.

ignorer *vt* to be ignorant of; to be unaware of; to ignore.

il *pn* he, it.

île *f* island, isle.

illégal *adj* illegal; unlawful.

illégitime *adj* illegitimate; unwarranted.

illettré *adj* illiterate.

illicite *adj* illicit.

illimité *adj* unlimited; limitless.

illisible *adj* illegible, unreadable.

illogique *adj* illogical.

illumination *f* illumination, lighting.

illusion *f* illusion

illusoire *adj* illusory; illusive.

illustration *f* illustration.

illustre *adj* illustrious, renowned.

illustrer *vt* to illustrate.

îlot *m* islet; block (flats).

image *f* image, picture; reflection.

imagé *adj* colourful; full of imagery.

imaginaire *adj* imaginary.

imagination *f* imagination.

imaginer *vt* to imagine; to suppose; to devise; **s'~** *vr* to imagine o.s.; to think.

imbattable *adj* unbeatable.

imbécile *mf* idiot, imbecile; * *adj* stupid, idiotic.

imbiber *vt* to soak, moisten.

imbriquer *vt* to fit into; to overlap; **s'~** *vr* to be linked.

imitation *f* imitation; mimicry; forgery.

imiter *vt* to imitate.

immaculé *adj* spotless, immaculate.

immangeable *adj* inedible.

immatriculation *f* registration.

immatriculer *vt* to register.

immédiat *adj* immediate; instant; **~ement** *adv* immediately, instantly.

immense *adj* immense, boundless.

immersion *f* immersion; submersion.

immeuble *m* building; block of flats; real estate.

immigrant *m* -e *f* immigrant.

immigration *f* immigration.

immigré *m* -e *f* immigrant.

imminent *adj* imminent, impending.

immobile *adj* motionless, still.

immobilier *adj* property; * *m* property business.

immobiliser *vt* to immobilise; to bring to a standstill; **s'~** *vr* to stop, stand still.

immobilité *f* stillness; immobility; permanence.

immonde *adj* squalid; base, vile.

immoral *adj* immoral.

immoralité *f* immorality.

immortaliser *vt* to immortalise.

immortel *adj* immortal.

immuniser *vt* to immunise.

immunité *f* immunity.

impact *m* impact.

impair *adj* odd, uneven.

impardonnable *adj* unforgivable, unpardonable.

imparfait *adj* imperfect.

impartial *adj* impartial.

impartialité *f* impartiality.

impasse *f* dead end, cul-de-sac; impasse.

impatience *f* impatience.

impatient *adj* impatient.

impatienter *vt* to irritate, annoy; **s'~** *vr* to grow, get impatient.

impeccable *adj* perfect; faultless, impeccable.

impénétrable *adj* impenetrable; inscrutable.

impensable *adj* unthinkable.

impératif *adj* imperative; mandatory; * *m* requirement; demand; constraint.

impératrice *f* empress.

imperceptible *adj* imperceptible.

imperfection *f* imperfection.

impérial *adj* imperial.

impérialisme *m* imperialism.

impersonnel *adj* impersonal.

impertinence *f* impertinence.

impertinent *adj* impertinent.

imperturbable *adj* unshakeable; imperturbable.

impétueux *adj* impetuous.

impitoyable *adj* merciless, pitiless.

implacable *adj* implacable.

implantation *f* implantation; establishment; introduction.

implanter *vt* to introduce; to establish; to implant; **s'~** *vr* to be established; to become implanted.

implication *f* implication; involvement.

implicite *adj* implicit.

impliquer *vt* to imply; to necessitate; to implicate; **s'~** *vr* to get involved in one's work.

impoli *adj* impolite, rude.

impopulaire *adj* unpopular.

importance *f* importance, significance; size.

important *adj* important, significant; sizeable.

importateur *m* **-trice** *f* importer; * *adj* importing.

importer *vt* to import; * *vi* to matter; **que m'importe que** what does it matter to me that; **peu importe** whatever; **n'im-porte qui** anybody; **n'importe quoi** anything; **n'importe comment** anyhow; **n'importe quel** any.

imposant *adj* imposing; stately.

imposer *vt* to impose, lay down; **s'~** *vr* to be essential; to assert o.s.

impossibilité *f* impossibility.

impossible *adj* impossible.

imposteur *m* impostor.

impôt *m* tax, duty.

impotent *adj* disabled, crippled.

imprégner *vt* impregnate; to permeate; to imbue.

impression *f* feeling, impression.

impressionnant *adj* impressive; upsetting.

impressionner *vt* to impress; to upset.

imprévisible *adj* unforeseeable; unpredictable.

imprévu *adj* unforeseen, unexpected.

imprimante *f* printer.

imprimé *adj* printed; * *m* printed form; printed material.

imprimerie *f* printing works; printing house.

imprimeur *m* printer.

improbable *adj* improbable, unlikely.

improductif *adj* unproductive.

improvisation *f* improvisation.

improviser *vt* to improvise.

improviste *adv*: **à l'~** unexpectedly.

imprudence *f* carelessness, imprudence.

impudence *f* impudence; shamelessness.

impudique *adj* immodest, shameless.

impuissance *f* powerlessness, helplessness.

impuissant *adj* powerless, helpless.

impulsif *adj* impulsive.

impulsion *f* impulse; impetus.

impunément *adv* with impunity.

impur *adj* impure; mixed.

impureté *f* impurity.

inacceptable *adj* unacceptable.

inaccessible *adj* inaccessible; obscure; incomprehensible.

inaccoutumé *adj* unusual.

inachevé *adj* unfinished, uncompleted.

inactif *adj* inactive, idle.

inaction *f* inactivity, idleness.

inactivité *f* inactivity.

inadapté *adj* unsuitable; maladjusted.

inadéquat *adj* inadequate.

inaltérable *adj* stable; unchanging, permanent.

inanimé *adj* inanimate; unconscious.

inaperçu *adj*: unnoticed.

inappréciable *adj* invaluable, inestimable.

inapte *adj* unfit.

inattaquable *adj* unassailable; irrefutable.

inattendu *adj* unexpected, unforeseen.

inattention *f* inattention, lack of attention.

inauguration *f* inauguration, opening.

inavouable *adj* shameful; undisclosable.

incapable *adj* incapable; incompetent.

incapacité *f* incompetence; disability; **être dans l'~ de** to be unable to do.

incendiaire *adj* incendiary; inflammatory; * *mf* arsonist.

incendie *m* fire, blaze.

incendier *vt* to set alight; to kindle.

incertain *adj* uncertain, unsure.

incertitude *f* uncertainty; **être dans l'~** to feel uncertain.

incessant *adj* incessant, ceaseless.

inceste *m* incest.

incident *m* incident, point of law.

incinération *f* incineration; cremation.

incitation *f* incitement; incentive.

inciter *vt* to incite, urge.

inclinaison *f* incline; gradient.

incliner *vt* to bend; to slope; to bow.

inclure *vt* to include; to insert.

inclus *adj* enclosed; included; **ci-~** herein enclosed.

incohérence *f* incoherence; inconsistency.

incohérent *adj* incoherent; inconsistent.

incolore *adj* colourless; clear.

incommode *adj* inconvenient; awkward.

incommoder *vt* to disturb, bother.

incomparable *adj* incomparable.

incompétence *f* incompetence.

incompétent *adj* incompetent; inexpert.

incomplet *adj* incomplete.

incompréhensible *adj* incomprehensible.

incompréhension *f* lack of understanding.

inconcevable *adj* inconceivable.

inconciliable *adj* irreconcilable.

inconditionnel *adj* unconditional; unreserved; unquestioning.

inconfortable *adj* uncomfortable; awkward.

incongru *adj* unseemly; incongruous.

inconnu *m* -**e** *f* stranger, unknown person; * *adj* unknown.

inconsciemment *adv* unconsciously; thoughtlessly.

inconscience *f* unconsciousness; thoughtlessness.

inconscient *adj* unconscious; thoughtless, reckless; * *m* subconscious, unconscious.

inconsidéré *adj* inconsiderate; thoughtless.

inconsistant *adj* flimsy; colourless; watery.

inconsolable *adj* disconsolate; inconsolable.

inconstant *adj* fickle; variable, inconstant.

incontestable *adj* incontestable, unquestionable.

inconvénient *m* drawback, inconvenience.

incorporer *vt* to incorporate, integrate.

incorrect *adj* faulty, incorrect.

incorrigible *adj* incorrigible.

incorruptible *adj* incorruptible.

incrédule *adj* incredulous; * *mf* unbeliever, non-believer.

incroyable *adj* incredible; unbelievable.

inculpé *m* -**e** *f* accused; * *adj* accused.

incurable *adj* incurable; ~**ment** *adv* incurably, hopelessly.

indéchiffrable *adj* indecipherable; incomprehensible.

indécis *adj* indecisive; unsettled; undefined.

indéfini *adj* undefined; indefinite.

indéfinissable *adj* indefinable.

indemne *adj* unharmed, unhurt.

indéniable *adj* undeniable, indisputable.

indépendance *f* independence.

indépendant *adj* independent.

indestructible *adj* indestructible.

indéterminé *adj* undetermined; unspecified; undecided.

index *m* index; index finger.

indexer *vt* to index.

indication *f* indication; piece of information; instruction.

indice *m* indication; clue; sign.

indifférence *f* indifference.

indifférent *adj* indifferent; immaterial.

indigène *mf* native; local; * *adj* indigenous, native.

indigeste *adj* indigestible.

indigestion *f* indigestion.

indigne *adj* unworthy; undeserving.

indigner *vt* to annoy, make indignant; **s'~** *vr* to be indignant.

indiquer *vt* to indicate, point out; to tell.

indirect *adj* indirect; circumstantial; collateral.

indiscipliné *adj* undisciplined.

indiscret *adj* indiscreet; inquisitive.

indiscutable *adj* indisputable; unquestionable.

indispensable *adj* indispensable; essential.

indisponible *adj* unavailable.

indistinct *adj* indistinct, vague.

individu *m* individual.

individuel *adj* individual.

indolore *adj* painless.

indubitable *adj* indubitable; certain.

indulgence *f* indulgence; le-niency.

indulgent *adj* indulgent; lenient.

industrialisation *f* industrialisation.

industrie *f* industry; dexterity, ingenuity.

industriel *m* **-le** *f* industrialist, manufacturer; * *adj* industrial.

inébranlable *adj* steadfast, unwavering.

inefficace *adj* ineffective; inefficient.

inefficacité *f* ineffectiveness; inefficiency.

inégal *adj* unequal; uneven; irregular.

inégalité *f* inequality; difference, disparity.

inépuisable *adj* inexhaustible.

inerte *adj* inert; lifeless.

inertie *f* inertia, apathy.

inespéré *adj* unexpected.

inestimable *adj* inestimable, invaluable.

inévitable *adj* inevitable, unavoidable.

inexact *adj* inexact, inaccurate.

inexactitude *f* inaccuracy.

inexistant *adj* nonexistent.

inexpérimenté *adj* inexperienced; inexpert.

infaillible *adj* infallible.

infâme *adj* infamous; base, vile.

infantile *adj* infantile, childish.

infatigable *adj* indefatigable, tireless.

infect *adj* vile; revolting; filthy.

infecter *vt* to infect; to contaminate; **s'~** *vr* to become infected.

infection *f* infection.

inférieur *adj* inferior; lower.

infériorité *f* inferiority.

infester *vt* to infest, overrun.

infidélité *f* infidelity.

infiltration *f* infiltration.

infini *adj* infinite; interminable.

infirme *adj* feeble; crippled, disabled.

infirmerie *f* infirmary; sick bay.

infirmier *m* **-ière** *f* nurse.

infirmité *f* disability; infirmity.

inflammation *f* inflammation.

inflation *f* inflation.

inflexible *adj* inflexible, rigid.

infliger *vt* to inflict; to impose.

influence *f* influence.

influencer *vt* to influence, sway.

informaticien *m* **-ne** *f* computer scientist.

informatique *f* computing; data processing; * *adj* computer.

informer *vt* to inform, tell.

infrarouge *adj* infrared.

infructueux *adj* fruitless, unsuccessful.

ingénieur *m* engineer.

ingénieux *adj* ingenious, clever.

ingénu *adj* ingenuous, naive.

ingrat *adj* ungrateful; unprofitable.

ingratitude *f* ingratitude.

ingrédient *m* ingredient; component.

inhabité *adj* uninhabited, unoccupied.

inhabituel *adj* unusual, unaccustomed.

inhumain *adj* inhuman.

inimaginable *adj* unimaginable.

inimitable *adj* inimitable.

initial *adj* initial.

initiation *f* initiation.

initiative *f* initiative; enterprise.

injecter *vt* to inject.

injection *f* injection.

injure *f* injury; insult.

injurier *vt* to abuse; insult.

injuste *adj* unjust, unfair.

injustice *f* injustice.

injustifié *adj* unjustified.

inné *adj* innate, inborn.

innocence *f* innocence.

innocent *m* -e *f* innocent person; simpleton; * *adj* innocent.

innocenter *vt* to clear, prove innocent.

innovation *f* innovation.

inoffensif *adj* inoffensive, harmless.

inonder *vt* to flood, inundate.

inoubliable *adj* unforgettable.

inouï *adj* unprecedented, unheard of.

inox *m* stainless steel.

inqualifiable *adj* unspeakable.

inquiet *adj* worried, anxious, uneasy.

inquiéter *vt* to worry, disturb; **s'~** *vr* to get worried.

insaisissable *adj* elusive; imperceptible.

insalubre *adj* insalubrious; unhealthy.

insatiable *adj* insatiable.

insatisfaction *f* dissatisfaction.

inscription *f* inscription; registration; matriculation.

inscrire *vt* to inscribe; to enter; to set down; to register; **s'~** *vr* to join; to register, enrol.

insecte *m* insect.

insecticide *m* insecticide.

insensé *adj* insane, demented.

inséparable *adj* inseparable.

insérer *vt* to insert.

insertion *f* insertion, inserting.

insignifiant *adj* insignificant, trifling.

insinuer *vt* to insinuate, imply; **s'~** *vr* to insinuate o.s. into; to creep into.

insipide *adj* insipid, tasteless.

insister *vi* to insist, be insistent; to stress.

insolence *f* insolence.

insolent *adj* insolent; brazen.

insomnie *f* insomnia.

insouciance *f* unconcern; carelessness.

insouciant *adj* carefree; careless.

inspecter *vt* to inspect, examine.

inspecteur *m* -trice *f* inspector

inspection *f* inspection.

inspiration *f* inspiration; suggestion.

inspirer *vt* to inspire; to breathe in; **s'~** *vr:* **s'~ de** to be inspired by.

instable *adj* unstable; unsettled.

installer *vt* to install; to fit out; **s'~** *vr* to set o.s. up; to settle down.

instant *m* moment, instant.

instantané *adj* instant, instantaneous.

instaurer *vt* to institute; to impose.

instinct *m* instinct.

instinctif *adj* instinctive.

institut *m* institute; school.

instituteur *m* **-trice** *f* teacher.

institution *f* institution; establishment.

instructif *adj* instructive.

instruction *f* instruction; education; inquiry.

instruire *vt* to instruct; to teach; to conduct an inquiry; **s'~** *vr* to educate o.s.; to obtain information.

instrument *m* instrument, implement.

insuffisant *adj* insufficient, inadequate.

insuline *f* insulin.

insulte *f* insult.

insulter *vt* to insult, affront.

insupportable *adj* unbearable, intolerable.

intact *adj* intact.

intégral *adj* integral; uncut; complete.

intégralité *f* whole; entirety.

intégrer *vt* to integrate; **s'~** *vr* to become integrated; to fit in.

intégrité *f* integrity.

intellectuel *m* **-le** *f* intellectual; * *adj* intellectual, mental.

intelligence *f* intelligence; understanding.

intelligent *adj* intelligent, shrewd, bright.

intelligible *adj* intelligible.

intense *adj* intense; severe.

intensif *adj* intensive.

intensifier *vt* to intensify; **s'~** *vr* to intensify.

intensité *f* intensity; severity.

intention *f* intention; purpose, intent.

intercepter *vt* to intercept.

interchangeable *adj* interchangeable.

interdire *vt* to forbid, ban, prohibit.

interdit *adj* forbidden, prohibited; dumbfounded.

intéressant *adj* interesting; attractive, worthwhile.

intéresser *vt* to interest; to concern; *vr:* **s'~ à** to be interested in.

intérêt *m* interest; significance, importance.

interférence *f* interference; conjunction.

intérieur *adj* interior, internal, inland; **à l'~** inside; within.

intermède *m* interlude.

interminable *adj* interminable; endless.

intermittent *adj* intermittent, sporadic.

international *adj* international.

interpeller *vt* to call out to; (*police*) to interpellate.

interprétation *f* interpretation, rendering.

interprète *mf* interpreter.

interpréter *vt* to interpret; to perform.

interrogation *f* interrogation, questioning; question.

interrogatoire *m* questioning; cross-examination.

interroger *vt* to question; to interrogate; **s'~** *vr* to wonder.

interrompre *vt* to interrupt, break; **s'~** *vr* to break off, interrupt o.s.

interrupteur *m* switch.

interruption *f* interruption, break.

intervalle *m* interval; space, distance.

intervenir *vi* to intervene; to take part in.

intervention *f* intervention; operation.

intestin *m* intestine.

intime *adj* intimate; private; * *mf* close friend.

intimider *vt* to intimidate.

intimité *f* intimacy; privacy.

intituler *vt* to call, entitle; **s'~** *vr* to be called; to call o.s.

intolérable *adj* intolerable.

intolérance *f* intolerance.

intolérant *adj* intolerant.

intonation *f* intonation.

intoxication *f* poisoning; indoctrination.

intransigeant *adj* intransigent, uncompromising.

intrépide *adj* intrepid, fearless.

intrigant *adj* scheming.

introduction *f* introduction; launching; (*jur*) institution.

introduire *vt* to introduce, insert; to present; **s'~** *vr* to find one's way in; to be introduced.

introverti *m* -e *f* introvert; * *adj* introverted.

intrus *m* -e *f* intruder; * *adj* intruding, intrusive.

intuitif *adj* intuitive.

intuition *f* intuition.

inutile *adj* useless; unavailing; pointless; **~ment** *adv* uselessly, needlessly.

inutilisable *adj* unusable.

invalide *adj* disabled; (*jur*) invalid.

invasion *f* invasion.

inventaire *m* inventory; stocklist.

inventer *vt* to invent; to devise; to make up.

inventeur *m* -**trice** *f* inventor.

invention *f* invention; inventiveness.

investir *vt* to invest; to surround.

invincible *adj* invincible, indomitable.

invisible *adj* invisible; unseen.

invitation *f* invitation.

invité *m* -e *f* guest.

inviter *vt* to invite, ask.

involontaire *adj* involuntary; unintentional.

invraisemblable *adj* unlikely, improbable.

iode *m* iodine.

ion *m* ion.

Irlandais *m* Irishman, -**e** *f* Irishwoman

irlandais *adj* Irish.

ironie *f* irony.

ironique *adj* ironic.

irradiation *f* irradiation; radiation.

irrationnel *adj* irrational.

irrécupérable *adj* irretrievable.

irréel *adj* unreal.

irréfléchi *adj* unconsidered; hasty.

irrégulier *adj* irregular; varying; uneven.

irrémédiable *adj* irreparable; incurable.

irremplaçable *adj* irreplaceable.

irrésistible *adj* irresistible.

irresponsable *adj* irresponsible

irréversible *adj* irreversible.

irrigation *f* irrigation.

irriguer *vt* to irrigate.

irriter *vt* to irritate; to provoke.

Islam *m* Islam.

isolement *m* loneliness; isolation; insulation.

isoler *vt* to isolate; to insulate; **s'~** *vr* to cut o.s. off.

issue *f* outlet; solution; outcome.

ivoire *m* ivory.

ivre *adj* drunk, inebriated.

ivresse *f* drunkenness.

ivrogne *mf* drunkard.

J

jadis *adv* formerly, long ago.

jaguar *m* jaguar.

jaillir *vi* to spout, gush; to spring.

jalon *m* staff; landmark, milestone.

jalonner *vt* to mark out.

jalousie *f* jealousy, envy.

jaloux *m* **-ouse** *f* jealous person; * *adj* jealous, envious.

jamais *adv* never, not ever; **à ~** for ever.

jambe *f* leg.

jambon *m* ham.

janvier *m* January.

jardin *m* garden.

jardinage *m* gardening.

jardiner *vi* to garden.

jardinier *m* **-ière** *f* gardener.

jargon *m* jargon, slang; gibberish.

jaser *vi* to chatter; to twitter; to babble.

jauge *f* gauge; capacity; tonnage.

jauger *vt* to gauge the capacity of; to size up.

jaune *adj* yellow; * *m* yellow.

jaunir *vi* to yellow, turn yellow; * *vt* to make yellow.

jaunisse *f* jaundice.

je, j' *pn* I.

jet *m* jet, spurt; throwing.

jetable *adj* disposable.

jetée *f* pier.

jeter *vt* to throw; to discard; to give out; **se ~** *vr* to throw o.s.; to rush at.

jeton *m* token; counter.

jeu *m* play; game; gambling.

jeudi *m* Thursday.

jeune *adj* young; junior; new; youthful; * *m* youth, young man; *f* young girl.

jeûne *m* fast.

jeûner *vi* to fast.

jeunesse *f* youth, youthfulness.

joaillerie *f* jewellery.

joaillier *m* **-ière** *f* jeweller.

joindre *vt* to join, link; to attach; **se ~** *vr* to join, join in.

joint *m* joint; join.

jointure *f* joint *(anat)*.

joli *adj* pretty; good, handsome.

jonction *f* junction.

jongler *vi* to juggle.

jongleur *m* **-euse** *f* juggler.

joue *f* cheek.

jouer *vi* to play; to gamble; to act.

jouet *m* toy.

joueur *m* **-euse** *f* player; gambler.

jouir *vi* to enjoy; to delight in.

jouissance *f* enjoyment; use.

our *m* day; daylight; **à ~ up** to date; **vivre au ~ le ~** to live from day to day; **~ férié** public holiday; **mise à ~** up-dating; update; **du ~ au lendemain** overnight.

ournal *m* newspaper; bulletin, journal; **~ télévisé** television news.

ournalisme *m* journalism.

ournaliste *mf* journalist.

ournée *f* day; day's work.

ovial *adj* jovial, jolly.

ovialité *f* joviality.

oyau *m* jewel, gem.

oyeux *adj* joyful, cheerful.

udaïsme *m* Judaism.

udicieusement *adv* judiciously

udicieux *adj* judicious.

udo *m* judo.

uge *m* judge.

ugement *m* judgment; sentence; opinion.

uger *vt* to judge; to decide; to consider.

uif *m* Jew.

uillet *m* July.

juin *m* June.

jumeau *m* **-elle** *f* twin; ***** *adj* twin; double.

jumelle(s) *f(pl)* binoculars.

jument *f* mare.

jungle *f* jungle.

jupe *f* skirt.

jurer *vt* to swear, pledge.

juridiction *f* jurisdiction; court of law.

juron *m* oath, curse.

jury *m* jury; board of examiners.

jus *m* juice.

jusque, jusqu' *prép* to, as far as; until.

juste *adj* just, fair; exact; sound.

justesse *f* accuracy; aptness; soundness.

justice *f* justice, fairness.

justification *f* justification; proof.

justifier *vt* to justify, prove; **se ~** *vr* to justify o.s.

juteux *adj* juicy; lucrative.

juvénile *adj* young, youthful.

juxtaposition *f* juxtaposition.

K

kaki *adj* khaki.

kaléidoscope *m* kaleidoscope.

kangourou *m* kangaroo.

karaté *m* karate.

kayac, kayak *m* kayak.

képi *m* kepi.

kermesse *f* fair; bazaar.

kilogramme *m* kilogram.

kilohertz *m* kilohertz.

kilomètre *m* kilometre.

kinésithérapeute *mf* physiotherapist.

kiosque *m* kiosk, stall.

kiwi *m* kiwi, Chinese gooseberry.

klaxon *m* horn.

kleptomane *mf* kleptomaniac.

kleptomanie *f* kleptomania.

koala *m* koala.

L

la *art pn: see* **le**.

là *adv* there; over there; then; **par ~** that way; **~-dedans** inside, in there; **~-dessous** underneath, under there; thereupon; **~-haut** up there, up on top; **celui-~** that one.

label *m* label; seal.

labeur *m* labour, toil.

laboratoire *m* laboratory.

laborieux *adj* laborious, toilsome.

labourer *vt* to plough; to dig over; to rip open.

lac *m* lake.

lacer *vt* to lace up; to tie up.

lacet *m* lace.

lâche *adj* slack; loose; lax; cowardly; * *mf* coward.

lâcher *vt* to loosen; to release.

lâcheté *f* cowardice; meanness.

laconique *adj* laconic.

lagon *m* lagoon.

laïc *m* layman, **laïque** *f* laywoman; * **laïque** *adj* lay, civil.

laid *adj* ugly, unsightly.

laideur *f* ugliness, unsightliness.

lainage *m* woollen article.

laine *f* wool.

laisse *f* leash, string, lead.

laisser *vt* to leave; to let; **~ tomber** to drop; **se ~ aller** to let o.s. go.

laisser-passer *m invar* pass, permit.

lait *m* milk

laitage *m* milk; milk products.

laiton *m* brass.

laitue *f* lettuce.

lambeau *m* shred; tatter.

lambris *m* plastering; panelling.

lame *f* blade; strip; metal plate.

lamentable *adj* lamentable, distressing.

lamenter (se) *vr* to lament, bewail.

lampadaire *m* standard-lamp; street lamp.

lampe *f* lamp, light; bulb.

lance *f* lance, spear.

lance-flammes *m invar* flamethrower.

lance-pierres *m invar* catapult.

lancer *vt* to throw; to launch; **se ~** to leap, jump; to embark on.

lancinant *adj* nagging; haunting.

lande *f* moor.

langage *m* language, speech.

langue *f* tongue; language.

languir *vi* to languish; to linger.

lanière *f* thong; lash.

lanoline *f* lanolin.

lanterne *f* lantern; lamp.

lapin *m* **-e** *f* rabbit.

lapsus *m* slip, mistake.

lard *m* fat; bacon.

large *adj* wide; generous; lax; great.

largeur *f* width, breadth.

larguer *vt* to loose, release; cast off.

larme *f* tear.

larmoyant *adj* tearful, weeping.

larve *f* larva, grub.

laryngite *f* laryngitis.

las *adj*, *f* **-se** weary, tired.

lasagne *f* lasagne.

laser *m* laser.

lasser *vt* to tire; **se ~** *vr* to grow tired.

lassitude *f* tiredness, weariness.

latent *adj* latent.

latéral *adj* lateral, side.

latex *m* latex.

latin *adj* Latin; * *m* Latin.

latitude *f* latitude; margin.

lauréat *m* **-e** *f* prize winner.

lavabo *m* washbasin.

lavage *m* washing; bathing.

lavande *f* lavender.

lave *f* lava.

laver *vt* to wash; to cleanse; **se ~** *vr* to wash o.s.

laverie *f* laundry.

lave-vaisselle *m invar* dishwasher.

laxatif *adj* laxative; * *m* laxative.

le *art*, *f* **la**, *devant voyelle* **l'**, *pl* **les** the; * *pn* him, her, them.

lécher *vt* to lick.

leçon *f* lesson; reading; class.

lecteur *m* **-trice** *f* reader.

lecture *f* reading; perusal.

légal *adj* legal, lawful.

légaliser *vt* to legalise.

légalité *f* legality, lawfulness.

légendaire *adj* legendary.

légende *f* legend; inscription.

léger *adj* light; slight; faint; inconsiderate.

légèreté *f* lightness; nimbleness; thoughtlessness.

législation *f* legislation, laws.

légitime *adj* legitimate, lawful.

légitimité *f* legitimacy.

léguer *vt* to bequeath; (*jur*) to devise.

légume *m* vegetable.

lendemain *m* next day, day after.

lent *adj* slow; tardy; sluggish.

lenteur *f* slowness.

lentille *f* lentil; lens.

léopard *m* leopard.

lèpre *f* leprosy.

lépreux *m* **-euse** *f* leper; * *adj* leprous.

lequel *pn*, *f* **laquelle**, *pl* **lesquels**, **lesquelles** who, whom, which.

lesbienne *f* lesbian.

léser *vt* to wrong; to damage.

lésion *f* wrong; lesion, wound.

lessive *f* washing powder.

leste *adj* nimble, agile.

léthargie *f* lethargy.

léthargique *adj* lethargic.

lettre *f* letter, note; literature; **en toutes ~s** in black and white; **suivre à la ~** to carry out to the letter; **avant la ~** in advance, premature.

leucémie *f* leukaemia.

leur *pn* them; **le ~, la ~, les ~s** theirs.

leurrer *vt* to deceive; to lure; **se ~** *vr* to delude o.s.

lever *vt* to lift, raise; to levy; **se ~** *vr* to get up; * *m* rising; getting up.

levier *m* lever.

lèvre *f* lip.

lévrier *m* greyhound.

levure *f* yeast.

lézard *m* lizard.

lézarde *f* crack.

liaison *f* affair; connection; liaison, link.

liasse *f* bundle.

libellule *f* dragonfly.

libéral *adj* liberal.

libéraliser *vt* to liberalise.

libéralisme *m* liberalism.

libération *f* release, liberation.

libérer *vt* to release; to liberate; **se ~** *vr* to free o.s.

liberté *f* liberty, freedom.

libraire *mf* bookseller.

librairie *f* bookshop; bookselling.

libre *adj* free; independent.

licence *f* degree; permit; licentiousness.

licenciement *m* redundancy; dismissal.

licencier *vt* to make redundant; to dismiss.

lichen *m* lichen.

licorne *f* unicorn.

lie *f* dregs, sediment.

liège *m* cork.

lien *m* bond; link, connection; tie.

lier *vt* to bind; to link; **se ~** *vr*: **se ~ avec** to make friends.

lierre *m* ivy.

lieu *m* place, position; cause; occasion; **avoir ~** to take place; **en premier ~** in the first place; **au ~ de** instead of.

lieutenant *m* (*mil*) lieutenant.

lièvre *m* hare.

ligature *f* ligature; tying up.

ligne *f* line; row; range.

lignée *f* lineage; offspring.

ligue *f* league.

lilas *m* lilac; * *adj* lilac.

limace *f* slug.

limande *f* dab.

lime *f* file.

limer *vt* to file down.

limitation *f* limitation, restriction.

limite *f* boundary, limit; **à la ~** ultimately.

limiter *vt* to limit, restrict; **se ~** *vr* to limit o.s. to.

limitrophe *adj* border.

limon *m* silt.

limonade *f* lemonade.

lin *m* flax; linen.

linceul *m* shroud.

linge *m* linen; washing.

lingerie *f* linen room; underwear, lingerie.

linguiste *mf* linguist.

linguistique *f* linguistics; * *adj* linguistic.

lion *m* lion, **lionne** *f* lioness.

lionceau *m* lion cub.

lipide *m* lipid.

liquéfier *vt* to liquefy; **se ~** *vr* to liquefy.

liqueur *f* liqueur; liquid.

liquidation *f* liquidation; winding up; elimination.

liquide *m* liquid.

lire *vt* to read.

lis *m* lily.

lisible *adj* legible; readable.

lisse *adj* smooth, glossy.

lisser *vt* to smooth, gloss.

liste *f* list; (*jur*) schedule.

lit *m* bed; layer.

literie *f* bedding.

litière *f* litter.

litre *m* litre.

littéraire *adj* literary.

littéral *adj* literal.

littérature *f* literature; writing.

littoral *m* coast; * *adj* coastal, littoral.

livide *adj* livid, pale.

livraison *f* delivery; number, issue.

livre *m* book; * *f* pound (weight, currency).

livrer *vt* to deliver, hand over; to give away; **se ~** *vr* to abandon o.s.

lobe *m* lobe.

local *adj* local.

localisation *f* localisation.

localiser *vt* to localise.

localité *f* locality; town.

locataire *mf* tenant; lodger.

location *f* renting; lease, leasing.

locomotive *f* locomotive, engine; dynamo.

logarithme *m* logarithm.

loge *f* lodge; dressing room; box.

logement *m* housing; accommodation.

loger *vt* to accommodate; to billet; * *vi* to live in.

logiciel *m* software.

logique *f* logic; * *adj* logical.

logistique *f* logistics.

loi *f* law; act, statute; rule.

loin *adv* far, a long way; * *m*: distance; background **au ~** in the distance; **de ~** from a distance.

lointain *adj* distant, remote; * *m* distance; background.

loisir *m* leisure, spare time.

long *adj*, *f* **-ue** long, lengthy.

longer *vt* to border; to walk along.

longévité *f* longevity.

longitude *f* longitude.

longtemps *adv* for a long time.

longueur *f* length.

longue-vue *f* telescope.

loque *f* rag.

loquet *m* latch; clasp.

lorgner *vt* to leer, ogle.

lors *adv* then; **~ de** at the time of; **dès** from that time.

lorsque *conj* when.

losange *m* lozenge, diamond.

lot *m* prize; lot; portion.

loterie *f* lottery; raffle.

lotion *f* lotion.

lotissement *m* allotment; site, housing development.

lotus *m* lotus.

louange *f* praise, commendation.

louche *adj* dubious; suspicious, shady.

loucher *vi* to squint; to ogle.

louer *vt* to rent, lease; to book.

loup *m* wolf.

loupe *f* magnifying glass.

louper *vt* (*fam*) to botch, bungle; to flunk.

lourd *adj* heavy; sultry; unwieldy.

lourdeur *f* heaviness.

loutre *f* otter.

loyal *adj* loyal, faithful.

loyauté *f* loyalty.

loyer *m* rent.

lubrifier *vt* to lubricate.

lubrique *adj* lustful, lecherous.

lucarne *f* skylight.

lucide *adj* lucid, clear.

lucidité *f* lucidity, clearness.

lucratif *adj* lucrative.

lueur *f* glimmer, gleam; glimpse.

lui *pn* him, her, it; **c'est à ~** it is his; **~même** himself, itself.

luire *vt* to shine, gleam.

luisant *adj* gleaming, shining.

lumière *f* light; daylight; lamp; insight.

lumineux *adj* luminous; illuminated.

lunaire *adj* lunar, moon.

lunatique *adj* fantastical, whimsical, quirky.

lundi *m* Monday.

lune *f* moon.

lunette *f* telescope; **~s** glasses.

lustré *adj* glossy; shiny.

luth *m* lute.

lutin m imp;goblin.
lutte f struggle; contest; strife.
lutter vi to struggle, fight.
lutteur m **-euse** f wrestler, fighter.
luxe m luxury, excess.
luxueux adj luxurious.
luxure f lust.
luxuriant adj luxuriant.

lycée m secondary school.
lycéen m secondary school boy, **-ne** f
secondary school girl.
lyncher vt to lynch.
lynx m lynx.
lyre f lyre.
lyrique adj lyric.

M

macabre adj macabre.
macadam m tarmac.
mâcher vt to chew.
machin m (fam) gadget; thingamajig.
machinal adj mechanical, automatic.
machine f machine; engine; apparatus.
machinerie f machinery, plant.
machiniste m machinist; driver; stage-
hand.
mâchoire f jaw.
madame f Madam; Mrs; lady.
mademoiselle f Miss; young lady.
magasin m shop, store; warehouse.
magazine m magazine.
magicien m **-ne** f magician.
magie f magic
magique adj magic; magical.
magistrat m magistrate.
magnanime adj magnanimous.
magnat m magnate.
magnésium m magnesium.
magnétique adj magnetic.
magnétiser vt to magnetise; to hypnotise.
magnétisme m magnetism; hypno-
tism.

magnétophone m tape recorder.
magnétoscope m video recorder
videotape.
magot m (fam) savings, hoard, nest egg
magouille f (fam) fiddle, scam; schem
ing.
mai m May.
maigre adj thin; meagre, scarce.
maigreur f thinness; meagreness
sparseness.
maigrir vi to get thinner; to waste away
maille f stitch; mesh; link.
maillet m mallet.
maillon m link; shackle.
maillot m jersey; leotard.
main f hand; **avoir la ~** to have the
lead; **passer la ~** to make way for so.
main-d'œuvre f workforce.
maintenance f maintenance, servic
ing.
maintenant adv now; **à partir de ~**
from now on.
maintenir vt to keep, maintain; pre
serve; **se ~** vr to persist; to hold one'
own.

maintien *m* maintenance; preservation; keeping up.

maire *m* mayor, *f* mayoress.

mais *conj* but.

mais *m* maize; corn.

maison *f* house; home; building; premises.

maître *m* **-esse** *f* master; ruler; lord; proprietor.

maîtresse *f* mistress; teacher.

maîtrise *f* mastery; control; expertise.

maîtriser *vt* to control; to master; **se ~** *vr* to control o.s.

majesté *f* majesty, grandeur.

majestueux *adj* majestic.

majeur *adj* major; main; chief; superior; * *m* major *mf* adult.

majoration *f* increased charge; overestimation.

majorer *vt* to increase, raise.

majoritaire *adj* majority.

majorité *f* majority.

majuscule *f* capital letter.

mal *adv* wrong, badly; * *m* evil, wrong; harm; pain.

malade *adj* sick, ill; diseased; * *mf* invalid, sick person.

maladie *f* illness; malady, complaint; disorder.

maladresse *f* clumsiness; awkwardness.

maladroit *adj* clumsy, awkward.

malchance *f* ill luck; misfortune; mishap.

malchanceux *adj* unlucky, unfortunate.

mâle *m* male; * *adj* male; manly, virile.

maléfique *adj* hurtful; malignant; baleful.

malencontreux *adj* unfortunate, untoward.

malentendu *m* misunderstanding.

malfaisant *adj* malevolent; harmful; wicked.

malgré *prép* in spite of; despite.

malheur *m* misfortune; calamity.

malheureux *adj* unfortunate; unlucky; unhappy.

malhonnête *adj* dishonest, crooked; uncivil.

malhonnêteté *f* dishonesty; incivility.

malice *f* malice, spite; mischievousness.

malicieux *adj* malicious, spiteful; mischievous.

malin *adj* shrewd, cunning, crafty; malignant.

malle *f* trunk.

malmener *vt* to ill-treat, maltreat.

malnutrition *f* malnutrition.

malsain *adj* unhealthy, unwholesome; immoral.

malveillant *adj* malevolent, spiteful.

maman *f* mother, mummy, mum.

mamelle *f* breast; udder.

mamelon *m* nipple, teat.

mammifère *m* mammal.

manche *f* sleeve; game, round; * *m* handle, shaft.

mandataire *mf* proxy; representative.

manège *m* roundabout, merry-go-round.

manette *f* lever, tap.

mangeable *adj* edible.

manger *vt* to eat; to consume.

mangue *f* mango.

maniable *adj* handy, workable, tractable; amenable.

maniaque *adj* eccentric; fussy.; * *mf* maniac; fusspot; fanatic.

manie *f* mania.

maniement m handling; management, use.

manier vt to handle; to manipulate.

manière f manner, way, style.

maniéré adj affected.

manifestation f demonstration; expression, manifestation.

manifeste adj manifest, evident, obvious; * m manifesto.

manifester vt to display, make known; to demonstrate; **se ~** vr to make o.s. known; to appear; to express o.s.

manigancer vt to contrive; to scheme.

manipuler vt to handle; to manipulate

manivelle f crank.

mannequin m model; dummy.

manœuvre f manoeuvre, operation; scheme; * m labourer.

manœuvrer vt to manoeuvre; to operate; * vi to manoeuvre, move.

manoir m manor.

manquant adj missing.

manque m lack, shortage; shortcoming, deficiency.

manquer vt to miss; to fail; to be absent.

manteau m coat; mantle, blanket; cloak.

manuel m manual, handbook; * adj manual.

manufacture f factory; manufacture.

manufacturier m -**ière** f factory owner; manufacturer; * adj manufacturing.

manuscrit m manuscript; typescript; * adj handwritten.

manutention f handling.

mappemonde f map of the world.

maquereau m mackerel.

maquette f model; mock-up; dummy; sketch.

maquillage m make-up.

maquiller vt to make up; to fake; to fiddle; **se ~** vr to put make-up on.

marais m marsh, swamp.

marasme m stagnation; depression, slump.

marbre m marble; marble statue.

marbré adj marbled; mottled, blotchy.

marchand m -**e** f shopkeeper; dealer; merchant; * adj market, trade.

marchandage m bargaining, haggling.

marchander vi to bargain over, haggle.

marchandise f merchandise, commodity; goods.

marche f walk; journey; progress; movement.

marché m market; transaction, contract.

marcher vi to walk, march; to progress; to work.

marcheur m -**euse** f walker, pedestrian.

mardi m Tuesday.

mare f pool, pond.

marécage m marsh, swamp.

marée f tide.

margarine f margarine.

marge f margin; latitude, freedom; mark-up.

marginal adj marginal.

mari m husband.

mariage m marriage.

marié m bridegroom; * adj married.

marier vt to marry; blend, harmonise; **se ~** vr to get married.

marine f navy; seascape; marine.

mariner vi to marinate; to hang about; * vt to marinate.

marionnette f puppet; puppet show.

maritime *adj* maritime; seaboard.

marmite *f* pot.

marmonner *vt* to mumble, mutter.

marquant *adj* outstanding, vivid.

marque *f* mark, sign; brand; make.

marquer *vt* to mark; to note down; to score.

marquis *m* marquis **-e** *f* marchioness.

marraine *f* godmother.

marron *m* chestnut; brown; * *adj* brown.

mars *m* March.

marsouin *m* porpoise.

marteau *m* hammer; knocker.

marteler *vt* to hammer; to beat.

martial *adj* martial, warlike.

martyriser *vt* to torture, martyrise.

mascarade *f* farce, mascarade.

masculin *adj* masculine.

masochisme *m* masochism.

masochiste *mf* masochist; * *adj* masochistic.

masquer *vt* to mask, conceal; to disguise.

massacre *m* massacre; slaughter.

massacrer *vt* to massacre, slaughter.

massage *m* massage.

masse *f* mass, heap; bulk; mob.

masser *vt* to mass, assemble; to massage.

massif *adj* massive, solid, heavy; * *m* massif; clump.

massivement *adv* en masse, massively, heavily.

massue *f* club.

masturbation *f* masturbation.

masturber *vi* se ~ *vr* to masturbate.

mat *adj* matt, dull; dead, dull-sounding.

mât *m* mast; pole.

match *m* match; game.

matelas *m* mattress.

matelassé *adj* stuffed; padded, cushioned.

matelot *m* sailor; seaman.

mater *vt* to subdue; to control, curb; to spy on; to ogle.

matériaux *mpl* material, materials.

matériel *adj* material, physical; practical.

maternel *adj* maternal, motherly.

mathématique *adj* mathematical; * *f* mathematics.

matière *f* material, matter; subject; ~ **première** raw material.

matin *m* morning; dawn.

matinal *adj* morning.

matinée *f* morning; matinée.

matricule *m* reference number; * *f* roll, register.

matrimonial *adj* matrimonial, marriage.

maudire *vt* to curse.

maudit *adj* cursed; blasted, damned.

maussade *adj* sulky, sullen.

mauvais *adj* bad; wicked; faulty; hurtful; poor.

mauve *adj* mauve; * *f* mallow.

maxime *f* maxim.

maximum *m* maximum.

mayonnaise *f* mayonnaise.

me, m' *pn* me; myself.

mécanicien *m* **-ne** *f* mechanic; engineer.

mécanique *f* mechanics; mechanical engineering; * *adj* mechanical.

mécanisme *m* mechanism, working.

mécène *m* patron.

méchanceté f spitefulness; wickedness; mischievousness.

méchant adj spiteful; wicked; mischievous.

mèche f wick, fuse; tuft.

méconnaissable adj unrecognisable.

méconnu adj unrecognised; misunderstood.

mécontent adj discontent, displeased.

mécontentement m discontent; displeasure.

médaille f medal; stain, mark.

médaillon m medallion; locket.

médecin m doctor, physician.

médecine f medicine

médical adj medical; **~ement** adv medically.

médicament m medicine, drug.

médicinal adj medicinal.

médiéval adj medieval.

médiocre adj mediocre; passable; indifferent.

médisant adj slanderous.

méditation f meditation.

méditer vi to meditate; * vt to contemplate, have in mind.

médium m medium.

méduse f jellyfish.

méfiance f distrust, mistrust.

méfiant adj distrustful, mistrustful.

méfier (se) vr to mistrust, distrust; to be suspicious.

mégaphone m megaphone.

mégot m cigarette-end, stub.

meilleur adj better, preferable; **le ~, la ~e** the best.

mélancolie f melancholy, gloom.

mélancolique adj melancholy; melancholic.

mélange m mixing, blending; mixture.

mélanger vt to mix, blend; to muddle.

mêler vt to mix; to combine; **se ~** vr to mix, mingle; **se ~ à** to join; **se ~ de** to meddle in.

mélodie f melody, tune.

mélodieux adj melodious, tuneful.

melon m melon.

membre m member; limb.

même adv even; **tout de ~** nevertheless, all the same; * adj same, identical; * pn: **le ~, la ~, les ~s** the same, the same ones.

mémoire f memory; * m memorandum, report.

mémoriser vt to memorise.

menace f threat; intimidation; danger.

menacer vt to threaten, menace; to impend.

ménage m housework, housekeeping; household.

ménager vt to treat with caution; to manage; to arrange.; **se ~** vr to take care of o.s.; * adj household, domestic.

ménagère f housewife.

mendier vt to beg; to implore.

mener vt to lead, guide; to steer; to manage.

meneur m -**euse** f leader; agitator.

méningite f meningitis.

ménopause f menopause.

menottes fpl handcuffs.

mensonge m lie, falsehood; error, illusion.

mensuel adj monthly.

mental adj mental.

mentalité f mentality.

menteur m -**euse** f liar; * adj lying, deceitful.

menthe *f* mint.

menthol *m* menthol.

mention *f* mention; comment; grade.

mentionner *vt* to mention.

mentir *vi* to lie; to be deceptive.

menton *m* chin.

menu *m* menu; meal; * *adj* slender, thin; petty, minor.

menuisier *m* joiner, carpenter.

mépris *m* contempt, scorn.

méprisant *adj* contemptuous, scornful.

mépriser *vt* to scorn, despise.

mer *f* sea; tide.

merci *m* thank you; * *f* mercy; **sans ~** merciless; **être à la ~ de** to be at the mercy of.

mercredi *m* Wednesday.

mercure *m* mercury.

mère *f* mother.

méridional *adj* southern.

merisier *m* wild cherry.

mérite *m* merit, worth; quality.

mériter *vt* to deserve, merit.

merle *m* blackbird.

merveille *f* marvel, wonder.

merveilleux *adj* marvellous, wonderful.

mésange *f* tit (*orn*).

mésentente *f* misunderstanding.

mesquin *adj* mean, niggardly; petty.

message *m* message.

messager *m* -**ère** *f* messenger.

messe *f* mass.

mesure *f* measure; gauge; measurement; moderation; step; **dans la mesure où** insofar as; **en ~** in time.

mesurer *vt* to measure; to assess; to limit; **se ~** *vr* to try one's strength; **se ~**

à to pit o.s. against, measure one's strength against.

métabolisme *m* metabolism.

métal *m* metal.

métallique *adj* metallic.

météore *m* meteor.

météorite *m*/*f* meteorite.

méthode *f* method, way.

méthodique *adj* methodical.

méticuleux *adj* meticulous

métier *m* job; occupation; **~ à tricoter** knitting machine; **~ à tisser** weaving loom.

métis *m* -**se** *f* half-caste; hybrid; mongrel; * *adj* half-caste; hybrid, mongrel.

mètre *m* metre.

métro *m* underground, metro.

métropole *f* metropolis.

métropolitain *adj* metropolitan; underground.

mets *m* dish.

metteur en scène *m* (*cin*) director.

mettre *vt* to put, place; to put on; **~ en marche** to start up; **se ~** *vr* to place o.s.; to sit down; **se ~ à** to begin to; **se ~ en route** to start off.

meuble *m* piece of furniture.

meubler *vt* to furnish.

meurtrier *m* murderer, -**ière** *f* murderess.

meurtrir *vt* to bruise.

meute *f* pack.

mi- *adj* half; **à ~chemin** halfway; **~clos** half-closed; **à ~jambe** up to the knees; **à ~voix** in a low voice.

microbe *m* germ, microbe.

microbien *adj* microbial, microbic.

microfilm *m* microfilm.

micro-onde *f* microwave; * *m* **micro-**

ondes microwave oven.

micro-ordinateur *m* microcomputer.

microphone *m* microphone.

microscope *m* microscope.

microscopique *adj* microscopic.

midi *m* midday, noon.

miel *m* honey.

mien *pn*, *f* **mienne: le ~, la mienne, les ~s, les miennes** mine, my own.

miette *f* crumb; remnant; morsel.

mieux *m* improvement; **le ~** the best; **de ~ en ~** better and better.

mignon *adj* sweet, pretty.

migraine *f* headache; migraine.

migrateur *m* migrant.

migration *f* migration.

mijoter *vi* to simmer, be brewing; * *vt* to simmer; to scheme, plot.

milice *f* militia.

militaire *m* serviceman; * *adj* military, army.

militant *m* -**e** *f* militant; * *adj* militant.

mille *m* one thousand; * *adj* one thousand.

millénaire *m* millennium, a thousand years; thousandth anniversary; * *adj* thousand-year-old; millennial.

mille-pattes *m* millipede, centipede.

millésime *m* year, date; vintage.

milliard *m* thousand million; billion.

milliardaire *adj* worth (many) millions; * *mf* multimillionaire.

milliardième *adj* thousand millionth; * *m* thousand millionth.

millier *m* thousand.

millimètre *m* millimetre.

million *m* million.

millionnaire *adj* millionaire; worth millions; * *mf* millionaire.

mime *m* mime; * *mf* mimic.

mimer *vt* to mime; to mimic, imitate.

mimétisme *m* mimicry; mimetism.

mimosa *m* mimosa.

minable *adj* seedy, shabby.

mince *adj* thin, slender; meagre, trivial.

mincir *vi* to get slimmer, get thinner.

mine *f* expression; appearance; mine; **avoir bonne ~** to look good.

minerai *m* ore.

minéral *adj* mineral; inorganic; * *m* mineral.

mineur *m* -**e** *f* minor; * *adj* minor; * *m* miner.

miniature *f* miniature.

mini-jupe *f* miniskirt.

minimal *adj* minimal, minimum.

minime *adj* minor, minimal.

ministère *m* ministry; agency.

ministériel *adj* ministerial.

ministre *m* minister; clergyman.

minoritaire *adj* minority.

minorité *f* minority.

minuit *m* midnight.

minuscule *adj* minuscule, tiny, minute.

minute *f* minute, moment.

minuterie *f* time switch; regulator.

minutieux *adj* meticulous.

mirabelle *f* mirabelle.

miracle *m* miracle, wonder.

miraculeux *adj* miraculous.

miroir *m* mirror, reflection.

mise *f* putting, placing; stake; deposit; investment; **~ en scène** production, staging; **~ en liberté** release; **~ en ordre** ordering, arrangement; **~ en œuvre** implementation.

miser *vt* to stake, to bet.

misérable *adj* miserable; destitute; pitiable.

misère *f* misery; poverty; destitution.

miséricorde *f* mercy, forgiveness.

missile *m* missile.

mission *f* mission, assignment.

missionnaire *m* missionary.

mi-temps *f* half-time; half.

miteux *adj* dingy, shabby, poverty-stricken.

mitigé *adj* mitigated; lukewarm.

mitoyen *adj* common; semi-detached.

mitrailleuse *f* machine gun.

mixer *vt* to mix; to blend.

mixte *adj* mixed; joint; combined.

mixture *f* mixture, concoction.

mobile *adj* moving; movable; mobile; nimble; * *m* motive; moving body.

mobilier *m* furniture; * *adj* movable; personal; transferable.

mobilisation *f* mobilisation, calling up.

mobilité *f* mobility.

mobylette *f* moped.

moche *adj* (*fam*) ugly, lousy.

mode *f* fashion; custom; * *m* form, mode; way.

modèle *m* model; pattern; design; example.

modeler *vt* to model; to shape.

modem *m* modem.

modération *f* moderation; diminution.

modéré *adj* moderate.

modérer *vt* moderate, restrained; **se ~** *vr* to control o.s., keep one's temper.

moderne *adj* modern, up-to-date.

moderniser *vt* to modernise.

modeste *adj* modest, simple; unassuming;.

modestie *f* modesty.

modification *f* modification.

modifier *vt* to modify, alter; **se ~** *vr* to be modified.

moelle *f* marrow; core.

moelleux *adj* mellow; soft; smooth.

mœurs *fpl* morals; customs.

moi *pn* me, I; **c'est à ~** it is mine, it is my turn; **~-même** myself.

mois *m* month.

moisir *vi* to go mouldy.

moisson *f* harvest.

moissonner *vt* to reap, harvest.

moite *adj* moist, damp.

moitié *f* half.

molaire *f* molar.

molécule *f* molecule.

mollusque *m* mollusc.

moment *m* moment, instant, while; time; opportunity.

momentané *adj* momentary; brief.

momie *f* mummy.

mon *pn*, *f* **ma**, *pl* **mes** my, my own.

monastère *m* monastery.

mondain *adj* worldly, mundane; society, fashionable.

monde *m* world, earth; society, company; **il y a du ~** there are some people there.

mondial *adj* world, world-wide.

moniteur *m* **-trice** *f* instructor, coach; supervisor.

monnaie *f* currency; coin; change.

monopoliser *vt* to monopolise.

monotone *adj* monotonous.

monotonie *f* monotony, sameness.

monsieur *m* sir, gentleman, Mr, *pl* **messieurs** gentlemen, Messrs.

monstre *m* monster.

monstrueux *adj* monstrous.

mont *m* mountain; mount.

montagne *f* mountain.

montagneux *adj* mountainous.

montant *m* upright; total, total sum; * *adj* upward, rising; upstream.

montée *f* climb, climbing; ascent; rise.

monter *vi* to go up, ascend; get into (vehicle); * *vt* to go up; to carry/bring up.

montre *f* watch.

montrer *vt* to show, point to; to prove; **se ~** *vr* to appear; to prove o.s.

monture *f* mount; setting; frame.

monument *m* monument, memorial.

monumental *adj* monumental, colossal.

moquer (se) *vr* to make fun, jeer, laugh at.

moqueur *m* **-euse** *f* mocker, scoffer; * *adj* mocking.

moral *adj* moral, ethical; intellectual.

moralité *f* morals, morality.

morbide *adj* morbid, unhealthy.

morceau *m* piece, morsel, fragment; extract.

mordre *vt* to bite, gnaw; to grip.

morne *adj* gloomy, dismal.

morose *adj* sullen, morose.

morse *m* Morse; walrus.

morsure *f* bite.

mort *m* dead man, **-e** *f* dead woman; * *adj* dead; * *f* death.

mortalité *f* mortality; death rate.

mortel *adj* mortal; fatal.

mortier *m* mortar.

morue *f* cod.

mosaïque *f* mosaic.

mosquée *f* mosque.

mot *m* word; saying; **~s croisés** crossword.

moteur *m* engine, motor; * *adj* motor, driving.

motif *m* motive, grounds; motif, design.

motion *f* motion.

motivation *f* motivation.

motiver *vt* to justify; to motivate.

moto *f* motorbike.

motte *f* clod, lump; slab.

mou *adj,* *f* **molle** soft; gentle; muffled.

mouche *f* fly.

moucher *vt* to wipe sb's nose; **se ~** *vr* to blow one's nose.

moucheron *m* midge, gnat.

moucheté *adj* speckled; flecked.

mouchoir *m* handkerchief.

moudre *vt* to mill, grind.

mouette *f* gull.

moufle *f* mitten.

mouillé *adj* wet, soaked.

mouiller *vt* to wet; to water down; **se ~** *vr* to get wet.

mouler *vt* to mould; to model.

moulin *m* mill.

moulu *adj* ground; bruised.

mourir *vi* to die.

mousse *f* moss; foam, froth.

mousser *vi* to froth, foam.

mousseux *adj* sparkling; frothy; * *m* sparkling wine.

moustique *m* mosquito.

moutarde *f* mustard.

mouton *m* sheep.

mouvement *m* movement, motion; animation.

mouvementé *adj* eventful; turbulent.

mouvoir *vt* to drive, power; **se ~** *vr* to move.

moyen *m* means; way; * *adj* average, medium, moderate.

moyenne *f* average.

mue *f* moulting; shedding.

muer *vi* to moult; to slough.

muet *m* mute (man), **muette** *f* mute (woman); * *adj* dumb; silent, mute.

mufle *m* muffle; muzzle.

muguet *m* lily-of-the-valley; (*med*) thrush.

mulet *m* mule.

multicolore *adj* multicoloured.

multiple *adj* numerous, multiple; * *m* multiple.

multiplier *vt* **se ~** *vr* to multiply, increase.

multitude *f* multitude, crowd.

municipal *adj* municipal; local.

munir *vt* to provide, equip with; **se ~** *vr* to equip o.s.

mur *m* wall.

mûr *adj* ripe, mature; worn out.

mûrir *vi* to ripen, mature.

murmure *m* murmur; muttering; grumbling.

murmurer *vi* to murmur; to whisper; grumble; to babble * *vt* to murmur.

musclé *adj* muscular, brawny.

musculaire *adj* muscular.

musée *m* art gallery, museum.

musicien *m* **-ne** *f* musician; * *adj* musical.

musique *f* music.

musulman *m* **-e** *f* Moslem; * *adj* Moslem.

mutant *m* **-e** *f* mutant; * *adj* mutant.

mutation *f* transfer; transformation; mutation.

muter *vt* to transfer, move.

mutilation *f* mutilation, maiming.

mutiler *vt* to mutilate; **se ~** *vr* to injure o.s.

mutuel *adj* mutual; **~lement** *adv* mutually.

mystère *m* mystery.

mystérieux *adj* mysterious.

mystifier *vt* to mystify; to hoax.

mythe *m* myth.

mythologie *f* mythology.

N

nacre *f* mother-of-pearl.

nacré *adj* nacreous, pearly, iridescent.

nageoire *f* fin, flipper.

nager *vi* to swim.

nageur *m* **-euse** *f* swimmer; rower.

naïf *adj* naïve, artless, ingenuous.

nain *m* **-e** *f* dwarf.

naissance *f* birth, extraction; dawn, beginning.

naître *vi* to be born; to arise, spring up.

naïveté *f* naïvety, artlessness, gullibility.

nappe *f* tablecloth; layer; sheet, expanse.

napper *vt* to top with.

napperon *m* tablemat.

narcisse *m* narcissus.

narcotique *m* drug, narcotic; * *adj* narcotic.

narguer *vt* to flout, defy; to cheek.

narine *f* nostril.

narrateur *m* **-trice** *f* narrator.

narration *f* narration, narrative.

naseau *m* nostril.

natalité *f* birth rate.

natation *f* swimming.

nation *f* nation.

national *adj* national; domestic.

nationaliser *vt* to nationalise.

nationaliste *mf* nationalist; * *adj* nationalist.

nationalité *f* nationality.

natte *f* plait, braid.

nature *f* nature; kind, sort; temperament.

naturel *adj* natural; native; unsophisticated.

naufrage *m* shipwreck; ruin, foundering.

nausée *f* nausea.

nautique *adj* nautical, water.

naval *adj* naval, shipbuilding.

navet *m* turnip.

navette *f* shuttle; **faire la ~** to shuttle between.

navigateur *m* navigator, sailor.

navigation *f* sailing, navigation.

navire *m* ship, vessel.

navrant *adj* distressing, upsetting.

ne *adv* no, not.

né *adj* born.

néanmoins *adv* nevertheless.

néant *m* nothing, nothingness, emptiness.

nécessaire *adj* necessary; requisite; indispensable.

nécessité *f* necessity; need; inevitability.

nectarine *f* nectarine.

néfaste *adj* harmful; unlucky; ill-fated.

négatif *adj* negative.

négation *f* negation; negative.

négligence *f* negligence, carelessness.

négligent *adj* negligent, careless; nonchalant.

négliger *vt* to neglect; to be negligent about.

négociant *m* **-e** *f* merchant.

négociation *f* negotiation.

négocier *vi* to negotiate; to trade; * *vt* to negotiate.

neige *f* snow.

neiger *vi* to snow, be snowing.

nerf *m* nerve.

nerveux *adj* nervous; vigorous; excitable.

nervosité *f* nervousness; excitability.

nervure *f* nervure, vein; rib.

net *adj*, *f* **-te** clean; clear; plain; sharp; net.

netteté *f* neatness; clearness; sharpness.

nettoyage *m* cleaning; clearing up.

nettoyer *vt* to clean; to ruin, clean out.

neuf *adj* nine; * *m* nine.

neutraliser *vt* to neutralise.

neutralité *f* neutrality.

neutre *adj* neutral; neuter.

neuvième *adj* ninth * *mf* ninth.

neveu *m* nephew.

névrose *f* neurosis.

nez *m* nose; flair.

niais *adj* silly, simple.

niche f niche, nook; kennel; trick.

nicotine *f* nicotine.

nid *m* nest; den; berth.

nièce *f* niece.

nier *vt* to deny; to repudiate.

nigaud *m* **-e** *f* simpleton.

niveau *m* level; standard; par; gauge.

niveler *vt* to level; to even out, equalise.

noblesse *f* nobleness, nobility.

noce *f* wedding, wedding feast; marriage ceremony.

nocif *adj* noxious, harmful.

noctambule *mf* night reveller, night owl; sleepwalker.

nocturne *adj* nocturnal, night; * *f* evening fixture; late night opening.

nodule *m* nodule.

Noël *m* Christmas.

nœud *m* knot, bow; crux.

noir *adj* black; dark; * *m* black; darkness; black man.

noircir *vt* to blacken; to dirty; **se ~** *vr* to darken, grow black.

noire *f* black woman.

noisette *f* hazel.

noix *f* walnut.

nom *m* name; fame; noun.

nomade *mf* nomad.

nombre *m* number, quantity.

nombreux *adj* numerous, frequent.

nombril *m* navel.

nominal *adj* nominal; noun.

nommer *vt* to appoint; nominate.

non *adv* no; not.

nonchalance *f* nonchalance.

nonchalant *adj* nonchalant.

non-sens *m* nonsense.

nord *m* north, northerly (wind).

nordique *adj* Nordic; Scandina-vian.

normal *adj* normal, usual; standard-sized.

norme *f* norm; standard.

nostalgie *f* nostalgia.

nostalgique *adj* nostalgic.

notable *adj* notable; noteworthy.

note *f* note; minute; mark; bill.

noter *vt* to note down; to notice; to mark.

notice *f* note; directions; instructions.

notion *f* notion, idea.

notoire *adj* notorious; well-known, acknowledged.

notre *adj, pl* **nos** ours, our own.

nôtre *pn*: **le ~, la ~, les ~s** ours, our own.

nouer *vt* to tie, knot; **se ~** *vr* to join together.

nouille *f* (piece of) pasta.

nourrice *f* child-minder, nanny.

nourrissant *adj* nourishing, nutritious.

nourriture *f* food; sustenance.

nous *pn* we; us; **c'est à ~** it's ours; it's our turn; **~-mêmes** ourselves.

nouveau *adj* new; recent; additional.

nouveau-né *m* **-e** *f* new-born child.

nouveauté *f* novelty; newness.

nouvelle *f* piece of news; short story.

novembre *m* November.

noyade *f* drowning, drowning incident.

noyer *vt* to drown; to flood; **se ~** *vr* to drown, drown o.s.; * *m* walnut (tree).

nu *adj* naked, nude; plain, unadorned.

nuage *m* cloud.

nuageux *adj* cloudy, overcast.

nucléaire *adj* nuclear; * *m* nuclear energy.

nudiste *mf* nudist; * *adj* nudist.

nudité *f* nakedness, nudity.

nuée *f* dense cloud; horde, swarm.

nuire *vi* to harm, injure; to prejudice.

nuisible *adj* harmful; noxious.

nuit *f* night, darkness.

nul *adj* no; nil; null and void; nonexistent; **~lement** *adv* not at all, not in the least.

nullité *f* nullity; uselessness.

numéral *adj* numeral; * *m* numeral.

numérique *adj* numerical; digital.

numéro *m* number; issue.
numérotation *f* numbering, numeration.
numéroter *vt* to number.

nuque *f* nape (of the neck).
nutritif *adj* nutritious, nourishing.
nutrition *f* nutrition.
nylon *m* nylon.

O

obéir *vt* to obey, be obedient; to comply.
obéissance *f* obedience; compliance.
obéissant *adj* obedient.
obèse *adj* obese.
obésité *f* obesity.
objecter *vt* to object.
objectif *adj* objective, unbiased; * *m* objective, target.
objection *f* objection.
objet *m* object, thing; purpose; matter.
obligation *f* obligation, duty; bond.
obligatoire *adj* obligatory, compulsory.
obligé *adj* obliged, compelled; inevitable; necessary.
obliger *vt* to oblige, require; (*jur*) to bind.
oblique *adj* oblique, sidelong.
oblitérer *vt* to obliterate; to cancel (stamp).
obscène *adj* obscene.
obscénité *f* obscenity.
obscur *adj* obscure, dark, gloomy.
obscurité *f* obscurity; darkness.
obséder *vt* to obsess, haunt.
obsèques *fpl* funeral.
observateur *m* **-trice** *f* observer; * *adj* observant.
observer *vt* to observe, watch; to notice; to comply with.
obsession *f* obsession.

obstacle *m* obstacle, hindrance.
obstétrique *f* obstetrics.
obstination *f* obstinacy, stubbornness.
obstiné *adj* obstinate, stubborn.
obstiner (s') *vr* to insist, persist.
obtenir *vt* to obtain, procure, get; to achieve.
obturation *f* stopping, closing up, obturation.
obus *m* shell.
occasion *f* occasion, opportunity; cause; bargain; **d'~** second-hand.
occident *m* west.
occidental *adj* western; Occidental.
occulte *adj* occult.
occupant *m* **-e** *f* occupant, occupier.
occupation *f* occupation, pursuit; work; occupancy.
occuper *vt* to occupy; to employ; to inhabit; **s'~** *vr* to keep busy.
océan *m* ocean.
octet *m* byte.
octobre *m* October.
octroyer *vt* to grant, bestow; **s'~** *vr* to allow oneself.
odeur *f* smell, odour.
odorat *m* smell (sense).
œil *m*, *pl* **yeux** eye; look; bud.
œillet *m* carnation.

œuf *m* egg.

œuvre *f* work; action, deed; production.

offense *f* offence; injury, wrong.

offenser *vt* to offend; to injure, shock; **s'~** *vr* to take offence.

offensif *adj* offensive; forceful, aggressive.

offensive *f* offensive, attack.

office *m* office, bureau; duty; function.

officiel *adj* official.

officier *m* officer.

offrande *f* offering.

offre *f* offer, tender, bid.

offrir *vt* to offer.

offusquer *vt* to offend; **s'~** *vr* to take offence; to be offended.

ogre *m* ogre, **-sse** *f* ogress.

oie *f* goose.

oignon *m* onion; bulb.

oiseau *m* bird.

oisif *adj* idle.

oisiveté *f* idleness.

oléagineux *adj* oily.

oléoduc *m* oil pipeline.

olive *f* olive.

olivier *m* olive tree.

olympique *adj* Olympic.

ombragé *adj* shaded, shady.

ombre *f* shade, shadow.

omelette *f* omelette.

omettre *vt* to leave out, miss out.

omission *f* omission.

omoplate *f* shoulder blade.

on *pn* one; someone, anyone.

once *f* ounce.

oncle *m* uncle.

onctueux *adj* smooth, creamy.

onde *f* wave.

ondoyant *adj* undulating, flowing; changeable.

ondulation *f* undulation; wave.

onduler *vi* to undulate; to ripple.

onéreux *adj* onerous; expensive, costly.

ongle *m* nail; claw, talon; hoof.

onze *adj* eleven; * *m* eleven.

onzième *adj* eleventh; * *mf* eleventh.

opale *f* opal.

opaque *adj* opaque; impenetrable.

opéra *m* opera.

opération *f* operation, performance; transaction, deal.

opératoire *adj* operating; operative, surgical.

opérer *vt* to operate; to carry out, implement.

opérette *f* operetta, light opera.

opiniâtre *adj* stubborn; persistent.

opinion *f* opinion, view.

opposant *m* **-e** *f* opponent; * *adj* opposing.

opposé *adj* opposite, contrary; facing; * *m* opposite; **à l'~** contrary to.

opposer *vt* to oppose; to contrast; to object; **s'~** *vr* to be opposed to; to clash, conflict.

opposition *f* opposition; conflict.

oppresser *vt* to oppress, weigh down.

oppressif *adj* oppressive.

oppression *f* oppression.

opprimer *vt* to oppress, crush.

opticien *m* **-ne** *f* optician.

optimisme *m* optimism.

optimiste *mf* optimist; * *adj* optimistic.

option *f* option, choice.

optionnel *adj* optional.

optique *adj* optical.

opulence *f* opulence, wealth.

or *m* gold; * *conj* now.

orage *m* storm, tempest, thunderstorm.

orageux *adj* stormy.
oral *adj* oral, verbal.
orange *f* orange; ***** *adj invar* orange.
orateur *m* **-trice** *f* orator.
orbite *f* orbit; socket; sphere.
orchestre *m* orchestra.
orchestrer *vt* to orchestrate, score.
orchidée *f* orchid.
ordinaire *adj* ordinary, common, usual;
* *m* custom, usual routine.
ordinateur *m* computer.
ordonnance *f* prescription, order.
ordre *m* order, command; class.
ordure *f* filth, dirt; excrement; rubbish.
oreille *f* ear; hearing; wing; handle.
oreiller *m* pillow.
oreillons *mpl* mumps.
organe *m* organ; instrument; medium.
organique *adj* organic.
organisateur *m* **-trice** *f* organiser.
organisation *f* organisation.
organiser *vt* to organise, arrange.
organisme *m* organism.
organiste *mf* organist.
orgasme *m* orgasm.
orge *f* barley.
orgie *f* orgy.
orgue *m* (*mus*) organ.
orgueil *m* pride, arrogance.
orgueilleux *adj* proud, arrogant.
orient *m* orient, east.
oriental *adj* eastern, oriental.
orientation *f* orientation; positioning;
directing; trend.
orienter *vt* to orientate; to position; to
direct; **s'~** *vr* to ascertain one's position;
to turn towards.
orifice *m* orifice; aperture, opening.
original *adj* original, novel; peculiar,

bizarre; ***** *m* original; top copy.
origine *f* origin, source, derivation; **à
l'~** originally.
originel *adj* original, primitive.
orme *m* elm.
ornement *m* ornament, embellishment.
ornemental *adj* ornamental.
orner *vt* to adorn, decorate.
ornière *f* rut.
ornithologiste, ornithologue *mf* or-
nithologist.
orphelin *m* **-e** *f* orphan.
orphelinat *m* orphanage.
orteil *m* toe.
orthodoxe *adj* orthodox; ***** *mf* orthodox.
orthopédique *adj* orthopaedic.
ortie *f* nettle.
os *m* bone.
oscillation *f* oscillation, swinging.
osciller *vi* to oscillate, swing.
oser *vt* to dare.
ossature *f* skeleton; framework.
ossements *mpl* bones.
ostensible *adj* open, conspicuous.
ostentation *f* ostentation.
ostracisme *m* ostracism.
otage *m* hostage.
otarie *f* sea-lion.
ôter *vt* to take away, remove; to deprive, deduct.
otite *f* ear infection.
ou *conj* or
où *adv* where, in which; *pn* where.
ouate *f* cotton wool.
oubli *m* forgetfulness; oblivion; oversight, omission.
oublier *vt* to forget; to omit, neglect.
ouest *m* west; *adj* west.
oui *adv* yes.

ouïe f hearing (sense).

ouragan m hurricane, whirlwind.

ourlet m hem.

ours m **-e** f bear.

ourson m bear cub.

outil m tool, implement.

outillage m (set of) tools; equipment.

outiller vt to equip; to provide with tools.

outrage m outrage, insult, wrong.

outrageant adj outrageous, insulting.

outre prép as well as, besides; **en ~** moreover; **~ mesure** to excess, inordinately; **passer ~** to go on, to take no notice.

outré adj excessive, exaggerated.

outrepasser vt to exceed; to transgress.

ouvert adj open; exposed; frank.

ouverture f opening; mouth; overture; means, way.

ouvrage m work; piece of work.

ouvre-boîte m tin-opener.

ouvre-bouteille m bottle-opener.

ouvrier m **-ière** f worker; * adj working-class; industrial; labour.

ouvrir vt to open; to unlock; to broach; **s'~** vr to open; to open one's mind; to cut o.s.

ovaire m ovary.

ovale adj oval; * m oval.

ovation f ovation.

ovulation f ovulation.

ovule m ovum; ovule.

oxygène m oxygen.

ozone f ozone.

P

pacifiste mf pacifist; * adj pacifist.

pacte m pact, treaty.

pagaie f paddle.

pagayer vi to paddle.

page f page; passage.

pagne m loincloth.

paiement m payment.

païen m **-ne** f pagan; * adj pagan.

paillasse f straw mattress.

paillasson m doormat.

paille f straw.

paillette f sequin; spangle.

pain m bread; loaf; bar.

pair adj even; * m peer; par; **hors ~** outstanding, matchless.

paire f pair; yoke; brace.

paisible adj peaceful; calm.

paître vi to graze.

paix f peace; quiet; stillness; tranquility.

palais m palace; law courts; palate.

palan m hoist.

pâle adj pale, pallid.

palette f palette; pallet; paddle.

pâleur f paleness, pallor.

palier m landing; level; degree.

pâlir vi to turn pale; to dim; to fade.

palliatif m palliative; * adj palliative.

pallier vt to palliate; to offset.

palme f palm leaf; palm.

palmé adj palmate; webbed.

palmier m palm tree.

palpable *adj* palpable.

palper *vt* to feel, touch; to palpate.

palpitation *f* palpitation; throbbing; quivering.

palpiter *vi* to palpitate; to beat; to race.

paludisme *m* malaria.

pamplemousse *m* grapefruit.

panaché *adj* variegated; motley.

pancarte *f* sign, notice; placard.

panda *m* panda.

panier *m* basket; pannier (mode).

panique *f* panic.

paniquer *vi* to panic, get panicky.

panne *f* breakdown; fault, problem.

panneau *m* panel; sign, notice.

panoplie *f* outfit; display.

panorama *m* panorama.

pansement *m* dressing, bandage.

panser *vt* to dress, bandage.

pantalon *m* trousers; pants; knickers.

panthère *f* panther.

pantomime *f* pantomime; mime.

pantoufle *f* slipper.

paon *m* peacock.

papa *m* dad; daddy.

papaye *f* papaya.

pape *m* pope.

papeterie *f* stationery; stationer's shop; paper mill.

papetier *m* **-ière** *f* stationer

papier *m* paper; article; wrapper.

papillon *m* butterfly.

papillote *f* sweet wrapper.

papoter *vi* to chatter.

Pâques *fpl* Easter.

paquebot *m* liner, steamer.

pâquerette *f* daisy.

paquet *m* packet, pack; bag; parcel.

par *prép* by, with, through; from; along;

~-ci, ~-là here and there, now and then; **~-derrière** round the back; **~-dessous** underneath; **~-dessus** over, above.

parachever *vt* to perfect; to complete.

parachute *m* parachute.

parade *f* parade, show; parry.

paradis *m* paradise; (*thea*) gallery.

paraffine *f* paraffin.

paragraphe *m* paragraph; section.

paraître *vi* to appear; to be published; to look, seem.

parallèle *adj* parallel; **~ment** *adv* parallel; at the same time.

paralyser *vt* to paralyse.

paralysie *f* paralysis.

paralytique *mf* paralytic; * *adj* paralytic.

paranoïaque *adj* paranoiac, paranoid; * *mf* paranoiac, paranoid.

parapluie *m* umbrella.

parasite *m* parasite, sponger.

paratonnerre *m* lightning conductor.

paravent *m* folding screen, partition.

parc *m* park; grounds; depot.

parcelle *f* fragment, particle; parcel.

parce que *conj* because.

parchemin *m* parchment.

parcmètre *m* meter (parking).

parcourir *vt* to travel through; to scour; to traverse.

pardon *m* pardon, forgiveness.

pardonner *vt* to pardon; to excuse, overlook.

pare-brise *m invar* windscreen.

pare-chocs *m invar* bumper.

pareil *m* **-le** *f* equal; match; **sans ~** unparalleled, unequalled; * *adj* like, equal, similar; identical.

parent *m* **-e** *f* relative, relation; **~s** (*pl*) parents.

parental *adj* parental.

parer *vt* to adorn, deck out; to ward off; to parry; ~ **à** to deal with, overcome.

paresse *f* laziness; sluggishness.

paresseux *m* **-euse** *f* lazy person, loafer; * *adj* lazy.

parfait *adj* perfect, flawless;.

parfois *adv* sometimes, occasionally.

parfumer *vt* to perfume, scent.

parfumerie *f* perfumery.

parfumeur *m* **-euse** *f* perfumer.

pari *m* bet, wager.

parier *vt* to bet, wager.

parking *m* car park; parking.

parlement *m* Parliament.

parlementaire *adj* parliamentary; * *mf* member of parliament.

parler *vi* to talk, speak; * *vt* to speak.

parmi *prép* among.

paroi *f* wall; surface.

paroisse *f* parish.

parole *f* word; speech; voice; lyrics.

parquer *vt* to park; to enclose, pen.

parquet *m* floor, floorboards.

parrain *m* godfather; patron; promoter.

parrainer *vt* to sponsor; propose.

parsemer *vt* to sprinkle, strew.

part *f* part; share; portion; **prendre ~ à** to participate in; **faire ~ de** to announce; **de sa part** for his part; **autre ~** elsewhere; **nulle ~** nowhere; **d'autre ~** moreover.

partage *m* sharing, distribution; portion.

partager *vt* to divide up, share out.

partenaire *mf* partner.

parti *m* party; option; match.

partial *adj* partial, biased.

participant *m* **-e** *f* participant, member; * *adj* participating.

participation *f* participation; involvement.

participer *vi* to take part in, participate.

particulier *adj* particular, specific; peculiar, characteristic.

partie *f* part; subject; game; party; **faire ~ de** to be a part of.

partiel *adj* part, partial.

partir *vi* to leave, set off; to start up; **à ~ de** from.

partisan *m* **-e** *f* partisan, supporter, proponent.

partout *adv* everywhere.

parvenir *vi:* ~ **à** to reach; to achieve.

pas *m* step; pace; footprint; gait; * *adv* no, not.

passage *m* passage, passing by; transit.

passager *m* **-ère** *f* passenger.

passant *m* **-e** *f* passer-by, wayfarer; * *adj* much-frequented, busy.

passe *f* pass; permit; channel.

passé *m* past.

passeport *m* passport.

passer *vi* to pass; to elapse; to disappear, fade; **se ~** *vr* to pass; to take place; **se ~ de** to do without.

passerelle *f* footbridge; bridge; gangway.

passe-temps *m invar* pastime.

passif *adj* passive; * *m* passive.

passion *f* passion; fondness.

passionné *adj* passionate, impassioned.

passionner *vt* to fascinate; to interest deeply, impassion; **se ~** *vr* to be fascinated by, have a passion for.

passivité *f* passivity, passiveness.

pastel *m* pastel.

pastèque *f* watermelon.

pasteur *m* minister, pastor.

pasteuriser *vt* to pasteurise.

patate f (fam) spud; sweet potato.

patauger vi to wade about, splash about.

pâte f pastry, pasta, dough, batter.

paternel adj paternal, fatherly.

paternité f paternity; fatherhood.

pathétique adj pathetic.

patience f patience, endurance.

patient adj patient, enduring.

patienter vi to wait.

patin m skate; ~ à glace iceskate; ~ à roulettes roller skate.

patinage m skating; slipping; spinning.

patiner vi to skate; to slip; to spin.

patineur m -euse f skater.

patinoire f ice rink.

patois m patois, provincial dialect.

patrie f homeland, country.

patriote mf patriot; * adj patriotic.

patron m -ne f owner, boss, proprietor.

patronner vt to patronise, sponsor.

patrouille f patrol.

patte f leg, paw, foot.

pâturage m pasture, pasturage, grazing.

pâture f pasture; food.

paume f palm.

paumer vt (fam) to lose; se ~ vr to get lost.

paupière f eyelid.

pause f pause; half-time.

pauvre adj poor; indigent; scanty; weak; * mf poor person, pauper.

pavot m poppy.

paye f pay, wages.

payer vt to pay, settle; to reward.

pays m country; region; village; land.

paysage m landscape; scenery.

paysan m countryman, farmer; -ne f countrywoman.

péage m toll; tollgate.

peau f skin; hide, pelt.

pêche f peach; fishing.

pécher vi to sin.

pêcher vt to fish; to catch; * m peach tree.

pécheur m -eresse f sinner.

pêcheur m fisherman, -euse f fisherwoman.

pédale f pedal; treadle.

pédaler vi to pedal.

pédestre adj pedestrian.

pédicure mf chiropodist.

peigne m comb.

peigner vt to comb; to card; se ~ vr to comb one's hair.

peignoir m dressing gown.

peindre vt to paint; to depict, portray.

peine f effort; sadness; pain; punishment; difficulty.

peiner vi to toil; to struggle.

peintre m painter.

peinture f painting, picture; paintwork.

péjoratif adj pejorative.

pelage m coat, fur.

peler vi to peel.

pèlerin m pilgrim.

pèlerinage m pilgrimage.

pélican m pelican.

pelle f shovel; spade.

pellicule f film; thin layer.

pelote f ball.

peloton m pack; squad; platoon.

pelouse f lawn, field; ground.

pelure f peeling, piece of peel.

pénal adj penal; criminal.

pénaliser vt to penalise.

pénalité f penalty.

penalty m penalty (kick).

pencher *vi* to lean; to tilt; (*mar*) to list; * *vt* to tip up; tilt; **se ~** *vr* to bend down; to study, look at.

pendant *prép* during; for; **~ que** while, whilst.

pendentif *m* pendant.

pendre *vi* to hang, dangle; * *vt* to hang.

pendule *f* clock; * *m* pendulum.

pénétrant *adj* penetrating, piercing; searching; acute.

pénétration *f* penetration; perception.

pénétrer *vi* to enter, penetrate; * *vt* to penetrate, pierce; to pervade.

pénible *adj* hard, tiresome; difficult; laborious.

péniche *f* barge.

péniciline *f* penicillin.

péninsule *f* peninsula.

pénis *m* penis.

pénitence *f* penitence, penance; punishment.

pensée *f* thought; thinking; mind.

penser *vt* to think, suppose, believe; * *vi* to think.

pensif *adj* pensive, thoughtful.

pension *f* pension; boarding house.

pensionnaire *mf* boarder; lodger.

pensionnat *m* boarding school.

pente *f* slope; gradient.

pépère *m* granddad, grandpa.

pépin *m* pip; snag, hitch.

perçant *adj* piercing, shrill.

percée *f* opening, clearing; breach; breakthrough.

perce-oreille *m* earwig.

perception *f* perception; collection.

percer *vt* to pierce; to drill; to see through.

percevoir *vt* to perceive, detect; to collect.

percher *vt* to stick; to place on; **se ~** *vr* to perch.

percuter *vt* to strike; to crash into.

perdant *m* -e *f* loser; * *adj* losing.

perdre *vt* to lose; to waste; to miss; * *vi* to lose; **se ~** *vr* to lose one's way.

perdrix *f* partridge.

perdu *adj* lost; wasted; missed.

père *m* father; sire.

péremptoire *adj* peremptory.

perfection *f* perfection.

perfectionnement *m* perfection, perfecting; improvement.

perfectionner *vt* to improve, perfect; **se ~** *vr* to improve, improve o.s.

perfectionniste *mf* perfectionist; * *adj* perfectionist.

perforation *f* perforation.

performance *f* result, performance.

péricliter *vi* to collapse; to be in jeopardy.

péril *m* peril, danger.

périlleux *adj* perilous.

périmé *adj* out-of-date; expired.

période *f* period; epoch, era; wave, spell.

périodique *adj* periodic.

péripétie *f* event, episode.

périple *m* voyage; journey.

périr *vi* to perish, die.

perle *f* pearl; bead; gem.

permanence *f* permanence.

permanent *adj* permanent, continuous.

permanente *f* perm.

permanenter *vt* to perm.

permettre *vt* to allow, permit.

permis *adj* permitted; * *m* permit, licence.

permission *f* permission; leave.

permuter *vt* to change, switch round; to permutate.

perpendiculaire *adj* perpendicular;

perpétuel *adj* perpetual; permanent.

perpétuer *vt* to perpetuate, carry on; **se ~** *vr* to be perpetuated; to survive.

perplexe *adj* perplexed, confused.

perplexité *f* perplexity, confusion.

perquisition *f* search.

perroquet *m* parrot.

perruche *f* budgerigar; chatterbox.

perruque *f* wig.

persécuter *vt* to persecute; to harass.

persécution *f* persecution.

persévérance *f* perseverance.

persévérer *vi* to persevere; to persist in.

persil *m* parsley.

persistance *f* persistence.

persistant *adj* persistent; evergreen.

persister *vi* to persist, keep up.

personnage *m* character, individual.

personnalité *f* personality.

personne *f* person; self; appearance; * *pn* anyone, anybody; nobody.

personnel *adj* personal; selfish.

personnifier *vt* to personify.

perspective *f* perspective; view; angle.

perspicace *adj* shrewd.

persuader *vt* to persuade; to convince.

persuasif *adj* persuasive; convincing.

persuasion *f* persuasion; conviction.

perte *f* loss, losing; ruin.

perturber *vt* to disrupt, disturb.

pervers *adj* perverse; perverted.

perversité *f* perversity.

pesant *adj* heavy, weighty.

pesanteur *f* gravity; heaviness.

pèse-personne *m* scales.

peser *vt* to weigh; to press; to evalu-

ate; * *vi* to weigh, weigh down; to hang over; **se ~** to weigh o.s.

pessimisme *m* pessimism.

pessimiste *mf* pessimist; * *adj* pessimistic.

peste *f* pest, nuisance; plague.

pesticide *m* pesticide.

pétale *f* petal.

pétillant *adj* bubbly, fizzy.

pétiller *vi* to crackle; to bubble; to sparkle.

petit *adj* small, tiny; slim; young.

petitesse *f* smallness, modesty; meanness.

petit-fils *m* grandson.

petite-fille *f* granddaughter.

pétition *f* petition.

petits-enfants *mpl* grandchildren.

pétrifié *adj* petrified; transfixed; fossilised.

pétrir *vt* to knead; to mould, shape.

pétrole *m* oil, petroleum.

pétrolier *m* oil tanker; * *adj* petroleum, oil, oil-producing.

peu *adv* little, not much, few; **un petit ~** a little bit; **quelque ~** a little; **pour ~ que** however little; **~ de** little, few.

peuplade *f* tribe, people.

peuple *m* people, nation; crowd.

peupler *vt* to populate, stock; to plant.

peuplier *m* poplar.

peur *f* fear, terror, apprehension; **avoir ~** to be afraid.

peureux *adj* fearful, timorous.

peut-être *adv* perhaps.

phallocrate *m* male chauvinist.

phare *m* lighthouse; headlight.

pharmacie *f* pharmacy.

pharmacien *m* **-ne** *f* pharmacist; chemist.

phase *f* phase, stage.

phénoménal *adj* phenomenal.

phénomène *m* phenomenon; freak; character.

philanthrope *mf* philanthropist.

philosophe *mf* philosopher; * *adj* philosophical.

philosophie *f* philosophy.

philosophique *adj* philosophical.

phobie *f* phobia.

phonétique *f* phonetics; * *adj* phonetic.

phoque *m* seal; sealskin.

photo *f* photo.

photocopie *f* photocopy.

photocopier *vt* to photocopy.

photocopieur *m*, **-euse** *f* photocopier.

photogénique *adj* photogenic.

photographe *mf* photograph.

photographie *f* photography.

photographier *vt* to photograph.

photographique *adj* photographic.

phrase *f* sentence; phrase.

physiothérapie *f* physiotherapy.

physique *f* physics; * *adj* physical.

pianiste *mf* pianist.

piano *m* piano.

pic *m* peak; **à ~** vertically, sheer.

pichet *m* pitcher, jug.

picorer *vt* to peck; to nibble.

picotement *m* tickle; prickling.

picoter *vt* to tickle; to prickle; to smart, sting.

pie *f* magpie; chatterbox.

pièce *f* piece; object; component; room; paper, document.

pied *m* foot; track; hoof; bottom; **à ~** on foot; **être sur ~** to be underway.

piédestal *m* pedestal.

piège *m* trap; pit; snare.

piéger *vt* to trap, set a trap.

pierre *f* stone.

piétiner *vi* to stamp (one's foot); * *vt* to trample on.

piéton *m* pedestrian; * *adj* pedestrian.

pieu *m* post, stake, pile.

pieux *adj* pious, devout.

pigeon *m* pigeon; dupe, mug.

pigment *m* pigment.

pignon *m* gable; cogwheel.

pile *f* pile; pier; battery; * *adv* dead; just, right, exactly.

piler *vt* to crush, pound.

pilier *m* pillar.

pillage *m* pillaging, looting.

piller *vt* to pillage, loot.

pilon *m* pestle; wooden leg.

pilote *m* pilot; driver.

piloter *vt* to pilot, fly; to drive.

pilule *f* pill.

piment *m* hot pepper, capsicum.

pin *m* pine.

pince *f* pliers, crowbar; pincer; dart.

pinceau *m* brush, paintbrush.

pincée *f* pinch.

pincer *vt* to pinch, nip; to grip.

pingouin *m* penguin.

ping-pong *m* table tennis.

pinte *f* pint.

pioche *f* pick, pickaxe.

piolet *m* ice axe.

pion *m* pawn; draught.

pionnier *m* pioneer.

pipe *f* pipe.

piquant *adj* prickly; pungent; piquant; * *m* quill, spine; prickle.

pique *f* pike, lance.

pique-nique *m* picnic.

piquer *vt* to sting, bite; to goad; to puncture.

piquet *m* post, picket.

piqûre *f* prick; sting; bite.

pirate *m* pirate.

pire *adj* worse; **le ~, la ~, les ~s** the worst.

pirouette *f* pirouette; about-turn.

pis *m* udder.

pis-aller *m invar* last resort, stopgap.

piscine *f* swimming pool.

piste *f* track, trail; course; runway; lead, clue.

pistolet *m* pistol, gun.

piston *m* piston.

piteux *adj* pitiful, pathetic.

pitié *f* pity, mercy.

pitoyable *adj* pitiful, pitiable.

pittoresque *adj* picturesque.

pivoter *vi* to revolve, pivot.

placard *m* cupboard; poster, notice.

place *f* place; square; seat; space; position; **à la ~ de** instead of.

placement *m* placing; investment.

placer *vt* to place, put; to fit; to seat; to sell; to invest; **se ~** *vr* to take up position; to stand; to find a job.

placide *adj* placid, calm.

placidité *f* placidity, calmness.

plafond *m* ceiling; roof.

plage *f* beach.

plaider *vt* to plead; to defend; * *vi* to plead for, go to court.

plaie *f* wound, cut; scourge.

plaindre *vt* to pity; to begrudge; **se ~** *vr* to complain.

plaine *f* plain.

plainte *f* complaint; moan, groan.

plaintif *adj* plaintive, complaining.

plaire *vi* to please, be pleasant; **se ~** *vr* to enjoy, take pleasure in.

plaisant *adj* pleasant, agreeable.

plaisanter *vi* to joke, jest.

plaisanterie *f* joking; pleasantry; humour.

plaisir *m* pleasure; delight; entertainment; **faire ~** to please.

plan *m* plan, scheme, project; plane, level.

planche *f* plank, board; plate; shelf.

plancher *m* floor.

planchette *f* small board, small shelf.

plancton *m* plankton.

planer *vi* to glide, soar; to hover over.

planète *f* planet.

planeur *m* glider.

planifier *vt* to plan.

planning *m* programme, schedule.

plantation *f* plantation; planting.

plante *f* plant.

planter *vt* to plant; to hammer in; to stick, dump.

plantureux *adj* copious, ample.

plaquer *vt* to plate, veneer; to jilt; tackle.

plaquette *f* plaque; tablet; slab.

plastique *m* plastic; * *adj* plastic.

plat *adj* flat; straight; dull, insipid.

platane *m* plane tree.

plateau *m* tray; turntable; plateau; stage.

plate-forme *f* platform.

platine *m* platinum; * *f* deck; turntable; stage.

platonique *adj* platonic.

plâtre *m* plaster.

plâtrer *vt* to plaster; to set in plaster.

plausible *adj* plausible.

plein *adj* full; entire, whole; busy.

plénitude *f* plenitude, fullness.

pleur *m* tear, sob; **en ~s** in tears.

pleurer *vi* to cry, weep; * *vt* to mourn for, lament.

pleuvoir *vi* to rain; to shower down, rain down.

pli *m* fold; crease; wrinkle; envelope.

plier *vt* to fold; to bend; * *vi* to bend; to yield; **se ~** *vr* to fold up; to submit.

plissement *m* creasing, folding; puckering.

plisser *vt* to pleat, fold; to pucker; * *vi* to become creased.

pliure *f* fold; bend.

plomb *m* lead; sinker; fuse.

plombage *m* weighting; leading; filling.

plomber *vt* to weight; to fill.

plomberie *f* plumbing.

plombier *m* plumber.

plongée *f* diving, dive.

plongeoir *m* diving board.

plongeon *m* dive.

plonger *vi* to dive; to plunge, dip sharply.

ployer *vi* to bend, to sag.

pluie *f* rain; shower.

plumage *m* plumage, feathers.

plume *f* feather.

plumeau *m* feather duster.

plumer *vt* to pluck.

plupart *f* most, most part, majority; **la ~ de** most of.

pluriel *m* plural; * *adj* plural.

plus *adv* more, most; **~ grand que** bigger than; **de ~ en ~** more and more; **de ~** besides, moreover; **non ~** neither, not either.

plusieurs *adj* several.

plus-value *f* appreciation; increase in value.

plutôt *adv* rather, quite, fairly; sooner.

pluvieux *adj* rainy, wet.

pneu *m* tyre.

pneumatique *adj* pneumatic; * *m* tyre.

pneumonie *f* pneumonia.

poche *f* pocket; pouch; bag.

pocher *vt* to poach.

pochette *f* pocket handkerchief; wallet; envelope.

pochoir *m* stencil.

poêle *m* stove; * *f* frying pan.

poème *m* poem.

poésie *f* poetry.

poète *m* poet.

poétique *adj* poetic.

poids *m* weight, influence; **~ lourd** heavyweight; **~ plume** featherweight.

poignard *m* dagger.

poignarder *vt* to stab.

poigne *f* grip; hand.

poignée *f* handful; **~ de mains** handshake.

poignet *m* wrist; cuff.

poil *m* hair; coat; bristle.

poilu *adj* hairy.

poinçon *m* hallmark, style; awl.

poinçonner *vt* to stamp; to hallmark.

poindre *vi* to break, dawn.

poing *m* fist; **coup de ~** punch.

point *m* point, spot; stage; full stop; **mettre au ~** to finalise; to perfect; **à~** medium, just right, when due; **~~virgule** semicolon; **~ de vue** point of view.

pointage *m* checking off; sighting; scrutiny.

pointe *f* point, head; spike, tack; **tailler en ~** to cut to a point; **sur la ~ des pieds** on tiptoe.

pointer *vi* to clock in; to soar up; to peep out; * *vt* to check off; to clock in; to stick into.

pointilleux *adj* particular, fastidious.

pointu *adj* pointed, sharp; subtle.

pointure *f* size, number.

poire *f* pear.

poireau *m* leek.

pois *m* pea; ~ **chiche** chickpea; **petits ~** garden peas.

poison *m* poison.

poisseux *adj* sticky.

poisson *m* fish.

poitrail *m* breast, chest.

poitrine *f* chest, breast; bosom.

poivre *m* pepper.

poivrière *f* pepperpot.

poivron *m* green pepper, capsicum.

polaire *adj* polar.

polariser *vt* to polarise; to attract.

pôle *m* pole; centre.

poli *adj* polite; polished, smooth.

police *f* police; policing; regulations.

policier *m* policeman, **-ière** *f* policewoman.

polir *vt* to polish; to refine.

politicien *m* **-ne** *f* politician.

politique *f* politics; policy; * *adj* political.

pollen *m* pollen.

polluant *adj* polluting; * *m* pollutant.

pollution *f* pollution.

polo *m* polo.

poltron *m* **-ne** *f* coward; * *adj* cowardly, craven.

polycopier *vt* to duplicate, stencil.

polyester *m* polyester.

pomme *f* apple.

pomme de terre *f* potato.

pommette *f* cheekbone.

pompe *f* pump.

pomper *vt* to pump.

pompeux *adj* pompous; pretentious.

pompier *m* fireman.

poncer *vt* to sand down, rub down.

ponction *f* (*med*) puncture.

ponctualité *f* punctuality.

ponctuation *f* punctuation.

ponctuel *adj* punctual.

pondéré *adj* weighted; levelheaded.

pondre *vt* to lay; to produce.

poney *m* pony.

pont *m* bridge; deck; axle.

ponte *f* laying; clutch.

populaire *adj* popular; working-class; vernacular.

popularité *f* popularity.

population *f* population.

porc *m* pig; pork.

porcelaine *f* porcelain, china.

porc-épic *m* porcupine.

porche *m* porch.

porcherie *f* pigsty.

pore *m* pore.

poreux *adj* porous.

pornographique *adj* pornographic.

port *m* port, harbour; carrying, wearing.

portatif *adj* portable.

porte *f* door; gate; threshold.

porte-avions *m invar* aircraft carrier.

porte-bagages *m invar* luggage rack.

porte-bonheur *m invar* lucky charm.

porte-clefs, porte-clés *m invar* key ring.

porte-documents *m invar* briefcase.

portée *f* reach, range; capacity; impact; significance; **à la ~ de** within reach.

porte-jarretelles *m invar* suspender belt.

portemanteau *m* coat hanger; hat stand.

porter *vt* to carry; to take; to wear; to hold, keep; **se ~** *vr* to put o.s. forward; to go.

porteur *m* **-euse** *f* porter; carrier; * *adj* booster; strong, buoyant.

portier *m* commissionaire.

portière *f* door.

portillon *m* gate, barrier.

portion *f* portion, share.

portrait *m* portrait.

pose *f* pose, posture; laying, fitting, setting.

poser *vt* to put; to install; to set out; to ask; **se ~** *vr* to land, settle; to come up, arise.

positif *adj* positive, definite.

position *f* position; situation; state; stance.

positionner *vt* to position, locate.

posséder *vt* to possess, have; to know inside out.

possessif *adj* possessive.

possession *f* possession, ownership.

possibilité *f* possibility; potential.

possible *adj* possible, feasible; potential.

postal *adj* postal, mail.

poste *f* post office, post; * *m* post, position; station; job.

poster *vt* to post, mail; to station; **se ~** *vr* to take up a position.

postérieur *adj* later, subsequent; back, posterior.

postérité *f* posterity; descendants.

postiche *m* hairpiece; toupee.

postulant *m* **-e** *f* applicant.

postuler *vt* to apply for; to postulate.

posture *f* posture, position.

pot *m* jar; pot; can.

potable *adj* drinkable; passable.

potage *m* soup.

pot-au-feu *m invar* stew.

pot-de-vin *m* bribe.

poteau *m* post, stake.

potelé *adj* plump, chubby.

potence *f* gallows; bracket.

potentiel *adj* potential; * *m* potential.

poterie *f* pottery, piece of pottery.

potion *f* potion.

potiron *m* pumpkin.

pou *m* louse.

poubelle *f* dustbin.

pouce *m* thumb; big toe; inch.

poudre *f* powder, dust.

poudrer *vt* to powder.

poulain *m* foal; protegé.

poule *f* hen, fowl.

poulet *m* chicken.

poulpe *m* octopus.

pouls *m* pulse.

poumon *m* lung.

poupe *f* stern.

poupée *f* doll.

poupon *m* baby.

pouponnière *f* day nursery, crèche.

pour *prép* for; to; in favour of; on account of; in order; **~ que** so that, in order that; **être ~** to be in favour of.

pourboire *m* tip.

pourceau *m* pig, swine.

pourcentage *m* percentage.

pourchasser *vt* to pursue; to harry.

pourparlers *mpl* talks, negotiations.

pourpre *adj* crimson; * *m* crimson.

pourquoi *adv* why; **~ pas?** why not?; * *m* reason, question.

pourrir *vi* to rot, go rotten; to deteriorate.

pourriture f rot, rottenness.

poursuite f pursuit; prosecution.

poursuivant m -e f pursuer; plaintiff.

poursuivre vt to pursue; to seek; to prosecute.

pourtant adv however, yet, nevertheless.

pourvoir vt to provide, equip.

pourvu conj: ~ que provided that.

pousse f shoot; sprouting.

poussée f pressure, pushing; thrust; upsurge.

pousser vt to push; to drive; to incite; * vi to push; to grow, expand; **se ~** vr to move, shift.

poussette f pushchair.

poussière f dust.

poussiéreux adj dusty.

poutre f beam.

pouvoir vi can, be able; may, be allowed; * m power, ability; authority; proxy.

praline f sugared almond.

pratiquant m -e f churchgoer; * adj practising.

pratique f practice; exercise; observance; * adj practical.

pratiquer vt to practise, exercise; to carry out.

pré m meadow.

préalable adj preliminary; previous.

préavis m notice, advance warning.

précaire adj precarious.

précaution f precaution; care.

précautionneux adj cautious, careful.

précédent adj previous, preceding; * m precedent.

précéder vt to precede, go before.

prêcher vt to preach; * vi to preach, sermonise.

prêcheur m -euse f preacher.

précieux adj precious; invaluable.

précipice m precipice; abyss.

précipitation f haste.

précis adj precise, exact.

préciser vt to specify; to clarify; **se ~** vr to become clear.

précision f precision, preciseness.

précoce adj precocious, premature.

préconçu adj preconceived.

préconiser vt to recommend; to advocate.

précurseur m forerunner, precursor.

prédateur m predator.

prédécesseur m predecessor.

prédestiné adj predestined, fated.

prédiction f prediction.

prédire vt to predict, foretell.

prédisposition f predisposition.

prédominance f predominance.

prédominant adj predominant.

préfabriqué adj prefabricated.

préface f preface, prelude.

préférable adj preferable; better.

préféré m -e f favourite; adj favourite, preferred.

préférer vt to prefer.

préhistorique adj prehistoric.

préjudice m loss; harm; wrong; damage.

préjugé m prejudice.

prélasser (se) vr to sprawl, lounge.

prélever vt to take; to levy; to deduct.

préliminaire m preliminary; * adj preliminary.

prélude m prelude; warm-up.

prématuré adj premature; untimely.

préméditation f premeditation.

prémédité adj premeditated.

premier m first, first floor, **-ière** f first,

first gear; * *adj* first; former; chief; early; primary.

première *f* première.

prémonition *f* premonition.

prendre *vt* to take; to pick up; to catch; * *vi* to take root; to harden; to start; **se ~** *vr* to consider o.s.; **s'y ~ mal** to set about the wrong way; **s'en ~ à** to set upon, take it out on.

préoccuper *vt* to worry; to preoccupy; **se ~** *vr* to concern o.s.

préparatif *m* preparation.

préparation *f* preparation; making up; training.

préparatoire *adj* preparatory.

préparer *vt* to prepare, get ready; to train.

préposition *f* preposition.

prérogative *f* prerogative.

près *adv* near, close; nearly, almost; **de ~** closely; **à peu ~** just about, near enough; **à peu de choses ~** more or less.

présage *m* omen; harbinger.

présence *f* presence.

présent *m* present, gift; * *adj* present; * *m* present; **à ~** just now.

présentateur *m* -**trice** *f* host, compère; presenter.

présentation *f* presentation; introduction; **faire les ~s** to make the introductions.

présenter *vt* to introduce; to present; to explain; **se ~** *vr* to appear; to come forward; to introduce o.s.

présentoir *m* display shelf.

préservatif *m* condom.

préserver *vt* to preserve; to protect.

président *m* -**e** *f* president.

présidentiel *adj* presidential.

présider *vt* to preside, chair; to direct.

présomption *f* presumption, assumption.

présomptueux *adj* presump-tuous.

presque *adv* almost, nearly; hardly, scarcely.

presqu'île *f* peninsula.

pressant *adj* urgent, pressing.

presse *f* press, newspapers; throng.

pressé *adj* hurried, urgent.

pressentiment *m* presentiment, fore-boding, premonition.

pressentir *vt* to have a presentiment of.

presse-papiers *m invar* paperweight.

presser *vt* to press; to squeeze; to hurry up; **se ~** *vr* to hurry; to crowd around.

pression *f* pressure.

prestation *f* benefit; service; payment; allowance.

prestidigitateur *m* -**trice** *f* conjurer; magician.

prestigieux *adj* prestigious.

présumer *vt* to presume, assume.

prêt *adj* ready; prepared, willing; * *m* loan, lending.

prétendant *m* -**e** *f* candidate.

prétendre *vt* to claim, maintain; to want; to intend, mean.

prétentieux *adj* pretentious.

prétention *f* pretension, claim; preten-tiousness.

prêter *vt* to lend; to attribute; to give.

prétexte *m* pretext, excuse.

prêtre *m* priest.

preuve *f* proof, evidence.

prévenant *adj* considerate, thoughtful.

prévenir *vt* to prevent; to warn, in-form; to anticipate.

prévention *f* prevention.

prévisible *adj* foreseeable.

prévision *f* prediction; forecast.

prévoir *vt* to anticipate; to plan; to provide for.

prévoyance *f* foresight, forethought.

prévoyant *adj* provident.

prier *vi* to pray; * *vt* to pray to; to beg; to invite.

prière *f* prayer; entreaty.

primaire *adj* primary; elementary.

prime *f* premium, subsidy; free gift.

primer *vi* to dominate; to take first place; * *vt* to outdo, prevail.

primevère *f* primrose.

primordial *adj* primordial, essential.

prince *m* prince.

princesse *f* princess.

principal *m* principal; headmaster; * *adj* main, principal.

principe *m* principle; origin; element; **en ~** in principle.

printemps *m* spring.

prioritaire *adj* having priority, priority.

priorité *f* priority.

pris *adj* taken; busy, engaged.

prise *f* hold, grip; catch; plug; dose; **lâcher ~** to let go one's hold; **~ de sang** blood sample; **~ de courant** plug, power point; **~ de conscience** awareness, realisation.

prisme *m* prism.

prison *f* prison; jail.

prisonnier *m* **-ière** *f* prisoner; * *adj* captive.

privation *f* deprivation.

privatiser *vt* to privatise.

privé *adj* private; unofficial; independent.

priver *vt* to deprive; **se ~** *vr* to go without.

privilège *m* privilege.

privilégier *vt* to favour.

prix *m* price, cost; prize.

probabilité *f* probability, likelihood.

probable *adj* probable, likely.

problème *m* problem, issue.

procédé *m* process; behaviour.

procéder *vi* to proceed.

procédure *f* procedure; proceedings.

procès *m* proceedings; lawsuit, trial.

processus *m* process; progress.

prochain *adj* next; imminent; * *m* neighbour.

proche *adj* nearby; close, imminent.

proclamer *vt* to proclaim, declare.

procurer *vt* to procure, provide; **se ~** *vr* to procure, obtain for o.s.

prodige *m* marvel, wonder.

prodigieux *adj* prodigious.

prodiguer *vt* to be lavish, be unsparing; to squander

producteur *m* **-trice** *f* producer; * *adj* producing, growing.

productif *adj* productive.

production *f* production; generation; output.

produire *vt* to produce; to grow; to generate; **se ~** *vr* to happen, take place.

produit *m* product; goods; yield, profit.

proférer *vt* to utter, pronounce.

professeur *m* teacher, professor.

profession *f* profession; occupation, trade.

professionnel *m* **-le** *f* professional; skilled worker; * *adj* professional; occupational; technical.

profil *m* profile, outline.

profiler *vt* to profile; to streamline; **se ~** *vr* to stand out, be profiled.

profit *m* profit; advantage, benefit.

profiter *vi* to profit; to thrive.

profiteur *m* **-euse** *f* profiteer.

profond *adj* deep, profound; heavy.

profondeur *f* depth; profundity.

profusion *f* profusion, wealth; **à ~** plenty, in profusion.

programme *m* program; syllabus; schedule.

programmer *vt* to program; to schedule.

progrès *m* progress; improvement; advance.

progresser *vi* to progress; to advance.

progression *f* progress; progression, spread.

prohiber *vt* to prohibit, ban.

proie *f* prey, victim.

projecteur *m* projector; spotlight, floodlight.

projectile *m* projectile; missile.

projection *f* projection, casting; showing.

projet *m* plan; draft.

projeter *vt* to plan; to throw out; to cast, project.

prolifération *f* proliferation.

proliférer *vi* to proliferate.

prologue *m* prologue.

prolongement *m* continuation, extension.

prolonger *vt* to prolong, extend; **se ~** *vr* to go on, persist.

promenade *f* walk, stroll; drive, spin.

promener *vt* to take out for a walk; **se ~** *vr* to go for a walk.

promesse *f* promise.

prometteur *adj* promising.

promettre *vt* to promise.

promontoire *m* promontory, headland.

promoteur *m* **-trice** *f* promoter, instigator.

promotion *f* promotion; advancement.

promouvoir *vt* to promote, upgrade.

prompt *adj* prompt; swift; ready.

promptitude *f* promptness; swiftness.

pronom *m* pronoun.

prononcer *vt* to pronounce, utter; **se ~** *vr* to reach a verdict.

prononciation *f* pronunciation.

propagande *f* propaganda.

propagation *f* propagation; spreading.

propager *vt* to propagate, spread; **se ~** *vr* to spread, be propagated.

prophète *m* prophet.

prophétie *f* prophecy.

prophétiser *vt* to prophesy.

propice *adj* propitious, favourable.

proportion *f* proportion, ratio.

proportionnel *adj* proportional.

propos *m* talk, remarks; intention; **à ~ de** about, on the subject of; **hors de ~** irrelevant.

proposer *vt* to propose, suggest; **se ~** *vr* to offer one's services; to intend to.

proposition *f* proposition, suggestion.

propre *adj* clean, neat; honest; own; peculiar; suitable.

propreté *f* cleanliness; tidiness.

propriétaire *mf* owner; landlord.

propriété *f* ownership, property; appropriateness, suitability.

propulser *vt* to propel, power.

propulsion *f* propulsion.

proscrire *vt* to proscribe; to prohibit.

prose *f* prose.

prospecter *vt* to prospect; to canvass.

prospère *adj* prosperous, flourishing.

prospérer *vi* to prosper, flourish.

prospérité *f* prosperity.

prostituée f prostitute.

prostitution f prostitution.

protecteur m **-trice** f protector; patron; * adj protective; patronising.

protection f protection; patronage.

protectionnisme m protectionism.

protégé m **-e** f favourite, protégé; * adj protected, sheltered.

protéger vt to protect; to patronise; **se ~** vr to protect o.s.

protéine f protein.

protestant m **-e** f Protestant; * adj Protestant.

protestation f protest, protestation.

protester vi to protest; to affirm.

protocole m protocol; etiquette.

protubérance f protuberance, bulge.

proue f prow; bows.

prouesse f prowess.

prouver vt to prove; to demonstrate.

provenir vi to come from; to be due to.

proverbe m proverb.

providence f providence.

providentiel adj providential.

province f province.

provincial m **-e** f provincial; * adj provincial.

provision f provision; supply, stock.

provisoire adj provisional, temporary.

provocant adj provocative.

provocation f provocation.

provoquer vt to provoke; to cause.

proximité f proximity, closeness; imminence.

prudence f prudence, care.

prudent adj prudent, careful.

prune f plum.

prunelle f pupil, eye.

psaume m psalm.

pseudonyme m pseudonym; pen name; alias.

psychanalyse f psychoanalysis.

psychanalyser vt to psychoanalyse.

psychanalyste mf psychoanalyst.

psychédélique adj psychedelic.

psychiatre mf psychiatrist.

psychiatrie f psychiatry.

psychique adj psychic, mental.

psychologie f psychology.

psychologique adj psychological.

psychologue mf psychologist; * adj psychological.

psychopathe mf psychopath; mentally ill person.

puberté f puberty.

public adj, f **publique** public, state; * m public, audience; public sector.

publication f publication, publishing.

publicité f publicity.

publier vt to publish; to make public.

puce f flea.

pudeur f modesty, decency.

pudique adj modest; chaste.

puer vi to stink; * vt to stink.

puis adv then, next.

puiser vt to draw from, extract.

puisque conj since; as, seeing that.

puissance f power, strength; output; force.

puissant adj powerful; potent.

puits m well; shaft.

pulpe f pulp.

pulsation f beat; beating; pulsation.

pulsion f drive, urge.

pulvériser vt to pulverise; to powder.

puma m puma.

punaise f bug; drawing pin.

punir vt to punish.

punition *f* punishment.
pupille *f* pupil; ward.
pupitre *m* desk; console; lectern.
pur *adj* pure; neat; clear.
pureté *f* purity, pureness.
purge *f* purge; purgative; draining.
purger *vt* to purge; to drain.
purifier *vt* to purify, cleanse.
puritain *m* -e *f* puritan; * *adj* puritan.
puritanisme *m* puritanism.

pur-sang *m invar* thoroughbred.
pus *m* pus.
putois *m* polecat; skunk.
putréfier *vt* to putrefy, rot.
pyjama *m* pyjamas.
pylône *m* pylon.
pyramide *f* pyramid.
pyrex *m* Pyrex.
python *m* python.

Q

quadrangle *m* quadrangle.
quadrillage *m* covering, control; check pattern.
quadriller *vt* to mark out in squares; to cover, control.
quai *m* quay, wharf; platform.
qualificatif *adj* qualifying.
qualification *f* qualification.
qualifier *vt* to describe; to qualify; **se ~** *vr* to qualify for; to call o.s.
qualité *f* quality; skill; position.
quand *conj* when, whenever, while.
quant *prép*: **~ à lui** as for him/it.
quantité *f* quantity, amount.
quarantaine *f* about forty; **avoir la ~** to be in one's forties.
quarante *adj, m inv* forty.
quarantième *adj, mf* fortieth.
quart *m* quarter; beaker; watch.
quartette *m* quartet.
quartier *m* district, neighbourhood; quarters; quarter.
quasi *adv* almost, nearly.

quatorze *adj, m* fourteen.
quatorzième *adj, mf* fourteenth.
quatre *adj, m* four.
quatre-vingt(s) *adj, m* eighty.
quatre-vingt-dix *adj, m* ninety.
quatre-vingtième *adj, mf* eightieth.
quatrième *adj, mf* fourth.
quatuor *m* quartet.
que *conj* that; than; * *pn* that; whom; what; which.
quel, *f* **quelle** *adj* who, what, which.
quelconque *adj* some, any; least, slight; poor, indifferent.
quelque *adj* some; **~ part** somewhere.
quelque chose *pn* something.
quelquefois *adv* sometimes
quelqu'un, *f* **-une** someone, somebody, *pl* **quelques-uns, -unes** *pn* some, a few.
quémander *vt* to beg for.
querelle *f* quarrel; row; debate.
quereller (se) *vr* to quarrel, squabble.
question *f* question; matter, issue.

questionnaire *m* questionnaire.

questionner *vt* to question.

quête *m* quest, search; collection.

quêter *vi* to seek; to collect money.

queue *f* tail; stalk; queue; **faire la ~** to queue.

qui *pn* who, whom; which.

quiconque *pn* whoever, whosoever.

quiétude *f* quiet; peace; tranquillity.

quille *f* skittle; (*mar*) keel.

quintette *m* quintet.

quinzaine *f* about fifteen; fortnight.

quinze *adj, m* fifteen.

quinzième *adj, mf* fifteenth.

quiproquo *m* mistake; misunderstanding.

quittance *f* receipt; bill.

quitter *vt* to leave; to give up; **se ~** *vr* to part company, separate.

quoi *pn* what; **~ que** whatever.

quoique *conj* although, though.

quolibet *m* gibe, jeer.

quote-part *f* share.

quotidien *adj* daily, everyday; * *m* everyday life.

R

rabâcher *vi* to harp on, keep on; * *vt* to rehearse, harp on.

rabais *m* reduction, discount; **au ~** at a reduced price.

rabaisser *vt* to humble, disparage; to reduce; **se ~** *vr* to belittle o.s.

rabattre *vt* to close; to pull down; to reduce; **se ~** *vr* to cut across, pull in front of; **se ~ sur** to fall back on.

rabbin *m* rabbi.

rabot *m* plane.

raboter *vt* to plane; to scrape.

rabougri *adj* stunted, puny.

racaille *f* rabble, scum.

raccommoder *vt* to mend, repair.

raccord *m* join; link; pointing.

raccordement *m* linking; joining; connecting.

raccorder *vt* to link up, join up; **se ~** *vr* to link, join up.

raccourci *m* shortcut; **en ~** in short.

raccourcir *vt* to shorten, curtail; * *vi* to shrink; to grow shorter.

raccrocher *vt* to ring off; to hang up; to grab; **se ~** *vr* to catch; to cling to.

race *f* race; stock; breed.

racial *adj* racial.

racine *f* root; **~ carrée** square root.

racisme *m* racism.

raciste *mf* racist; * *adj* racist.

racler *vt* to scrape; to rake.

racoler *vt* to accost; to solicit.

raconter *vt* to tell, recount.

radar *m* radar.

rade *f* (*mar*) harbour, roads.

radeau *m* raft.

radiateur *m* radiator; heater.

radiation *f* radiation.

radical *adj* radical.

radieux *adj* radiant, dazzling.

radin *m* -e *f* skinflint; * *adj* mean, stingy.

radio *f* radio; X-ray.

radioactif *adj* radioactive.

radioactivité *f* radioactivity.

radiodiffuser *vt* to broadcast (radio).

radiodiffusion *f* broadcasting (radio).

radiographie *f* radiography; X-ray photography.

radiologie *f* radiology.

radio-taxi *m* radio taxi.

radis *m* radish.

radium *m* radium.

radoter *vi* to ramble; to dote.

radoucir *vt* to soften; **se ~** *vr* to calm down; to mellow.

rafale *f* gust, blast; flurry.

raffermir *vt* to harden; to strengthen; **se ~** *vr* to become strengthened.

raffiné *adj* refined, sophisticated.

raffinement *m* refinement, sophistication.

raffiner *vt* to refine.

raffoler *vi*: **~ de** to be crazy about.

rafle *f* raid, round-up.

rafraîchir *vt* to cool, freshen, chill; **se ~** *vr* to freshen up; to get colder.

rafraîchissant *adj* refreshing, cooling.

rafraîchissement *m* cooling; cold drink.

rage *f* rage, fury; mania; rabies.

rageur *adj* quick-tempered; bad-tempered.

ragot *m* (*fam*) malicious gossip.

ragoût *m* ragout; stew.

raid *m* raid; trek.

raide *adj* stiff; steep; rough; (*col*) broke.

raideur *f* stiffness; steepness; roughness.

raidir *vt* to stiffen; to tighten; to harden.

raie *f* line; furrow; scratch.

raifort *m* horseradish.

rail *m* rail; railway.

railler *vt* to scoff at, mock.

raillerie *f* mockery, scoffing.

railleur *adj* mocking, scoffing.

raisin *m* grape.

raison *f* reason; motive; sense; ground; ratio; **avoir ~** to be right; **en ~ de** because of.

raisonnable *adj* reasonable, sensible.

raisonnement *m* reasoning; argument.

raisonner *vi* to reason; to argue.

rajeunir *vi* to feel younger; to be modernised; * *vt* to rejuvenate.

rajouter *vt* to put in; to add; **en ~** to exaggerate.

rajuster *vt* to readjust, rearrange; to tidy up.

ralenti *adj* slow; slackened; * *m* slow motion; **au ~** ticking over, idling.

ralentir *vi* to slow down, let up; * *vt* to slow down, check.

ralentissement *m* slowing down; slowing up.

râler *vi* to groan, moan.

rallumer *vt* to relight; to switch on again; to revive.

ramage *m* song; foliage.

ramassage *m* collection; gathering.

ramasser *vt* to pick up; to collect, gather.

rambarde *f* guardrail.

rame *f* oar; underground train; stake.

rameau *m* branch; ramification.

ramener *vt* to bring back, restore.

ramer *vi* to row.

ramollir *vt* to soften; to weaken; **se ~** *vr* to go soft.

ramoner *vt* to sweep.

ramoneur *m* chimney sweep.

rampant *adj* crawling, creeping.

rampe *f* ramp, slope; gradient.

ramper *vi* to crawl, slither.

rance *adj* rancid, rank.

rancœur *f* rancour, resentment.

rançon *f* ransom.

rancune *f* grudge, resentment.

rancunier *adj* rancorous, spiteful.

randonnée *f* drive; ride; ramble.

randonneur *m* **-euse** *f* hiker, rambler.

rang *m* row, line; rank; class.

rangée *f* row, range, tier.

ranger *vt* to arrange, array; to put in order; **se ~** *vr* to line up; to make room; to park.

rapace *m* bird of prey.

râpe *f* rasp, rough file.

râper *vt* to grate; to rasp.

râpeux *adj* rough.

rapide *adj* rapid, quick; steep.

rapiécer *vt* to patch up.

rappel *m* recall; reminder.

rappeler *vt* to recall; to remind; **se ~** *vr* to remember.

rapport *m* report; relation; reference; profit; **en ~ avec** in touch with.

rapporter *vt* to report; to bring back; to yield; **se ~** *vr*: **se ~ à** to relate to.

rapporteur *m* **-euse** *f* reporter; tell-tale; ***** *adj* tell-tale; ***** *m* (*math*) protractor.

rapprochement *m* drawing closer; reconciliation.

rapprocher *vt* to bring nearer; to reconcile; **se ~** *vr* to approach; to come together, be reconciled.

rapt *m* abduction.

raquette *f* racket.

rare *adj* rare; few, odd; exceptional.

ras *adj* close-shaven, shorn; **à ~ bords** to the brim; **en avoir ~ le bol** (*fam*) to be fed up.

rasage *m* shaving; shearing.

raser *vt* to shave off; to scrape; **se ~** *vr* to have a shave.

rasoir *m* razor.

rassasier *vt* to fill sb up.

rassemblement *m* assembling; crowd; political group.

rassembler *vt* to rally, gather together; **se ~** *vr* to gather, assemble.

rasseoir (se) *vr* to sit down again.

rassis *adj* settled; calm; stale.

rassurer *vt* to reassure; to comfort; **se ~** *vr* to be reassured.

rat *m* rat.

ratatiner *vt* to shrivel; to wrinkle; **se ~** *vr* to become wrinkled.

rate *f* spleen.

raté *m* **-e** *f* failure; ***** *m* misfire.

râteau *m* rake.

râtelier *m* rack; denture.

rater *vt* to miss; to spoil; to fail; ***** *vi* misfire; to miss.

ration *f* ration, allowance.

rationnel *adj* rational.

rationnement *m* rationing.

rationner *vt* to ration, put on rations.

ratisser *vt* to rake; to comb.

rattraper *vt* to catch again, retake; to recover; **se ~** *vr* to catch hold of; to make up for.

raturer *vt* to cross out.

rauque *adj* hoarse, raucous.

ravage *m* havoc; ravaging, laying waste.

ravager *vt* to ravage; devastate.

ravaler *vt* to swallow again; to restore.

ravi *adj* delighted.

ravin *m* ravine, gully.

raviser (se) *vr* to think better of it, change one's mind.

ravissant *adj* ravishing, delightful.

raviver *vt* to revive, reanimate; **se ~** *vr* to be revived.

rayer *vt* to scratch; to cross out.

rayon *m* ray, beam; spoke; shelf.

rayonnant *adj* radiant, beaming.

rayonner *vi* to radiate, shine; to be influential.

rayure *f* stripe; streak; groove.

réaccoutumer *vt* to reaccustom; **se ~** *vr* to become reaccus-tomed.

réacteur *m* reactor; jet-engine.

réaction *f* reaction.

réactionnaire *adj* reactionary; * *mf* reactionary.

réactiver *vt* to reactivate.

réadaptation *f* rehabilitation; read-justment.

réadapter *vt* to readjust; to rehabili-tate.

réagir *vi* to react.

réalisateur *m* **-trice** *f* director, film-maker.

réalisation *f* realisation; carrying out; achievement.

réaliser *vt* to realise; to carry out; to achieve; **se ~** *vr* to be realised, come true.

réalisme *m* realism.

réaliste *adj* realistic; * *mf* realist.

réalité *f* reality; **en ~** in fact, in reality.

réanimation *f* resuscitation.

réanimer *vt* to reanimate; to resusci-tate.

réapparaître *vi* to reappear.

rébarbatif *adj* stern, grim, forbidding.

rebattu *adj* hackneyed.

rebelle *mf* rebel; * *adj* rebel, rebellious.

rebeller (se) *vr* to rebel.

rébellion *f* rebellion.

rebord *m* rim, edge; hem.

rebrousser *vt* to brush back; **~ chemin** to turn back.

rebut *m* scrap; repulse, rebuff.

récalcitrant *adj* recalcitrant, stub-born.

récapituler *vt* to recapitulate, sum up.

receler *vt* to receive; to harbour.

recensement *m* census, inventory.

recenser *vt* to make a census of; to record.

récent *adj* recent; new.

récépissé *m* receipt.

récepteur *m* receiver.

réceptif *adj* receptive.

réception *f* reception, welcome; re-ceipt.

réceptionniste *mf* receptionist.

récession *f* recession.

recette *f* recipe; formula.

receveur *m* **-euse** *f* recipient; collec-tor.

recevoir *vt* to receive, welcome; to take, collect.

rechange *m*: change; spare.

recharge *f* recharging; reloading.

recharger *vt* to recharge; to reload; to refill.

réchaud *m* stove; dish-warmer.

réchauffer *vt* to reheat; to warm up; **se ~** *vr* to get warmer.

rêche *adj* rough, harsh.

recherche *f* search; inquiry; investigation; research; **être à la ~ de** to be in search of.

recherché *adj* sought after, in demand; choice, exquisite.

rechercher *vt* to seek; to investigate.

rechute *f* relapse; lapse.

récidiviste *mf* recidivist, habitual criminal.

récif *m* reef.

récipient *m* container, receptacle.

réciproque *adj* reciprocal, mutual.

récit *m* account, story.

récital *m*, *pl* -als recital.

récitation *f* recitation; recital.

réciter *vt* to recite.

réclamation *f* complaint; demand; claim.

réclame *f* advertisement; publicity; **en ~** on offer.

réclamer *vt* to claim, demand, ask for; * *vi* to complain.

reclus *adj* shut up, secluded.

réclusion *f* reclusion; confinement.

recoiffer *vt* to do sb's hair; **se ~** *vr* to do one's hair.

recoin *m* corner, nook.

récolte *f* harvest; collection; result.

récolter *vt* to harvest; to collect.

recommandation *f* recommendation, reference.

recommander *vt* to recommend; to commend; to register (letter).

recommencement *m* renewal; fresh beginning.

récompense *f* reward; award.

réconciliation *f* reconciliation.

réconcilier *vt* to reconcile; **se ~** *vr* to become reconciled.

reconduire *vt* to bring back; to see home, escort.

réconfort *m* comfort.

réconforter *vt* to comfort; to fortify; **se ~** *vr* to take some refreshment.

reconnaissance *f* recognition; acknowledgement; gratitude.

reconnaissant *adj* grateful.

reconnaître *vt* to recognise; to acknowledge; to be grateful.

reconnu *adj* recognised, accepted.

reconsidérer *vt* to reconsider.

reconstituer *vt* to reconstitute; rebuild, restore.

reconstitution *f* reconstitution; rebuilding, restoration.

reconversion *f* reconversion, redeployment.

recoupement *m* crosscheck.

recourbé *adj* curved, hooked.

recourir *vi* to run again; **~ à** to resort to.

recours *m* recourse; redress; (*jur*) appeal.

recouvrir *vt* to cover again; to cover up.

récréation *f* recreation; break.

récrimination *f* recrimination, remonstration.

récriminer *vi* to recriminate, remonstrate.

recroqueviller (se) *vr* to shrivel up.

recrue *f* recruit.

recruter *vt* to recruit.

recteur *m* priest, rector.

rectificatif *m* correction; * *adj* corrected, rectified.

reçu *p.p.* **recevoir** accepted, successful; * *m* receipt.

recueil *m* collection, miscellany.

recueillement *m* meditation.

recueillir *vt* to gather, collect; to record; **se ~** *vr* to collect one's thoughts.

recul *m* retreat; recession; decline.

reculer *vi* to fall back, retreat; * *vt* to move back; to defer.

récupération *f* recovery; retrieval.

récupérer *vt* to recover, retrieve; to recuperate; * *vi* to recover.

récurer *vt* to scour.

recycler *vt* to recycle.

rédacteur *m* **-trice** *f* editor, compiler.

redevable *adj* indebted, owing; liable.

redevance *f* rent; tax; fees.

rédiger *vt* to write; to compile; to draft.

redoubler *vt* to increase, intensify; * *vi* to increase, intensify; **~ de** to redouble.

redoutable *adj* redoubtable, formidable.

redouter *vt* to dread, fear.

redresser *vt* to rectify; to true; to set up again; **se ~** *vr* to stand up; to right oneself.

réduction *f* reduction; discount; mitigation.

réduire *vt* to reduce, diminish; **se ~** *vr*: **se ~ à** to boil down to.

réduit *adj* reduced, limited; miniature; * *m* retreat; recess; small room.

réel *adj* real, genuine.

refaire *vt* to redo; to remake; to renew.

référence *f* reference.

référendum *m* referendum.

refermer *vt* to close again.

réfléchi *adj* well-considered; reflective, thoughtful.

réfléchir *vi* to think, reflect; * *vt* to realise; to mirror.

reflet *m* reflection; reflex.

refléter *vt* to reflect, mirror.

réflexion *f* thought, reflection; remark; **à la ~** on reflection; **~ faite** all things considered.

réforme *f* reform, amendment; discharge.

réformer *vt* to reform, correct; to invalid out; to scrap.

refouler *vt* to drive back, repel.

refrain *m* refrain, chorus.

réfréner *vt* to curb, hold in check.

réfrigérateur *m* refrigerator.

réfrigérer *vt* to refrigerate.

refroidir *vt* to cool; * *vi* to cool down, get cold.

refroidissement *m* cooling; chill.

refuge *m* refuge, shelter; lay-by.

réfugié *m* **-e** *f* refugee; * *adj* refugee.

réfugier (se) *vr* to take refuge.

refus *m* refusal.

refuser *vt* to refuse; to reject; to deny; **se ~** *vr* to deny o.s.; **se ~ à** to reject.

regagner *vt* to regain, win back.

regain *m* renewal; revival.

régal *m* delight, treat.

regard *m* look; glance; expression; peephole.

regardant *adj* particular, meticulous; stingy.

regarder *vt* to look at; to glance; to be opposite; to concern; **~ à** to think about.

régenter *vt* to rule over, domineer.

régie *f* administration; state control.

régime *m* system, régime; scheme; diet; rate, speed.

région *f* region, area.

régir *vt* to govern, rule.

registre *m* register, record; style; compass.

réglable *adj* adjustable.

réglage *m* regulation, adjustment; tuning.

règle *f* rule; order; regularity; period.

règlement *m* regulation, rules; settlement.

réglementaire *adj* regulation; statutory.

réglementation *f* regulations; control.

réglementer *vt* to regulate, control.

régler *vt* to settle, pay; to regulate.

réglisse *f* liquorice.

règne *m* reign.

régner *vi* to reign; to prevail.

regorger *vi*: ~ de to overflow with, abound in.

régression *f* regression.

regret *m* regret, yearning.

regrettable *adj* regrettable.

regretter *vt* to regret, be sorry; to miss. together.

régulariser *vt* to regularise; straighten out.

régulier *adj* regular; consistent; steady; even; legitimate.

réhabilitation *f* rehabilitation; discharge; reinstatement.

rehausser *vt* to heighten, raise.

rein *m* kidney.

reine *f* queen.

réintégrer *vt* to reinstate; to return to.

réitérer *vt* to reiterate, repeat.

rejet *m* rejection, dismissal; throwing up.

rejeter *vt* to reject, dismiss; throw up.

rejoindre *vt* to rejoin; to catch up with.

rejouer *vt* to replay; to perform again; * *vi* to play again.

réjouir *vt* to delight; to entertain; **se ~** *vr* to rejoice, be delighted.

réjouissance *f* rejoicing, merry-making.

relâche *f* intermission, respite; **faire ~** to be closed; **sans ~** relentlessly.

relâchement *m* relaxation, loosening; laxity.

relâcher *vt* to relax, slacken; **se ~** *vr* to relax; to become lax.

relais *m* relay; shift.

relatif *adj* relative; relating to.

relation *f* relation, relationship; reference; acquaintance; account; **être en ~ avec** to be in contact with.

relaxer *vt* to relax; to acquit; to release; **se ~** *vr* to relax.

relayer *vt* to relieve, take the place of; to relay; **se ~** *vr* to take turns.

reléguer *vt* to relegate; to banish.

relève *f* relief; relief party.

relevé *m* statement; list; bill; * *adj* turned up, rolled up; elevated.

relever *vt* to set up again, raise again; to rebuild; to relieve; **se ~** *vr* to stand up again; to get up.

relief *m* relief; contours; depth.

relier *vt* to link up, connect; to bind.

religieux *m* monk, **-euse** *f* nun; * *adj* religious.

religion *f* religion.

relique *f* relic.

reliure *f* binding; bookbinding.

reluire *vi* to gleam, shine.

remarquable *adj* remarkable, notable.

remarque *f* remark, comment.

remarquer *vt* to remark; to notice.

rembourrer *vt* to stuff; to pad.

rembourser *vt* to reimburse, pay back.

remède *m* remedy, cure.

remédier *vi*: ~ **à** to remedy, cure.

remerciement *m* thanks; thanking.

remercier *vt* to thank.

remettre *vt* to put back; to replace; to restart; to revive; **se ~** *vr* to recover, get better; **se ~ à** to start doing sth again; **se ~ de** to get over sth.

réminiscence *f* reminiscence.

remise *f* delivery; discount; ~ **en état** repairing; ~ **à neuf** restoration; ~ **en jeu** throw-in; ~ **en question** calling into question.

remmener *vt* to take back.

remontant *m* tonic; * *adj* invigorating, fortifying.

remonte-pente *m* ski tow.

remonter *vi* to go up again; to rise, increase; to return; * *vt* to go up; to take up.

remontrance *f* remonstrance.

remords *m* remorse.

remorque *f* trailer; towrope.

remorquer *vt* to tow.

remorqueur *m* tug.

rémouleur *m* knife-grinder.

remous *m* back-wash; eddy, swirl.

rempart *m* rampart; defence.

remplaçant *m* **-e** *f* substitute.

remplacement *m* replacing; substitution.

remplacer *vt* to replace, stand in for.

remplir *vt* to fill; to fill in; to fulfil; **se ~** *vr* to fill up.

remporter *vt* to take away.

remuant *adj* restless, fidgety.

remue-ménage *m invar* commotion; hullabaloo.

remuer *vi* to move; to fidget; * *vt* to move, shift; to stir; **se ~** *vr* to move; to shift o.s.

rémunération *f* remuneration, payment.

renaissance *f* rebirth, Renaissance.

renard *m* fox.

renchérir *vi* to go further, go one better; to bid higher.

rencontre *f* meeting, encounter; conjuncture; collision.

rencontrer *vt* to meet; to find; to strike; **se ~** *vr* to meet each other.

rendement *m* yield; output.

rendez-vous *m* appointment; date; meeting place.

rendre *vt* to render; to give back, return; to yield; **se ~** *vr* to surrender; to give way.

rêne *f* rein.

renfermé *adj* withdrawn, close.

renfermer *vt* to contain, hold.

renflement *m* bulge.

renfoncement *m* recess.

renforcer *vt* to strengthen, reinforce.

renfort *m* reinforcement; help.

renfrogné *adj* frowning, glum.

renier *vt* to repudiate, disown.

renifler *vt* to sniff, snuffle.

renne *m* reindeer.

renom *m* renown, fame.

renommée *f* renowned, famed.

renoncer *vi* to renounce, give up.

renouer *vt* to retie; to renew.

renouveau *m* spring; renewal.

renouveler *vt* to renew; to revive; **se ~** *vr* to be renewed.

renouvellement *m* renewal; revival.

rénovation *f* renovation; renewal.

renseignement *m* information; intelligence.

renseigner *vt* to inform, give information to; **se ~** *vr* to ask for information.

rentabiliser *vt* to make profitable.

rentable *adj* profitable.

rente *f* rent; profit; annuity.

rentrée *f* reopening; reassembly; reappearance.

rentrer *vi* to re-enter; to return home; to begin again; * *vt* to bring in.

renversement *m* inversion; reversal; overturning.

renverser *vt* to turn upside down; to reverse; to overturn.

renvoi *m* sending back; returning; dismissal.

renvoyer *vt* to send back; to return; to dismiss.

repaire *m* den, lair.

répandre *vt* to pour out; to scatter, spread; **se ~** *vr* to spread; to be spilled.

répandu *adj* widespread.

réparer *vt* to repair; to restore; to make up for.

repartir *vi* to set off again; to start up again.

répartir *vt* to share out; to distribute; **se ~** *vr* to share out.

repas *m* meal.

repassage *m* ironing; grinding, sharpening.

repasser *vt* to iron; to cross again; to resit; * *vi* to go past again.

repêcher *vt* to fish out, retrieve.

repenti *adj* repentant.

repentir *m* repentance, contrition.

repentir (se) *vr* to repent, rue.

répercuter *vt* to reverberate; to echo; **se ~** *vr* to reverberate; to echo.

repère *m* line, mark; **point de ~** indication, reference mark.

repérer *vt* to spot, pick out; to mark out.

répertoire *m* index, catalogue; repertory.

répéter *vt* to repeat; to rehearse; **se ~** *vr* to repeat o.s.; to reoccur.

répétitif *adj* repetitive.

répétition *f* repetition; rehearsal.

repiquer *vt* to plant out, transplant.

répit *m* respite, rest.

repli *m* fold, coil.

replier *vt* to fold up; **se ~** *vr* to coil up.

réplique *f* reply, retort; counterattack.

répliquer *vt* to reply; to retaliate.

répondant *m* **-e** *f* guarantor; bail, surety.

répondeur *m* answering machine.

répondre *vt* to answer, reply.

réponse *f* response, reply.

report *m* postponement, deferment; carrying forward.

reportage *m* report; commentary; reporting.

reporter *vt* to postpone; to carry forward; to transfer; * *m* reporter.

reposant *adj* restful, refreshing.

repoussant *adj* repulsive; repellent.

repousser *vt* to push back; to repel.

représailles *fpl* reprisals; retaliation.

représentant *m* representative.

représentatif *adj* representative.

représentation *f* representation; performance.

représenter *vt* to represent, depict; to perform; to symbolise.

répression f repression.

réprimande f reprimand, rebuke.

réprimander vt to reprimand, rebuke.

reprise f resumption; recapture, taking back; **à plusieurs ~s** several times.

reproche m reproach; objection.

reprocher vt to reproach, blame.

reproduction f reproduction; copy; duplicate.

reproduire vt to reproduce, copy; to repeat; **se ~ vr** to reproduce, breed.

républicain m -e f republican; * adj republican.

république f republic.

répudier vt to repudiate; to renounce.

répugnance f repugnance, disgust.

répugnant adj repugnant, disgusting, revolting.

réputation f reputation; character; fame.

réputé adj reputable, renowned; supposed, reputed.

requérir vt to call for, request.

requête f petition, request.

requin m shark.

requis adj required, requisite.

réquisitionner vt to requisition; to conscript.

rescapé m -e f survivor.

réseau m network, net.

réservation f reservation, booking.

réserve f reserve; reservation, caution.

réserver vt to reserve, save; to book; to lay by.

résidence f residence; apartment block.

résidentiel adj residential.

résider vi to reside, dwell.

résidu m residue.

résignation f resignation.

résigner (se) vr to resign o.s.

résilier vt to terminate; to annul.

résistance f resistance.

résistant adj resistant; tough, unyielding.

résister vi to resist, withstand.

résolu adj resolved, determined.

résolution f resolution, determination.

résonner vi to resound, resonate.

résorber vt to reduce; to absorb; **se ~ vr** to be reduced.

résoudre vt to solve; to resolve; to annul.

respect m respect, regard, deference.

respecter vt to respect; to comply with.

respectueux adj respectful.

respiration f breathing, respiration.

respirer vi to breathe, respire; to rest; * vt to breathe in.

resplendissant adj shining, radiant.

responsabilité f responsibility; liability.

responsable adj responsible; liable; * mf official, manager.

ressemblance f resemblance, likeness; similarity.

ressemblant adj lifelike.

ressembler vi to resemble, be like; **se ~ vr** to be alike.

ressentiment m resentment.

ressentir vt to feel, experience; **se ~ vr: se ~ de** to feel the effects of.

resserrement m contraction, tightening; narrowing.

ressort m spring; motivation.

ressource f resource, resort, expedient.

ressusciter vi to revive, reawaken; to

come back to life; * *vt* to resuscitate; to revive.

restant *adj* remaining; * *m* rest, remainder.

restaurant *m* restaurant.

restaurateur *m* **-trice** *f* restaurateur; restorer.

restauration *f* restoration, rehabilitation; catering.

restaurer *vt* to restore; to feed.

reste *m* rest, left-over, remainder; **du ~** besides; **être en ~** to be outdone.

rester *vi* to remain, stay; to be left; to continue; to pause.

restituer *vt* to return, restore; to refund.

restreindre *vt* to restrict, curtail.

restreint *adj* restricted, limited.

restriction *f* restriction, limitation; reserve.

résultat *m* result, outcome; profit.

résulter *vi*: **~ de** to result, follow from, ensue.

résumé *m* summary, recapitulation; **en ~** in brief.

résumer *vt* to sum up; **se ~** *vr*: **se ~ à** to amount to.

rétablir *vt* to re-establish, restore; **se ~** *vr* to recover, get well again.

retard *m* lateness; delay; **être en ~** to be late; to be behind; to be backward.

retardataire *mf* latecomer; * *adj* obsolete.

retardé *adj* backward, slow.

retarder *vt* to delay; to hinder; to put back; * *vi* to be out of touch.

retenir *vt* to hold back, retain; to remember; **se ~** *vr* to control o.s.

rétention *f* retention; withholding.

retentir *vi* to resound; to ring.

retenue *f* discretion; deduction, stoppage; reservoir.

retiré *adj* remote, isolated.

retirer *vt* to take off; to take out, withdraw; to redeem; **se ~** *vr* to retire, withdraw; to stand down.

retomber *vi* to fall again; to have a relapse; **~ sur** to come across again.

rétorquer *vt* to retort.

retoucher *vt* to touch up; to alter.

retour *m* return; recurrence; vicissitude, reversal.

retournement *m* reversal; turnaround.

retourner *vt* to reverse, turn over; to return; * *vi* to return, go back; **se ~** *vr* to turn over; to overturn.

rétracter *vt* to retract, take back; **se ~** *vr* to retract, withdraw one's evidence.

retrait *m* ebb; retreat; withdrawal; **être en ~** to be set back.

retraite *f* retreat; retirement; refuge; **à la ~** retired.

retraité *m* **-e** *f* pensioner; * *adj* retired.

rétrécir *vi* to narrow; to shrink; * *vt* to take in, make narrower; **se ~** *vr* to narrow; to shrink.

rétrécissement *m* narrowing; shrinking.

rétribution *f* retribution.

rétroactif *adj* retrospective; retroactive.

rétrograde *adj* reactionary, backward.

rétroprojecteur *m* overhead projector.

rétrospectif *adj* retrospective.

rétrospective *f* retrospective.

retrousser *vt* to roll up, hitch up.

retrouvailles *fpl* reunion.

retrouver *vt* to find again, to regain;

to recover; to recognise; **se ~** *vr* to meet up; to end up in.

rétroviseur *m* rear-view mirror.

réunion *f* reunion, gathering.

réunir *vt* to unite; to collect, gather; to combine; **se ~** *vr* to meet; to assemble.

réussir *vi* to succeed, be a success; * *vt* to make a success of.

réussite *f* success, successful outcome.

revanche *f* revenge; **en ~** on the other hand.

rêvasser *vi* to daydream.

rêve *m* dream, dreaming; illusion.

réveil *m* waking, awaking; alarm clock.

réveiller *vt* to wake; **se ~** *vr* to awaken.

réveillon *m* midnight feast.

révélation *f* revelation, disclosure; developing.

révéler *vt* to reveal, disclose; **se ~** *vr* to be revealed; to prove to be.

revenant *m* **-e** *f* ghost.

revendeur *m* **-euse** *f* retailer; dealer.

revendication *f* claiming; claim; demand.

revendiquer *vt* to claim; to demand.

revenir *vi* to come back, reappear; to happen again; **~ à soi** to come round.

revenu *m* income, revenue.

rêver *vi* to dream; to muse; * *vt* to dream of.

réverbère *m* street lamp.

révérence *f* bow, curtsey.

revers *m* back, reverse; counterpart.

revêtement *m* coating, surface.

revêtir *vt* to don; to assume.

rêveur *m* **-euse** *f* dreamer; * *adj* dreamy.

revigorer *vt* to invigorate; to revive.

revirement *m* change of mind; reversal; turnaround.

réviser *vt* to review; to revise.

révision *f* review; auditing; revision.

revivre *vt* to relive; * *vi* to live again; come alive again.

revoir *vt* to see again; **se ~** *vr* to meet each other again.

révolte *f* revolt, rebellion.

révolter *vt* to revolt, outrage; **se ~** *vr* to rebel, revolt.

révolu *adj* past, bygone.

révolutionnaire *mf* revolutionary; * *adj* revolutionary.

révoquer *vt* to revoke; to dismiss.

revue *f* review; inspection.

rez-de-chaussée *m invar* ground floor.

rhubarbe *f* rhubarb.

rhum *m* rum.

rhumatisme *m* rheumatism.

rhume *m* cold.

riant *adj* smiling; cheerful.

ribambelle *f* swarm, herd.

ricanement *m* snigger, sniggering.

ricaner *vi* to snigger, giggle.

riche *adj* rich, wealthy; abundant; * *mf* rich person.

richesse *f* richness; wealth; abundance.

ricochet *m* ricochet; rebound.

rictus *m* grin; grimace.

ride *f* wrinkle; ripple; ridge.

ridé *adj* wrinkled.

rideau *m* curtain.

ridicule *adj* ridiculous; * *m* ridiculousness; absurdity; ridicule.

ridiculiser *vt* to ridicule.

rien *pn* nothing; **de ~** don't mention it; **il n'en est ~** it's nothing of the sort;

* *m* nothingness; mere nothing; pinch, shade; **en un ~ de temps** in no time.

rieur *adj* cheerful; laughing.

rigidité *f* rigidity, stiffness.

rigole *f* channel; rivulet.

rigoler *vi* (*fam*) to have a good laugh.

rigoureux *adj* rigorous, harsh.

rigueur *f* rigour; harshness, severity.

rime *f* rhyme.

rimer *vi* to rhyme (with).

rince-doigts *m invar* finger-bowl.

rincer *vt* to rinse out; to rinse.

ring *m* boxing ring.

riposte *f* riposte, retort.

riposter *vi* to answer back, retaliate.

rire *vi* to laugh; to smile; to joke; ***** *m* laughter, laugh.

risée *f* laugh; ridicule; mockery, derision.

risible *adj* laughable, ridiculous.

risque *m* risk, hazard.

risqué *adj* risky, hazardous; risqué.

risquer *vt* to risk; to venture; **se ~** *vr* to venture, dare.

ristourne *f* discount, rebate.

rite *m* rite.

rituel *adj* ritual.

rivage *m* shore.

rival *m* **-e** *f* rival; **sans ~** unrivalled; ***** *adj* rival.

rivaliser *vi* to rival, compete with; **~ de** to vie with.

rivalité *f* rivalry.

rive *f* shore, bank.

river *vt* to clinch; to rivet.

rivière *f* river.

riz *m* rice.

robe *f* dress; gown; **~ de chambre** dressing gown.

robinet *m* tap.

robuste *adj* robust.

roc *m* rock.

rocaille *f* loose stones; rocky ground.

rocailleux *adj* rocky.

roche *f* rock.

rocher *m* rock, boulder.

roder *vt* to grind; to run in.

rôder *vi* to roam; to prowl about.

rôdeur *m* **-euse** *f* prowler.

rogner *vt* to pare, prune, clip.

rognon *m* kidney.

roi *m* king.

rôle *m* role, character; roll, catalogue.

roman *m* novel; romance.

romancier *m* **-ière** *f* novelist.

romanesque *adj* fabulous; storybook; fictional.

romantique *adj* romantic.

rompre *vt* to break; to snap; to dissolve; ***** *vi* to break; to burst.

rond *m* circle, ring; slice, round; ***** *adj* round; chubby, plump; frank.

ronde *f* patrol; round; beat.

rondelle *f* slice, round; disc.

rondin *m* log.

rond-point *m* roundabout.

ronflement *m* snore, snoring; humming; roaring.

ronfler *vi* to snore; to hum; to roar.

ronger *vt* to gnaw.

ronronner *vi* to purr; to hum.

rosbif *m* roast beef.

rose *f* rose; ***** *adj* pink; ***** *m* pink.

roseau *m* reed.

rosée *f* dew.

rossignol *m* nightingale.

rot *m* belch, burp.

roter *vi* to belch, burp.

rôti *m* joint, roast.

rôtir *vt* to roast.

rouage *m* cog; gearwheel.

roucouler *vi* to coo; to bill.

roue *f* wheel.

rouge *adj* red; * *m* red; ~ **à lèvres** lipstick.

rouge-gorge *m* robin.

rougeole *f* measles.

rougir *vi* to blush, go red; * *vt* to make red, redden.

rouille *f* rust.

rouiller *vi* to rust; * *vt* to make rusty.

roulant *adj* on wheels; moving.

rouleau *m* roll; roller.

rouler *vt* to wheel, roll along; * *vi* to go, run (train); to drive.

roulette *f* castor; trundle; roulette.

roulotte *f* caravan.

rouquin *m* -e *f* redhead; * *adj* red-haired.

route *f* road; way; course, direction.

routier *adj* road; * *m* lorry driver; transport café.

routinier *adj* humdrum, routine.

roux *m*, **rousse** *f* redhead; * *adj* red, auburn.

royaume *m* kingdom.

royauté *f* monarchy.

ruban *m* ribbon; tape, band.

rubis *m* ruby.

ruche *f* hive.

rude *adj* rough; hard; unrefined.

rudiment *m* rudiment; principle.

rudimentaire *adj* rudimentary.

rudoyer *vt* to treat harshly.

rue *f* street.

ruelle *f* alley.

ruer *vi* to kick (horse); **se ~** *vr* to pounce on.

rugir *vi* to roar.

rugissement *m* roar, roaring.

rugueux *adj* rough; coarse.

ruine *f* ruin; wreck.

ruiner *vt* to ruin.

ruisseau *m* stream, brook.

ruisseler *vi* to stream, flow.

rumeur *f* rumour; murmur; hum.

ruminer *vt* to ruminate; to brood over.

rupture *f* break, rupture; breach; split.

rural *adj* rural, country.

ruse *f* cunning, slyness.

rusé *adj* cunning, crafty.

rythme *m* rhythm; rate, speed.

rythmique *adj* rhythmic.

S

sable *m* sand.

sablé *m* shortbread biscuit; * *adj* sandy, sanded.

sablier *m* hourglass.

sabot *m* clog; hoof.

saboter *vt* to sabotage; to mess up.

saboteur *m* -euse *f* saboteur; bungler.

sac *m* bag, sack; ~ **à main** handbag; ~ **de voyage** travelling bag.

saccade *f* jerk, jolt.

saccadé *adj* jerky, broken, staccato.

saccager *vt* to sack; to wreck, devastate.

sacerdoce *m* priesthood.

sachet *m* bag; sachet; packet.

sacoche *f* saddlebag, satchel.

sacre *m* coronation; consecration.

sacré *adj* sacred, holy; damned, confounded.

sacrer *vt* to crown; to consecrate.

sacrifier *vt* to sacrifice; to give up.

sacrilège *m* sacrilege.

sadique *adj* sadistic; * *mf* sadist.

sadisme *m* sadism.

sagace *adj* sagacious, shrewd.

sagacité *f* sagacity, shrewdness.

sage *adj* wise, sensible; well-behaved; * *m* sage, wise man.

sage-femme *f* midwife.

sagesse *f* wisdom, sense; good behaviour.

saignant *adj* bleeding; underdone.

saignement *m* bleeding.

saigner *vi* to bleed; * *vt* to bleed; to stick.

saillant *adj* prominent, protruding.

saillie *f* projection; sally; flash of wit.

saillir *vi* to gush out; to project, jut.

sain *adj* healthy; sound; sane.

saindoux *m* lard.

saint *m* -e *f* saint; * *adj* holy, saintly.

sainteté *f* saintliness; holiness.

saisie *f* (*jur*) seizure, distraint; capture.

saisir *vt* to take hold of; (*jur*) to seize, distrain; to capture.

saisissant *adj* gripping, startling, striking.

saison *f* season.

salade *f* salad; jumble, miscellany.

salaire *m* salary, pay; reward.

sale *adj* dirty, filthy; obscene; nasty.

salé *adj* salty, salted; savoury.

saler *vt* to salt.

saleté *f* dirtiness, dirt; rubbish; obscenity.

salière *f* saltcellar.

salir *vt* to make dirty, soil; **se ~** *vr* to get dirty.

saliver *vi* to salivate; to drool.

salle *f* room; hall; theatre; audience; **~ de séjour** living room; **~ à manger** dining room; **~ de bain** bathroom; **~ de cinéma** cinema.

salon *m* lounge, sitting room; exhibition.

salopette *f* overalls.

saluer *vt* to greet; to salute.

salut *m* safety, salvation; welfare; wave (hand); salute.

salutaire *adj* salutary; profitable; healthy.

salutation *f* salutation, greeting.

samedi *m* Saturday.

sanction *f* sanction, penalty; approval.

sanctionner *vt* to punish; to sanction, approve.

sanctuaire *m* sanctuary.

sandale *f* sandal.

sang *m* blood; race; kindred.

sangle *f* strap; girth.

sanglier *m* wild boar.

sanglot *m* sob.

sangloter *vi* to sob.

sangsue *f* leech.

sanitaire *adj* health, sanitary.

sans-abris *mf invar* homeless person.

sans-gêne *adj* inconsiderate; * *m invar* inconsiderate type.

santal *m* sandalwood.

santé *f* health, healthiness.

saper *vt* to undermine, sap.

sapeur-pompier *m* fireman.

saphir *m* sapphire.

sapin *m* fir tree, fir.

sarcasme *m* sarcasm.

sarcastique *adj* sarcastic.

sarcler *vt* to weed; to hoe.

sardonique *adj* sardonic.

satanique *adj* satanic, diabolical.

satellite *m* satellite.

satiété *f* satiety, satiation; **à ~** ad nauseam.

satin *m* satin.

satiné *adj* satiny, satin-smooth; glazed.

satire *f* satire, lampoon.

satirique *adj* satirical.

satisfaction *f* satisfaction; gratification; appeasement.

satisfaire *vt* to satisfy; to gratify; to appease.

satisfaisant *adj* satisfactory; satisfying.

satisfait *adj* satisfied.

saturé *adj* saturated; overloaded, jammed.

saturer *vt* to saturate; to surfeit; to congest.

sauce *f* sauce, dressing.

saucière *f* sauceboat.

saucisse *f* sausage.

saucisson *m* large sausage; salami.

sauf *prép* save, except; unless; * *adj* safe, unhurt.

sauge *f* sage.

saugrenu *adj* preposterous, absurd.

saule *m* willow.

saumon *m* salmon.

saupoudrer *vt* to sprinkle; to dust.

saut *m* jump, bound; waterfall.

sauter *vi* to jump, leap; to blow up; to get sacked.

sauterelle *f* grasshopper.

sautiller *vi* to hop, skip.

sauvage *adj* savage, wild; unsociable.

sauvegarde *f* safeguard; backup.

sauvegarder *vt* to safeguard.

sauver *vt* to save, rescue; to preserve; **se ~** *vr* to save o.s.; to escape.

sauvetage *m* rescue; salvage.

sauveteur *m* rescuer.

savant *adj* learned; expert; skilled; * *m* scientist, scholar.

savoir *vt* to know; to be aware; to understand; to be able; * *m* learning, knowledge.

savoir-faire *m* know-how.

savoir-vivre *m* good manners, good breeding.

savon *m* soap.

savonner *vt* to soap, lather.

savonnette *f* bar of soap.

savoureux *adj* tasty, savoury.

scandale *m* scandal.

scandaleux *adj* scandalous.

scandaliser *vt* to scandalise, shock deeply; **se ~** *vr* to be scandalised.

scanner *m* scanner.

sceau *m* seal.

scélérat *m* -e *f* villain, rascal; * *adj* villainous, wicked.

sceller *vt* to seal.

scénario *m* scenario; screenplay.

scénariste *mf* scriptwriter.

scène *f* stage; scenery, scene.

scepticisme *m* scepticism.

sceptique *adj* sceptical; * *mf* sceptic.

schéma *m* diagram, sketch; outline.

schizophrène *mf* schizophrenic; * *adj* schizophrenic.

schizophrénie *f* schizophrenia.

scie *f* saw; bore.

sciemment *adv* knowingly, on purpose.

science *f* science; skill; knowledge.

science-fiction *f* science fiction.

scientifique *adj* scientific.

scinder *vt* to split, divide up.

scintillant *adj* sparkling, glistening.

scintillement *m* sparkling, glistening.

scintiller *vi* to sparkle, glisten.

sciure *f* sawdust.

scolarité *f* schooling.

scorpion *m* scorpion.

scout *m* scout, boy scout.

script *m* printing; script.

scrupule *m* scruple, qualm, doubt.

scrupuleux *adj* scrupulous.

scruter *vt* to scrutinise, scan.

scrutin *m* ballot, poll.

sculpter *vt* to sculpt; to carve.

sculpteur *m* sculptor.

sculpture *f* sculpture.

se *pn* oneself, himself, herself, itself, themselves.

séance *f* meeting, sitting, session; seat.

seau *m* bucket, pail.

sec *adj, f* **sèche** dry, arid; barren; unfeeling; curt; neat.

séchage *m* drying; seasoning.

sèche-cheveux *m invar* hair-drier

sèchement *adv* dryly; curtly.

sécher *vi* to dry, dry out; * *vt* to dry, wipe.

sécheresse *f* drought; dryness.

second *adj* second, in second place; * *m* second; second floor; second in command; * *f* second.

secondaire *adj* secondary.

seconder *vt* to assist, help.

secouer *vt* to shake, toss; **se ~** *vr* to shake o.s.

secourir *vt* to help, assist.

secouriste *mf* first-aid worker.

secours *m* help, assistance; relief; rescue.

secousse *f* jolt, bump.

secret *m* secret; privacy; mystery; * *adj* secret; private; discreet.

secrétaire *mf* secretary; * *m* writing desk.

secrétariat *m* office of secretary; secretariat.

sécrétion *f* secretion.

secte *f* sect.

secteur *m* sector, section, district.

section *f* section, division; branch.

sectionner *vt* to sever; to divide into sections.

sécurisant *adj* reassuring, lending security.

sécurité *f* security; safety.

sédatif *m* sedative; * *adj* sedative.

sédentaire *adj* sedentary; * *m* sedentary.

sédiment *m* sediment.

séducteur *m* seducer **-trice** *f* seductress.

séduction *f* seduction; captivation.

séduire *vt* to seduce; to charm, captivate.

séduisant *adj* seductive; enticing, attractive.

segmenter *vt* to segment.

ségrégation *f* segregation.

seigle *m* rye.

seigneur *m* lord, nobleman; master.

sein *m* breast, bosom; womb; **au ~ de** within.

seize *adj, m* sixteen.

seizième *adj, mf* sixteenth.

séjour *m* stay, sojourn; abode; **salle de ~** living room.

séjourner *vi* to stay, sojourn.

sel *m* salt; wit.

sélecteur *m* selector; gear lever.

sélectif *adj* selective.

sélection *f* choosing, selection.

sélectionner *vt* to select, pick.

selle *f* saddle.

selon *prép* according to; pursuant to.

semaine *f* week.

semblable *adj* like, similar, alike; such.

semblant *m* appearance, look; pretence; **faire ~ (de)** to pretend to.

sembler *vi* to seem, appear.

semelle *f* sole.

semence *f* seed; semen.

semer *vt* to sow; to scatter, strew.

semestre *m* half-year; semester.

semestriel *adj* half-yearly; semestral.

semis *m* seedling; sowing; seedbed.

semoule *f* semolina.

sénat *m* senate.

sénateur *m* senator.

sénile *adj* senile.

sénilité *f* senility.

sens *m* sense; judgement; consciousness; meaning; direction; **bon ~** good sense.

sensation *f* sensation, feeling.

sensationnel *adj* fantastic, sensational.

sensé *adj* sensible.

sensibiliser *vt* to make sensitive to, heighten awareness of.

sensibilité *f* sensitivity, sensitiveness.

sensoriel *adj* sensory.

sensualité *f* sensuality.

sensuel *adj* sensual.

sentier *m* path, track.

sentiment *m* feeling, sentiment; emotion.

sentimentalisme *m* sentimentalism.

sentinelle *f* sentry, sentinel.

sentir *vt* to feel; to perceive, guess; to smell.

séparation *f* separation; division; pulling apart.

séparer *vt* to separate, divide; to pull off; to split; **se ~** *vr* to separate, divide; to part with.

sept *adj, m* seven.

septembre *m* September

septième *adj, mf* seventh.

séquelle *f* after-effect.

séquence *f* sequence.

serein *adj* serene, calm.

sérénade *f* serenade.

sérénité *f* serenity, calmness.

sergent *m* sergeant; **~ de ville** police constable.

série *f* series, string; class; rank.

sérieux *adj* serious; responsible.

serment *m* oath; pledge.

sermonner *vt* to lecture, reprimand.

séropositif *adj* HIV positive.

serpent *m* serpent, snake.

serpenter *vi* to meander, wind.

serre *f* greenhouse; claw.

serré *adj* tight; close, compact.

serrer *vt* to tighten, fasten; to clench; **se ~** *vr* to crowd, huddle.

serrure *f* lock.

serrurier *m* locksmith.

serveur *m* waiter, **-euse** *f* waitress.

serviable *adj* obliging, helpful.

service *m* service; function; department; operation; **~ militaire** national service.

serviette *f* towel; serviette, napkin.

servile *adj* servile, slavish.

servilité *f* servility.

servir *vi* to be of use, be useful; * *vt* to serve, attend to; **se ~** *vr* to help o.s.; **se ~ de** to use, make use of.

seuil *m* threshold.

seul *adj* alone; single; sole.

sève *f* sap; pith, vigour.

sévère *adj* severe, austere.

sévérité *f* severity; strictness.

sévir *vi* to deal severely; to rage, hold sway.

sevrer *vt* to wean; to deprive.

sexe *m* sex; genitals.

sexualité *f* sexuality.

sexuel *adj* sexual, sex.

si *adv* so, so much, however much; yes; * *conj* if; whether.

sida *m* Aids.

sidérer *vt* to flabbergast, stagger.

sidérurgique *adj* steel-making.

sidérurgiste *mf* steel maker.

siècle *m* century; period.

siège *m* seat, bench; head office.

siéger *vi* to sit; to be located.

sien *pn, f* **sienne: le ~** his, its, his own, its own, **la sienne** her, its, her own, its own, **les ~s, les siennes** their, their own.

sieste *f* nap, snooze; siesta.

sifflement *m* whistling; hissing.

siffler *vi* to whistle; to hiss; * *vt* to whistle for; to hiss, boo.

sifflet *m* whistle.

sigle m abbreviation; acronym.

signal *m* signal, sign.

signalement *m* description, particulars.

signature *f* signature; signing.

signe *m* sign; mark; indication; symptom.

signer *vt* to sign; to hallmark.

signet *m* bookmark.

significatif *adj* significant, revealing.

signification *f* significance; meaning.

signifier *vt* to mean, signify; to make known; to serve notice.

silence *m* silence; stillness.

silencieux *adj* silent; still.

silhouette *f* silhouette, outline.

sillage *m* wake; slipstream; trail.

sillon *m* furrow; fissure.

sillonner *vt* to plough, furrow; to criss-cross.

similaire *adj* similar.

similarité *f* similarity.

similitude *f* similitude.

simple *adj* simple; mere; single; common.

simplicité *f* simplicity; simpleness.

simplifier *vt* to simplify.

simulation *f* simulation.

simuler *vt* to simulate, feign.

simultané *adj* simultaneous.

sincère *adj* sincere, honest.

sincérité *f* sincerity, honesty.

singe *m* monkey.

singulier *adj* singular; peculiar; remarkable.

sinistre *m* disaster; accident; * *adj* sinister.

sinistré *m* -e *f* disaster victim; * *adj* disaster-stricken.

sinon *conj* otherwise, if not; except.

sinus *m* sinus; (*math*) sine.

siphon *m* siphon.

sirène *f* mermaid; siren, hooter.

sirop *m* syrup.

sirupeux *adj* syrupy.

sismique *adj* seismic.

site *m* setting, beauty spot.

sitôt *adv* so soon, as soon; **pas de ~** not for a while; **~ que** as soon as.

situation *f* situation, position; state of affairs.

situer *vt* to site, situate; **se ~** *vr* to place o.s.; to be situated.

six *adj*, *m* six.

sixième *adj*, *mf* sixth.

ski *m* ski, skiing.

skier *vi* to ski.

skieur *m* **-euse** *f* skier.

slip *m* briefs, panties, swimming trunks.

snob *adj* snobbish.

snobisme *m* snobbery, snobbishness.

sobre *adj* sober, temperate.

sobriété *f* sobriety, temperance.

sobriquet *m* nickname.

sociable *adj* sociable; social.

social *adj* social.

social-démocrate *mf* social democrat; * *adj* social democrat.

socialisme *m* socialism.

socialiste *mf* socialist; * *adj* socialist.

sociétaire *mf* member.

société *f* society; company; partnership.

sociologie *f* sociology.

sociologue *mf* sociologist.

socquette *f* ankle sock.

sœur *f* sister; nun.

soi *pn* one(self); self; **~-même** oneself, himself, herself, itself; **~-disant** so called.

soie *f* silk.

soif *f* thirst.

soigné *adj* neat, well-kept.

soigner *vt* to look after, care for; **se ~** *vr* to take care of o.s.

soigneusement *adv* neatly; carefully.

soigneux *adj* neat; careful.

soin *m* care; attention; trouble.

soir *m* evening; night.

soirée *f* evening; evening party.

soit *conj* either; or; whether; * *adv* granted; that is to say.

soixantaine *f* about sixty.

soixante *adj*, *m* sixty.

soixantième *adj*, *mf* sixtieth.

soja *m* soya.

sol *m* ground; floor; soil.

soldat *m* soldier.

solde *f* pay; * *m* balance; clearance sale.

solder *vt* to pay; to settle, discharge; **se ~** *vr*: **se ~ par** to show (profit, loss).

sole *f* sole; hearth.

soleil *m* sun, sunshine; sunflower.

solennel *adj* solemn.

solidarité *f* solidarity.

solide *adj* solid; stable; sound.

solidifier *vt* **se ~** *vr* to solidify.

soliste *mf* soloist.

solitaire *mf* recluse, hermit; * *adj* solitary, lone; **~ment** *adv* alone.

solitude *f* solitude; loneliness.

solliciter *vt* to seek, solicit; to appeal to.

solo *m* solo.

soluble *adj* soluble, solvable.

solution *f* solution; solving; answer.

solvable *adj* solvent; creditworthy.

solvant *m* solvent.

sombre *f* dark; gloomy, dismal.

sombrer *vi* to sink, founder.

sommaire *m* summary, argument; * *adj* basic, brief, summary.

sommation *f* summons; demand.

somme *m* nap, snooze.

sommeil *m* sleep; sleepiness, drowsiness.

sommeiller *vi* to slumber, doze.

sommelier *m* wine waiter.

sommet *m* summit; top; crest; apex.

sommité *f* leading light, eminent person.

somnifère *m* sleeping pill.

somnoler *vi* to doze, drowse.

somptueux *adj* sumptuous, lavish.

son *m* sound; * *adj*, *f* **sa**; *pl* **ses** his, her, its.

sonate *f* sonata.

sonde *f* sounding line; probe; drill.

sonder *vt* to sound; to probe; to drill.

songe *m* dream.

songer *vt* to dream; to imagine; to consider.

songeur *adj* pensive.

sonner *vi* to ring; to go off; * *vt* to ring, sound.

sonnerie *f* ringing, bells; chimes.

sonnette *f* small bell; house-bell.

sonore *adj* resonant, deep-toned.

sonorisation *f* sound recording; sound system.

sonorité *f* sonority, tone; resonance.

sophistiqué *adj* sophisticated.

soporiphique *m* sleeping drug.

sorcellerie f witchcraft, sorcery.

sordide *adj* sordid, squalid.

sort *m* fate, destiny, lot.

sortant *adj* outgoing, retiring.

sorte *f* sort, kind, manner.

sortie *f* exit, way out; trip; sortie; outburst; export.

sortilège *m* spell (magical).

sortir *vi* to go out, emerge; to result; to escape; **se ~** *vr* to get out of; to extri-

cate o.s.; **s'en ~** to get over, pull through.

sosie *m* double, second self.

sot *adj*, *f* **-te** silly, foolish.

sottise *f* stupidity; stupid remark, action.

soubresaut *m* jolt; start.

souche *f* stump; stock.

souci *m* worry; concern.

soucier (se) *vr*: **se ~ de** to care about.

soucieux *adj* concerned, worried.

soucoupe *f* saucer.

soudain *adj* sudden, unexpected.

soude *f* soda.

souder *vt* to solder; to weld.

soudeur *m* **-euse** *f* solderer; welder.

soudoyer *vt* to bribe, buy over.

soudure *f* soldering, welding.

souffle *m* blow, puff; breath.

soufflé *m* soufflé; *adj* flabbergasted.

souffler *vi* to blow; to breathe; to puff.

soufflerie *f* bellows.

soufflet *m* slap in the face; affront; bellows.

souffrance *f* suffering; pain.

souffrant *adj* suffering; in pain.

souffrir *vi* to suffer, be in pain.

souhait *m* wish.

souhaitable *adj* desirable.

souhaiter *vt* to wish for, desire.

souiller *vt* to soil, dirty; to tarnish.

soulagement *m* relief.

soulager *vt* to relieve, soothe.

soulèvement *m* uprising.

soulever *vt* to lift, raise; to excite, stir up; **se ~** *vr* to rise; to revolt.

soulier *m* shoe.

souligner *vt* to underline.

soumettre *vt* to subdue, subjugate; to submit, deliver.

soumis *adj* submissive.

soumission *f* submission.

soupape *f* valve; safety valve.

soupçon *m* suspicion, conjecture; hint.

soupçonner *vt* to suspect, surmise.

soupçonneux *adj* suspicious.

soupe *f* soup.

soupeser *vt* to feel the weight of; to weigh up.

soupière *f* soup tureen.

soupir *m* sigh; gasp.

soupirer *vi* to sigh; to gasp.

souple *adj* supple; pliable.

souplesse *f* suppleness; flexibility.

source *f* source; origin; spring.

sourcil *m* eyebrow.

sourd *m* -e *f* deaf person; * *adj* deaf; muted; veiled.

sourdine *f* mute.

sourd(e)-muet(te) *m(f)* deaf-mute; * *adj* deaf and dumb.

souriant *adj* smiling, cheerful.

sourire *m* smile, grin.

souris *f* mouse.

sournois *adj* deceitful; sly.

sous *prép* under, beneath, below.

sous-alimenté *adj* undernourished.

sous-bois *m* undergrowth.

sous-chef *m* second-in-command.

souscrire *vi* to subscribe.

sous-directeur *m* -**trice** *f* sub-manager.

sous-entendre *vt* to imply, infer.

sous-louer *vt* to sublet.

sous-marin *m* submarine; * *adj* underwater.

sous-officier *m* non-commissioned officer.

soussigné *adj* undersigned.

sous-sol *m* subsoil; basement.

sous-titre *m* subtitle.

sous-titrer *vt* to subtitle.

soustraction *f* subtraction.

soustraire *vt* to subtract; to remove; **se ~** *vr:* **se ~ à** to escape, elude.

sous-traitance *f* subcontracting.

sous-traitant *m* subcontractor.

sous-traiter *vi* to subcontract.

sous-vêtement *m* undergarment.

soute *f* hold; baggage hold.

soutenir *vt* to hold up; to sustain; to endure.

souterrain *m* underground passage; * *adj* underground.

soutien *m* support.

soutien-gorge *m* bra.

souvenir *m* memory; recollection; reminder.

souvenir (se) *vr* to remember, recollect.

souvent *adv* often, frequently.

souverain *m* -e *f* sovereign; * *adj* sovereign; supreme.

soyeux *adj* silky.

spacieux *adj* spacious, roomy.

spaghetti *mpl* spaghetti.

sparadrap *m* sticking plaster.

spasme *m* spasm.

spatial *adj* spatial; space.

spatule *f* spatula.

spécial *adj* special, particular.

spécialiser *vt* to specialise; **se ~** *vr* to be a specialist in sth.

spécialiste *mf* specialist.

spécialité *f* speciality; specialism.

spécification *f* specification.

spécifier *vt* to specify, determine.

spécifique *adj* specific.

spécimen *m* specimen; sample.

spectacle *m* spectacle, scene.

spectaculaire *adj* spectacular.

spectateur *m* **-trice** *f* spectator.

spectre *m* ghost.

spéculation *f* speculation.

spéculer *vi* to speculate.

sperme *m* sperm, semen.

sphère *f* sphere.

sphérique *adj* spherical.

spirale *f* spiral.

spiritisme *m* spiritualism.

spirituel *adj* witty; spiritual.

splendeur *f* splendour, brilliance.

splendide *adj* splendid, magnificent.

sponsoriser *vt* to sponsor.

spontané *adj* spontaneous.

sporadique *adj* sporadic.

sportif *m* sportsman, **-ive** *f* sportswoman; * *adj* sports; competitive; athletic.

squelette *m* skeleton.

squelettique *adj* skeleton-like, scrawny.

stabiliser *vt* to stabilise, consolidate; **se ~** *vr* to stabilise, become stabilised.

stable *adj* stable, steady.

stade *m* stadium; stage.

stage *m* training course; probation.

stagiaire *mf* trainee.

standard *m* standard; switchboard; * *adj* standard.

standardiser *vt* to standardise.

standardiste *mf* switchboard operator.

starter *m* choke.

station *f* station; stage, stop; resort; posture.

stationnaire *adj* stationary.

stationnement *m* parking.

stationner *vi* to park.

statique *adj* static.

statistique *f* statistics; * *adj* statistical.

statuer *vt* to rule, give a verdict.

statu quo *m* status quo.

statut *m* statute, ordinance; status.

stéréo(phonique) *adj* stereophonic.

stéréotype *m* stereotype.

stérile *adj* sterile, infertile.

stérilet *m* coil, IUD.

stériliser *vt* to sterilise.

stérilité *f* sterility.

sternum *m* breastbone, sternum.

stimulant *adj* stimulating; * *m* stimulant, stimulus.

stimulation *f* stimulation.

stimuler *vt* to stimulate, spur on.

stipuler *vt* to stipulate, specify.

stock *m* stock, supply.

stockage *m* stocking; stockpiling.

stocker *vt* to stock, stockpile.

stop *m* stop; stop sign; brake-light.

stopper *vt* to stop, halt; * *vi* to stop, halt.

store *m* blind, shade.

strabisme *m* squinting.

stratégie *f* strategy.

stratégique *adj* strategic.

stratifié *adj* stratified.

stress *m* stress.

stressant *adj* stressful.

stresser *vt* to cause stress to.

strict *adj* strict, severe.

strident *adj* strident, shrill.

strié *adj* streaked, striped, ridged.

structure *f* structure.

structurel *adj* structural.

structurer *vt* to structure; **se ~** *vr* to develop a structure.

studieux *adj* studious.

studio *m* studio; film theatre.

stupéfaction *f* stupefaction, amazement.

stupéfait *adj* astounded, dumbfounded.

stupéfiant *adj* astounding, amazing; * *m* drug, narcotic.

stupéfier *vt* to stupefy; to astound.

stupeur *f* amazement; stupor.

stupide *adj* stupid, foolish.

stupidité *f* stupidity.

style *m* style; stylus.

stylet *m* stiletto.

styliste *mf* designer; stylist.

stylo *m* pen.

su *m* knowledge.

subalterne *mf* subordinate; * *adj* subordinate.

subconscient *m* subconscious; * *adj* subconscious.

subdiviser *vt* to subdivide.

subdivision *f* subdivision.

subir *vt* to sustain, support; to undergo, suffer.

subit *adj* sudden.

subjectif *adj* subjective.

subjectivité *f* subjectivity.

submerger *vt* to submerge, flood; to engulf.

submersible *m* submersible; * *adj* submersible.

subordination *f* subordination.

subordonné *m* **-e** *f* subordinate; * *adj* subordinate.

subreptice *adj* surreptitious.

subséquent *adj* subsequent.

subside *m* grant.

subsidiaire *adj* subsidiary.

substance *f* substance.

substantiel *adj* substantial.

substituer *vt* to substitute, replace.

substitut *m* substitute.

substitution *f* substitution.

subtil *adj* subtle.

subtiliser *vt* to steal, spirit away.

subtilité *f* subtlety.

subvenir *vi*: ~ **à** to provide for.

subvention *f* grant, subsidy.

subventionner *vt* to subsidise.

subversif *adj* subversive.

suc *m* sap; juice.

succéder *vi*: ~ **à** to succeed, follow; * **se** ~ *vr* to succeed one another.

succès *m* success; hit.

successeur *m* successor.

successif *adj* successive.

succession *f* succession; inheritance, estate.

succinct *adj* succinct.

succomber *vi* to succumb, give way.

succulent *adj* succulent, delicious.

succursale *f* branch.

sucer *vt* to suck.

sucette *f* lollipop; dummy.

suçon *m* love bite.

sucre *m* sugar.

sucrer *vt* to sugar, sweeten.

sucrerie *f* sugar refinery.

sucrier *m* sugar bowl; * *adj* sugar; sugar-producing.

sud *m* south.

suer *vi* to sweat, perspire.

sueur *f* sweat.

suffire *vi* to suffice, be sufficient; **il suffit de** it is enough to, it only takes.

suffisant *adj* sufficient, adequate.

suffoquer *vi* to choke, suffocate; * *vt* to choke, stifle.

suggérer *vt* to suggest, put forward.

suggestion *f* suggestion.

suicidaire *adj* suicidal.

suicide *m* suicide.

suicider (se) *vr* to commit suicide.

suie *f* soot.

suintement *m* oozing; sweating.

suinter *vi* to ooze; to sweat.

suite *f* rest; sequel; continuation; series; connection; progress; **tout de ~** at once; **deux fois de ~** two times in a row; **et ainsi de ~** and so on; **à la suite de** after, behind; **par la ~** afterwards; **donner ~ à** to follow up.

suivant *m* -e *f* next one; attendant; * *adj* following, next; * *prép* according to; **~ que** according to whether.

suivi *adj* steady, regular; widely adopted; * *m* follow-up.

suivre *vt* to follow; to attend, accompany; to exercise; **~ son cours** to take its course; **à suivre** to be continued; **se ~** *vr* to follow each other; to be continuous.

sujet *m* subject, topic; ground; reason; * *adj*: **être ~ à** to be subject to, liable to.

sujétion *f* subjection; constraint.

sulfure *m* sulphur.

sultan *m* sultan, **-e** *f* sultana.

summum *m* climax, height.

super *m* super, four-star petrol; * *adj* (*fam*) ultra, super.

superbe *adj* superb, splendid.

supercherie *f* trick, trickery.

superficie *f* area, surface.

superficiel *adj* superficial.

superflu *adj* superfluous.

supérieur *adj* upper; superior; higher, greater.

supériorité *f* superiority.

superposer *vt* to superimpose; **se ~** *vr* to be superimposed.

superposition *f* superimposition.

supersonique *adj* supersonic.

superstitieux *adj* superstitious.

superviser *vt* to supervise.

supplanter *vt* to supplant, oust.

suppléant *m* **-e** *f* substitute, understudy; * *adj* substitute.

supplément *m* supplement; extra charge.

supplémentaire *adj* supplementary, additional.

supplice *m* corporal punishment; torture.

support *m* support, prop; stand.

supporter *vt* to support; to endure, bear.

supposer *vt* to suppose; to assume; to imply.

supposition *f* supposition, surmise.

suppression *f* suppression; deletion; cancellation.

supprimer *vt* to suppress; to cancel.

suprématie *f* supremacy.

suprême *adj* supreme.

sur *prép* on; over, above; into; out of, from.

sûr *adj* sure, certain; secure; **~ de soi** self-assured; **bien ~** of course; **à coup ~** for sure; **~ement** *adv* surely, certainly.

suranné *adj* outmoded, outdated.

surcharge *f* overloading; excess; surcharge.

surcharger *vt* to overload.

surchauffe *f* overheating.

surcroît *m*: surplus, excess; **de ~** in addition.

surdité *f* deafness.

surélever *vt* to raise, heighten.

surenchérir *vi* to outbid.

surestimer *vt* to overestimate; to over-value.

sûreté *f* safety; guarantee, surety; **être en ~** to be safe.

surexcité *adj* overexcited.

surgeler *vt* to deep-freeze.

surgir *vi* to rise, appear; to arise, crop up.

surhomme *m* superman.

surintendant *m* superintendent.

surlendemain *m* day after tomorrow.

surmenage *m* overwork.

surmener *vt* to overwork; **se ~** *vr* to overwork.

surmonter *vt* to surmount, overcome.

surnager *vi* to float.

surnaturel *adj* supernatural.

surnom *m* nickname.

surnommer *vt* to nickname.

surpasser *vt* to surpass, outdo.

surplomber *vt* to overhang.

surplus *m* surplus, remainder, excess.

surpopulation *f* overpopulation.

surprendre *vt* to surprise, amaze.

surproduction *f* overproduction.

surréalisme *m* surrealism.

surréaliste *mf* surrealist; * *adj* surrealistic.

sursaut *m* start, jump.

sursauter *vi* to start, jump.

sursis *m* reprieve; deferment.

surtaxe *f* surcharge.

surtout *adv* especially; above all.

surveillant *m* -e *f* warder, guard.

surveiller *vt* to watch; to supervise; to inspect.

survêtement *m* tracksuit.

survie *f* survival.

survivant *m* -e *f* survivor; * *adj* surviving.

survivre *vi* to survive.

survoler *vt* to fly over.

susceptible *adj* sensitive; susceptible; capable; likely; **être ~ de** to be liable to.

susciter *vt* to arouse, incite.

suspect *m* -e *f* suspect; * *adj* suspicious, suspect.

suspecter *vt* to suspect.

suspendre *vt* to hang up; to suspend, defer.

suspendu *adj* hanging; suspended.

suspens *m*: **en ~** in abeyance; shelved.

suspense *m* suspense.

suspension *f* suspension; deferment; adjournment.

suspicieux *adj* suspicious.

susurrer *vt* to whisper.

svelte *adj* svelte, slim.

syllabe *f* syllable.

sylvestre *adj* forest.

symbole *m* symbol.

symbolique *adj* symbolic; token; nominal.

symboliser *vt* to symbolise.

symbolisme *m* symbolism.

symétrique *adj* symmetrical.

sympa *adj invar* (*fam*) nice, friendly.

sympathie *f* liking; fellow feeling; sympathy.

sympathique *adj* likeable, nice; friendly.

sympathisant *m* -e *f* sympathiser; * *adj* sympathising.

sympathiser *vi* to get on well with.

symphonie *f* symphony.

symptomatique *adj* symptomatic.

symptôme *m* symptom.
synagogue *f* synagogue.
synchroniser *vt* to synchronise.
syncope *f* blackout.
syndical *adj* trade-union.
syndicalisme *m* trade unionism.
syndicat *m* trade union; association.

syndiquer *vt* to unionise.
syndrome *m* syndrome.
synonyme *m* synonym; * *adj* synonymous.
syphilis *f* syphilis.
systématique *adj* systematic.
système *m* system.

T

tabac *m* tobacco.
tabatière *f* snuffbox; skylight.
table *f* table; ~ **de nuit** bedside table;
~ **ronde** round-table conference.
tableau *m* table; chart; timetable;
scene; ~ **de bord** dashboard.
tablette *f* bar; tablet; block.
tablier *m* apron; pinafore; overall.
tabou *m* taboo.
tabouret *m* stool.
tache *f* mark; stain; spot.
tâche *f* task; assignment; work.
taché *adj* stained, blemished.
tâcher *vi* to endeavour.
tacheté *adj* spotted; freckled.
tacite *adj* tacit.
taciturne *adj* taciturn, silent.
tact *m* tact; **avoir du** ~ to have tact,
be tactful.
tactile *adj* tactile.
tactique *f* tactics; * *adj* tactical.
tagliatelles *fpl* tagliatelli.
taillader *vt* to slash, gash.
taille *f* waist; height, stature, size; **de**
~ considerable, sizeable; **être de** ~ **à**
to be up to it.

taille-crayons *m* pencil sharpener.
tailler *vt* to cut; to carve; to sharpen;
se ~ *vr* (*fam*) to clear off, split.
tailleur *m* tailor.
taillis *m* copse, coppice.
taire *vt* to hush up; to conceal; **se** ~ *vr*
to be quiet; to fall silent.
talc *m* talc, talcum powder.
talent *m* talent, ability.
talentueux *adj* talented.
talon *m* heel; end; pile.
talonner *vt* to follow closely; to hound.
talus *m* embankment.
tambour *m* drum; barrel.
tambourin *m* tambourine.
tambouriner *vi* to drum; to beat, hammer.
tamis *m* sieve; riddle.
tamiser *vt* to sieve; to sift.
tampon *m* stopper, plug; tampon;
buffer.
tamponner *vt* to mop up; to stamp.
tandem *m* tandem; duo.
tandis *conj* ~ **que** while; whereas.
tangent *adj* tangent, tangential.
tango *m* tango.

tanguer *vi* to pitch (ship).

tanière *f* den, lair.

tank *m* tank.

tanner *vt* to tan, weather.

tanneur *m* tanner.

tant *adv* so much; **~ que** as long as; **~ soit peu** ever so slightly; **~ mieux** so much the better; that's a good job; **~ pis** too bad; **~ bien que mal** as well as can be expected.

tante *f* aunt.

tantôt *adv* sometimes; this afternoon; shortly.

tapage *m* din, uproar, racket.

tape *f* slap.

taper *vi* to hit, tap, stamp; to beat down; * *vt* to beat; to slap; to type.

tapioca *m* tapioca.

tapir (se) *vr* to crouch; to hide away.

tapis *m* carpet; rug; cloth.

tapisser *vt* to wallpaper; to cover; to carpet.

tapisserie *f* tapestry; **faire ~** to be a wallflower.

tapoter *vt* to pat; to tap; to strum.

taquin *adj* teasing.

taquiner *vt* to tease; to plague.

tarauder *vt* to tap; to torment.

tard *adv* late.

tarder *vi* to delay, put off; to dally.

tardif *adj* late; tardy; slow; backward.

tari *adj* dried up.

tarif *m* tariff; price-list.

tarir *vt* to dry up; to exhaust; **se ~** *vr* to dry up.

tarte *f* tart, flan.

tartelette *f* tartlet, tart.

tartine *f* slice of buttered bread.

tartre *m* tartar; fur, scale.

tas *m* heap, pile; lot, set.

tasse *f* cup.

tassement *m* settling, sinking.

tasser *vt* to heap up; **se ~** *vr* to sink; subside.

tata *f* auntie.

tâter *vt* to feel, try; **se ~** *vr* to feel o.s.

tâtonnement *m* trial and error; experimentation.

tâtonner *vi* to feel one's way, grope along.

tatouage *m* tattooing; tattoo.

taudis *m* hovel, slum.

taupe *f* mole.

taureau *m* bull.

tauromachie *f* bullfighting.

taux *m* rate; ratio; **~ de change** exchange rate.

taverne *f* tavern.

taxe *f* tax; duty; rate.

taxer *vt* to tax; to fix the price of.

taxi *m* taxi.

tchin-tchin! *interj* cheers!

te *pn* you, yourself.

technicien *m* **-ne** *f* technician.

technique *f* technique; * *adj* technical.

technologie *f* technology.

teigne *f* moth; ringworm.

teindre *vt* to dye.

teint *m* complexion, colouring.

teinte *f* tint, colour, shade.

teinter *vt* to tint; to stain.

teinture *f* dye; dyeing.

teinturier *m* **-ère** *f* dyer; dry cleaner.

tel *adj* such; like, similar; **~ quel** such as it is; **en tant que ~** as such, in such a capacity; **il n'y a rien de ~** there's nothing like...

télé *f* TV, telly.

télécarte f phonecard.

télécommande f remote control.

télécopie f fax.

télécopieur m fax machine.

téléphérique m cableway; cable-car.

télégramme m telegram; cable.

téléguider vt to radio-control.

téléobjectif m telephoto lens.

télépathie f telepathy.

téléphone m telephone.

téléphoner vi to telephone.

télescope m telescope.

télescopique adj telescopic.

télésiège m chairlift.

téléski m lift, ski tow.

téléviseur m television set.

télévision f television.

télex m telex.

tellement adv so, so much; ~ **de** so many, so much.

téméraire adj rash, reckless.

témérité f rashness; recklessness.

témoignage m testimony; evidence; certificate.

témoigner vi to testify.

témoin m witness; evidence; proof.

tempérament m constitution; temperament; character.

température f temperature.

tempérer vt to temper; to assuage, soothe.

tempo m tempo, pace.

temporaire adj temporary.

temporel adj worldly, temporal.

temporiser vi to temporise, delay.

temps m time; while; tense; beat; weather; **de** ~ **en** ~ from time to time; **entre** ~ meanwhile.

tenace adj tenacious, stubborn, persistent.

ténacité f tenacity; stubbornness.

tenaille f pincers; tongs.

tenailler vt to torture; to rack.

tendance f tendency; leaning; trend.

tendancieux adj tendentious.

tendinite f tendinitis.

tendon m tendon, sinew.

tendre adj tender, soft; delicate.

tendu adj tight; stretched; concentrated; delicate, fraught.

ténèbres fpl darkness, gloom.

ténébreux adj dark, gloomy.

teneur f terms; content; grade.

tenir vt to hold, keep; to stock; to run; * vi to hold, stay in place; ~ **à** to value, care about; ~ **de** to take after; **se** ~ vr to hold on to; to behave; **s'en** ~ **à** to limit o.s. to, stick to.

tennis m tennis; ~ **de table** table tennis.

ténor m tenor; leading light.

tentacule m tentacle.

tentation f temptation.

tentative f attempt, bid.

tente f tent.

tenter vt to tempt.

tenture f hanging; curtain.

tenue f holding; session; deportment, good behaviour; dress, appearance.

tergiverser vi to procrastinate, beat about the bush.

terme m term; termination, end; word, expression; **au** ~ **de** at the end of.

terminaison f ending.

terminal adj terminal; * m terminal.

terminer vt to terminate; to finish off; **se** ~ vr to terminate; to come to an end.

terne adj colourless; lustreless, drab; spiritless.

ternir vt to tarnish, dull.

terrain *m* ground, soil, earth; plot; position; site; field.

terrasse *f* terrace.

terrasser *vt* to floor, knock down; to strike down, overcome.

terre *f* earth; world; ground, land.

terrer (se) *vr* to crouch down; to lie low, go to ground.

terrestre *adj* land; terrestrial.

terreur *f* terror, dread.

terreux *adj* earthy; dirty; ashen.

terrible *adj* terrible, dreadful; terrific, great.

terrien *m* countryman; earthling; **-ne** *f* countrywoman; earthling.

terrier *m* burrow; earth; terrier.

terrifier *vt* to terrify.

territoire *m* territory, area.

territorial *adj* land, territorial.

terroir *m* land.

terroriser *vt* to terrorise.

terroriste *mf* terrorist; * *adj* terrorist.

test *m* test.

testament *m* will, testament.

tester *vt* to test; to make out one's will.

testicule *m* testicle, testis.

tétard *m* tadpole.

tête *f* head; face; front; top; sense, judgment; **tenir ~** to stand up to sb; **faire la ~** to pout, sulk; **~ de turc** whipping boy; **~ de mort** skull and crossbones; **être en ~** to head.

tête à tête *m* private conversation; **en ~** in the lead.

téter *vt* to suck.

tétine *f* teat; udder; dummy.

téton *m* breast.

têtu *adj* headstrong, stubborn.

texte *m* text.

textuel *adj* textual, literal, exact.

thé *m* tea.

théâtral *adj* theatrical, dramatic.

théâtre *m* theatre; drama.

théière *f* teapot.

thématique *adj* thematic.

thème *m* theme.

théologie *f* theology.

théorie *f* theory.

théorique *adj* theoretical.

thérapeute *mf* therapist.

thérapie *f* therapy.

thermal *adj* thermal.

thermique *adj* thermal; thermic.

thermomètre *m* thermometer.

thermos *f/m* thermos.

thermostat *m* thermostat.

thèse *f* thesis.

thon *m* tuna.

thrombose *f* thrombosis.

thym *m* thyme.

thyroïde *f* thyroid.

tic *m* twitch, tic; mannerism.

tiède *adj* lukewarm, tepid.

tien *pn, f* **tienne: le ~, la tienne, les ~s, les tiennes** yours, your own.

tiers *adj* third; * *m* third.

tige *f* stem, stalk.

tigre *m* tiger.

tigresse *f* tigress.

tilleul *m* lime, linden.

timbre *m* stamp; postmark; bell; tone, timbre.

timbrer *vt* to stamp; to postmark.

timide *adj* timid, shy.

tintamarre *m* hubbub, uproar.

tintement *m* ringing; chiming; toll.

tinter *vi* to ring, toll; to chime.

tique *f* tick.

tiquer *vi* to wince.

tir *m* shooting, firing, fire; shot; **~ à l'arc** archery.

tirage *m* drawing, drawing off; printing; circulation; friction.

tirailler *vt* to tug; to plague; to pester.

tire-bouchon *m* corkscrew.

tire-fesses *m* ski tow.

tirelire *f* moneybox.

tirer *vt* to pull; to draw; to extract; **se ~** *vr* (*fam*) to clear off; **bien s'en ~** to make a good job of sth.

tiret *m* dash; hyphen.

tireur *m* -**euse** *f* gunner, sharpshooter; printer; drawer (cheque).

tiroir *m* drawer.

tison *m* brand.

tisonnier *m* poker.

tisser *vt* to weave.

tissu *m* texture, fabric; tissue.

titanesque *adj* titanic.

titre *m* title; heading; denomination; claim, right; deed; **à ~ de** by right of; **à juste ~** deservedly, justly; **en ~** titular, acknowledged.

tituber *vi* to stagger.

toast *m* slice of toast; toast.

toc *m* tap, knock; sham jewellery etc.; **en ~** imitation, fake.

toi *pn* you; **~-même** yourself; **c'est à ~** it's your's; it's your turn.

toile *f* cloth; canvas; sheet

toilette *f* cleaning, grooming; washstand; **faire sa ~** to wash oneself; **cabinet de ~** bathroom.

toiser *vt* to survey; to evaluate.

toison *f* fleece.

toit *m* roof; home.

tôle *f* sheet metal.

tolérance *f* tolerance.

tolérant *adj* tolerant.

tolérer *vt* to tolerate; to put up with.

tomate *f* tomato.

tombe *f* tomb; grave.

tombeau *m* tomb.

tomber *vi* to fall; to sink; to decay; **laisser ~** to drop; **~ amoureux** to fall in love; **~ sur** to come across; **bien/ mal ~** to be lucky/unlucky.

tome *m* book; volume.

ton *adj*, *f* **ta**, *pl* **tes** your; * *m* tone; pitch; shade.

tonalité *f* tonality; key.

tondeuse *f* clippers, shears; mower.

tondre *vt* to shear, clip; mow.

tonifier *vt* to tone up; to invigorate.

tonique *adj* tonic; fortifying; invigorating *m* tonic.

tonne *f* ton.

tonneau *m* barrel, cask.

tonnerre *m* thunder.

tonton *m* (*fam*) uncle.

tonus *m* tone; energy.

top *m* pip, stroke.

toquade *f* infatuation; fad, craze.

toque *f* fur hat; cap.

toquer *vi* to tap, rap.

torche *f* torch.

torcher *vt* to wipe, mop up; **se ~** *vr* to wipe oneself.

torchon *m* cloth; duster.

tordre *vt* to twist, contort; **se ~** *vr* to bend, twist; to sprain.

tordu *adj* twisted, crooked, bent.

tornade *f* tornado.

torpeur *f* torpor.

torpille *f* torpedo.

torpiller *vt* to torpedo.

torrentiel *adj* torrential.

torsade *f* twist; cable moulding.

torse *m* chest; torso.

tort *m* fault; wrong; prejudice; **avoir ~** to be wrong; **à ~ ou à raison** wrongly or rightly; **faire du ~** to harm; **à ~ et à travers** wildly; here, there and everywhere.

tortiller *vt* to twist; **se ~** *vr* to wriggle; to squirm.

tortionnaire *mf* torturer; * *adj* pertaining to torture.

tortue *f* tortoise.

tortueux *adj* tortuous, winding, meandering.

tôt *adv* early; soon, quickly; **au plus ~** as soon as possible.

totaliser *vt* to totalise, add up.

touchant *adj* touching, moving.

touche *f* touch; trial; stroke; key.

toucher *vt* to touch; to feel; * *m* touch, feeling.

touffu *adj* bushy, thick.

toujours *adv* always; still; all the same; **pour ~** for ever; **~ est-il que** the fact remains that.

toupie *f* spinning top.

tour *f* tower; * *m* turn, round; circuit; tour; trick; **faire un ~** to take a stroll; **faire le tour de** to go around; **fermer à double ~** to double-lock; **jouer un ~** to play a trick; **~ à ~** by turns.

tourbe *f* peat.

tourbillon *m* whirlwind, whirlpool.

tourbillonner *vi* to whirl, eddy.

tourisme *m* tourism.

touriste *mf* tourist.

tourment *m* torment, agony.

tourmente *f* storm, tempest.

tourmenter *vt* to rack, torment; **se ~** *vr* to fret; to worry.

tournage *m* turning; *(cin)* shooting.

tournant *m* bend; turning point; * *adj* revolving, swivel; winding.

tournedos *m* fillet steak.

tournée *f* tour; round.

tourner *vt* to turn; to round; * *vi* to turn; to work; to change; **se ~** *vr* to turn round; to change.

tournesol *m* sunflower.

tourneur *m* turner.

tournevis *m* screwdriver.

tournoi *m* tournament.

tournoyer *vi* to whirl, swirl.

tournure *f* turn; turn of phrase.

tourte *f* pie.

tousser *vi* to cough.

tout *adj*, *pl* **tous**, **toutes** all; whole; every; **~ le monde** everybody; * *pn* everything; all; * *m* whole, only thing; **pas du ~** not at all; **du ~ au ~** completely; * *adv* entirely, quite; **~ droit** straight on; **~ à fait** completely, quite; **~ de suite** immediately.

toutefois *adv* however.

toux *f* cough.

toxicomane *mf* drug addict; * *adj* drug addicted.

toxicomanie *f* drug addiction.

toxique *adj* toxic.

trac *m* nerves, stage fright.

tracas *m* bustle, turmoil; worry.

tracasser *vt* to worry; to harass.

trace *f* track, impression; outline, sketch; vestige, trace.

tracé *m* layout, plan.

tracer *vt* to draw, trace; to open up.

tractation *f* transaction; bargaining.

tracteur *m* tractor.

traditionnel *adj* traditional; usual.

traducteur *m* -**trice** *f* translator.

traduction *f* translation.

traduire *vt* to translate.

trafic *m* traffic; trading; dealings.

trafiquer *vi* to fiddle, tamper with.

tragique *adj* tragic.

trahir *vt* to betray.

trahison *f* betrayal, treason.

train *m* train; pace, rate; **être en ~ de** to be in the act of doing sth.

traînasser *vi* to dawdle; to loiter.

traîne *f* dragging; train; **être à la ~** to be in tow.

traîneau *m* sledge.

traînée *f* trail, track; drag.

traîner *vi* to lag, dawdle; to drag on; * *vt* to drag, pull; to protract.

train-train *m* humdrum routine.

traire *vt* to milk.

trait *m* trait, feature; deed; relation; **avoir ~ à** to have reference; **~ d'union** hyphen, connecting link.

traite *f* trade; draft, bill; milking.

traité *m* treaty; treatise, tract.

traitement *m* treatment; salary; processing.

traiter *vt* to treat; to process; * *vi* to treat, negotiate.

traiteur *m* caterer; trader.

traître *m* traitor.

traîtrise *f* treachery.

trajet m distance; journey; course, path.

trame *f* framework; web.

tramer *vt* to plot; to weave.

tranchant *adj* sharp, cutting.

tranche *f* slice; edge; section.

tranchée *f* trench; cutting.

trancher *vt* to cut, sever; to conclude; to settle; * *vi* to cut; to resolve; to stand out.

tranquille *adj* quiet, tranquil.

tranquillisant *m* tranquilliser; * *adj* soothing, tranquillising.

tranquilliser *vt* to reassure.

tranquillité *f* tranquillity.

transaction *f* transaction, arrangement.

transatlantique *m* transatlantic liner; * *adj* transatlantic.

transcription *f* transcription; copy.

transcrire *vt* to transcribe; copy out.

transe *f* trance.

tranférer *vt* to transfer.

transfert *m* transfer; conveyance.

transfuge *mf* defector.

transfusion *f* transfusion.

transgresser *vt* to transgress, infringe.

transgression *f* transgression, infringement.

transi *adj* numb, paralysed.

transiger *vi* to compromise, come to terms.

transistor *m* transistor.

transit *m* transit.

transiter *vi* to pass in transit.

translucide *adj* translucent.

transmettre *vt* to transmit; to pass on, hand down.

transmission *f* transmission; passing on; handing down.

transparaître *vi* to show through.

transparence *f* transparency.

transpercer *vt* to pierce; to penetrate.

transplanter *vt* to transplant.

transport *m* carrying; transport; conveyance; transfer.

transporter *vt* to carry; to transport.

transporteur *m* haulier; carrier.

transvaser *vt* to decant.

trapèze *m* trapeze.

trapéziste *mf* trapeze artist.

trappeur *m* trapper.

trapu *adj* squat; thickset.

traquer *vt* to track; to hunt down.

traumatisant *adj* traumatising.

traumatiser *vt* to traumatise.

travail *m* work; job, occupation; labour; *pl* **travaux** work, labour.

travailler *vi* to work; to endeavour; * *vt* to work, shape; to cultivate; to fatigue.

travailleur *m* **-euse** *f* worker; * *adj* diligent; hard-working.

travers *m* breadth; irregularity; fault; **à ~** through, across; **de ~** obliquely, askew; **en ~** across, crosswise.

traversée *f* crossing, going through; traverse.

traverser *vt* to cross, traverse.

travesti *m* drag artist; transvestite; * *adj* disguised.

trébucher *vi* to stumble, trip up.

trèfle *m* clover.

tréfonds *m* subsoil, bottom.

treille *f* climbing vine.

treillis *m* trellis; wire mesh.

treize *adj*, m thirteen.

treizième *adj*, *mf* thirteenth.

tremblant *adj* trembling, shaking.

trembler *vi* to tremble, shake.

trembloter *vi* to tremble slightly, flicker.

trémousser (se) *vr* to wriggle.

tremper *vt* to soak; to dip; * *vi* to soak; to take part in.

tremplin *m* springboard; ski-jump.

trentaine *f* about thirty.

trente *adj*, m thirty.

trentième *adj*, *mf* thirtieth.

trépasser *vi* to pass away.

trépidant *adj* pulsating, quivering.

trépied *m* tripod.

trépigner *vi* to stamp one's feet.

très *adv* very; most; very much.

trésor *m* treasure.

trésorerie *f* treasury.

trésorier *m* **-ière** *f* treasurer.

tressaillir *vi* to thrill; to shudder.

tressauter *vi* to start, jump.

tresse *f* plait, braid.

tresser *vt* to plait, braid.

trêve *f* truce; respite, rest.

tri *m* sorting out; selection; grading.

triage *m* sorting out.

triangle *m* triangle.

triangulaire *adj* triangular.

tribal *adj* tribal.

tribord *m* starboard.

tribu *f* tribe.

tribunal *m* court, tribunal.

tribune *f* gallery, stand; rostrum.

tribut *m* tribute.

tributaire *adj* dependent, tributary.

tricher *vi* to cheat.

tricheur *m* **-euse** *f* cheater.

tricot *m* jumper; knitting.

tricoter *vt* to knit.

tridimensionnel *adj* three-dimensional.

trier *vt* to sort out; to pick over.

trifouiller *vi* (*fam*) to rummage about; * *vt* to rummage about in.

trimer *vi* to slave away.

trimestre *m* quarter; term.

trimestriel *adj* quarterly; three-monthly.

tringle *f* rod.

trinquer *vi* to toast; to booze.

trio *m* trio.

triomphant *adj* triumphant.

triomphe *m* triumph, victory.

triompher *vi* to triumph.

triple *adj* triple, treble.

tripler *vi* to triple; * *vt* to triple, treble.

tripoter *vt* to play with, speculate with.

trique *f* cudgel.

triste *adj* sad, melancholy.

tristesse *f* sadness; melancholy.

trivial *adj* mundane, trivial; coarse, crude.

trivialité *f* triviality; crudeness.

troc *m* exchange; barter.

trognon *m* core; stalk.

trois *adj, m* three.

troisième *adj, mf* third.

trombe *f*: ~ **d'eau** cloudburst, downpour; **entrer/sortir en** ~ to dash in/out.

trombone *m* trombone.

trompe *f* trumpet; trunk, snout.

tromper *vt* to deceive, trick; **se** ~ *vr* to be mistaken.

tromperie *f* deception, deceit.

trompette *f* trumpet.

trompeur *adj* deceitful; deceptive.

tronc *m* trunk, shaft.

tronçon *m* section, part.

tronçonneuse *f* chain saw.

trône *m* throne.

trop *adv* too; too much, unduly; *m* ~ too much, too many.

trophée *m* trophy.

tropical *adj* tropical.

tropique *m* tropic.

trop-plein *m* overflow; excess.

troquer *vt* to barter, swap.

trot *m* trot.

trotter *vi* to trot; to run about; to toddle.

trottiner *vi* to jog along; to trot along.

trottinette *f* scooter.

trottoir *m* pavement.

trou *m* hole; gap; cavity.

troublant *adj* disturbing, disquieting.

trouble *adj* unclear; murky, suspicious; * *m* disturbance, confusion; disorder.

trouble-fête *mf* spoilsport, killjoy.

troubler *vt* to disturb, disconcert; to cloud, darken; **se** ~ *vr* to become cloudy; to become flustered.

trouer *vt* to make a hole in; to pierce.

trouille *f*: **avoir la** ~ to have the wind up.

troupeau *m* herd, drove.

trousse *f* case, kit; wallet.

trouver *vt* to find, detect; to think; **se** ~ *vr* to find o.s.; to be located; **il se trouve que** it happens that.

truand *m* (*fam*) gangster; tramp.

truc *m* (*fam*) trick; gadget, thingummy.

truculent *adj* truculent; colourful, vivid.

truelle *f* trowel.

truie *f* sow.

truite *f* trout.

truquage *m* rigging, fixing; fiddling.

truquer *vt* to rig, fix; to fiddle.

tu *pn* you.

tuant *adj* exhausting; exasperating.

tuba *m* tuba, snorkel.

tube *m* tube, pipe; duct.

tuer *vt* to kill; **se** ~ *vr* to be killed; to kill o.s.

tuerie *f* slaughter.

tueur *m* **-euse** *f* killer.

tuile *f* tile.

tulipe *f* tulip.

tuméfié *adj* puffed-up, swollen.

tumeur *f* tumour.

tumulte *m* tumult, commotion.

tumultueux *adj* tumultuous, stormy.

tunique *f* tunic; smock.

tunnel *m* tunnel.

turbulence *f* turbulence; excitement.

turbulent *adj* turbulent.

tutelle *f* guardianship, supervision.

tuteur *m* **-trice** *f* guardian; * *m* stake, prop.

tuyau *m* pipe.

tympan *m* eardrum.

type *m* type; model; sample; bloke, chap.

typé *adj* typical.

typhoïde *f* typhoid; * *adj* typhoid.

typhon *m* typhoon.

typhus *m* typhus.

typique *adj* typical.

tyran *m* tyrant.

U

ulcère *m* ulcer.

ulcérer *vt* to sicken; to embitter.

ultérieur *adj* later, subsequent.

ultimatum *m* ultimatum.

ultime *adj* ultimate, final.

ultra-violet *m* ultraviolet ray; * *adj* ultraviolet.

un, une *art* a, an; (number) one; **l'~ l'autre, les ~s les autres** one another.

unanime *adj* unanimous.

uni *adj* plain, self-coloured; close; smooth.

unification *f* unification; standardisation.

unifier *vt* to unify; to standardise.

uniforme *adj* uniform, regular; * *m* uniform.

uniformité *f* uniformity; regularity.

union *f* union; combination, blending.

unique *adj* only, single; unique.

unir *vt* to unite; to join; to combine; **s'~** *vr* to unite; to be joined in marriage.

unisson *m* unison; **à l'~** in unison.

unité *f* unity; unit.

univers *m* universe; world.

universel *adj* universal; all-purpose.

universitaire *adj* university; * *mf* academic.

université *f* university.

uranium *m* uranium.

urbain *adj* urban, city.

urbanisme *m* town planning.

urbaniste *mf* town planner.

urgence *f* urgency; emergency.

urgent *adj* urgent.

urine *f* urine.

uriner *vi* to urinate.

urne *f* ballot box; urn.

usage *m* use; custom; usage; practice; wear; **faire ~ de** to exercise; to make use of.

usager *m* **-ère** *f* user.

usé *adj* worn; threadbare; banal, trite.

user *vt* to make use of, enjoy; to wear

out; **~ de** to exercise; to employ; **s'~** *vr* to wear out.

usine *f* factory.

usiner *vt* to machine; to manufacture.

usité *adj* in common use, common.

ustensile *m* implement; utensil.

usuel *adj* ordinary; everyday.

usurper *vt* to usurp.

utérus *m* womb, uterus.

utile *adj* useful.

utilisateur *m*, **-trice** *f* user.

utilisation *f* use.

utiliser *vt* to use, utilise; to make use of.

V

vacance *f* vacancy; **~s** holiday.

vacancier *m* **-ière** *f* holidaymaker.

vacant *adj* vacant, unoccupied.

vacarme *m* racket, row.

vaccin *m* vaccine.

vaccination *f* vaccination.

vacciner *vt* to vaccinate.

vache *f* cow.

vachement *adv (fam)* damned, bloody.

vacherie *f (fam)* rottenness, meanness; nasty remark/trick.

vaciller *vi* to sway, totter; to falter.

va-et-vient *m invar* comings and goings; to and fro.

vagabond *m* **-e** *f* tramp, vagabond.

vagabondage *m* wandering, roaming; *(jur)* vagrancy.

vagabonder *vi* to wander, roam.

vagin *f* vagina.

vague *adj* vague, hazy, indistinct; * *m* vagueness; * *f* wave.

vaguer *vi* to wander, roam.

vaillant *adj* brave, courageous.

vain *adj* vain.

vaincre *vt* to defeat, overcome.

vainqueur *m* conqueror, victor.

vaisseau *m* vessel; ship.

vaisselle *f* crockery; dishes; **faire la ~** to do the washing up.

valable *adj* valid, legitimate; worthwhile.

valeur *f* value, worth; security, share; meaning.

valide *adj* able, able-bodied.

valider *vt* to validate.

validité *f* validity.

valise *f* suitcase.

vallée *f* valley.

vallon *m* vale, dale.

vallonné *adj* undulating, hilly.

valoir *vt* to be worth; to be valid; **il vaut mieux** it is better to; **~ la peine** to be worth the trouble.

valoriser *vt* to develop; to enhance.

valse *f* waltz.

valser *vi* to waltz.

vandale *mf* vandal.

vandalisme *m* vandalism.

vanille *f* vanilla.

vanité *f* vanity, conceit.

vaniteux *adj* vain, conceited.

vanne *f* gate, sluice.

vannerie *f* basketry; wickerwork.

vantard *adj* boastful, bragging.

vantardise *f* boastfulness; boast.

vanter *vt* to praise, vaunt; **se ~** *vr* to boast, brag.

vapeur *f* haze, vapour.

vaporeux *adj* filmy, vaporous.

vaporisateur *m* spray, atomiser.

vaporiser *vt* to spray; to vaporise.

variable *adj* variable, changeable.

variante *f* variant; variation.

variation *f* variation, change.

varice *f* varicose vein.

varicelle *f* chickenpox.

varié *adj* varied; variegated; various.

varier *vi* to vary, change; * *vt* to vary.

variété *f* variety, diversity.

variole *f* smallpox.

vasculaire *adj* vascular.

vase *m* vase, bowl; * *f* silt, mud.

vasistas *m* fanlight.

vaste *adj* vast, huge.

vaudou *m* voodoo.

vaurien *m* **-ne** *f* good-for-nothing.

vautour *m* vulture.

vautrer (se) *vr* to wallow in.

veau *m* calf; veal.

vecteur *m* vector.

vécu *adj* real, true-life; lived; * *m* real-life.

vedette *f* star; (*mar*) launch.

végétal *adj* vegetable.

végétarien *m* **-ne** *f* vegetarian; * *adj* vegetarian.

végétatif *adj* vegetative.

végétation *f* vegetation.

végéter *vi* to vegetate; to stagnate.

véhémence *f* vehemence.

véhément *adj* vehement.

véhicule *m* vehicle.

veille *f* wakefulness; watch; eve.

veillée *f* evening; evening meeting.

veiller *vi* to stay up, sit up.

veilleur *m* watchman.

veilleuse *f* night light; sidelight.

veinard *m* **-e** *f* lucky person; * *adj* lucky, jammy.

veine *f* vein, seam; inspiration; luck.

velléité *f* vague desire, vague impulse.

vélo *m* bike.

velours *m* velvet.

velouté *adj* velvety, downy.

velu *adj* hairy.

vendanger *vt* to harvest grapes from; * *vi* to harvest the grapes.

vendeur *m* **-euse** *f* seller, salesperson.

vendre *vt* to sell.

vendredi *m* Friday.

vénéneux *adj* poisonous.

vénérien *adj* venereal.

vengeance *f* vengeance, revenge.

venger *vt* to avenge; **se ~** *vr* to avenge o.s.

venimeux *adj* venomous, poisonous; vicious.

venin *m* venom; poison.

venir *vi* to come; to happen; to grow; **~ de** to come from; to derive from; **~ au monde** to be born.

vent *m* wind; breath; emptiness.

vente *f* sale; selling; auction; **en ~** for sale.

ventilateur *m* ventilator, fan.

ventiler *vt* to ventilate; to divide up.

ventouse *f* sucker; suction disc.

ventre *m* stomach, belly; womb.

ventricule *m* ventricle.

ventriloque *mf* ventriloquist.

venue *f* coming.

ver *m* worm; grub.

véracité *f* veracity; truthfulness.

véranda *f* veranda.

verbal *adj* verbal.

verbe *m* verb; language, word.

verbiage *m* verbiage.

verdeur *f* vigour, vitality.

verdir *vi* to go green; * *vt* to turn green.

verge *f* stick, cane.

verger *m* orchard.

verglas *m* black ice.

véridique *adj* truthful, veracious.

vérification *f* check; verification.

vérifier *vt* to verify, check; to audit.

véritable *adj* real, genuine.

vérité *f* truth; truthfulness, sincerity; **en ~** really, actually.

vermine *f* vermin.

verni *adj* varnished.

vernis *m* varnish; glaze; shine.

vernissage *m* varnishing; glazing.

verre *m* glass; lens; drink.

verrerie *f* glassworks; glass-making.

verrière *f* window; glass roof.

verrou *m* bolt.

verrouiller *vt* to bolt; to lock.

verrue *f* wart, verruca.

vers *prép* towards; around; about; * *m* line, verse.

verse *f*: **pleuvoir à ~** to pour down.

verser *vt* to pour, shed; to pay; (*mil*) to assign.

verset *m* verse.

verso *m* back.

vert *m* green; * *adj* green; **langue ~e** slang; **~ement** *adv* sharply, brusquely.

vertical *adj* vertical.

vertu *f* virtue; courage; **en ~ de** in accordance with.

vertueux *adj* virtuous.

vessie *f* bladder.

veste *f* jacket.

vestiaire *m* cloakroom; changing-room.

vestibule *m* hall, vestibule.

vestige *m* relic; trace, vestige.

veston *m* jacket.

vêtement *m* garment.

vétéran *m* veteran.

vétérinaire *mf* veterinary surgeon; * *adj* veterinary.

vêtir *vt* to clothe, dress; **se ~** *vr* to dress o.s.

vêtu *adj* dressed; clad, wearing.

vétuste *adj* dilapidated, ancient.

veuf *m* widower; * *adj* widowed.

veule *adj* spineless.

veuve *f* widow; * *adj* widowed.

vexant *adj* annoying, vexing.

vexer *vt* to annoy; to hurt.

viande *f* meat.

vibrer *vi* to vibrate; to quiver.

vibromasseur *m* vibrator.

vicaire *m* curate, vicar.

vice *m* vice; fault, defect.

vice-versa *adv* vice versa.

vicieux *adj* licentious; dissolute; incorrect.

vicomte *m* viscount.

victime *f* victim, casualty; **être ~ de** to be the victim of.

victoire *f* victory.

victorieux *adj* victorious.

vidange *f* emptying; waste outlet.

vidanger *vt* to empty; to drain off.

vide *adj* empty, vacant, devoid; * *m* vacuum; gap; void.

vidéo *f* video; * *adj invar* video.
vidéocassette *f* videocassette.
vider *vt* to empty; to drain; to vacate; to gut.
videur *m* bouncer.
vie *f* life; living; **être en ~** to be alive.
vieillard *m* old man.
vieillesse *f* old age; the elderly; oldness.
vieillir *vi* to get old; * *vt* to age; to put years on.
vieillissement *m* ageing; obsolescence.
vierge *f* virgin; * *adj* virgin; blank; unexposed.
vieux *adj*, *f* **vieille** old; ancient; obsolete.
vif *adj* alive, lively; quick; eager, passionate.
vigile *m* vigil.
vigne *f* vine; vineyard.
vignoble *m* vineyard.
vigoureux *adj* vigorous.
vigueur *f* vigour, strength, energy.
vil *adj* vile; lowly.
vilain *m* naughty boy, **-e** *f* naughty girl.
villa *f* villa, detached house.
village *m* village.
ville *f* town, city.
vin *m* wine.
vinaigre *m* vinegar.
dressing.
vindicatif *adj* vindictive.
vingt *adj*, *m* twenty.
vingtaine *f* about twenty; score.
vingtième *adj*, *mf* twentieth.
vinicole *adj* wine, wine-growing.
viol *m* rape.
violation *f* violation; transgression.
violence *f* violence; force, duress.
violent *adj* violent; considerable, excessive.

violer *vt* to violate, desecrate; to rape.
violet *adj* purple, violet; * *m* purple, violet.
violette *f* (*bot*) violet.
violeur *m* rapist.
violon *m* violin.
violoncelle *m* cello.
vipère **f** viper, adder.
virage *m* turn, bend; tacking.
viral *adj* viral.
virement *m* turning, tacking; transfer, clearance.
virer *vt* to transfer; * *vi* to turn, tack.
virevolter *vi* to spin round, pirouette.
virginité *f* virginity; purity.
virgule *f* comma; (*math*) point.
viril *adj* virile; male, masculine.
virilité *f* virility; masculinity.
virtuel *adj* virtual; potential.
virtuose *mf* virtuoso, master.
vis *f* screw.
visage *m* face; expression.
vis-à-vis *prép*: opposite; **~ de** towards; as regards; * *m* encounter; person opposite; **en ~** opposite each other.
viscéral *adj* visceral; deep-rooted.
viser *vt* to aim, target; to visa.
visibilité *f* visibility.
visible *adj* visible; evident, obvious.
visière *f* peak; eyeshade; visor.
vision *f* eyesight; vision.
visionnaire *mf* visionary; * *adj* visionary.
visite *f* visit; visiting, inspection; visitor.
visiter *vt* to visit; to examine, inspect.
visiteur *m* **-euse** *f* visitor; representative.
vison *m* mink.
visqueux *adj* viscous, thick.
visser *vt* to screw on.

visuel *adj* visual.

vital *adj* vital.

vitalité *f* energy, vitality.

vitamine *f* vitamin.

vite *adv* quickly, fast; soon; * *adj* swift; quick.

vitesse *f* speed, swiftness; gear.

viticole *adj* wine, wine-growing.

viticulteur *m* wine grower.

vitrage *m* glazing; windows.

vitrail *m* stained-glass window.

vitre *f* pane, window.

vitreux *adj* glassy, glazed, vitreous.

vitrier *m* glazier.

vitrine *f* shop window; display cabinet.

vivacité *f* vivacity, liveliness; vividness; acuteness.

vivant *adj* alive, living; lively.

vivement *adv* quickly, briskly; keenly, acutely.

vivier *m* fishpond.

vivifiant *adj* refreshing, invigorating.

vivifier *vt* to enliven, invigorate, refresh.

vivre *vi* to live, be alive; to last, endure; **vive la mariée!** three cheers for the bride; * *vt* to live, spend; to live through.

vocabulaire *m* vocabulary.

vocal *adj* vocal.

vocation *f* vocation, calling.

vœu *m* vow; wish.

vogue *f* fashion, vogue.

voici *prép* here is, here are; ago, past.

voie *f* way, road; means; process; ~ **ferrée** railway; ~ **d'eau** leak; **en ~ de** in the process of.

voilà *prép* there is, there are; ago; **et ~!** so there!

voile *f* sail; * *m* veil.

voiler *vt* to veil, shroud; **se ~** *vr* to wear a veil; to mist over.

voilier *m* sailing boat, yacht.

voir *vt* to see; to deal with; to understand; **avoir à ~ avec** to have to do with; **se ~** *vr* to find o.s.; to show.

voisin *m* **-e** *f* neighbour; fellow; * *adj* neighbouring, next.

voisinage *m* neighbourhood, vicinity.

voiture *f* car; carriage; cart.

voix *f* voice; vote.

vol *m* flight; flock; **à ~ d'oiseau** as the crow flies.

volaille *f* fowl, poultry.

volant *m* steering wheel; * *adj* flying.

volcan *m* volcano.

volcanique *adj* volcanic.

volée *f* flight; volley; **à la ~** in mid-air; rashly, at random; **demi-~** half-volley.

voler *vi* to fly; ~ **en éclats** to smash into pieces; * *vt* to steal; to rob.

volet *m* shutter; flap, paddle.

voleur *m* **-euse** *f* thief; * *adj* dishonest, thieving.

volontaire *adj* voluntary; intentional.

volonté *f* will, wish; willingness; willpower.

volontiers *adv* willingly; gladly.

volt *m* volt.

voltiger *vi* to flutter about.

volumineux *adj* voluminous, bulky.

voluptueux *adj* voluptuous.

vomir *vi* to vomit, be sick; * *vt* to vomit, bring up.

vomissement *m* vomiting.

vos = *pl* **votre**.

votant *m* **-e** *f* voter.

vote *m* vote; voting.

voter *vi* to vote.

votre *adj*, *pl* **vos** your, your own.

vôtre *pn*: **le ~, la ~, les ~s** yours, your own.

vouer *vt* to vow; to devote, dedicate.

vouloir *vt* to want, wish; to require; to try; **~ du mal à** to wish sb harm; **en ~ à** to bear a grudge against sb.

voulu *adj* required; deliberate.

vous *pn* you, yourself.

voûte *f* vault.

voûté *adj* vaulted.

voyage *m* journey, trip; travelling.

voyager *vi* to travel, journey.

voyageur *m* **-euse** *f* traveller, passenger.

voyant *m* **-e** *f* seer; * *m* signal light; * *adj* gaudy, showy.

voyelle *f* vowel.

voyou *m* lout, loafer, hoodlum.

vrac *adv*: **en ~** in bulk.

vrai *adj* true, genuine.

vraisemblable *adj* likely, probable.

vrille *f* tendril; spiral; **descendre en ~** to come down in a spin.

vrombir *vi* to roar, hum.

vu *adj* seen; considered, regarded; **être bien/mal ~** to be well/ poorly thought of; **ni ~ ni connu** you won't discover anything; * *prép* in view of.

vue *f* sight, eyesight; **en ~ de** with a view to; **avoir des ~s sur** to have designs on.

vulgaire *adj* vulgar, crude.

vulgarité *f* vulgarity, coarseness.

vulnérable *adj* vulnerable.

WXYZ

wagon-citerne *m* tanker.

wagon-lit *m* sleeper.

wagon-restaurant *m* restaurant car.

xylophone *m* xylophone.

yacht *m* yacht.

yaourt *m* yoghurt.

yard *m* yard.

yeux *pl* = **œil**.

yin *m* yin.

yoga *m* yoga.

yoghurt *m* = **yaourt**.

yuppie *mf* yuppy.

zèbre *m* zebra.

zèle *m* zeal.

zélé *adj* zealous.

zéro *m* zero, nought, nothing.

zézayer *vi* to lisp.

zigzaguer *vi* to zigzag.

zinc *m* zinc.

zizanie *f* ill-feeling.

zizi *m* (*fam*) willy.

zodiaque *m* zodiac.

zona *m* shingles.

zone *f* zone, area.

zoologie *f* zoology.

zoom *m* zoom; zoom lens.

zozoter *vi* (*fam*) to lisp.

zut *interj* damn! rubbish! shut up!

ENGLISH-FRENCH
DICTIONARY

A

a *art* un, une.
aback *adv* **to be taken ~** *vi* être décontenancé.
abandon *vt* abandonner, laisser.
abash *vt* couvrir de honte.
abate *vt* baisser; * *vi* baisser; se calmer.
abbey *n* abbaye *f.*
abbreviate *vt* abréger, raccourcir.
abbreviation *n* abréviation *f.*
abdicate *vt* abdiquer; renoncer à.
abdication *n* abdication *f;* renonciation *f.*
abdomen *n* abdomen *m.*
abdominal *adj* abdominal.
abduct *vt* kidnapper, enlever.
abductor *n* abducteur *m.*
aberration *n* aberration *f.*
abet *vt:* **to aid and ~** être complice de.
abeyance *n* suspension *f.*
abhor *vt* abhorrer, exécrer.
abhorrence *n* exécration, horreur *f.*
abide *vt* supporter, souffrir.
ability *n* capacité, aptitude *f;* **abilities** *pl* talents *mpl.*
abject *adj* misérable; abject, méprisable; **~ly** *adv* misérablement.
ablaze *adj* enflammé.
able *adj* capable; **to be ~** pouvoir.
able-bodied *adj* robuste.
ably *adv* habilement.
abnormal *adj* anormal.
abnormality *n* anomalie *f.*
aboard *adv* à bord.
abolish *vt* abolir, supprimer.
abolition *n* abolition, suppression *f.*

abominable *adj* abominable; **~bly** *adv* abominablement.
abomination *n* abomination *f.*
aborigines *npl* aborigènes *mpl.*
abort *vi* avorter.
abortion *n* avortement *m.*
abortive *adj* raté.
abound *vi* abonder; **~ with** abonder en.
about *prep* au sujet de; vers; * *adv* çà et là; **to be ~ to** être sur le point de; **to go ~ a thing** entreprendre quelque chose.
above *prep* au-dessus de; * *adv* au-dessus; **~ all** surtout, principalement; **~ mentioned** mentionné ci-dessus.
aboveboard *adj* franc.
abrasion *n* écorchure *f.*
abrasive *adj* abrasif.
abreast *adv* de front.
abridge *vt* abréger, raccourcir.
abroad *adv* à l'étranger; **to go ~** se rendre à l'étranger.
abrupt *adj* abrupt; brusque; **~ly** *adv* brusquement; rudement.
abscess *n* abcès *m.*
abscond *vi* s'enfuir.
absence *n* absence *f.*
absent *adj* absent; * *vi* s'absenter.
absentee *n* absent *m* -e *f.*
absenteeism *n* absentéisme *m.*
absent-minded *adj* distrait.
absolute *adj* absolu; **~ly** *adv* absolument.
absolutism *n* absolutisme *m.*
absolve *vt* absoudre.

absorb *vt* absorber.

absorbent *adj* absorbant.

absorption *n* absorption *f.*

abstain *vi* s'abstenir.

abstemious *adj* sobre.

abstinence *n* abstinence *f.*

abstract *adj* abstrait; * *n* abrégé *m*; **in the ~** dans l'abstrait.

abstruse *adj* abstrus, obscur.

absurd *adj* absurde; **~ly** *adv* absurdement.

absurdity *n* absurdité *f.*

abundance *n* abondance *f.*

abundant *adj* abondant; **~ly** *adv* abondamment.

abuse *vt* abuser de; insulter; maltraiter; * *n* abus *m*; injures *fpl*; mauvais traitements *mpl.*

abusive *adj* injurieux.

abysmal *adj* abominable.

academic *adj* universitaire; scolaire; théorique.

academy *n* académie *f.*

accelerate *vt* accélérer.

accelerator *n* accélérateur *m.*

acceleration *n* accélération *f.*

accent *n* accent *m*; * *vt* accentuer.

accentuate *vt* accentuer.

accept *vt* accepter.

acceptable *adj* acceptable.

acceptance *n* acceptation *f.*

access *n* accès *m.*

accessible *adj* accessible.

accessory *n* accessoire *m*; (*law*) complice *m.*

accident *n* accident *m*; hasard *m.*

accidental *adj* accidentel; **~ly** *adv* par hasard.

acclaim *vt* acclamer.

accommodate *vt* loger; accommoder.

accommodating *adj* obligeant.

accommodation *n* logement *m.*

accompaniment *n* (*mus*) accompagnement *m.*

accompanist *n* (*mus*) accompagnateur *m* -trice *f.*

accompany *vt* accompagner.

accomplice *n* complice *mf.*

accomplish *vt* accomplir.

accomplished *adj* accompli.

accomplishment *n* accomplissement *m*; **~s** *pl* talents *mpl.*

accord *n* accord *m*; **of one's own ~** de son propre chef.

accordance *n*: **in ~ with** conformément à.

according *prep* selon; **~ly** *adv* en conséquence.

accordion *n* (*mus*) accordéon *m.*

accost *vt* accoster.

account *n* compte *m*; **on no ~** en aucun cas; **on ~ of** en raison de; **to call to ~** demander des comptes; * *vt* **~ for** expliquer; représenter.

accountable *adj* responsable.

accountancy *n* comptabilité *f.*

accountant *n* comptable *mf.*

accumulate *vt* accumuler; * *vi* s'accumuler.

accumulation *n* accumulation *f.*

accuracy *n* exactitude *f.*

accurate *adj* exact; **~ly** *adv* exactement.

accursed *adj* maudit.

accusation *n* accusation *f.*

accusatory *adj* accusateur.

accuse *vt* accuser.

accustomed *adj* accoutumé.

ace *n* as *m.*

acerbic *adj* acerbe.

acetate *n* (*chem*) acétate *m*.

ache *n* douleur *f*; * *vi* faire mal.

achieve *vt* réaliser; obtenir.

achievement *n* réalisation *f*, exploit *m*.

acid *adj* acide; aigre; * *n* acide *m*.

acidity *n* acidité *f*.

acknowledge *vt* reconnaître, admettre.

acknowledgment *n* reconnaissance *f*.

acne *n* acné *f*.

acorn *n* gland *m*.

acoustics *n* acoustique *f*.

acquaint *vt* informer, aviser.

acquaintance *n* connaissance *f*.

acquiescent *adj* consentant.

acquire *vt* acquérir.

acquisition *n* acquisition *f*.

acquit *vt* acquitter.

acquittal *n* acquittement *m*.

acre *n* acre *f*.

acrid *adj* âcre; acerbe.

acrimonious *adj* acrimonieux.

across *adv* en travers, d'un côté à l'autre; * *prep* à travers; **to come ~** tomber sur.

act *vt* jouer; * *vi* agir; jouer la comédie; * *n* acte *m*.

acting *adj* intérimaire.

action *n* action *f*; combat *m*.

action replay *n* répétition *f*.

activate *vt* activer.

active *adj* actif; **~ly** *adv* activement.

activity *n* activité *f*.

actor *n* acteur *m*.

actress *n* actrice *f*.

actual *adj* réel; concret; **~ly** *adv* en fait; réellement.

acumen *n* perspicacité *f*.

acute *adj* aigu; perspicace; **~ accent** *n*

accent aigu *m*; **~ angle** *n* angle aigu *m*; **~ly** *adv* vivement; avec perspicacité.

ad *n* annonce *f*.

adamant *adj* inflexible.

adapt *vt* adapter, ajuster.

adaptable *adj* adaptable.

adaptation *n* adaptation *f*.

adaptor *n* adaptateur *m*.

add *vt* ajouter; **~ up** additionner.

adder *n* vipère *f*.

addict *n* intoxiqué *m* -e *f*.

addiction *n* dépendance *f*.

addictive *adj* qui crée une dépendance.

addition *n* addition *f*.

additional *adj* additionnel; **~ly** *adv* de plus.

additive *n* additif *m*.

address *vt* adresser; s'adresser à; * *n* adresse *f*; discours *m*.

adept *adj* expert.

adequacy *n* suffisance *f*; capacité *f*.

adequate *adj* adéquat; suffisant; **~ly** *adv* convenablement; suffisamment.

adhere *vi* adhérer.

adherence *n* adhérence *f*.

adhesion *n* adhérence *f*; adhésion *f*.

adhesive *adj* adhésif.

adjacent *adj* adjacent, contigu.

adjective *n* adjectif *m*.

adjoining *adj* contigu.

adjourn *vt* reporter, remettre.

adjournment *n* ajournement *m*.

adjudicate *vt* décider; juger.

adjust *vt* ajuster, adapter.

adjustable *adj* ajustable, adaptable.

adjustment *n* ajustement *m*; réglage *m*.

adjutant *n* (*mil*) adjudant *m*.

ad lib *vt* improviser.

administer *vt* administrer; distribuer.

administration *n* administration *f*; gouvernement *m*.

administrative *adj* administratif.

administrator *n* administrateur *m* -trice *f*.

admirable *adj* admirable; **~bly** *adv* admirablement.

admiral *n* amiral *m*.

admiralty *n* ministère de la Marine *m*.

admiration *n* admiration *f*.

admire *vt* admirer.

admirer *n* admirateur *m* -trice *f*.

admiringly *adv* avec admiration.

admission *n* admission, entrée *f*.

admit *vt* admettre; **~ to** recon-naître, avouer.

admittance *n* admission *f*.

admittedly *adv* il est vrai (que).

admonish *vt* admonester, réprimander.

admonition *n* admonestation *f*; con-seil *m*.

ad nauseam *adv* à saturation.

ado *n* agitation *f*.

adolescence *n* adolescence *f*.

adopt *vt* adopter.

adopted *adj* adoptif.

adoption *n* adoption *f*.

adoptive *adj* adoptif.

adorable *adj* adorable.

adoration *n* adoration *f*.

adore *vt* adorer.

adorn *vt* orner.

adrift *adv* à la dérive.

adroit *adj* adroit, habile.

adulation *n* adulation *f*.

adult *adj* adulte; * *n* adulte *mf*.

adulteration *n* falsification *f*.

adulterous *adj* adultère.

adultery *n* adultère *m*.

advance *vt* avancer; * *vi* avancer; faire des progrès; * *n* avance *f*.

advanced *adj* avancé.

advancement *n* avancement *m*.

advantage *n* avantage *m*; **to take ~ of** profiter de.

advantageous *adj* avantageux.

advent *n* venue *f*; **Advent** *n* Avent *m*.

adventure *n* aventure *f*.

adventurous *adj* aventureux.

adverb *n* adverbe *m*.

adversary *n* adversaire *mf*.

adverse *adj* défavorable, contraire.

adversity *n* adversité *f*; malheur *m*.

advertise *vt* faire de la publicité pour; mettre une annonce pour.

advertisement *n* publicité *f*; annonce *f*.

advertising *n* publicité *f*.

advice *n* conseil *m*; avis *m*.

advisable *adj* prudent, conseillé.

advise *vt* conseiller; aviser.

advisedly *adv* de manière avisée.

advisory *adj* consultatif.

advocate *n* avocat *m*; * *vt* plaider pour.

aerial *n* antenne *f*.

aerobics *npl* aérobic *m*.

aeroplane *n* avion *m*.

aerosol *n* aérosol *m*.

afar *adv* au loin; **from ~** de loin.

affable *adj* affable; **~bly** *adv* affablement.

affair *n* affaire *f*.

affect *vt* toucher; affecter.

affectation *n* affectation *f*.

affected *adj* affecté.

affection *n* affection *f*.

affectionate *adj* affectueux; **~ly** *adv* affectueusement.

affidavit n déclaration sous serment f.

affiliate vt affilier.

affiliation n affiliation f.

affinity n affinité f.

affirm vt affirmer, déclarer.

affirmative adj affirmatif.

afflict vt affliger.

affliction n affliction f.

affluence n abondance f.

affluent adj riche; abondant.

afford vt fournir; **to be able to ~** avoir les moyens d'acheter.

affray n (law) rixe f.

affront n affront m, injure f; * vt affronter; insulter.

aflame adv en flammes.

afloat adv à flot.

afraid adj apeuré; **I am ~** j'ai peur.

afresh adv à nouveau.

aft adv (mar) en poupe.

after prep après; * adv après; **~ all** après tout.

afterbirth n placenta m.

after-effects npl répercussions fpl.

afterlife n vie après la mort f.

aftermath n conséquences fpl.

afternoon n après-midi mf.

aftershave n après-rasage m.

aftertaste n arrière-goût m.

afterward(s) adv ensuite.

again adv à nouveau; **~ and ~** de nombreuses fois; **as much ~** encore autant.

against prep contre; **~ the grain** à contre fil; de mauvaise volonté.

age n âge m; vieillesse f; **under ~** mineur; * vt vieillir.

aged adj âgé.

agency n agence f.

agenda n ordre du jour m.

agent n agent m.

aggravate vt aggraver; énerver.

aggravation n aggravation f; énervement m.

aggregate n agrégat m.

aggression n agression f.

aggressive adj agressif.

aggressor n agresseur m.

aggrieved adj offensé.

aghast adj horrifié.

agile adj agile; adroit.

agility n agilité f; adresse f.

agitate vt agiter.

agitation n agitation f.

ago adv: **how long ~?** il y a combien de temps?

agog adj en émoi; impatient.

agonising adj atroce, angoissant.

agony n douleur f atroce; angoisse f.

agree vt convenir; * vi être d'accord.

agreeable adj agréable; **~bly** adv agréablement.

agreed adj convenu; **~!** adv d'accord!

agreement n accord m.

agricultural adj agricole.

agriculture n agriculture f.

ahead adv en avant; à l'avance.

aid vt aider, secourir; * n aide f, secours m; aide mf.

aide-de-camp n (mil) aide de camp m.

AIDS n SIDA m.

ail vt affliger.

ailing adj souffrant.

ailment n maladie f.

aim vt pointer; viser; aspirer à; * n but m; cible f.

aimless adj sans but; **~ly** à la dérive, sans but.

air n air m; * vt aérer.

airborne adj aéroporté.

air-conditioned adj climatisé.

air-conditioning n climatisation f.

aircraft n avion m.

air force n armée de l'air f.

air freshener n appareil de conditionnement d'air m.

air gun n carabine à air comprimé f.

airless adj mal aéré, mal ventilé.

airline n ligne aérienne f.

airmail n: by ~ par avion.

airport n aéroport m.

airsick adj: to be ~ avoir le mal de l'air.

airstrip n piste d'atterrissage f.

air terminal n aérogare f.

airtight adj hermétique.

airy adj aéré; léger.

aisle n nef d'église f.

ajar adj entrouvert.

akimbo adj les poings sur les hanches.

akin adj ressemblant.

alabaster n albâtre m; * adj d'albâtre.

alacrity n vivacité f.

alarm n alarme f; * vt alarmer; inquiéter.

alarmist n alarmiste mf.

alas adv hélas.

albeit conj bien que.

album n album m.

alcohol n alcool m.

alcoholic adj alcoolisé; * n alcoolique mf.

alcove n alcôve f.

ale n bière f.

alert adj vigilant; vif; * n alerte f.

algae npl algues fpl.

algebra n algèbre f.

alias adj alias.

alibi n (law) alibi m.

alien adj étranger; * n étranger m -ère f; extra-terrestre mf.

alienate vt aliéner.

alienation n aliénation f.

alight vi mettre pied à terre; * adj en feu.

align vt aligner.

alike adj semblable, égal; * adv de la même façon.

alimony n (law) pension f alimentaire.

alive adj en vie, vivant; actif.

alkali n alcali m.

alkaline adj alcalin.

all adj tout; * adv totalement; ~ at once, ~ of a sudden soudain; ~ the same cependant; ~ the better tant mieux; not at ~! pas du tout!; il n'y a pas de quoi!; * n tout m.

allay vt apaiser.

all clear n feu vert m.

allegation n allégation f.

allege vt alléguer.

allegiance n loyauté, fidélité f.

allergy n allergie f.

alleviate vt alléger.

alleviation n allègement m.

alley n ruelle f.

alliance n alliance f.

allied adj allié.

alligator n alligator m.

all-night adj ouvert toute la nuit.

allocate vt allouer.

allocation n allocation f.

allot vt assigner.

allow vt permettre; accorder; ~ for tenir compte de.

allowance n allocation f, concession f.

alloy n alliage m.

all right *adv* bien.
all-round *adj* complet.
allude *vi* faire allusion à.
allure *n* charme, attrait *m*.
alluring *adj* attrayant.
allusion *n* allusion *f*.
ally *n* allié *n* -e *f*; * *vt* allier.
almanac *n* almanach *m*.
almighty *adj* omnipotent, tout-puissant.
almond *n* amande *f*.
almost *adv* presque.
aloft *prep* en l'air; en haut.
alone *adj* seul; * *adv* seul; **to leave ~** laisser tranquille.
along *adv* le long (de).
aloof *adj* distant.
aloud *adj* à voix haute.
alphabet *n* alphabet *m*.
alphabetical *adj* alphabétique; **~ly** *adv* par ordre alphabétique, alphabétiquement.
alpine *adj* alpin.
already *adv* déjà.
also *adv* aussi.
altar *n* autel *m*.
alter *vt* modifier.
alteration *n* modification *f*.
altercation *n* altercation *f*.
alternate *adj* alterné; * *vt* alterner; **~ly** *adv* alternativement.
alternative *n* alternative *f*; * *adj* alternatif; **~ly** *adv* sinon.
although *conj* bien que, malgré.
altitude *n* altitude *f*.
altogether *adv* complètement.
aluminium *n* aluminium *m*.
always *adv* toujours.
a.m. *adv* du matin.

amalgamate *vt* amalgamer; *vi* s'amalgamer.
amalgamation *n* amalgamation *f*.
amass *vt* accumuler, amasser.
amateur *n* amateur *m*.
amateurish *adj* d'amateur.
amaze *vt* stupéfier.
amazement *n* stupéfaction *f*.
amazing *adj* stupéfiant; **~ly** *adv* incroyablement.
amazon *n* amazone *f*.
ambassador *n* ambassadeur *m*.
amber *n* ambre *m*; * *adj* ambré.
ambidextrous *adj* ambidextre.
ambiguity *n* ambiguïté *f*.
ambiguous *adj* ambigu.
ambition *n* ambition *f*.
ambitious *adj* ambitieux.
amble *vi* marcher tranquillement.
ambulance *n* ambulance *f*.
ambush *n* embuscade *f*; **to lie in ~** être embusqué; * *vt* tendre une embuscade à.
amelioration *n* amélioration *f*.
amenable *adj* responsable.
amend *vt* modifier; amender.
amendment *n* modification *f*; amendement *m*.
amends *npl* compensation *f*.
amenities *npl* commodités *fpl*.
America *n* Amérique *f*.
American *adj* américain.
amethyst *n* améthyste *f*.
amiable *adj* aimable.
amicable *adj* amical.
amid(st) *prep* entre, parmi.
amiss *adv*: **something's ~** quelque chose ne va pas.
ammonia *n* ammoniaque *m*.
ammunition *n* munitions *fpl*.

amnesia n amnésie f.

amnesty n amnistie f.

among(st) prep entre, parmi.

amoral adj amoral.

amorous adj amoureux.

amount n montant m; quantité f; * vi s'élever (à).

amp(ere) n ampère m.

amphibian n amphibie m.

amphitheatre n amphithéâtre m.

ample adj spacieux; abondant, gros.

amplifier n amplificateur m.

amply adv amplement.

amputate vt amputer.

amputation n amputation f.

amulet n amulette f.

amuse vt distraire, divertir.

amusement n distraction f, divertissement m.

amusing adj divertissant.

an art un, une.

anachronism n anachronisme m.

anaemia n anémie f.

anaemic adj (med) anémique.

anaesthetic n anesthésique m.

analog adj (comput) analogique.

analogous adj analogue.

analogy n analogie f.

analyse vt analyser.

analysis n analyse f.

analyst n analyste mf.

analytical adj analytique.

anarchist n anarchiste mf.

anarchy n anarchie f.

anatomy n anatomie f.

ancestor n ancêtre mf.

ancestral adj ancestral.

ancestry n ascendance f.

anchor n ancre f; * vi jeter l'ancre.

anchovy n anchois m.

ancient adj ancien, antique.

ancillary adj auxiliaire.

and conj et.

anecdote n anecdote f.

anemone n (bot) anémone f.

anew adv de nouveau.

angel n ange m.

angelic adj angélique.

anger n colère f; * vt mettre en colère, irriter.

angle n angle m.

angler n pêcheur à la ligne m.

angling n pêche à la ligne f.

angrily adv avec colère.

angry adj en colère, irrité.

anguish n angoisse f.

angular adj angulaire.

animal n adj animal m.

animated adj animé.

animation n animation f.

animosity n animosité f.

aniseed n graine d'anis f.

ankle n cheville f.

annals n annales fpl.

annex vt annexer; * n annexe f.

annihilate vt annihiler, anéantir.

annihilation n anéantissement m.

anniversary n anniversaire (de) m.

annotate vt annoter.

annotation n annotation f.

announce vt annoncer.

announcement n annonce f.

announcer n présentateur m -trice f.

annoy vt ennuyer.

annoyance n ennui m.

annoying adj ennuyeux.

annual adj annuel; **~ly** adv annuellement.

annuity n rente viagère f.

annul vt annuler, abroger.

annulment n annulation f.

anoint vt oindre.

anomalous adj anormal.

anomaly n anomalie, irrégularité f.

anonymity n anonymat m.

anonymous adj anonyme; **~ly** adv anonymement.

anorexia n anorexie f.

another adj un autre; **one ~** l'un l'autre.

answer vt répondre à; **~ for** répondre de; **~ to** répondre à; * n réponse f.

answerable adj responsable.

answering machine n répondeur téléphonique m.

ant n fourmi f.

antagonise vt provoquer.

antagonism n antagonisme m; rivalité f.

antagonist n antagoniste mf.

antarctic adj antarctique.

anteater n fourmilier m.

antelope n antilope f.

antenna n antenne f.

anthem n hymne m.

anthology n anthologie f.

anthropology n anthropologie f.

antiaircraft adj antiaérien.

antibiotic n antibiotique m.

antibody n anticorps m.

Antichrist n Antéchrist m.

anticipate vt prévoir.

anticipation n attente f; prévision f.

anticlockwise adv dans le sens contraire des aiguilles d'une montre.

antidote n antidote m.

antifreeze n antigel m.

antipathy n antipathie f.

antiquated adj vieux; suranné.

antique n meuble m ancien.

antiseptic adj antiseptique.

antisocial adj antisocial.

antithesis n antithèse f.

antler n corne f.

anvil n enclume f.

anxiety n anxiété f; désir m.

anxious adj anxieux; **~ly** adv anxieusement.

any adj pn n'importe quel, n'importe quelle; un, une; tout; **~body** quelqu'un; n'importe qui; personne; **~how** de toute façon; de n'importe quelle manière; **~more** plus; **~place** n'importe où; nulle part; **~thing** quelque chose; n'importe quoi; rien.

apart adv séparément.

apartment n appartement m.

apathetic adj apathique.

apathy n apathie f.

ape n singe m; * vt singer.

aperture n ouverture f.

apex n sommet m; apex m.

aplomb n aplomb m.

apologetic adj d'excuse.

apologise vt excuser.

apology n apologie, défense f.

apoplexy n apoplexie f.

apostle n apôtre m.

apostrophe n apostrophe f.

appall vt horrifier, atterrer.

appalling adj horrible.

apparatus n appareil m.

apparel n vêtements mpl.

apparent adj évident, apparent; **~ly** adv apparemment.

apparition n apparition, vision f.

appeal vi faire appel; * n (law) appel m.

appealing *adj* attrayant.

appear *vi* paraître.

appearance *n* apparence *f*.

appease *vt* apaiser.

appendage *n* appendice *m*.

appendicitis *n* appendicite *f*.

appendix *n* appendice *m*.

appetising *adj* appétissant.

appetite *n* appétit *m*.

applaud *vt vi* applaudir.

applause *n* applaudissements *mpl*.

apple *n* pomme *f*.

apple pie *n* tourte aux pommes *f*.

appliance *n* appareil *m*.

applicable *adj* applicable.

applicant *n* candidat *m* -e *f*.

application *n* application *f*; candidature *f*.

apply *vt* appliquer; * *vi* s'adresser.

appoint *vt* nommer.

appointment *n* rendez-vous *m*; nomination *f*.

apportion *vt* répartir.

apposite *adj* approprié, juste.

appraisal *n* estimation *f*.

appraise *vt* évaluer.

appreciable *adj* appréciable, sensible.

appreciably *adv* sensiblement.

appreciate *vt* apprécier; être conscient de.

appreciation *n* appréciation *f*.

appreciative *adj* reconnaissant.

apprehend *vt* appréhender.

apprehension *n* appréhension *f*; arrestation *f*.

apprehensive *adj* appréhensif.

apprentice *n* apprenti *m*; * *vt* mettre en apprentissage.

apprenticeship *n* apprentissage *m*.

apprise *vt* informer.

approach *vi* (s')approcher; * *vt* (s')approcher de; * *n* approche *f*.

approachable *adj* accessible, approchable.

approbation *n* approbation *f*.

appropriate *vt* s'approprier; * *adj* approprié, adéquat.

approval *n* approbation *f*.

approve (of) *vt* approuver.

approximate *vi* s'approcher; * *adj* approximatif; **~ly** *adv* approximativement.

approximation *n* approximation *f*.

apricot *n* abricot *m*.

April *n* avril *m*.

apron *n* tablier *m*.

apt *adj* idéal; susceptible; **~ly** *adv* opportunément.

aptitude *n* aptitude *f*.

aquarium *n* aquarium *m*.

aquatic *adj* aquatique.

arbitrary *adj* arbitraire.

arbitration *n* arbitrage *m*.

arcade *n* galerie *f*.

arch *n* arc *m*; * *adj* malicieux.

archaeological *adj* archéologique.

archaeology *n* archéologie *f*.

archaic *adj* archaïque.

archangel *n* archange *m*.

archbishop *n* archevêque *m*.

archer *n* archer *m*.

archery *n* tir à l'arc *m*.

architect *n* architecte *mf*.

architectural *adj* architectural.

architecture *n* architecture *f*.

archives *npl* archives *fpl*.

archly *adv* malicieusement.

archway *n* arcade, voûte *f*.

arctic *adj* arctique.

ardent *adj* ardent; **~ly** *adv* ardemment.

ardour *n* ardeur *f*.

arduous *adj* ardu, difficile.

area *n* région *f*; domaine *m*.

arena *n* arène *f*.

arguably *adv* peut-être, sans doute.

argue *vi* se disputer; * *vt* soutenir.

argument *n* argument *m*; dispute *f*.

argumentative *adj* raisonneur.

aria *n* (*mus*) aria *f*.

arid *adj* aride.

aridity *n* aridité *f*.

arise *vi* se lever; survenir.

aristocracy *n* aristocratie *f*.

aristocrat *n* aristocrate *mf*.

aristocratic *adj* aristocratique.

arithmetic *n* arithmétique *f*.

ark *n* arche *f*.

arm *n* bras *m*; arme *f*; * *vt* armer; * *vi* (s')armer.

armament *n* armement *m*.

armchair *n* fauteuil *m*.

armful *n* brassée *f*.

armistice *n* armistice *m*.

armour *n* armure *f*.

armoury *n* arsenal *m*.

armpit *n* aisselle *f*.

army *n* armée *f*.

aroma *n* arôme *m*.

aromatic *adj* aromatique.

around *prep* autour de; * *adv* autour.

arouse *vt* éveiller; exciter.

arrange *vt* arranger, organiser.

arrangement *n* arrangement *m*.

arrant *adj* fieffé.

array *n* série *f*.

arrears *npl* arriéré *m*; retard *m*.

arrest *n* arrestation *f*; * *vt* arrêter.

arrival *n* arrivée *f*.

arrive *vi* arriver.

arrogance *n* arrogance *f*.

arrogant *adj* arrogant.

arrow *n* flèche *f*.

arsenal *n* (*mil*) arsenal *m*.

arsenic *n* arsenic *m*.

arson *n* incendie criminel *m*.

art *n* art *m*.

arterial *adj* artériel.

artery *n* artère *f*.

artful *adj* malin, astucieux.

art gallery *n* musée d'art *m*.

arthritis *n* arthrite *f*.

artichoke *n* artichaut *m*.

article *n* article *m*.

articulated *adj* articulé.

artifice *n* artifice *m*.

artificial *adj* artificiel; **~ly** *adv* artificiellement.

artillery *n* artillerie *f*.

artisan *n* artisan *m*.

artist *n* artiste *mf*.

artistic *adj* artistique.

artistry *n* habileté *f*.

artless *adj* naturel, simple; **~ly** *adv* naturellement, simplement.

art school *n* école des beaux-arts *f*.

as *conj* comme; pendant que; aussi; **~ for**, **~ to** quant à.

asbestos *n* asbeste *m*, amiante *f*.

ascend *vi* monter.

ascendancy *n* ascendant *m*.

ascension *n* ascension *f*.

ascent *n* montée *f*.

ascertain *vt* établir.

ash *n* (*bot*) frêne *m*; cendre *f*.

ashamed *adj* honteux.

ashore *adv* à terre.

ashtray *n* cendrier *m*.

Ash Wednesday *n* mercredi des Cendres *m*.

aside *adv* de côté.

ask *vt* demander; **~ after** demander des nouvelles de; **~ for** demander.

askew *adv* de côté.

asleep *adj* endormi; **to fall ~** s'endormir.

asparagus *n* asperge *f*.

aspect *n* aspect *m*.

aspersion *n* calomnie *f*.

asphalt *n* asphalte *m*.

asphyxiation *n* asphyxie *f*.

aspiration *n* aspiration *f*.

aspire *vi* aspirer, désirer.

aspirin *n* aspirine *f*.

ass *n* âne *m*.

assail *vt* assaillir, attaquer.

assailant *n* assaillant, agresseur *m*.

assassin *n* assassin *m*.

assassinate *vt* assassiner.

assassination *n* assassinat *m*.

assault *n* assaut *m*; agression *f*; * *vt* agresser.

assemble *vt* assembler; * *vi* s'assembler.

assembly *n* assemblée *f*.

assent *n* assentiment *m*; * *vi* donner son assentiment.

assert *vt* soutenir; affirmer.

assertion *n* assertion *f*.

assertive *adj* péremptoire.

assess *vt* évaluer.

assessment *n* évaluation *f*.

assets *npl* biens *mpl*.

assiduous *adj* assidu; **~ly** *adv* assidûment.

assign *vt* assigner.

assignation *n* rendez-vous *m*; (*law*) cession *f*.

assignment *n* (*law*) cession *f*; mission *f*.

assist *vt* assister, aider; secourir.

assistance *n* assistance, aide *f*, secours *m*.

assistant *n* aide *mf*, assistant *m* -e *f*.

associate *vt* associer; * *adj* associé; * *n* associé *m* -e *f*.

association *n* association *f*.

assorted *adj* assorti.

assortment *n* assortiment *m*.

assume *vt* assumer; supposer.

assumption *n* supposition *f*.

assurance *n* assurance *f*.

assure *vt* assurer.

asterisk *n* astérisque *m*.

asthma *n* asthme *m*.

asthmatic *adj* asthmatique.

astonish *vt* surprendre, stupéfier.

astonishing *adj* stupéfiant.

astonishment *n* surprise, stupéfaction *f*.

astound *vt* ébahir.

astray *adv*: **to lead ~** détourner du droit chemin.

astrologer *n* astrologue *mf*.

astrological *adj* astrologique.

astrology *n* astrologie *f*.

astronaut *n* astronaute *mf*.

astronomer *n* astronome *mf*.

astronomical *adj* astronomique.

astronomy *n* astronomie *f*.

astute *adj* malin.

asylum *n* asile, refuge *m*.

at *prep* à; en; **~ once** tout de suite; **~ all** du tout; **~ all events** en tout cas; **~ first** au début, d'abord; **~ last** enfin.

atheist *n* athée *mf*.

athlete *n* athlète *mf*.

athletic *adj* athlétique.

atlas *n* atlas *m*.

atmosphere *n* atmosphère *f*.

atmospheric *adj* atmosphérique.

atom *n* atome *m*.

atom bomb *n* bombe atomique *f*.

atomic *adj* atomique.

atone *vt* expier.

atrocious *adj* atroce.

atrocity *n* atrocité, énormité *f*.

attach *vt* joindre.

attaché *n* attaché *m* -e *f*.

attachment *n* attachement *m*.

attack *vt* attaquer; * *n* attaque *f*.

attacker *n* attaquant *m* -e *f*.

attempt *vt* essayer; * *n* essai *m*, tentative *f*.

attend *vt* servir; assister à; ~ **to** s'occuper de; * *vi* faire attention.

attendance *n* service *m*; assistance *f*; présence *f*.

attendant *n* serviteur *m*.

attention *n* attention *f*; soin *m*.

attentive *adj* attentif.

attic *n* grenier *m*.

attire *n* atours *mpl*.

attitude *n* attitude *f*.

attract *vt* attirer.

attraction *n* attraction *f*; attrait *m*.

attractive *adj* attrayant.

attribute *vt* attribuer; * *n* attribut *m*.

auburn *adj* auburn.

auction *n* vente aux enchères *f*.

auctioneer *n* commissaire-priseur *m*.

audacious *adj* audacieux, téméraire; ~**ly** *adv* audacieusement.

audacity *n* audace, témérité *f*.

audible *adj* audible; ~**ly** *adv* audiblement.

audience *n* audience *f*; auditoire *m*.

auditor *n* vérificateur(-trice) de comptes *m(f)*; auditeur *m* -trice *f*.

augment *vt vi* augmenter.

August *n* août *m*.

aunt *n* tante *f*.

au pair *n* (jeune fille) au pair *f*.

aura *n* aura *f*.

auspices *npl* auspices *mpl*.

auspicious *adj* favorable, propice; ~**ly** *adv* favorablement.

austere *adj* austère, sévère.

austerity *n* austérité *f*.

authentic *adj* authentique.

authenticate *vt* légaliser.

authenticity *n* authenticité *f*.

author *n* auteur *m*.

authorisation *n* autorisation *f*.

authorise *vt* autoriser.

authoritarian *adj* autoritaire.

authoritative *adj* autoritaire.

authority *n* autorité *f*.

autocratic *adj* autocratique.

autograph *n* autographe *m*.

automated *adj* automatisé.

automatic *adj* automatique.

automaton *n* automate *m*.

autopsy *n* autopsie *f*.

autumn *n* automne *m*.

autumnal *adj* automnal.

auxiliary *adj* auxiliaire.

avail *vt*: **to ~ oneself of** profiter de; * *n*: **to no ~** en vain.

available *adj* disponible.

avalanche *n* avalanche *f*.

avarice *n* avarice *f*.

avaricious *adj* avare.

avenge *vt* venger.

avenue *n* avenue *f*.

average *vt* atteindre la moyenne de; * *n* moyenne *f*, moyen terme *m*.

aversion *n* aversion *f*, dégoût *m*.

avert *vt* détourner, écarter.

aviary n volière f.

avoid vt éviter; échapper à.

avoidable adj évitable.

await vt attendre.

awake vt réveiller; * vi se réveiller; * adj éveillé.

award vt attribuer; * n prix m; décision f.

aware adj conscient; au courant.

away adv absent; loin.

awe n peur, crainte f.

awe-inspiring, awesome adj terrifiant; imposant.

awful adj horrible, terrible; ~ly adv horriblement, terriblement.

awkward adj gauche, maladroit; délicat; ~ly adv maladroitement.

awry adv de travers.

axe n hache f; * vt licencier; supprimer.

axis n axe m.

axle n axe m.

B

babble vi bavarder, babiller.

babe, baby n bébé, enfant en bas-âge m; nourrisson m.

baboon n babouin m.

babyish adj enfantin; puéril.

bachelor n célibataire m; (diplôme) licencié m -e f.

back n dos m; * adv en arrière, à l'arrière; * vt soutenir, appuyer, renforcer.

backbite vt médire de, sur.

backbone n colonne vertébrale, épine dorsale f.

backdate vt antidater.

backer n partisan m -e f.

backgammon n (jeu de) jacquet m.

background n fond m.

backlash n réaction violente f.

backlog n accumulation de travail en retard f.

back number n vieux numéro (magazine, journal) m.

backpack n sac à dos m.

back payment n rappel de salaire m.

backside n derrière m.

backward adj rétrograde; retardé; lent; * adv en arrière.

bacon n lard m.

bad adj mauvais, de mauvaise qualité; méchant; malade; ~ly adv mal.

badge n plaque f, insigne m, badge m; symbole m; signe m.

badger n blaireau m; * vt harceler.

badminton n badminton m.

baffle vt déconcerter, confondre.

bag n sac m; valise f.

baggage n bagages mpl; équipement m.

bagpipe n cornemuse f.

bail n mise en liberté sous caution, caution f.

bait vt tourmenter; appâter; * n appât m; amorce f.

baize n serge f.

bake vt faire cuire au four.

baker n boulanger m -ère f.

bakery n boulangerie f.

baking n cuisson f; fournée f.

baking powder n levure f.

balance n balance f; équilibre m; solde d'un compte m; **to lose one's ~** perdre l'équilibre; * vt peser; peser le pour et le contre; solder; équilibrer.

balance sheet n bilan m.

balcony n balcon m.

bald adj chauve.

baldness n calvitie f.

bale n balle f.

baleful adj sinistre, funeste, maléfique.

ball n balle f; boule f; ballon m.

ballad n ballade f.

ballerina n ballerine f.

ballet n ballet m.

ballistic adj balistique.

balloon n montgolfière f, aérostat m.

ballot n scrutin m; vote m.

ballpoint (pen) n stylo à bille m.

ballroom n salle de bal f.

bamboo n bambou m.

bamboozle vt (fam) embobiner.

ban n interdiction f; * vt interdire.

banal adj banal.

banana n banane f.

band n bande f; reliure f; courroie de transmission f; orchestre m.

bandage n bande f, bandage m; * vt bander.

bandit n bandit m.

bandstand n kiosque à musique m.

bandy vt avoir des mots.

bandy-legged adj aux jambes arquées.

bang n coup violent, claquement m, détonation f; * vt frapper violemment; claquer.

bangle n bracelet m.

banish vt bannir, exiler, chasser, expatrier.

banister(s) n(pl) rampe d'escalier f.

banjo n banjo m.

bank n rive f; remblai m; banque f; banc m; digue f; * vt déposer de l'argent à la banque; **~ on** compter sur.

bank account n compte en banque m.

banker n banquier m -ière f.

banking n opérations bancaires fpl.

banknote n billet de banque m.

bankrupt adj failli; * n failli m.

bank statement n relevé de compte m.

banner n bannière f; étendard m.

banquet n banquet m.

baptise vt baptiser.

baptism n baptême m.

bar n bar m; barre f; obstacle m; (law) barreau m; * vt empêcher; interdire; exclure.

barbarian n barbare mf; * adj barbare, cruel.

barbaric adj barbare.

barbecue n barbecue m.

barber n coiffeur (pour hommes) m.

bar code n code barres m.

bard n barde m; poète m.

bare adj nu, dépouillé; simple; pur; * vt dénuder, découvrir.

barefaced adj éhonté, impudent.

barefoot(ed) adj aux pieds nus.

barely adv à peine, tout juste.

bargain n affaire f; contrat, marché m; occasion f; * vi conclure un marché; négocier.

barge n péniche f.

baritone n (mus) baryton m.

bark n écorce f; aboiement m; * vi aboyer.

barley n orge m.

barmaid n serveuse f.

barman n barman m.

barn n grange f; étable f.

barometer n baromètre m.

baron n baron m.

baroness n baronne f.

barracks npl caserne f.

barrage n barrage m; (fig) torrent m.

barrel n tonneau, fût m; canon de fusil m.

barren adj stérile, infertile, improductif.

barricade n barricade f; barrière f; * vt barricader, barrer.

barrier n barrière f; obstacle m (rail) portillon d'accès m.

barring adv excepté, sauf.

barrow n brouette f.

barter vi faire du troc; * vt troquer, échanger.

base n base f; partie inférieure f, pied m; point de départ m; * vt fonder sur; * adj vil, abject.

baseball n baseball m.

basement n sous-sol m.

bash vt frapper.

basic adj fondamental, de base; **~ally** adv fondamentalement.

basin n cuvette f; lavabo m.

basis n base f; fondement m.

bask vi se prélasser.

basket n panier m, corbeille f.

basketball n basket-ball m.

bass n (mus) contrebasse f.

bassoon n basson m.

bastard n, adj bâtard m.

baste vt arroser la viande de son jus; bâtir.

bat n chauve-souris f.

batch n fournée f.

bath n bain m.

bathe vt (vi) (se) baigner.

bathing suit n maillot de bain m.

bathroom n salle de bain f.

baths npl piscine f.

baton n matraque f.

battalion n (mil) bataillon m.

batter vt battre; frapper, martyriser; * n pâte à frire f.

battering ram n (mil) bélier m.

battery n pile, batterie f.

battle n bataille f; combat m; * vi se battre, combattre.

battlefield n champ de bataille m.

battleship n cuirassé m.

bawdy adj paillard m.

bawl vi brailler, (fam) gueuler.

bay n baie f; laurier m; * vi aboyer, hurler; * adj bai.

bayonet n baïonnette f.

bazaar n bazar m.

be vi être.

beach n plage f.

beacon n phare, signal lumineux m.

bead n perle f; **~s** npl chapelet m.

beak n bec m.

beaker n gobelet m.

beam n rayon m; poutre f; * vi rayonner, resplendir.

bean n haricot m; **French ~** haricot m vert.

beansprouts npl germes de soja mpl.

bear vt porter, supporter, produire; * vi se diriger.

bear n ours m.

beard n barbe f.

bearing n relation f; maintien, port m.

beast n bête f; brute f.

beastly adj bestial, brutal; abominable.

beat vt battre; * vi battre, palpiter; * n battement m; pulsation f.

beating n correction, raclée f; battement m.

beautiful adj beau, belle, magnifique.

beautify vt embellir; décorer.

beauty n beauté f; ~ **salon** n institut de beauté m; ~ **spot** n site touristique m.

beaver n castor m.

because conj parce que; * prép: ~ **of** en raison de.

beckon vi faire signe.

become vt convenir, aller à; * vi devenir, se faire.

becoming adj convenable, seyant.

bed n lit m.

bedclothes npl couvertures et draps mpl.

bedding n literie f.

bedlam n maison f de fous; chahut m.

bedridden adj cloué au lit; grabataire.

bedroom n chambre f.

bedtime n heure d'aller au lit f.

bee n abeille f.

beech n hêtre m.

beef n bœuf (viande) m.

beefburger n hamburger m.

beehive n ruche f.

beeline n ligne droite f.

beer n bière f.

beetle n scarabée m.

beetroot n betterave f.

befit vt convenir à.

before adv, prep avant; devant; * conj avant de, avant que.

beforehand adv à l'avance, au préalable.

befriend vt traiter en ami; aider.

beg vt mendier; solliciter; supplier; * vi demander la charité.

beggar n mendiant m -e f.

begin vt vi commencer.

beginner n débutant m -e f; novice mf.

beginning n commencement, début m, origine f.

begrudge vt donner à contrecœur; envier.

behalf n faveur f, intérêt m; nom m, part f.

behave vi se comporter, se conduire.

behaviour n conduite f; comportement m.

behead vt décapiter.

behind prep derrière; * adv derrière, par-derrière, en arrière.

beige adj beige.

being n existence f; être m.

belated adj tardif.

belch vi éructer; * vt vomir; * n éructation f, rot m.

belfry n beffroi, clocher m.

belief n foi, croyance f; conviction, opinion f, credo m.

believable adj croyable.

believe vt croire; * vi penser, croire.

belittle vt rabaisser.

bell n cloche f.

belligerent adj belligérant.

bellow vi beugler, mugir; hurler.

bellows npl soufflet m.

belly n ventre m.

belong vi appartenir à.

belongings npl affaires fpl.

beloved adj chéri, bien-aimé.

below adv en dessous, en bas; * prep sous, au-dessous de, en dessous.

belt n ceinture f.

bemoan vt déplorer; pleurer.

bemused adj déconcerté.

bench n banc m.

end *vt* courber, plier; incliner; * *vi* se courber, s'incliner; * *n* courbe *f*.

beneath *adv* au-dessous; * *prep* sous, au-dessous de.

benefactor *n* bienfaiteur *m* -trice *f*.

beneficial *adj* profitable, salutaire, utile.

beneficiary *n* bénéficiaire *mf*.

benefit *n* intérêt, avantage *m*; profit *m*; bienfait *m*; * *vt* profiter à; * *vi* bénéficier.

benevolent *adj* bienveillant; de bienfaisance.

benign *adj* bienveillant, doux, affable; bénin.

bent *n* penchant *m*.

bequeath *vt* léguer à.

bereavement *n* perte *f*; deuil *m*.

beret *n* béret *m*.

berry *n* baie *f*.

berserk *adj* fou furieux.

berth *n* (*mar*) couchette *f*.

beside(s) *prep* à côté de; excepté; * *adv* de plus, en outre.

besiege *vt* assiéger, assaillir.

best *adj* le meilleur, la meilleure; * *adv* le mieux; * *n* le meilleur, le mieux *m*.

bestial *adj* bestial, brutal.

bestow *vt* accorder, conférer; consacrer.

bestseller *n* best-seller *m*.

bet *n* pari *m*; * *vt* parier.

betray *vt* trahir.

betrayal *n* trahison *f*.

betroth *vt* promettre en mariage.

better *adj adv* meilleur, mieux; **so much the ~** tant mieux; * *vt* améliorer.

betting *n* pari *m*.

between *prep* entre;* *adv* au milieu.

beverage *n* boisson *f*.

bevy *n* bande *f*, groupe *m*.

beware *vi* prendre garde.

bewilder *vt* déconcerter, dérouter.

bewilderment *n* perplexité *f*.

bewitch *vt* ensorceler, enchanter.

beyond *prep* au-delà de; au-dessus de; plus de; sauf; * *adv* au-delà, plus loin.

bias *n* préjugé *m*; tendance, inclination *f*.

bib *n* bavoir *m*.

Bible *n* Bible *f*.

biblical *adj* biblique.

bibliography *n* bibliographie *f*.

bicker *vi* se chamailler.

bicycle *n* bicyclette *f*.

bid *vt* ordonner, commander; offrir; * *n* offre, tentative *f*.

bidding *n* ordre *m*; enchère, offre *f*.

bifocals *npl* verres à double foyer *mpl*.

big *adj* grand, gros; important.

bigamist *n* bigame *mf*.

bigamy *n* bigamie *f*.

bigheaded *adj* frimeur.

bigot *n* fanatique *mf*.

bigoted *adj* fanatique.

bike *n* vélo *m*.

bikini *n* bikini *m*.

bile *n* bile *f*.

bilingual *adj* bilingue.

bilious *adj* bilieux.

bill *n* bec (d'oiseau) *m*; addition *f*; billet *m*.

billboard *n* panneau d'affichage *m*.

billet *n* logement *m*.

billiards *npl* billard *m*.

billion *n* milliard *m*.

bin *n* coffre *m*.

bind *vt* attacher; lier; entourer; relier.

binding *n* reliure *f*, extra-fort *m*.

binge *n* beuverie, bringue *f*.

bingo *n* loto *m*.

binoculars *npl* jumelles *fpl*.

biochemistry n biochimie f.
biographer n biographe mf.
biographical adj biographique.
biography n biographie f.
biological adj biologique.
biology n biologie f.
birch n bouleau m.
bird n oiseau m.
bird's-eye view n vue d'ensemble f.
bird-watcher n ornithologue mf.
birth n naissance f.
birth certificate n extrait de naissance m.
birth control n limitation des naissances f.
birthday n anniversaire m.
birthplace n lieu de naissance m.
biscuit n biscuit m.
bishop n évêque m.
bison n bison m.
bit n morceau m; peu m.
bitch n chienne f, (fig) plainte f.
bite vt mordre; * n morsure f.
bitter adj amer, âpre; cuisant, acerbe; glacial; ~ly adv amèrement; avec amertume; âprement.
bizarre adj étrange, bizarre.
black adj noir, obscur; * n noir m.
blackberry n mûre f.
blackbird n merle m.
blackboard n tableau (noir) m.
blacken vt noircir, ternir.
blacklist n liste noire f.
blackmail n chantage m; * vt faire chanter.
black market n marché noir m.
black sheep n brebis galeuse f.
bladder n vessie f.
blade n lame f.
blame vt blâmer; * n faute f.

blameless adj irréprochable.
bland adj affable, suave; doux; apaisant.
blank adj blanc; vide, déconcerté.
blank cheque n chèque en blanc m.
blanket n couverture f.
blare vi retentir.
blasphemous adj blasphématoire.
blasphemy n blasphème m.
blast n souffle d'air m; explosion f; * vt faire sauter.
blast-off n lancement m, mise à feu f.
blatant adj flagrant.
blaze n flamme f; * vi flamber; resplendir.
bleach vt blanchir; décolorer; * vi blanchir; * n eau de Javel f.
bleak adj morne, lugubre, glacial, désolé.
bleary(-eyed) adj larmoyant.
bleat vi bêler.
bleed vt vi saigner.
bleeding n saignement m.
bleeper n bip m.
blemish vt gâter; ternir; * n tache f, infamie f.
blend vt mélanger.
bless vt bénir.
blessing n bénédiction f; bienfait m.
blight vt détruire.
blind adj aveugle; ~ alley n impasse f; * vt aveugler; éblouir; * n (Venetian) ~ store vénitien m.
blindfold vt bander les yeux de.
blindly adv à l'aveuglette, aveuglément.
blindness n cécité f.
blind spot n angle mort m.
blink vi clignoter.
blinkers npl clignotants mpl.

bliss n bonheur extrême m; félicité f.

blissful adj heureux; béat, bienheureux; **~ly** adv heureusement.

blister n ampoule f, cloque f; * vi se couvrir de cloques.

blitz n bombardement aérien m.

blizzard n tempête de neige f.

bloated adj gonflé, boursouflé, bouffi.

blob n goutte, tache f.

bloc n bloc m.

block n bloc m; encombrement, blocage m; pâté de maisons m; **~ (up)** vt bloquer.

blockade n blocus m; * vt faire le blocus, bloquer.

blockage n obstruction f.

blockbuster n grand succès m.

blond adj blond; * n blond m -e f.

blood n sang m.

blood donor n donneur(-euse) de sang m(f).

blood group n groupe sanguin m.

bloodhound n limier m.

bloodless adj exangue, anémié; sans effusion de sang.

blood poisoning n empoisonnement du sang m.

blood pressure n pression artérielle f.

bloodshed n effusion de sang f; carnage m.

bloodshot adj injecté de sang.

bloodstream n système sanguin m.

blood test n analyse de sang f.

bloodthirsty adj sanguinaire.

blood transfusion n transfusion sanguine f.

blood vessel n veine f; vaisseau sanguin m.

bloody adj sanglant, ensanglanté;

cruel; **~ minded** adj pas commode, buté.

bloom n fleur f; (also fig); * vi éclore, fleurir.

blossom n fleur f.

blot vt tacher; sécher; effacer; * n tache f.

blotchy adj marbré; couvert de taches.

blouse n chemisier m.

blow vi souffler; sonner; * vt souffler; faire voler; jouer de; **~ up** exploser; * n coup m.

blubber n blanc de baleine m; * vi pleurnicher.

bludgeon n gourdin m; matraque f.

blue adj bleu.

bluebottle n (bot) bleuet m; mouche bleue f.

blueprint n (fig) projet m.

bluff n esbrouffe f; * vt faire de l'esbrouffe.

blunder n gaffe f; * vi faire une gaffe.

blunt adj émoussé, obtus; direct.

bluntly adv carrément; sans ménagements.

blur n image f floue; * vt brouiller.

blurt out vt laisser échapper.

blush n rougeur f; fard à joues m; * vi rougir.

blustery adj de tempête, violent.

boa n boa m (serpent).

boar n verrat m.

board n planche f; table f; conseil m; * vt monter à bord de.

boarding card n carte d'embarquement f.

boarding school n pensionnat m.

boast vi se vanter; * n vantardise f; rodomontade f.

boastful *adj* vantard.

boat *n* bateau *m*; canot *m*; barque *f*.

boating *n* canotage *m*; promenade en bateau *f*.

bodice *n* corsage *m*.

bodily *adj adv* physique(ment).

body *n* corps *m*; cadavre *m*.

body-building *n* culturisme *m*.

bodyguard *n* garde du corps *m*.

bodywork *n* (*auto*) carrosserie *f*.

bog *n* marécage *m*.

bogus *adj* faux.

boil *vi* bouillir; * *vt* faire bouillir; * *n* furoncle *m*; ébullition *f*.

boiler *n* casserole *f*; chaudière *f*.

boiling point *n* point d'ébullition *m*.

boisterous *adj* bruyant; turbulent; tumultueux.

bold *adj* audacieux, téméraire, osé, hardi.

bolster *vt* soutenir.

bolt *n* verrou *m*; * *vt* verrouiller, fermer au verrou.

bomb *n* bombe *f*.

bombard *vt* (*phys*) bombarder.

bombardier *n* bombardier *m*.

bombshell *n* (*fig*) bombe *f*.

bond *n* lien *m*; attache *f*; engagement *m*; obligation *f*.

bondage *n* esclavage, asservissement *m*.

bone *n* os *m*; * *vt* désosser.

bonfire *n* feu (de joie) *m*.

bonnet *n* bonnet *m*.

bonus *n* prime *f*.

bony *adj* osseux.

boo *vt* huer.

booby trap *n* mine *f*.

book *n* livre *m*.

bookcase *n* bibliothèque *f*.

bookkeeping *n* comptabilité *f*.

bookshop *n* librairie *f*.

bookworm *n* rat de bibliothèque *m*.

boom *n* grondement *m*; essor *m*; * *v* gronder.

boon *n* bienfait *m*, aubaine *f*; faveur *f*.

boorish *adj* rustre, rustique.

boost *n* stimulation *f*; * *vt* stimuler.

boot *n* botte *f*; coffre *m*; **to ~** *adv* de plus, de surcroît.

booth *n* cabine *f*, baraque *f*.

booze *vi* se saôuler; * *n* alcool *m*.

border *n* bord *m*; bordure *f*; lisière *f*; frontière *f*; * *vt* border, avoisiner.

borderline *n* limite *f*.

bore *vt* forer, percer; ennuyer; * *n* perceuse *f*; calibre *m*; raseur *m*.

boredom *n* ennui *m*.

boring *adj* ennuyeux.

born *adj* né; originaire.

borrow *vt* emprunter.

borrower *n* emprunteur *m* -euse *f*.

bosom *n* sein *m*, poitrine *f*.

bosom friend *n* ami(e) intime *m(f)*.

boss *n* chef *m*; patron(ne) *m(f)*.

botanic(al) *adj* botanique.

botanist *n* botaniste *mf*.

botany *n* botanique *f*.

botch *vt* cochonner.

both *pn* tou(te)s les deux, l'un(e) et l'autre; * *adj* les deux.

bother *vt* ennuyer, déranger; * *n* ennui, problème *m*.

bottle *n* bouteille *f*; * *vt* mettre en bouteille.

bottleneck *n* embouteillage *m*; goulot *m*.

bottle-opener *n* ouvre-bouteille *m* invar.

bottom n fond m; fondement m; * adj du bas; dernier.

bottomless adj sans fond, insondable; inépuisable.

bough n branche f; rameau m.

boulder n gros galet m.

bounce vi rebondir; bondir, faire des bonds; * n bond, rebond m.

bound n limite f; saut m; répercussion f; * vi bondir; sauter; * adj à destination de.

boundary n limite f; frontière f.

boundless adj illimité, infini.

bout n attaque f; accès m; combat m.

bow vt incliner, baisser; * vi se courber; faire une révérence; * n salut m, révérence f.

bow n arc m; archet m; nœud m.

bowels npl intestins mpl; entrailles fpl.

bowl n bol, saladier m; boule f; * vi jouer aux boules.

bowling n boules fpl.

bowling alley n bowling m.

bow tie n nœud papillon m.

box n boîte, caisse f; loge f.

boxer n boxeur m.

boxing n boxe f.

boxing gloves npl gants de boxe mpl.

boxing ring n ring m.

box office n guichet m.

boy n garçon m.

boycott vt boycotter; * n boycottage m.

boyfriend n petit ami m.

boyish adj d'enfant, puéril; de garçon.

bra n soutien-gorge m.

brace n attache f; bretelle f; appareil dentaire m.

bracelet n bracelet m

bracken n (bot) fougère f.

bracket n tranche f; parenthèse f; crochet m; * ~ **with** vt réunir par une accolade; mettre ensemble.

bracing adj vivifiant, tonifiant.

brag n fanfaronnade f; * vi se vanter, fanfaronner.

braid n tresse f; * vt tresser.

brain n cerveau m; tête f; * vt assommer, défoncer le crâne à.

brainwash vt faire un lavage de cerveau à.

brainwave n idée lumineuse f.

brainy adj intelligent.

brake n frein m; * vi freiner.

bran n son m.

branch n branche f; ramification f; * vi se ramifier.

brand n marque f; marque au fer f; * vt marquer au fer.

brandish vt brandir.

brand-new adj flambant-neuf.

brandy n cognac m.

brash adj grossier; impertinent.

brass n cuivre m.

brassiere n soutien-gorge m.

brat n môme, gosse mf.

bravado n bravade f.

brave adj courageux, brave, vaillant; * vt braver; * n brave m.

bravery n bravoure f; courage m; magnificence f.

brawl n bagarre, rixe f; * vi se bagarrer.

brawn n muscle m.

brazen adj de cuivre; impudent, effronté.

breach n rupture f; brèche f; violation f.

bread n pain m; (also fig).

breadcrumbs npl chapelure f.

breadth n largeur f.

breadwinner n soutien de famille m.

break *vt* casser; briser; violer; interrompre; * *vi* se casser; ~ **into** entrer par effraction; ~ **out** s'échapper; * *n* cassure, rupture *f*; interruption *f*.

breakdown *n* panne *f*; dépression nerveuse *f*.

breakfast *n* petit déjeuner *m*.

breakthrough *n* percée, innovation *f*.

breast *n* poitrine *f*, sein *m*; cœur *m*.

breaststroke *n* brasse *f*.

breath *n* haleine *f*; respiration *f*; souffle *m*.

breathe *vt vi* respirer; exhaler.

breathing *n* respiration *f*; souffle *m*.

breathing space *n* moment de répit *m*.

breathless *adj* hors d'haleine.

breathtaking *adj* stupéfiant.

breed *n* race, espèce *f*; * *vt* élever, engendrer; produire; éduquer; * *vi* se reproduire.

breeding *n* élevage *m*; éducation *f*.

breeze *n* brise *f*.

breezy *adj* frais.

brevity *n* brièveté *f*; concision *f*.

brew *vt* faire infuser; brasser; comploter * *vi* infuser; se tramer; * *n* infusion *f*.

brewery *n* brasserie *f*.

bribe *n* pot-de-vin *m*; * *vt* acheter, soudoyer.

bribery *n* corruption *f*.

brick *n* brique *f*.

bricklayer *n* maçon *m*.

bridal *adj* de noces, nuptial.

bride *n* mariée *f*.

bridegroom *n* marié *m*.

bridesmaid *n* demoiselle d'honneur *f*.

bridge *n* pont *m*; arête du nez *f*; che-

valet *m*.

bridle *n* bride *f*; frein *m*; * *vt* brider; réfréner.

brief *adj* bref, concis, succinct; * *n* affaire *f*; résumé *m*.

briefcase *n* serviette *f*.

briefly *adv* brièvement, en peu de mots.

brigade *n* (*mil*) brigade *f*.

brigadier *n* (*mil*) général de brigade *m*.

bright *adj* clair, brillant, éclatant.

brighten *vt* faire briller; * *vi* s'éclairer.

brilliance *n* éclat *m*.

brilliant *adj* éclatant; génial.

brim *n* bord *m*.

brimful *adj* plein jusqu'au bord.

bring *vt* apporter; amener; persuader; ~ **about** entraîner, provoquer; ~ **up** élever.

brink *n* bord *m*.

brisk *adj* vif, rapide, frais.

bristle *n* poil *m*; soie *f*; * *vi* se hérisser.

brittle *adj* cassant, fragile.

broach *vt* aborder.

broad *adj* large.

broadbeans *npl* fèves *fpl*.

broadcast *n* émission *f*; * *vt vi* diffuser, émettre.

broadcasting *n* radiodiffusion *f*; émission de télévision *f*.

broaden *vt* élargir; * *vi* s'élargir.

broadly *adv* généralement.

broad-minded *adj* tolérant, aux idées larges.

brocade *n* brocart *m*.

broccoli *n* brocoli *m*.

brochure *n* brochure *f*, dépliant *m*.

brogue *n* accent *m* du terroir.

broken *adj* cassé; interrompu.

broker *n* courtier *m*.

ronchitis n bronchite f.

ronze n bronze m; * vt bronzer, bru-
air.

rooch n broche f.

rood vi couver; ruminer; * n couvée
; nichée f.

room n genêt m; balai m.

roomstick n manche à balai m.

roth n bouillon de viande et de légu-
nes m.

rothel n bordel m.

rother n frère m.

rotherhood n fraternité f.

rother-in-law n beau-frère m.

row n sourcil m; front m; sommet m.

rowbeat vt intimider.

rown adj marron; brun; ~ **paper** n
apier d'emballage m; ~ **sugar** n
assonnade f; * n marron m; * vt brunir.

rowse vt parcourir; * vi paître.

ruise vt faire un bleu à; * n bleu m,
cchymose f.

runette n brune f.

runt n choc m.

rush n brosse f; pinceau m; accro-
hage m; * vt brosser.

russels sprout n chou de Bruxelles m.

rutal adj brutal.

rutality n brutalité f.

rute n brute f; * adj bestial, féroce.

rutish adj brutal, bestial; féroce.

ubble n bulle f; * vi faire des bulles,
ouillonner; pétiller.

ucket n seau m.

uckle n boucle f; * vt attacher, bou-
ler; * vi se déformer.

ud n bourgeon, bouton m; * vi bour-
eonner.

uddhism n bouddhisme m.

budding adj en bouton.

budge vi bouger, remuer; céder.

budgerigar n perruche f.

budget n budget m.

buff n mordu m.

buffalo n bison m.

buffet n buffet m; * vt gifler; frapper.

bug n punaise f.

bugle(horn) n clairon m.

build vt construire, bâtir.

builder n constructeur m; entrepreneur
m.

building n bâtiment m; immeuble, édifice m.

bulb n bulbe m; oignon m.

bulge vi se renfler; * n gonflement, renflement m.

bulk n masse f; volume m; grosseur f;
majeure partie f.

bulky adj volumineux; encombrant.

bull n taureau m.

bulldog n bouledogue m.

bulldozer n bulldozer m.

bullet n balle f.

bulletin board n panneau d'affichage
m.

bulletproof adj pare-balles, blindé.

bullfight n corrida f.

bullfighter n torero m.

bullion n or en barre m.

bullring n arène f.

bull's-eye n centre de la cible m.

bully n tyran m; * vt tyraniser.

bum n clochard m.

bump n heurt m; secousse f; bosse f; *
vt heurter.

bumpy adj cahoteux, bosselé.

bun n petit pain m; chignon m.

bunch n botte f; groupe m.

bundle n paquet m, liasse f; ballot m; fagot m.

bungalow n bungalow m.

bungle vt bousiller; * vi faire mal les choses.

bunion n (med) oignon m.

bunk n couchette f.

bunker n abri m; bunker m.

buoy n (mar) bouée f.

buoyancy n flottabilité f; optimisme m.

buoyant adj flottable; gai, enjoué.

burden n charge f; fardeau m; * vt charger.

bureaucracy n bureaucratie f.

bureaucrat n bureaucrate mf.

burglar n cambrioleur m -euse f.

burglar alarm n signal d'alarme, signal antivol m.

burglary n cambriolage m.

burial n enterrement m; obsèques fpl.

burlesque n caricature, parodie f.

burn vt brûler; incendier; mettre le feu à; * vi brûler; * n brûlure f.

burner n brûleur m.

burning adj brûlant.

burrow n terrier m; * vi se terrer.

burst vi éclater; ~ **into tears** éclater en sanglots; ~ **out laughing** éclater de rire; * vt ~ **into** faire irruption dans.

bury vt enterrer, inhumer.

bus n (auto)bus m.

bush n buisson, taillis m.

bushy adj touffu, plein de buissons.

business n entreprise f; commerce m; affaires fpl; activité f.

businesslike adj sérieux.

businessman n homme d'affaires m.

businesswoman n femme d'affaires f.

bust n buste m.

bus-stop n arrêt d'autobus m.

bustle vi s'affairer; s'activer; * n remue-ménage m; animation f.

bustling adj animé.

busy adj occupé; actif.

busybody n mouche du coche f.

but conj mais; sauf, excepté, seulement.

butcher n boucher m -ère f; * vt abattre, massacrer.

butler n majordome m.

butt n butte f; mégot m.

butter n beurre m; * vt beurrer.

buttercup n (bot) bouton d'or m.

butterfly n papillon m.

buttocks npl fesses fpl.

button n bouton m; * vt boutonner.

buttonhole n boutonnière f.

buttress n contre-fort m; soutien m; * vt soutenir.

buxom adj bien en chair.

buy vt acheter.

buyer n acheteur m -euse f.

buzz n bourdonnement, murmur m; * vi bourdonner.

buzzard n buse f.

buzzer n interphone m.

by prep à côté de, près de; par; de; ~ **and** ~ bientôt; ~ **the** ~ à propos; ~ **all means** certainement.

bygone adj passé.

by-product n sous-produit m.

bystander n spectateur m -trice f; badaud m -e f.

byte n (comput) octet m.

byword n proverbe, dicton m.

C

cab n taxi m.

cabbage n chou m.

cabin n cabine f; cabane f.

cabinet n conseil des ministres m; meuble de rangement m; console f.

cable n (mar) câble m.

cable car n téléphérique m.

cable television n télévision par câble f.

cache n cachette f.

cackle vi caqueter, jacasser.

cactus n cactus m.

cadet n cadet m.

Caesarean section, ~ operation n med) césarienne f.

cafeteria n cafétéria f.

caffein(e) n caféine f.

cage n cage f; prison f; * vt mettre en cage; emprisonner.

cagey adj circonspect.

cajole vt cajoler.

cake n gâteau m.

calamity n calamité f, désastre m.

calculate vt calculer, compter.

calculation n calcul m.

calculator n calculatrice f.

calculus n (math, med) calcul m.

calendar n calendrier m.

calf n veau m; vachette f; mollet m.

calibre n calibre m.

call vt appeler; appeler au téléphone; convoquer; ~ for demander, nécessiter; aller chercher quelqu'un; ~ on rendre visite à; ~ names insulter; * n appel m; cri m; visite f; nomination f; vocation f; profession f.

caller n visiteur m -euse f.

calling n profession, vocation f.

callous adj dur; insensible.

calm n calme m, tranquillité f; * adj calme, tranquille; * vt calmer; apaiser.

calorie n calorie f.

camel n chameau m.

cameo n camée m.

camera n appareil photographique m; caméra f.

cameraman n cameraman, cadreur m.

camomile n camomille f.

camouflage n camouflage m.

camp n camp m; * vi camper.

campaign n campagne f; * vi faire campagne.

campaigner n militant, candidat en campagne électorale m.

camper n campeur m -euse f.

campsite n camping m.

can v aux pouvoir; * n boîte de conserve f.

canal n conduit m; canal m.

cancel vt annuler.

cancellation n annulation f.

cancer n cancer m.

candid adj candide, simple, sincère.

candidate n candidat(e) m(f).

candle n bougie f; cierge m.

candlelight n lueur d'une bougie f.

candlestick n bougeoir m.

candour n candeur f, sincérité f.

candy n bonbon m.

cane n canne f; bâton m.

canine adj canin.

cannabis n cannabis m.

cannibal n cannibale mf; anthropophage mf.

cannon n canon m; ~ **ball** n boulet de canon m.

canoe n canoë m.

canonise vt canoniser.

can opener n ouvre-boîte m.

canopy n baldaquin m, marquise f.

cantankerous adj acariâtre, atrabilaire.

canteen n cantine f.

canvas n toile f.

canvass vt sonder, examiner; débattre; * vi solliciter des voix; faire du démarchage.

canvasser n prospecteur m -trice f, démarcheur m -euse f.

canyon n canyon m.

cap n casquette f.

capability n capacité, aptitude, faculté f; potentiel m.

capable adj capable.

capacity n capacité, aptitude f; potentiel m.

cape n cap, promontoire m.

caper n cabriole f; gambade f; * vi cabrioler; gambader.

capital adj capital; principal; * n capital m; capitale f; majuscule f.

capitalise vt: ~ **on** profiter de.

capitalist n capitaliste mf.

capital punishment n peine de mort, peine capitale f.

capitulate vi capituler.

capitulation n capitulation f.

caprice n caprice m.

capricious adj capricieux.

capsize vt (mar) chavirer.

capsule n capsule f.

captain n capitaine m.

captivate vt captiver.

captive n captif m -ive f, prisonnier m - ière f.

captivity n captivité f.

capture n capture f; * vt prendre, capturer.

car n voiture f, automobile f; wagon m.

caramel n caramel m.

carat n carat m.

caravan n caravane f.

carbohydrates npl hydrates de carbone mpl.

carbon n carbone m.

carbon copy n copie carbone f, double carbone m.

carbon paper n papier carbone m.

carbuncle n escarboucle f; furoncle m, tumeur maligne f.

carburettor n carburateur m.

carcass n cadavre m.

card n carte f.

cardboard n carton m.

card game n jeu de cartes m.

cardiac adj cardiaque.

cardinal adj cardinal, principal; * n cardinal m.

care n soin m; souci m; * vi se soucier de, être concerné par; **what do I ~?** qu'est-ce que cela peut me faire?; ~ **for** vt soigner; aimer.

career n carrière f; cours m; * vi aller à toute vitesse.

carefree n insouciant.

careful adj soigneux, consciencieux, prudent.

careless adj insouciant, négligent; indolent.

caress n caresse f; * vt caresser.

caretaker n gardien m -ne f, concierge mf.

cargo n cargaison de navire f.

car hire n location de voiture f.

caricature n caricature f; * vt caricaturer.

caring adj aimant; humanitaire.

carnal adj charnel; sensuel.

carnation n œillet m.

carnival n carnaval m.

carnivorous adj carnivore.

carol n chant m (de Noël).

carpenter n charpentier m.

carpet n tapis m.

carriage n port m; voiture f; wagon m.

carrier pigeon n pigeon voyageur m.

carrion n charogne f.

carrot n carotte f.

carry vt porter; transporter; conduire; * vi porter; ~ on continuer.

cart n charrette f; chariot m.

cartilage n cartilage m.

cartload n charretée f.

carton n pot m; boîte f.

cartoon n dessin animé m.

cartridge n cartouche f.

carve vt tailler, sculpter; ciseler.

carving knife n couteau à découper m.

car wash n station de nettoyage pour voitures f.

case n boîte f; valise f; cas m; étui m; enveloppe f; **in** ~ au cas où.

cash n espèces fpl; * vt encaisser.

cash dispenser n distributeur automatique de billets m.

cashier n caissier m -ière f.

cashmere n cachemire m.

casing n chambranle m; enveloppe f.

casino n casino m.

cask n tonneau, fût m.

casket n cercueil m.

casserole n cocotte f.

cassette n cassette f.

cassette player, recorder n lecteur de cassettes, magnétophone m.

cassock n soutane f.

cast vt jeter, lancer; couler; * n coup m; moule m.

castaway n réprouvé, paria m.

castigate vt punir sévèrement.

casting vote n voix prépondérante f.

cast iron n fonte f.

castle n château m.

castor oil n huile de ricin f.

castrate vt castrer.

castration n castration f.

casual adj accidentel, fortuit; ~ly adv par hasard, fortuitement.

casualty n victime f, mort m -e f.

cat n chat m, chatte f.

catalogue n catalogue m.

catalyst n catalyseur m.

catapult n catapulte f.

cataract n cataracte f.

catarrh n rhume m; catarrhe m.

catastrophe n catastrophe f.

catch vt attraper, saisir; prendre; surprendre; ~ **fire** prendre feu; * n prise f; capture f; (mus) canon m; attrape f.

catchphrase n rengaine f.

catchy adj qui attire l'attention; accrocheur.

catechism n catéchisme m.

categorical adj catégorique; ~ly adv catégoriquement.

categorise vt classer par catégories.

category n catégorie f.

cater vi approvisionner en nourriture.

caterer n fournisseur, traiteur m.

catering n restauration f.

caterpillar n chenille f.

cathedral n cathédrale f.

catholic *adj n* catholique *mf*.

Catholicism *n* catholicisme *m*.

cattle *n* bétail *m*.

cauliflower *n* chou-fleur *m*.

cause *n* cause *f*; raison *f*; motif *m*; procès *m*; * *vt* causer.

caution *n* prudence, précaution *f*; avertissement *m*; * *vt* avertir.

cautious *adj* prudent, circonspect.

cavalry *n* cavalerie *f*.

cave *n* grotte *f*; caverne *f*.

cavern *n* caverne *f*.

cavernous *adj* caverneux.

cavity *n* cavité *f*.

cease *vt* cesser, arrêter; * *vi* cesser.

ceasefire *n* cessez-le-feu *m*.

cedar *n* cèdre *m*.

ceiling *n* plafond *m*.

celebrate *vt* célébrer, fêter.

celebration *n* fête *f*.

celebrity *n* célébrité *f*.

celery *n* céleri *m*.

celestial *adj* céleste, divin.

celibacy *n* célibat *m*.

celibate *adj* célibataire.

cell *n* cellule *f*.

cellar *n* cave *f*; cellier *m*.

cello *n* violoncelle *m*.

cellophane *n* cellophane *f*.

cellular *adj* cellulaire.

cellulose *n* (*chem*) cellulose *f*.

cement *n* ciment *m*; (*also fig*).

cemetery *n* cimetière *m*.

cenotaph *n* cénotaphe *m*.

censor *n* censeur *m*, critique *mf*.

censorious *adj* sévère, critique.

censorship *n* censure *f*.

censure *n* censure, critique *f*; * *vt* censurer, condamner; critiquer.

census *n* recensement *m*.

cent *n* centime *m*.

centenary *n* centenaire *m*; * *adj* centenaire.

centennial *adj* centenaire.

centigrade *n* centigrade *m*.

centilitre *n* centilitre *m*.

centimetre *n* centimètre *m*.

centipede *n* mille-pattes *m invar*.

central *adj* central.

centralise *vt* centraliser.

centre *n* centre *m*; * *vt* centrer; concentrer; * *vi* se concentrer.

centrifugal *adj* centrifuge.

century *n* siècle *m*.

ceramic *adj* en céramique.

cerebral *adj* cérébral.

ceremonial *adj n* cérémonial *m*; rituel *m*.

ceremonious *adj* cérémonieux.

ceremony *n* cérémonie *f*; cérémonies *fpl*.

certain *adj* certain, sûr; ~**ly** *adv* certainement, sans aucun doute.

certainty, certitude *n* certitude, conviction *f*.

certificate *n* certificat, acte *m*.

certify *vt* certifier, assurer.

cervical *adj* cervical.

chagrin *n* dépit *m*.

chain *n* chaîne *f*; série, suite *f*; * *vt* en chaîner; attacher avec une chaîne.

chain reaction *n* réaction en chaîne *f*.

chainstore *n* grand magasin à succursales *m*.

chair *n* chaise *f*; * *vt* présider.

chairman *n* président *m*.

chalk *n* craie *f*.

challenge *n* défi *m*; * *vt* défier.

challenging *adj* provocateur.

chambermaid *n* femme de chambre *f*.

chameleon n caméléon m.

chamois leather n peau de chamois f.

champion n champion m -ne f; * vt défendre.

championship n championnat m.

chance n hasard m; chance f; occasion f; **by ~** par hasard; * vt faire par hasard.

chandelier n lustre m.

change vt changer; * vi changer, se transformer; * n changement m, modification f; variété f; change m.

changeable adj changeant, variable; inconstant.

changing adj variable, changeant.

channel n canal m; chaîne f, * vt canaliser.

chant n chant m scandé; * vt scander.

chaos n chaos m.

chaotic adj chaotique.

chapel n chapelle f.

chaplain n chapelain m.

chapter n chapitre m.

char vt carboniser.

character n caractère m; personnage m.

characterise vt caractériser.

characteristic adj caractéristique; **~ally** adv typiquement.

charcoal n charbon de bois m.

charge vt charger; accuser; * n fardeau m; accusation f; (mil) attaque f; prix m.

charge card n carte de crédit f.

charitable adj caritatif; charitable; **~bly** adv charitablement.

charity n charité, bienfaisance f; aumône f.

charm n charme m; attrait m; * vt charmer, enchanter.

charming adj charmant.

chart n carte de navigation f; diagramme m.

charter n charte f; privilège m; * vt affréter.

charter flight n vol charter m.

chase vt donner la chasse à; poursuivre; * n chasse f.

chaste adj chaste; pur; sobre.

chastise vt châtier, punir, corriger.

chastity n chasteté, pureté f.

chat vi causer; * n petite conversation f, bavardage m.

chatter vi bavarder; jacasser; * n bavardage m; jacasserie f.

chatterbox n moulin à paroles m, pipelette f.

chatty adj bavard.

chauvinist n chauvin m -e f.

cheap adj bon marché, peu cher.

cheapen vt baisser le prix de.

cheat vt tromper, frauder; * n fraude, tricherie f; tricheur m -euse f.

check vt vérifier; contrôler; réprimer, enrayer; stopper; enregistrer; * n contrôle m.

checkmate n échec et mat m.

checkout n caisse f.

checkpoint n poste de contrôle m.

checkroom n (US) consigne f.

checkup n bilan de santé m.

cheek n joue f; culot (fam) m.

cheekbone n pommette f.

cheer n gaieté f, joie f; applaudissement m.

cheerful adj gai, enjoué, joyeux.

cheese n fromage m.

chef n chef (de cuisine) m.

chemical adj chimique.

chemist n chimiste mf; pharmacien m -ne f.

chemistry n chimie f.

cheque n chèque m.

cherish vt chérir, aimer.

cherry n cerise f; * adj vermeil.

cherub n chérubin m.

chess n échecs mpl.

chessboard n échiquier m.

chessman n pièce de jeu d'échecs f.

chest n poitrine f; cage thoracique f; ~ **of drawers** commode f.

chestnut n châtaigne f.

chew vt mâcher, mastiquer.

chick n poussin m; (fig) poulette (fam) f, nana (fam) f.

chicken n poulet m.

chickenpox n varicelle f.

chief adj principal, en chef; ~**ly** adv principalement; * n chef m.

chiffon n mousseline de soie f.

chilblain n engelure f.

child n enfant m.

childbirth n accouchement m.

childhood n enfance f.

childish adj enfantin, puéril.

childless adj sans enfants.

childlike adj d'enfant.

children npl de **child**: enfants mpl.

chill adj froid, frais, f fraîche; * n froid m; * vt refroidir; glacer.

chilly adj froid, très frais.

chime n carillon m; harmonie f; * vi sonner; s'accorder.

chimney n cheminée f.

chimpanzee n chimpanzé m.

chin n menton m.

china(ware) n porcelaine f.

chink n fente f; tintement m; * vi tinter.

chip vt ébrécher; * vi s'ébrécher; * n fragment, éclat m; puce f; frite f.

chiropodist n pédicure mf.

chirp vi pépier, gazouiller; * n pépiement, gazouillis m.

chisel n ciseau m; * vt ciseler.

chitchat n bavardage, papotage m.

chivalrous adj chevaleresque.

chivalry n chevalerie f.

chives npl ciboulette f.

chlorine n chlore m.

chloroform n chloroforme m.

chocolate n chocolat m.

choice n choix m, préférence f; assortiment m; sélection f; * adj de choix, de qualité.

choir n chœur m.

choke vt étrangler; étouffer.

cholera n choléra m.

choose vt choisir, élire.

chop vt trancher, couper, hacher; * n côtelette f; ~**s** pl (sl) babines fpl.

chopper n hélicoptère m.

chopsticks npl baguettes fpl.

chord n corde f, (mus) accord m.

chore n corvée f; travail routinier m.

chorus n chœur m.

christen vt baptiser.

Christendom n christianisme m; chrétienté f.

christening n baptême m.

Christian adj n chrétien m -ne f; ~ **name** prénom m.

Christianity n christianisme m; chrétienté f.

Christmas n Noël f.

Christmas card n carte de Noël f.

Christmas Eve n veille de Noël f.

chrome n chrome m.

chronic adj chronique.

chronicle n chronique f.

chronological adj chronologique.

chubby adj potelé.

chuck vt lancer, jeter.

chuckle *vi* rire, glousser.
chum *n* copain *m*, copine *f*.
chunk *n* gros morceau *m*.
church *n* église *f*.
churlish *adj* fruste, grossier; hargneux.
churn *n* baratte *f*; * *vt* baratter.
cider *n* cidre *m*.
cigar *n* cigare *m*.
cigarette *n* cigarette *f*.
cigarette case *n* étui à cigarettes *m*.
cinder *n* braise *f*.
cinema *n* cinéma *m*.
cinnamon *n* cannelle *f*.
cipher *n* chiffre *m* (code).
circle *n* cercle *m*; groupe *m*; * *vt* encercler; tourner autour de * *vi* décrire des cercles.
circuit *n* circuit *m*; tour *m*; tournée *f*.
circuitous *adj* détourné, indirect.
circular *adj* circulaire; * *n* circulaire *f*.
circulate *vi* circuler.
circulation *n* circulation *f*.
circumcise *vt* circoncire.
circumcision *n* circoncision *f*.
circumference *n* circonférence *f*.
circumflex *n* accent circonflexe *m*.
circumspect *adj* circonspect.
circumstance *n* circonstance, situation *f*.
circumstantial *adj* circonstancié; accessoire.
circus *n* cirque *m*.
cistern *n* citerne *f*.
citizen *n* citoyen *m* -ne *f*.
city *n* ville *f*.
civic *adj* civique.
civil *adj* civil, courtois.
civilian *n* civil *m* -e *f*.
civilisation *n* civilisation *f*.

civilise *vt* civiliser.
civility *n* civilité, courtoisie *f*.
civil war *n* guerre civile *f*.
clad *adj* vêtu, habillé.
claim *vt* revendiquer, réclamer; * *n* demande *f*; réclamation *f*.
claimant *n* demandeur *m*.
clairvoyant *n* voyant *m* -e *f*.
clamber *vi* grimper (avec difficulté).
clammy *adj* moite.
clamour *n* clameur *f*, cris *mpl*; * *vi* vociférer, crier.
clamp *n* attache *f*; * *vt* serrer; imposer;
~ **down on** resserrer le contrôle.
clan *n* clan, groupe *m*.
clandestine *adj* clandestin.
clang *n* bruit métallique *m*; * *vi* faire un bruit métallique.
clap *vt vi* applaudir.
claret *n* vin rouge de Bordeaux *m*.
clarification *n* clarification *f*, éclaircissement *m*.
clarify *vt* clarifier, éclaircir.
clarinet *n* clarinette *f*.
clarity *n* clarté *f*.
clash *vi* se heurter; s'entrechoquer; * *n* choc *m*; affrontement *m*.
clasp *n* fermoir *m*; boucle *f*; étreinte *f*;
* *vt* agrafer; étreindre.
class *n* classe *f*; catégorie *f*; * *vt* classer, classifier.
classic(al) *adj* classique; * *n* auteur classique *m*.
classification *n* classification *f*.
classify *vt* classifier, classer.
classmate *n* camarade de classe *mf*.
classroom *n* salle de classe *f*.
clatter *vi* résonner; cliqueter; * *n* cliquetis *m*.

clause n (gram) proposition f; clause f.

claw n griffe f; serre f; pince f; * vt griffer; agripper.

clay n argile m.

clean adj propre; net; * vt nettoyer.

cleanliness n propreté, pureté f.

cleanse vt nettoyer.

clear adj clair; net; transparent; évident; * adv distinctement; * vt clarifier, éclaircir; dégager; disculper; * vi s'éclaircir.

clearance n déblaiement m; autorisation f.

clear-cut adj net.

cleft n fissure, crevasse f.

clemency n clémence f.

clenched adj serré.

clergy n clergé m.

clergyman n ecclésiastique m.

clerical adj clérical, ecclésiastique.

clerk n ecclésiastique m; employé m.

clever adj intelligent; habile; astucieux.

click vt claquer; * vi faire un bruit sec.

client n client m -e f.

cliff n falaise f.

climate n climat m.

climax n point culminant m, apogée m.

climb vt grimper, escalader; * vi grimper, escalader.

climber n alpiniste mf.

climbing n alpinisme m.

clinch vt serrer fort.

cling vi s'accrocher (à), se cramponner (à); adhérer, (se) coller.

clinic n clinique f.

clink vt faire tinter; * vi tinter, résonner; * n tintement m.

clip vt couper; * n clip m; pince f.

clipping n coupure f.

clique n clique f.

cloak n cape f; prétexte m; * vt masquer.

cloakroom n vestiaire m.

clock n horloge f.

clockwork n mécanisme d'horloge m; * adj précis.

cloister n cloître m.

close vt fermer; clore, conclure; terminer; * vi se fermer; * n fin f; conclusion f; * adj proche; étroit; ajusté; dense; réservé; * adv de près; ~ **by** tout près.

closet n placard m.

close-up n gros plan m.

closure n fermeture f; clôture f.

clot n caillot m; grumeau m.

cloth n tissu m; chiffon m; toile f; clergé m.

clothe vt habiller, vêtir.

clothes npl vêtements mpl; linge m.

clothing n vêtements mpl.

cloud n nuage m; nuée f; * vt rendre trouble; assombrir; * vi se couvrir; s'obscurcir.

cloudy adj nuageux, nébuleux; obscur, sombre, trouble.

clout n coup de poing m.

clove n clou de girofle m.

clover n trèfle m.

clown n clown m.

club n matraque f; club m.

clue n indice m, indication f; idée f.

clump n massif m.

clumsy adj gauche, maladroit; lourd.

cluster n bouquet m; grappe f; groupe m; * vt grouper; * vi se rassembler.

clutch n prise f; embrayage m; * vt empoigner, agripper.

clutter vt encombrer.

coach n autocar m; wagon m; entraîneur m; * vt entraîner, donner des cours particuliers à.

coagulate vt coaguler; agglutiner; * vi se coaguler; s'agglutiner.

coal n charbon m.

coalition n coalition f.

coalmine n mine de charbon, houillère f.

coarse adj rude; grossier.

coast n côte f.

coastal adj côtier.

coastguard n gendarmerie maritime f, garde-côte m.

coastline n littoral m.

coat n manteau m; pelage m; couche f; * vt enduire, revêtir.

coat hanger n cintre m.

coating n revêtement m.

coax vt cajôler.

cobbler n cordonnier m.

cobbles, cobblestones npl pavés ronds mpl.

cobweb n toile d'araignée f.

cocaine n cocaïne f.

cock n coq m; (zool) mâle m; * vt armer; dresser.

cockerel n jeune coq m.

cockfight(ing) n combat de coqs m.

cockpit n cabine de pilotage f.

cockroach n cafard m.

cocktail n cocktail m.

cocoa n cacao m.

coconut n noix de coco f.

cocoon n cocon m.

cod n morue f.

code n code m; indicatif m.

cod-liver oil n huile de foie de morue f.

coercion n coercition, contrainte f.

coffee n café m.

coffee break n pause-café f.

coffeepot n cafetière f.

coffee table n table basse f.

coffin n cercueil m.

cog n dent d'engrenage f.

cognac n cognac m.

cohabit vi cohabiter.

cohabitation n cohabitation f.

coherent adj cohérent; logique.

cohesion n cohésion f.

coil n rouleau m; bobine f; * vt enrouler.

coin n pièce de monnaie f; * vt frapper.

coincide vi coïncider.

coincidence n coïncidence f.

coke n coke m.

colander n passoire f.

cold adj froid; indifférent; ~ly adv froidement; avec froideur; * n froid m; rhume m.

cold-blooded adj insensible.

coldness n froideur f.

cold sore n bouton de fièvre m.

coleslaw n salade de chou cru f.

colic n coliques fpl.

collaborate vi collaborer.

collaboration n collaboration f.

collapse vi s'écrouler; * n écroulement; (med) évanouissement m.

collapsible adj pliant.

collar n col m.

collarbone n clavicule f.

collate vt collationner, confronter.

collateral adj concomitant; parallèle; * n nantissement m.

colleague n collègue mf, confrère m, consœur f.

collect vt rassembler; collectionner.

collection n collection f.

collective *adj* collectif.

collector *n* collectionneur *m* -euse *f*.

college *n* faculté *f*.

collide *vi* entrer en collision, se heurter.

collision *n* collision *f*, heurt *m*.

colloquial *adj* familier; parlé.

colon *n* deux-points *m invar*; (*med*) colon *m*.

colonel *n* (*mil*) colonel *m*.

colonial *adj* colonial.

colonise *vt* coloniser.

colony *n* colonie *f*.

colossal *adj* colossal.

colour *n* couleur *f*; prétexte *m*; * *vt* colorer; * *vi* se colorer.

colour-blind *adj* daltonien.

colourful *adj* coloré.

colouring *n* teint *m*; coloris *m*.

colourless *adj* sans couleur, incolore.

colt *n* poulain *m*.

column *n* colonne *f*.

columnist *n* chroniqueur *m*.

coma *n* coma *m*.

comatose *adj* comateux.

comb *n* peigne *m*; * *vt* peigner.

combat *n* combat *m*; * *vt* combattre.

combination *n* combinaison, association *f*.

combine *vt* combiner; * *vi* s'unir.

combustion *n* combustion *f*.

come *vi* venir; ~ **across,** ~ **upon** *vt* rencontrer par hasard, tomber sur; ~ **by** *vt* obtenir; ~ **down** *vi* descendre; se résumer à, baisser (prices); ~ **from** *vt* provenir de; être originaire de; ~ **in for** *vt* être l'objet de; ~ **into** *vt* hériter de; ~ **round,** ~ **to** *vi* revenir à soi; ~ **up with** *vt* suggérer.

comedian *n* comédien *m*; comique *m*.

comedy *n* comédie *f*.

comet *n* comète *f*.

comfort *n* confort *m*; aises *fpl*; commodités *fpl*; consolation *f*; * *vt* réconforter; soulager; consoler.

comfortable *adj* confortable; réconfortant.

comic(al) *adj* comique.

coming *n* venue, arrivée *f*; * *adj* à venir.

comma *n* (*gr*) virgule *f*.

command *vt* ordonner, commander; * *n* ordre *m*.

commander *n* commandant *m*.

commandment *n* commandement *m*.

commando *n* commando *m*.

commemorate *vt* commémorer.

commemoration *n* commémoration *f*.

commence *vt vi* commencer.

commend *vt* recommander, confier à; louer.

commendable *adj* louable.

commensurate *adj* proportionné.

comment *n* commentaire *m*; * *vt* commenter.

commentary *n* commentaire *m*; observation *f*.

commentator *n* commentateur *m* -trice *f*.

commerce *n* commerce *m*, affaires *fpl*; relations *fpl*.

commercial *adj* commercial.

commiseration *n* commisération, pitié *f*.

commission *n* commission *f*; * *vt* commissionner; commander.

commit *vt* commettre; confier à; engager.

commitment n engagement m.

committee n comité m.

commodity n produit m, denrée f.

common adj commun; ordinaire; **in ~** en commun.

commoner n roturier m -ière f.

commonly adv communément, généralement.

commonplace n lieux communs mpl; * adj banal.

common sense n bon sens m.

commotion n vacarme m; perturbation f.

communicable adj communicable, transmissible.

communicate vt communiquer, transmettre; * vi communiquer.

communication n communication f.

communicative adj communicatif.

communion n communion f.

communism n communisme m.

communist n communiste mf.

community n communauté f.

community centre n centre social m.

commute vt échanger.

compact adj compact, serré, dense; * n accord, contrat m.

compact disc n disque compact m.

companion n compagnon m, compagne f.

company n compagnie, fréquentation f; société f.

comparable adj comparable.

comparative adj comparatif; ~ly adv comparativement.

compare vt comparer.

comparison n comparaison f.

compartment n compartiment m.

compass n boussole f.

compassion n compassion f.

compassionate adj compatissant.

compatible adj compatible.

compel vt contraindre, obliger, forcer.

compelling adj irrésistible.

compensate vt compenser.

compensation n compensation f; dédommagement m.

compère n animateur m -trice f.

compete vi rivaliser (avec), faire concurrence (à).

competence n compétence f; aptitude f.

competent adj compétent; suffisant; ~ly adv avec compétence.

competition n compétition f; concurrence f.

competitive adj concurrentiel, compétitif.

competitor n concurrent m -e f.

compilation n compilation f.

compile vt compiler.

complacency n suffisance f.

complacent adj suffisant.

complain vi se plaindre; déposer une plainte.

complaint n plainte f; réclamation f.

complement n complément m.

complete adj complet; achevé; * vt achever, mener à bien, compléter.

completion n achèvement m.

complex adj complexe.

complexion n teint m; aspect m.

complexity n complexité f.

complicate vt compliquer.

complication n complication f.

compliment n compliment m; * vt complimenter.

complimentary adj flatteur; à titre gracieux.

comply *vi* se soumettre, se plier, se conformer.

component *adj* composant.

compose *vt* composer; constituer.

composed *adj* calme, posé.

composer *n* auteur *m*; compositeur *m* -trice *f*.

composite *adj* composite, composé.

composition *n* composition *f*.

compost *n* compost *m*.

composure *n* maîtrise de soi *f*, calme *m*, sang-froid *m*.

compound *vt* composer, combiner; * *adj n* composé *m*.

comprehensive *adj* global; complet; compréhensif.

compress *vt* comprimer, concentrer; * *n* compresse *f*.

comprise *vt* comprendre, embrasser.

compromise *n* compromis *m*; * *vt* compromettre; * *vi* adopter un compromis.

compulsion *n* contrainte *f*; compulsion *f*.

compulsive *adj* compulsif.

compulsory *adj* obligatoire.

compunction *n* remords, scrupule *m*.

compute *vt* calculer.

computer *n* ordinateur *m*.

computerise *vt* traiter par ordinateur, informatiser.

computer programming *n* programmation *f*.

computer science *n* informatique *f*.

comrade *n* camarade *mf*; compagnon *m*, compagne *f*.

con *vt* duper; * *n* duperie *f*.

concave *adj* concave.

conceal *vt* cacher, dissimuler.

concede *vt* concéder, accorder.

conceit *n* vanité *f*; trait d'esprit *m*.

conceited *adj* vaniteux, prétentieux.

conceivable *adj* concevable.

conceive *vt* concevoir; * *vi* concevoir.

concentrate *vt* concentrer.

concentration *n* concentration *f*.

concentration camp *n* camp de concentration *m*.

concept *n* concept *m*.

conception *n* conception *f*.

concern *vt* concerner, toucher; * *n* affaire *f*; souci *m*.

concerning *prep* en ce qui concerne, concernant.

concession *n* concession *f*.

conciliatory *adj* conciliateur, conciliant.

concise *adj* concis, succinct.

conclude *vt* conclure; décider; déduire.

conclusion *n* conclusion, déduction *f*; fin *f*.

conclusive *adj* décisif, concluant.

concoction *n* préparation *f*; élaboration *f*.

concord *n* entente, harmonie *f*.

concourse *n* rassemblement *m*; carrefour *m*; foule *f*.

concrete *n* béton *m*; * *vt* bétonner.

concubine *n* concubine *f*.

concurrently *adv* simultanément.

concussion *n* commotion *f*.

condemn *vt* condamner; désapprouver.

condemnation *n* condamnation *f*.

condensation *n* condensation *f*.

condense *vt* condenser.

condescend *vi* condescendre; daigner.

condescending *adj* condescendant.

condescension n condescendance f.

condition vt conditionner; * n condition, situation f; état m.

conditional adj conditionnel, hypothétique.

conditioner n après-shampooing m.

condolences npl condoléances fpl.

condom n préservatif m.

condone vt pardonner, fermer les yeux sur.

conducive adj propice, opportun.

conduct n conduite f; comportement m; * vt conduire, mener.

conductor n receveur m; chef d'orchestre m; conducteur m.

cone n cône m.

confectioner's (shop) n confiserie f; pâtisserie f.

confederacy n confédération f.

confederate adj n confédéré m.

confer vt vi conférer.

conference n conférence f.

confess vt confesser; * vi se confesser.

confession n confession f.

confessional n confessionnal m.

confessor n confesseur m.

confidant n confident m -e f.

confide vt confier; ~ in se confier à.

confidence n confiance f; assurance f.

confident adj confiant, assuré, sûr (de soi).

confidential adj confidentiel.

confine vt limiter; emprisonner.

confinement n détention f; alitement m.

confirm vt confirmer; ratifier.

confirmation n confirmation f; ratification f; corroboration f.

confirmed adj invétéré, endurci.

confiscate vt confisquer.

conflict n conflit m; lutte f; dispute f.

conflicting adj contradictoire.

conform vt conformer, adapter; * vi se conformer (à), s'adapter (à).

confound vt confondre.

confront vt confronter; affronter.

confrontation n affrontement m, confrontation f.

confuse vt confondre; embarrasser; embrouiller.

confusing adj déroutant.

confusion n confusion f; désordre m.

congeal vt solidifier, congeler; * vi se solidifier, se congeler.

congenial adj sympathique; similaire.

congestion n encombrement m, congestion f.

congratulate vt complimenter, féliciter.

congratulations npl félicitations fpl.

congratulatory adj de félicitations.

congregate vt rassembler, réunir.

congregation n assemblée f, rassemblement m.

congress n congrès m; conférence f.

congressman n membre du Congrès m.

conic(al) adj conique.

conifer n conifère m.

coniferous adj (bot) conifère.

conjecture n conjecture, supposition f; * vt conjecturer, supposer.

conjunction n conjonction f, union f.

conjure vt conjurer; exorciser.

conjurer n magicien m -ne f, illusionniste mf.

con man n escroc m.

connect vt relier, joindre, rattacher.

connection n liaison, connexion f.

connivance n connivence f.

connive vi fermer les yeux (sur); être de connivence.

connoisseur n connaisseur m -euse f.

conquer vt conquérir; vaincre.

conqueror n vainqueur m; conquérant m.

conquest n conquête f.

conscience n conscience f.

conscientious adj consciencieux; de conscience; ~ly adv consciencieusement.

conscious adj conscient; intentionnel.

conscript n conscrit m.

consecutive adj consécutif.

consensus n consensus m.

consent n consentement m; assentiment m; * vi consentir.

consequence n conséquence f; importance f.

conservation n conservation f.

conservative adj conservateur.

conservatory n conservatoire m.

conserve vt conserver; * n conserve f.

consider vt considérer, examiner; * vi penser, délibérer.

considerable adj considérable; important; ~bly adv considérablement.

considerate adj prévenant, attentionné; prudent; ~ly adv avec prévenance; prudemment.

consideration n considération f; réflexion f; estime f; rémunération f.

considering conj étant donné que; ~ that vu que; étant donné que.

consignment n expédition f, envoi m.

consist vi consister (en).

consistency n consistance f; cohérence f; constance f.

consistent adj constant; cohérent; compatible; ~ly adv régulièrement.

consolation n consolation f; réconfort m.

console vt consoler.

consonant adj en accord; * n (gr) consonne f.

consort n consort m; associé m -e f.

conspicuous adj voyant, manifeste; notable.

conspiracy n conspiration f.

constancy n constance, fermeté d'âme f; persévérance f.

constant adj constant; persévérant.

constellation n constellation f.

constipated adj constipé.

constituency n électorat m; circonscription f.

constituent n composant m; * adj constituant.

constitute vt constituer; établir.

constitution n constitution f.

constitutional adj constitutionnel.

constrain vt contraindre, forcer, obliger.

constraint n contrainte f.

constrict vt serrer; gêner.

construct vt construire, bâtir.

construction n construction f.

construe vt interpréter, analyser.

consul n consul m.

consult vt consulter; * vi (se) consulter.

consultation n consultation, délibération f.

consume vt consommer; dissiper; consumer, brûler; * vi se consommer.

consumer n consommateur m, -trice f.

consummate vt consommer, accomplir; perfectionner; * adj accompli, consommé.

consummation n consommation f; perfection f.

consumption n consommation f.

contact n contact m.

contact lenses npl lentilles de contact fpl.

contagious adj contagieux.

contain vt contenir, renfermer; refréner.

container n récipient m.

contaminate vt contaminer.

contamination n contamination f.

contemplate vt contempler.

contemplation n contemplation f.

contemporaneous,contempo-rary adj contemporain.

contempt n mépris, dédain m.

contemptible adj méprisable, vil.

contemptuous adj méprisant, dédaigneux.

content adj content, satisfait; * vt contenter, satisfaire; * n contentement m; **~s** pl contenu m; table des matières f.

contention n querelle, altercation f.

contentment n contentement m, satisfaction f.

contest vt contester, discuter; disputer; * n concours m; altercation f.

contestant n concurrent m -e f.

context n contexte m.

continent adj continent, chaste; * n continent m.

continental adj continental.

contingency n contingence f; événement imprévu m; éventualité f.

contingent n contingent m; * adj contingent, éventuel.

continual adj continuel.

continuation n continuation, reprise, suite f.

continue vt vi continuer.

continuous adj continu.

contortion n contorsion f.

contour n contour m.

contraband n contrebande f; * adj de contrebande.

contraception n contraception f.

contraceptive n contraceptif m; * adj contraceptif.

contract vt contracter; * vi se contracter; * n contrat m.

contraction n contraction f.

contractor n entrepreneur m.

contradict vt contredire.

contradiction n contradiction f.

contradictory adj contradictoire.

contrary adj contraire, opposé; * n contraire m; **on the ~** au contraire.

contrast n contraste m; * vt contraster, mettre en contraste.

contrasting adj contrasté, opposé.

contravention n infraction f.

contribute vt contribuer.

contribution n contribution f; cotisation f.

contributor n souscripteur (-trice), collaborateur(-trice) m(f).

contributory adj contribuant.

contrite adj contrit, repentant.

contrition n contrition f, repentir m.

contrivance n dispositif m; invention f.

contrive vt inventer, combiner; trouver le moyen de.

control n contrôle m; maîtrise f; autorité f; * vt maîtriser; réguler; contrôler; gouverner.

controversial *adj* polémique.

controversy *n* polémique *f*.

conundrum *n* énigme *f*.

convalescence *n* convalescence *f*.

convalescent *adj* convalescent.

convene *vt* convoquer; réunir; * *vi* se réunir.

convenience *n* commodité, convenance *f*.

convenient *adj* commode, pratique; qui convient; ~**ly** *adv* commodément.

convent *n* couvent *m*.

convention *n* convention *f*; contrat *m*; assemblée *f*.

conventional *adj* conventionnel.

converge *vi* converger.

convergence *n* convergence *f*.

conversant *adj* au courant; compétent.

conversation *n* conversation *f*.

converse *vi* converser.

conversely *adv* inversement, réciproquement.

conversion *n* conversion; transformation *f*.

convert *vt* convertir; * *n* converti *m* -e *f*.

convertible *adj* convertible; * *n* décapotable *f*.

convex *adj* convexe.

convey *vt* transporter; transmettre, communiquer.

conveyance *n* transport *m*; transfert *m*; cession *f*.

convict *vt* déclarer coupable; * *n* détenu *m* -e *f*.

conviction *n* condamnation *f*; conviction *f*.

convince *vt* convaincre, persuader.

convoy *n* convoi *m*.

convulsion *n* convulsion *f*; bouleversement *m*; forte agitation *f*.

cook *n* cuisinier *m* -ière *f*; * *vt* cuire; falsifier; * *vi* faire la cuisine, cuisiner.

cookbook *n* livre de cuisine *m*.

cooker *n* cuisinière *f*.

cookery *n* cuisine *f*.

cool *adj* frais; calme; * *n* fraîcheur *f*; * *vt* rafraîchir, refroidir.

coolly *adv* fraîchement; de sang-froid.

cooperate *vi* coopérer.

cooperation *n* coopération *f*.

cooperative *adj* coopératif.

coordinate *vt* coordonner.

coordination *n* coordination *f*.

cop *n* (*fam*) flic *m*.

cope *vi* se débrouiller.

copier *n* photocopieuse *f*.

copious *adj* copieux, abondant.

copper *n* cuivre *m*.

copulate *vi* copuler.

copy *n* copie *f*; reproduction *f*; exemplaire *m*; * *vt* copier; imiter.

copyright *n* droit d'auteur *m*.

coral *n* corail *m*.

coral reef *n* récif de corail *m*.

cord *n* cordon *m*, corde *f*.

cordial *adj* cordial, chaleureux.

corduroy *n* velours côtelé *m*.

core *n* trognon *m*; noyau, centre, cœur *m*.

cork *n* liège *m*; bouchon *m*; * *vt* boucher.

corkscrew *n* tire-bouchon *m*.

corn *n* maïs *m*; grain *m*; blé *m*.

corncob *n* épi de maïs *m*.

corner *n* coin *m*; angle *m*.

cornet *n* cornet *m*.

cornfield *n* champ de maïs *m*.

cornflakes *npl* flocons de maïs, cornflakes *mpl*.

cornice *n* corniche *f*.

coronary *n* infarctus *m*.

coronation *n* couronnement *m*.

coroner *n* coroner *m*.

corporal *n* caporal *m*.

corporate *adj* en commun; d'entreprise.

corporation *n* corporation *f*; société
par actions *f*.

corps *n* (*mil*) corps *m*.

corpse *n* cadavre *m*.

corpuscle *n* corpuscule *m*; électron *m*.

correct *vt* corriger; rectifier; * *adj* correct, juste; **~ly** *adv* correctement.

correction *n* correction *f*, rectification *f*.

correlation *n* corrélation *f*.

correspond *vi* correspondre.

correspondence *n* correspondance *f*.

correspondent *adj* correspondant; *
n correspondant *m* -e *f*.

corridor *n* couloir, corridor *m*.

corroborate *vt* corroborer.

corroboration *n* corroboration *f*.

corrode *vt* corroder.

corrosion *n* corrosion *f*.

corrosive *adj n* corrosif *m*.

corrugated iron *n* tôle ondulée *f*.

corrupt *vt* corrompre; * *vi* se corrompre, se pourrir; * *adj* corrompu; dépravé.

corruption *n* corruption *f*; dépravation
f.

corset *n* corset *m*, gaine *f*.

cortege *n* cortège *m*.

cosily *adv* confortablement, douillette-
ment.

cosmetic *adj n* cosmétique *m*.

cosmic *adj* cosmique.

cosmonaut *n* cosmonaute *mf*.

cosmopolitan *adj* cosmopolite.

cosset *vt* dorloter.

cost *n* prix, coût *m*; * *vi* coûter.

costly *adj* coûteux, cher.

costume *n* costume *m*.

cosy *adj* douillet.

cottage *n* cottage *m*.

cotton *n* coton *m*.

cotton wool *n* coton hydrophile *m*.

couch *n* canapé, divan *m*.

cough *n* toux *f*; * *vi* tousser.

council *n* conseil *m*.

councillor *n* membre du conseil *m*;
conseiller *m* -ère *f*.

counsel *n* conseil *m*; avocat *m*.

counsellor *n* conseiller *m* -ère *f*; avocat *m*.

count *vt* compter, dénombrer; calculer;
~ on compter sur; * *n* compte *m*; calcul
m; chef d'accusation *m*; comte *m*.

countdown *n* compte à rebours *m*.

countenance *n* visage *m*; aspect *m*;
mine *f*.

counter *n* comptoir *m*; pion *m*.

counteract *vt* contrecarrer; neutraliser; contrebalancer.

counterbalance *vt* contrebalancer;
compenser; * *n* contrepoids *m*.

counterfeit *vt* contrefaire; * *adj* faux.

countermand *vt* annuler.

counterpart *n* contrepartie *f*; homo-
logue *mf*.

counterproductive *adj* qui va à l'en-
contre du but visé.

countersign *vt* contresigner.

countess *n* comtesse *f*.

countless *adj* innombrable.

country n pays m; patrie f; campagne f; région f; * adj rustique; campagnard.

county n comté m.

couple n couple m; **a ~ of** deux; * vt unir, associer.

coupon n coupon m, bon m.

courage n courage m.

courageous adj courageux.

courier n messager m; guide m.

course n cours m; route f; chemin m; plat m; marche à suivre f; **of ~** bien sûr, naturellement.

court n cour f; tribunal m; * vt courtiser; solliciter.

courteous adj courtois; poli.

courtesy n courtoisie f.

court-martial n conseil de guerre m.

courtyard n cour f.

cousin n cousin m -e f.

cove n (mar) crique, anse f.

cover n couverture f; abri m; prétexte m; * vt (re)couvrir; dissimuler; protéger.

coverage n reportage m, couverture f.

covering n couverture f; couche f.

covert adj voilé; caché, secret.

cover-up n dissimulation f.

covet vt convoiter.

covetous adj avide, cupide.

cow n vache f.

coward n lâche mf.

cowardice n lâcheté f.

cowardly adj lâche; adv lâchement.

cower vi se tapir.

coy adj timide; coquet; évasif.

crab n crabe m.

crack n craquement m; fente, fissure f; * vt fêler, craquer; **~ down on** sévir; * vi se fêler; craquer.

cracker n pétard m; biscuit salé m.

crackle vi crépiter, pétiller.

cradle n berceau m; * vt bercer.

craft n habileté f; métier manuel m; barque f.

craftsman n artisan m.

crafty adj astucieux, rusé.

cram vt bourrer; fourrer; * vi s'entasser.

cramp n crampe f; * vt entraver.

cramped adj à l'étroit.

crane n grue f.

crash vi s'écraser; * n fracas m; collision f.

crash helmet n casque m.

crash landing n atterrissage en catastrophe m.

crass adj grossier, crasse.

crate n caisse f; cageot m.

crater n cratère m.

cravat n foulard m, cravate f.

crave vt avoir extrêmement besoin de.

craving n désir extrême m, soif f.

crawl vi ramper; **~ with** grouiller de.

crayon n crayon de couleur m.

craze n manie f, engouement m.

crazy adj fou.

creak vi grincer, craquer.

cream n crème f; * adj crème.

creamy adj crémeux.

crease n pli m; * vt froisser.

create vt créer; causer.

creation n création f.

creative adj créatif.

creator n créateur m -trice f.

creature n créature f.

credentials npl lettres de créance fpl; preuves d'identité fpl.

credibility n crédibilité f.

credible adj crédible.

credit n crédit m; honneur m; reconnaissance *f*; * *vt* croire, reconnaître; créditer.

credit card *n* carte de crédit *f*.

creditor *n* créancier *m* -ière *f*.

credulous *adj* crédule.

creed *n* credo *m*.

creep *vi* ramper; avancer lentement.

creeper *n* (*bot*) plante grimpante *f*.

creepy *adj* terrifiant, qui donne la chair de poule.

cremate *vt* incinérer.

cremation *n* incinération, crémation *f*.

crematorium *n* crématoire *m*.

crescent *adj* croissant; * *n* croissant de lune *m*.

cress *n* cresson *m*.

crest *n* crête *f*.

crested *adj* à crête.

crestfallen *adj* découragé, abattu.

crevice *n* fissure, lézarde *f*.

crew *n* bande, équipe *f*; équipage *m*.

cricket *n* grillon *m*.

crime *n* crime *m*; délit *m*.

criminal *adj* criminel; * *n* criminel *m* -le *f*.

crimson *adj n* cramoisi *m*.

cripple *n*, *adj* invalide *mf*; * *vt* estropier; (*fig*) paralyser.

crisis *n* crise *f*.

crisp *adj* frais; croquant.

criss-cross *adj* entrecroisé.

criterion *n* critère *m*.

critic *n* critique *m*.

critical *adj* critique; exigeant, sévère.

criticise *vt* critiquer.

criticism *n* critique *f*.

croak *vi* coasser, croasser.

crochet *n* crochet *m*; * *vt* faire au crochet; *vi* faire du crochet.

crockery *n* poterie *f*.

crocodile *n* crocodile *m*.

crook *n* escroc *m*; filou *m*.

crooked *adj* tordu; malhonnête.

crop *n* culture *f*; récolte *f*; * *vt* récolter.

cross *n* croix *f*; croisement *m*; * *adj* de mauvaise humeur, fâché; * *vt* traverser, croiser; ~ **over** traverser.

crossbar *n* barre transversale *f*.

crossbreed *n* hybride *m*.

cross-examine *vt* soumettre à un contre-interrogatoire.

crossing *n* traversée *f*; passage pour piétons *m*.

cross-purpose *n*: be at ~s comprendre (quelqu'un) de travers.

cross-reference *n* renvoi *m*, référence *f*.

crossroad *n* carrefour *m*.

crotch *n* entre-jambes *m*.

crouch *vi* s'accroupir, se tapir.

crow *n* corbeau *m*; chant du coq *m*; * *vi* chanter victoire.

crowd *n* foule *f*; monde *m*; * *vt* entasser; * *vi* s'entasser.

crown *n* couronne *f*; sommet *m*; * *vt* couronner.

crucial *adj* crucial.

crucifix *n* crucifix *m*.

crucifixion *n* crucifixion *f*.

crucify *vt* crucifier.

crude *adj* brut, grossier.

cruel *adj* cruel.

cruelty *n* cruauté *f*.

cruise *n* croisière *f*; * *vi* croiser.

cruiser *n* croiseur *m*.

crumb *n* miette *f*.

crumble *vt* émietter; effriter; * *vi* s'émietter; se désintégrer.

crumple *vt* froisser.

crunch *vt* croquer; * *n* (*fig*) crise *f.*

crusade *n* croisade *f.*

crush *vt* écraser; opprimer; * *n* cohue *f.*

crust *n* croûte *f.*

crutch *n* béquille *f.*

cry *vt vi* crier; pleurer; * *n* cri *m*; sanglot *m.*

cryptic *adj* énigmatique.

crystal *n* cristal *m.*

crystallise *vi* se cristalliser; * *vt* cristalliser.

cub *n* petit *m* (animal).

cube *n* cube *m.*

cubic *adj* cubique.

cuckoo *n* coucou *m.*

cucumber *n* concombre *m.*

cuddle *vt* embrasser; * *vi* s'enlacer; * *n* étreinte *f*, câlin *m.*

cue *n* queue de billard *f.*

cuff *n* manchette *f*; revers de pantalon *m.*

culinary *adj* culinaire.

cull *vt* sélectionner; éliminer.

culminate *vi* culminer.

culmination *n* point culminant *m.*

culpable *adj* coupable; blâmable.

culprit *n* coupable *mf.*

cult *n* culte *m.*

cultivate *vt* cultiver; améliorer, perfectionner.

cultivation *n* culture *f.*

cultural *adj* culturel.

culture *n* culture *f.*

cumbersome *adj* encombrant; lourd, pesant.

cunning *adj* astucieux, rusé; * *n* astuce, finesse *f.*

cup *n* tasse, coupe *f*; (*bot*) corolle *f.*

cupboard *n* placard *m.*

curator *n* conservateur *m*; curateur *m.*

curb *n* frein *m*; bord du trottoir *m*; * *vt* freiner, juguler, modérer.

curdle *vt* cailler, figer; *vi* se cailler, se figer.

cure *n* remède *m*; cure *f*; * *vt* guérir.

curfew *n* couvre-feu *m.*

curiosity *n* curiosité *f.*

curious *adj* curieux.

curl *n* boucle de cheveux *f*; * *vt* boucler; friser; * *vi* friser.

curly *adj* frisé, bouclé.

currant *n* raisin *m* sec.

currency *n* monnaie *f*; circulation *f*; cours *m.*

current *adj* courant; actuel; * *n* cours *m*; tendance *f*, courant *m.*

current affairs *npl* actualité *f*; problèmes actuels *mpl.*

currently *adv* actuellement.

curse *vt* maudire; * *vi* jurer; * *n* malédiction *f.*

cursor *n* curseur *m.*

cursory *adj* superficiel; hâtif.

curt *adj* succinct; sec.

curtail *vt* réduire; écourter.

curtain *n* rideau *m.*

curtsy *n* révérence *f*; * *vi* faire une révérence.

curve *vt* courber; * *n* courbe *f.*

cushion *n* coussin *m.*

custard *n* crème anglaise *f.*

custodian *n* gardien *m* -ne *f.*

custody *n* garde *f*; emprisonnement *m.*

custom *n* coutume *f*, usage *m.*

customary *adj* habituel, coutumier, ordinaire.

customer *n* client *m* -e *f.*

customs *npl* douane *f.*

cut *vt* découper; couper; tailler; réduire; blesser; * *vi* couper; se couper; * *n* coupe *f*; coupure *f*; réduction *f*; **~ and dried** *adj* arrangé.

cutback *n* réduction *f.*

cute *adj* mignon.

cutlery *n* couverts *mpl.*

cut-rate *adj* à prix réduit.

cutting *n* coupure *f*; * *adj* coupant; tranchant.

cyanide *n* cyanure *m.*

cycle *n* cycle *m*; bicyclette *f*; * *vi* aller à bicyclette.

cycling *n* cyclisme *m.*

cyclist *n* cycliste *mf.*

cyclone *n* cyclone *m.*

cylinder *n* cylindre *m*; rouleau *m.*

cylindric(al) *adj* cylindrique.

cymbals *n* cymbale *f.*

cynic(al) *adj* cynique; sceptique; * *n* cynique *mf.*

cynicism *n* cynisme *m.*

cyst *n* kyste *m.*

D

dabble *vi* barboter.

dad(dy) *n* papa *m.*

daddy-long-legs *n* (*zool*) cousin *m.*

daffodil *n* narcisse *m*, jonquille *f.*

dagger *n* poignard *m.*

daily *adj* quotidien; * *adv* quotidiennement, tous les jours; * *n* quotidien *m.*

dainty *adj* délicat; élégant.

dairy *n* laiterie *f.*

dairy farm *n* laiterie *f.*

dairy produce *n* produits laitiers *mpl.*

daisy *n* marguerite *f.*

dam *n* barrage *m*; * *vt* endiguer.

damage *n* dommage *m*; tort *m*; * *vt* endommager; faire du tort à.

dame *n* dame *f*, fille *f.*

damn *vt* condamner; * *adj* maudit.

damnable *adj* maudit.

damnation *n* damnation *f.*

damning *adj* accablant.

damp *adj* humide; * *n* humidité *f*; * *vt* humidifier.

dampen *vt* humidifier.

dampness *n* humidité *f.*

dance *n* danse *f*; soirée dansante *f*; * *vt vi* danser.

dance hall *n* dancing *m.*

dancer *n* danseur *m* -euse *f.*

dandelion *n* pissenlit *m.*

dandruff *n* pellicules *fpl.*

danger *n* danger *m.*

dangerous *adj* dangereux.

dangle *vi* pendre.

dapper *adj* soigné.

dappled *adj* tacheté.

dare *vi* oser; * *vt* défier.

daredevil *n* casse-cou *m invar.*

daring *n* audace *f*; * *adj* audacieux.

dark *adj* sombre, obscur; * *n* obscurité *f*; ignorance *f.*

darken *vt* assombrir, obscurcir; * *vi* s'assombrir, s'obscurcir.

darkness n obscurité f.
darkroom n chambre noire f.
darling n, adj chéri m -e f.
darn vt repriser.
dart n dard m.
darts n jeu de fléchettes m.
dash vi se dépêcher; * n goutte f; tiret, trait m.
dashboard n tableau de bord m.
dashing adj impétueux; élégant.
dastardly adj infâme.
data n données fpl.
database n base de données f.
data processing n traitement de données m.
date n date f; rendez-vous m; (bot) datte f; * vt dater; sortir avec.
dated adj démodé.
daughter n fille f;
daughter-in-law n belle-fille f.
daunting adj décourageant.
dawdle vi traîner.
dawn n aube f; * vi se lever.
day n jour m, journée f.
daylight n lumière du jour, lumière naturelle f.
daytime n journée f, jour m.
dazed adj étourdi.
dazzling adj éblouissant.
dead adj mort.
dead heat n arrivée ex-aequo f.
deadline n date limite f.
deadlock n impasse f.
deadly adj mortel; * adv terriblement.
deaf adj sourd.
deafen vt assourdir.
deaf-mute n sourd(e)-muet(te) mf.
deafness n surdité f.
deal n accord m; marché m; **a great ~**

beaucoup; **a good ~** pas mal; * vt distribuer, donner; * vi **~ in** être dans le commerce de; **~ with** avoir affaire à.
dealer n commerçant m; trafiquant m; donneur m.
dealings npl rapports mpl; transactions fpl.
dean n doyen m.
dear adj **~ly** adv cher.
dearth n pénurie f.
death n mort f.
deathbed n lit de mort m.
death certificate n acte de décès m.
death penalty n peine de mort f.
debar vt exclure.
debase vt dégrader.
debatable adj discutable.
debate n débat m; * vt discuter; examiner.
debauched adj débauché.
debauchery n débauche f.
debilitate vt débiliter.
debit n débit m; * vt (com) débiter.
debt n dette f; **to get into ~** s'endetter.
debtor n débiteur m -trice f.
debunk vt démystifier.
decade n décennie f.
decadence n décadence f.
decaffeinated adj décaféiné.
decanter n carafe f.
decapitate vt décapiter.
decay vi décliner; pourrir; * n déclin m; pourrissement m; carie f.
deceased adj décédé.
deceit n tromperie f.
deceitful adj trompeur; **~ly** adv faussement.
deceive vt tromper.

218

December n décembre m.

decency n décence f; pudeur f.

decent adj décent; bien, bon.

deception n tromperie f.

deceptive adj trompeur.

decide vt decider; * vi se décider.

decidedly adv décidément.

deciduous adj (bot) à feuilles caduques.

decimal adj décimal.

decipher vt déchiffrer.

decision n décision, détermination f.

decisive adj décisif.

deck n pont m; * vt orner.

deckchair n chaise longue f.

declaration n déclaration f.

declare vt déclarer.

decline vt (gr) décliner; refuser; * vi décliner; * n déclin m; décadence f.

decode vt décoder.

decompose vt décomposer.

decomposition n décomposition f.

decor n décor m; décoration f.

decorate vt décorer, orner.

decoration n décoration f.

decorative adj décoratif.

decorator n décorateur m -trice f.

decorous adj bienséant, convenable.

decorum n décorum m.

decoy n leurre m.

decrease vt diminuer; * n diminution f.

decree n décret m; * vt décréter; ordonner.

decrepit adj décrépit.

dedicate vt dédier; consacrer.

dedication n dédicace f; consacration f.

deduce vt déduire, conclure.

deduct vt déduire, soustraire.

deduction n déduction f.

deed n action f; exploit m.

deep adj profond.

deep-freeze n congélateur m.

deer n cerf m.

deface vt défigurer.

defamation n diffamation f.

default n défaut m; manque m; * vi manquer à ses engagements.

defeat n défaite f; * vt vaincre; frustrer.

defect n défaut m.

defection n désertion f.

defective adj défectueux.

defend vt défendre; protéger.

defendant n accusé m -e f.

defense n défense f; protection f.

defenseless adj sans défense.

defensive adj défensif.

deferential adj respectueux.

defiance n défi m.

defiant adj provocant.

deficiency n défaut m; manque m.

deficient adj insuffisant.

deficit n déficit m.

define vt définir.

definite adj sûr; précis; ~ly adv sans aucun doute.

definition n définition f.

definitive adj définitif.

deflate vt dégonfler.

deflect vt dévier.

deform vt déformer.

deformity n déformité f.

defraud vt escroquer.

defrost vt dégivrer; décongeler.

deft adj habile.

defunct adj défunt.

defuse vt désamorcer.

degenerate vi dégénérer; * adj dégénéré.

degradation n dégradation f.

degrade vt dégrader.

degree n degré m; diplôme m.

dehydrated adj déshydraté.

de-ice vt dégivrer.

deign vi daigner.

deity n divinité f.

dejected adj découragé.

delay vt retarder; * n retard m.

delectable adj délectable.

delegate vt déléguer; * n délégué m -e f.

delegation n délégation f.

delete vt effacer.

deliberate vt examiner; * adj délibéré.

deliberation n délibération f.

delicacy n délicatesse f.

delicate adj délicat.

delicious adj délicieux, exquis.

delight n délice m; enchantement m; *. vt enchanter; * vi adorer.

delighted adj enchanté.

delightful adj charmant.

delinquency n délinquance f.

delinquent n délinquant m -e f.

delirious adj délirant.

delirium n délire m.

deliver vt livrer; délivrer; prononcer.

delivery n livraison f, accouchement m.

delude vt tromper.

deluge n déluge m.

delusion n tromperie f, illusion f.

demand n demande f; * vt exiger; réclamer.

demanding adj exigeant.

demarcation n démarcation f.

demeanour n conduite f, comportement m.

demented adj dément.

demise n disparition f.

democracy n démocratie f.

democrat n démocrate mf.

democratic adj démocratique.

demolish vt démolir.

demolition n démolition f.

demon n démon, diable m.

demonstrable adj démontrable.

demonstrate vt démontrer, prouver; * vi manifester.

demonstration n démonstration f; manifestation f.

demonstrative adj démonstratif.

demonstrator n manifestant m -e f.

demoralise vt démoraliser.

demote vt rétrograder.

demure adj réservé.

den n antre m.

denial n dénégation f.

denims npl jean m.

denomination n valeur f; dénomination f.

denote vt dénoter, indiquer.

denounce vt dénoncer.

dense adj dense, épais.

density n densité f.

dent n bosse f; * vt cabosser.

dental adj dentaire.

dentist n dentiste mf.

dentistry n dentisterie f.

denture n dentier m.

denude vt dénuder, dépouiller.

denunciation n dénonciation f.

deny vt nier.

deodorant n déodorant m.

depart vi partir.

department n département m; service m.

department store n grand magasin m.

departure n départ m.

departure lounge n salle d'embarquement f.

depend *vi* dépendre; ~ **on/upon** compter sur.

dependable *adj* fiable; sûr.

depict *vt* dépeindre, décrire.

depleted *adj* réduit.

deplorable *adj* déplorable, lamentable.

deplore *vt* déplorer, lamenter.

deport *vt* déporter; expulser.

deportation *n* déportation *f*, expulsion *f*.

deportment *n* comportement *m*.

deposit *vt* déposer; * *n* dépôt *m*; caution *f*.

depositor *n* déposant *m* -e *f*.

depot *n* dépôt *m*.

depraved *adj* dépravé.

depravity *n* dépravation *f*.

depreciation *n* dépréciation *f*.

depress *vt* déprimer.

depressed *adj* déprimé.

depression *n* dépression *f*.

deprivation *n* privation *f*.

deprive *vt* priver.

deprived *adj* défavorisé.

depth *n* profondeur *f*.

deputation *n* députation *f*.

deputise *vi* remplacer.

deputy *n* remplaçant *m* -e *f*; député *m*; délégué *m* -e *f*.

deranged *adj* dérangé.

derelict *adj* abandonné, en ruines.

deride *vt* se moquer de.

derision *n* dérision *f*.

derisive *adj* ridicule; moqueur.

derivation *n* dérivation *f*.

derivative *n* dérivé *m*.

derive *vt vi* dériver.

derogatory *adj* désobligeant.

descend *vi* descendre.

descendant *n* descendant *m* -e *f*.

descent *n* descente *f*.

describe *vt* décrire.

description *n* description *f*.

descriptive *adj* descriptif.

desert *n* désert *m*; * *adj* désert; * *vt* abandonner; déserter.

deserter *n* déserteur *m*.

desertion *n* désertion *f*.

deserve *vt* mériter.

deservedly *adv* à juste titre.

design *vt* concevoir; dessiner; * *n* dessein *m*; design *m*; dessin *m*.

designate *vt* désigner.

designer *n* créateur *m* -trice *f*, styliste *mf*.

desirable *adj* désirable.

desire *n* désir *m*; * *vt* désirer.

desist *vi* abandonner.

desk *n* bureau *m*.

desolate *adj* désert, désolé.

desolation *n* désolation *f*.

despair *n* désespoir *m*; * *vi* se désespérer.

despatch = **dispatch**.

desperate *adj* désespéré; ~**ly** *adv* désespérément; extrêmement.

desperation *n* désespoir *m*.

despicable *adj* méprisable.

despise *vt* mépriser.

despite *prep* malgré.

despondent *adj* abattu.

despotic *adj* despotique.

dessert *n* dessert *m*.

destination *n* destination *f*.

destine *vt* destiner.

destiny *n* destin, sort *m*.

destitute *adj* indigent.

destitution *n* indigence *f*.

destroy *vt* détruire.

destruction *n* destruction *f*.

destructive *adj* destructeur.

desultory *adj* irrégulier; sans méthode.

detach *vt* séparer, détacher.

detachment *n* (*mil*) détachement *m*.

detail *n* détail *m*; **in ~** en détail; * *vt* détailler.

detain *vt* retenir; détenir.

detect *vt* détecter.

detection *n* détection *f*; découverte *f*.

detective *n* détective *m*.

detention *n* détention *f*.

deter *vt* dissuader.

detergent *n* détergent *m*.

deteriorate *vt* détériorer.

deterioration *n* détérioration *f*.

determination *n* détermination *f*.

determine *vt* déterminer, décider.

determined *adj* déterminé.

deterrent *n* force de dissuasion *f*.

detest *vt* détester.

detestable *adj* détestable.

detonate *vi* détoner.

detonation *n* détonation *f*.

detour *n* déviation *f*.

detract *vi* nuire à.

detriment *n* détriment *m*.

detrimental *adj* préjudiciable.

devaluation *n* dévaluation *f*.

devastating *adj* dévastateur.

devastation *n* dévastation *f*.

develop *vt* développer.

development *n* développement *m*.

deviate *vi* dévier.

deviation *n* déviation *f*.

device *n* mécanisme *m*.

devil *n* diable, démon *m*.

devilish *adj* diabolique.

devious *adj* tortueux.

devise *vt* inventer; concevoir.

devoid *adj* dépourvu.

devote *vt* consacrer.

devoted *adj* dévoué.

devotee *n* partisan *m* -e *f*.

devotion *n* dévotion *f*.

devour *vt* dévorer.

devout *adj* dévot, pieux.

dew *n* rosée *f*.

dexterity *n* dextérité *f*.

dexterous *adj* adroit, habile.

diabetes *n* diabète *m*.

diabetic *n* diabétique *mf*.

diagnosis *n* (*med*) diagnostic *m*.

diagonal *adj* diagonal; **~ly** *adv* diagonalement; * *n* diagonale *f*.

diagram *n* diagramme *m*.

dial *n* cadran *m*.

dialect *n* dialecte *m*.

dialogue *n* dialogue *m*.

diameter *n* diamètre *m*.

diametrical *adj* diamétral; **~ly** *adv* diamétralement.

diamond *n* diamant *m*; **~s** *npl* (cards) carreaux *mpl*.

diaper *n* couche *f*.

diarrhoea *n* diarrhée *f*.

diary *n* journal *m*.

dice *npl* dés *mpl*.

dictate *vt* dicter; * *n* ordre *m*.

dictation *n* dictée *f*.

dictatorial *adj* dictatorial.

diction *n* diction *f*

dictionary *n* dictionnaire *m*.

die *vi* mourir; **~ away** s'affaiblir; **~ down** s'éteindre.

die *n* (*sing de* **dice**) dé *m*.

diehard *n* réactionnaire *mf*.

diesel *n* diesel *m*.

diet *n* diète *f*; régime *m*; * *vi* être au régime.

differ *vi* différer.

difference *n* différence *f*.

different *adj* différent.

differentiate *vt* différencier.

difficult *adj* difficile.

difficulty *n* difficulté *f*.

diffidence *n* timidité *f*; manque d'assurance *m*.

diffident *adj* timide; mal assuré.

diffuse *vt* diffuser, répandre; * *adj* diffus.

diffusion *n* diffusion *f*.

dig *vt* creuser; * *n* coup *m*.

digest *vt* digérer.

digestion *n* digestion *f*.

digestive *adj* digestif.

digger *n* excavatrice *f*.

digit *n* chiffre *m*.

digital *adj* digital; numérique.

dignified *adj* digne.

dignitary *n* dignitaire *m*.

dignity *n* dignité *f*.

digress *vi* faire une digression.

dilapidated *adj* délabré.

dilate *vt* dilater; * *vi* se dilater.

dilemma *n* dilemme *m*.

diligence *n* assiduité *f*.

diligent *adj* assidu; ~**ly** *adv* avec assiduité.

dilute *vt* diluer.

dim *adj* indistinct; faible; sombre; * *vt* affaiblir; troubler.

dime *n* pièce de dix cents *f*.

dimension *n* dimension *f*.

diminish *vt vi* diminuer.

diminution *n* diminution *f*.

diminutive *n* diminutif *m*.

dimmer *n* interrupteur d'intensité *m*.

dimple *n* fossette *f*.

din *n* vacarme *m*.

dine *vi* dîner.

dinghy *n* canot pneumatique *f*.

dingy *adj* sale; miteux.

dinner *n* dîner *m*.

dinosaur *n* dinosaure *m*.

dip *vt* tremper.

diphtheria *n* diphtérie *f*.

diphthong *n* diphtongue *f*.

diploma *n* diplôme *m*.

diplomacy *n* diplomatie *f*.

diplomat *n* diplomate *m*.

diplomatic *adj* diplomatique.

dire *adj* atroce, affreux.

direct *adj* direct; * *vt* diriger.

direction *n* direction *f*; instruction *f*.

directly *adv* directement; immédiatement.

director *n* directeur *m* -trice *f*.

directory *n* annuaire *m*.

dirt *n* saleté *f*.

dirty *adj* sale.

disability *n* incapacité *f*; infirmité *f*.

disabled *adj* infirme.

disadvantage *n* désavantage *m*; * *vt* désavantager.

disadvantageous *adj* désavantageux.

disagree *vi* ne pas être d'accord.

disagreeable *adj* désagréable.

disagreement *n* désaccord *m*.

disappear *vi* disparaître.

disappearance *n* disparition *f*.

disappointed *adj* déçu.

disappointing *adj* décevant.

disappointment *n* déception *f*.

disapproval *n* désapprobation *f*.

disapprove *vt* désapprouver.

disarmament *n* désarmement *m*.

disarray *n* désordre *m*.

disaster *n* désastre *m*.

disastrous adj désastreux.

disbelief n incrédulité f.

disc n disque m.

discard vt jeter.

discernible adj perceptible.

discerning adj perspicace.

discernment n perspicacité f.

discharge vt décharger; régler (une dette); remplir; * n décharge f; règlement m.

disciple n disciple m.

discipline n discipline f; * vt discipliner.

disclaimer n dénégation f.

disclose vt révéler.

disclosure n révélation f.

disco n discothèque f.

discoloration n décoloration f.

discolour vt décolorer.

discomfort n incommodité f.

disconcert vt déconcerter.

disconnect vt débrancher.

disconsolate adj inconsolable.

discontented adj mécontent.

discontinue vt interrompre.

discord n discorde f.

discordant adj discordant.

discount n escompte m; remise f; * vt escompter.

discourage vt décourager.

discouraging adj décourageant.

discourse n discours m.

discourteous adj discourtois.

discover vt découvrir.

discovery n découverte f.

discredit vt discréditer.

discreet adj discret.

discrepancy n contradiction f.

discretion n discrétion f.

discriminate vt distinguer; discriminer.

discrimination n discrimination f.

discuss vt discuter.

discussion n discussion f.

disdain vt dédaigner; * n dédain, mépris m.

disdainful adj dédaigneux, méprisant.

disease n maladie f.

diseased adj malade.

disembark vt vi débarquer.

disenchanted adj désenchanté.

disenchantment n désenchantement m.

disengage vt dégager.

disentangle vt démêler.

disfigure vt défigurer.

disgrace n honte f; scandale m; * vt déshonorer.

disgraceful adj honteux; scandaleux; **~ly** adv honteusement.

disgruntled adj mécontent.

disguise vt déguiser; * n déguisement m.

disgust n dégoût m; * vt dégoûter.

disgusting adj dégoûtant.

dish n plat m; assiette f; * vt servir dans un plat; **~ up** servir.

dishearten vt démoraliser.

dishevelled adj ébouriffé.

dishonest adj malhonnête.

dishonesty n malhonnêteté f.

dishonour n déshonneur m; * vt déshonorer.

dishonourable adj déshono-rable.

dishtowel n torchon à vaisselle m.

dishwasher n lave-vaisselle m; plongeur m -euse f.

disillusioned adj désillusionné.

disinclination n aversion f.

disinclined adj peu enclin.

disinfect *vt* désinfecter.

disinfectant *n* désinfectant *m*.

disinherit *vt* déshériter.

disintegrate *vi* se désintégrer.

disinterested *adj* désintéressé.

disjointed *adj* déréglé; décousu.

disk *n* disque *m*; disquette *f*.

diskette *n* disque *m*, disquette *f*.

dislike *n* aversion *f*; * *vt* ne pas aimer.

dislocate *vt* disloquer.

dislocation *n* dislocation *f*.

dislodge *vt* déloger.

disloyal *adj* déloyal.

disloyalty *n* déloyauté *f*.

dismal *adj* triste, lugubre.

dismantle *vt* démonter.

dismay *n* consternation *f*.

dismember *vt* démembrer.

dismiss *vt* renvoyer; écarter.

dismissal *n* renvoi *m*; rejet *m*.

disobedience *n* désobéissance *f*.

disobedient *adj* désobéissant.

disobey *vt* désobéir.

disorder *n* désordre *m*.

disorderly *adj* en désordre, confus.

disorganised *adj* désorganisé.

disorientated *adj* désorienté.

disown *vt* renier.

disparaging *adj* désobligeant.

disparity *n* disparité *f*.

dispassionate *adj* impartial; calme.

dispatch *vt* envoyer; * *n* envoi *m*; dépêche *f*.

dispel *vt* dissiper.

dispense *vt* dispenser; distribuer.

disperse *vt* disperser.

displace *vt* déplacer.

display *vt* exposer; faire preuve de; * *n* exposition *f*; déploiement *m*.

displeased *adj* mécontent.

displeasure *n* mécontentement *m*.

disposable *adj* à jeter.

disposal *n* disposition *f*.

dispose *vt* disposer.

disposition *n* disposition *f*.

disproportionate *adj* disproportionné.

disprove *vt* réfuter.

dispute *n* dispute *f*; controverse *f*; * *vt* mettre en cause.

disqualify *vt* exclure; disqualifier.

disregard *vt* ne pas tenir compte de; mépriser; * *n* dédain *m*.

disreputable *adj* de mauvaise réputation.

disrespect *n* irrévérence *f*.

disrespectful *adj* irrespectueux.

disrupt *vt* interrompre.

disruption *n* interruption *f*.

dissatisfaction *n* mécontentement *m*.

dissatisfied *adj* mécontent.

dissect *vt* disséquer.

dissection *n* dissection *f*.

disseminate *vt* disséminer.

dissent *vi* être en dissension; * *n* dissension *f*.

dissertation *n* thèse *f*.

dissident *n* dissident *m* -e *f*.

dissipate *vt* dissiper.

dissipation *n* dissipation *f*.

dissolute *adj* dissolu.

dissolution *n* dissolution *f*.

dissolve *vt* dissoudre; * *vi* se dissoudre.

dissuade *vt* dissuader.

distance *n* distance *f*; **at a ~** de loin; * *vt* distancer.

distant *adj* distant.

distaste *n* dégoût *m*.

distasteful *adj* désagréable.

distil *vt* distiller.

distillery *n* distillerie *f*.

distinct *adj* distinct.

distinction *n* distinction *f*.

distinctive *adj* distinctif.

distinguish *vt* distinguer; discerner.

distort *vt* déformer.

distortion *n* distortion *f*.

distract *vt* distraire.

distracted *adj* distrait.

distraction *n* distraction *f*; confusion *f*.

distraught *adj* éperdu.

distress *n* souffrance *f*; détresse *f*; * *vt* désoler; affliger.

distribute *vt* distribuer, répartir.

distribution *n* distribution *f*.

distrustful *adj* méfiant.

disturb *vt* déranger.

disturbance *n* dérangement *m*; trouble *m*.

disturbed *adj* troublé.

disturbing *adj* troublant.

disuse *n* désuétude *f*.

disused *adj* abandonné.

ditch *n* fossé *m*.

dither *vi* hésiter.

ditto *adv* idem.

dive *vi* plonger.

diver *n* plongeur *m* -euse *f*.

divergence *n* divergence *f*.

divergent *adj* divergent.

diverse *adj* divers, différent.

diversion *n* diversion *f*.

diversity *n* diversité *f*.

divert *vt* dévier; divertir.

divide *vt* diviser; * *vi* se diviser.

dividend *n* dividende *m*.

divine *adj* divin.

divinity *n* divinité *f*.

diving *n* plongeon *m*.

diving board *n* plongeoir *m*.

division *n* (*math*) division *f*.

divorce *n* divorce *m*; * *vi* divorcer.

divorced *adj* divorcé.

divulge *vt* divulguer.

dizzy *adj* pris de vertige.

do *vt* faire.

docile *adj* docile.

dock *n* dock *m*; * *vi* entrer aux docks.

dockyard *n* chantier *m* naval.

doctor *n* docteur *m*.

doctrine *n* doctrine *f*.

document *n* document *m*.

dodge *vt* esquiver.

doe *n* biche *f*.

dog *n* chien *m*.

dogged *adj* tenace.

dogmatic *adj* dogmatique.

doings *npl* faits *mpl*.

do-it-yourself *n* bricolage *m*.

doleful *adj* lugubre, triste.

doll *n* poupée *f*.

dollar *n* dollar *m*.

dolphin *n* dauphin *m*.

domain *n* domaine *m*.

dome *n* dôme *m*.

domestic *adj* domestique.

domesticate *vt* domestiquer.

domestication *n* domestication *f*.

domesticity *n* domesticité *f*.

domicile *n* domicile *m*.

dominant *adj* dominant.

dominate *vi* dominer.

domination *n* domination *f*.

domineering *adj* autoritaire.

dominoes *npl* domino *m*.

donate *vt* donner, faire don de.

donation n donation f.

done p, adj fait; cuit.

donkey n âne m.

donor n donneur m; donateur m.

doodle vi gribouiller.

doom n sort m.

door n porte f.

doorbell n sonnette f.

doorman n portier m.

doorway n entrée f.

dormant adj latent; dormant.

dormitory n dortoir m.

dose n dose f; * vt doser; donner une dose à.

dossier n dossier m.

dot n point m.

dote vi adorer.

double adj double; * vt doubler; * n double m.

double bed n lit m à deux places.

double-breasted adj croisé.

double chin n double menton m.

double room n chambre pour deux f.

doubly adv doublement.

doubt n doute m; * vt douter de.

doubtful adj douteux.

doubtless adv indubitablement.

dough n pâte f.

douse vt éteindre.

dove n colombe f.

dowdy adj mal habillé.

down n duvet m; * prep en bas; **to sit ~** s'asseoir; **upside ~** à l'envers.

downcast adj démoralisé; baissé.

downfall n ruine f.

downhearted adj découragé.

downhill adv en descendant, dans la descente.

down payment n acompte m.

downpour n grosse averse f.

downright adj manifeste.

downstairs adv en bas.

down-to-earth adj pratique; terre à terre.

downward(s) adv vers le bas.

dowry n dot f.

doze vi somnoler.

dozen n douzaine f.

dozy adj somnolent.

drab adj gris; morne.

draft n brouillon m; traite f.

drag vt tirer; * n drague f; ennui m.

dragon n dragon m.

dragonfly n libellule f.

drain vt drainer; vider; * n tuyau d'écoulement m.

drainpipe n tuyau d'écoulement m.

drake n canard mâle m.

drama n drame m.

dramatic adj dramatique.

dramatise vt dramatiser.

dramatist n dramaturge mf.

drape vt draper.

drastic adj radical.

draught n courant d'air m.

draughts npl jeu de dames m.

draughty adj exposé aux courants d'air.

draw vt tirer; dessiner.

drawback n désavantage, inconvénient m.

drawer n tiroir m.

drawing n dessin m.

drawing board n planche à dessin f.

drawl vi parler d'une voix traînante.

dread n terreur f; * vt redouter, craindre.

dreadful adj horrible.

dream n rêve m; * vt vi rêver.

dreary adj triste, morne.

dredge vt draguer.

dregs npl lie f.

drench vt tremper.

dress vt habiller; panser; * vi s'habiller; * n robe f.

dressing n pansement m; sauce f.

dressing gown n peignoir m.

dressing room n loge f, garde-robe f.

dressing table n coiffeuse f.

dressmaker n couturier m -ière f.

dressy adj élégant.

dribble vi tomber goutte à goutte.

drift n amoncellement m; courant m; sens m; * vi aller à la dérive.

drill n perceuse f; (mil) exercice m; * vt percer.

drink vt vi boire; * n boisson f.

drip vi goutter; * n goutte f, goutte-à-goutte m.

drive vt conduire; pousser; * vi conduire; * n promenade en voiture f, allée, entrée f.

drivel n imbécilités fpl; * vi baver; dire des imbécilités.

driver n conducteur m -trice f; chauffeur m.

driveway n allée, entrée f.

driving n conduite f.

driving instructor n moniteur (-trice) d'auto-école m(f).

driving licence n permis m de conduire.

driving test n examen m du permis de conduire.

drizzle vi bruiner.

droll adj drôle.

drone n bourdonnement m.

droop vi tomber.

drop n goutte f; * vt laisser tomber; * vi tomber.

dross n scories fpl.

drought n sécheresse f.

drove n: in ~s en troupe.

drown vt noyer; * vi se noyer.

drowsy adj somnolent.

drudgery n corvée f.

drug n drogue f; * vt droguer.

drug addict n drogué m -e f.

drum n tambour m; * vi jouer du tambour.

drummer n batteur m.

drumstick n baguette de tambour f.

drunk adj ivre.

drunkard n ivrogne mf.

drunken adj ivre.

dry adj sec; * vt faire sécher; * vi sécher.

dry-cleaning n nettoyage à sec m.

dual adj double.

dubbed adj doublé.

dubious adj douteux.

duck n canard m; * vt vi plonger.

duckling n caneton m.

dud adj nul; faux.

due adj dû, f due; * adv exactement; * n droit m; chose due f.

duel n duel m.

duet n (mus) duo m.

dull adj terne; insipide; gris; * vt ternir; atténuer.

duly adv dûment; en temps voulu.

dumb adj muet.

dumbfounded adj interloqué.

dummy n mannequin m; prête-nom m.

dump n tas m; * vt jeter; laisser tomber.

dumpy *adj* boulot;-te *f*.
dunce *n* cancre *m*.
dune *n* dune *f*.
dung *n* fumier *m*.
dungarees *npl* salopette *f*.
dungeon *n* donjon *m*; cachot *m*.
dupe *n* dupe *f*; * *vt* duper.
duplicate *n* duplicata *m*; copie *f*; * *vt* dupliquer.
duplicity *n* duplicité *f*.
durable *adj* durable.
duration *n* durée *f*.
during *prep* pendant.
dusk *n* crépuscule *m*.
dust *n* poussière *f*; * *vt* épousseter.
duster *n* chiffon *m*.
dusty *adj* poussiéreux.

Dutch courage *n* courage puisé dans la boisson *m*.
dutiful *adj* obéissant, soumis.
duty *n* devoir *m*; obligation *f*.
duty-free *adj* hors taxe.
dwarf *n* nain *m*, naine *f*; * *vt* rapetisser.
dwelling *n* habitation *f*; domicile *m*.
dwindle *vi* diminuer.
dye *vt* teindre; * *n* teinture *f*.
dyeing *n* teinturerie *f*; teinture *f*.
dying *adj* mourant, agonisant; * *n* mort *f*.
dynamic *adj* dynamique.
dynamics *n* dynamique *f*.
dynamite *n* dynamite *f*.
dynamo *n* dynamo *f*.
dynasty *n* dynastie *f*.
dysentery *n* dysenterie *f*.

E

each *pn* chacun(e); ~ **other** les un(e)s les autres.
eager *adj* enthousiaste; ardent.
eagle *n* aigle *m*.
ear *n* oreille *f*; ouïe *f*; **by ~** en improvisant.
earache *n* mal d'oreille *m*.
eardrum *n* tympan *m*.
early *adj* premier; *adv* tôt, de bonne heure.
earmark *vt* (*fig*) désigner.
earn *vt* gagner.
earnest *adj* sérieux.
earnings *npl* revenus *mpl*.
earring *n* boucle d'oreille *f*.
earth *n* terre *f*; * *vt* brancher à la terre.

earthenware *n* poterie *f*.
earthquake *n* tremblement de terre *m*.
earthy *adj* terreux; truculent.
earwig *n* perce-oreille *m*.
ease *n* aise *f*; facilité *f*; **at ~** à l'aise; * *vt* apaiser; soulager.
easel *n* chevalet *m*.
easily *adv* facilement.
east *n* est *m*; orient *m*.
Easter *n* Pâques *fpl*.
Easter egg *n* œuf de Pâques *m*.
eastern *adj* de l'est, oriental.
eastward(s) *adv* vers l'est.
easy *adj* facile; commode; ~ **going** décontracté.
eat *vt vi* manger.

eau de Cologne n eau f de Cologne.

eavesdrop vt espionner; écouter discrètement.

ebb n reflux m; * vi refluer; décliner.

ebony n ébène f.

eccentric adj excentrique.

eccentricity n excentricité f.

echo n écho m; * vi résonner.

eclipse n éclipse f; * vt éclipser.

ecology n écologie f.

economic(al) adj économique; économe.

economics npl économie f.

economise vt économiser.

economist n économiste mf.

economy n économie f.

ecstasy n extase f.

ecstatic adj extatique.

eczema n eczéma m.

edge n fil m; pointe f; bord m; acrimonie f; * vt border; affiler.

edgeways, edgewise adv de côté.

edgy adj nerveux.

edible adj mangeable; comestible.

edification n édification f.

edifice n édifice m.

edit vt diriger; rédiger; couper.

edition n édition f.

editor n directeur m -trice f; rédacteur m -trice f.

educate vt éduquer; instruire.

education n éducation f; instruction f.

eel n anguille f.

eerie adj inquiétant; surnaturel.

effect n effet m; réalité f; ~s npl biens mpl; * vt effectuer.

effective adj efficace; effectif.

effectual adj efficace.

effeminate adj efféminé.

effervescence n effervescence f.

effete adj (bot) stérile; faible.

efficacy n efficacité f.

efficiency n efficacité f.

efficient adj efficace.

effigy n effigie f.

effort n effort m.

effortless adj sans effort.

effrontery n effronterie f.

effusive adj chaleureux; expansif.

egg n œuf m; * ~ on vt encourager.

eggcup n coquetier m.

eggshell n coquille d'œuf f.

ego(t)istical adj égoïste.

eight adj n huit m.

eighteen adj n dix-huit m.

eighteenth adj n dix-huitième mf.

eighth adj n huitième mf.

eightieth adj n quatre-vingtième mf.

eighty adj n quatre-vingt.

either pn n'importe lequel, n'importe laquelle; * conj ou, soit.

eject vt éjecter, expulser.

ejection n éjection, expulsion f.

eke vt augmenter; prolonger.

elaborate vt élaborer; * adj élaboré; compliqué; ~ly adv avec soin.

elapse vi s'écouler.

elastic adj élastique.

elasticity n élasticité f.

elated adj exultant.

elation n exultation f.

elbow n coude m; * vt pousser du coude.

elbow-room n espace m; (fig) liberté, latitude f.

elder n sureau m; * adj aîné.

elderly adj d'un âge avancé.

elders npl anciens mpl.

eldest adj aîné.

elect vt élire; choisir; * adj élu; choisi.

election n élection f; choix m.

electioneering n propagande électorale f.

electorate n électorat m.

electric(al) adj électrique.

electric fire n radiateur électrique m.

electrician n électricien m.

electricity n électricité f.

electrify vt électriser.

electron n électron m.

electronic adj électronique; ~s npl électronique f.

elegance n élégance f.

elegant adj élégant; ~ly adv élégamment.

elegy n élégie f.

element n élément m.

elemental, elementary adj élémentaire.

elephant n éléphant m.

elevate vt élever, hausser.

elevation n élévation f; hauteur f.

eleven adj n onze m.

eleventh adj n onzième mf.

elf n elfe m.

elicit vt tirer, obtenir.

eligible adj éligible.

eliminate vt éliminer, écarter.

elk n élan m.

elliptic(al) adj elliptique.

elm n orme m.

elocution n élocution f.

elongate vt allonger.

elope vi s'échapper, s'enfuir.

eloquence n éloquence f.

eloquent adj éloquent.

else pn autre.

elsewhere adv ailleurs.

elusive, elusory adj insaisissable.

emaciated adj émacié.

emanate (from) vi émaner (de).

emancipation n émancipation f; affranchissement m.

embalm vt embaumer.

embankment n talus m; quai m.

embargo n embargo m.

embark vt embarquer.

embarrass vt embàrrasser.

embarrassment n embarras m.

embassy n ambassade f.

embellishment n ornement m.

ember n braise f.

embezzle vt détourner.

embezzlement n détournement de fonds m.

embitter vt rendre amer.

emblem n emblème m.

embodiment n (law) incorporation f; incarnation f.

embody vt (law) incorporer; incarner.

embrace vt étreindre; comprendre; * n étreinte f.

embroider vt broder.

embroidery n broderie f.

embroil vt impliquer.

embryo n embryon m.

emerald n émeraude f.

emerge vi émerger; apparaître.

emergency n urgence f.

emergency exit n sortie de secours f.

emergency landing n atterrissage forcé m.

emery n émeri m.

emigrate vi émigrer.

emigration n émigration f.

eminence n hauteur f; éminence, excellence f.

eminent *adj* élevé; éminent, distingué;
~ly *adv* éminemment.
emission *n* émission *f.*
emit *vt* émettre.
emotion *n* émotion *f.*
emotional *adj* émotionnel; ému.
emperor *n* empereur *m.*
emphasis *n* emphase *f.*
emphasise *vt* souligner, accentuer.
emphatic *adj* emphatique; **~ally** *adv*
avec emphase.
empire *n* empire *m.*
employ *vt* employer.
employee *n* employé *m* -e *f.*
employer *n* employeur *m.*
employment *n* emploi, travail *m.*
empress *n* impératrice *f.*
emptiness *n* vide *m;* futilité *f.*
empty *adj* vide; vain; * *vt* vider.
empty-handed *adj* les mains vides.
emulate *vt* imiter.
emulsion *n* émulsion *f.*
enable *vt* permettre.
enamel *n* émail *m;* * *vt* émailler.
enamour *vt* s'éprendre de.
encase *vt* entourer.
enchant *vt* enchanter.
enchanting *adj* enchanteur.
enchantment *n* enchantement *m.*
encircle *vt* encercler.
enclose *vt* entourer; inclure, joindre.
enclosure *n* clôture *f;* enceinte *f.*
encompass *vt* comprendre.
encounter *n* rencontre *f;* combat *m;* *
vt rencontrer.
encourage *vt* encourager.
encouragement *n* encouragement *m.*
encroach *vi* empiéter (sur).
encrusted *adj* incrusté.

encyclopedia *n* encyclopédie *f.*
end *n* fin *f;* extrémité *f;* bout *m;* dessein
m; * *vi* terminer.
endanger *vt* mettre en danger.
endearing *adj* attachant.
endearment *n* expression de tendresse *f.*
endeavour *vi* s'efforcer, tenter; * *n* effort *m.*
ending *n* fin, conclusion *f;* dénouement *m;* terminaison *f.*
endless *adj* infini, perpétuel; **~ly** *adv*
sans fin, perpétuellement.
endorse *vt* endosser; approuver.
endorsement *n* endos *m;* approbation *f.*
endow *vt* doter.
endurance *n* endurance *f;* patience *f.*
endure *vt* supporter; * *vi* durer.
endways, endwise *adv* debout.
enemy *n* ennemi *mf.*
energetic *adj* énergique, vigoureux.
energy *n* énergie, force *f.*
enfold *vt* envelopper.
enforce *vt* mettre en vigueur.
enforced *adj* forcé.
engaged *adj* fiancé; occupé.
engagement *n* engagement *m;* combat *m;* fiançailles *fpl;* **~ ring** *n* bague de
fiançailles *f.*
engine *n* moteur *m;* locomotive *f.*
engine driver *n* conducteur *m.*
engineer *n* ingénieur *m;* mécanicien *m.*
engineering *n* ingénierie *f.*
engrave *vt* graver.
engraving *n* gravure *f.*
engrossed *adj* absorbé.
engulf *vt* submerger.
enhance *vt* améliorer; réhausser.
enigma *n* énigme *f.*
enjoy *vt* aimer; jouir de; **~ o.s.** s'amuser.

enjoyable *adj* agréable; amusant.

enjoyment *n* plaisir *m*; jouissance *f*.

enlarge *vt* agrandir; étendre; dilater.

enlargement *n* agrandissement *m*; extension *f*; dilatation *f*.

enlighten *vt* éclairer.

enlightened *adj* éclairé.

enlist *vt* recruter.

enlistment *n* recrutement *m*.

enmity *n* inimitié *f*; haine *f*.

enormity *n* énormité *f*; atrocité *f*.

enormous *adj* énorme.

enough *adv* suffisamment; assez; * *n* assez *m*.

enquire *vt* = **inquire**.

enrage *vt* rendre furieux.

enrich *vt* enrichir; orner.

enrol *vt* enrôler; inscrire.

enrolment *n* inscription *f*.

enslave *vt* asservir.

ensue *vi* s'ensuivre.

ensure *vt* assurer.

entail *vt* impliquer, entraîner.

entangle *vt* emmêler, embrouiller.

entanglement *n* emmêlement *m*.

enter *vt* entrer dans; inscrire; ~ **for** se présenter à; ~ **into** commencer; faire partie de.

enterprise *n* entreprise *f*.

enterprising *adj* entreprenant.

entertain *vt* divertir; recevoir; avoir.

entertainer *n* artiste *mf*.

entertaining *adj* divertissant, amusant.

entertainment *n* divertissement, passe-temps *m*.

enthralled *adj* captivé.

enthralling *adj* captivant.

enthusiasm *n* enthousiasme *m*.

enthusiast *n* enthousiaste *mf*.

enthusiastic *adj* enthousiaste.

entice *vt* tenter; séduire.

entire *adj* entier, complet; parfait; ~**ly** *adv* entièrement.

entirety *n* intégralité *f*.

entitle *vt* intituler; conférer un droit à.

entitled *adj*: **to be ~ to** avoir le droit de.

entity *n* entité *f*.

entrails *npl* entrailles *fpl*.

entrance *n* entrée *f*; admission *f*.

entrance fee *n* droit d'inscription *m*.

entrant *n* participant *m* -e *f*; candidat *m* -e *f*.

entreat *vt* implorer, supplier.

entreaty *n* supplication, prière *f*.

entrust *vt* confier.

entry *n* entrée *f*.

entwine *vt* entrelacer.

enumerate *vt* énumérer.

enunciation *n* énonciation *f*.

envelop *vt* envelopper.

envelope *n* enveloppe *f*.

enviable *adj* enviable.

envious *adj* envieux; ~**ly** *adv* avec envie.

environment *n* environnement *m*.

environmental *adj* relatif à l'environnement.

envisage *vt* envisager.

envoy *n* envoyé *m* -e *f*.

envy *n* envie *f*; * *vt* envier.

ephemeral *adj* éphémère.

epic *adj* épique; * *n* récit épique *m*.

epidemic *n* épidémie *f*.

epilepsy *n* épilepsie *f*.

epileptic *adj* épileptique.

epilogue *n* épilogue *m*.

episode *n* épisode *m*.

epistle *n* épître *f*.

epitome *n* modèle *m*; résumé *m*.

epitomise *vt* incarner; résumer.

epoch *n* époque *f*.

equal *adj* égal; semblable; * *n* égal *m* -e *f*; * *vt* égaler.

equalise *vt* égaliser.

equaliser *n* point égalisateur *m*.

equality *n* égalité *f*.

equally *adv* également.

equate *vt* comparer; assimiler.

equation *n* équation *f*.

equator *n* équateur *m*.

equatorial *adj* équatorial.

equestrian *adj* équestre.

equilibrium *n* équilibre *m*.

equip *vt* équiper.

equipment *n* équipement *m*.

equity *n* équité, justice, impartialité *f*.

equivalent *adj* *n* équivalent *m*.

equivocal *adj* équivoque, ambigu.

era *n* ère *f*.

eradicate *vt* supprimer; extirper.

erase *vt* effacer; gommer.

eraser *n* gomme *f*.

erect *vt* ériger; élever; * *adj* droit, debout.

erection *n* érection *f*; structure *f*.

ermine *n* hermine *f*.

erode *vt* éroder; ronger.

erotic *adj* érotique.

errand *n* message *m*; commission *f*.

errand boy *n* garçon de courses, messager *m*.

erratic *adj* changeant; irrégulier.

erroneous *adj* erroné, faux.

error *n* erreur *f*.

erudite *adj* érudit.

erupt *vi* entrer en éruption; faire éruption.

eruption *n* éruption *f*.

escalate *vi* monter en flèche; s'intensifier.

escalation *n* montée en flèche *f*; intensification *f*.

escalator *n* escalier roulant *m*.

escapade *n* fredaine *f*.

escape *vt* éviter; échapper à; * *vi* s'évader, s'échapper; * *n* évasion, fuite *f*; **to make one's** ~ prendre la fuite.

escapism *n* évasion de la réalité *f*.

escort *n* escorte *f*; * *vt* escorter.

especial *adj* spécial; ~**ly** *adv* spécialement.

espionage *n* espionnage *m*.

essay *n* essai *m*.

essence *n* essence *f*.

essential *n* essentiel *m*; * *adj* essentiel, principal; ~**ly** *adv* essentiellement.

establish *vt* établir; fonder; démontrer.

establishment *n* établissement *m*; fondation *f*; institution *f*.

estate *n* état *m*; domaine *m*; biens *mpl*.

esteem *vt* estimer; apprécier; * *n* estime *f*; considération *f*.

estimate *vt* estimer; évaluer.

estimation *n* estimation, évaluation *f*; opinion *f*.

estranged *adj* séparé.

estuary *n* estuaire *m*.

etch *vt* graver à l'eau forte.

etching *n* gravure à l'eau forte *f*.

eternal *adj* éternel, perpétuel.

eternity *n* éternité *f*.

ether *n* éther *m*.

ethical *adj* éthique, moral.

ethics *npl* éthique *f*.

ethnic *adj* ethnique.

etiquette *n* étiquette *f*.

eulogy *n* éloge *m*.

euphemism *n* euphémisme *m*.

evacuate *vt* évacuer.

evacuation n évacuation f.

evade vt éviter; échapper à.

evaluate vt évaluer.

evangelic(al) adj évangélique.

evangelist n évangéliste m.

evaporate vt faire évaporer; * vi s'évaporer; se volatiliser.

evaporation n évaporation f.

evasion n dérobade f.

evasive adj évasif.

eve n veille f.

even adj égal; uni; pair; * adv même; encore; * vt égaliser; unir; * vi: ~ **out** s'égaliser.

evening n soir m, soirée f.

evening class n cours du soir m.

evening dress n robe du soir f; tenue de soirée f.

evenly adv également; uniment.

event n événement m; épreuve f.

eventful adj mouvementé.

eventual adj final; **~ly** adv finalement, en fin de comptes.

eventuality n éventualité f.

ever adv toujours; jamais; déjà; **for ~ and ~** pour toujours; **~ since** depuis.

evergreen adj à feuilles persistantes; * n arbre à feuilles persistantes m.

everlasting adj éternel.

every adj chacun, chacune; **~ where** partout; **~ thing** tout; **~ one, ~ body** tout le monde.

evict vt expulser.

eviction n expulsion f.

evidence n évidence f; témoignage m; preuve f; * vt témoigner de.

evident adj évident; manifeste; **~ly** adv manifestement, de toute évidence.

evil adj mauvais; malveillant; * n mal m.

evocative adj évocateur.

evolution n évolution f.

ewe n brebis f.

exact adj exact; * vt exiger.

exactly adv exactement.

exaggerate vt exagérer.

exaggeration n exagération f.

exalted adj exalté; élevé.

examination n examen m.

examine vt examiner.

examiner n examinateur m -trice f.

example n exemple m.

exasperate vt exaspérer, irriter.

exasperation n exaspération, irritation f.

excavate vt exhumer, creuser.

excavation n excavation f.

exceed vt excéder, dépasser.

exceedingly adv trop; extrêmement.

excel vt surpasser; vi exceller.

excellence n excellence f, supériorité f.

excellent adj excellent.

except vt excepter, exclure; **~(ing)** prep excepté, à l'exception de.

exception n exception f.

exceptional adj exceptionnel.

excerpt n extrait m.

excess n excès m.

excessive adj excessif.

exchange vt échanger; permuter; * n échange m; change m.

exchange rate n taux de change m.

excitable adj excitable.

excite vt exciter; animer; enthousiasmer; stimuler.

excited adj animé, enthousiaste; excité.

excitement n animation f, enthousiasme m.

exciting adj passionnant; stimulant.

exclaim *vi* s'exclamer.

exclamation *n* exclamation *f*.

exclamation mark *n* point d'exclamation *m*.

exclude *vt* exclure.

exclusion *n* exclusion *f*; exception *f*.

exclusive *adj* exclusif.

excommunicate *vt* excommunier.

excrement *n* excrément *m*.

excruciating *adj* atroce, horrible.

excursion *n* excursion *f*; digression *f*.

excuse *vt* excuser; pardonner; * *n* excuse *f*.

execute *vt* exécuter.

execution *n* exécution *f*.

executioner *n* bourreau *m*.

exemplary *adj* exemplaire.

exemplify *vt* exemplifier.

exempt *adj* exempt.

exemption *n* exemption *f*.

exercise *n* exercice *m*; * *vi* prendre de l'exercice; * *vt* exercer; montrer.

exercise book *n* cahier *m*.

exert *vt* employer, exercer; ~ **o.s.** s'efforcer.

exertion *n* effort *m*.

exhale *vt* exhaler; expirer.

exhaust *n* échappement *m*; * *vt* épuiser.

exhaustion *n* épuisement *m*.

exhibit *vt* exhiber; montrer; * *n* (*law*) pièce à conviction *f*.

exhibition *n* exposition, présentation *f*.

exhilarating *adj* stimulant, grisant.

exhilaration *n* joie *f* intense.

exile *n* exil *m*; * *vt* exiler, déporter.

exist *vi* exister.

existence *n* existence *f*.

exit *n* sortie *f*; * *vi* sortir.

exodus *n* exode *m*.

exonerate *vt* disculper; décharger.

exoneration *n* disculpation *f*; décharge *f*.

exorbitant *adj* exorbitant, excessif.

exorcise *vt* exorciser.

exorcism *n* exorcisme *m*.

exotic *adj* exotique.

expand *vt* étendre; dilater.

expanse *n* étendue *f*.

expansion *n* expansion *f*.

expansive *adj* expansif.

expect *vt* attendre; espérer; penser.

expectancy *n* attente *f*; espoir *m*.

expectant mother *n* femme enceinte *f*.

expectation *n* expectative *f*; attente *f*.

expedient *adj* opportun; * *n* expédient *m*.

expedite *vt* accélérer; expédier.

expedition *n* expédition *f*.

expel *vt* expulser.

expend *vt* dépenser; utiliser.

expendable *adj* jetable; consommable.

expenditure *n* dépense *f*.

expense *n* dépense *f*; coût *m*.

expense account *n* frais *mpl* de représentation.

expensive *adj* cher; coûteux.

experience *n* expérience *f*; pratique *f*; * *vt* ressentir, éprouver; connaître.

experienced *adj* expérimenté.

experiment *n* expérience *f*; * *vi* expérimenter.

experimental *adj* expérimental.

expert *adj* expert.

expertise *n* compétences *fpl*.

expire *vi* expirer.

explain *vt* expliquer.

explanation *n* explication *f*.

explanatory *adj* explicatif.

explicit adj explicite.

explode vt faire exploser; vi exploser.

exploit vt exploiter; * n exploit m.

exploitation n exploitation f.

exploration n exploration f.

exploratory adj exploratoire.

explore vt explorer, examiner; sonder.

explorer n explorateur m -trice f.

explosion n explosion f.

explosive adj n explosif m.

export vt exporter.

export, exportation n exportation f.

exporter n exportateur m -trice f.

expose vt exposer; dévoiler.

exposition n exposition f; interprétation f.

expostulate vi faire des remontrances.

exposure n exposition f; temps de pose m; cliché m.

expound vt exposer; interpréter.

express vt exprimer; * adj exprès; * n exprès m; (rail) rapide m.

expression n expression f, locution f.

expressionless adj inexpressif.

expressive adj expressif; ~ly adv d'une manière expressive.

expressly adv expressément.

expulsion n expulsion f.

exquisite adj exquis.

extend vt étendre; élargir; * vi s'étendre.

extension n extension f.

extensive adj étendu; important; ~ly adv considérablement.

extent n extension f.

extenuating adj atténuant.

exterior adj n extérieur m.

exterminate vt exterminer; supprimer.

extermination n extermination f; suppression f.

external adj externe.

extinct adj disparu; éteint.

extinction n extinction f.

extinguish vt éteindre; supprimer.

extinguisher n extincteur m.

extortion n extorsion f.

extortionate adj exorbitant.

extra adv particulièrement; n supplément m.

extract vt extraire; * n extrait m.

extraction n extraction f; origine f.

extradition n (law) extradition f.

extramarital adj extérieur au mariage.

extraordinary adj extraordinaire.

extravagance n extravagance f; gaspillage m.

extravagant adj extravagant; exorbitant; gaspilleur; ~ly adv de manière extravagante; en gaspillant.

extreme adj extrême; suprême; ultime; * n extrême m; ~ly adv extrêmement.

extremist adj n extrémiste mf.

extremity n extrémité f.

extricate vt extirper, démêler.

extrovert adj n extraverti m -e f.

exuberance n exubérance f.

exuberant adj exubérant.

eye n œil m; * vt regarder, observer; lorgner.

eyeball n globe oculaire m.

eyebrow n sourcil m.

eyelash n cil m.

eyelid n paupière f.

eyesight n vue f.

eyesore n monstruosité f.

eyetooth n canine f.

eyewitness n témoin oculaire m.

F

fable n fable f; légende f.

fabric n tissu m.

fabricate vt fabriquer; inventer.

fabrication n fabrication f; invention f.

fabulous adj fabuleux.

face n visage m, figure f; surface f; façade f; mine f; apparence f; * vt faire face à; affronter; ~ **up to** faire face à.

face-lift n lifting m.

facet n facette f.

facetious adj facétieux, plaisant, spirituel.

face value n valeur nominale f.

facial adj facial.

facile adj facile; superficiel.

facility n facilité f; équipement m, infrastructure f.

facing n revers m; * prep en face de.

fact n fait m; réalité f; **in ~** en fait.

faction n faction f; dissension f.

factor n facteur m.

factory n usine f.

factual adj factuel, basé sur les faits.

faculty n faculté f; le corps enseignant m.

fad n engouement m.

fade vi se faner; perdre son éclat.

fail vt échouer à; omettre; manquer à ses engagements envers; * vi échouer; faiblir; manquer.

failing n défaut m.

failure n échec m; panne f; raté m; faillite f; manquement m.

faint vi s'évanouir, défaillir; * n évanouissement m; * adj faible.

fair adj beau; blond; clair; favorable; juste, équitable; considérable; passable; * adv loyalement; * n foire f.

fairly adv équitablement; absolument.

fair play n fair-play, franc-jeu m.

fairy n fée f.

fairy tale n conte de fées m.

faith n foi f; croyance f; fidélité f.

faithful adj fidèle, loyal.

fake n falsification f; imposteur m; * adj faux; * vt feindre; falsifier.

falcon n faucon m.

fall vi tomber; s'effondrer; diminuer, baisser; ~ **asleep** s'endormir; ~ **back on** avoir recours à; ~ **behind** être à la traîne; ~ **for** se faire avoir; tomber amoureux de; ~ **in love** tomber amoureux; ~ **out** se produire; se quereller; * n chute f; automne m.

fallacy n erreur f; sophisme m; tromperie f.

fallible adj faillible.

fallout n retombées fpl.

fallout shelter n abri antiatomique m.

false adj faux.

false alarm n fausse alerte f.

falsehood, falseness n mensonge m; fausseté f.

falsify vt falsifier.

faltering adj chancelant.

fame n réputation f; renommée, notoriété f.

famed adj célèbre.

familiar adj familier; domestique; ~**ly** adv familièrement.

familiarise vt familiariser.

familiarity n familiarité f.

family n famille f.

famine n famine f; disette f.

famished adj affamé.

famous adj célèbre, fameux; **~ly** adv fameusement.

fan n éventail m; ventilateur m; jeune admirateur m -trice f; * vt éventer; attiser.

fanatic adj n fanatique mf.

fanaticism n fanatisme m.

fan belt n courroie de ventilateur f.

fanciful adj fantasque, capricieux.

fancy n fantaisie, imagination f; caprice m; * vt avoir envie de; s'imaginer.

fancy-dress ball n bal masqué m.

fanfare n (mus) fanfare f.

fang n croc m.

fantastic adj fantastique; excentrique.

fantasy n imagination f.

far adv loin; * adj lointain, éloigné.

farce n farce f.

farcical adj grotesque.

fare n prix (du voyage) m; tarif m; nourriture f; voyageur m -euse f; client m -e f.

farewell n adieu m.

farm n ferme f, exploitation agricole f; * vt cultiver.

farmer n fermier m; agriculteur m.

farmhand n ouvrier agricole m.

farmhouse n ferme f.

farming n agriculture f.

farmyard n cour de ferme f.

far-reaching adj d'une grande portée, considérable.

fart n (sl) pet m; * vi péter.

farther adv plus loin; * adj plus éloigné.

farthest adv le plus lointain; le plus loin; au plus.

fascinate vt fasciner, captiver.

fascination n fascination f, charme m.

fascism n fascisme.

fashion n manière, façon f, forme f; coutume f, mode f; style m.

fashionable adj à la mode; chic; **~bly** adv à la mode.

fashion show n défilé de mode m.

fast vi jeûner; * n jeûne m; * adj rapide; ferme, stable; * adv rapidement; fermement; solidement.

fasten vt attacher; fixer; attribuer; * vi se fixer, s'attacher.

fastener, fastening n attache f; fermoir m.

fast food n restauration rapide f.

fastidious adj minutieux, méticuleux.

fat adj gros, gras; * n graisse f.

fatal adj mortel; néfaste.

fatality n accident mortel m, fatalité f.

fate n destin, sort m.

fateful adj fatidique.

father n père m.

father-in-law n beau-père m.

fathom vt sonder; pénétrer.

fatigue n fatigue f; * vt fatiguer, lasser.

fatuous adj imbécile, stupide, niais.

fault n défaut m, faute f, délit m; faille f.

faultless adj irréprochable.

faulty adj défectueux.

fauna n faune f.

faux pas n impair m.

favour n faveur f; approbation f; avantage m; * vt favoriser, préférer.

favourable adj favorable, propice.

favourite n favori m; * adj favori.

favouritism n favoritisme m.

fawn n faon m; * vi flatter servilement.

fax n télécopieur, fax m; télécopie f, fax m; * vt envoyer par fax, télécopier.

fear *vt* craindre; * *n* crainte *f.*

fearful *adj* effrayant; craintif, peureux; **~ly** *adv* terriblement; craintivement.

fearless *adj* intrépide, courageux.

feasible *adj* faisable, réalisable.

feast *n* festin, banquet *m*; fête *f*; * *vi* banqueter.

feat *n* exploit *m*; prouesse *f.*

feather *n* plume *f.*

feature *n* caractéristique *f*; trait *m*; * *vi* figurer.

feature film *n* long métrage *m.*

February *n* février *m.*

federal *adj* fédéral.

fed-up *adj:* **to be ~** en avoir marre.

fee *n* honoraires *mpl*; frais *mpl.*

feeble *adj* faible, frêle.

feed *vt* nourrir; alimenter; * *vi* manger; se nourrir; * *n* nourriture *f*, alimentation *f.*

feedback *n* réaction *f*, répercussion *f.*

feel *vt* sentir; toucher; croire; * *n* sensation *f*; toucher *m.*

feeler *n* antenne *f*; (*fig*) tentative *f.*

feeling *n* sensation *f*; sentiment *m.*

feign *vt* inventer; feindre, simuler.

feline *adj* félin.

fellow *n* homme, type *m*; membre *m.*

fellow citizen *n* concitoyen *m* -enne *f.*

fellow countryman *n* compatriote *m.*

fellow feeling *n* sympathie *f.*

fellow men *npl* semblables *mpl.*

fellowship *n* camaraderie *f*; association *f.*

felon *n* criminel *m* -le *f.*

felony *n* crime *m.*

felt *n* feutre *m.*

felt-tip pen *n* feutre *m.*

female *n* femelle *f*; * *adj* de sexe féminin, femelle.

feminine *adj* féminin.

feminist *n* féministe *mf.*

fence *n* barrière *f*; clôture *f*; * *vt* clôturer; * *vi* faire de l'escrime.

fencing *n* escrime *f.*

fennel *n* (*bot*) fenouil *m.*

ferment *n* agitation *f*; * *vt* fermenter.

fern *n* (*bot*) fougère *f.*

ferocious *adj* féroce.

ferocity *n* férocité *f.*

ferret *n* furet *m*; * *vt* fureter; **~ out** découvrir, dénicher.

ferry *n* bac *m*; ferry *m*; * *vt* transporter.

fertile *adj* fertile, fécond.

fertilise *vt* fertiliser.

fertiliser *n* engrais *m.*

fertility *n* fertilité, fécondité *f.*

fervent *adj* fervent; ardent.

fervour *n* ferveur, ardeur *f.*

fester *vi* suppurer; s'envenimer.

festival *n* fête *f*; festival *m.*

festive *adj* de fête.

festivity *n* fête *f*, réjouissances *fpl.*

fetch *vt* aller chercher.

fetus *n* fœtus *m.*

feud *n* rivalité *f*, dissension *f.*

fever *n* fièvre *f.*

feverish *adj* fiévreux.

few *adj* peu; **a ~** quelques; **~ and far between** rares.

fewer *adj* moins (de); * *adv* moins.

fewest *adj* le moins (de).

fib *n* bobard *m*; * *vi* raconter des bobards.

fibre *n* fibre *f.*

fibreglass *n* fibre de verre *f.*

fickle *adj* volage, inconstant.

fiction n fiction f; invention f.
fictional adj fictif.
fictitious adj fictif, imaginaire; feint.
fiddle n violon m; combine f; * vi jouer du violon.
fidelity n fidélité, loyauté f.
fidget vi s'agiter, s'impatienter.
fidgety adj agité, remuant.
field n champ m; étendue f; domaine m.
field day n (mil) jour de grandes manœuvres m.
fiend n démon m; mordu m.
fiendish adj diabolique.
fierce adj féroce, violent; acharné, furieux.
fiery adj ardent; fougueux.
fifteen adj n quinze m.
fifteenth adj n quinzième mf.
fifth adj n cinquième mf; ~ly adv cinquièmement.
fiftieth adj n cinquantième mf.
fifty adj n cinquante m.
fig n figue f.
fight vt vi se battre (contre); combattre; lutter; * n bataille f; combat m; lutte f.
fighter n combattant m; lutteur m; chasseur m.
fighting n combat m.
figurative adj figuratif.
figure n figure f; forme, silhouette f; image f; chiffre m; * vi figurer; avoir du sens; ~ out comprendre.
figurehead n figure de proue f.
file n file f; liste f; (mil) colonne, rangée f; lime f; dossier m; fichier m; * vt enregistrer; limer; classer; déposer; * vi ~ in/out entrer/sortir en file; ~ past défiler devant.
filing cabinet n classeur (meuble) m.

fill vt remplir.
fillet n filet m.
fillet steak n filet de bœuf m.
filly n pouliche f.
film n pellicule f; film f; cellophane m; * vt filmer; * vi s'embuer.
film star n vedette de cinéma f.
filter n filtre m; * vt filtrer.
filter-tipped adj à bout filtre.
filth(iness) n immondice, ordure f; saleté, crasse f.
filthy adj crasseux, dégoûtant.
fin n nageoire f.
final adj dernier; définitif; ~ly adv finalement.
finale n finale m.
finalise vt parachever, rendre définitif.
finalist n finaliste mf.
finance n finance f.
financial adj financier.
find vt trouver, découvrir; ~ out découvrir; démasquer.
findings npl résultats mpl, conclusions fpl; verdict m.
fine adj fin; pur; aigu; raffiné; beau, f belle; délicat; subtil; élégant; * n amende f; * vt infliger une amende à.
fine arts npl beaux arts mpl.
finery n parure f.
finesse n finesse, subtilité f.
finger n doigt m; * vt toucher, manier.
fingernail n ongle m.
fingerprint n empreinte digitale f.
fingertip n bout du doigt m.
finish vt finir, terminer, achever.
fir n sapin m
fire n feu m; incendie m; * vt mettre le feu à; incendier; tirer; * vi s'enflammer, faire feu.

fire alarm n alarme d'incendie f.
firearm n arme à feu f.
fire engine n voiture de pompiers f.
fire escape n escalier de secours m.
fire extinguisher n extincteur m.
fireman n pompier m.
fireplace n cheminée f, foyer m.
fireproof adj ignifugé.
fire station n caserne de pompiers f.
fireworks npl feu d'artifice m.
firing squad n peloton d'exécution m.
firm adj ferme, solide; constant; * n (com) compagnie f; **~ly** adv fermement.
firmness n fermeté f; résolution f.
first adj premier; * adv premièrement; **at ~** d'abord; **~ly** adv en premier lieu.
first aid n premiers secours mpl.
first-aid kit n trousse de premiers secours f.
first-class adj de première classe, de première catégorie.
first-hand adj de première main.
fish n poisson m; * vi pêcher.
fishbone n arête f.
fisherman n pêcheur m.
fish farm n entreprise de pisciculture f.
fishing n pêche f.
fishing line n ligne de pêche f.
fishing rod n canne à pêche f.
fishing tackle n attirail de pêche m.
fishy adj (fig) suspect.
fissure n fissure, crevasse f.
fist n poing m.
fit n accès m, attaque f; crise f; * adj en forme; capable; adapté à, qui convient; * vt aller à; ajuster, adapter; * vi (bien) aller; **~ in** s'accorder avec; être en harmonie avec.
fitness n forme physique f; aptitude f.

fitted carpet n moquette f.
fitted kitchen n cuisine encastrée f.
fitter n monteur m.
fitting adj qui convient, approprié, juste; * n accessoire m; **~s** pl installations fpl.
five adj cinq m.
fix vt fixer, établir; **~ up** arranger.
fixation n obsession f.
fixture n (sport) rencontre f.
fizz vi pétiller.
fizzy adj gazeux.
flabbergasted adj abasourdi.
flabby adj mou, f molle, flasque.
flaccid adj flasque, mou, f molle.
flag n drapeau m; (bot) iris m; * vi s'affaiblir.
flagrant adj flagrant.
flair n flair m; talent m.
flak n tir antiaérien m; critiques fpl.
flake n flocon m; paillette f; * vi s'effriter, s'écailler.
flaky adj floconneux; friable.
flamboyant adj flamboyant; ostentatoire.
flame n flamme f; ardeur f.
flamingo n flamant m.
flank n flanc m; (also mil); * vt flanquer.
flannel n flanelle f.
flap n battement m; rabat m; * vt vi battre.
flare vi luire, briller; **~ up** s'embraser; se mettre en colère; éclater; * n flamme f.
flash n éclat m; éclair m; * vt faire briller; allumer.
flashbulb n ampoule de flash f.
flashy adj tape-à-l'œil, voyant.
flask n flasque f; flacon m.
flat adj plat; uniforme; insipide; * n

plaine *f*; plat *m*; (*mus*) bémol *m*; ~**ly** *adv* horizontalement; platement; également; catégoriquement.

flatten *vt* aplanir; aplatir.

flatter *vt* flatter.

flattering *adj* flatteur.

flattery *n* flatterie *f*.

flatulence *n* (*med*) flatulence *f*.

flaunt *vt* étaler, afficher.

flavour *n* saveur *m*; * *vt* parfumer; assaisonner.

flaw *n* défaut *m*; imperfection *f*.

flawless *adj* parfait.

flea *n* puce *f*.

fleck *n* petite tache *f*; particule *f*.

flee *vt* fuir de; * *vi* s'enfuir; fuir.

fleece *n* toison *f*; * *vt* (*sl*) tondre.

fleet *n* flotte *f*; (autos) parc *m*.

fleeting *adj* fugace, fugitif.

flesh *n* chair *f*.

fleshy *adj* charnu.

flex *n* cordon *m*; * *vt* fléchir.

flexible *adj* flexible, souple.

flick *n* petit coup *m*; * *vt* donner un petit coup à.

flicker *vt* vaciller; trembloter.

flier *n* aviateur *m* -trice *f*.

flight *n* vol *m*; suite *f*; volée *f*; (*fig*) envolée *f*.

flimsy *adj* léger; fragile.

flinch *vi* sourciller.

fling *vt* lancer, jeter.

flip *vt* lancer.

flippant *adj* désinvolte, cavalier.

flipper *n* nageoire *f*.

flirt *vi* flirter; * *n* charmeur *m* -euse *f*.

flirtation *n* flirt *f*.

flit *vi* voler, voleter.

float *vt* faire flotter; lancer; * *vi* flotter; * *n* flotteur *m*; char (de carnaval) *m*; provision *f*.

flock *n* troupeau *m*; volée *f*; foule *f*; * *vi* affluer.

flood *n* inondation *f*; marée haute *f*; déluge *m*; * *vt* inonder.

flooding *n* inondation *f*.

floodlight *n* projecteur *m*.

floor *n* sol *m*; plancher *m*; étage *m*; * *vt* parqueter; déconcerter.

floorboard *n* planche *f*.

flop *n* four, fiasco *m*.

floppy *adj* lâche; * *n* disquette *f*.

flora *n* flore *f*.

floral *adj* floral.

florid *adj* fleuri.

florist *n* fleuriste *mf*.

flotilla *n* (*mar*) flotille *f*.

flounder *n* flet *m*; * *vi* patauger.

flour *n* farine *f*.

flourish *vi* fleurir; prospérer; * *n* fioriture *f*; (*mus*) fioriture *f*.

flourishing *adj* florissant.

flout *vt* mépriser, se moquer de.

flow *vi* couler; circuler; monter (marée); ondoyer; * *n* flux *m*; écoulement *m*; flot *m*.

flower *n* fleur *f*; * *vi* fleurir.

flowerbed *n* parterre de fleurs *m*.

flowerpot *n* pot de fleurs *m*.

flowery *adj* fleuri.

fluctuate *vi* fluctuer.

fluctuation *n* fluctuation *f*.

fluency *n* aisance *f*.

fluent *adj* coulant; facile; ~**ly** *adv* couramment.

fluff *n* peluche *f*; ~**y** *adj* duveteux.

fluid *adj n* fluide *m*.

fluke n (sl) veine f.

fluoride n fluorure m.

flurry n rafale f; agitation f.

flush vt: **to ~ out** nettoyer à grande eau; * vi rougir; * n rougeur f; éclat m.

flushed adj rouge.

flustered adj énervé.

flute n flûte f.

flutter vi voleter; s'agiter; * n agitation f; émoi m.

flux n flux m.

fly vt piloter; transporter par avion; * vi voler; fuir; * n mouche f; braguette f.

flying n aviation f.

flying saucer n soucoupe volante f.

foal n poulain m.

foam n écume f; * vi écumer.

foam rubber n caoutchouc mousse m.

focus n foyer m; centre m.

fodder n fourrage m.

foe n ennemi m -e f, adversaire mf.

fog n brouillard m.

foggy adj brumeux.

fog light n feu de brouillard m.

foible n point faible m.

foil vt déjouer; * n papier d'aluminium m; fleuret m.

fold n pli m; parc à moutons m; * vt plier.

folder n chemise f; dépliant m.

foliage n feuillage m.

folk n gens mpl.

folklore n folklore m.

folk song n chant folklorique m.

follow vt suivre; **~ up** suivre; exploiter; * vi suivre, s'ensuivre, résulter.

follower n serviteur m; disciple mf, partisan m -e f; adhérent m -e f, admirateur m -trice f.

following adj suivant; * n partisans mpl.

folly n folie, extravagance f.

fond adj affectueux; **to be ~ of** aimer; **~ly** adv affectueusement.

fondle vt caresser.

fondness n prédilection f; affection f.

food n nourriture f.

food mixer n mixer m.

food poisoning n intoxication alimentaire f.

food processor n robot m ménager.

fool n imbécile mf, idiot m -e f; * vt duper.

foolhardy adj téméraire.

foolish adj idiot, insensé; **~ly** adv bêtement.

foolproof adj infaillible.

foot n pied m; patte f.

football n football m; ballon de football m.

footballer n footballeur m -euse f.

footbrake n frein à pied m.

foothold n prise (pour le pied) f.

footing n prise (pour le pied) f; statut m; situation f; plan m.

footnote n note (de bas de page) f.

footpath n sentier m.

footprint n empreinte (de pas) f.

footstep n pas m.

footwear n chaussures fpl.

for prep pour; en raison de; pendant; * conj car; **as ~ me** quant à moi; **what ~?** pourquoi?; pourquoi faire?

forbid vt interdire, défendre; empêcher; **God ~!** pourvu que non!

forbidding adj menaçant; sévère.

force n force f; puissance, vigueur f; violence f; **~s** pl forces armées fpl; * vt forcer, obliger, contraindre; imposer.

forceful adj énergique.

forceps *n* forceps *m*.

forcible *adj* énergique, vigoureux, puissant.

ford *n* gué *m*; * *vt* passer à gué.

fore *n*: **to the ~** en évidence.

forearm *n* avant-bras *m*.

foreboding *n* pressentiment *m*.

forecast *vt* prévoir; * *n* prévision *f*.

forefinger *n* index *m*.

forefront *n*: **in the ~ of** au premier plan de.

foregone *adj* passé; anticipé.

foreground *n* premier plan *m*.

forehead *n* front *m*.

foreign *adj* étranger.

foreigner *n* étranger *m* -ère *f*.

foreign exchange *n* devises *fpl*.

foreman *n* contremaître *m*; (*law*) premier juré *m*.

foremost *adj* principal.

forensic *adj* médico-légal.

forerunner *n* précurseur *m*; signe avant-coureur *m*.

foresight *n* prévoyance *f*; prescience *f*.

forest *n* forêt *f*.

forestry *n* sylviculture *f*.

foretaste *n* avant-goût *m*.

forever *adv* toujours; un temps infini.

foreword *n* préface *f*.

forfeit *n* amende *f*; confiscation *f*; * *vt* perdre.

forge *n* forge *f*; usine métallurgique *f*; * *vt* forger; contrefaire * *vi*: **~ ahead** aller de l'avant.

forger *n* faussaire *mf*.

forgery *n* contrefaçon *f*.

forget *vt* *vi* oublier.

forgetful *adj* étourdi; négligent.

forgive *vt* pardonner.

forgiveness *n* pardon *m*; indulgence *f*.

fork *n* fourchette *f*; fourche *f*; * *vi* bifurquer; **~ out** (*sl*) casquer.

forked *adj* fourchu.

fork-lift truck *n* chariot élévateur *m*.

forlorn *adj* malheureux, abandonné.

form *n* forme *f*; formule *f*; formulaire *m*; formalité *f*; moule *m*; * *vt* former.

formal *adj* formel; méthodique; cérémonieux.

formality *n* formalité *f*; cérémonie *f*.

format *n* format *m*; * *vt* formater.

formation *n* formation *f*.

former *adj* précédent, ancien; **~ly** *adv* autrefois, jadis.

formidable *adj* effrayant, terrible.

formula *n* formule *f*.

formulate *vt* formuler.

forsake *vt* abandonner, renoncer à.

fort *n* fort *m*.

forte *n* fort *m*.

forthcoming *adj* prochain; sociable.

forthright *adj* franc.

fortieth *adj n* quarantième *mf*.

fortify *vt* fortifier, renforcer.

fortnight *n* quinze jours *mpl*; deux semaines *fpl*; * *adj* **~ly** bimensuel; * *adv* **~ly** tous les quinze jours.

fortress *n* (*mil*) forteresse *f*.

fortunate *adj* chanceux; **~ly** *adv* heureusement.

fortune *n* chance *f*, sort *m*; fortune *f*.

fortune-teller *n* diseuse de bonne aventure *f*.

forty *adj n* quarante *m*.

forward *adj* avancé; précoce; présomptueux; **~(s)** *adv* en avant, vers l'avant; * *vt* transmettre; promouvoir; expédier.

fossil *adj* fossilisé; * *n* fossile *m.*

foster *vt* encourager.

foster child *n* enfant adoptif *m.*

foster father *n* père adoptif *m.*

foster mother *n* mère adoptive *f.*

foul *adj* infect, ignoble; vil, déloyal; * *vt* polluer.

foul play *n* jeu déloyal *m;* meurtre *m.*

found *vt* fonder, créer; établir, édifier; fondre.

foundation *n* foundation *f,* fondement *m.*

founder *n* fondateur *m* -trice *f;* fondeur *m;* * *vi (mar)* couler.

foundry *n* fonderie *f.*

fountain n **fonta**ine *f.*

four *adj n* quatre *m.*

foursome *n* groupe de quatre personnes *m.*

fourteen *adj n* quatorze *m.*

fourteenth *adj n* quatorzième *mf.*

fourth *adj n* quatrième *mf;* * *n* quart *m.*

fowl *n* volaille *f.*

fox *n* renard *f;* *(fig)* rusé *m.*

foyer *n* vestibule *m.*

fracas *n* rixe *f.*

fraction *n* fraction *f.*

fracture *n* fracture *f,* * *vt* fracturer.

fragile *adj* fragile; frêle.

fragility *n* fragilité *f;* faiblesse, délicatesse *f.*

fragment *n* fragment *m.*

fragrance *n* parfum *m.*

fragrant *adj* parfumé, odorant.

frail *adj* frêle, fragile.

frailty *n* fragilité *f;* faiblesse *f.*

frame *n* charpente *f;* châssis *m,* armature *f;* cadre *m;* structure *f;* monture *f;* * *vt* encadrer; concevoir; construire; former.

frame of mind *n* état d'esprit *m.*

framework *n* charpente *f;* structure *f,* cadre *m.*

franchise *n* droit de vote *m;* franchise *f.*

frank *adj* franc, direct.

frantic *adj* frénétique, effréné.

fraternise *vi* fraterniser.

fraud *n* fraude, tromperie *f.*

fraudulence *n* caractère frauduleux *m.*

fraudulent *adj* frauduleux.

fraught *adj* accablé, tendu.

fray *n* rixe, bagarre, querelle *f.*

freak *n* caprice *m;* phénomène *m.*

freckle *n* tache de rousseur *f.*

free *adj* libre; autonome; gratuit; dégagé; * *vt* affranchir; libérer; débarrasser.

freedom *n* liberté *f.*

free-for-all *n* mêlée générale *f.*

freelance *adj* indépendant; * *adv* en indépendant.

freely *adv* librement; franchement; libéralement.

freemason *n* franc-maçon *m.*

freepost *n* port payé *m.*

free-range *adj* de plein air.

freewheel *vi* rouler en roue libre.

free will *n* libre arbitre *m.*

freeze *vi* geler; * *vt* congeler; geler.

freeze-dried *adj* lyophilisé.

freezer *n* congélateur *m.*

freezing *adj* gelé.

freezing point *n* point de congélation *m.*

freight *n* cargaison *f;* fret *m.*

freighter *n* affréteur *m.*

freight train *n* train de marchandises *m.*

French bean *n* haricot vert *m.*

French window *n* porte-fenêtre *f.*
frenzied *adj* fou, frénétique.
frenzy *n* frénésie *f*; folie *f.*
frequency *n* fréquence *f.*
frequent *adj* fréquent; **~ly** *adv* fréquemment; * *vt* fréquenter.
fresh *adj* frais; nouveau, récent.
freshen *vt* rafraîchir; * *vi* se rafraîchir.
freshly *adv* nouvellement; récemment.
freshness *n* fraîcheur *f.*
freshwater *adj* d'eau douce.
fret *vi* s'agiter, se tracasser.
friar *n* moine *m.*
friction *n* friction *f.*
Friday *n* vendredi *m.*
friend *n* ami *m* -e *f.*
friendly *adj* amical.
friendship *n* amitié *f.*
fright *n* peur, frayeur *f.*
frighten *vt* effrayer.
frightened *adj* effrayé, apeuré.
frightening *adj* effrayant.
frightful *adj* épouvantable, effroyable; **~ly** *adv* affreusement, effroyablement.
frigid *adj* froid, glacé; frigide.
fringe *n* frange *f.*
fringe benefits *npl* avantages *mpl* en nature.
frisk *vt* fouiller.
frisky *adj* vif, fringant.
fritter *vt*: **to ~ away** gaspiller.
frivolity *n* frivolité *f.*
frivolous *adj* frivole, léger.
frizzy *adj* frisé.
fro *adv*: **to go to and ~** aller et venir.
frock *n* robe *f.*
frog *n* grenouille *f.*
frolic *vi* folâtrer, gambader.
from *prep* de; depuis; à partir de.

front *n* avant, devant *m*; façade *f*; front *m*; * *adj* de devant; premier.
front door *n* porte d'entrée *f.*
frontier *n* frontière *f.*
front page *n* première page *f.*
frost *n* gel *m*; gelée *f*; * *vt* geler.
frostbite *n* engelure *f.*
frostbitten *adj* gelé.
frosty *adj* glacial; givré.
froth *n* écume *f*; * *vi* écumer.
frothy *adj* mousseux, écumeux.
frown *vt* froncer les sourcils; * *n* froncement de sourcils *m.*
frozen *adj* gelé.
frugal *adj* frugal; économique; simple.
fruit *n* fruit *m.*
fruitful *adj* fécond, fertile; fructueux, utile.
fruition *n* réalisation *f.*
fruit juice *n* jus de fruit *m.*
fruitless *adj* stérile; infécond.
fruit salad *n* salade de fruits *f.*
frustrated *adj* frustré.
frustration *n* frustration *f.*
fry *vt* frire.
frying pan *n* poêle *f.*
fuchsia *n* (*bot*) fuchsia *m.*
fudge *n* caramel *m* mou.
fuel *n* combustible, carburant *m.*
fuel tank *n* réservoir à carburant *m.*
fugitive *adj n* fugitif *m* -ive *f.*
fulfil *vt* accomplir; réaliser.
fulfilment *n* accomplissement *m.*
full *adj* plein, rempli; complet; * *adv* pleinement, entièrement.
full-blown *adj* complet.
full-length *adj* en pied; de long métrage.
full moon *n* pleine lune *f.*
full-time *adj* à plein temps.

fully *adv* pleinement, entièrement.

fumble *vi* manier gauchement; far-fouiller.

fume *vi* exhaler des vapeurs; rager, fumer; * **~s** *npl* exhalaisons *fpl*.

fumigate *vt* fumiger.

fun *n* amusement *m*; plaisir *m*; **to have ~** (bien) s'amuser.

function *n* fonction *f*.

functional *adj* fonctionnel.

fund *n* fonds *m*; * *vt* financer.

fundamental *adj* fondamental.

funeral *n* enterrement *m*.

fungus *n* champignon *m*; moisissure *f*.

funnel *n* entonnoir *m*; cheminée *f*.

funny *adj* amusant; curieux.

fur *n* fourrure *f*.

fur coat *n* manteau de fourrure *m*.

furious *adj* furieux; déchaîné.

furnace *n* fourneau *m*; chaudière *f*.

furnish *vt* meubler; fournir; pourvoir.

furniture *n* meubles *mpl*.

furrow *n* sillon *m*; * *vt* sillonner; rider.

furry *adj* à poil.

further *adj* supplémentaire; plus lointain; * *adv* plus loin, plus avant; en outre; de plus; * *vt* faire avancer; favoriser; promouvoir.

further education *n* formation *f* postscolaire.

furthest *adv* le plus loin, le plus éloigné.

furtive *adj* furtif; secret.

fury *n* fureur *f*; furie *f*; colère *f*.

fuse *vt* fondre; faire sauter; * *vi* fondre, sauter; * *n* fusible *m*; amorce *f*.

fuse box *n* boîte à fusibles *f*.

fusion *n* fusion *f*.

fuss *n* tapage *m*; histoires *fpl*.

fussy *adj* tatillon, chipoteur.

futile *adj* futile, vain.

futility *n* futilité *f*.

future *adj* futur; * *n* futur *m*; avenir *m*.

fuzzy *adj* flou, confus; crépu.

G

gable *n* pignon *m*.

gadget *n* gadget *m*.

gag *n* bâillon *m*; blague *f*; * *vt* bâillonner.

gaiety *n* gaieté *f*.

gaily *adv* gaiement.

gain *n* gain *m*; bénéfice *m*; * *vt* gagner; atteindre.

galaxy *n* galaxie *f*.

gale *n* grand vent *m*.

gall *n* bile *f*; fiel *m*.

gallant *adj* galant.

gall bladder *n* vésicule biliaire *f*.

gallery *n* galerie *f*.

gallon *n* gallon *m* (mesure).

gallop *n* galop *m*; * *vi* galoper.

gallows *n* potence *f*.

gallstone *n* calcul biliaire *m*.

galore *adv* en abondance.

galvanise *vt* galvaniser.

gambit *n* stratagème *m*.

gamble *vi* jouer; spéculer; * *n* risque *m*; pari *m*.

gambler n joueur m -euse f.

gambling n jeu m (d'argent).

game n jeu m; divertissement m; partie f; gibier m; * vi jouer.

gamekeeper n garde-chasse m.

gammon n jambon m.

gang n gang m, bande f.

gangrene n gangrène f.

gangster n gangster m.

gangway n passerelle f.

gap n trou m; vide m; intervalle, écart m.

gape vi être bouche bée; bâiller.

gaping adj béant.

garage n garage m.

garbled adj confus.

garden n jardin m.

gardener n jardinier m -ière f.

gardening n jardinage m.

gargle vi se gargariser.

gargoyle n gargouille f.

garish adj tapageur.

garland n guirlande f.

garlic n ail m.

garment n vêtement m.

garnish vt garnir, décorer; * n garniture f.

garrison n (mil) garnison f.

garrulous adj locace, bavard.

garter n jarretelle f.

gas n gaz m; essence f.

gas fire n radiateur à gaz m.

gash n entaille f, fente f; * vt entailler.

gasp vi haleter; * n halètements mpl.

gas mask n masque à gaz m.

gas meter n compteur à gaz m.

gassy adj gazeux.

gastric adj gastrique.

gastronomic adj gastronomique.

gasworks npl usine à gaz f.

gate n porte f; portail m.

gateway n porte f.

gather vt rassembler; ramasser; comprendre; * vi se rassembler.

gathering n réunion f; récolte f.

gaudy adj criard.

gauge n calibre m; écartement m; * vt mesurer; calibrer.

gaunt adj décharné.

gauze n gaze f.

gay adj gai; vif; homosexuel.

gaze vi contempler, considérer; * n regard m.

gazelle n gazelle f.

gear n équipement m, matériel m; appareil m; affaires fpl; vitesse f.

gearbox n boîte de vitesses f.

gear wheel n roue d'engrenage f.

gel n gel m.

gelatin(e) n gélatine f.

gelignite n gélignite f.

gem n pierre précieuse f, perle f.

gender n genre m.

gene n gène m.

general adj général; commun, usuel; in ~ en général; ~ly adv généralement; * n général m; générale f.

general election n élections générales fpl.

generalisation n généralisation f.

generalise vt généraliser.

generality n généralité; majeure partie f.

generate vt engendrer; produire; causer.

generation n génération f.

generator n générateur m.

generic adj générique.

generosity n générosité, libéralité f.

generous adj généreux.

genetics npl génétique f.

genial adj cordial; doux.

genitals *npl* organes génitaux *mpl*.

genius *n* génie *m*.

genteel *adj* distingué.

gentle *adj* doux, *f* douce, modéré.

gentleman *n* gentleman *m*.

gently *adv* doucement.

gents *n* toilettes pour hommes *fpl*.

genuine *adj* authentique; sincère.

genus *n* genre *m*.

geography *n* géographie *f*.

geologist *n* géologue *mf*.

geology *n* géologie *f*.

geometry *n* géométrie *f*.

geranium *n* (*bot*) géranium *m*.

geriatric *n* malade gériatrique *mf*; * *adj* gériatrique.

germ *n* (*bot*) germe *m*.

gesticulate *vi* gesticuler.

gesture *n* geste *m*.

get *vt* avoir; obtenir; atteindre; gagner; attraper; * *vi* devenir; aller.

ghastly *adj* affreux; sinistre.

ghost *n* fantôme, spectre *m*.

ghostly *adj* spectral.

giant *n* géant *m* -e *f*.

gibberish *n* charabia *m*; sornettes *fpl*.

gibe *vi* se moquer; * *n* moquerie *f*.

giblets *npl* abattis (de volaille) *mpl*.

giddy *adj* vertigineux.

gift *n* cadeau *m*; don *m*; talent *m*.

gifted *adj* talentueux; doué.

gigantic *adj* gigantesque.

giggle *vi* rire bêtement.

gill *n* quart de pinte *m*; ~s *pl* branchies *fpl*.

gimmick *n* truc *m*.

gin *n* gin *m*.

ginger *n* gingembre *m*.

gingerbread *n* pain d'épice *m*.

ginger-haired *adj* roux, *f* rousse.

giraffe *n* girafe *f*.

girder *n* poutre *f*.

girdle *n* gaine *f*; ceinture *f*.

girl *n* fille *f*.

girlfriend *n* amie *f*; petite amie *f*.

girlish *adj* de fille.

giro *n* virement *m*.

girth *n* sangle *f*; circonférence *f*.

gist *n* essence *f*.

give *vt* donner; offrir; prononcer; faire; consacrer; ~ **away** offrir; trahir; révéler; ~ **back** rendre; ~ **in** *vi* céder; *vt* remettre; ~ **off** dégager; ~ **out** distribuer; ~ **up** *vi* abandonner; *vt* renoncer à.

glacier *n* glacier *m*.

glad *adj* joyeux, content; ~**ly** *adv* avec joie, avec plaisir.

gladiator *n* gladiateur *m*.

glamorous *adj* attrayant, séduisant.

glamour *n* attrait *m*, séduction *f*.

glance *n* regard *m*; * *vi* regarder; jeter un coup d'œil.

gland *n* glande *f*.

glare *n* éclat *m*; regard féroce *m*; * *vi* éblouir, briller; lancer des regards indignés.

glaring *adj* éclatant; évident; furieux.

glass *n* verre *m*; longue-vue *f*; miroir *m*; ~**es** *pl* lunettes *fpl*; * *adj* en verre.

glassy *adj* vitreux, cristallin.

glaze *vt* vitrer; vernisser.

glazier *n* vitrier *m*.

gleam *n* rayon *m*; * *vi* rayonner, briller.

gleaming *adj* brillant.

glee *n* joie *f*; exultation *f*.

glib *adj* facile; volubile.

glide *vi* glisser; planer.

gliding *n* vol plané *m*.

glimpse n aperçu m; vision f; * vt entrevoir.

glint vi briller, scintiller.

glisten, glitter vi luire, briller.

gloat vi exulter.

global adj global; mondial.

globe n globe m; sphère f.

gloom, gloominess n obscurité f; mélancolie, tristesse.

gloomy adj sombre, obscur; triste, mélancolique.

glorify vt glorifier, célébrer.

glorious adj glorieux, illustre.

glory n gloire, célébrité f.

gloss n glose f; lustre m; * vt gloser, interpréter; lustrer; ~ **over** passer sur.

glossy adj lustré, brillant.

glove n gant m.

glow vi rougeoyer; rayonner; * n rougeoiment m; éclat m; feu m.

glower vi lancer des regards noirs.

glue n colle f; * vt coller.

glum adj abattu, triste.

glut n surabondance f.

glutton n glouton m -ne f.

gluttony n gloutonnerie f.

glycerine n glycérine f.

gnarled adj noueux.

gnash vt: **to** ~ **one's teeth** grincer des dents.

gnat n moucheron m.

gnaw vt ronger.

gnome n gnome m.

go vi aller; s'en aller, partir; disparaître; se perdre; ~ **ahead** continuer; ~ **away** s'en aller; ~ **back** repartir; ~ **by** passer; ~ **for** vt se lancer sur; aimer; ~ **in** entrer; ~ **off** s'en aller, partir; se passer; se gâter; ~ **on** continuer; se passer;

~ **out** sortir; s'éteindre; ~ **up** monter.

goad n aiguillon m; * vt aiguillonner; stimuler.

go-ahead adj entreprenant; * n feu vert m.

goal n but, objectif m.

goalkeeper n gardien de but m.

goalpost n poteau de but m.

gobble vt engloutir, avaler.

go-between n intermédiaire mf.

goblet n coupe f.

goblin n lutin m.

God n Dieu m.

godchild n filleul m -e f.

goddess n déesse f.

godfather n parrain m.

godforsaken adj perdu.

godmother n marraine f.

godsend n don du ciel m.

goggles npl lunettes fpl; lunettes de plongée fpl.

gold n or m.

golden adj doré; d'or; excellent.

goldfish n poisson rouge m.

gold-plated adj plaqué or.

goldsmith n orfèvre m.

golf n golf m.

golfer n golfeur m -euse f.

gone adj parti; perdu; passé; fini; mort, disparu.

gong n gong m.

good adj bon; bienveillant; favorable; valable; * adv bien; * n bien m; avantage m; ~**s** pl biens mpl; marchandises fpl.

goodbye ! excl au revoir!

Good Friday n Vendredi Saint m.

good-looking adj beau.

good-natured adj qui a bon caractère.

goodness n bonté f, qualité f.

goodwill n bienveillance f.

goose *n* oie *f*.

gooseberry *n* groseille à maquereau *f*.

gore *n* sang *m*; * *vt* blesser d'un coup de corne.

gorge *n* (*geogr*) gorge *f*; * *vt* engloutir, avaler.

gorgeous *adj* merveilleux.

gorilla *n* gorille *m*.

gorse *n* ajonc *m*.

gory *adj* sanglant.

gospel *n* évangile *m*.

gossamer *n* gaze *f*; toile d'araignée *f*.

gossip *n* commérages, cancans *mpl*; * *vi* cancaner, faire des commérages.

gout *n* goutte *f* (maladie).

govern *vt* gouverner, diriger.

government *n* gouvernement *m*; administration publique *f*.

governor *n* gouverneur *m*.

gown *n* toge *f*; robe *f*; robe de chambre *f*.

grab *vt* saisir.

grace *n* grâce *f*; faveur *f*; pardon *m*; grâces *fpl*; **to say ~** dire le bénédicité; * *vt* orner; honorer.

graceful *adj* gracieux.

gracious *adj* gracieux; favorable.

grade *n* grade *m*; degré *m*; classe *f*.

gradual *adj* graduel.

graduate *vi* obtenir son diplôme.

graduation *n* remise des diplômes *f*.

graffiti *n* graffiti *mpl*.

graft *n* greffe *f*; * *vt* greffer.

grain *n* grain *m*; graine *f*; céréales *fpl*.

gram *n* gramme *m*.

grammar *n* grammaire *f*.

grammatical *adj* **~ly** *adv* grammatical(lement).

grand *adj* grandiose; magnifique.

grandchild *n* petit-fils *m*; petite-fille *f*;

grandchildren *pl* petits-enfants *mpl*.

grandad *n* pépé *m*.

granddaughter *n* petite-fille *f*.

grandeur *n* grandeur *f*; pompe *f*.

grandfather *n* grand-père *m*.

grandiose *adj* grandiose.

grandmother *n* grand-mère *f*.

grandparents *npl* grands-parents *mpl*.

grand piano *n* piano à queue *m*.

grandson *n* petit-fils *m*.

grandstand *n* tribune *f*.

granite *n* granit *m*.

granny *n* mamie *f*.

grant *vt* accorder; **to take for ~ed** considérer comme acquis; * *n* bourse *f*; allocation *f*.

granule *n* granule *m*.

grape *n* grain *m* de raisin.

grapefruit *n* pamplemousse *m*.

graph *n* graphe, graphique *m*.

graphic(al) *adj* graphique; pittoresque.

graphics *n* art graphique *m*; graphiques *mpl*.

grasp *vt* saisir, empoigner; comprendre; * *n* poigne *f*, compréhension *f*; prise *f*.

grasping *adj* avide.

grass *n* herbe *f*.

grasshopper *n* sauterelle *f*.

grass-roots *adj* populaire; de base.

grass snake *n* couleuvre *f*.

grassy *adj* herbeux.

grate *n* grille *f*; * *vt* râper; grincer (des dents); * *vi* grincer.

grateful *adj* reconnaissant.

gratification *n* satisfaction *f*.

gratifying *adj* réjouissant.

grating *n* grillage *m*; grincement *m*; * *adj* grinçant; énervant.

gratis *adv* gratis, gratuitement.

gratitude *n* gratitude, reconnaissance *f*.

gratuitous *adj* gratuit; volontaire.

gratuity *n* gratification *f*.

grave *n* tombe *f*; * *adj* grave, sérieux.

grave digger *n* fossoyeur *m*.

gravel *n* gravier *m*.

gravestone *n* pierre tombale *f*.

graveyard *n* cimetière *m*.

gravitate *vi* graviter.

gravity *n* gravité *f*.

gravy *n* jus de viande *m*; sauce *f*.

graze *vt* paître; effleurer; * *vi* paître.

grease *n* graisse *f*; * *vt* graisser.

greaseproof *adj* (papier) sulfurisé.

greasy *adj* gras.

great *adj* grand; important; fort; **~ly** *adv* énormément.

greatness *n* grandeur *f*; importance *f*; pouvoir *m*; noblesse *f*.

greediness, greed *n* avidité *f*; gloutonnerie *f*.

greedy *adj* avide; glouton.

Greek *n* grec *m*; Grec *m* Grecque *f*.

green *adj* vert; inexpérimenté; * *n* vert *m*; verdure *f*.

greengrocer *n* marchand(e) de fruits et légumes *m(f)*.

greenhouse *n* serre *f*.

greet *vt* saluer; accueillir.

greeting *n* salutation *f*; accueil *m*.

greeting(s) card *n* carte de vœux *f*.

grenade *n* (*mil*) grenade *f*.

grenadier *n* grenadier *m*.

grey *adj* gris; * *n* gris *m*.

greyhound *n* lévrier *m*.

grid *n* grille *f*; réseau *m*.

grief *n* chagrin *m*, douleur, peine *f*.

grievance *n* grief *m*; doléance *f*; différend *m*; injustice *f*; tort *m*.

grieve *vt* peiner, affliger; * *vi* se chagriner, s'affliger.

grievous *adj* douloureux; grave, atroce.

grill *n* gril *m*; grillade *f*; * *vt* faire griller; interroger, cuisiner.

grim *adj* peu engageant; sinistre.

grimace *n* grimace *f*; moue *f*.

grime *n* saleté *f*.

grin *n* grimace *f*, sourire *m*; * *vi* grimacer; sourire.

grind *vt* moudre; piler, broyer; affûter, aiguiser; * *vi* grincer.

grip *n* prise *f*; poignée *f*; sac *m* de voyage; * *vt* saisir, agripper.

gripping *adj* passionnant.

grisly *adj* horrible; sinistre.

gristle *n* cartilage *m*.

grit *n* gravillon *m*; cran *m*.

groan *vi* gémir; grogner; * *n* gémissement *m*; grognement *m*.

groceries *npl* épicerie *f*, provisions *fpl*.

groggy *adj* sonné, étourdi.

groin *n* aine *f*.

groom *n* palefrenier *m*; valet *m*; marié *m*; * *vt* panser; préparer.

groove *n* rainure *f*.

grope *vt* chercher à tâtons; * *vi* tâtonner.

gross *adj* gros, corpulent; épais; grossier; brut; **~ly** *adv* énormément.

grotto *n* grotte *f*.

ground *n* terre *f*, sol *m*; terrain, territoire *m*; fondement *m*; raison fondamentale *f*, fond *m*; * *vt* retenir au sol; fonder; mettre une prise de terre à.

ground floor *n* rez-de-chaussée *m*.

grounding *n* connaissances de base *fpl*.

groundless *adj* sans fondement.

groundwork *n* travaux de préparation *mpl*.

group *n* groupe *m*; * *vt* regrouper.

grouse n grouse f, coq de bruyère m; * vi grogner.

grove n bosquet m.

grovel vi se traîner; ramper.

grow vt cultiver; faire pousser; * vi pousser; grandir; augmenter; ~ up grandir.

growl vi grogner; * n grognement m.

grown-up n adulte mf.

growth n croissance f, augmentation f; poussée f.

grub n asticot m.

grubby adj sale.

grudge n rancune f; * vt accorder à contrecœur; vi avoir de la rancune.

grudgingly adv à contrecœur.

gruelling adj difficile, pénible.

gruesome adj horrible.

gruff adj brusque.

grumble vi grogner; grommeler.

grumpy adj ronchon, grincheux.

grunt vi grogner; * n grognement m.

guarantee n garantie f; * vt garantir.

guard n garde f; garde m; * vt garder; défendre.

guarded adj prudent; surveillé.

guardian n tuteur m -trice f; gardien m -ne f.

guerrilla n guérillero m.

guess vt deviner; supposer; * vi deviner; * n conjecture f.

guesswork n conjectures fpl.

guest n invité m -ée f; client m -e f.

guffaw n éclat de rire m.

guidance n guidage m; direction f.

guide vt guider, diriger; * n guide m.

guidebook n guide m.

guide dog n chien d'aveugle m.

guidelines npl directives fpl.

guile n astuce f.

guillotine n guillotine f; * vt guillotiner.

guilt n culpabilité f.

guilty adj coupable.

guinea pig n cochon d'Inde, cobaye m.

guise n apparence f.

guitar n guitare f.

gulf n golfe m; abîme m.

gull n mouette f.

gullet n œsophage m.

gullible adj crédule.

gulp n gorgée f; * vt vi avaler.

gum n gomme f, gencive f; chewing-gum m; * vt coller.

gun n pistolet m; fusil m.

gunfire n coups de feu mpl.

gunpoint n: at ~ sous la menace d'une arme à feu.

gunpowder n poudre à canon f.

gurgle vi gargouiller.

guru n gourou m.

gush vi jaillir; bouillonner; * n jaillissement m.

gushing adj jaillissant; très exubérant.

gusset n soufflet m.

gust n rafale f; bouffée f.

gusto n plaisir m, délectation f.

gut n intestin m; ~s npl cœur au ventre m; * vt vider.

gutter n gouttière f; caniveau m.

guy n mec, type m.

guzzle vt bouffer, engloutir; avaler.

gym(nasium) n gymnase m.

gymnast n gymnaste mf.

gymnastic adj gymnastique; ~s npl gymnastique f.

gypsy n gitan m -e f.

gyrate vi tourner.

H

habit n habitude f.
habitat n habitat m.
habitual adj habituel.
hack vt entailler, couper.
hackneyed adj rebattu.
haddock n aiglefin m.
haemorrhage n hémorragie f.
hag n sorcière f.
haggard adj exténué; défait.
haggle vi marchander.
hail n grêle f; * vt saluer; * vi grêler.
hailstone n grêlon m.
hair n cheveux mpl; poil m.
hairbrush n brosse à cheveux f.
haircut n coupe de cheveux f.
hairdresser n coiffeur m -euse f.
hairdryer n séchoir à cheveux m.
hair remover n crème dépilatoire f.
hairspray n laque à cheveux f.
hairstyle n coiffure f.
hairy adj chevelu; poilu.
hale adj vigoureux.
half n moitié f; * adj demi; * adv à moitié.
half-hearted adj peu enthousiaste.
half-hour n demi-heure f.
half-price adj à moitié prix.
half-time n mi-temps f.
halfway adv à mi-chemin.
hall n vestibule m.
hallmark n marque f.
hallucination n hallucination f.
halo n halo m.
halt vi s'arrêter; * n arrêt m; halte f.
halve vt couper en deux.
ham n jambon m.

hammer n marteau m; * vt marteler.
hammock n hamac m.
hamper n panier m; * vt embarrasser, entraver.
hand n main f; ouvrier m -ière f; aiguille f; **at ~** à portée de main; * vt donner, passer.
handbag n sac à main m.
handbrake n frein à main m.
handcuff n menotte f.
handful n poignée f.
handicap n handicap m.
handicapped adj handicapé.
handicraft n artisanat m.
handiwork n travail manuel m.
handkerchief n mouchoir m.
handle n manche m, queue f; anse f; poignée f; * vt manier; traiter, prendre.
handlebars npl guidon m.
handshake n poignée de mains f.
handsome adj beau; **~ly** adv élégamment.
handwriting n écriture f.
handy adj pratique; adroit.
hang vt accrocher; pendre; * vi pendre, être accroché; être pendu.
hanger n cintre m.
hanger-on n parasite m.
hangover n gueule de bois f.
hang-up n complexe m.
hanker vi avoir envie.
haphazard adj fortuit.
hapless adj malheureux.
happen vi se passer; **I ~ to have one** il se trouve que j'en ai un.

happily *adv* heureusement; gaiement.

happiness *n* bonheur *m*.

happy *adj* heureux.

harangue *n* harangue *f*; * *vt* haranguer.

harass *vt* harceler; tourmenter.

harbinger *n* précurseur *m*.

harbour *n* port *m*; * *vt* héberger; entretenir, nourrir.

hard *adj* dur; pénible; sévère, rigide; ~ **of hearing** dur d'oreille.

harden *vt vi* durcir.

hard-headed *adj* réaliste.

hard-hearted *adj* au cœur dur, insensible.

hardly *adv* à peine; ~ **ever** presque jamais.

hardship *n* épreuve(s) *f(pl)*.

hard-up *adj* fauché, sans le sou.

hardware *n* matériel *m*; quincaillerie *f*.

hardwearing *adj* résistant.

hardy *adj* fort, robuste; résistant.

hare *n* lièvre *m*.

hare-brained *adj* écervelé.

harm *n* mal *m*; tort *m*; * *vt* faire du mal à; nuire à.

harmful *adj* nuisible.

harmless *adj* inoffensif.

harmonious *adj* harmonieux.

harmonise *vt* harmoniser.

harmony *n* harmonie *f*.

harness *n* harnais *m*; * *vt* harnacher.

harp *n* harpe *f*.

harpoon *n* harpon *m*.

harpsichord *n* clavecin *m*.

harrow *n* herse *f*.

harry *vt* harceler; dévaster.

harsh *adj* dur; austère; rude.

harvest *n* récolte *f*; moisson *f*; * *vt* récolter; moissonner.

harvester *n* moissonneur *m* -euse *f*; moissonneuse *f* (machine).

haste *n* hâte *f*.

hastily *adv* à la hâte, précipitamment.

hasty *adj* hâtif; irréfléchi.

hat *n* chapeau *m*.

hatch *vt* couver; faire éclore; tramer; * *n* écoutille *f*.

hatchback *n* (*auto*) voiture à hayon arrière *f*.

hatchet *n* hachette *f*.

hate *n* haine *f*; * *vt* haïr, détester.

hateful *adj* odieux, détestable.

hatred *n* haine *f*.

haughtiness *n* orgueil *m*; hauteur *f*.

haughty *adj* hautain, orgueil-leux.

haul *vt* tirer; * *n* prise *f*; butin *m*.

haunt *vt* hanter; fréquenter; * *n* repaire *m*.

have *vt* avoir; posséder.

haven *n* refuge *m*.

havoc *n* ravages *mpl*.

hawk *n* faucon *m*; * *vi* chasser au faucon.

hawthorn *n* aubépine *f*.

hay *n* foin *m*.

hay fever *n* rhume des foins *m*.

hazard *n* risque, danger *m*; * *vt* risquer.

hazardous *adj* risqué, dangereux.

haze *n* brume *f*.

hazel *adj* noisette.

hazelnut *n* noisette *f*.

hazy *adj* brumeux.

he *pn* il.

head *n* tête *f*; chef *m*; esprit *m*; * *vt* conduire; ~ **for** se diriger vers.

headache *n* mal de tête *m*.

headlight *n* phare *m*.

headline *n* titre *m*.

headlong *adv* à toute allure.

headmaster *n* directeur *m*.

head office n siège social m.

headphones npl écouteurs mpl.

headquarters npl (mil) quartier général m; siège social m.

headstrong adj têtu.

headway n progrès m(pl).

heal vt vi guérir.

health n santé f.

healthy adj en bonne santé; sain.

heap n tas m; * vt entasser.

hear vt entendre; écouter; * vi entendre; avoir des nouvelles.

hearing n ouïe f.

hearing aid n audiophone m.

hearsay n rumeur f.

hearse n corbillard m.

heart n cœur m; **by ~** par cœur; **with all my ~** de tout cœur.

heart attack n crise cardiaque f.

heartbreaking adj à fendre le cœur.

heartburn n acidité f gastrique.

heartfelt adj sincère.

hearth n foyer m.

heartily adv sincèrement, cordialement.

heartless adj cruel.

heat n chaleur f; * vt chauffer.

heater n radiateur m.

heather n (bot) bruyère f.

heathen n païen m, païenne f.

heating n chauffage m.

heatwave n onde de chaleur f.

heave vt lever; tirer; * n effort m.

heaven n ciel m.

heavenly adj divin.

heavy adj lourd, pesant; considérable.

Hebrew n hébreu m (langue).

heckle vt interrompre.

hectic adj agité.

hedge n haie f; * vt entourer d'une haie.

hedgehog n hérisson m.

heed vt tenir compte de; * n soin m; attention f.

heel n talon m.

hefty adj costaud, puissant.

height n hauteur f; altitude f.

heighten vt rehausser; augmenter; intensifier.

heir n héritier m.

heiress n héritière f.

heirloom n héritage m.

helicopter n hélicoptère m.

hell n enfer m.

hellish adj infernal.

helmet n casque m.

help vt aider, secourir; **I cannot ~ it** je n'y peux rien; je ne peux pas m'en empêcher; * n aide f; secours m.

helpful adj utile; qui rend service.

helping n portion f.

helpless adj impuissant; **~ly** adv désespérément; sans pouvoir rien faire.

helter-skelter adv n'importe comment, en désordre.

hem n ourlet m; * vt ourler.

hemisphere n hémisphère m.

hemp n chanvre m.

hen n poule f.

henchman n acolyte m.

henceforth, henceforward adv dorénavant.

hepatitis n hépatite f.

her pn son, sa, ses; elle; la; lui.

herb n herbe f; **~s** pl fines herbes fpl.

herbaceous adj herbacé.

herd n troupeau m.

here adv ici.

hereditary adj héréditaire.

heredity n hérédité f.

heresy n hérésie f.

heretic n, adj hérétique mf.

heritage n patrimoine, héritage m.

hermit n ermite m.

hernia n hernie f.

hero n héros m.

heroic adj héroïque.

heroine n héroïne f.

heroism n héroïsme m.

heron n héron m.

herring n hareng m.

hers pn le sien, la sienne, le(s) sien(ne)s, à elle.

herself pn elle-même.

hesitant adj hésitant.

hesitate vi hésiter.

hesitation n hésitation f.

heterosexual adj n hétérosexuel m -le f.

hew vt tailler; couper.

heyday n apogée m.

hi excl salut!

hibernate vi hiberner.

hiccup n hoquet m; * vi avoir le hoquet.

hide vt cacher; * n cuir m; peau f.

hideaway n cachette f.

hideous adj hideux; horrible.

hiding-place n cachette f.

hierarchy n hiérarchie f.

hieroglyphic n hiéroglyphe m.

hi-fi n hi-fi f invar.

higgledy-piggledy adv pêle-mêle.

high adj haut; élevé.

high chair n chaise haute f.

high-handed adj tyrannique.

highlight n point fort m.

highly adv extrêmement, hautement.

high school n lycée m.

high-strung adj nerveux, tendu.

hike vi faire une randonnée.

hijack vt détourner.

hijacker n pirate de l'air m.

hilarious adj hilarant; hilare.

hill n colline f.

hillock n petite colline f.

hillside n coteau m.

hilly adj montagneux.

hilt n poignée f.

him pn lui; le.

himself pn lui-même; soi.

hind adj derrière.

hinder vt gêner, entraver.

hindrance n gêne f, obstacle m.

hindmost adj dernier.

hindsight n: with ~ rétrospectivement.

hinge n charnière f, gond m.

hint n allusion f; insinuation f; * vt insinuer; suggérer.

hip n hanche f.

hippopotamus n hippopotame m.

hire vt louer; * n location f.

his pn son, sa, ses; le sien, la sienne, les sien(ne)s; à lui.

Hispanic adj hispanique.

hiss vt vi siffler.

historic(al) adj historique.

history n histoire f.

hit vt frapper; atteindre; heurter; * n coup m; succès m.

hitch vt accrocher; * n nœud m; anicroche f.

hitchhike vi faire du stop.

hive n ruche f.

hoard n stock m; trésor caché m; * vt accumuler, amasser.

hoarse adj rauque.

hoax n canular m; * vt faire un canular à.

hobble *vi* boitiller.

hobby *n* passe-temps *m invar*.

hobbyhorse *n* cheval de bataille *m*.

hockey *n* hockey *m*.

hoe *n* binette *f*; * *vt* biner.

hoist *vt* hisser; * *n* grue *f*.

hold *vt* tenir; détenir; contenir; ~ **on to** se tenir à; * *vi* valoir; * *n* prise *f*; pouvoir *m*.

holdup *n* hold-up *m*; retard *m*.

hole *n* trou *m*.

holiday *n* jour de congé *m*; jour férié *m*; ~s *pl* vacances *fpl*.

hollow *adj* creux; * *n* creux *m*; * *vt* creuser, vider.

holly *n* (*bot*) houx *m*.

holocaust *n* holocauste *m*.

holster *n* étui de révolver *m*.

holy *adj* saint; bénit; sacré.

holy water *n* eau bénite *f*.

homage *n* hommage *m*.

home *n* maison *f*; patrie *f*; domicile *m*; ~**ly** *adj* simple.

homeless *adj* sans abri.

home-made *adj* fait maison.

homesick *adj* nostalgique, qui a le mal du pays.

hometown *n* ville natale *f*.

homeward *adj* vers chez soi; vers son pays.

homework *n* devoirs *mpl*.

homicidal *adj* homicide.

homicide *n* homicide *m*; homicide *mf*.

homoeopathy *n* homéopathie *f*.

homosexual *adj n* homosexuel *m* -le *f*.

honest *adj* honnête.

honesty *n* honnêteté *f*.

honey *n* miel *m*.

honeycomb *n* rayon de miel *m*.

honeymoon *n* lune de miel *f*.

honeysuckle *n* (*bot*) chèvrefeuille *m*.

honorary *adj* honoraire.

honour *n* honneur *m*; * *vt* honorer.

honourable *adj* honorable.

honourably *adv* honorablement.

hood *n* capot *m*; capuche *f*.

hoof *n* sabot *m*.

hook *n* crochet *m*; hameçon *m*; * *vt* accrocher.

hooligan *n* vandale *m*.

hoop *n* cerceau *m*.

hop *n* (*bot*) houblon *m*; saut *m*; * *vi* sauter.

hope *n* espoir *m*, espérance *f*; * *vi* espérer.

hopeful *adj* plein d'espoir; prometteur.

hopeless *adj* désespéré.

horde *n* horde *f*.

horizon *n* horizon *m*.

horizontal *adj* horizontal.

hormone *n* hormone *f*.

horn *n* corne *f*.

hornet *n* frelon *m*.

horoscope *n* horoscope *m*.

horrendous *adj* horrible.

horrible *adj* horrible.

horribly *adv* horriblement; énormément.

horrid *adj* horrible.

horrific *adj* horrible, affreux.

horrify *vt* horrifier.

horror *n* horreur *f*.

horror film *n* film d'horreur *m*.

horse *n* cheval *m*.

horseback *adv*: on ~ à cheval.

horse chestnut *n* marron d'Inde *m*.

horsepower *n* cheval-vapeur *m*; puissance en chevaux *f*.

horse race *n* course de chevaux *f*.

horseradish *n* raifort *m*.

horseshoe n fer à cheval m.
horticulture n horticulture f.
horticulturist n horticulteur m -trice f.
hose-pipe n tuyau m.
hosiery n bonneterie f.
hospitable adj hospitalier.
hospitably adv avec hospitalité.
hospital n hôpital m.
hospitality n hospitalité f.
host n hôte m; hostie f.
hostage n otage m.
hostess n hôtesse f.
hostile adj hostile.
hostility n hostilité f.
hot adj chaud; épicé.
hotel n hôtel m.
hotheaded adj exalté.
hotline n téléphone rouge m.
hotplate n plaque chauffante f.
hound n chien de chasse m.
hour n heure f.
hourly adv toutes les heures.
house n maison f, maisonnée f; * vt loger.
houseboat n péniche f.
housebreaking n cambriolage m.
household n famille f, ménage m.
housekeeper n gouvernante f.
house-warming party n pendaison de crémaillère f.
housewife n ménagère f.
housework n travaux ménagers mpl.
housing n logement m.
hovel n taudis m.
hover vi planer.
how adv comme; comment; ~ **do you do!** enchanté.
however adv de quelque manière que; cependant, néanmoins.
howl vi hurler; * n hurlement m.

hub n centre m; moyeu m.
hubbub n vacarme m.
hubcap n enjoliveur m.
huff n: in a ~ fâché.
hug vt étreindre; * n étreinte f.
huge adj énorme.
hulk n (mar) carcasse f; ponton m.
hull n (mar) coque f.
hum vi chantonner.
human adj humain.
humane adj humain.
humanitarian adj humanitaire.
humanity n humanité f.
humble adj humble, modeste; * vt humilier.
humdrum adj monotone.
humid adj humide.
humidity n humidité f.
humiliate vt humilier.
humiliation n humiliation f.
humility n humilité f.
humorist n humoriste mf.
humorous adj humoristique.
humour n sens de l'humour m, humour m; * vt complaire à.
hump n bosse f.
hunch n intuition f; ~**backed** adj bossu.
hundred adj cent; * n centaine f.
hundredth adj centième.
hundredweight n quintal m.
hunger n faim f; * vi avoir faim.
hunger strike n grève de la faim f.
hungrily adv avidement.
hungry adj qui a faim, affamé.
hunt vt chasser; poursuivre; chercher; * vi chasser; * n chasse f.
hunter n chasseur m.
hunting n chasse f.
hurdle n haie f.

hurl *vt* lancer avec violence, jeter.

hurricane *n* ouragan *m*.

hurried *adj* fait à la hâte; précipité; **~ly** *adv* hâtivement; précipitamment.

hurry *vt* presser; * *vi* se presser, se dépêcher; * *n* hâte *f*.

hurt *vt* faire mal à; blesser.

hurtful *adj* blessant.

husband *n* mari *m*.

husk *n* coque *f* (graine).

husky *adj* rauque.

hustle *vt* pousser avec force, bousculer.

hut *n* cabane, hutte *f*.

hutch *n* clapier *m*.

hyacinth *n* jacinthe *f*.

hydraulic *adj* hydraulique; **~s** *npl* hydraulique *f*.

hydroelectric *adj* hydroélectrique.

hydrofoil *n* hydroptère *m*.

hydrogen *n* hydrogène *m*.

hyena *n* hyène *f*.

hygiene *n* hygiène *f*.

hygienic *adj* hygiénique.

hymn *n* hymne *m*.

hyphen *n* (*gr*) trait d'union *m*.

hypochondriac *adj n* hypocondriaque *mf*.

hypocrisy *n* hypocrisie *f*.

hypocrite *n* hypocrite *mf*.

hypocritical *adj* hypocrite.

hypothetical *adj* **~ly** *adv* hypothétique(ment).

hysterical *adj* hystérique.

hysterics *npl* hystérie *f*; crise de nerfs *f*.

I

I *pn* je, j'; moi

ice *n* glace *f*; * *vt* glacer; geler.

ice-axe *n* piolet *m*.

iceberg *n* iceberg *m*.

ice cream *n* glace *f*.

ice rink *n* patinoire *f*.

ice skating *n* patinage sur glace *m*.

icicle *n* stalactite *f*, glaçon *m*.

icy *adj* glacé.

idea *n* idée *f*.

ideal *adj* idéal.

idealist *n* idéaliste *mf*.

identical *adj* identique.

identification *n* identification *f*.

identify *vt* identifier.

identity *n* identité *f*.

ideology *n* idéologie *f*.

idiom *n* expression idiomatique *f*.

idiomatic *adj* idiomatique.

idiosyncrasy *n* idiosyncrasie *f*.

idiot *n* imbécile *mf*.

idiotic *adj* idiot, bête.

idle *adj* désœuvré; au repos; inutile.

idleness *n* paresse *f*; oisiveté *f*.

idol *n* idole *f*.

idolise *vt* idôlatrer.

idyllic *adj* idyllique.

i.e. *adv* c.-à-d., c'est-à-dire.

if *conj* si; **~ not** sinon.

ignite *vt* allumer, enflammer.

ignition *n* (*chem*) ignition *f*; allumage *m*.

ignition key *n* clé de contact *f*.

ignoble *adj* infâme; bas.

ignominious *adj* ignominieux.

ignoramus *n* ignorant *m* -e *f*.

ignorance *n* ignorance *f*.

ignorant *adj* ignorant.

ignore *vt* ne pas tenir compte de.

ill *adj* malade; * *n* mal *m*; dommage *m*; * *adv* mal.

ill-advised *adj* malavisé.

illegal *adj* ~ly *adv* illégal(ement).

illegible *adj* illisible.

illegibly *adv* illisiblement.

illegitimate *adj* illégitime.

ill feeling *n* rancœur *f*.

illicit *adj* illicite.

illiterate *adj* analphabète, illettré.

illness *n* maladie *f*.

illogical *adj* illogique.

illumination *n* illumination *f*.

illusion *n* illusion *f*.

illusory *adj* illusoire.

illustrate *vt* illustrer.

illustration *n* illustration *f*.

illustrious *adj* illustre.

ill-will *n* malveillance *f*.

image *n* image *f*.

imagery *n* images *fpl*.

imaginable *adj* imaginable.

imaginary *adj* imaginaire.

imagination *n* imagination *f*.

imaginative *adj* imaginatif.

imagine *vt* imaginer.

imbalance *n* déséquilibre *m*.

imbecile *adj* imbécile, idiot.

imitate *vt* imiter.

imitation *n* imitation *f*.

immaculate *adj* immaculé.

immaterial *adj* insignifiant.

immature *adj* pas mûr.

immediate *adj* immédiat; ~ly *adv* immédiatement.

immense *adj* immense; énorme.

immerse *vt* immerger.

immersion *n* immersion *f*.

immigrant *n* immigrant *m* -e *f*.

immigration *n* immigration *f*.

imminent *adj* imminent.

immobile *adj* immobile.

immobility *n* immobilité *f*.

immodest *adj* immodeste.

immoral *adj* immoral.

immorality *n* immoralité *f*.

immortal *adj* immortel.

immortalise *vt* immortaliser.

immortality *n* immortalité *f*.

immune *adj* immunisé.

immunise *vt* immuniser.

immunity *n* immunité *f*.

imp *n* lutin *m*.

impact *n* impact *m*.

impair *vt* diminuer; affaiblir.

impale *vt* empaler.

impart *vt* communiquer.

impartial *adj* ~ly *adv* impartial(ement).

impartiality *n* impartialité *f*.

impassable *adj* impraticable; infranchissable.

impasse *n* impasse *f*.

impatience *n* impatience *f*.

impatient *adj* impatient.

impeach *vt* (*law*) mettre en accusation.

impeccable *adj* impeccable.

impediment *n* obstacle *m*.

impending *adj* imminent.

impenetrable *adj* impénétrable.

imperative *adj* impératif.

imperceptible *adj* imperceptible.

imperfect *adj* ~ly impar-fait(ement); *
n (*gr*) imparfait *m*.

imperfection *n* imperfection *f*; défaut *m*.

imperial *adj* impérial.

imperialism *n* impérialisme *m*.

imperious *adj* impérieux.

impersonal *adj* ~ly *adv* impersonel(lement).

impersonate *vt* se faire passer pour;
imiter.

impertinence *n* impertinence *f*.

impertinent *adj* impertinent.

imperturbable *adj* imperturbable.

impervious *adj* imperméable; indifférent.

impetuous *adj* impétueux.

impetus *n* élan *m*.

impinge (on) *vi* affecter; empiéter (sur).

implacable *adj* implacable.

implant *vt* implanter.

implement *n* outil *m*; ustensile *m*.

implicate *vt* impliquer.

implication *n* implication *f*.

implicit *adj* implicite.

implore *vt* supplier.

imply *vt* supposer.

impolite *adj* impoli.

import *vt* importer; * *n* importation *f*.

importance *n* importance *f*.

important *adj* important.

importer *n* importateur *m* -trice *f*.

impose *vt* imposer.

imposing *adj* imposant.

imposition *n* imposition *f*.

impossibility *n* impossibilité *f*.

impossible *adj* impossible.

impostor *n* imposteur *m*.

impotence *n* impotence *f*.

impotent *adj* impotent.

impound *vt* confisquer.

impoverished *adj* appauvri.

impracticable *adj* impraticable.

impractical *adj* peu pratique.

imprecise *adj* imprécis.

impregnable *adj* inexpugnable.

impregnate *vt* imprégner; féconder.

impregnation *n* fécondation *f*; imprégnation *f*.

impress *vt* impressionner.

impression *n* impression *f*; édition *f*.

impressionable *adj* impressionnable.

impressive *adj* impressionnant.

imprint *n* empreinte *f*.

imprison *vt* emprisonner.

imprisonment *n* emprisonnement *m*.

improbable *adj* improbable.

impromptu *adj* impromptu.

improper *adj* indécent; déplacé; impropre.

impropriety *n* impropriété *f*; inconvenance *f*.

improve *vt* améliorer; * *vi* s'améliorer.

improvement *n* amélioration *f*.

improvise *vt* improviser.

imprudence *n* imprudence *f*.

imprudent *adj* imprudent.

impudence *n* impudence *f*.

impudent *adj* impudent.

impulse *n* impulsion *f*.

impulsive *adj* impulsif.

impunity *n* impunité *f*.

impure *adj* impur.

impurity *n* impureté *f*.

in *prep* dans; en.

inability *n* incapacité *f*.

inaccessible *adj* inaccessible.

inaccuracy *n* inexactitude *f*.

inaccurate *adj* inexact.

inaction *n* inaction *f*.

inactive *adj* inactif.

inactivity *n* inactivité *f.*

inadequate *adj* inadéquat.

inadvertently *adv* par inadvertance.

inane *adj* inepte.

inanimate *adj* inanimé.

inapplicable *adj* inapplicable.

inappropriate *adj* impropre.

inattentive *adj* inattentif.

inaudible *adj* inaudible.

inauguration *n* inauguration *f.*

in-between *adj* intermédiaire.

inborn, inbred *adj* inné.

incalculable *adj* incalculable.

incandescent *adj* incandescent.

incapable *adj* incapable.

incapacitate *vt* mettre dans l'incapacité.

incapacity *n* incapacité *f.*

incarcerate *vt* incarcérer.

incautious *adj* imprudent.

incendiary *n* bombe incendiaire *f;* incendiaire *mf*

incense *n* encens *m;* * *vt* exaspérer.

incentive *n* stimulant *m;* prime, aide *f*

incessant *adj* incessant, continuel.

incest *n* inceste *m.*

incestuous *adj* incestueux.

inch *n* pouce *m;* ~ **by** ~ petit à petit.

incidence *n* fréquence *f.*

incident *n* incident *m.*

incidental *adj* fortuit; **~ly** *adv* incidemment.

incinerator *n* incinérateur *m.*

incision *n* incision *f.*

incisive *adj* incisif.

incisor *n* incisive *f.*

incite *vt* inciter, encourager.

inclement *adj* inclément.

inclination *n* inclination, propension *f.*

incline *vt* incliner; * *vi* s'incliner.

include *vt* inclure, comprendre.

including *prep* inclus, y compris.

inclusion *n* inclusion *f.*

inclusive *adj* inclus; tout compris.

incognito *adv* incognito.

incoherence *n* incohérence *f.*

incoherent *adj* incohérent.

income *n* revenu *m;* recettes *fpl.*

income tax *n* impôt sur le revenu *m.*

incoming *adj* entrant; nouveau.

incomparable *adj* incomparable.

incompatible *adj* incompatible.

incompetence *n* incompétence *f.*

incompetent *adj* incompétent.

incomplete *adj* incomplet.

incomprehensible *adj* incompréhensible.

inconceivable *adj* inconcevable.

inconclusive *adj* peu concluant; * *adv* d'une manière peu concluante.

incongruous *adj* incongru.

inconsequential *adj* inconséquent.

inconsiderate *adj* sans considération; inconsidéré.

inconsistency *n* inconsistance *f.*

inconsistent *adj* inconsistant.

inconsolable *adj* inconsolable.

inconspicuous *adj* discret.

incontinence *n* incontinence *f.*

incontinent *adj* incontinent.

incontrovertible *adj* indéniable.

inconvenience *n* inconvénient, désagrément *m;* * *vt* incommoder.

inconvenient *adj* incommode.

incorporate *vt* incorporer; * *vi* s'incorporer.

incorrect *adj* incorrect, inexact.

incorrigible *adj* incorrigible.

incorruptible *adj* incorruptible.

increase *vt vi* augmenter; * *n* augmentation *f.*

increasing *adj* croissant; *adv* ~**ly** de plus en plus.
incredible *adj* incroyable.
incredulity *n* incrédulité *f*.
incredulous *adj* incrédule.
increment *n* augmentation *f*.
incriminate *vt* incriminer.
incubator *n* couveuse *f*.
incumbent *adj* en exercice; * *n* titulaire *mf*.
incur *vt* encourir.
incurable *adj* incurable.
incursion *n* incursion *f*.
indebted *adj* endetté; redevable.
indecency *n* indécence *f*.
indecent *adj* indécent.
indecision *n* indécision, irrésolution *f*.
indecisive *adj* indécis, irrésolu.
indecorous *adj* inconvenant.
indeed *adv* vraiment.
indefatigable *adj* infatigable.
indefinite *adj* ~**ly** *adv* indéfini(ment).
indelible *adj* indélébile.
indemnity *n* indemnité *f*.
indent *vt* bosseler; renfoncer.
independence *n* indépendance *f*.
independent *adj* indépendant.
indescribable *adj* indescriptible.
indestructible *adj* indestructible.
indeterminate *adj* indéterminé.
index *n* (*math*) indice *m*; index *m*.
index finger *n* index *m*.
indicate *vt* indiquer.
indication *n* indication *f*; indice *m*.
indicator *n* indicateur *m*.
indictment *n* accusation *f*.
indifference *n* indifférence *f*.
indifferent *adj* indifférent.
indigenous *adj* indigène.
indigestible *adj* indigeste.

indigestion *n* indigestion *f*.
indignant *adj* indigné.
indignation *n* indignation *f*.
indignity *n* indignité *f*.
indigo *n* indigo *m*.
indirect *adj* indirect.
indiscreet *adj* indiscret.
indiscretion *n* indiscrétion *f*.
indiscriminate *adj* ~**ly** *adv* sans discernement.
indispensable *adj* indispensable.
indisposed *adj* indisposé.
indisposition *n* indisposition *f*.
indisputable *adj* indiscutable.
indistinct *adj* indistinct, confus.
indistinguishable *adj* indiscernable.
individual *adj* ~**ly** *adv* individuel(lement); * *n* individu *m*.
individuality *n* individualité *f*.
indivisible *adj* indivisible.
indoctrinate *vt* endoctriner.
indoctrination *n* endoctrinement *m*.
indolence *n* indolence *f*.
indolent *adj* indolent.
indomitable *adj* indomptable.
indoors *adv* à l'intérieur.
indubitably *adv* indubitablement.
induce *vt* persuader; causer, provoquer.
inducement *n* encouragement *m*; incitation *f*.
induction *n* induction *f*.
indulge *vt* céder à; *vi* se permettre, se laisser aller.
indulgence *n* indulgence *f*.
indulgent *adj* indulgent.
industrial *adj* industriel.
industrialise *vt* industrialiser.
industrialist *n* industriel *m*.
industrious *adj* travailleur.

industry *n* industrie *f.*

inebriated *vt* ivre.

inedible *adj* non comestible.

ineffable *adj* ineffable.

ineffective, ineffectual *adj* inefficace.

inefficiency *n* inefficacité *f.*

inefficient *adj* inefficace.

ineligible *adj* inéligible.

inept *adj* inepte; déplacé.

ineptitude *n* ineptie *f;* manque d'à-propos *m.*

inequality *n* inégalité *f.*

inert *adj* inerte.

inertia *n* inertie *f.*

inescapable *adj* inévitable.

inestimable *adj* inestimable.

inevitable *adj* inévitable.

inevitably *adv* inévitablement.

inexcusable *adj* inexcusable.

inexhaustible *adj* inépuisable.

inexorable *adj* inexorable.

inexpensive *adj* bon marché.

inexperienced *adj* inexpérimenté.

inextricably *adv* inextricablement.

infallible *adj* infaillible.

infamous *adj* vil, infâme.

infancy *n* enfance *f.*

infant *n* bébé *m;* enfant *mf.*

infantile *adj* infantile.

infantry *n* infanterie *f.*

infatuated *adj* fou.

infatuation *n* folie *f;* obsession *f.*

infect *vt* infecter.

infection *n* infection *f.*

infectious *adj* contagieux; infectieux.

infer *vt* inférer.

inference *n* inférence *f.*

inferior *adj* inférieur; * *n* subordonné *m*-e *f.*

inferiority *n* infériorité *f.*

inferno *n* enfer *m.*

infest *vt* infester.

infidelity *n* infidélité *f.*

infiltrate *vi* s'infiltrer.

infinite *adj* ~**ly** *adv* infini(ment).

infinity *n* infini *m;* infinité *f.*

infirm *adj* infirme.

infirmary *n* infirmerie *f.*

infirmity *n* infirmité *f.*

inflame *vt* enflammer; * *vi* s'enflammer.

inflammation *n* inflammation *f.*

inflammatory *adj* inflammatoire.

inflatable *adj* gonflable.

inflate *vt* gonfler.

inflation *n* inflation *f.*

inflexible *adj* inflexible.

inflict *vt* infliger.

influence *n* influence *f;* * *vt* influencer.

influential *adj* influent.

influenza *n* grippe *f.*

inform *vt* informer.

informal *adj* informel; simple; familier.

informality *n* simplicité *f.*

informant *n* informateur *m* -trice *f*

information *n* information *f.*

infrared *adj* infrarouge.

infringe *vt* enfreindre.

infringement *n* infraction *f.*

infuriate *vt* rendre furieux.

ingenious *adj* ingénieux.

ingenuity *n* ingéniosité *f.*

ingenuous *adj* ~**ly** *adv* ingénu(ment); sincère(ment).

ingrained *adj* invétéré.

ingratiate *vi:* ~ **with sb** chercher à entrer dans les bonnes grâces de qn.

ingratitude *n* ingratitude *f.*

ingredient *n* ingrédient *m.*

inhabit *vt vi* habiter.

inhabitable *adj* habitable.

inhabitant *n* habitant *m* -e *f*.

inhale *vt* inhaler.

inherent *adj* inhérent.

inherit *vt* hériter.

inheritance *n* héritage *m*.

inhibited *adj* inhibé.

inhibition *n* inhibition *f*.

inhospitable *adj* inhospitalier.

inhospitality *n* inhospitalité *f*.

inhuman *adj* inhumain.

inhumanity *n* inhumanité, cruauté *f*.

inimitable *adj* inimitable.

initial *adj* initial; * *n* initiale *f*.

initially *adv* au début.

initiation *n* début, commencement *m*; initiation *f*.

initiative *n* initiative *f*.

inject *vt* injecter.

injection *n* injection *f*.

injunction *n* injonction *f*, ordre *m*.

injure *vt* blesser.

injury *n* blessure *f*; tort *m*.

injury time *n* arrêts de jeu *mpl*.

injustice *n* injustice *f*.

ink *n* encre *f*.

inkling *n* soupçon *m*.

inland *adj* intérieur; * *adv* vers l'intérieur, dans les terres.

in-laws *npl* belle-famille *f*.

inlet *n* entrée *f*; bras de mer *m*.

inmate *n* détenu *m* -e *f*.

inn *n* auberge *f*; hôtel *m*.

innate *adj* inné.

inner *adj* intérieur.

innermost *adj* le plus profond.

inner tube *n* chambre à air *f*.

innkeeper *n* aubergiste *mf*, hôtelier *m* -ière *f*.

innocence *n* innocence *f*.

innocent *adj* innocent.

innocuous *adj* inoffensif.

innovation *n* innovation *f*.

innuendo *n* allusion *f*; insinuation *f*.

innumerable *adj* innombrable.

inoculation *n* inoculation *f*.

inoffensive *adj* inoffensif.

inopportune *adj* inopportun.

inordinately *adv* démesurément.

input *n* entrée *f*; consommation *f*.

inquest *n* enquête *f*.

inquire *vt vi* demander.

inquiry *n* demande de renseignements *f*; enquête *f*.

inquisitive *adj* curieux.

inroad *n* incursion *f*.

insane *adj* fou, *f* folle.

insanity *n* folie *f*.

insatiable *adj* insatiable.

inscribe *vt* inscrire; dédier.

inscription *n* inscription *f*; dédicace *f*.

inscrutable *adj* impénétrable.

insect *n* insecte *m*.

insecticide *n* insecticide *m*.

insecure *adj* peu assuré.

insecurity *n* insécurité *f*.

insensitive *adj* insensible.

inseparable *adj* inséparable.

insert *vt* introduire, insérer.

insertion *n* insertion *f*.

inside *n* intérieur *m*; * *adv* à l'intérieur.

inside out *adv* à l'envers; à fond.

insidious *adj* insidieux.

insight *n* perspicacité *f*.

insignia *npl* insignes *mpl*.

insignificant *adj* insignifiant.

insincere *adj* peu sincère.

insincerity *n* manque de sincérité *m*.

insinuate *vt* insinuer.

insinuation *n* insinuation *f*.

insipid *adj* insipide.

insist *vi* insister.

insistence *n* insistance *f*.

insistent *adj* insistant.

insolence *n* insolence *f*.

insolent *adj* insolent.

insoluble *adj* insoluble.

insolvency *n* insolvabilité *f*.

insomnia *n* insomnie *f*.

inspect *vt* examiner, inspecter.

inspection *n* inspection *f*.

inspector *n* inspecteur *m* -trice *f*.

inspiration *n* inspiration *f*.

inspire *vt* inspirer.

instability *n* instabilité *f*.

instal *vt* installer.

installation *n* installation *f*.

instalment *n* installation *f*; versement *m*.

instance *n* exemple *m*; **for ~** par exemple.

instant *adj* instantané; **~ly** *adv* immédiatement; * *n* instant, moment *m*.

instantaneous *adj* **~ly** *adv* instantané(ment).

instead (of) *pr* au lieu, à la place (de).

instep *n* cou-de-pied *m*.

instigate *vt* inciter; susciter.

instigation *n* incitation *f*.

instil *vt* instiller; inspirer.

instinct *n* instinct *m*.

instinctive *adj* instinctif; **~ly** *adv* instinctivement, d'instinct.

institute *vt* instituer; * *n* institut *m*.

institution *n* institution *f*.

instruct *vt* instruire.

instruction *n* instruction *f*.

instructive *adj* instructif.

instructor *n* professeur *m*; moniteur *m* -trice *f*.

instrument *n* instrument *m*.

instrumental *adj* instrumental.

insubordination *n* insubordination *f*.

insufferable *adj* insupportable.

insufficient *adj* insuffisant.

insular *adj* insulaire; borné.

insulation *n* isolation *f*, insonorisation *f*.

insulin *n* insuline *f*.

insult *vt* insulter; * *n* insulte *f*.

insuperable *adj* insurmontable.

insurance *n* (com) assurance *f*.

insure *vt* assurer.

insurmountable *adj* insurmontable.

intact *adj* intact.

intake *n* admission *f*, consommation *f*.

integral *adj* intégrant; (chem) intégral; * *n* intégrale *f*.

integrate *vt* intégrer.

integration *n* intégration *f*.

integrity *n* intégrité *f*.

intellect *n* intellect *m*.

intellectual *adj* intellectuel.

intelligence *n* intelligence *f*.

intelligent *adj* intelligent.

intelligible *adj* intelligible.

intend *vt* avoir l'intention de.

intended *adj* voulu.

intense *adj* intense.

intensify *vt* intensifier.

intensity *n* intensité *f*.

intensive *adj* intensif.

intensive care unit *n* service de soins intensifs *m*.

intent *adj* résolu; attentif; **~ly** *adv* attentivement; * *n* intention *f*, dessein *m*.

intention *n* intention *f*, dessein *m*.

intentional adj intentionnel; **~ly** adv à dessein, intentionnellement.

interaction n interaction f.

intercept vt intercepter.

interchange n échange m.

intercom n interphone m.

intercourse n relations sexuelles fpl.

interest vt intéresser; * n intérêt m.

interesting adj intéressant.

interest rate n taux d'intérêt m.

interfere vi s'ingérer.

interference n ingérence f, interférence f.

interim adj intérimaire.

interior adj intérieur.

interior designer n décorateur (-trice) d'intérieur m(f).

interloper n intrus m -e f.

interlude n intermède m.

intermediary n intermédiaire mf.

intermediate adj intermédiaire.

interminable adj interminable.

intermingle vt entremêler; * vi s'entremêler.

intermission n entracte m; interruption f.

intermittent adj intermittent.

internal adj intérieur; interne.

international adj international.

interpret vt interpréter.

interpretation n interprétation f.

interpreter n interprète mf.

interrogate vt interroger.

interrogation n interrogatoire m.

interrupt vt interrompre.

interruption n interruption f.

intersection n croisement m.

intersperse vt parsemer.

intertwine vt entrelacer.

interval n intervalle m; mi-temps f.

intervene vi intervenir.

intervention n intervention f.

interview n entrevue f; interview f; * vt faire passer une entrevue à; interviewer.

interviewer n interviewer m.

intestine n intestin m.

intimacy n intimité f.

intimate n intime mf; * adj **~ly** adv intime(ment); * vt insinuer, laisser entendre.

intimidate vt intimider.

into prep dans, en.

intolerable adj intolérable.

intolerance n intolérance f.

intolerant adj intolérant.

intonation n intonation f.

intoxicate vt enivrer.

intoxication n ivresse f.

intravenous adj intraveineux.

intrepid adj intrépide; **~ly** adv intrépidement.

intricacy n complexité f.

intricate adj complexe, compliqué.

intrigue n intrigue f; * vi intriguer.

intriguing adj intrigant.

introduce vt introduire.

introduction n introduction f.

introductory adj d'introduction.

introvert n introverti m -ie f.

intrude vi s'ingérer, s'immiscer.

intruder n intrus m -e f.

intrusion n intrusion f.

intuition n intuition f.

intuitive adj intuitif.

inundate vt inonder.

invade vt envahir.

invader n envahisseur m -euse f.

invalid adj invalide; * n invalide mf.

invalidate vt invalider, annuler.

invaluable adj inappréciable.

invariably *adv* invariablement.

invasion *n* invasion *f.*

inveigle *vt* persuader, entraîner.

invent *vt* inventer.

invention *n* invention *f.*

inventive *adj* inventif.

inventor *n* inventeur *m* -trice *f.*

inventory *n* inventaire *m.*

invest *vt* investir.

investigate *vt* faire des recherches sur; examiner.

investigation *n* investigation *f;* recherches *fpl.*

investigator *n* investigateur *m* -trice *f;* chercheur *m* -euse *f.*

investment *n* investissement *m.*

inveterate *adj* invétéré.

invigorating *adj* vivifiant.

invincible *adj* invincible.

inviolable *adj* inviolable.

invisible *adj* invisible.

invitation *n* invitation *f.*

invite *vt* inviter.

inviting *adj* attrayant, tentant.

invoice *n* (*com*) facture *f.*

involuntary *adj* involontaire.

involve *vt* impliquer, entraîner.

involved *adj* compliqué; impliqué.

involvement *n* implication *f;* confusion *f.*

inward *adj* intérieur; intime; **~, ~s** *adv* vers l'intérieur.

iodine *n* (*chem*) iode *m.*

irascible *adj* irascible.

irate *adj* irrité.

iron *n* fer *m;* * *adj* de fer; * *vt* repasser.

ironic *adj* ironique.

ironing *n* repassage *m.*

ironing board *n* table *f* à repasser.

iron ore *n* minerai de fer *m.*

ironwork *n* ferronnerie *f;* **~s** *pl* ferronneries *fpl.*

irony *n* ironie *f.*

irrational *adj* irrationnel.

irreconcilable *adj* irréconciliable; inconciliable.

irregular *adj* irrégulier.

irrelevant *adj* hors de propos.

irreplaceable *adj* irremplaçable.

irresistible *adj* irrésistible.

irresolute *adj* **~ly** *adv* irré-solu(ment).

irresponsible *adj* irresponsable.

irreverence *n* irrévérence *f.*

irreverent *adj* irrévérencieux.

irrigate *vt* irriguer.

irrigation *n* irrigation *f.*

irritable *adj* irritable.

irritate *vt* irriter.

irritating *adj* irritant.

irritation *n* irritation *f.*

Islam *n* Islam *m.*

island *n* île *f.*

islander *n* insulaire *mf.*

isle *n* île *f.*

isolate *vt* isoler.

isolation *n* isolement *m.*

issue *n* sujet *m,* question *f;* * *vt* publier; distribuer; fournir.

it *pn* il, elle; le, la; cela, ça, ce, c'.

italic *n* italique *m.*

itch *n* démangeaison *f;* * *vi* avoir des démangeaisons.

item *n* article *m.*

itemise *vt* détailler.

itinerary *n* itinéraire *m.*

its *pn* son, sa, ses.

itself *pn* lui-même, elle-même.

ivory *n* ivoire *m.*

ivy *n* lierre *m.*

J

jab *vt* planter, enfoncer.

jackal *n* chacal *m.*

jackboots *npl* bottes de militaire *fpl.*

jackdaw *n* choucas *m.*

jacket *n* veste *f;* couverture *f.*

jackpot *n* gros lot *m.*

jade *n* jade *m.*

jagged *adj* dentelé.

jaguar *n* jaguar *m.*

jail *n* prison *f.*

jailbird *n* prisonnier *m,* -ière *f.*

jailer *n* geôlier *m* -ière *f.*

jam *n* confiture *f;* embouteillage *m.*

jangle *vi* cliqueter.

January *n* janvier *m.*

jar *vi* se heurter; (*mus*) détonner; grincer; * *n* pot *m.*

jargon *n* jargon *m.*

jasmine *n* jasmin *m.*

jaundice *n* jaunisse *f.*

javelin *n* javelot *m.*

jaw *n* mâchoire *f.*

jealous *adj* jaloux.

jealousy *n* jalousie *f.*

jeans *npl* jean *m.*

jeer *vi* se moquer, railler; * *n* raillerie, moquerie *f.*

jelly *n* gelée *f.*

jellyfish *n* méduse *f.*

jeopardise *vt* risquer, mettre en péril.

jerk *n* secousse *f;* * *vt* donner une secousse à.

jerky *adj* saccadé.

jersey *n* jersey *m,* tricot *m.*

jest *n* blague, plaisanterie *f.*

jet *n* avion à réaction *m;* jet *m;* gicleur *m.*

jet engine *n* moteur à réaction *m.*

jettison *vt* se défaire de.

jetty *n* jetée *f.*

Jew *n* Juif *m.*

jewel *n* bijou *m.*

jeweller *n* bijoutier *m* -ière *f.*

jewellery *n* bijoux *mpl.*

Jewish *adj* juif.

jibe *n* raillerie, moquerie *f.*

jigsaw *n* puzzle *m.*

jilt *vt* laisser tomber.

jinx *n* porte-malheur *m invar.*

job *n* travail *m.*

jockey *n* jockey *m.*

jocular *adj* joyeux; facétieux.

jog *vi* faire du jogging.

join *vt* joindre, unir; ~ **in** participer à; * *vi* se réunir; se joindre.

joiner *n* menuisier *m.*

joint *n* articulation *f;* * *adj* commun.

jointly *adv* conjointement.

joke *n* blague, plaisanterie *f;* * *vi* blaguer, plaisanter.

joker *n* blagueur *m* -euse *f.*

jolly *adj* gai, joyeux.

jolt *vt* secouer; * *n* secousse *f.*

jostle *vt* bousculer.

journal *n* revue *f.*

journalism *n* journalisme *m.*

journalist *n* journaliste *mf.*

journey *n* voyage *m;* * *vi* voyager.

jovial *adj* jovial, gai.

joy *n* joie *f.*

joyful, joyous *adj* joyeux, gai.

jubilant *adj* réjoui.

Judaism *n* judaïsme *m*.

judge *n* juge *m*; * *vt* juger.

judgment *n* jugement *m*.

judicial *adj* judiciaire.

judicious *adj* judicieux.

judo *n* judo *m*.

jug *n* cruche *f*.

juggle *vi* jongler.

juggler *n* jongleur *m* -euse *f*.

juice *n* jus *m*; suc *m*.

juicy *adj* juteux.

jukebox *n* juke-box *m*.

July *n* juillet *m*.

jumble *vt* mélanger; * *n* mélange *m*; fouillis *m*.

jump *vi* sauter; * *n* saut *m*.

jumper *n* pull *m*.

juncture *n* joncture *f*.

June *n* juin *m*.

jungle *n* jungle *f*.

junior *adj* plus jeune.

junk *n* cochonnerie *f*; bric-à-brac *m invar*.

jurisdiction *n* juridiction *f*.

juror *n* juré *m*.

jury *n* jury *m*.

just *adj* juste; * *adv* justement, exactement; ~ **now** tout de suite.

justice *n* justice *f*.

justifiably *adv* légitimement.

justification *n* justification *f*.

justify *vt* justifier.

jut *vi*: **to ~ out** faire saillie, dépasser.

juvenile *adj* juvénile; pour enfants.

juxtaposition *n* juxtaposition *f*.

K

kaleidoscope *n* kaléidoscope *m*.

kangaroo *n* kangourou *m*.

karate *n* karaté *m*.

kebab *n* brochette *f*.

keel *n* (*mar*) quille *f*.

keen *adj* aiguisé; vif; enthousiaste.

keep *vt* garder, conserver; tenir.

keepsake *n* souvenir *m*.

keg *n* baril *m*.

kennel *n* niche *f*.

kernel *n* amande *f*; noyau *m*.

kettle *n* bouilloire *f*.

key *n* clé, clef *f*; (*mus*) ton *m*; touche *f*.

keyboard *n* clavier *m*.

keyhole *n* trou de la serrure *m*.

key ring *n* porte-clefs *m invar*.

khaki *n* kaki *m*.

kick *vi* (*vt*) donner un coup de pied (à); * *n* coup de pied *m*; plaisir *m*.

kid *n* gamin *m* -e *f*.

kidnap *vt* kidnapper.

kidnapper *n* kidnappeur *m* -euse *f*.

kidney *n* rein *m*; rognon *m*.

killer *n* assassin *m*.

killing *n* assassinat *m*.

kilo *n* kilo *m*.

kilobyte *n* kilo-octet *m*.

kilogram *n* kilogramme *m*.

kilometre *n* kilomètre *m*.

kin *n*: **next of ~** parent proche *m*.

kind *adj* gentil; * *n* genre *m*, sorte *f*.

kind-hearted *adj* bon.

kindle *vt* allumer; * *vi* s'allumer.

kindliness *n* gentillesse, bonté *f*.

kindness *n* bonté *f*.

kindred *adj* apparenté.

kinetic *adj* cinétique.

king *n* roi *m*.

kingdom *n* royaume *m*.

kingfisher *n* martin-pêcheur *m*.

kiosk *n* kiosque *m*.

kiss *n* baiser *m*; * *vt* embrasser.

kit *n* équipement *m*.

kitchen *n* cuisine *f*.

kite *n* cerf-volant *m*.

kitten *n* chaton *m*.

knack *n* don, chic *m*.

knee *n* genou *m*.

knee-deep *adj* jusqu'aux genoux.

kneel *vi* s'agenouiller.

knife *n* couteau *m*.

knight *n* chevalier *m*.

knit *vt vi* tricoter.

knitwear *n* tricots *mpl*.

knob *n* bouton *m*; nœud *m* (du bois).

knock *vt vi* cogner, frapper; ~ **down** abattre; * *n* coup *m*.

knocker *n* heurtoir *m*.

knock-kneed *adj* aux genoux cagneux.

knock-out *n* knock-out *m*.

knot *n* nœud *m*; * *vt* nouer.

know *vt vi* savoir; connaître.

know-all *n* je-sais-tout *m*.

know-how *n* savoir-faire *m*.

knowing *adj* entendu; ~**ly** *adv* en connaissance de cause.

knowledge *n* connaissances *fpl*.

knowledgeable *adj* bien informé.

knuckle *n* articulation *f*.

L

label *n* étiquette *f*.

laboratory *n* laboratoire *m*.

laborious *adj* laborieux; pénible.

labour *n* travail *m*; **to be in ~** être en train d'accoucher; * *vi* travailler.

labourer *n* ouvrier *m*.

labyrinth *n* labyrinthe *m*.

lace *n* lacet *m*; dentelle *f*; * *vt* lacer.

lack *vt* manquer de; * *vi* manquer; * *n* manque *m*.

lackadaisical *adj* nonchalant.

lacquer *n* laque *f*.

lad *n* garçon *m*.

ladder *n* échelle *f*.

ladle *n* louche *f*.

lady *n* dame *f*.

ladybird *n* coccinelle *f*.

ladylike *adj* distingué.

lag *vi* se laisser distancer.

lager *n* bière blonde *f*.

laidback *adj* décontracté.

lair *n* repaire *m*.

lake *n* lac *m*.

lamb *n* agneau *m*; * *vi* agneler.

lame *adj* boiteux.

lament *vt* se lamenter sur; * *vi* se

lamenter; * n lamentation f.

lamentable adj lamentable, déplorable.

laminated adj laminé.

lamp n lampe f.

lampoon n satire f.

lampshade n abat-jour m invar.

lance n lance f; bistouri m; * vt inciser.

land n pays m; terre f; * vt débarquer; * vi atterrir, débarquer.

landing n atterrissage m.

landlady n propriétaire f.

landlord n propriétaire m.

landmark n point de repère m.

landowner n propriétaire terrien m.

landscape n paysage m.

landslide n glissement de terrain m.

lane n allée, ruelle f; file f.

language n langue f; langage m.

languid adj languissant.

languish vi languir.

lanky adj grand et maigre.

lantern n lanterne f.

lap n genoux mpl; * vt laper.

lapel n revers m.

lapse n laps m; défaillance f; * vi expirer, se périmer; se relâcher.

larceny n vol m.

larch n mélèze m.

lard n saindoux m.

larder n garde-manger m invar.

large adj grand; **at ~** en liberté; **~ly** adv en grande partie.

large-scale adj à grande échelle.

lark n alouette f.

larva n larve f.

laryngitis n laryngite f.

lascivious adj lascif.

laser n laser m.

lash n coup de fouet m; * vt fouetter; attacher.

last adj dernier; **at ~** enfin; **~ly** adv finalement; * n dernier m, dernière f; forme f (de cordonnier); * vi durer.

lasting adj durable.

last-minute adj de dernière minute.

latch n loquet m.

late adj en retard; défunt; * adv tard; **~ly** adv récemment.

latecomer n retardataire mf.

latent adj latent.

lather n mousse f.

latitude n latitude f.

latter adj dernier; **~ly** adv récemment.

lattice n treillis m.

laudably adv louablement.

laugh vi rire; **~ at** vt rire de, se moquer de; * n rire m.

laughable adj risible; dérisoire.

laughing stock n risée f.

laughter n rires mpl.

launch vt lancer; * vi se lancer; * n (mar) vedette f.

launching pad n rampe de lancement f.

launder vt laver.

laundrette n laverie automatique f.

laundry n lessive f.

laurel n laurier m.

lava n lave f.

lavatory n toilettes fpl.

lavender n (bot) lavande f.

lavish adj prodigue; **~ly** adv avec prodigalité; * vt prodiguer.

law n loi f; droit m.

law-abiding adj respectueux de la loi.

law court n tribunal m.

lawful adj légal; légitime; **~ly** adv légalement.

lawmaker n législateur m -trice f.

lawn n pelouse f, gazon m.

lawnmower n tondeuse à gazon f.

law suit n procès m.

lawyer n avocat m; juriste m.

lax adj relâché.

laxative n laxatif m.

lay vt coucher; mettre; pondre; ~ **claim** réclamer; prétendre (à); * vi pondre.

layabout n paresseux m -euse f.

layer n couche f.

layman n laïc m.

layout n disposition f; présentation f.

laze vi paresser.

lazily adv paresseusement.

laziness n paresse f.

lazy adj paresseux.

lead n plomb m; * vt vi conduire, mener.

leader n chef m.

leadership n direction f.

leading adj principal; premier.

leaf n feuille f.

leaflet n feuillet m; prospectus m.

league n ligue f, lieue f.

leak n fuite f; * vi (mar) faire eau.

lean vt appuyer; * vi s'appuyer; * adj maigre.

leap vi sauter; * n saut m.

leapfrog n saute-mouton m.

leap year n année bisextile f.

learn vt vi apprendre.

learned adj instruit.

learner n élève mf; débutant m, -e f.

lease n bail m; * vt louer.

leash n laisse f.

least adj moindre; **at ~** au moins.

leather n cuir m.

leave n permission f; congé m; **to take ~** prendre congé; * vt laisser.

lecherous adj lascif, lubrique.

lecture n conférence f; * vi faire une conférence.

lecturer n conférencier m -ière f.

ledge n rebord m.

ledger n (com) registre m.

leech n sangsue f.

leek n (bot) poireau m.

leer vt regarder d'un œil lascif.

leeway n liberté d'action f.

left adj gauche; **on the ~** à gauche.

left-handed adj gaucher.

left-luggage office n consigne f.

leftovers npl restes mpl.

leg n jambe f, patte f.

legacy n héritage, legs m.

legal adj légal, légitime.

legalise vt légaliser.

legality n légalité, légitimité f.

legal tender n monnaie légale f.

legend n légende f.

legendary adj légendaire.

legible adj lisible.

legislation n législation f.

legislature n corps législatif m.

legitimacy n légitimité f.

legitimate adj légitime.

leisure n loisir m; **~ly** adj tranquille.

lemon n citron m.

lemonade n limonade f.

lemon tea n thé au citron m.

lend vt prêter.

length n longueur f; durée f.

lengthways, lengthwise adv dans le sens de la longueur.

lengthy adj long.

lenient adj indulgent.

lens n lentille f (optique).

Lent n Carême m.

lentil n lentille f.

leopard n léopard m.

leotard n justaucorps m.

leper n lépreux m -euse f.

leprosy n lèpre f.

lesbian n lesbienne f.

less adj moins; * adv moins.

lesson n leçon f.

lest conj de crainte que.

let vt laisser, permettre; louer.

lethal adj mortel.

lethargic adj léthargique.

lethargy n léthargie f.

letter n lettre f.

letter box boite aux lettres f.

lettering n inscription f.

lettuce n salade f.

leukaemia n leucémie f.

level adj plat, égal; à niveau; * n niveau m; * vt niveler.

lever n levier m.

leverage n effet de levier m; prise f.

levity n légèreté f.

levy n levée f, prélèvement m; * vt prélever.

lewd adj obscène.

liability n responsabilité f.

liable adj sujet (à); responsable.

liaise vi effectuer une liaison.

liaison n liaison f.

liar n menteur m -euse f.

libel n diffamation f; * vt diffamer.

libellous adj diffamatoire.

liberal adj libéral; généreux.

liberate vt libérer.

liberation n libération f.

liberty n liberté f.

librarian n bibliothécaire mf.

library n bibliothèque f.

licence n licence f, permis m; permission f.

licentious adj licencieux.

lichen n (bot) lichen m.

lick vt lécher.

lid n couvercle m.

lie n mensonge m; * vi mentir; être allongé.

lieu n: **in ~ of** au lieu de.

lieutenant n lieutenant m.

life n vie f, **for ~** pour toute la vie.

life belt n gilet de sauvetage m.

lifeboat n canot de sauvetage m.

lifeguard n maître nageur m; garde du corps m.

life jacket n gilet de sauvetage m.

lifeless adj mort; sans vie.

lifelike adj naturel.

life-sized adj grandeur nature.

lifespan n durée de vie f.

lifestyle n style de vie m.

lifetime n vie f.

lift vt lever.

light n lumière f; * adj léger; clair; * vt allumer; éclairer.

light bulb n ampoule f.

lighten vi s'éclaircir; * vt éclairer; éclaircir; alléger.

lighter n briquet m.

light-headed adj étourdi.

lighthouse n (mar) phare m.

lighting n éclairage m.

lightly adv légèrement.

lightning n éclair m.

lightweight adj léger.

light year n année-lumière f.

like adj pareil; * adv comme; * vt vi aimer.

likeable adj sympathique.

likelihood n probabilité f.

likely adj probable, vraisemblable.

likeness n ressemblance f.

likewise adv pareillement.

liking n goût m.

lilac n lilas m.

lily n lis m; **~ of the valley** muguet m.

limb n membre m.

lime n chaux f; lime f; **~ tree** tilleul m.

limestone n pierre à chaux f.

limit n limite f; * vt limiter.

limitation n limitation f; restriction f.

limitless adj illimité.

limo(usine) n limousine f.

limp vi boiter; * n boitement m; * adj mou.

line n ligne f, ride f; * vt rayer; rider.

linen n lin m; linge m de maison.

liner n transatlantique m.

linesman n juge de ligne m.

linger vi traîner.

lingerie n lingerie f.

lingering adj long.

linguist n linguiste mf.

linguistic adj linguistique.

linguistics n linguistique f.

lining n doublure f.

link n chaînon m; * vt relier.

linoleum n linoléum m.

lint n peluche f.

lion n lion m.

lioness n lionne f.

lip n lèvre f, bord m.

lip-read vi lire sur les lèvres.

lip salve n pommade pour les lèvres f.

lipstick n rouge à lèvres m.

liqueur n liqueur f.

liquid adj liquide; * n liquide m.

liquidation n liquidation f.

liquidise vt liquéfier.

liquorice n réglisse m/f.

lisp vi zézayer; * n zézaiement m.

list n liste f; * vt faire une liste de.

listen vi écouter.

listless adj indifférent.

literal adj **~ly** adv littéral(ement).

literary adj littéraire.

literate adj cultivé.

literature n littérature f.

lithe adj agile.

litre n litre m.

litter n litière f; ordures fpl; * vt recouvrir, joncher.

little adj petit; * n peu m.

live vi vivre; habiter; **~ on** vt se nourrir de; **~ up to** vt faire honneur à; * adj vivant.

livelihood n moyens de subsistance mpl.

lively adj vif.

liven up vt animer.

liver n foie m.

livestock n bétail m.

livid adj livide; furieux.

living n vie f; * adj vivant.

living room n salle de séjour f.

lizard n lézard m.

load vt charger; * n charge f.

loaf n pain m.

loam n terreau m.

loan n prêt m.

loathe vt détester.

loathing n aversion f.

loathsome adj répugnant.

lobby n vestibule m.

lobe n lobe m.

lobster n langouste f.

local adj local.

local anaesthetic n anesthésique local m.

local government n administration f municipale, administration f locale.

localise vt localiser.

locality n localité f.

locate vt localiser.

location n situation f.

lock n serrure f; * vt fermer à clé.

locker n casier m.

locket n médaillon m.

locksmith n serrurier m.

locomotive n locomotive f.

locust n sauterelle f.

lodge n loge du gardien f; * vi se loger.

lodger n locataire mf.

loft n grenier m.

lofty adj haut.

log n bûche f.

logic n logique f.

logical adj logique.

loins npl reins mpl.

loiter vi s'attarder.

lollipop n sucette f.

lonely adj seul, solitaire.

loneliness n solitude f.

long adj long, f longue; * vi désirer.

long-distance n: ~ **call** appel interurbain m.

longevity n longévité f.

long-haired adj aux cheveux longs.

longing n désir m.

longitude n longitude f.

long jump n saut en longueur m.

long-range adj à longue portée.

long-term adj à long terme.

long-winded adj prolixe.

look vi regarder; sembler; ~ **after** vt s'occuper de; garder; ~ **for** vt chercher; ~ **forward to** vt attendre avec impatience; * n aspect m; regard m.

look-out n (mil) sentinelle f; vigie f.

loom n métier à tisser m; * vi menacer.

loop n boucle f.

loophole n échappatoire f.

loose adj lâché; desserré; ~**ly** adv approxi-

mativement; ~, **loosen** vt lâcher; desserrer.

loot vt piller; * n butin m.

lopsided adj de travers; déséquilibré.

lord n seigneur m.

lose vt vi perdre.

loss n perte f; **to be at a ~** ne pas savoir que faire.

lot n sort f, lot m; **a ~** beaucoup.

lotion n lotion f.

lottery n loterie f.

loud adj fort, bruyant.

loudspeaker n haut-parleur m.

lounge n salon m.

louse n (pl **lice**) pou m.

lousy adj minable.

lout n vaurien m.

lovable adj sympathique.

love n amour m; **to fall in ~** tomber amoureux; * vt aimer.

love letter n lettre d'amour f.

love life n vie sentimentale f.

lovely adj beau.

lover n amant m.

loving adj affectueux.

low adj bas; * vi meugler.

lower vt baisser.

loyal adj loyal, fidèle.

loyalty n loyauté f; fidélité f.

lozenge n pastille f.

lubricate vt lubrifier.

lucid adj lucide.

luck n chance f.

luckily adv heureusement, par chance.

lucky adj chanceux, qui a de la chance.

lucrative adj lucratif.

ludicrous adj absurde.

lug vt traîner.

luggage n bagages mpl.

lukewarm adj tiède.

lull *vt* bercer; * *n* répit *m*.

lullaby *n* berceuce *f*.

lumbago *n* lumbago *m*.

lumberjack *n* bûcheron *m*.

luminous *adj* lumineux.

lump *n* bosse *f*; grosseur *f*; morceau *m*; * *vt* réunir.

lump sum *n* somme globale *f*.

lunacy *n* folie *f*.

lunar *adj* lunaire.

lunatic *adj* fou, *f* folle.

lunch, luncheon *n* déjeuner *m*.

lungs *npl* poumons *mpl*.

lurch *n* embardée *f*.

lure *n* leurre *m*; attrait *m*; * *vt* séduire, attirer.

lurid *adj* criard (couleur); horrible.

lurk *vi* être tapi.

luscious *adj* délicieux.

lush *adj* luxuriant.

lust *n* luxure *f*; sensualité *f*; désir *m*; * *vi* désirer; **~ after** *vt* convoiter.

lustful *adj* luxurieux, voluptueux.

lute *n* luth *m*.

luxuriance *n* exubérance, luxuriance *f*.

luxuriant *adj* exubérant, luxuriant.

luxuriate *vi* pousser de manière exubérante.

luxurious *adj* luxueux.

luxury *n* luxe *m*.

lying *n* mensonges *mpl*.

lynch *vt* lyncher.

lynx *n* linx *m*.

lyrical *adj* lyrique.

lyrics *npl* paroles *fpl*.

M

macaroni *n* macaronis *mpl*.

macaroon *n* macaron *m*.

machine *n* machine *f*.

machine gun *n* mitrailleuse *f*.

machinery *n* machinerie *f*; mécanisme *m*.

mackerel *n* maquereau *m*.

mad *adj* fou, *f* folle; furieux; insensé.

Madam *n* madame *f*.

madden *vt* rendre fou; rendre furieux.

madly *adv* à la folie; comme un fou.

madman *n* fou *m*.

madness *n* folie *f*.

magazine *n* magazine *m*, revue *f*; (*mil*) magasin *m*.

maggot *n* asticot *m*.

magic *n* magie *f*; * *adj* **~ally** *adv* magique(ment).

magician *n* magicien *m* -ne *f*.

magistrate *n* magistrat *m*.

magnanimous *adj* **~ly** *adv* magnanime(ment).

magnet *n* aimant *m*.

magnetic *adj* magnétique.

magnetism *n* magnétisme *m*.

magnificence *n* magnificence *f*.

magnificent *adj* **~ly** *adv* magnifique(ment).

magnify *vt* grossir; exagérer.

magnifying glass *n* loupe *f*.

magpie *n* pie *f*.

mahogany *n* acajou *m*.

maid n bonne f.

maiden n jeune fille f.

maiden name n nom de jeune fille m.

mail n courrier m.

mail-order n vente par correspondance f.

maim vt mutiler.

main adj principal; essentiel.

mainland n continent m.

mainly adv principalement, essentiellement.

main street n rue principale f.

maintain vt maintenir; soutenir.

maintenance n entretien m.

maize n maïs m.

majestic adj majestueux.

majesty n majesté f.

major adj majeur; * n (mil) commandant m.

majority n majorité f.

make vt faire; ~ **up** inventer; ~ **up for** compenser; * n marque f.

make-believe n invention f.

make-up n maquillage m.

malady n maladie f.

malaria n malaria f.

malcontent adj n mécontent m -e f.

male adj mâle; masculin; * n mâle m.

malevolent adj malveillant; ~**ly** adv avec malveillance.

malfunction n mauvais fonctionnement m.

malice n méchanceté f.

malicious adj méchant.

malign adj nocif; * vt calomnier.

malignant adj malfaisant.

mall n centre commercial m.

malleable adj malléable.

mallet n maillet m.

malnutrition n malnutrition f.

malpractice n malversations fpl.

mammal n mammifère m.

mammoth adj gigantesque.

man n homme m; * vt (mar) équiper en personnel.

manacle n entrave f; ~**s** pl menottes fpl.

manage vt diriger; réussir; * vi réussir.

manageable adj maniable.

management n direction f.

manager n directeur m.

managing director n directeur m général.

mandatory n obligatoire.

mane n crinière f.

manfully adv vaillamment.

mangle n essoreuse f; * vt mutiler.

manhandle vt maltraiter; manutentionner.

manhood n âge d'homme m; virilité f.

mania n manie f.

maniac n maniaque mf.

manic adj obsessionnel.

manicure n manucure f.

manifest adj manifeste; * vt manifester.

manifestation n manifestation f.

manifesto n manifeste m.

manipulate vt manipuler.

manly adj viril.

man-made adj artificiel.

manner n manière f; attitude f; ~**s** pl manières fpl.

manoeuvre n manœuvre f.

mansion n château m.

manslaughter n homicide involontaire m.

mantelpiece n manteau de cheminée m.

manual adj n manuel m.

manufacture n fabrication f; * vt fabriquer.

manufacturer n fabricant m.

manure n fumier m; engrais m; purin m; * vt fumer.

manuscript n manuscrit m.

many adj beaucoup de; **how ~?** combien?; **as ~ as** autant que.

map n carte f; plan m; * vt dessiner un plan de.

maple n érable m.

mar vt gâter, gâcher.

marathon n marathon m.

marble n marbre m; * adj marbré.

March n mars m.

march n marche f; * vi marcher.

mare n jument f.

margarine n margarine f.

margin n marge f; bord m.

marginal adj marginal.

marijuana n marijuana f.

marinate vt mariner.

marine adj marin; * n fusilier m marin.

marital adj matrimonial.

maritime adj maritime.

marjoram n marjolaine f.

mark n marque f; signe m; * vt marquer.

marker n marque f; marqueur m.

market n marché m.

marketing n marketing m.

market research n étude de marché f.

marksman n tireur d'élite m.

marmalade n confiture d'oranges f.

maroon adj marron rouge.

marquee n tente f.

marriage n mariage m.

marriage certificate n acte de mariage m.

married adj marié; conjugal.

marrow n moelle f.

marry vi se marier.

marsh n marécage m.

marshy adj marécageux.

martial adj martial; **~ law** n loi martiale f.

marvel n merveille f; * vi s'émer-veiller.

marvellous adj merveilleux.

marzipan n massepain m, pâte d'amandes f.

mascara n mascara m.

masculine adj masculin, viril.

mash n bouillie, purée f.

mask n masque m; * vt masquer.

masochist n masochiste mf.

masquerade n mascarade f.

mass n masse f; messe f; multitude f.

massacre n massacre m; * vt massacrer.

massage n massage m.

massive adj énorme.

mass media npl média mpl.

mast n mât m.

master n maître m; * vt maîtriser.

masterly adj magistral.

mastermind vt diriger.

masterpiece n chef-d'œuvre m.

mastery n maîtrise f.

mat n tapis m.

match n allumette f; match m; * vt égaler; * vi bien aller ensemble.

matchbox n boîte d'allumettes f.

matchmaker n marieur m -euse f.

mate n camarade mf; * vt accoupler.

material adj matériel.

maternal adj maternel.

mathematical adj mathématique.

mathematician n mathématicien m -ne f.

mathematics npl mathématiques fpl.

maths n maths fpl.

matinee n matinée f.

matrimonial *adj* matrimonial.

mat(t) *adj* mat.

matted *adj* emmêlé.

matter *n* matière, substance *f*; sujet *m*; affaire *f*; **what is the ~?** que se passe-t-il?; **a ~ of fact** un fait; * *vi* importer.

mattress *n* matelas *m*.

mature *adj* mûr; * *vi* mûrir.

maturity *n* maturité *f*.

maul *vt* meurtrir.

mausoleum *n* mausolée *m*.

mauve *adj* mauve.

maxim *n* maxime *f*.

maximum *n* maximum *m*.

may *v aux* pouvoir; **~be** peut-être.

May *n* mai *m*.

mayor *n* maire *m*.

maze *n* labyrinthe *m*.

me *pn* moi; me.

meadow *n* prairie *f*, pré *m*.

meagre *adj* pauvre.

meal *n* repas *m*; farine *f*.

mean *adj* avare, mesquin; moyen; **in the ~time, ~while** pendant ce temps-là; **~s** *npl* moyens *mpl*; * *vt vi* signifier.

meaning *n* sens *m*, signification *f*.

meaningful *adj* significatif.

meaningless *adj* vide de sens.

meanness *n* avarice, mesquinerie *f*.

meantime, meanwhile *adv* pendant ce temps-là.

measles *npl* rougeole *f*.

measure *n* mesure *f*; * *vt* mesurer.

measurement *n* mesure *f*.

meat *n* viande *f*.

meatball *n* boulette de viande *f*.

mechanic *n* mécanicien *m*.

mechanical *adj* **~ly** *adv* mécanique(ment).

mechanics *npl* mécanique *f*.

mechanism *n* mécanisme *m*.

medal *n* médaille *f*.

medallion *n* médaillon *m*.

meddle *vi* se mêler des affaires des autres.

meddler *n* fouineur *m* -euse *f*, indiscret *m* -ète *f*.

media *npl* média *mpl*.

medical *adj* médical.

medicated *adj* médical.

medicinal *adj* médicinal.

medicine *n* médecine *f*; médicament *m*.

medieval *adj* médiéval.

mediocre *adj* médiocre.

mediocrity *n* médiocrité *f*.

meditate *vi* méditer.

meditation *n* méditation *f*.

meditative *adj* méditatif.

medium *n* milieu *m*; médium *m*; * *adj* moyen.

medley *n* mélange *m*.

meek *adj* docile.

meet *vt* rencontrer; * *vi* se rencontrer; se retrouver.

meeting *n* réunion *f*; congrès *m*.

megaphone *n* mégaphone *m*.

melancholy *n* mélancolie *f*; * *adj* mélancolique.

mellow *adj* moelleux; doux; * *vi* mûrir.

melodious *adj* mélodieux.

melody *n* mélodie *f*.

melon *n* melon *m*.

melt *vt* faire fondre; * *vi* fondre.

member *n* membre *m*.

membership *n* adhésion *f*.

membrane *n* membrane *f*.

memento *n* mémento *m*.

memo *n* note de service *f*.

memoir n mémoire m.

memorable adj mémorable.

memorial n monument commémoratif, mémorial m.

memorise vt mémoriser.

memory n mémoire f; souvenir m.

menace n menace f; * vt menacer.

menacing adj menaçant.

menagerie n ménagerie f.

mend vt réparer; raccommoder.

mending n réparation f, raccommodage m.

menial adj vil.

meningitis n méningite f.

menopause n ménopause f.

mental adj mental.

mentality n mentalité f.

mention n mention f; * vt mentionner.

menu n menu m.

mercenary adj n mercenaire m.

merchandise n marchandise f.

merchant n négociant m -e f.

merciful adj miséricordieux.

merciless adj ~ly adv impitoyable(ment).

mercury n mercure m.

mercy n pitié f.

mere adj ~ly adv simple(ment).

merge vt vi fusionner.

merger n fusion f.

merit n mérite m; * vt mériter.

mermaid n sirène f.

merrily adv joyeusement.

merriment n divertissement m; réjouissance f.

merry adj joyeux.

merry-go-round n manège m.

mesh n maille f.

mesmerise vt hypnotiser.

mess n désordre m; confusion f; (mil) mess m; ~ **up** vt mettre en désordre.

message n message m.

messenger n messager m -ère f.

metabolism n métabolisme m.

metal n métal m.

metallic adj métallique.

meteor n météore m.

meter n compteur m.

method n méthode f.

methodical adj ~ly adv méthodique(ment).

Methodist n méthodiste mf.

metre n mètre m.

metric adj métrique.

metropolis n métropole f.

metropolitan adj métropolitain.

mezzanine n mezzanine f.

microbe n microbe m.

microphone n microphone m.

microchip n microprocesseur m, puce f.

microscope n microscope m.

microscopic adj microscopique.

microwave n four à micro-ondes m.

mid adj demi; mi-.

midday n midi m.

middle adj moyen; du milieu; * n milieu m.

middleweight n poids moyen m.

middling adj moyen, passable.

midge n moucheron m.

midget n nain m -e f.

midnight n minuit m.

midriff n diaphragme m; estomac m.

midst n milieu m.

midsummer n milieu de l'été m.

midway adv à mi-chemin.

midwife n sage-femme f.

midwifery n obstétrique f.

might n force f.

mighty adj fort, puissant.

migraine n migraine f.

migrate vi émigrer.

migration n émigration f.

migratory adj migratoire.

mike n micro m.

mild adj doux; modéré.

mildness n douceur f.

mile n mile m.

mileage n kilométrage m.

militant adj militant.

military adj militaire.

militia n milice f.

milk n lait m; * vt traire; exploiter.

milkshake n milk-shake m.

milky adj laiteux; **M~ Way** n Voie lactée f.

mill n moulin m; * vt moudre.

millennium n millénaire m.

miller n meunier m.

millimetre n millimètre m.

million n million m.

millionaire n millionaire mf.

millionth adj n millionième mf.

mime n mime m.

mimic vt mimer.

mimicry n mimique f.

mince vt hacher.

mind n esprit m; * vt prendre soin de; * vi: **do you ~?** est-ce que cela vous dérange?

mindful adj soucieux; attentif.

mindless adj insouciant.

mine pn le mien, la mienne, les miens, les miennes; à moi; * n mine f; * vi exploiter la mine.

minefield n champ de mines m.

miner n mineur m.

mineral adj n minéral m.

mineral water n eau minérale f.

mingle vt mêler.

miniature n miniature f.

minimal adj minime.

minimise vt minimiser.

minimum n minimum m.

mining n exploitation minière f.

minister n ministre m; * vt servir.

ministerial adj ministériel.

ministry n ministère m.

mink n vison m.

minnow n vairon m.

minor adj mineur; * n mineur m -e f.

minority n minorité f.

minstrel n ménestrel m.

mint n (bot) menthe f; hôtel de la Monnaie m; * vt frapper la monnaie.

minus adv moins.

minute adj minuscule.

minute n minute f.

miracle n miracle m.

miraculous adj miraculeux.

mirror n miroir m.

mirth n allégresse f.

misadventure n mésaventure f.

misanthropist n misanthrope mf.

misapply vt mal appliquer.

misapprehension n méprise f.

misbehave vi se conduire mal.

misbehaviour n mauvaise conduite f.

miscalculate vt mal calculer.

miscarriage n fausse couche f.

miscarry vi faire une fausse couche; échouer.

miscellaneous adj divers, varié.

mischief n mal, tort m.

mischievous adj mauvais; espiègle.

misconception n méprise f.

misconduct n mauvaise conduite f.

misconstrue vt mal interpréter.

misdeed n méfait m.

misdemeanour n délit m.

miser n avare mf.

miserable adj malheureux.

miserly adj mesquin, avare.

misery n malheur m; misère f.

misfit n inadapté m -e f.

misfortune n infortune f.

misgiving n doute m.

misguided adj malencontreux; mala-visé.

mishap n mésaventure f.

mislay vt égarer.

mislead vt induire en erreur.

mismanagement n mauvaise administration f.

misnomer n (law) nom inapproprié m.

misogynist n misogyne mf.

misprint vt mal imprimer; * n coquille f.

Miss n Mlle, Mademoiselle f.

miss vt rater; s'ennuyer de.

misshapen adj déformé.

missile n missile m.

missing adj perdu; absent.

mission n mission f.

missionary n missionnaire mf.

mist n brouillard m.

mistake vt confondre; * vi se tromper; **to be mistaken** se tromper; * n méprise f, erreur f.

Mister n monsieur m.

mistletoe n (bot) gui m.

mistress n maîtresse f.

mistrust vt se méfier de; * n méfiance f.

mistrustful adj méfiant.

misty adj brumeux.

misunderstand vt mal comprendre.

misunderstanding n malentendu m.

mitigation n atténuation f.

mittens npl moufles fpl.

mix vt mélanger.

mixed adj mélangé; mixte.

mixed-up adj confus.

mixer n mixeur m.

mixture n mélange m.

mix-up n confusion f.

moan n gémissement m; * vi gémir; se plaindre.

moat n fossé m.

mob n foule f; masse f.

mobile adj mobile.

mobility n mobilité f.

mock vt se moquer de.

mockery n moquerie f.

mode n mode m.

model n modèle m; * vt modeler.

moderate adj ~ly adv modé-ré(ment). * vt modérer.

moderation n modération f.

modern adj moderne.

modernise vt moderniser.

modest adj ~ly adv modes-te(ment).

modesty n modestie f.

modification n modification f.

modify vt modifier.

moist adj humide.

moisten vt humidifier.

moisture n humidité f.

molar n molaire f.

mole n taupe f.

molecule n molécule f.

molest vt importuner.

mollify vt apaiser.

mollusc n mollusque m.

mollycoddle *vt* dorloter.

molten *adj* fondu.

moment *n* moment *m*.

momentarily *adv* momentanément.

momentary *adj* momentané.

momentous *adj* capital.

momentum *n* vitesse *f*; élan *m*.

monarch *n* monarque *m*.

monarchy *n* monarchie *f*.

monastery *n* monastère *m*.

Monday *n* lundi *m*.

monetary *adj* monétaire.

money *n* argent *m*; pièce de monnaie *f*.

mongrel *adj n* bâtard *m* -e *f*.

monitor *n* moniteur *m* -trice *f*.

monk *n* moine *m*.

monkey *n* singe *m*.

monologue *n* monologue *m*.

monopolise *vt* monopoliser.

monopoly *n* monopole *m*.

monosyllable *n* monosyllabe *m*.

monotonous *adj* monotone.

monotony *n* monotonie *f*.

monster *n* monstre *m*.

monstrosity *n* monstruosité *f*.

monstrous *adj* monstrueux.

month *n* mois *m*.

monthly *adj* mensuel; *adv* mensuellement.

monument *n* monument *m*.

monumental *adj* monumental.

mood *n* humeur *f*.

moody *adj* de mauvaise humeur; lunatique.

moon *n* lune *f*.

moonlight *n* clair de lune *m*.

moor *n* lande *f*; * *vt* (*mar*) amarrer.

moose *n* élan *m*, orignal *m*.

mop *n* lavette *f*; * *vt* éponger.

mope *vi* se morfondre.

moped *n* vélomoteur *m*.

moral *adj* ~**ly** *adv* moral(ement); ~**s** *npl* moralité *f*.

morale *n* moral *m*.

morality *n* moralité *f*.

morbid *adj* morbide.

more *adj adv* plus; **never** ~ plus jamais; **once** ~ encore une fois; ~ **and** ~ de plus en plus.

moreover *adv* de plus, en outre.

morning *n* matin *m*; **good** ~ bonjour.

moron *n* imbécile *mf*.

morose *adj* morose.

morse *n* morse *m*.

morsel *n* bouchée *f*; morceau *m*.

mortal *adj* ~**ly** *adv* mortel(lement); * *n* mortel *m* -le *f*.

mortality *n* mortalité *f*.

mortar *n* mortier *m*.

mortgage *n* hypothèque *f*; * *vt* hypothéquer.

mortify *vt* mortifier.

mortuary *n* morgue *f*.

mosaic *n* mosaïque *f*.

mosque *n* mosquée *f*.

mosquito *n* moustique *m*.

moss *n* (*bot*) mousse *f*.

most *adj pn* la plupart de; * *adv* extrêmement; **at** ~ au maximum; ~**ly** *adv* surtout, essentiellement.

moth *n* papillon de nuit *m*; mite *f*.

mothball *n* boule de naphtaline *f*.

mother *n* mère *f*.

motherhood *n* maternité *f*.

mother-in-law *n* belle-mère *f*.

motherly *adj* maternel.

mother-of-pearl *n* nacre *f*.

mother-to-be *n* future maman *f*.

motif n (art, mus) motif m.
motion n mouvement m.
motionless adj immobile.
motion picture n film m.
motivated adj motivé.
motive n motif m.
motley adj bigarré.
motor n moteur m.
motorbike n moto f.
motorboat n canot à moteur m.
motorcycle n motocyclette f.
mottled adj marbré, tacheté.
motto n devise f.
mould n moule m; * vt mouler.
mouldy adj moisi.
moult vi muer.
mound n monticule m.
mount n mont m; * vt gravir.
mountain n montagne f.
mountaineering n alpinisme m.
mountainous adj montagneux.
mourn vt pleurer.
mourner n personne en deuil f.
mournful adj ~ly adv triste(ment).
mourning n deuil m.
mouse n (pl mice) souris f.
mouth n bouche f; embouchure f.
mouth organ n harmonica m.
mouthwash n eau dentifrice f.
move vt déplacer; toucher, émouvoir; * vi bouger; * n mouvement m.
movement n mouvement m.
moving adj touchant, émouvant.
Mrs n Mme, Madame f.
much adj pn beaucoup; adv beaucoup, très.
muck n saleté f.
mud n boue f.
muddle vt confondre; embrouiller; * n confusion f; désordre m.

muddy adj boueux.
muffle vt assourdir.
mug n tasse f.
mule n mulet m; mule f.
mull vt méditer.
multiple adj multiple.
multiplication n multiplication f.
multiply vt multiplier.
multitude n multitude f.
mumble vt vi grommeler.
mummy n momie f.
mumps npl oreillons mpl.
munch vt mâcher.
mundane adj banal.
municipal adj municipal.
mural n mural m.
murder n assassinat, meurtre m; homicide volontaire m; * vt assassiner.
murderer n assassin, meurtrier m.
murderous adj meurtrier.
murmur n murmure m; * vt vi murmurer.
muscle n muscle m.
muscular adj musculaire.
muse vi méditer, rêver.
museum n musée m.
mushroom n (bot) champignon m.
music n musique f.
musical adj musical; mélodieux.
musician n musicien m -ne f.
musk n musc m.
muslin n mousseline f.
must v aux devoir.
mustard n moutarde f.
muster vt rassembler.
musty adj moisi.
mute adj muet, silencieux.
muted adj assourdi.
mutilate vt mutiler.

mutilation *n* mutilation *f.*

mutiny *n* mutinerie *f; vi* se mutiner, se révolter.

mutter *vt vi* grommeler, marmonner; * *n* grommellement *m.*

mutual *adj* ~**ly** *adv* mutuel(le-ment), réciproque(ment).

muzzle *n* muselière *f;* museau *m;* * *vt* museler.

my *pn* mon, ma, mes.

myself *pn* moi-même.

mysterious *adj* mystérieux.

mystery *n* mystère *m.*

mystic(al) *adj* mystique.

mystify *vt* mystifier; laisser perplexe.

myth *n* mythe *m.*

mythology *n* mythologie *f.*

N

nag *n* bourrin *m;* * *vt* harceler.

nagging *adj* persistant.

nail *n* ongle *m;* clou *m;* * *vt* clouer.

nailbrush *n* brosse à ongles *f.*

nailfile *n* lime à ongles *f.*

nail polish *n* vernis à ongles *m.*

naive *adj* naïf.

naked *adj* nu; dénudé; pur, simple.

name *n* nom *m;* réputation *f;* * *vt* nommer; mentionner.

nameless *adj* anonyme.

namely *adv* à savoir.

namesake *n* homonyme *m.*

nanny *n* nourrice *f.*

nap *n* sieste *f,* somme *m.*

nape *n* nuque *f.*

napkin *n* serviette *f.*

narcissus *n* (*bot*) narcisse *m.*

narcotic *adj n* narcotique *m.*

narrate *vt* narrer, raconter.

narrative *adj* narratif; * *n* narration *f.*

narrow *adj* ~**ly** *adv* étroit(ement); * *vt* resserrer; limiter.

narrow-minded *adj* à l'esprit étroit.

nasty *adj* méchant; mauvais; sale.

nation *n* nation *f.*

national *adj* ~**ly** *adv* national(e-ment).

nationalise *vt* nationaliser.

nationalism *n* nationalisme *m.*

nationalist *adj n* nationaliste *mf.*

nationality *n* nationalité *f.*

native *adj* natal; * *n* autochtone *mf.*

natural *adj* ~**ly** *adv* naturel(le-ment).

nature *n* nature *f,* sorte *f.*

naughty *adj* méchant.

nausea *n* nausée, envie de vomir *f.*

nauseate *vt* donner des nausées à.

nauseous *adj* écœurant.

nautic(al), naval *adj* nautique.

navel *n* nombril *m.*

navigate *vi* naviguer.

navigation *n* navigation *f.*

navy *n* marine *f.*

Nazi *n* nazi *m* -e *f.*

near *prep* près de; * *adv* près; à côté; * *adj* proche.

nearby *adj* proche.

nearly *adv* presque.

neat *adj* soigné; net, propre.

necessary *adj* nécessaire.

necessity *n* nécessité *f.*

neck *n* cou *m;* * *vi* se bécoter.

necklace *n* collier *m.*

née *adj:* ~ **Brown** née Brown.

need *n* besoin *m;* pauvreté *f;* * *vt* avoir besoin de, nécessiter.

needle *n* aiguille *f.*

needlework *n* couture *f.*

needy *adj* nécessiteux, pauvre.

negation *n* négation *f.*

negative *adj* négatif; * *n* négative *f;* négation *f;* négatif *m.*

neglect *vt* négliger; * *n* négligence *f.*

negligee *n* négligé, déshabillé *m.*

negligence *n* négligence *f;* manque de soin *m.*

negligent *adj* négligent.

negotiate *vt vi* négocier.

negotiation *n* négociation *f.*

neighbour *n* voisin *m,* -e *f;* * *vt* être voisin de.

neighbouring *adj* voisin.

neighbourly *adj* sociable.

neither *conj* ni; * *pn* aucun(e), ni l'un(e) ni l'autre.

neon light *n* lumière au néon *f.*

nephew *n* neveu *m.*

nerve *n* nerf *m;* courage *m;* toupet *m.*

nerve-racking *adj* exaspérant.

nervous *adj* nerveux.

nervous breakdown *n* dépression nerveuse *f.*

nest *n* nid *m;* nichée *f.*

nest egg *n* (*fig*) économies *fpl.*

nestle *vt vi* se blottir.

net *n* filet *m.*

net curtain *n* voile *m.*

netting *n* filet *m.*

nettle *n* ortie *f.*

network *n* réseau *f.*

neurosis *n* névrose *f.*

neurotic *adj n* névrosé *m* -e *f.*

neuter *adj* (*gr*) neutre.

neutral *adj* neutre.

neutralise *vt* neutraliser.

neutrality *n* neutralité *f.*

never *adv* jamais; ~ **mind** ça ne fait rien.

never-ending *adj* interminable.

nevertheless *adv* cependant, néanmoins.

new *adj* neuf; nouveau; dernier; ~**ly** *adv* nouvellement.

newborn *adj* nouveau-né, *f* nouvelle-née.

newcomer *n* nouveau venu *m,* nouvelle venue *f.*

news *npl* nouvelles, informations *fpl.*

news agency *n* agence de presse *f.*

newscaster *n* présentateur *m* -trice *f.*

news flash *n* flash d'information *m.*

newsletter *n* bulletin *m.*

newspaper *n* journal *m.*

newsreel *n* actualités *fpl.*

New Year *n* Nouvel An *m.*

next *adj* prochain; **the ~ day** le jour suivant; * *adv* ensuite, après.

nib *n* pointe *f;* plume *f.*

nibble *vt* mordiller.

nice *adj* gentil(le) *m(f);* agréable; joli.

nice-looking *adj* beau, *f* belle.

nick *n* entaille *f;* * *vt* (*sl*) faucher.

nickel *n* nickel *m.*

nickname *n* surnom *m;* * *vt* surnommer.

niece *n* nièce *f.*

niggling *adj* insignifiant.

night *n* nuit *f.*

nightclub *n* boîte de nuit *f.*

nightingale *n* rossignol *m.*

nightly *adv* tous les soirs; toutes les nuits; * *adj* nocturne.

nightmare *n* cauchemar *m.*

night school *n* cours du soir *mpl.*

night shift *n* équipe de nuit *f.*

night-time *n* nuit *f.*

nimble *adj* léger; agile, souple.

nine *adj n* neuf *m.*

nineteen *adj n* dix-neuf *m.*

nineteenth *adj n* dix-neuvième *mf.*

ninetieth *adj n* quatre-vingt-dixième *mf.*

ninety *adj n* quatre-vingt-dix *m.*

ninth *adj n* neuvième *mf.*

nip *vt* pincer; mordre.

nipple *n* mamelon *m*; tétine *f.*

no *adv* non; * *adj* aucun; pas de.

nobility *n* noblesse *f.*

noble *adj* noble; * *n* noble *mf.*

nobody *pn* personne.

nocturnal *adj* nocturne.

nod *n* signe de tête *m*; * *vi* faire un signe de la tête; somnoler.

noise *n* bruit *m.*

noisy *adj* bruyant.

nominal *adj* ~**ly** *adv* nominal(ement).

nominate *vt* nommer.

nonchalant *adj* nonchalant.

noncommittal *adj* réservé.

nondescript *adj* quelconque.

none *pn* aucun; personne.

nonentity *n* nullité *f.*

nonexistent *adj* inexistant.

nonfiction *n* ouvrages non romanesques *mpl.*

nonplussed *adj* perplexe.

nonsense *n* absurdité *f.*

nonsensical *adj* absurde.

nonsmoker *n* non-fumeur *m.*

nonstick *adj* anti-adhérent.

nonstop *adj* direct; * *adv* sans s'arrêter.

noodles *npl* nouilles *fpl.*

noon *n* midi *m.*

noose *n* nœud coulant *m.*

nor *conj* ni.

normal *adj* normal.

north *n* nord *m*; * *adj* du nord.

northerly, northern *adj* du nord.

North Pole *n* pôle Nord *m.*

nose *n* nez *m.*

nosebleed *n* saignement de nez *m.*

nostalgia *n* nostalgie *f.*

nostril *n* narine *f.*

not *adv* pas; non.

notable *adj* notable.

notch *n* cran *m*, dent *f*; * *vt* denteler.

note *n* note *f*; billet *m*; mot *m*; marque *f*; * *vt* noter, marquer; remarquer.

notebook *n* carnet *m.*

noted *adj* célèbre, connu.

notepad *n* bloc-notes *m.*

notepaper *n* papier à lettres *m.*

nothing *n* rien *m.*

notice *n* notice *f*; avis *m*; * *vt* remarquer.

noticeable *adj* visible.

notification *n* notification *f.*

notify *vt* notifier.

notion *n* notion *f*; opinion *f*; idée *f.*

notorious *adj* notoire.

noun *n* (*gr*) nom, substantif *m.*

nourishing *adj* nourrissant.

nourishment *n* nourriture *f*, aliments *mpl.*

novel *n* roman *m.*

novelist *n* romancier *m* -ière *f.*

novelty n nouveauté f.

November n novembre m.

now adv maintenant; **~ and then** de temps en temps.

nowadays adv de nos jours, à l'heure actuelle.

nowhere adv nulle part.

nozzle n douille f.

nuclear adj nucléaire.

nude adj nu.

nudge vt donner un coup de coude à.

nudist n nudiste mf.

nudity n nudité f.

nuisance n ennui m; gêne f.

null adj nul.

numb adj engourdi; * vt engourdir.

number n numéro, nombre m; quantité f; * vt numéroter; compter.

numberplate n plaque d'immatriculation f.

numbness n engourdissement m.

numeral n chiffre m.

numerical adj numérique.

numerous adj nombreux.

nun n religieuse f.

nurse n infirmière f; * vt soigner; ménager.

nursery n crèche f; chambre d'enfant f.

nursery rhyme n comptine f.

nursery school n (école) maternelle f.

nursing home n maison de repos f.

nut n noix f.

nutmeg n noix de muscade f.

nutritious adj nutritif.

nylon n nylon m; * adj en nylon.

O

oak n chêne m.

oar n rame f.

oath n serment m.

oatmeal n flocons d'avoine mpl.

oats npl avoine f.

obedience n obéissance f.

obedient adj obéissant; **~ly** adv avec obéissance.

obese adj obèse.

obesity n obésité f.

obey vt obéir à.

obituary n nécrologie f.

object n objet m; * vt objecter.

objection n objection f.

objectionable adj désagréable.

objective adj n objectif m.

obligation n obligation f.

obligatory adj obligatoire.

oblige vt obliger; rendre service à.

obliging adj obligeant.

oblique adj oblique; indirect.

obliterate vt effacer.

oblivion n oubli m.

oblivious adj oublieux.

obnoxious adj odieux.

oboe n hautbois m.

obscene adj obscène.

obscenity n obscénité f.

obscure adj obscur.

obscurity n obscurité f.

observant *adj* observateur; respectueux.

observation *n* observation *f.*

observe *vt* observer.

observer *n* observateur *m* -trice *f.*

obsess *vt* obséder.

obsessive *adj* obsédant.

obsolete *adj* désuet.

obstacle *n* obstacle *m.*

obstinate *adj* obstiné.

obstruct *vt* obstruer; entraver.

obstruction *n* obstruction *f;* encombrement *m.*

obtain *vt* obtenir.

obtrusive *adj* importun.

obvious *adj* évident.

occasion *n* occasion *f.*

occasional *adj* occasionnel.

occupant, occupier *n* occupant *m* -e *f;* locataire *mf.*

occupation *n* occupation *f;* emploi *m.*

occupy *vt* occuper.

occur *vi* se produire, arriver.

occurrence *n* incident *m.*

ocean *n* océan *m.*

October *n* octobre *m.*

octopus *n* poulpe *m.*

odd *adj* impair; étrange; quelconque; ~ly *adv* étrangement.

oddity *n* singularité, particularité *f.*

odds *npl* chances *fpl.*

odour *n* odeur *f;* parfum *m.*

of *prep* de; à.

off *adj* éteint; fermé; annulé; en congé.

offence *n* offense *f;* injure *f.*

offend *vt* offenser, blesser; choquer; * *vi* pécher.

offender *n* délinquant *m* -e *f.*

offensive *adj* offensant; injurieux\.

offer *vt* offrir; * *n* offre *f.*

offering *n* offrande *f;* offre *f.*

offhand *adj* désinvolte; * *adv* soudainement.

office *n* bureau *m;* poste *m,* fonctions *fpl;* service *m.*

officer *n* officier *m;* fonctionnaire *mf.*

official *adj* ~ly *adv* officiel(lement); * *n* employé *m* -e *f.*

officiate *vi* officier.

off-peak *adj* aux heures creuses.

offset *vt* compenser; décaler.

offshoot *n* ramification *f.*

offside *adj* hors jeu.

offspring *n* progéniture *f;* descendance *f.*

offstage *adv* en coulisses.

ogle *vt* lorgner.

oil *n* huile *f;* * *vt* huiler.

oil painting *n* peinture à l'huile *f.*

oil rig *n* derrick *m.*

oil tanker *n* pétrolier *m.*

oil well *n* puits pétrolifère *m.*

oily *adj* huileux; gras.

ointment *n* onguent *m.*

OK, okay *excl* O.K., d'accord; * *adj* bien; * *vt* approuver.

old *adj* vieux, *f* vieille.

old age *n* vieillesse *f.*

old-fashioned *adj* démodé.

olive *n* olivier *m;* olive *f.*

olive oil *n* huile d'olive *f.*

omelet(te) *n* omelette *f.*

omen *n* augure, présage *m.*

ominous *adj* menaçant.

omission *n* omission *f;* négligence *f.*

omit *vt* omettre.

on *prep* sur, dessus; en; pour; * *adj* allumé; branché; ouvert; de service.

once *adv* une fois; **at ~** tout de suite; **all at ~** tout d'un coup; **~ more** encore une fois.

oncoming *adj* qui arrive.

one *adj* un, une; **~ by ~** un par un.

one-man *adj* individuel.

onerous *adj* lourd; (*law*) dur.

oneself *pn* soi-même.

one-sided *adj* partial.

one-to-one *adj* face à face.

ongoing *adj* continu; en cours.

onion *n* oignon *m*.

on-line *adj adv* en ligne.

onlooker *n* spectateur *m* -trice *f*.

only *adj* seul, unique; * *adv* seulement.

onset, onslaught *n* début *m*; attaque *f*.

onward(s) *adv* en avant.

ooze *vi* suinter.

open *adj* ouvert; public; déclaré; sincère, franc; **~ly** *adv* ouvertement; * *vt* ouvrir; * *vi* s'ouvrir; commencer.

opening *n* ouverture *f*; (*com*) débouché *m*; inauguration *f*; commencement *m*.

open-minded *adj* aux idées larges.

openness *n* clareté *f*, franchise, sincérité *f*.

opera *n* opéra *m*.

operate *vi* fonctionner; opérer.

operation *n* fonctionnement *m*; opération *f*.

operator *n* opérateur *m* -trice *f*; téléphoniste *mf*.

opinion *n* opinion *f*; jugement *m*.

opinionated *adj* entêté.

opinion poll *n* sondage *m*.

opponent *n* opposant *m* -e *f*; adversaire *mf*.

opportunity *n* occasion *f*.

oppose *vt* s'opposer à.

opposite *adj* opposé; contraire; * *adv* en face; *prep* en face de; * *n* contraire *m*.

opposition *n* opposition *f*; résistance *f*.

oppress *vt* opprimer.

oppression *n* oppression *f*.

oppressive *adj* oppressif.

oppressor *n* oppresseur *m*.

optic(al) *adj* optique.

optician *n* opticien *m* -ne *f*.

optimist *n* optimiste *mf*.

optimistic *adj* optimiste.

option *n* option *f*.

optional *adj* optionnel; facultatif.

or *conj* ou.

oral *adj* oral, verbal.

orange *n* orange *f*.

orator *n* orateur *m* -trice *f*.

orbit *n* orbite *f*.

orchard *n* verger *m*.

orchestra *n* orchestre *m*.

orchid *n* orchidée *f*.

ordeal *n* épreuve *f*.

order *n* ordre *m*; commande *f*; mandat *m*; classe *f*; * *vt* ordonner; commander; mettre en ordre.

orderly *adj* ordonné; réglé.

ordinary *adj* ordinaire.

ore *n* minerai *m*.

organ *n* organe *m*; orgue *m*.

organic *adj* organique.

organisation *n* organisation *f*.

organise *vt* organiser.

organism *n* organisme *m*.

organist *n* organiste *mf*.

orgasm *n* orgasme *m*.

oriental *adj* oriental.

orifice *n* orifice *m*.

origin *n* origine *f*.

original *adj* original; originel.

originality *n* originalité *f*.

originate *vi* provenir (de); être originaire (de).

ornament *n* ornement *m*; * *vt* ornementer, décorer.

ornamental *adj* ornemental.

ornate *adj* ornementé.

orphan *adj n* orphelin *m* -e *f*.

orphanage *n* orphelinat *m*.

orthodox *adj* orthodoxe.

osprey *n* balbuzard pêcheur *m*.

ostensibly *adv* selon les apparences.

ostentatious *adj* ostentatoire.

ostracise *vt* frapper d'ostracisme.

ostrich *n* autruche *f*.

other *pn* autre.

otherwise *adv* autrement.

otter *n* loutre *f*.

ought *v aux* devoir; falloir.

ounce *n* once *f*.

our *pn* notre, *pl* nos.

ours *pn* le nôtre, la nôtre, les nôtres; à nous.

ourselves *pn pl* nous-mêmes.

oust *vt* évincer; déposséder.

out *adv* dehors; éteint.

outback *n* intérieur *m*.

outboard *adj*: ~ **motor** (moteur) hors-bord *m*.

outbreak *n* éruption *f*; explosion *f*.

outburst *n* explosion *f*.

outcast *n* paria *m*.

outcome *n* résultat *m*.

outcry *n* protestations *fpl*.

outdated *adj* démodé; périmé.

outdo *vt* surpasser.

outdoor *adj* de plein air, ~s *adv* à l'extérieur.

outer *adj* extérieur.

outermost *adj* extrême; le plus à l'extérieur.

outfit *n* tenue *f*; équipement *m*.

outgoing *adj* extroverti; sortant.

outing *n* excursion *f*.

outlandish *adj* bizarre.

outlaw *n* hors-la-loi *m*; * *vt* proscrire.

outlet *n* sortie *f*; débouché *m*.

outline *n* contour *m*; grandes lignes *fpl*.

outlook *n* perspective *f*.

outmoded *adj* démodé.

outnumber *vt* être plus nombreux que.

out-of-date *adj* périmé; démodé.

out-patient *n* patient(e) en consultation externe *m(f)*.

output *n* rendement *m*; sortie *f*.

outrage *n* outrage *m*; * *vt* outrager.

outrageous *adj* outrageant; atroce.

outright *adv* absolument, complètement; * *adj* absolu, complet.

outset *n* commencement *m*.

outshine *vt* éclipser.

outside *n* surface *f*; extérieur *m*; apparence *f*; * *adv* dehors; * *prep* en dehors de.

outsize *adj* grande taille.

outskirts *npl* périphérie *f*, alentours *mpl*.

outspoken *adj* franc.

outstanding *adj* exceptionnel; en suspens.

outward *adj* extérieur; vers l'extérieur; d'aller.

outwit *vt* être plus spirituel que.

oval *n*, *adj* ovale *m*.

ovary *n* ovaire *m*.

oven *n* four *m*.

over *prep* sur, dessus; plus de; pendant; all ~ de tous côtés; * *adj* fini; en trop, en plus.

overall *adj* total; * *adv* dans l'ensemble; ~s *npl* salopette *f*.

overawe *vt* impressionner.

overbearing *adj* despotique.

overboard *adv* (mar) par-dessus bord.

overcast *adj* couvert.

overcharge *vt* surcharger; faire payer un prix excessif à.

overcoat *n* pardessus *m*.

overcome *vt* vaincre; surmonter.

overcrowded *adj* bondé; surpeuplé.

overdraft *n* découvert *m*.

overdrawn *adj* à découvert.

overdue *adj* en retard; arriéré.

overeat *vi* trop manger.

overestimate *vt* surestimer.

overflow *vt* déborder de; * *vi* déborder; * *n* inondation *f*; surplus *m*.

overgrown *adj* envahi.

overgrowth *n* végétation envahissante *f*.

overhang *vt* surplomber.

overhaul *vt* réviser; * *n* révision *f*.

overhead *adv* en l'air, au-dessus.

overhear *vt* entendre par hasard.

overjoyed *adj* fou de joie.

overlap *vi* se chevaucher.

overlook *vt* dominer; donner sur; oublier; laisser passer, tolérer; négliger.

overnight *adv* pendant la nuit; * *adj* de nuit.

overpowering *adj* écrasant.

overrate *vt* surévaluer.

overriding *adj* prédominant.

overrule *vt* rejeter; annuler.

overrun *vt* envahir; infester; dépasser.

overseas *adv* à l'étranger; outre-mer; * *adj* étranger.

overseer *n* contremaître *m*.

overshadow *vt* éclipser.

oversight *n* oubli *m*; erreur *f*.

oversleep *vi* se réveiller en retard.

overspill *n* excédent de population *m*.

overstep *vt* dépasser.

overt *adj* ouvert; public.

overtake *vt* doubler.

overthrow *vt* renverser; détruire; * *n* renversement *m*; ruine, déroute *f*.

overtime *n* heures supplémentaires *fpl*.

overture *n* ouverture *f*.

overturn *vt* renverser.

overweight *adj* trop lourd.

overwhelming *adj* écrasant; irrésistible.

overwork *vi* se surmener, trop travailler.

owe *vt* devoir; être redevable de.

owing *adj* dû; ~ **to** en raison de.

owl *n* chouette *f*.

own *adj* propre; **my ~** mon, ma, mes propre(s); * *vt* posséder; ~ **up** *vi* confesser.

owner *n* propriétaire *mf*.

ownership *n* possession *f*.

ox *n* bœuf *m*; **~en** *pl* bœufs *mpl*.

oxygen *n* oxygène *m*.

oyster *n* huître *f*.

ozone *n* ozone *m*.

P

pace *n* pas *m*; allure *f*; * *vt* arpenter; * *vi* marcher.

pacemaker *n* meneur *m* -euse *f* de train; (*med*) pacemaker *m*.

pack *n* paquet *m*; jeu de cartes *m*; bande *f*; * *vt* empaqueter; remplier; * *vi* faire ses valises.

package *n* paquet *m*; accord *m*.

package tour *n* voyage organisé *m*.

packet *n* paquet *m*.

packing n emballage m.

pact n pacte m.

pad n bloc m; coussinet, tampon m; plateforme f; (sl) piaule f; * vt rembourrer.

padding n rembourrage m.

paddle vi ramer; * n pagaie f.

pagan adj n païen m, païenne f.

page n page f; page m.

pageant n grand spectacle m.

pail n seau m.

pain n douleur f; mal m; peine f; * vt peiner.

painful adj douloureux; pénible; ~ly adv douloureusement; péniblement; à grand-peine.

painkiller n analgésique m.

painless adj indolore; sans peine.

painstaking adj soigneux.

paint vt peindre.

paintbrush n pinceau m.

painter n peintre m.

painting n peinture f; tableau m.

paintwork n peinture f.

pair n pair m.

pal n copain m, copine f, pote m.

palatable adj savoureux.

palate n palais m.

palatial adj grandiose.

pale adj pâle; clair.

palette n palette f.

pall n nuage m (de fumée); * vi perdre sa saveur.

pallet n palette f.

palliative adj n palliatif m.

pallid adj pâle.

pallor n pâleur f.

palm n (bot) palme f, palmier m.

palmistry n chiromancie f.

palpable adj palpable; évident.

palpitation n palpitation f.

paltry adj dérisoire; mesquin.

pamper vt gâter, dorloter.

pamphlet n pamphlet m; brochure f.

pan n casserole f; poêle f.

pancake n crêpe f.

pandemonium n pandémonium m.

pane n vitre f.

panel n panneau m; comité m.

pang n angoisse f; tourment m.

panic adj n (de) panique f.

panicky adj paniqué, affolé.

panic-stricken adj pris de panique.

pansy n (bot) pensée f.

pant vi haleter.

panther n panthère f.

pantry n placard m.

pants npl slip m; pantalon m.

paper n papier m; journal m; épreuve f d'examen; exposé m, étude f; ~s pl documents mpl; (com) fonds mpl; * adj en papier; * vt garnir de papier; tapisser.

paperback n livre de poche m.

paper clip n trombone m.

paperweight n presse-papiers m.

paprika n paprika m.

par n équivalence f; égalité f; pair m.

parable n parabole f.

parachute n parachute m; * vi sauter en parachute.

parade n parade f; (mil) défilé m; * vt faire défiler, faire parader; * vi défiler, parader; se pavaner.

paradise n paradis m.

paragraph n paragraphe m.

parallel adj parallèle; * n parallèle f; * vt mettre en parallèle; comparer.

paralyse vt paralyser.

paralysis n paralysie f.

paralytic(al) adj paralytique.

paramount adj suprême, supérieur.

paranoid adj paranoïaque.

paraphernalia n affaires fpl; attirail m.

parasite n parasite m.

paratrooper n parachutiste m.

parcel n paquet m; parcelle f; * vt empaqueter, emballer.

parched adj desséché.

parchment n parchemin m.

pardon n pardon m; * vt pardonner.

parent n parent m -e f; ~s parents mpl.

parish n paroisse f; * adj paroissial.

park n parc m; * vt garer; vi se garer.

parking n stationnement m.

parking meter n parcomètre m.

parking ticket n amende pour stationnement interdit f.

parliament n parlement m.

parliamentary adj parlementaire.

parlour n parloir m; salon m.

parody n parodie f; * vt parodier.

parole n: on ~ sur parole.

parrot n perroquet m.

parry vt parer.

parsley n (bot) persil m.

parsnip n (bot) navet m.

part n partie f; part f; rôle (d'acteur) m; raie f; * vt séparer; diviser; * vi se séparer; se diviser; ~ with céder; se défaire de; donner; ~ly adv en partie.

partial adj partial; ~ly adv avec partialité; partiellement.

participant n participant m -e f.

participate vi participer (à).

participation n participation f.

particular adj particulier, singulier; * n particulier m; particularité f.

parting n séparation f; raie (dans les cheveux) f.

partisan n partisan m -e f.

partition n partition, séparation f; * vt diviser en plusieurs parties, partager,

partner n associé m -e f.

partridge n perdrix f.

party n parti m; fête f.

pass vt passer; dépasser; adopter; être admis à; * vi passer; * n permis m; passage m; ~ away vi mourir; ~ by vi passer; vt négliger, oublier; ~ on vt transmettre; passer.

passage n passage m; traversée f; couloir m.

passenger n passager m -ère f.

passer-by n passant m -e f.

passing adj passager.

passion n passion f; amour m; emportement m.

passionate adj passionné; ~ly adv passionnément; ardemment.

passive adj passif.

Passover n Pâque f juive.

passport n passeport m.

password n mot de passe m.

past adj passé; * n (gr) prétérit m; passé m; * prep au-delà de; après.

pasta n pâtes fpl.

paste n pâte f; colle f; * vt coller.

pasteurised adj pasteurisé.

pastime n passe-temps m invar; divertissement m.

pastor n pasteur m.

pastry n pâtisserie f.

pasture n pâture f.

pat vt tapoter.

patch n pièce f; tache f; terrain m; * vt rapiécer; ~ up réparer; se réconcilier.

patent adj breveté; évident; * n brevet m; * vt faire breveter.

patent leather n cuir verni m.

paternal adj paternel.

paternity n paternité f.

path n chemin, sentier m.

pathetic adj ~**ally** adv pathétique(ment); lamentable(ment).

pathology n pathologie f.

pathos n pathétique m.

patience n patience f.

patient adj patient; * n patient m, -e f.

patriot n patriote mf.

patriotic adj patriotique.

patrol n patrouille f; * vi patrouiller.

patron n protecteur m; client m -e f.

patronise vt patronner, protéger.

patter n trottinement m; bavardage m; * vi trottiner.

pattern n motif m; modèle m.

paunch n panse f; ventre m.

pauper n pauvre mf.

pause n pause f; * vi faire une pause; hésiter.

pave vt paver; carreler.

pavement n trottoir m.

paw n patte f; * vt tripoter.

pawn n pion m; gage m; * vt engager.

pay vt payer; ~ **back** vt rembourser; ~ **for** payer; ~ **off** vt liquider; vi payer; rapporter; * n paie f; salaire m.

pay day n jour de paie m.

payment n paiement m.

pay-phone n téléphone public m.

pea n pois m.

peace n paix f.

peaceful adj paisible; pacifique.

peach n pêche f.

peacock n paon m.

peak n pic m; maximum m.

peal n carillon m; grondement m.

peanut n cacahuète f.

pear n poire f.

pearl n perle f.

peasant n paysan m -ne f.

peat n tourbe f.

pebble n caillou m; galet m.

peck n coup de bec m; * vt picoter.

peculiar adj étrange, singulier.

peculiarity n particularité, singularité f.

pedal n pédale f; * vi pédaler.

pedestal n piédestal m.

pedestrian n piéton m -ne f; * adj pédestre.

pedigree n généalogie f; pedigree m; * adj de race.

peek vi regarder à la dérobée.

peel vt peler; éplucher; * vi peler; * n peau f; pelure f.

peer n pair m.

peerless adj incomparable.

peeved adj fâché.

peg n cheville f; piquet m; * vt cheviller.

pellet n boulette f.

pelt n fourrure f; * vt arroser; * vi pleuvoir à verse.

pen n stylo m; plume f; enclos m.

penalty n peine f; sanction f; amende f.

penance n pénitence f.

pence n = pl of **penny**.

pencil n crayon m.

pencil case n trousse f.

pendant n pendentif m.

pendulum n pendule m.

penetrate vt pénétrer (dans).

penicillin n pénicilline f.

peninsula n péninsule f.

penis n pénis m.

penitence n pénitence f.

penknife n canif m.

penniless adj sans le sou.

penny n penny m.

penpal n correspondant m -e f.

pension n pension f.

pensive adj pensif.

penthouse n appartement situé sur le toit d'un immeuble m.

pent-up adj reprimé, refoulé.

people n peuple m; nation f; gens mpl; * vt peupler.

pep n énergie f; ~ **up** vt animer.

pepper n poivre m; * vt poivrer.

peppermint n menthe poivrée f.

per prep par.

per annum adv par an.

per capita adj adv par habitant.

perceive vt percevoir.

percentage n pourcentage m.

perception n perception f; notion f.

perch n perche f.

percolator n percolateur m.

percussion n percussion f.

peremptory adj péremptoire; décisif.

perfect adj parfait; idéal; ~**ly** adv parfaitement; * vt parfaire, perfectionner.

perfection n perfection f.

perforation n perforation f.

perform vt exécuter; effectuer; * vi donner une représentation, tenir un rôle.

performance n exécution f; accomplissement m; rendement m; représentation f.

performer n exécutant m -e f, acteur m -trice f.

perfume n parfum m; * vt parfumer.

perhaps adv peut-être.

peril n péril, danger m.

perimeter n périmètre m.

period n période f; époque f; règles fpl.

periodic(al) adj périodique.

periodical n journal m.

perish vi périr.

perjure vt parjurer.

perjury n parjure m.

perk n extra, à-côté m.

permanent adj permanent.

permissible adj permis.

permission n permission f.

permissive adj permissif.

permit vt permettre; * n permis m.

perpendicular adj ~**ly** adv perpendiculaire(ment).

perpetrate vt perpétrer, commettre.

perpetual adj perpétuel.

perpetuate vt perpétuer, éterniser.

perplex vt confondre, laisser perplexe.

persecute vt persécuter; importuner.

persecution n persécution f.

perseverance n persévérance f.

persevere vi persévérer.

persist vi persister.

persistence n persistance f.

persistent adj persistant.

person n personne f.

personal adj ~**ly** adv personnel-(lement).

personal assistant n secrétaire mf de direction.

personal column n annonces personnelles fpl.

personal computer n ordinateur individuel m.

personality n personnalité f.

personnel n personnel m.

perspective n perspective f.

perspiration n transpiration f.

perspire vi transpirer.

persuade vt persuader.

persuasion n persuasion f.

persuasive adj persuasif; ~**ly** adv de manière persuasive.

pert adj plein d'entrain.

perturb vt perturber.

pervade vt pénétrer, traverser.

perverse adj pervers, dépravé; ~ly adv perversement.

pervert vt pervertir, corrompre.

pessimist n pessimiste mf.

pest n insecte nuisible m; casse-pieds (fam) mf invar.

pester vt importuner, fatiguer.

pestilence n peste f.

pet n animal domestique m; préféré m -e f; * vt gâter; * vi se peloter (fam).

petal n (bot) pétale m.

petite adj menue.

petition n pétition f; * vt présenter une pétition à; supplier.

petrified adj pétrifié.

petroleum n pétrole m.

petticoat n jupon m.

pettiness n insignifiance f.

petty adj mesquin; insignifiant.

petty cash n argent destiné aux dépenses courantes m.

petulant adj pétulant.

pew n banc m.

pewter n étain m.

phantom n fantôme m.

pharmacist n pharmacien m, -ienne f.

pharmacy n pharmacie f.

phase n phase f.

pheasant n faisan m.

phenomenal adj phénoménal.

phenomenon n phénomène m.

philanthropist n philanthrope mf.

philanthropy n philanthropie f.

philosopher n philosophe mf.

philosophical(ly)   adj   (adv) philosophique(ment).

philosophy n philosophie f.

phobia n phobie f.

phone n téléphone m; * vt téléphoner à; ~ back vt vi rappeler; ~ up vt appeler au téléphone.

phone book n annuaire m.

phone box, phone booth n cabine téléphonique f.

phone call n coup de téléphone m.

photocopier n photocopieuse f.

photocopy n photocopie f.

photograph n photo(graphie) f; * vt photographier.

photographer n photographe mf.

photographic adj photographique.

photography n photo(graphie) f.

phrase n phrase f, locution f; * vt exprimer.

phrase book n guide de conversation m.

physical adj ~ly adv physi-que(ment).

physician n médecin m.

physiotherapy n physiothérapie f.

physique n physique m.

pianist n pianiste mf.

piano n piano m.

pick vt choisir; cueillir; gratter; ~ on vt s'en prendre à; ~ out vt choisir; ~ up vi s'améliorer; se remettre; * vt ramasser; décrocher; arrêter; acheter; * n pic m; choix m.

picket n piquet m.

pickpocket n pickpocket m.

picnic n pique-nique m.

pictorial adj pictural; illustré.

picture n image f; peinture f; photo f; * vt dépeindre; se figurer.

picturesque adj pittoresque.

pie n gâteau m; tarte f; pâté en croûte m.

piece n morceau m; pièce f; tranche f; * vt raccommoder.

pier n jetée f.

pierce vt percer, transpercer.

pig n cochon m.

pigeon n pigeon m.

pigeonhole n casier m.

pigheaded adj têtu.

pigsty n porcherie f.

pigtail n natte f.

pile n tas m; pile f; amas m; poil m; **~s** pl hémorroïdes fpl; * vt entasser, empiler.

pilgrim n pèlerin m.

pilgrimage n pèlerinage m.

pill n pilule f.

pillage vt piller, mettre à sac.

pillar n pilier m.

pillion n siège arrière m.

pillow n oreiller m.

pillow case n taie d'oreiller f.

pilot n pilote m; * vt piloter; (fig) mener.

pimp n proxénète, maquereau (fam) m.

pimple n bouton m.

pin n épingle f; goupille f; **~s and needles** npl fourmis fpl; * vt épingler; goupiller.

pinafore n tablier m.

pinball n flipper m.

pincers n tenailles fpl.

pinch vt pincer; (sl) piquer, faucher; * vi serrer; * n pincement m; pincée f.

pincushion n pelote à épingles f.

pine n (bot) pin m; * vi languir.

pineapple n ananas m.

pink adj n rose m.

pinnacle n sommet m.

pinpoint vt préciser; souligner.

pint n pinte f.

pioneer n pionnier m.

pious adj pieux, dévot.

pip n pépin m.

pipe n tube, tuyau m; pipe f; **~s** tuyauterie f.

piper n joueur de cornemuse m.

pique n pique f; dépit m.

piracy n piraterie f.

pirate n pirate m.

pirouette n pirouette f; vi pirouetter.

pistol n pistolet m.

piston n piston m.

pit n noyau m; mine f; fosse f.

pitch n lancement m; ton m; * vt lancer, jeter; * vi tomber; piquer du nez.

pitcher n cruche f.

pitchfork n fourche f.

pitfall n piège m.

pithy adj moelleux; vigoureux.

pitiable adj pitoyable; déplorable.

pitiful adj pitoyable; lamentable.

pittance n salaire de misère m; pitance f.

pity n pitié f; * vt avoir pitié de.

pivot n pivot, axe m.

pizza n pizza f.

placard n affiche f.

placate vt apaiser.

place n endroit, lieu m; place f; * vt placer; mettre.

placid adj placide, calme.

plagiarism n plagiat m.

plague n peste f; * vt tourmenter; infester.

plaice n carrelet m.

plain adj uni; simple; clair, sincère; commun; évident; **~ly** adv simplement; clairement; * n plaine f.

plait n tresse f; * vt tresser.

plan n plan m; projet m; * vt projeter.

plane n avion m; plan m; rabot m; * vt aplanir; raboter.

planet n planète f.

plank n planche f.

plant n plante f; usine f; machinerie f; * vt planter.

plantation n plantation f.

plaster n plâtre m; emplâtre m; * vt plâtrer; emplâtrer.

plastered adj (sl) bourré, soûl.

plastic adj plastique.

plastic surgery n chirurgie esthétique f.

plate n assiette f; plaque f; lame f.

plateau n (geol) plateau m.

plate glass n vitre f.

platform n plateforme f.

platinum n platine m.

platoon n (mil) peloton m.

platter n écuelle f; plat m.

plausible adj plausible.

play n jeu m; pièce de théâtre f; * vt vi jouer; (also mus) ~ **down** vt rabaisser; minimiser.

player n joueur m -euse f; acteur m -trice f.

playful adj enjoué, amusé; ~ly adv d'une manière enjouée; pour s'amuser.

playground n cour de récréation f; jardin d'enfants m.

playgroup n halte-garderie f.

playpen n parc pour enfant m.

playwright n dramaturge mf.

plea n appel m; excuse f, prétexte m.

plead vt plaider; prétexter.

pleasant adj agréable; plaisant; aimable.

please vt faire plaisir à.

pleased adj content.

pleasing adj agréable, plaisant.

pleasure n plaisir m; gré m, volonté f.

pleat n pli m.

pledge n promesse f; gage m; * vt engager; promettre.

plentiful adj copieux; abondant.

plenty n abondance f; ~ **of** beaucoup de.

pliers npl pinces fpl.

plight n épreuve f; situation difficile f.

plod vi se traîner, avancer péniblement.

plot n petit morceau de terrain m; complot m; intrigue f; * vt tracer; comploter; conspirer.

plough n charrue f; * vt labourer.

ploy n truc m.

pluck vt tirer; arracher; déplumer; * n courage m.

plug n tampon m; bouchon m; bougie f; prise f; * vt boucher.

plum n prune f.

plumage n plumage m.

plumber n plombier m.

plume n plume f, panache m.

plump adj rondouillet, dodu.

plunder vt mettre à sac, piller; * n pillage m; butin m.

plunge vi plonger; s'élancer.

plunger n piston m.

plural adj n pluriel m.

plus n signe plus m; * prep plus.

plush adj en peluche.

ply vt manier avec vigueur; * vi s'appliquer.

plywood n contreplaqué m.

pneumatic drill n marteau pneumatique m.

pneumonia n pneumonie f.

poach vt pocher; braconner; vi braconner.

poacher n braconnier m.

pocket n poche f; * vt empocher.

pocket money n argent de poche m.

pod n cosse f.

podgy adj boudiné.

poem n poème m.

poet n poète m.

poetic adj poétique.

poetry n poésie f.

point n pointe f; point m; promon-toire m; **~ of view** n point de vue m; ***** vt pointer; tailler en pointe; indiquer.

point-blank adv à bout portant; directement.

pointed adj pointu; acéré; **~ly** adv subtilement.

pointer n auguille f; pointer m.

pointless adj inutile.

poise n attitude f; équilibre m.

poison n poison m; ***** vt empoisonner.

poisoning n empoisonnement m.

poisonous adj vénéneux.

poke vt attiser; donner un coup de coude à; pousser du doigt.

poker n tison m; poker m.

polar adj polaire.

pole n pôle m; mât m; perche f.

pole vault n saut à la perche m.

police n police f.

police car n voiture de police f.

policeman n agent de police m.

police station n commissariat m.

policewoman n femme agent de police f.

policy n politique f; police d'assurance f.

polio n polio f.

polish vt polir; cirer; **~ off** vt parachever; expédier; ***** n poli m.

polished adj poli; ciré; élégant.

polite adj **~ly** adv poli(ment), courtois(ement).

political adj politique.

politician n homme (femme) politique m(f).

politics npl politique f.

polka n polka f; **~ dot** n pois m.

poll n liste électorale f; vote m; sondage m.

pollen n (bot) pollen m.

pollution n pollution, contamination f.

polyester n polyester m.

polystyrene n polystyrène m.

pomegranate n grenade f.

pomp n pompe f; splendeur f.

pompom n pompon m.

pompous adj pompeux.

pond n mare f; étang m.

ponder vt considérer; réfléchir à.

ponderous adj lourd, pesant.

pontoon n ponton m.

pony n poney m.

ponytail n queue de cheval f.

pool n flaque d'eau f; piscine f; ***** vt grouper.

poor adj pauvre; mauvais.

pop n pop m; papa m; boisson gazeuse f; éclatement m; *** ~ in/out** vi entrer/sortir un instant.

popcorn n popcorn m.

Pope n pape m.

poplar n peuplier m.

poppy n (bot) pavot m.

popular adj **~ly** adv popu-laire(ment).

popularity n popularité f.

population n population f.

porcelain n porcelaine f.

porch n porche m.

porcupine n porc-épic m.

pore n pore m.

pork n porc m (viande).

pornography n pornographie f.

porous adj poreux.

porpoise n marsouin m.

porridge n porridge m, flocons d'avoine mpl.

port n port m; (mar) sabord m; babord m; porto (vin) m.

portable adj portable, portatif.

porter n portier m; garçon m.

porthole n hublot m.

portion n portion, part f.

portrait n portrait m.

portray *vt* faire le portrait de; dépeindre.

pose *n* posture *f*; pose *f*; * *vt vi* poser.

posh *adj* chic; bourgeois.

position *n* position *f*; situation *f*; * *vt* mettre en position.

positive *adj* positif; réel; favorable; **~ly** *adv* positivement; assurément.

possess *vt* posséder.

possession *n* possession *f*.

possessive *adj* possessif.

possibility *n* possibilité *f*.

possible *adj* possible; **~ly** *adv* peut-être.

post *n* courrier *m*; poste *f*; emploi *m*; poste *m*; pieu *m*; * *vt* poster; fixer.

postage *n* affranchissement *m*.

postcard *n* carte postale *f*.

posterior *n* postérieur *m*.

posterity *n* postérité *f*.

postgraduate *n* licencié *m* -e *f*.

posthumous *adj* posthume.

postman *n* facteur *m*.

postmark *n* cachet de la poste *m*.

post office *n* poste *f*, bureau de poste *m*.

postpone *vt* remettre; différer.

postscript *n* post-scriptum *m*.

posture *n* posture *f*.

posy *n* petit bouquet de fleurs *m*.

pot *n* pot *m*; marmite *f*; (*sl*) marijuana *f*.

potato *n* pomme de terre, patate (*fam*) *f*.

potent *adj* puissant.

potential *adj* potentiel.

pothole *n* trou *m*.

potion *n* potion *f*.

pottery *n* poterie *f*.

pouch *n* sac *m*.

poultice *n* cataplasme *m*.

poultry *n* volaille *f*.

pound *n* livre *f*, livre sterling *f*; fourrière *f*; * *vt* concasser; * *vi* taper fort.

pour *vt* verser; servir; * *vi* couler; pleuvoir à verse.

pout *vi* faire la moue.

poverty *n* pauvreté *f*.

powder *n* poudre *f*; * *vt* saupoudrer.

powder puff *n* houppette *f*.

powdery *adj* poudreux.

power *n* pouvoir *m*; puissance *f*; empire *m*; autorité *f*; force *f*; * *vt* propulser.

powerful *adj* puissant.

power station *n* centrale électrique *f*.

practical *adj* **~ly** *adv* pratique(ment).

practicality *n* faisabilité *f*.

practical joke *n* farce *f*.

practice *n* pratique *f*; usage *m*; entraînement *m*; **~s** *pl* agissements *mpl*.

practise *vt* pratiquer, exercer; * *vi* s'exercer, s'entraîner.

prairie *n* prairie *f*.

praise *n* éloge *m*; louange *f*; * *vt* louer.

praiseworthy *adj* digne d'éloges.

prance *vi* cabrioler.

prank *n* folie, extravagance *f*.

prawn *n* crevette *f*.

pray *vi* prier.

prayer *n* prière *f*.

preach *vt* prêcher.

preacher *n* prédicateur *m*.

precarious *adj* précaire, incertain.

precaution *n* précaution *f*.

precede *vt* précéder.

precedent *adj n* précédent *m*.

precinct *n* limite *f*; enceinte *f*; circonscription *f*.

precious *adj* précieux.

precipice *n* (*fig*) précipice *m*.

precise *n* précis, exact.

precision *n* précision, exactitude *f*.

preclude *vt* exclure, empêcher.

precocious *adj* précoce, prématuré.

preconceive *vt* préconcevoir.

precursor *n* précurseur *m*.

predator *n* prédateur *m*.

predecessor *n* prédécesseur *m*.

predestination *n* prédestination *f*.

predicament *n* situation difficile *f*.

predict *vt* prédire.

predictable *adj* prévisible.

prediction *n* prédiction *f*.

predilection *n* prédilection *f*.

predominant *adj* prédominant.

preen *vt* nettoyer (ses plumes).

preface *n* préface *f*.

prefer *vt* préférer.

preferable *adj* préférable.

preferably *adv* de préférence.

preference *n* préférence *f*.

preferential *adj* préférentiel.

prefix *vt* préfixer; * *n* (*gr*) préfixe *m*.

pregnancy *n* grossesse *f*.

pregnant *adj* enceinte.

prehistoric *adj* préhistorique.

prejudice *n* (*law*) préjudice, tort *m*; préjugé *m*.

prejudiced *adj* qui a des préjugés; partial.

preliminary *adj* préliminaire.

prelude *n* prélude *m*.

premarital *adj* préconjugal.

premature *adj* **~ly** *adv* prématuré(ment).

premeditation *n* préméditation *f*.

première *n* (*thea*) première *f*.

premises *npl* locaux *mpl*.

premium *n* prix *m*; indemnité *f*; prime *f*.

premonition *n* pressentiment *m*, prémonition *f*.

preoccupied *adj* préoccupé; absorbé.

preparation *n* préparation *f*.

preparatory *adj* préparatoire.

prepare *vt* préparer; * *vi* se préparer.

preposition *n* préposition *f*.

preposterous *adj* ridicule, absurde.

prerequisite *n* condition requise *f*.

prerogative *n* prérogative *f*.

prescription *n* prescription *f*; ordonnance *f*.

presence *n* présence *f*.

present *n* cadeau *m*; * *adj* présent; actuel; **~ly** *adv* actuellement; * *vt* offrir, donner; présenter.

presentation *n* présentation *f*.

presenter *n* présentateur *m* -trice *f*.

presentiment *n* pressentiment *m*, prémonition *f*.

preservation *n* préservation *f*.

preservative *n* préservatif *m*.

preserve *vt* préserver; conserver; faire des conserves de.

preside *vi* présider; diriger.

president *n* président *m*.

presidential *adj* présidentiel.

press *vt* appuyer sur; serrer; pressurer; * *vi* se presser; * *n* presse *f*; pressoir *m*; pression *f*.

press conference *n* conférence de presse *f*.

pressing *adj* pressant; urgent.

pressure *n* pression *f*.

pressure group *n* groupe de pression *m*.

prestige *n* prestige *m*.

presumably *adv* vraisemblablement.

presume *vt* présumer, supposer.

presumptuous *adj* présomptueux.

presuppose *vt* présupposer.

pretence *n* prétexte *m*; simulation *f*; prétention *f*.

pretend *vi* prétendre; faire semblant.

pretentious *adj* prétentieux.

pretext *n* prétexte *m*.

pretty *adj* joli, mignon; * *adv* assez; plutôt.

prevalent *adj* prédominant.

prevent *vt* prévenir; empêcher; éviter.

prevention *n* prévention *f*.

preview *n* avant-première *f*.

previous *adj* précédent; antérieur; ~**ly** *adv* auparavant.

prey *n* proie *f*.

price *n* prix *m*.

priceless *adj* inappréciable.

prick *vt* piquer; exciter; * *n* piqûre *f*; pointe *f*.

prickle *n* picotement *m*; épine *f*.

prickly *adj* épineux.

pride *n* orgueil *m*; vanité *f*; fierté *f*.

priest *n* prêtre *m*.

priggish *adj* affecté, bégueule.

prim *adj* prude, affecté.

primarily *adv* principalement, surtout.

primary *adj* primaire; principal, premier.

primate *n* primate *m*.

prime *n* (*fig*) fleur *f*; commencement *m*; * *adj* premier; principal; excellent; * *vt* amorcer.

prime minister *n* premier ministre *m*.

primitive *adj* primitif.

primrose *n* (*bot*) primevère *f*.

prince *n* prince *m*.

princess *n* princesse *f*.

principal *adj* ~**ly** *adv* principal(ement); * *n* principal *m*.

principle *n* principe *m*.

print *vt* imprimer; * *n* impression *f*; estampe *f*; caractères imprimés *mpl*.

printer *n* imprimeur *m*; imprimante *f*.

printing *n* impression *f*.

prior *adj* antérieur, précédent.

priority *n* priorité *f*.

prism *n* prisme *m*.

prison *n* prison *f*.

prisoner *n* prisonnier *m* -ière *f*.

pristine *adj* d'origine; intact.

privacy *n* intimité *f*.

private *adj* privé; secret; particulier; ~**ly** *adv* en privé.

private eye *n* détective privé *m*.

privilege *n* privilège *m*.

prize *n* prix *m*; * *vt* apprécier, évaluer.

prizewinner *n* gagnant *m*, -e *f*.

pro *prep* pour.

probability *n* probabilité *f*; vraisemblance *f*.

probable *adj* probable, vraisemblable; ~**bly** *adv* probablement.

probation *n* essai *m*; probation *f*.

probe *n* sonde *f*; enquête *f*; * *vt* sonder; * *vi* faire des recherches.

problem *n* problème *m*.

procedure *n* procédure *f*.

proceed *vi* procéder; provenir; poursuivre; ~**s** *npl* produit *m*; montant *m*.

proceedings *n* procédure *f*; procédé *m*; procès *m*.

process *n* processus *m*; procédé *m*.

procession *n* procession *f*.

proclaim *vt* proclamer; promulguer.

proclamation *n* proclamation *f*; décret *m*.

procrastinate *vt* différer, retarder.

procure *vt* procurer.

prod *vt* pousser.

prodigal *adj* prodigue.

prodigious *adj* prodigieux.

prodigy *n* prodige *m*.

produce *vt* produire; créer; fabriquer; * *n* produit *m*.

producer n producteur m -trice f.

product n produit m; œuvre f; fruit m.

production n production f; produit m.

productive adj productif.

productivity n productivité f.

profane adj profane.

profess vt professer; exercer; déclarer.

profession n profession f.

professional adj professionnel.

professor n professeur m.

proficiency n capacité f.

proficient adj compétent.

profile n profil m.

profit n bénéfice, profit m; avantage m; * vi profiter (de).

profitability n rentabilité f.

profitable adj profitable, avantageux.

profound adj ~ly adv profond(ément).

profuse adj profus; prodigue; ~ly adv à profusion.

program(me) n programme m.

programming n programmation f.

programmer n programmeur m -euse f.

progress n progrès m; cours m; * vi progresser.

progression n progression f; avance f.

progressive adj progressif.

prohibit vt prohiber; défendre.

prohibition n prohibition f.

project vt projeter; * n projet m.

projectile n projectile m.

projection n projection f.

projector n projecteur m.

prolific adj prolifique, fécond.

prologue n prologue m.

prolong vt prolonger.

prominence n proéminence f; éminence f.

prominent adj proéminent.

promiscuous adj immoral, débauché.

promise n promesse f; * vt promettre.

promising adj prometteur.

promontory n promontoire m.

promote vt promouvoir.

promoter n promoteur m.

promotion n promotion f.

prompt adj ~ly adv prompt(ement).

prong n dent f (fourchette).

pronoun n pronom m.

pronounce vt prononcer; déclarer.

pronounced adj marqué, prononcé.

pronunciation n prononciation f.

proof n preuve f; * adj imperméable; résistant.

prop vt soutenir; * n appui, soutien m; tuteur m.

propaganda n propagande f.

propel vt propulser.

propeller n hélice f.

proper adj propre; convenable; exact; approprié; ~ly adv convenablement; correctement.

property n propriété f.

prophecy n prophétie f.

prophesy vt prophétiser, prédire.

prophet n prophète m.

proportion n proportion f; symétrie f.

proportional adj proportionnel.

proposal n proposition f; offre f.

propose vt proposer.

proposition n proposition f.

proprietor n propriétaire mf.

prose n prose f.

prosecution n poursuites fpl; accusation f.

prosecutor n (law) procureur m.

prospect n perspective f; espoir m; * vt vi prospecter.

prospective adj probable; futur.

prosper *vi* prospérer.

prosperity *n* prospérité *f.*

prosperous *adj* prospère.

prostitute *n* prostituée *f.*

prostitution *n* prostitution *f.*

protect *vt* protéger; abriter.

protection *n* protection *f.*

protective *adj* protecteur.

protector *n* protecteur *m* -trice *f.*

protégé *n* protégé *m* -e *f.*

protein *n* protéine *f.*

protest *vi* protester; * *n* protestation *f.*

Protestant *n* protestant *m* -e *f.*

protocol *n* protocole *m.*

prototype *n* prototype *m.*

protrude *vi* déborder, ressortir.

proud *adj* fier, orgueilleux.

prove *vt* prouver; justifier; * *vi* s'avérer; se révéler.

proverb *n* proverbe *m.*

provide *vt* fournir; ~ **for** pourvoir aux besoins de; prévoir.

provided *conj*: ~ **that** pourvu que.

providence *n* providence *f.*

province *n* province *f*; compétence *f.*

provincial *adj* *n* provincial *m* -e *f.*

provision *n* provision *f*; disposition *f.*

provisional *adj* **-ly** *adv* provi-soire(ment).

provocation *n* provocation *f.*

provocative *adj* provocateur.

provoke *vt* provoquer.

prow *n* (*mar*) proue *f.*

prowess *n* prouesse *f.*

prowl *vi* rôder.

prowler *n* rôdeur *m* -euse *f.*

proximity *n* proximité *f.*

prudence *n* prudence *f.*

prudent *adj* prudent, circonspect.

prudish *adj* prude.

prune *vt* tailler; * *n* pruneau *m.*

pry *vi* espionner.

psalm *n* psaume *m.*

pseudonym *n* pseudonyme *m.*

psychiatrist *n* psychiatre *mf.*

psychiatry *n* psychiatrie *f.*

psychic *adj* psychique.

psychoanalysis *n* psychanalyse *f.*

psychoanalyst *n* psychanaliste *mf.*

psychological *adj* psychologique.

psychologist *n* psychologue *mf.*

psychology *n* psychologie *f.*

puberty *n* puberté *f.*

public *adj* public; commun; * *n* public *m.*

publican *n* patron(ne) de pub *m(f).*

publication *n* publication *f*; édition *f.*

publicise *vt* faire de la publicité pour.

publicity *n* publicité *f.*

publish *vt* publier.

publisher *n* éditeur *m* -trice *f.*

publishing *n* édition *f.*

pucker *vt* plisser.

pudding *n* pudding *m*; dessert *m.*

puddle *n* flaque d'eau *f.*

puff *n* souffle *m*; bouffée *f*; * *vt* souffler; dégager; * *vi* souffler; bouffer.

pull *vt* tirer; arracher; ~ **down** faire descendre; abattre; ~ **in** *vi* s'arrêter; entrer en gare; ~ **off** enlever; ~ **out** *vi* partir; * *vt* arracher; ~ **through** *vi* s'en sortir; se remettre.

pulp *n* pulpe *f.*

pulpit *n* chaire *f.*

pulsate *vi* palpiter.

pulse *n* pouls *m*; légumes *mpl* secs.

pulverise *vt* pulvériser.

pummel *vt* marteler.

pump *n* pompe *f*; * *vt* pomper; puiser.

pun *n* jeu de mots *m*; * *vi* faire des jeux de mots.

punch n coup de poing m; poinçon m; punch m; * vt cogner; perforer; poinçonner.

punctual adj ponctuel, exact.

punctuate vt ponctuer.

punctuation n ponctuation f.

pungent adj piquant, âcre; mordant.

punish vt punir.

punishment n châtiment m, punition f; peine f.

punk n punk mf; minable mf; ~ (music) punk m.

puny adj chétif, maigrelet.

pup, puppy n chiot m; * vi avoir des chiots, mettre bas.

pupil n élève mf; pupille mf.

puppet n marionnette f.

purchase vt acheter; * n achat m; acquisition f.

pure adj pur.

purge vt purger.

purification n purification f.

purify vt purifier.

purist n puriste mf.

puritan n puritain m -e f.

purity n pureté f.

purple adj n pourpre, violet m.

purport vt: to ~ to prétendre.

purpose n intention f; but, dessein m; on ~ exprès, à dessein.

purr vi ronronner.

purse n sac à main m; porte-monnaie m invar.

pursue vi poursuivre; suivre.

pursuit n poursuite f; occupation f.

push vt pousser; presser; * n poussée f; impulsion f; effort m; énergie f.

pusher n trafiquant de drogues m.

push-up n (gymn) pompe f.

put vt mettre, poser; proposer; obliger; ~ **down** poser par terre; rabaisser; attribuer; ~ **forward** avancer; ~ **off** remettre; décourager; ~ **on** mettre; allumer; prendre; affecter; ~ **out** éteindre; faire sortir; déranger.

putrid adj putride.

putty n mastic m.

puzzle n énigme f; casse-tête m invar.

puzzling adj étrange, mystérieux.

pyjamas npl pyjama m.

pylon n pylône m.

pyramid n pyramide f.

python n python m.

Q

quadrangle n quadrilatère m.

quail n caille f.

quaint adj désuet; bizarre.

quake vi trembler.

qualification n qualification f; diplôme m.

qualified adj qualifié; diplômé.

qualify vt qualifier; modérer; * vi se qualifier.

quality n qualité f.

qualm n scrupule m.

quandary n incertitude f, doute m.

quantitative adj quantitatif.

quantity n quantité f.

quarantine *n* quarantaine *f*.
quarrel *n* dispute, querelle *f*; * *vi* se disputer, se quereller.
quarrelsome *adj* querelleur.
quarry *n* carrière *f*.
quarter *n* quart *m*; **a ~ of an hour** un quart d'heure; * *vt* diviser en quatre.
quarterly *adj* trimestriel; * *adv* tous les trimestres.
quartet *n* (*mus*) quartette *m*; quatuor *m*.
quash *vt* écraser; annuler.
quay *n* quai *m*.
queasy *adj* qui a des nausées; écœurant.
queen *n* reine *f*; dame *f* (cartes).
queer *adj* extrange; (*sl*) pédale *f*.
quell *vt* étouffer; apaiser.
quench *vt* assouvir; éteindre.
query *n* question *f*; * *vt* demander.
quest *n* recherche *f*.
question *n* question *f*; sujet *m*; doute *m*; * *vt* douter de; mettre en question; questionner.
questioner *n* interrogateur *m*.
question mark *n* point d'interrogation *m*.

questionnaire *n* questionnaire *m*.
quibble *vi* chicaner.
quick *adj* rapide; vif; prompt.
quicken *vt* presser; accélérer; * *vi* s'accélérer.
quicksand *n* sables mouvants *mpl*.
quicksilver *n* mercure *m*.
quiet *adj* calme; silencieux.
quintet *n* (*mus*) quintette *m*.
quip *n* sarcasme *m*; * *vt* railler.
quirk *n* particularité *f*.
quit *vt* arrêter de; quitter; * *vi* abandonner; démissionner; * *adj* quitte.
quite *adv* assez; complètement, absolument.
quiver *vi* trembler.
quiz *n* concours *m*; examen *m*; * *vt* interroger.
quizzical *adj* railleur.
quota *n* quota *m*.
quotation *n* citation *f*.
quotation marks *npl* guillemets *mpl*.
quote *vt* citer.

R

rabbi *n* rabbi, rabbin *m*.
rabbit *n* lapin *m*.
rabble *n* cohue *f*.
rabies *n* rage *f*.
race *n* course *f*; race *f*; * *vt* faire une course avec; * *vi* courir; faire une course; aller très vite; foncer.
racial *adj* racial.
racing *n* courses *fpl*.
rack *n* casier *m*; étagère *f*; * *vt* soumettre

au supplice du chevalet; tourmenter.
racket *n* vacarme *m*; raquette *f*.
racy *adj* piquant, plein de verve.
radiant *adj* rayonnant, radieux.
radiate *vt vi* rayonner, irradier.
radiation *n* irradiation *f*.
radiator *n* radiateur *m*.
radical(ly) *adj* (*adv*) radical(ement).
radio *n* radio *f*.
radioactive *adj* radioactif.

radish n radis m.

radius n radius m.

raffle n tombola f; * vt mettre en tombola.

raft n radeau, train de flottage m.

rafter n chevron m.

rag n lambeau m, loque f.

ragamuffin n va-nu-pieds m invar; galopin m.

rage n rage f; fureur f; * vi être furieux; faire rage.

ragged adj déguenillé.

raging adj furieux, déchaîné, enragé.

raid n raid m; * vt faire un raid sur.

raider n raider m, pillard m.

rail n rambarde f, garde-fou m; (rail) rail, chemin de fer m; * vt entourer d'une barrière.

railway n chemin de fer m.

rain n pluie f; * vi pleuvoir.

rainbow n arc-en-ciel m.

rainy adj pluvieux.

raise vt lever, soulever; ériger, édifier; élever.

raisin n raisin sec m.

rake n râteau m.

ram n bélier m; navire bélier m; * vt enfoncer.

ramble vi errer; faire une randonnée; * n excursion à pied, randonnée f.

ramp n rampe f.

rampant adj exubérant.

ramshackle adj délabré.

ranch n ranch m.

rancid adj rance.

rancour n rancœur f.

random adj fortuit, fait au hasard; **at ~** au hasard.

range vt ranger, classer; * vi s'étendre; * n rangée f; ordre m; portée f; chaîne f;

champ de tir m; fourneau de cuisine m.

rank adj exubérant; fétide; flagrant; * n rang m, classe f, grade m.

ransack vt saccager, piller.

ransom n rançon f.

rant vi déclamer.

rap vi donner un coup sec; * n petit coup sec m.

rapacious adj rapace.

rape n viol m; rapt m; (bot) colza m; * vt violer.

rapid adj **~ly** adv rapide(ment).

rapist n violeur m.

rapt adj extasié; absorbé.

rapture n ravissement m; extase f.

rapturous adj de ravissement.

rare adj **~ly** adv rare(ment).

rascal n vaurien m.

rash adj imprudent, téméraire; **~ly** adv sans réfléchir; * n vague f; éruption (cutanée) f.

rashness n imprudence f.

rasp n râpe f; * vt râper.

raspberry n framboise f.

rat n rat m.

rate n taux, prix, cours m; classe f; vitesse f; * vt estimer, évaluer.

rather adv plutôt; quelque peu.

rating n estimation f; classement m; indice m.

ratio n rapport m.

ration n ration f; (mil) vivres mpl.

rational adj rationnel; raisonnable; **~ly** adv rationnellement.

rattle vi s'entrechoquer; cliqueter * vt faire s'entrechoquer; * n fracas m; cliquetis m.

rattlesnake n serpent à sonnettes m.

ravage vt ravager, piller; dévaster; * n ravage m.

rave *vi* délirer.

raven *n* corbeau *m*.

ravenous *adj* ~**ly** *adv* vora-ce(ment).

ravine *n* ravin *m*.

ravishing *adj* enchanteur.

raw *adj* cru; brut; novice.

ray *n* rayon *m*; (*fish*) raie *f*.

razor *n* rasoir *m*.

reach *vt* atteindre; arriver à; * *vi* s'étendre, porter; * *n* portée *f*.

react *vi* réagir.

reaction *n* réaction *f*.

read *vt vi* lire.

reader *n* lecteur *m* -trice *f*.

readily *adv* volontiers; facilement.

reading *n* lecture *f*.

readjust *vt* réajuster, réadapter.

ready *adj* prêt; enclin; disposé.

real *adj* réel, vrai; ~**ly** *adv* vraiment.

realisation *n* réalisation *f*.

realise *vt* se rendre compte de; réaliser.

reality *n* réalité *f*.

reap *vt* moissonner.

reappear *vi* réapparaître.

rear *n* arrière *m*; derrière *m*; * *vt* élever, dresser.

reason *n* raison *f*, cause *f*; * *vt vi* raisonner.

reasonable *adj* raisonnable.

reassure *vt* rassurer; (*com*) réassurer.

rebel *n* rebelle *mf*; * *vi* se rebeller.

rebellion *n* rébellion *f*.

rebellious *adj* rebelle.

rebuff *n* rebuffade *f*; * *vt* repousser.

rebuke *vt* réprimander; * *n* réprimande *f*.

recalcitrant *adj* récalcitrant.

recall *vt* (se) rappeler; retirer; * *n* retrait *m*.

recant *vt* rétracter, désavouer.

recapitulate *vt vi* récapituler.

recapture *n* reprise *f*.

recede *vi* reculer.

receipt *n* reçu *m*; réception *f*.

receive *vt* recevoir; accueillir.

recent *adj* récent, neuf.

receptacle *n* récipient *m*.

reception *n* réception *f*.

recess *n* (*law*) vacance *f*; renfoncement *m*; recoin *m*.

recession *n* recul *m*; (*com*) récession *f*.

recipe *n* recette *f*.

recipient *n* destinataire *mf*.

reciprocal *adj* ~**ly** *adv* réciproque(ment).

reciprocate *vi* rendre la pareille.

recital *n* récit *m*; récital *m*.

recite *vt* réciter; exposer, énumérer.

reckless *adj* téméraire; ~**ly** *adv* imprudemment.

reckon *vt* compter, calculer; * *vi* calculer.

reckoning *n* compte *m*; calcul *m*.

reclaim *vt* assainir; récupérer.

recline *vt* reposer; * *vi* être allongé.

recluse *n* reclus *m* -e *f*.

recognise *vt* reconnaître.

recognition *n* reconnaissance *f*.

recoil *vi* reculer.

recollect *vt* se rappeler, se souvenir de.

recollection *n* souvenir *m*.

recommend *vt* recommander.

recommendation *n* recommandation *f*.

recompense *n* récompense *f*; * *vt* récompenser.

reconcile *vt* réconcilier.

reconciliation *n* réconciliation *f*.

reconnoitre *vt* (*mil*) reconnaître.

reconsider *vt* reconsidérer.

reconstruct *vt* reconstruire.

record *vt* enregistrer; consigner par écrit; * *n* rapport *m*, registre *m*; disque *m*; record *m*; ~**s** *pl* archives *fpl*.

recorder n magnétophone m, archiviste mf; (mus) flûte à bec f.

recourse n recours m.

recover vt retrouver; reprendre; récupérer; * vi se remettre, se rétablir.

recovery n guérison f, reprise f.

recreation n détente f, récréation f.

recriminate vi récriminer.

recrimination n récrimination f.

recruit vt recruter; * n (mil) recrue f.

rectangle n rectangle m.

rectitude n rectitude f.

rector n pasteur m.

recur vi se reproduire.

recurrence n répétition f.

recurrent adj répétitif.

red adj rouge; * n rouge m.

redden vt vi rougir.

redeploy vt réaffecter.

redhanded adj: **to catch sb ~** prendre quelqu'un la main dans le sac.

redhot adj brûlant, ardent.

red-letter day n jour à marquer d'une pierre blanche m.

redolent adj parfumé, odorant.

redouble vt vi redoubler.

redress vt réparer; corriger; redresser; * n réparation f, redressement m.

red tape n (fig) paperasserie f.

reduce vt réduire; diminuer; abaisser.

reduction n réduction f, baisse f.

redundancy n licenciement m.

redundant adj superflu; licencié.

reed n roseau m.

reef n (mar) ris m; récif m.

reek n puanteur f; * vi empester; puer.

reel n bobine f; bande f; dévidoir m; * vi chanceler.

re-enter vt rentrer.

refer vt soumettre, renvoyer; se référer à; * vi se référer.

referee n arbitre m.

reference n référence, allusion f.

refine vt raffiner, affiner.

refinement n raffinement m; raffinerie f; culture f.

refinery n raffinerie f.

reflect vt réfléchir, refléter; * vi réfléchir.

reflection n réflexion, pensée f.

reform vt réformer; * vi se réformer.

reform, reformation n réforme f.

reformer n réformateur m -trice f.

refraction n réfraction f.

refrain vi: **to ~ from sth** s'abstenir de qch.

refresh vt rafraîchir.

refreshment n rafraîchissement m.

refrigerator n glacière f; réfrigérateur m.

refuge n refuge, asile m.

refugee n réfugié m -e f.

refund vt rembourser; * n remboursement m.

refurbish vt rénover.

refusal n refus m.

refuse vt refuser; * n déchets mpl.

regain vt recouvrer, reprendre.

regal adj royal.

regard vt considérer; * n considération f; respect m.

regarding pr en ce qui concerne.

regardless adv quand même, malgré tout.

regatta n régate f.

regent n régent m.

regime n régime m.

regiment n régiment m.

region n région f.

register n registre m; * vt enregistrer; **~ed letter** n lettre recommandée f.

registrar *n* officier d'état civil *m*.

registration *n* enregistrement *m*.

registry *n* enregistrement *m*.

regret *n* regret *m* * *vt* regretter.

regretful *adj* plein de regrets.

regular *adj* régulier; ordinaire; ~ly *adv* régulièrement; * *n* habitué *m* -e *f*.

regulate *vt* régler, réglementer.

regulation *n* règlement *m*; réglementation *f*.

rehabilitation *n* réhabilitation *f*.

rehearsal *n* répétition *f*.

rehearse *vt* répéter; raconter.

reign *n* règne *m*; * *vi* régner.

reimburse *vt* rembourser.

rein *n* rêne *f*; * *vt* ~ **in** (*fig*) contenir.

reindeer *n* renne *m*.

reinforce *vt* renforcer.

reinstate *vt* réintégrer.

reiterate *vt* réitérer.

reiteration *n* réitération, répétition *f*.

reject *vt* rejeter.

rejection *n* refus, rejet *m*.

rejoice *vt* réjouir; * *vi* se réjouir.

rejoicing *n* réjouissance *f*.

relapse *vi* retomber; * *n* rechute *f*.

relate *vt* relater; rapprocher; * *vi* se rapporter.

related *adj* apparenté.

relation *n* rapport *m*; parent *m*.

relationship *n* lien de parenté *m*; relation *f*; rapport *m*.

relative *adj* relatif; * *n* parent *m* -e *f*.

relax *vt* relâcher; détendre; * *vi* se relâcher; se détendre.

relaxation *n* relâchement *m*; détente *f*.

relay *n* relais *m*; * *vt* retransmettre.

release *vt* libérer, relâcher; * *n* libération *f*, décharge *f*.

relegate *vt* reléguer.

relegation *n* relégation *f*.

relent *vi* s'adoucir.

relentless *adj* implacable.

relevant *adj* pertinent.

reliable *adj* fiable, digne de confiance.

reliance *n* confiance *f*.

relic *n* relique *f*.

relief *n* soulagement *m*; secours *m*.

relieve *vt* soulager, alléger; secourir.

religion *n* religion *f*.

religious *adj* religieux.

relinquish *vt* abandonner, renoncer à.

relish *n* saveur *f*; goût *m*; attrait *m*; * *vt* savourer, se délecter de.

reluctance *n* répugnance *f*.

reluctant *adj* peu disposé.

rely *vi* compter sur, avoir confiance en.

remain *vi* rester, demeurer.

remainder *n* reste, restant *m*.

remains *npl* restes, vestiges *mpl*; dépouille *f*.

remark *n* remarque, observation *f*; * *vt* (faire) remarquer, (faire) observer.

remarkable *adj* remarquable, notable.

remarry *vi* se remarier.

remedial *adj* de rattrapage.

remedy *n* remède, recours *m*; * *vt* remédier à.

remember *vt* se souvenir de; se rappeler.

remind *vt* rappeler.

reminiscence *n* réminiscence *f*.

remiss *adj* négligent.

remission *n* rémission *f*.

remnant *n* reste, restant *m*.

remorse *n* remords *m*.

remorseless *adj* implacable.

remote *adj* lointain, éloigné; ~ly *adv* au loin, de loin.

removal n suppression f; déménagement m.

remove vt enlever; * vi déménager.

render vt rendre, remettre; traduire; (law) rendre.

rendezvous n rendez-vous m; point de ralliement m.

renew vt renouveler.

renewal n renouvellement m.

renounce vt renoncer à.

renovation n rénovation f.

renown n renommée f; célébrité f.

renowned adj célèbre, renommé.

rent n loyer m; location f; * vt louer.

rental n loyer m.

renunciation n renonciation f.

reorganisation n réorganisation f.

reorganise vt réorganiser.

repair vt réparer; * n réparation f.

repartee n répartie, réplique f.

repay vt rembourser; rendre, récompenser.

repeal vt abroger, annuler; * n abrogation, annulation f.

repeat vt répéter.

repeatedly adv à plusieurs reprises.

repel vt repousser, rebuter.

repent vi se repentir.

repentance n repentir m.

repentant adj repentant.

repertory n répertoire m.

repetition n répétition, réitération f.

replace vt replacer; remplacer.

replenish vt remplir de nouveau.

replete adj rempli, rassasié.

reply n réponse f; * vi répondre.

report vt rapporter, relater; rendre compte de; * n rapport m; compte rendu m; rumeur f.

reporter n journaliste mf.

reprehensible adj répréhensible.

represent vt représenter.

representation n représentation f.

representative adj représentatif; * n représentant(e) m(f).

repress vt réprimer, contenir.

repression n répression f.

repressive adj répressif.

reprieve vt accorder un sursis ou un répit à; * n sursis m.

reprimand vt réprimander, blâmer; * n blâme m; réprimande f.

reprisal n représailles fpl.

reproach n reproche, opprobre m; * vt reprocher.

reproachful adj réprobateur.

reproduce vt reproduire.

reproduction n reproduction f.

reptile n reptile m.

republic n république f.

republican adj n républicain m, -e f.

repudiate vt renier.

repugnance n répugnance f, dégoût m.

repugnant adj répugnant.

repulsion n répulsion f.

repulsive adj répulsif.

reputation n réputation f.

request n demande, requête f; * vt demander.

require vt demander, nécessiter.

requirement n besoin m; exigence f.

requisite adj nécessaire, indispensable; * n objet(s) néces-saire(s) m(pl).

requisition n demande; (mil) réquisition f.

rescue vt sauver, secourir; * n secours m, délivrance f.

research   vt   faire   des/de   la

recherche(s); * n recherche(s) f(pl).

resemblance n ressemblance f.

resemble vt ressembler à.

resent vt être contrarié/irrité par.

resentful adj plein de ressentiment; amer.

resentment n ressentiment m.

reservation n réserve f; réservation f.

reserve vt réserver; * n réserve f.

reside vi résider.

residence n résidence f; séjour m.

resident n résident m, -e f.

residue n reste, résidu m.

resign vt démissionner de, renoncer à, céder; se résigner à; * vi démissionner.

resignation n démission f.

resist vt résister, s'opposer.

resistance n résistance f.

resolute adj ~ly adv résolu(ment).

resolution n résolution f.

resolve vt résoudre; * vi (se) résoudre, (se) décider.

resonance n résonance f.

resonant adj résonant.

resort vi recourir; * n lieu de vacances m; recours m.

resound vi résonner.

resource n ressource(s) f(pl); expédient m.

respect n respect m; égard m; rapport m; ~s pl respects mpl; * vt respecter.

respectability n respectabilité f.

respectable adj respectable; considérable.

respectful adj respectueux.

respiratory adj respiratoire.

respite n répit m; (law) sursis m.

resplendent adj resplendissant.

respond vi répondre; réagir.

response n réponse, réaction f.

responsibility n responsabilité f.

responsible adj responsable.

responsive adj sensible à, réceptif.

rest n repos m; (mus) pause f; reste, restant m; * vt faire/or laisser reposer; appuyer; * vi se reposer, reposer.

resting place n lieu de repos m.

restitution n restitution f.

restless adj agité; instable.

restoration n restauration f.

restore vt restituer, restaurer.

restrain vt retenir, contenir.

restraint n contrainte, entrave f.

restrict vt restreindre, limiter.

restriction n restriction f.

result vi résulter; * n résultat m.

resume vt reprendre.

resurrection n résurrection f.

resuscitate vt réanimer.

retail vt vendre au détail, détailler; * n vente au détail f.

retain vt retenir, conserver.

retaliate vi se venger.

retaliation n représailles fpl.

retarded adj retardé.

retch vi avoir des haut-le-cœur.

retention n rétention f.

reticence n réticence f.

retina n rétine f.

retire vt mettre à la retraite; * vi se retirer; prendre sa retraite.

retired adj retraité, à la retraite.

retirement n isolement m; retraite f.

retort vt rétorquer; * n réplique f.

retrace vt retracer.

retract vt rétracter; retirer.

retrain vt recycler.

retreat n repli m; * vi se retirer.

retribution n châtiment m; récompense f.

retrievable *adj* récupérable; réparable.

retrieve *vt* récupérer, recouvrer.

retriever *n* chien d'arrêt *m*.

retrograde *adj* rétrograde.

retrospect, retrospection *n* regard rétrospectif *m*.

retrospective *adj* rétrospectif.

return *vt* rendre; restituer; renvoyer; * *n* retour *m*; renvoi *m*; récompense *f*; revenu *m*; remboursement *m*.

reunion *n* réunion *f*.

reunite *vt* réunir; * *vi* se réunir.

reveal *vt* révéler.

revelation *n* révélation *f*.

revelry *n* fête *f*.

revenge *vt* venger; * *n* vengeance *f*.

revenue *n* revenu *m*; rente *f*.

reverberation *n* répercussion *f*; réverbération *f*.

reverence *n* vénération *f*; * *vt* révérer.

reverential *adj* révérenciel, respectueux.

reversal *n* renversement *m*; annulation *f*.

reverse *vt* renverser; annuler; * *vi* faire marche arrière; * *n* inverse *m*; contraire *m*; revers *m*.

reversible *adj* révocable; réversible.

revert *vi* revenir; retourner.

review *vt* revoir; (*mil*) passer en revue; * *n* revue *f*; examen *m*.

reviewer *n* critique *m*.

revise *vt* réviser; mettre à jour.

revision *n* révision *f*.

revisit *vt* retourner voir.

revival *n* reprise *f*; renouveau *m*.

revive *vt* ranimer; raviver; * *vi* reprendre connaissance; reprendre.

revolt *vi* se révolter; * *n* révolte *f*.

revolting *adj* exécrable.

revolution *n* révolution *f*.

revolutionary *adj n* révolutionnaire *mf*.

revolve *vt* (re)tourner; * *vi* tourner.

revolving *adj* tournant.

revulsion *n* écœurement *m*.

reward *n* récompense *f*; * *vt* récompenser.

rhapsody *n* r(h)apsodie *f*.

rheumatic *adj* rhumatisant.

rheumatism *n* rhumatisme *m*.

rhinoceros *n* rhinocéros *m*.

rhubarb *n* rhubarbe *f*.

rhyme *n* rime *f*; vers *mpl*; * *vi* rimer.

rhythm *n* rythme *m*.

rhythmical *adj* rythmique.

rib *n* côte *f*.

ribald *adj* paillard.

ribbon *n* ruban *m*; lambeaux *mpl*.

rice *n* riz *m*.

rich *adj* riche; sompteux; abondant.

riches *npl* richesse *f*.

rid *vt* débarrasser; se débarrasser de.

riddance *n*: **good ~!** bon débarras!

riddle *n* énigme *f*; crible *m*; * *vt* cribler.

ride *vi* monter à cheval; aller en voiture; * *n* promenade à cheval *ou* en voiture *f*.

rider *n* cavalier *m* -ière *f*.

ridge *n* arête, crête *f*; chaîne *f*; * *vt* rider, strier.

ridicule *n* ridicule *m*; raillerie *f*; * *vt* ridiculiser.

ridiculous *adj* ~**ly** *adv* ridicule(ment).

riding *n* équitation *f*; monte *f*.

rife *adj* répandu, abondant.

riffraff *n* racaille *f*.

rifle *vt* dévaliser, piller; strier, rayer; * *n* fusil *m*.

rig *vt* équiper; truquer; (*mar*) gréer; * *n* gréement *m*; plate-forme de forage *f*.

right *adj* droit, bien; juste; équitable; ~! bien!, bon!; **~ly** *adv* bien; correctement; à juste titre; * *n* justice *f*; raison *f*, droit *m*; droite *f*.

righteous *adj* droit, vertueux.

rigid *adj* rigide; sévère, strict.

rigidity *n* rigidité *f*, sévérité *f*.

rigmarole *n* galimatias *m*.

rigorous *adj* rigoureux.

rigour *n* rigueur *f*, sévérité *f*.

rim *n* bord *m*, monture *f*.

rind *n* peau, écorce *f*.

ring *n* anneau, cercle, rond *m*; bague *f*; tintement *m* de cloche; * *vt* sonner; * *vi* sonner, retentir.

ringleader *n* meneur *m*.

rink *n* (*also* **ice ~**) patinoire *f*.

rinse *vt* rincer.

riot *n* émeute *f*; * *vi* se livrer à une émeute.

rioter *n* émeutier *m*, -ière *f*.

riotous *adj* séditieux; dissolu.

rip *vt* déchirer, fendre.

ripe *adj* mûr.

ripen *vt* *vi* mûrir.

rip-off *n* (*sl*): **it's a ~!** c'est du vol!

ripple *vt* rider; * *vi* se rider; * *n* ondulation *f*, ride *f*.

rise *vi* se lever; naître; se soulever; monter; provenir de; s'élever; croître; ressusciter; * *n* hausse *f*, augmentation *f*; montée *f*; lever *m*; source *f*.

risk *n* risque, danger *m*; * *vt* risquer.

risky *adj* risqué.

rite *n* rite *m*.

ritual *adj* *n* rituel *m*.

rival *adj* rival; * *n* rival *m* -e *f*; * *vt* rivaliser avec, concurrencer.

rivalry *n* rivalité *f*.

river *n* rivière *f*.

rivet *n* rivet *m*; * *vt* riveter, river.

road *n* route *f*.

roadsign *n* panneau de signalisation *m*.

roadworks *npl* travaux routiers *mpl*.

roam *vt* parcourir; errer dans; * *vi* errer.

roar *vi* hurler, rugir; mugir; * *n* hurlement *m*; rugissement, mugissement *m*; grondement *m*.

roast *vt* rôtir; griller.

rob *vt* voler.

robber *n* voleur *m* -euse *f*.

robbery *n* vol *m*.

robe *n* robe (de cérémonie) *f*; peignoir de bain *m*; * *vt* revêtir d'une robe de cérémonie.

robin (redbreast) *n* rouge-gorge *m*.

robust *adj* robuste.

rock *n* roche *f*; rocher *m*; roc *m*; * *vt* bercer; balancer; ébranler; * *vi* (se) balancer.

rocket *n* fusée *f*.

rocking chair *n* fauteuil à bascule *m*.

rocky *adj* rocheux.

rod *n* baguette, tringle, canne *f*.

rodent *n* rongeur *m*.

roe *n* chevreuil *m*; œufs *mpl* de poisson.

rogue *n* coquin, polisson *m*; gredin *m*.

roguish *adj* coquin.

roll *vt* rouler; étendre; enrouler; * *vi* (se) rouler; * *n* roulement *m*; rouleau *m*; liste *f*; catalogue *m*; liasse *f*, petit pain *m*.

roller *n* rouleau, cylindre *m*.

roller skates *npl* patins à roulettes *mpl*.

rolling pin *n* rouleau à pâtisserie *m*.

romance *n* romance *f*; roman *m*; conte *m*; fable *f*.

romantic *adj* romantique.

roof *n* toit *m*; voûte *f*; * *vt* couvrir.

roofing n toiture f.

rook n freux m; tour f (aux échecs).

room n pièce, salle f; place f, espace m; chambre f.

roomy adj spacieux.

roost n perchoir m; * vi se percher.

root n racine f; origine f; * vt vi ~ out extirper; dénicher.

rope n corde f; cordage m; * vi attacher.

rosary n rosaire m.

rose n rose f.

rosebud n bouton de rose m.

rosemary n (bot) romarin m.

rosette n rosette f.

rosé wine n (vin) rosé m.

rosy adj rosé.

rot vi pourrir; * n pourriture f.

rotate vt faire tourner; * vi tourner.

rotation n rotation f.

rote n: by ~ par cœur.

rotten adj pourri; corrompu.

rotund adj rond, replet, arrondi.

rouge n rouge (à joues) m.

rough adj accidenté, inégal, rugueux; rude, brutal, brusque; houleux; ~ly adv rudement.

roughcast n crépi m.

roughness n rugosité f; rudesse, brusquerie f; agitation f.

round adj rond, circulaire; rondelet; franc; * n cercle m; rond m; tour m; tournée f; partie f; ronde f; canon m; série f; * adv autour de; environ; * vt contourner; arrondir.

roundabout adj détourné, indirect; * n rond-point m.

rouse vt réveiller; exciter.

rout n déroute, débâcle f; * vt mettre en déroute.

route n itinéraire m; route f.

routine adj habituel; * n routine f; numéro m.

rove vi vagabonder, errer.

row n querelle f; vacarme m.

row n rangée, file f; * vt (mar) ramer.

rowdy n hooligan, voyou m.

royal adj royal; princier.

royalist n royaliste mf.

royalty n royauté f; droits d'auteur mpl; royalties fpl; redevance f; membres de la famille royale mpl.

rub vt frotter; irriter.

rubber n caoutchouc m, gomme f; préservatif m.

rubber band n élastique m.

rubbish n détritus mpl; ordures fpl; bêtises fpl; décombres mpl.

ruby n rubis m.

rucksack n sac à dos m.

rudder n gouvernail m.

rude adj impoli, rude, brusque; grossier, primitif.

rudiment n rudiments mpl.

rue vt regretter amèrement; * n (bot) rue f.

rueful adj triste.

ruffian n voyou m, brute f; * adj brutal.

ruffle vt ébouriffer, déranger; rider.

rug n tapis m, carpette f.

rugged adj accidenté, déchiqueté; rude; robuste.

ruin n ruine f; perte f; ruines fpl; * vt ruiner; détruire.

rule n règle f; règlement m; pouvoir m; domination f; * vt gouverner, dominer; décider, régler, diriger.

ruler n dirigeant m -e f; règle f.

rum n rhum m.

rumble vi gronder, tonner.

ruminate *vt* ruminer.

rummage *vi* fouiller.

rumour *n* rumeur *f*; * *vt* faire courir le bruit.

run *vt* diriger; organiser; faire couler; passer; * *vi* courir; fuir, se sauver; filer; fonctionner; aller; couler; concourir.

runaway *n* fugitif *m* -ive *f*, fuyard *m*.

rung *n* barreau, échelon *m*.

runner *n* coureur *m*; concurrent *m* -e *f*; messager *m*.

runway *n* piste de décollage *f*.

rupture *n* rupture *f*; hernie *f*; * *vt* rompre; * *vi* se rompre.

rural *adj* rural, champêtre.

ruse *n* ruse *f*, stratagème *m*.

rush *n* jonc *m*; ruée *f*; hâte *f*; * *vt* pousser vivement; * *vi* se précipiter, s'élancer.

russet *adj* roux.

rust *n* rouille *f*, * *vi* se rouiller.

rustic *adj* rustique; * *n* paysan, rustaud *m*.

rustle *vi* bruire; * *vt* faire bruire; froisser.

rusty *adj* rouillé; roux.

rut *n* (*zool*) rut *m*; ornière *f*.

ruthless *adj* cruel, impitoyable.

rye *n* (*bot*) seigle *m*.

S

Sabbath *n* sabbat *m*; dimanche *m*.

sabre *n* sabre *m*.

saccharin *n* saccharine *f*.

sack *n* sac *m*; * *vt* mettre à sac; renvoyer.

sacrament *n* sacrement *m*; Eucharistie *f*.

sacred *adj* saint, sacré; inviolable.

sacrifice *n* sacrifice *m*; * *vt* sacrifier.

sacrificial *adj* sacrificiel.

sacrilege *n* sacrilège *m*.

sad *adj* triste, déprimé; attristant; regrettable.

sadden *vt* attrister.

saddle *n* selle *f*; col *m*; * *vt* seller.

saddlebag *n* sacoche de selle *f*.

sadness *n* tristesse *f*.

safe *adj* sûr; en sécurité; hors de danger; sans danger; ~ **and sound** sain et sauf; * *n* coffre-fort *m*.

safe-conduct *n* sauf-conduit *m*.

safeguard *n* sauvegarde *f*, * *vt* sauvegarder, protéger.

safety *n* sécurité *f*; sûreté *f*.

safety belt *n* ceinture de sécurité *f*.

safety pin *n* épingle de nourrice *f*.

sage *n* (*bot*) sauge *f*, sage *m*; * *adj* sage.

sail *n* voile *f*; * *vt* piloter; * *vi* aller à la voile, naviguer.

sailing *n* navigation *f*.

sailor *n* marin *m*.

saint *n* saint *m* -e *f*.

saintly *adj* saint.

sake *n* bien *m*, égard *m*; **for God's ~** pour l'amour de Dieu.

salad *n* salade *f*.

salad dressing *n* vinaigrette *f*.

salary *n* salaire *m*.

sale *n* vente *f*; solde *m*.

salesman *n* vendeur *m*.

saleswoman *n* vendeuse *f*.

salient *adj* saillant.

saline *adj* salin.

saliva *n* salive *f*.

sallow *adj* jaunâtre, cireux.

sally *n* (*mil*) sortie, saillie *f*; * *vi* saillir.

salmon *n* saumon *m*.

salt *n* sel *m*; * *vt* saler.

salt cellar *n* salière *f*.

salubrious *adj* salubre, sain.

salubrity *n* salubrité *f*.

salutary *adj* salutaire.

salutation *n* salutation(s) *f(pl)*.

salute *vt* saluer; * *n* salut *m*.

salvation *n* salut *m*.

salve *n* baume, onguent *m*.

same *adj* même, identique.

sample *n* échantillon *m*; prélèvement *m*; * *vt* goûter.

sanatorium *n* sanatorium *m*.

sanctimonious *adj* cagot.

sanction *n* sanction *f*; * *vt* sanctionner.

sanctity *n* sainteté *f*.

sanctuary *n* sanctuaire *m*; asile *m*.

sand *n* sable *m*; * *vt* sabler.

sandal *n* sandale *f*.

sandpit *n* carrière de sable *f*.

sandy *adj* sablonneux, sableux.

sane *adj* sain.

sanguine *adj* sanguin.

sanitary towel *n* serviette *f* hygiénique.

sanity *n* santé mentale, raison *f*.

sap *n* sève *f*; * *vt* miner.

sapient *adj* sage, prudent.

sapphire *n* saphir *m*.

sarcasm *n* sarcasme *m*.

sarcastic *adj* sarcastique, caustique.

sash *n* écharpe *f*; ceinture *f*.

satanic(al) *adj* satanique.

satchel *n* cartable *m*.

satellite *n* satellite *m*.

satiate, sate *vt* rassasier, assouvir.

satin *n* satin *m*; * *adj* en *ou* de satin.

satire *n* satire *f*.

satirical *adj* satirique.

satirise *vt* faire la satire de.

satirist *n* écrivain satirique *m*.

satisfaction *n* satisfaction *f*.

satisfactory *adj* satisfaisant.

satisfy *vt* satisfaire; convaincre.

saturate *vt* saturer.

Saturday *n* samedi *m*.

sauce *n* sauce *f*; assaisonnement *m*; * *vt* assaisonner.

saucepan *n* casserole *f*.

saucer *n* soucoupe *f*.

saucy *adj* impertinent.

saunter *vi* flâner, se balader.

sausage *n* saucisse *f*.

savage *adj* sauvage, barbare; * *n* sauvage *mf*.

savagery *n* sauvagerie, barbarie *f*.

save *vt* sauver; économiser; épargner; éviter; conserver; * *adv* sauf, à l'exception de; * *n* (*sport*) arrêt *m*.

saving *n* sauvetage *m*; ~s *pl* économies *fpl*, épargne *f*.

savings account *n* compte d'épargne *m*.

savings bank *n* caisse d'épargne *f*.

Saviour *n* Sauveur *m*.

savour *n* saveur *f*; goût *m*; * *vt* déguster, savourer.

savoury *adj* savoureux.

saw *n* scie *f*; * *vt* scier.

sawdust *n* sciure *f*.

saxophone *n* saxophone *m*.

say *vt* dire.

saying *n* dicton, proverbe *m*.

scab *n* gale *f*, croûte *f*.

scabbard n gaine f; fourreau m.

scaffold n échafaud m; échafaudage m.

scaffolding n échafaudage m.

scald vt échauder; * n brûlure f.

scale n balance f; échelle f; gamme f; écaille f; * vt escalader; écailler.

scallop n feston m; coquille f St Jacques; * vt festonner.

scalp n cuir chevelu m; * vt scalper.

scamper vi galoper.

scampi npl langoustines fpl.

scan vt scruter; explorer; scander.

scandal n scandale m; infamie f.

scandalise vt scandaliser.

scandalous adj scandaleux.

scant, scanty adj rare, insuffisant.

scantily adv pauvrement, insuffisamment.

scapegoat n bouc émissaire m.

scar n cicatrice f; * vt marquer d'une cicatrice.

scarce adj rare; ~ly adv à peine.

scarcity n rareté f; pénurie f.

scare vt effrayer; * n peur; panique f.

scarecrow n épouvantail m.

scarf n écharpe f.

scarlet n écarlate f; * adj écarlate.

scatter vt éparpiller; disperser.

scavenger n charognard m; éboueur m.

scenario n scénario m; (also fig).

scene n scène f; lieu m; spectacle m, vue f.

scenery n vue f; décor (de théâtre) m.

scenic adj scénique.

scent n parfum m, odeur f; odorat m; piste f; * vt parfumer.

sceptic n sceptique mf.

sceptic(al) adj sceptique.

scepticism n scepticisme m.

schedule n horaire m; programme m; liste f.

scheme n projet, plan m; schéma m; système m; machination f; * vt machiner; * vi intriguer.

schemer n conspirateur m -trice f, intrigant m -e f.

schism n schisme m.

schismatic n schismatique mf.

scholar n élève mf; érudit m -e f.

scholarship n savoir m, science f; bourse (d'études) f.

school n école f; * vt instruire.

schoolboy n écolier, élève m.

schoolgirl n écolière, élève f.

schoolteacher n instituteur/trice mf; professeur mf.

science n science f.

scientific adj   ~ally adv scientifique(ment).

scientist n scientifique mf.

scintillate vi scintiller, étinceler.

scintillating adj brillant, scintillant.

scissors npl ciseaux mpl.

scoff vi se moquer.

scold vt réprimander; * vi grogner.

scoop n louche f; pelle f; exclusivité f; * vt évider; écoper.

scooter n scooter m; trottinette f.

scope n portée, envergure, étendue f; zone de compétence f; liberté d'action f.

scorch vt brûler; roussir, griller; * vi se brûler, roussir.

score n score m; marque f; entaille, rayure f; titre, égard m; compte m; (mus) partition f; vingtaine f; * vt marquer; souligner; * vi marquer un/des point(s).

scorn vt mépriser; dédaigner; * n dédain, mépris m.

scornful adj dédaigneux.

scorpion n scorpion m.

Scotch n whisky m.

scoundrel n vaurien m.

scour vt récurer, frotter; nettoyer; * vi battre la campagne.

scourge n fouet m; châtiment m; * vt fouetter; châtier.

scout n (mil) éclaireur m -euse f; guetteur m; reconnaissance f; * vi aller en reconnaissance.

scowl vi se renfrogner; * n mine renfrognée f.

scraggy adj rugueux; famélique.

scramble vi avancer à quatre pattes; grimper; se battre; se disputer; * n bousculade, ruée f; ascension f.

scrap n bout m; restes mpl; petit morceau m; bagarre f; ferraille f.

scrape vt vi racler, gratter; * vt érafler; * n embarras m, ennui m.

scraper n racloir m.

scratch vt griffer, égratigner; gratter; griffonner; * n égratignure f.

scrawl vt vi gribouiller; * n griffonnage m.

scream, screech vi hurler, pousser des cris; * n cri perçant, hurlement m.

screen n écran m; paravent m; rideau m; écran de cheminée m; * vt abriter, cacher; projeter; passer au crible, sélectionner.

screenplay n scénario m.

screw n vis f; * vt visser; extorquer, soutirer.

screwdriver n tournevis m.

scribble vt gribouiller; * n gribouillage m.

scribe n scribe m.

script n scénario m; script m.

scriptural adj biblique.

Scripture n Écriture f sainte.

scroll n rouleau (de papier ou parchemin) m.

scrub vt nettoyer à la brosse, récurer; annuler; * n broussailles fpl.

scruffy adj mal soigné.

scruple n scrupule m.

scrupulous adj scrupuleux.

scrutinise vt étudier minutieusement, examiner.

scrutiny n examen minutieux m.

scuffle n échauffourée, rixe f; * vi se bagarrer.

scull n aviron m.

scullery n arrière-cuisine f.

sculptor n sculpteur m -trice f.

sculpture n sculpture f; * vt sculpter.

scum n écume f; crasse f; rebut m.

scurrilous adj injurieux; vil, ignoble.

scurvy n scorbut m.

scuttle vi courir précipitamment.

scythe n faux f.

sea n mer f; * adj marin.

sea breeze n brise de mer f.

seafood n fruits de mer mpl.

sea front n bord de mer m.

seagull n mouette f.

sea horse n hippocampe m.

seal n sceau m; phoque m; * vt sceller.

sealing wax n cire à cacheter f.

seam n couture f; * vt faire une couture.

seamanship n habileté à naviguer f.

seamstress n couturière f.

sea plane n hydravion m.

seaport n port de mer m.

sear vt cautériser.

search vt fouiller; inspecter; examiner; scruter, sonder; * n fouille f; recherche f; perquisition f.

searchlight n projecteur m.

seashore n rivage m, bord de mer m.

seasick adj sujet au mal de mer.

seasickness n mal de mer m.

seaside n bord de mer m.

season n saison f; moment opportun m; assaisonnement m; * vt assaisonner; dessécher.

seasoning n assaisonnement m.

season ticket n carte d'abonnement f.

seat n siège m; place f; derrière m; fond m; * vt (faire) asseoir; placer.

seat belt n ceinture de sécurité f.

seaweed n algue f.

secession n sécession f; séparation f.

seclude vt éloigner, isoler.

seclusion n solitude f; isolement m.

second adj ~(ly) adv deuxiè-me(ment); * n second m; seconde f; (mus) seconde f; * vt aider; seconder.

secondary adj secondaire.

secondary school n collège d'enseignement secondaire m.

secrecy n secret m; discrétion f.

secret adj n secret m.

secretary n secrétaire mf.

secrete vt cacher; (med) sécréter.

secretion n sécrétion f.

secretive adj secret, dissimulé.

sect n secte f.

sectarian n sectaire mf.

section n section f.

sector n secteur m.

secular adj séculaire.

secure adj sûr; en sûreté; * vt mettre en sûreté; assurer.

security n sécurité f; sûreté f; protection f; caution f.

sedate adj ~ly adv calme(ment), posé(ment).

sedative n sédatif m.

sedentary adj sédentaire.

sediment n sédiment m; lie f; dépôt m.

sedition n sédition f.

seduce vt séduire; corrompre.

seducer n séducteur m -trice f.

seduction n séduction f.

seductive adj séduisant.

see vt voir, remarquer, découvrir; connaître; juger; comprendre; * vi voir; comprendre; ~! regarde!; tu vois!

seed n graine, semence f; * vi monter en graine.

seedling n semis m.

seedy adj minable.

seeing conj: ~ that vu que.

seek vt chercher; demander.

seem vi paraître, sembler.

seer n prophète m.

seesaw n bascule f; * vi osciller.

seethe vi bouillir, bouillonner.

segment n segment m.

seize vt saisir; attraper; opérer la saisie de.

seizure n capture f; saisie f.

seldom adv rarement, peu souvent.

select vt sélectionner, choisir; * adj choisi, sélectionné.

selection n sélection f.

self n soi-même f; **the ~** le moi; * pref auto-.

self-confident adj sûr de soi.

self-defence n autodéfense f.

self-denial n abnégation de soi f.

self-employed adj indépendant.

self-evident adj évident, qui va de soi.

selfish adj ~ly adv égoïste(ment).

selfishness n égoïsme m.

self-pity n apitoiement sur soi-même m.

self-portrait n autoportrait m.

self-reliant *adj* indépendant.

self-respect *n* respect de soi *m*.

selfsame *adj* exactement le même, identique.

self-satisfied *adj* suffisant.

self-service *adj* libre-service.

self-styled *adj* autoproclamé.

self-sufficient *adj* autosuffisant.

self-taught *adj* autodidacte.

sell *vt* vendre; attraper; * *vi* se vendre.

seller *n* vendeur *m* -euse *f*.

selling-off *n* liquidation *f*.

semblance *n* semblant *m*, apparence *f*.

semen *n* sperme *m*.

semester *n* semestre *m*.

semicircle *n* demi-cercle *m*.

semicircular *adj* semi-circulaire.

semicolon *n* point-virgule *m*.

senate *n* sénat *m*.

senator *n* sénateur *m* -trice *f*.

send *vt* envoyer, expédier, adresser; émettre; pousser.

sender *n* expéditeur *m* -trice *f*.

senile *adj* sénile.

senility *n* sénilité *f*.

senior *n* aîné *m* -e *f*; * *adj* aîné; supérieur.

seniority *n* ancienneté *f*.

sensation *n* sensation *f*.

sense *n* sens *m*; sensation *f*; raison *f*; bon sens *m*; sentiment *m*.

senseless *adj* insensé; sans connaissance.

sensibility *n* sensibilité *f*.

sensible *adj* sensé, raisonnable; sensible.

sensitive *adj* sensible.

sensual, sensuous *adj* ~**ly** *adv* sensuel(lement).

sensuality *n* sensualité *f*.

sentence *n* phrase *f*; condamnation *f*; * *vt* condamner, prononcer une sentence contre.

sentientious *adj* sentencieux;.

sentiment *n* sentiment *m*; opinion *f*.

sentimental *adj* sentimental.

sentinel, sentry *n* sentinelle *f*.

separable *adj* séparable.

separate *vt* séparer; * *vi* se séparer; * *adj* séparé; distinct; ~**ly** *adv* séparément.

separation *n* séparation *f*.

September *n* septembre *m*.

sepulchre *n* sépulcre *m*.

sequel *n* conséquence *f*; suite *f*.

sequence *n* ordre *m*, série *f*.

serenade *n* sérénade *f*; * *vt* jouer une sérénade pour.

serene *adj* serein.

serenity *n* sérénité *f*.

serf *n* serf *m*, serve *f*.

sergeant *n* sergent *m*; (US) caporalchef *m*; brigadier *m*.

serial *adj* de/en série; * *n* feuilleton *m*; téléroman *m*.

series *n* série *f*.

serious *adj* sérieux, grave.

sermon *n* sermon *m*.

serpent *n* serpent *m*.

serrated *adj* en dents de scie.

serum *n* sérum *m*.

servant *n* domestique *mf*.

serve *vt* servir; desservir; faire; accomplir; * *vi* servir; être utile.

service *n* service *m*; office *m*; entretien *m*; * *vt* entretenir; réviser.

service station *n* station-service *f*.

servile *adj* servile.

session *n* séance, session *f*; réunion *f*.

set *vt* mettre, poser, placer; fixer, déterminer; * *vi* se coucher (soleil); se figer; se mettre; * *n* jeu *m*; service *m*; ensemble *m*; (*cine*) plateau *m*; set *m*; groupe *m*, bande *f*; * *adj* fixe, figé; prêt; déterminé.

settee *n* canapé *m*.

setting *n* disposition *f*; cadre *m*; monture *f*.

settle *vt* poser, installer, arranger; régler; calmer; * *vi* se poser; s'installer; se calmer.

settlement *n* règlement *m*; établissement *m*; accord *m*; résolution *f*; colonie *f*; colonisation *f*.

settler *n* colon *m*, colonisateur *m* -trice *f*.

set-to *n* lutte *f*; combat *m*.

seven *adj n* sept *m*.

seventeen *adj n* dix-sept *m*.

seventeenth *adj n* dix-septième *mf*.

seventh *adj n* septième *mf*.

seventieth *adj n* soixante-dixième *mf*.

seventy *adj n* soixante-dix *m*.

sever *vt* séparer.

several *adj pn* plusieurs.

severance *n* séparation *f*.

severe *adj* sévère, rigoureux, austère, dur.

severity *n* sévérité *f*.

sew *vt vi* coudre.

sewer *n* égout *m*.

sewing machine *n* machine à coudre *f*.

sex *n* sexe *m*.

sexist *adj n* sexiste *mf*.

sexual *adj* sexuel.

shabby *adj* miteux.

shackle *vt* enchaîner; ~**s** *npl* chaînes *fpl*.

shade *n* ombre, obscurité *f*; nuance *f*; abat-jour *m*; * *vt* ombrager; abriter; atténuer.

shadow *n* ombre *f*.

shadowy *adj* ombragé; sombre; indistinct.

shady *adj* ombreux, ombragé; sombre.

shaft *n* flèche *f*; fût *m*; puits *m*; (*tech*) arbre *m*; rayon *m*.

shag *n* tabac *m*; cormoran huppé *m*.

shaggy *adj* hirsute.

shake *vt* secouer; agiter; * *vi* trembler; chanceler; ~ **hands** se serrer la main; * *n* secousse *f*; tremblement *m*.

shaky *adj* tremblant.

shallow *adj* peu profond, superficiel; futile.

shallowness *n* manque de profondeur *m*; futilité *f*.

sham *vt* feindre; * *n* imitation *f*; imposture *f*; * *adj* feint, simulé.

shambles *npl* désordre *m*.

shame *n* honte *f*; * *vt* faire honte à, déshonorer.

shamefaced *adj* honteux, confus.

shameful *adj* honteux; scandaleux.

shameless *adj* ~**ly** *adv* effronté(ment).

shampoo *vt* faire un shampooing à; * *n* shampooing *m*.

shamrock *n* trèfle *m*.

shanty *n* baraque *f*.

shape *vt* former; façonner; modeler; * *vi* prendre forme; * *n* forme, figure *f*; modèle *m*.

shapeless *adj* informe.

shapely *adj* bien proportionné.

share *n* part, portion *f*; (*com*) action *f*; soc (de charrue) *m*; * *vt* partager; répartir; * *vi* partager.

shark *n* requin *m*.

sharp *adj* aigu, acéré; malin; fin; pénétrant; âpre, mordant, cinglant; per-

çant; vif, violent; * n (mus) dièse m; *
adv pile.

sharpen vt aiguiser, affûter.

sharpness n tranchant m; finesse,
acuité f; aigreur f.

shatter vt fracasser, détruire; * vi se fracasser.

shave vt raser, raboter; * vi se raser; n
rasage m.

shaver n rasoir électrique m.

shaving n rasage m.

shaving brush n blaireau m.

shaving cream n crème à raser f.

shawl n châle m.

she pn elle.

sheaf n gerbe f; liasse f.

sheath n fourreau m.

shed vt verser, répandre; perdre; * n
hangar m; cabane f.

sheen n lustre m.

sheep n mouton m.

sheepish adj penaud; timide.

sheepskin n peau de mouton f.

sheer adj pur, absolu, véritable; abrupt;
* adv abruptement.

sheet n drap m; plaque f; feuille (de
papier) f; (mar) écoute f.

sheet lightning n éclairs en nappes mpl.

shelf n étagère f; (mar) écueil m; saillie
f; **on the ~** au rancart.

shell n coquille f; carcasse f; écorce f;
obus m; * vt écosser, décortiquer; bombarder; * vi se décortiquer.

shellfish npl invar crustacé m; fruits de
mer mpl.

shelter n abri m; asile, refuge m; * vt
abriter; protéger; * vi s'abriter.

shelve vt mettre au rancart.

shepherd n berger m.

sherbet n sorbet m.

sherry n xérès m.

shield n bouclier m; écran protecteur
m; * vt protéger.

shift vi changer; se déplacer; * vt changer, bouger; transférer; * n changement
m; roulement m.

shinbone n tibia m.

shine vi briller, reluire, illuminer; * vt
cirer; * n éclat m.

shingle n galets mpl; ~s pl (med) zona m.

shining adj resplendissant.

shiny adj brillant, reluisant.

ship n bateau m; navire m; bâtiment
m; * vt embarquer; transporter.

shipbuilding n construction navale f.

shipment n cargaison f.

shipwreck n naufrage m.

shirt n chemise f.

shiver vi frissonner.

shoal n banc m (de poissons).

shock n choc m; décharge f; coup m; *
vt bouleverser; choquer.

shock absorber n amortisseur m.

shoddy adj de mauvaise qualité.

shoe n chaussure f; fer (à cheval) m; *
vt chausser; ferrer (un cheval.

shoehorn n chausse-pied m.

shoelace n lacet de chaussure m.

shoot vt tirer, lancer, décocher; * vi
pousser, bourgeonner; passer en flèche;
s'élancer; * n pousse f.

shop n magasin m; atelier m.

shoplifter n voleur(-euse) à l'étalage m(f).

shopper n acheteur m -euse f.

shopping n courses fpl.

shopping centre n centre commercial
m.

shore n rivage, bord m, côte f.

short *adj* court, bref, succinct, concis;
~ly *adv* brièvement; rapidement.

shortcoming *n* insuffisance *f*; défaut *m*.

shorten *vt* raccourcir; abréger.

short-sighted *adj* myope.

shot *n* coup *m*; décharge *f*; plomb *m*;
tentative *f*; prise *f*.

shotgun *n* fusil de chasse *m*.

shoulder *n* épaule *f*; accotement *m*; *
vt charger sur son épaule.

shout *vi* crier; * *vt* crier; * *n* cri *m*, acclamation *f*.

shove *vt vi* pousser; * *n* poussée *f*.

shovel *n* pelle *f*, * *vt* pelleter.

show *vt* montrer; faire voir, présenter;
prouver; expliquer; * *vi* se voir; * *n* exposition *f*; spectacle *m*; manifestation
f; salon *m*.

show business *n* monde du spectacle *m*.

shower *n* averse *f*; douche *f*; (*fig*) torrent *m*; * *vi* pleuvoir.

showy *adj* voyant, ostentatoire.

shred *n* lambeau *m*, parcelle *f*; * *vt*
mettre en lambeaux.

shrewd *adj* astucieux; perspicace.

shriek *vt vi* hurler; * *n* hurlement *m*.

shrill *adj* aigu, strident.

shrimp *n* crevette *f*; nabot *m* -e *f*, avor-
ton *m*.

shrine *n* lieu saint *m*.

shrink *vi* rétrécir; se réduire, rapetisser.

shrivel *vi* se ratatiner, se flétrir; * *vt*
ratatiner.

shroud *n* voile *m*; linceul *m*; * *vt* envelopper, voiler; ensevelir.

shrub *n* arbuste *m*.

shrubbery *n* massif d'arbustes *m*.

shrug *vt* hausser les épaules; * *n* haus-
sement d'épaules *m*.

shudder *vi* frissonner; * *n* frisson *m*.

shuffle *vt* mélanger; battre.

shun *vt* fuir, éviter.

shut *vt* fermer; *vi* (se) fermer.

shutter *n* volet *m*.

shuttle *n* navette *f*.

shuttlecock *n* volant *m*.

shy *adj* timide; réservé; embarrassé,
gauche.

sick *adj* malade; écœuré.

sicken *vt* rendre malade; * *vi* tomber
malade.

sick leave *n* congé de maladie *m*.

sickly *adj* maladif.

sickness *n* maladie *f*.

sick pay *n* indemnité de maladie *f*.

side *n* côté *m*; flanc *m*; camp *m*; parti
m; * *adj* latéral; secondaire; * *vi* se ranger du côté de.

sideboard *n* buffet *m*.

sidelong *adj* oblique.

sideways *adv* de côté, obli-quement.

sidle *vi* avancer de côté; avancer furtivement.

siege *n* (*mil*) siège *m*.

sieve *n* tamis *m*; crible *m*; passoire *f*; *
vt tamiser.

sift *vt* tamiser; passer au crible; dégager.

sigh *vi* soupirer, gémir; * *n* soupir *m*.

sight *n* vue *f*; mire *f*; spectacle *m*.

sightseeing *n* tourisme *m*.

sign *n* signe *m*, indication *f*; panneau
m; geste *m*; trace *f*; * *vt* signer.

signal *n* signal *m*.

signalman *n* (*rail*) aiguilleur *m*.

signature *n* signature *f*.

signet *n* sceau *m*.

significance *n* importance *f*.

significant *adj* considérable.

signify vt signifier.

signpost n poteau indicateur m.

silence n silence m; * vt imposer le silence à.

silent adj silencieux.

silicon chip n puce f électronique.

silk n soie f.

silkworm n ver à soie m.

silky adj soyeux; satiné.

sill n rebord m; seuil m.

silly adj bête, stupide.

silver n argent m; * adj en argent.

silversmith n orfèvre m.

similar adj semblable; similaire.

similarity n ressemblance f.

simmer vi cuire à feu doux, mijoter.

simper vi minauder; * n sourire affecté m.

simple adj simple; naïf.

simpleton n nigaud m -e f.

simplicity n simplicité f; naïveté f.

simplify vt simplifier.

simply adv simplement; seulement.

simulate vt simuler, feindre.

simulation n simulation f.

simultaneous adj simultané.

sin n péché m; * vi pécher.

since adv depuis; * prep depuis; * conj depuis que; puisque.

sincere adj ~ly adv sincère(ment); **yours ~ly** veuillez agréer, Monsieur/ Madame, l'expression de mes salutations distinguées.

sincerity n sincérité f.

sinew n tendon m.

sinful adj coupable, honteux.

sing vt vi chanter; (poet) vt célébrer.

singe vt roussir.

singer n chanteur m -euse f.

singing n chant m.

single adj seul, unique, simple; célibataire; * n aller simple m.

singly adv séparément.

singular adj singulier, rare; * n singulier m; ~ly adv singulièrement.

sinister adj sinistre; de mauvais augure, funeste.

sink vi couler; sombrer; s'affaisser; tomber très bas, baisser; * vt couler, faire sombrer; ruiner; * n évier m.

sinner n pécheur m; pécheresse f.

sinuous adj sinueux.

sinus n sinus m.

sip vt boire à petites gorgées; * n petite gorgée f.

siphon n siphon m.

sir n monsieur m.

siren n sirène f.

sirloin n aloyau (de bœuf) m.

sister n sœur f.

sisterhood n solidarité féminine f.

sister-in-law n belle-sœur f.

sit vi s'asseoir; se trouver; * vt se présenter à.

site n emplacement m; site m.

sitting n séance, réunion f; position assise f.

sitting room n salle de séjour f.

situated adj situé.

situation n situation f.

six adj n six m.

sixteen adj n seize m.

sixteenth adj n seizième mf.

sixth adj n sixième mf.

sixtieth adj n soixantième mf.

sixty adj n soixante m.

size n taille, grandeur f; volume m; dimension f; ampleur f; étendue f.

skate n patin m; * vi patiner.

skateboard n planche à roulettes f, skateboard m.

skating n patinage m.

skating rink n patinoire f.

skeleton n squelette m.

skeleton key n passe(-partout) m.

sketch n croquis m; esquisse f; * vt equisser, faire un croquis de.

skewer n broche f; brochette f.

ski n ski m; * vi skier.

skid n dérapage m; * vi déraper.

skier n skieur m -euse f.

skiing n ski m.

skilful adj ~ly adv adroit(ement), habile(ment).

skill n habileté, adresse, dextérité f.

skilled adj adroit; qualifié.

skim vt écrémer; effleurer.

skimmed milk n lait écrémé m.

skin n peau f; * vt écorcher.

skin diving n plongée sous-marine f.

skinny adj maigre, efflanqué.

skip vi sautiller, gambader; * vt sauter, passer; * n saut, bond m; benne f.

ski pants npl fuseau (de ski) m.

skipper n capitaine m.

skirmish n escarmouche f; * vi s'engager dans une escarmouche.

skirt n jupe f; bordure f; * vt contourner.

skittle n quille f.

skull n crâne m.

sky n ciel m.

skylight n lucarne f.

skyscraper n gratte-ciel m invar.

slab n dalle f.

slack adj lâche, mou, indolent, négligent.

slack(en) vt relâcher; ralentir; diminuer; * vi se relâcher; ralentir.

slam vt claquer violemment; * vi se refermer en claquant.

slander vt calomnier, dire du mal de; * n calomnie f.

slang n argot m.

slant vi pencher; être incliné; * n inclinaison f; point de vue m.

slanting adj en pente, incliné.

slap n claque f; (on the face) gifle f; * adv en plein; * vt donner une claque à, gifler.

slash vt entailler; * n entaille f.

slate n ardoise f.

slating n recouvrement en ardoises m.

slaughter n carnage, massacre m; * vt abattre; massacrer.

slaughterhouse n abattoir m.

slave n esclave mf; * vi travailler comme un nègre.

slavery n esclavage m.

slay vt tuer.

sleazy adj louche, sordide.

sledge n traîneau m.

sledgehammer n marteau de forgeron m.

sleek adj lisse et brillant, luisant.

sleep vi dormir; * n sommeil m.

sleeper n dormeur m -euse f.

sleeping bag n sac de couchage m.

sleeping pill n somnifère m.

sleepless adj sans sommeil.

sleepwalking n somnambulisme m.

sleepy adj qui a envie de dormir; endormi.

sleet n neige fondue f.

sleeve n manche f.

sleight n: ~ of hand tour de passepasse m.

slender adj svelte, mince, élancé; faible.

slice n tranche f; spatule f; * vt couper (en tranches).

slide *vi* glisser; faire des glissades; * *n* glissade *f*; coulisse *f*; diapositive *f*; toboggan *m*.

sliding *adj* glissant; coulissant.

slight *adj* léger, mince, petit; * *n* affront *m*; * *vt* manquer d'égards pour.

slim *adj* mince; * *vi* maigrir.

slime *n* vase *f*; dépôt visqueux *m*.

slimming *n* amaigrissement *m*.

slimy *adj* visqueux, gluant.

sling *n* fronde *f*; écharpe *f*; * *vt* lancer.

slink *vi* s'en aller furtivement; s'éclipser.

slip *vi* (se) glisser, se faufiler; * *vt* glisser; * *n* glissade *f*; faux pas *m*; oubli *m*; fiche *f*.

slipper *n* pantoufle *f*.

slippery *adj* glissant.

slipshod *adj* négligé.

slit *vt* fendre, inciser; * *n* fente, incision *f*.

slobber *n* bave *f*.

slogan *n* slogan *m*.

slop *n* fange *f*; bouillon *m*; **~s** *pl* eaux sales *fpl*.

slope *n* inclinaison *f*; pente *f*; déclivité *f*; versant *m*; * *vt* incliner.

sloping *adj* en pente; incliné.

sloppy *adj* négligé; peu soigné.

sloth *n* paresse *f*.

slouch *vi* manquer de tenue; se tenir d'une façon négligée.

slovenly *adj* négligé, sale, débraillé.

slow *adj* lent; lourd; ennuyeux.

slug *n* lingot *m*; limace *f*; jeton *m*; coup *m*.

sluggish *adj* paresseux; léthargique.

sluice *n* écluse *f*; * *vt* lâcher les vannes.

slum *n* taudis *m*; quartier pauvre *m*.

slumber *vi* dormir paisiblement; * *n* sommeil paisible *m*.

slump *n* effrondrement *m*.

slur *vt* dénigrer; calomnier; mal articuler; * *n* calomnie *f*.

slush *n* neige fondante *f*.

slut *n* traînée *f*.

sly *adj* rusé.

smack *n* léger goût *m*; claque *f*; gros baiser retentissant *m*; * *vi* sentir; embrasser bruyamment; * *vt* donner une claque à.

small *adj* petit, menu.

smallpox *n* variole *f*.

smalltalk *n* conversation *f* banale.

smart *adj* élégant; rapide; astucieux; vif; * *vi* brûler.

smash *vt* casser, briser; détruire; * *vi* se briser (en mille morceaux), se fracasser; * *n* fracas *m*; coup violent *m*.

smattering *n* connaissances superficielles *fpl*.

smear *n* (*med*) frottis *m*; * *vt* enduire; salir.

smell *vt vi* sentir; * *n* odorat *m*; odeur *f*; mauvaise odeur *f*.

smelly *adj* malodorant.

smelt *vt* fondre.

smile *vi* sourire; * *n* sourire *m*.

smirk *vi* sourire d'un air affecté.

smite *vt* frapper.

smith *n* forgeron *m*.

smithy *n* forge *f*.

smock *n* blouse *f*.

smoke *n* fumée *f*; vapeur *f*; * *vt vi* fumer.

smokeless *adj* sans fumée.

smoker *n* fumeur *m* -euse *f*.

smoking: 'no ~' 'interdiction de fumer'.

smoky *adj* enfumé; qui fume.

smooth *adj* lisse, uni, égal; doucereux; mielleux; * *vt* lisser; aplanir; adoucir.

smother *vt* étouffer; réprimer.

smoulder *vi* couver, se consumer.

smudge *vt* étaler; * *n* tache *f.*

smug *adj* suffisant.

smuggle *vt* passer en contrebande.

smuggler *n* contrebandier *m* -ière *f.*

smut *n* saleté *f*; trace de suie *f.*

smutty *adj* noirci; obscène.

snack *n* collation *f.*

snack bar *n* snack-bar *m.*

snag *n* obstacle *m.*

snail *n* escargot *m.*

snake *n* serpent *m.*

snap *vt* casser net; * *vi* se casser net; claquer; mordre; parler sèchement; * *n* claquement *m*; photographie *f.*

snare *n* piège *m*; collet *m.*

snarl *vi* gronder férocement.

snatch *vt* saisir; s'emparer de; * *n* geste vif *m*; vol *m*; fragment *m.*

sneak *vi* se glisser furtivement; * *n* faux-jeton *m.*

sneer *vi* parler d'un ton méprisant; ricaner.

sneeze *vi* éternuer.

sniff *vt* renifler; * *vi* renifler.

snigger *vi* ricaner.

snip *vt* donner de petits coups de ciseaux dans; * *n* petit coup de ciseaux *m*; petit bout *m.*

sniper *n* franc-tireur *m.*

snivel *n* pleurnicherie *f*; * *vi* pleurnicher.

snobbish *adj* snob.

snooze *n* petit somme *m*; * *vi* faire un somme.

snore *vi* ronfler.

snorkel *n* tube respiratoire *m.*

snort *vi* renifler fortement.

snout *n* museau *m*; groin *m.*

snow *n* neige *f*; * *vi* neiger.

snowball *n* boule de neige *f.*

snowdrop *n* (*bot*) perce-neige *m invar.*

snowman *n* bonhomme de neige *m.*

snowplough *n* chasse-neige *m invar.*

snowy *adj* neigeux; enneigé.

snub *vt* repousser, rejeter.

snub-nosed *adj* au nez retroussé.

snug *adj* confortable, douillet; bien abrité.

so *adv* si, tellement, aussi; ainsi.

soak *vi* tremper; * *vt* faire tremper.

soap *n* savon *m.*

soap opera *n* feuilleton à l'eau de rose *m.*

soap powder *n* lessive *f.*

soar *vi* monter en flèche.

sob *n* sanglot *m*; * *vi* sangloter.

sober *adj* sobre; sérieux.

sobriety *n* sobriété *f*; sérieux, calme *m.*

soccer *n* football *m.*

sociable *adj* sociable, liant.

social *adj* social, sociable.

socialism *n* socialisme *m.*

socialist *n* socialiste *mf.*

social work *n* assistance sociale *f.*

social worker *n* assistant(e) social(e) *m(f).*

society *n* société *f*; compagnie *f.*

sociologist *n* sociologue *mf.*

sociology *n* sociologie *f.*

sock *n* chaussette *f.*

socket *n* prise de courant *f.*

sod *n* gazon *m.*

soda *n* soude *f*; eau *f* de Seltz, soda *m.*

soft *adj* doux, moelleux; aimable, gentil.

soften *vt* (r)amollir, adoucir; atténuer.

soft-hearted *adj* compatissant.

soft-spoken *adj* à la voix douce.

software *n* logiciel *m.*

soil *vt* salir, souiller; * *n* salissure, souillure *f*; sol *m*; terre *f.*

sojourn *vi* séjourner; * *n* séjour *m.*

solace vt consoler, soulager; * n consolation f.

solder vt souder; * n soudure f.

soldier n soldat m.

sole n plante du pied f; semelle (de chaussure) f; sole f; * adj seul, unique.

solemn adj ~ly adv solen-nel(lement).

solemnity n solennité f.

solicit vt solliciter; quémander.

solicitor n notaire m.

solicitous adj plein de sollicitude.

solid adj solide, compact; * n solide m.

solidify vt solidifier.

solidity n solidité f.

soliloquy n soliloque m.

solitaire n solitaire m (jeu).

solitary adj solitaire, retiré; * n anachorète m.

solitude n solitude f.

solo n (mus) solo m.

soluble adj soluble.

solution n solution f.

solve vt résoudre.

solvency n solvabilité f.

solvent adj solvable; n (chem) solvant m.

some adj du, de la, de l', des; quelques; quelconque; certain(e)s; quelque.

somebody pn quelqu'un.

somehow adv d'une façon ou d'une autre.

something pn quelque chose.

sometimes adv quelquefois, parfois.

somewhat adv quelque peu.

somewhere adv quelque part.

son n fils m.

sonata n (mus) sonate f.

song n chanson f.

son-in-law n gendre m.

sonnet n sonnet m.

sonorous adj sonore.

soon adv bientôt; **as ~ as** dès que.

sooner adv plus tôt; plutôt.

soot n suie f.

soothe vt calmer, apaiser; flatter.

soothsayer n devin m.

sop n pain trempé m.

sophisticated adj sophistiqué.

soporific adj soporifique.

sorcery n sorcellerie f.

sordid adj sordide, sale.

sore n plaie, blessure f; * adj douloureux, sensible; contrarié; **-ly** adv fortement.

sorrow n peine f, chagrin m; * vi se lamenter.

sorrowful adj triste, affligé.

sorry adj désolé, navré; déplorable; **I am ~** je suis désolé.

sort n sorte f; genre m; espèce f; race f; manière f; * vt classer; trier.

soul n âme f; essence f; personne f.

sound adj sain; solide; valide; * n son m; bruit m; * vt sonner (de); * vi sonner, retentir; ressembler; sembler.

sound effects npl bruitage m.

soundtrack n bande sonore f.

soup n soupe f.

sour adj aigre, acide; acerbe; revêche.

source n source f; origine f.

sourness n acidité, aigreur f; acrimonie f.

south n sud m; * adj sud, du sud, au sud; * adv au sud; vers le sud.

southerly, southern adj du sud, sud, méridional.

sovereign adj n souverain m -e f.

sovereignty n souveraineté f.

sow n truie f.

sow vt semer; disperser.

soy n soja m.

space n espace m; intervalle m; * vt espacer.

spacecraft n vaisseau spatial m.

spaceman/woman n astronaute mf.

spacious adj spacieux, ample.

spade n bêche f; pique m (carte).

span n envergure f; * vt enjamber; embrasser.

spaniel n épagneul m.

Spanish adj espagnol; * n espagnol m; Espagnol m -e f.

spar n (mar) espar m; * vi s'en-traîner.

spare vt vi épargner; ménager; éviter; se passer de; * adj de trop; de réserve.

sparing adj limité, modéré, économe; ~ly adv frugalement, avec modération.

spark n étincelle f.

sparkle n scintillement m, étincelle f; * vi étinceler; briller.

spark plug n bougie f.

sparrow n moineau m.

sparse adj clairsemé; épars; ~ly adv faiblement.

spasm n spasme m.

spasmodic adj spasmodique.

spatter vt éclabousser; * vi gicler.

spatula n spatule f.

spawn n frai m; * vt pondre; engendrer.

speak vt parler; dire; * vi parler, s'entretenir; prendre la parole.

speaker n haut-parleur m; interlocuteur m -trice f; orateur m.

spear n lance f; harpon m; * vt transpercer d'un coup de lance.

special adj spécial, particulier.

speciality n spécialité f.

species n espèce f.

specific adj spécifique.

specification n spécification f.

specify vt spécifier.

specimen n spécimen m; exemple m.

speck(le) n grain, tache f; * vt tacheter, moucheter.

spectacle n spectacle m.

spectator n spectateur m -trice f.

spectre n spectre m.

speculate vi spéculer; méditer.

speculation n spéculation f; conjecture f; méditation f.

speculative adj spéculatif, méditatif.

speech n parole f; discours m; langage m; élocution f.

speechless adj muet.

speed n vitesse f; rapidité f; * vt presser; accélérer; * vi se presser.

speedboat n vedette f.

speed limit n limitation de vitesse f.

speedometer n compteur de vitesse m.

speedway n piste de course f.

speedy adj rapide, prompt.

spell n charme, sortilège m; période f; * vt écrire; épeler; ensorceler, envoûter; * s'écrire; s'épeler.

spelling n orthographe f.

spend vt dépenser; passer; épuiser; gaspiller.

sperm n sperme m.

spew vi (sl) vomir.

sphere n sphère f.

spherical adj sphérique.

spice n épice f.

spicy adj épicé.

spider n araignée f.

spike n pointe f; clou m; * vt clouter.

spill vt renverser, répandre; * vi se répandre.

spin vt filer; inventer, fabriquer; faire tourner; * vi tourner; * n tournoiement m; tour (en voiture) m.

spinach n épinard m.

spinal adj spinal.

spine n colonne vertébrale, épine dorsale f.

spinner n fileur m; fileuse f.

spinning wheel n rouet m.

spin-off n sous-produit m.

spinster n célibataire f.

spiral adj en spirale.

spire n flèche f; aiguille f; tige f.

spirit n esprit m; âme f, caractère m, disposition f; courage m; humeur f; * vt encourager; animer; ~ **away** faire disparaître comme par enchantement.

spirited adj vif, fougueux.

spirit lamp n lampe à alcool f.

spiritual adj ~**ly** adv spirituel(lement).

spiritualist n spiritualiste mf.

spit n crachat m; salive f; * vt vi cracher; crépiter.

spite n dépit m, rancune f; **in ~ of** en dépit de, malgré; * vt vexer.

spiteful adj rancunier, malveillant.

splash vt éclabousser, faire gicler; * vi barboter; * n éclaboussure f; tache f.

spleen n rate f, spleen m.

splendid adj splendide, magnifique.

splendour n splendeur f; magnificence f.

splint n éclisse f.

splinter n éclat m; esquille f; écharde f; * vt (vi) (se) fendre en éclats.

split n fente f; rupture f; * vt fendre, diviser; * vi se fendre.

spoil vt abîmer; gâter; gâcher.

spoke n rayon (de roue) m.

spokesman/woman n porte-parole mf.

sponge n éponge f; * vt éponger; * vi être un parasite.

sponger n parasite m.

sponsor n caution m; parrain m; marraine f.

spontaneity n spontanéité f.

spontaneous adj spontané.

spoon n cuiller f.

sporadic adj sporadique.

sport n sport m; jeu m; divertissement, amusement m.

sports car n voiture de sport f.

sportsman/woman n sportif m -ive f.

sportswear n vêtements de sport mpl.

spot n tache f; point m; endroit m; pois m; * vt apercevoir; tacher.

spotless adj impeccable, immaculé.

spotlight n feu de projecteur m.

spotted, spotty adj tacheté; à pois.

spouse n époux m, épouse f.

spout vi jaillir; gicler; déblatérer; * vt faire jaillir; * n bec m; gargouille f, jet m.

sprain vt fouler; * n entorse f.

sprawl vi s'étaler.

spray n spray m; pulvérisation f, embruns mpl.

spread vt étendre, étaler; répandre, propager; * vi s'étendre, se répandre; * n propagation, diffusion f.

spree n fête f.

sprightly adj alerte, vif, fringant.

spring vi bondir, sauter; provenir, découler; émaner, naître; * n printemps m; élasticité f; ressort m; saut m; source f.

sprinkle vt arroser.

sprinkling n arrosage m.

sprout n pousse f, germe m; ~**s** npl choux de Bruxelles mpl; * vi germer.

spruce adj net, impeccable; * vt se mettre sur son trente-et-un.

spur n éperon m; ergot (coq) m; stimulant m; * vt éperonner; stimuler.

spurious adj faux, feint; falsifié, de contrefaçon.

spurn *vt* repousser avec mépris.

spy *n* espion *m* -ne *f*; * *vt* apercevoir; espionner; *vi* espionner.

squabble *vi* se disputer, se quereller; * *n* querelle, dispute *f*.

squad *n* escouade *f*; brigade *f*; équipe *f*.

squadron *n* (*mil*) escadron *m*.

squalid *adj* misérable, sordide.

squall *n* rafale *f*; bourrasque *f*.

squalor *n* saleté *f*; misère *f*.

squander *vt* gaspiller, dilapider.

square *adj* carré; catégorique; honnête; * *n* carré *m*; place *f*, équerre *f*.

squash *vt* écraser; * *n* squash *m*.

squat *vi* s'accroupir; * *adj* accroupi; trapu, courtaud.

squeak *vi* grincer, crier; * *n* cri, couinement *m*.

squeal *vi* pousser un cri aigu, couiner.

squeamish *adj* impressionable; délicat.

squeeze *vt* presser, tordre; comprimer; * *n* pression *f*; serrement de main *m*; cohue *f*.

squid *n* calmar *m*.

squint *adj* atteint de strabisme; * *vi* loucher; * *n* strabisme *f*.

squirrel *n* écureuil *m*.

squirt *vt* faire gicler.

stab *vt* poignarder.

stability *n* stabilité, solidité *f*.

stable *n* écurie *f*; * *adj* stable.

staff *n* personnel *m*; bâton *m*; soutien *m*.

stag *n* cerf *m*.

stage *n* étape *f*; scène *f*; échafaudage *m*; théâtre *m*; stade *m*; estrade *f*.

stagger *vi* vaciller, tituber; hésiter; * *vt* stupéfier; échelonner.

stagnant *adj* stagnant.

staid *adj* posé, sérieux, guindé.

stain *vt* tacher; ternir; * *n* tache *f*.

stainless *adj* sans tache; immaculé.

stair *n* marche *f*; **~s** *pl* escalier *m*.

stake *n* pieu *m*; enjeu *m*.

stale *adj* rassis, rance.

stalk *vi* avancer d'un air majestueux; * *n* tige, queue *f*, trognon *m*.

stall *n* stalle *f*; stand, étalage *m*; (fauteuil d') orchestre *m*; emplacement *m*; * *vt* caler; * *vi* caler; atermoyer.

stallion *n* étalon *m*.

stamina *n* résistance *f*.

stammer *vi* bégayer; * *n* bégaiement *m*.

stamp *vt* trépigner; timbrer; affranchir; tamponner; * *vi* trépigner; * *n* timbre *m*; cachet *m*; tampon *m*; empreinte *f*; estampille *f*.

stampede *n* débandade *f*.

stand *vi* être debout, se tenir; se maintenir; résister; être situé, se trouver; rester, durer; s'arrêter, faire halte; * *vt* poser; résister; soutenir, supporter; * *n* position, prise de position *f*; pied, support *m*; étalage *m*; état *m*; tribune *f*, stand *m*.

standard *n* étendard *m*; modèle *m*; étalon *m*; norme *f*; * *adj* normal.

standstill *n* arrêt *m*; immobilisation *f*.

staple *n* agrafe *f*.

star *n* étoile *f*; astérisque *m*.

starboard *n* tribord *m*.

starch *n* amidon *m*.

stare *vi*: **to ~ at** regarder fixement; * *n* regard fixe *m*.

stark *adj* raide, rigide; cru; * *adv* complètement.

start *vi* commencer, débuter; sursauter, tressaillir; démarrer, se mettre en route; * *vt* commencer; amorcer; lancer; mettre en marche; * *n* début *m*; ouverture *f*, sursaut *m*; départ *m*; avance *f*.

starting point n point de départ m.

startling adj surprenant, alarmant.

starvation n inanition, faim f.

starve vi mourir de faim.

state n état m; condition f; pompe f, apparat m; * vt déclarer; exposer.

stately adj majestueux, imposant.

statement n déclaration, affirmation f.

statesman n homme d'État m.

static adj statique; * n parasites mpl.

station n station f; place, position f; condition f, rang m; situation f; condition f; (rail) gare f.

stationary adj stationnaire, immobile.

stationery n papeterie f.

statistical adj statistique.

statistics npl statistiques fpl.

statue n statue f.

stature n stature, taille f.

statute n statut m; loi f.

stay n séjour m; ~s npl corset m; * vi rester, demeurer; tenir; loger.

stead n place f, lieu m.

steadfast adj ferme, résolu, inébranlable.

steady adj stable, solide; * vt affermir.

steak n bifteck m; steak m.

steal vt vi voler.

stealth n discrétion f.

stealthy adj furtif.

steam n vapeur f; buée f; * vt cuire à la vapeur; * vi fumer.

steel n acier m; * adj d'acier.

steep adj abrupt; excessif; * vt tremper.

steeple n clocher m; flèche f.

steeplechase n steeple (course) m.

steer vt conduire; diriger; gouverner; * vi tenir le gouvernail.

steering wheel n volant m.

stem n tige f, tronc m; souche f; pied m; tuyau m; * vt endiguer.

stench n odeur fétide f.

stencil n stencil m, pochoir m.

step n pas m, marche f; trace f; * vi faire un pas; marcher.

stepdaughter n belle-fille f.

stepfather n beau-père m.

stepmother n belle-mère f.

stepping stone n pierre de gué f.

stepson n beau-fils m.

stereo n stéréo f.

stereotype n stéréotype m; * vt stéréotyper.

sterile adj stérile.

sterility n stérilité f.

sterling n livres sterling fpl.

stern adj sévère, rigide, strict; * n (mar) poupe f.

stethoscope n (med) stéthoscope m.

stew vt faire cuire à l'étouffée; * n ragoût m.

steward n intendant m; (mar) steward m.

stewardess n hôtesse de l'air f.

stick n bâton m; canne f; baguette f; * vt coller; piquer, planter; supporter; * vi tenir; se planter; rester fidèle.

sticky adj collant, poisseux.

stiff adj raide, rigide; inflexible; dur; entêté.

stiffen vt raidir, renforcer; * vi se raidir.

stifle vt étouffer.

stile n tourniquet m.

stiletto n stylet m; talon aiguille m.

still vt calmer, apaiser; faire taire; * adj silencieux, calme; * n alambic m; * adv encore; toujours; quand même, tout de même.

stillborn adj mort-né.

stilts *npl* échasses *fpl*.

stimulant *n* stimulant *m*.

stimulate *vt* stimuler.

stimulation *n* stimulant *m*; stimulation *f*.

stimulus *n* stimulant *m*.

sting *vt* piquer; * *vi* brûler; * *n* dard *m*; piqûre *f*, aiguillon *m*.

stingy *adj* mesquin, avare, pingre.

stink *vi* puer; * *n* puanteur *f*.

stipulate *vt* stipuler.

stipulation *n* stipulation *f*.

stir *vt* remuer; agiter; exciter; * *vi* remuer, bouger.

stirrup *n* étrier *m*.

stitch *vt* coudre; * *n* point *m*; point de suture *m*.

stoat *n* hermine *f*.

stock *n* réserve *f*; provision *f*; bouillon *m*; souche *f*, lignée *f*; capital *m*; fonds *mpl*; **~s** *pl* valeurs mobilières *fpl*; * *vt* approvisionner, stocker.

stockade *n* prison militaire *f*.

stockbroker *n* agent de change *m*.

stock exchange *n* Bourse *f*.

stocking *n* bas *m*.

stock market *n* Bourse *f*.

stole *n* étole *f*.

stomach *n* estomac *m*; ventre *m*; * *vt* digérer; endurer.

stone *n* pierre *f*; caillou *m*; noyau *m*; * *adj* de pierre; * *vt* lancer des pierres sur; dénoyauter; empierrer.

stony *adj* pierreux, rocailleux; dur.

stool *n* tabouret *m*; rebord, appui *m*.

stoop *vi* se baisser, se pencher; * *n* inclination en avant *f*.

stop *vt* arrêter, interrompre; boucher; * *vi* s'arrêter, cesser; * *n* arrêt *m*; halte *f*; pause *f*; point *m*.

stoppage, stopping *n* obstruction *f*; engorgement *m*; (*rail*) suppression *f*.

stopwatch *n* chronomètre *m*.

storage *n* emmagasinage *m*; entreposage *m*.

store *n* provision *f*; réserve *f*; entrepôt *m*, magasin *m*; * *vt* mettre en réserve, accumuler, emmagasiner.

storey *n* étage *m*.

stork *n* cigogne *f*.

storm *n* tempête *f*, orage *m*; assaut *m*; * *vt* prendre d'assaut; * *vi* faire rage.

stormily *adv* violemment.

stormy *adj* orageux; houleux.

story *n* histoire *f*; récit *m*.

stout *adj* corpulent, robuste, vigoureux; solide.

stove *n* poêle *m*; cuisinière *f*.

straggle *vi* être disséminé.

straight *adj* droit; direct; franc; * *adv* droit; directement.

straighten *vt* redresser.

straightforward *adj* honnête; franc; direct.

strain *vt* tendre; fouler; forcer; mettre à l'épreuve; * *vi* peiner; * *n* tension *f*; effort *m*; entorse *f*; contrainte *f*; lignée *f*, accent *m*; ton *m*.

strainer *n* passoire *f*.

strait *n* détroit *m*; embarras *m*; situation critique *f*.

strait-jacket *n* camisole de force *f*.

strand *n* brin *m*; rivage *m*, rive *f*.

strange *adj* inconnu; étrange.

stranger *n* inconnu(e) *m(f)*, étranger *m* -ère *f*.

strangle *vt* étrangler.

strangulation *n* strangulation *f*.

strap *n* lanière, sangle *f*; courroie *f*.

strapping *adj* robuste, charpenté.

stratagem *n* stratagème *m*.

strategic *adj* stratégique *m*.

strategy *n* stratégie *f*.

stratum *n* strate *f*.

straw *n* paille *f*.

strawberry *n* fraise *f*.

stray *vi* s'égarer; vagabonder; * *adj* perdu; errant.

streak *n* raie, bande *f*; filet *m*; * *vt* strier.

stream *n* ruisseau *m*, rivière *f*; torrent *m*; * *vi* ruisseler.

streamer *n* serpentin *m*.

street *n* rue *f*.

strength *n* force, puissance *f*; vigueur *f*; robustesse *f*.

strengthen *vt* fortifier; confirmer, renforcer.

strenuous *adj* ardu; vigoureux.

stress *n* pression *f*; stress *m*; tension *f*; contrainte *f*; importance *f*; accent *m*; * *vt* souligner; accentuer.

stretch *vt* étendre, étirer; élargir; forcer; * *vi* s'étendre, s'étirer.

stretcher *n* brancard *m*.

strict *adj* strict, sévère; exact, rigoureux, précis.

stride *n* grand pas *m*; * *vi* marcher à grandes enjambées.

strike *vt* frapper; heurter; attaquer; rayer; * *vi* frapper; se mettre en grève; sonner; * *n* coup *m*; grève *f*; découverte *f*.

striker *n* gréviste *mf*.

striking *adj* frappant; saisissant.

string *n* ficelle *f*; corde *f*; cordon *m*; rang *m*; fibre *f*.

strip *vt* déshabiller, dévêtir; * *vi* se déshabiller; * *n* bande *f*; langue *f*; bandelette *f*.

stripe *n* raie, rayure *f*; coup de fouet *m*; * *vt* rayer.

stroke *n* coup *m*; trait *m*; course *f*; caresse *f*; apoplexie *f*; * *vt* caresser.

stroll *n* petit tour *m*; * *vi* flâner.

strong *adj* fort, vigoureux, robuste; puissant; intense.

structure *n* structure *f*; construction *f*.

struggle *vi* lutter; se battre; se démener; * *n* lutte *f*.

strut *vi* se pavaner; * *n* démarche affectée *f*.

stub *n* souche *f*; bout *m*; talon *m*.

stubble *n* chaume *m*; barbe de plusieurs jours *f*.

stubborn *adj* entêté, obstiné.

stucco *n* stuc *m*.

stud *n* clou *m*; crampon *m*; écurie *f*.

student *n, adj* étudiant *m* -e *f*.

studio *n* studio, atelier *m*.

studious *adj* studieux; sérieux.

study *n* étude *f*; études *fpl*; méditation *f*; * *vt* étudier; observer; * *vi* étudier; faire des études.

stuff *n* matière *f*; matériaux *mpl*; étoffe *f*; * *vt* (rem)bourrer, remplir; empailler.

stuffing *n* rembourrage *m*.

stuffy *adj* mal aéré; collet monté.

stumble *vi* trébucher; * *n* faux pas, trébuchement *m*.

stumbling block *n* hésitation *f*; pierre d'achoppement *f*.

stump *n* souche *f*; moignon *m*; bout *m*.

stun *vt* étourdir; stupéfier.

stunt *n* cascade *f*; coup de publicité *m*; * *vt* empêcher de croître.

stuntman *n* cascadeur *m*.

stupefy *vt* hébéter; stupéfier.

stupendous *adj* prodigieux, remarquable.

stupid *adj* ~ly *adv* stupide(ment).

stupidity *n* stupidité *f*.

stupor *n* stupeur *f*.

sturdy *adj* vigoureux, robuste, fort; hardi, résolu.

stutter *vi* bégayer.

sty *n* porcherie *f*; taudis *m*.

stye *n* orgelet *m*.

style *n* style *m*; mode *f*; * *vt* appeler, dénommer; créer, dessiner.

stylish *adj* élégant, qui a du chic.

subdivide *vt* subdiviser.

subdivision *n* subdivision *f*.

subdue *vt* subjuguer, assujettir; contenir, réfréner; adoucir.

subject *adj* soumis; sujet à; * *n* sujet *m*; thème *m*; * *vt* soumettre; exposer.

subjection *n* sujétion *f*.

sublet *vt* sous-louer.

sublimate *vt* sublimer.

sublime *adj* sublime, suprême.

submachine gun *n* mitraillette *f*.

submarine *adj n* sous-marin *m*.

submerge *vt* submerger.

submission *n* soumission *f*.

submissive *adj* soumis, docile.

submit *vt* soumettre; * *vi* se soumettre.

subordinate *adj* subalterne, inférieur.

subordination *n* subordination *f*.

subscribe *vi* souscrire; * *vt* apposer; signer.

subscriber *n* souscripteur *m* -trice *f*.

subscription *n* souscription *f*.

subsequent *adj* ~**ly** *adv* ultérieur(ement).

subservient *adj* subordonné; utile.

subside *vi* s'affaisser, baisser.

subsidence *n* affaissement *m*.

subsidiary *adj* subsidiaire.

subsidise *vt* subventionner, fournir des subsides à.

subsidy *n* subvention *f*; subside *m*.

substance *n* substance *f*; fond *m*; essentiel *m*.

substantial *adj* considérable; réel, substantiel; solide.

substantiate *vt* justifier.

substitute *vt* substituer; * *n* remplaçant *m* -e *f*.

substitution *n* substitution *f*.

subterfuge *n* subterfuge *m*; faux-fuyant *m*.

subterranean *adj* souterrain.

subtitle *n* sous-titre *m*.

subtle *adj* subtile.

subtlety *n* subtilité *f*.

subtract *vt* (*math*) soustraire.

suburb *n* banlieue *f*.

suburban *adj* de banlieue.

subversive *adj* subversif.

subway *n* métro *m*.

succeed *vi* réussir; succéder; avoir du succès; * *vt* succéder à, suivre.

success *n* succès *m*.

successful *adj* couronné de succès, qui réussit.

succession *n* succession *f*.

successive *adj* successif.

successor *n* successeur *m*.

succinct *adj* succinct, concis.

succulent *adj* succulent.

succumb *vi* succomber.

such *adj* tel, pareil; ~ **as** tel que.

suck *vt vi* sucer; *vi* téter.

suction *n* succion *f*.

sudden *adj* ~**ly** *adv* soudain(ement), subit(ement).

suds *npl* mousse de savon *f*.

sue *vt* poursuivre en justice; supplier.

suede *n* daim *m*.

suffer *vt* souffrir, subir; tolérer, endurer; * *vi* souffrir.

suffering *n* souffrance *f*; douleur *f*.

suffice *vi* suffire, être suffisant.

sufficiency *n* quantité suffisante *f*; aisance *f*.

sufficient *adj* suffisant.

suffocate *vt vi* étouffer.

suffocation *n* suffocation *f*.

suffuse *vt* baigner, se répandre sur.

sugar *n* sucre *m*; * *vt* sucrer.

suggest *vt* suggérer.

suggestion *n* suggestion *f*.

suicidal *adj* suicidaire.

suicide *n* suicide *m*; suicidé *m* -e *f*.

suit *n* procès *m*; pétition *f*; costume *m*; tailleur *m*; requête *f*; * *vt* convenir à; aller à; arranger, adapter.

suitable *adj* qui convient, approprié.

suitcase *n* valise *f*.

suite *n* suite *f*; escorte *f*; mobilier *m*; cortège *m*.

suitor *n* plaideur *m*; prétendant *m*.

sulky *adj* boudeur, maussade.

sullen *adj* maussade; sombre.

sulphur *n* soufre *m*.

sultan *n* sultan *m*.

sultana *n* sultane *f*; raisin sec *m*.

sultry *adj* étouffant; chaud.

sum *n* somme *f*; total *m*; ~ **up** *vt* résumer; récapituler; * *vi* résumer.

summarily *adv* sommairement.

summary *adj n* résumé *m*.

summer *n* été *m*.

summit *n* sommet *m*; cime *f*.

summon *vt* convoquer, citer à comparaître; sommer; (*mil*) sommer de se rendre.

summons *n* convocation *f*, sommation *f*.

sumptuous *adj* somptueux.

sun *n* soleil *m*.

sunbathe *vi* prendre un bain de soleil, se faire bronzer.

sunburnt *adj* bronzé, hâlé.

Sunday *n* dimanche *m*.

sundial *n* cadran solaire *m*.

sundry *adj* divers, différent.

sunflower *n* tournesol *m*.

sunglasses *npl* lunettes de soleil *fpl*.

sunlight *n* lumière du soleil *f*.

sunny *adj* ensoleillé; radieux.

sunrise *n* lever de soleil *m*.

sunset *n* coucher de soleil *m*.

sunshade *n* parasol *m*.

sunshine *n* (lumière du) soleil *m*; ensoleillement *m*.

sunstroke *n* insolation *f*.

suntan *n* bronzage *m*.

super *adj* (*fam*) sensationnel.

superannuation *n* retraite, pension de retraite *f*.

superb *adj* ~**ly** *adv* super-be(ment).

supercilious *adj* hautain, dédaigneux.

superficial *adj* ~**ly** *adv* superficiel(lement).

superfluous *adj* superflu.

superhuman *adj* surhumain.

superintendent *n* directeur *m* -trice *f*.

superior *adj n* supérieur *m* -e *f*.

superiority *n* supériorité *f*.

superlative *adj n* superlatif *m*.

supermarket *n* supermarché *m*.

supernatural *adj* surnaturel.

superpower *n* superpuissance *f*.

supersede *vt* remplacer; supplanter.

supersonic *adj* supersonique.

superstition *n* superstition *f*.

superstitious *adj* superstitieux.

superstructure *n* superstructure *f*.

supervise *vt* surveiller, superviser.

supervision *n* surveillance *f*.

supervisor *n* surveillant *m* -e *f*.

supper *n* dîner *m*.

supplant *vt* supplanter.

supple *adj* souple, flexible; obséquieux.

supplement *n* supplément *m*.

supplementary *adj* supplémentaire.

supplier *n* fournisseur *m*.

supply *vt* fournir, approvisionner; suppléer à, remédier à; * *n* approvisionnement *m*; provision *f*.

support *vt* soutenir; supporter, appuyer; * *n* appui *m*.

supporter *n* partisan *m*; supporter *m*, adepte *mf*.

suppose *vt vi* supposer.

supposition *n* supposition *f*.

suppress *vt* supprimer.

suppression *n* suppression *f*.

supremacy *n* suprématie *f*.

supreme *adj* suprême.

surcharge *vt* surcharger; * *n* surtaxe *f*.

sure *adj* sûr, certain; infaillible; **to be ~** certainement; **~ly** *adv* sûrement, certainement, sans doute.

sureness *n* certitude, sûreté *f*.

surety *n* certitude *f*; caution *f*.

surf *n* (*mar*) ressac *m*.

surface *n* surface *f*; * *vt* revêtir; * *vi* remonter à la surface.

surfboard *n* planche (de surf) *f*.

surfeit *n* excès *m*.

surge *n* vague, montée *f*; * *vi* déferler.

surgeon *n* chirurgien *m*.

surgery *n* chirurgie *m*.

surgical *adj* chirurgical.

surly *adj* revêche, bourru.

surmise *vt* conjecturer; * *n* conjecture *f*.

surmount *vt* surmonter.

surname *n* nom de famille *m*.

surpass *vt* surpasser, dépasser.

surplice *n* surplis *m*.

surplus *n* excédent *m*; surplus *m*; * *adj* en surplus.

surprise *vt* surprendre; * *n* surprise *f*.

surrender *vt* rendre; céder; * *vi* se rendre; * *n* reddition *f*.

surreptitious *adj* **~ly** *adv* subreptice(ment).

surrogate *n* substitut *m*.

surrogate mother *n* mère porteuse *f*.

surround *vt* entourer, cerner, encercler.

survey *vt* examiner, inspecter; faire le relevé de; * *n* enquête *f*; relevé (des plans) *m*.

survive *vi* survivre; * *vt* survivre à.

survivor *n* survivant *m* -e *f*.

susceptible *adj* sensible.

suspect *vt* soupçonner; * *n* suspect *m* -e *f*.

suspend *vt* suspendre.

suspense *n* incertitude *f*; suspense *m*.

suspension *n* suspension *f*.

suspicion *n* soupçon *m*.

suspicious *adj* soupçonneux.

sustain *vt* soutenir, supporter, maintenir; subir.

sustenance *n* (moyens de) subsistance *f*.

swab *n* tampon *m*; prélèvement *m*.

swagger *vi* plastronner.

swallow *n* hirondelle *f*; * *vt* avaler.

swamp *n* marais *m*.

swan *n* cygne *m*.

swap *vt* échanger; * *n* échange *m*.

swarm *n* essaim *m*; grouillement *m*; nuée *f*; * *vi* fourmiller; grouiller de monde; pulluler.

swarthy *adj* basané.

sway *vt* balancer; * *vi* se balancer, osciller; * *n* balancement *m*; emprise, domination, puissance *f*.

swear *vt* jurer; faire prêter serment; * *vi* jurer.

sweat *n* sueur *f*; * *vi* suer, transpirer.

sweater, sweatshirt *n* pullover *m*.

sweep *vt* balayer; ramoner; * *vi* s'étendre; avancer rapidement, majestueusement; * *n* coup de balai *m*; grand geste *m*; champ *m*.

sweepstake *n* sweepstake *m*.

sweet *adj* sucré, doux, agréable; suave; gentil; mélodieux; adorable; * *adv* doux; sucré; * *n* bonbon *m*.

sweeten *vt* sucrer; adoucir; assainir; purifier.

sweetheart *n* petit(e) ami(e) *m(f)*; chéri *m* -e *f*.

sweetness *n* goût sucré *m*, douceur *f*.

swell *vi* gonfler; enfler; augmenter; * *vt* gonfler, enfler, grossir; * *n* houle *f*.

swelling *n* gonflement *m*; boursouflure, tuméfaction *f*.

swelter *vi* étouffer de chaleur.

swerve *vi* faire un écart; * *vt* dévier.

swift *adj* rapide, prompt, vif; * *n* martinet *m*.

swill *vt* boire avidement; * *n* pâtée *f*.

swim *vi* nager; * *vt* traverser à la nage; * *n* baignade *f*.

swimming *n* natation *f*, nage *f*; vertige *m*.

swimming pool *n* piscine *f*.

swimsuit *n* maillot de bain *m*.

swindle *vt* escroquer.

swindler *n* escroc *m*.

swine *n* pourceau, porc *m*.

swing *vi* se balancer, osciller; virer; * *vt* balancer; faire tourner; influencer; * *n* balancement *m*; rythme *m*.

swirl *n* tourbillon *m*.

switch *n* baguette *f*; interrupteur *m*; (*rail*) aiguille *f*; * *vt* changer de; **~ off** éteindre; **~ on** allumer.

switchboard *n* standard (téléphonique) *m*.

swivel *vt* faire pivoter.

swoon *vi* s'évanouir; * *n* évanouissement *m*, défaillance *f*.

swoop *vi* fondre sur; * *n* descente en piqué *f*; descente, rafle *f*.

sword *n* épée *f*.

swordfish *n* espadon *m*.

sycamore *n* sycomore *m*.

sycophant *n* sycophante *mf*.

syllable *n* syllabe *f*.

syllabus *n* programme *m* (d'un cours).

symbol *n* symbole *m*.

symbolic(al) *adj* symbolique.

symbolise *vt* symboliser.

symmetrical *adj* **~ly** *adv* symétrique(ment).

sympathetic *adj* compatissant.

sympathise *vi* compatir.

sympathy *n* compassion *f*.

symphony *n* symphonie *f*.

symptom *n* symptôme *m*.

synagogue *n* synagogue *f*.

syndicate *n* syndicat *m*.

syndrome *n* syndrome *m*.

synonym *n* synonyme *m*.

synonymous *adj* synonyme.

syringe *n* seringue *f*; * *vt* serin-guer.

system *n* système *m*.

systematic *adj* **~ally** *adv* systématique(ment).

systems analyst *n* analyste de systèmes *mf*.

T

tab n patte f; étiquette f.

table n table f.

tablecloth n nappe f.

tablespoon n grande cuiller f.

tablet n tablette f; comprimé m.

table tennis n ping-pong m.

taboo adj n tabou m.

tacit adj ~**ly** adv tacite(ment).

taciturn adj taciturne.

tack n broquette f; bordée f; * vt clouer; * vi tirer des bordées.

tackle n attirail, équipement, matériel m; plaquage m.

tactician n tacticien m.

tactics npl tactique f.

tadpole n têtard m.

tag n ferret m; étiquette f; * vt ferrer.

tail n queue f, basque f, * vt suivre, filer.

tailor n tailleur m.

tainted adj infecté; souillé.

take vt prendre, saisir; apporter, emporter; conduire; enlever, retirer; passer; * vi prendre; ~ **back** vt reprendre; raccompagner; ~ **down** vt descendre; prendre (notes); ~ **in** vt saisir, comprendre; recevoir; ~ **off** vi décoller; vt enlever; imiter; ~ **on** vt accepter; engager; s'attaquer à; ~ **to** vt se prendre d'amitié pour; ~ **up** vt monter; occuper; se mettre à.

takeoff n décollage m.

takeover n prise f de contrôle.

takings npl recette f.

talent n talent m; don m.

talented adj talentueux.

talk vi parler, bavarder; causer; * n conversation f; discussion f; entretien m.

talkative adj loquace.

tall adj grand, élevé; incroyable.

tally vi correspondre.

talon n serre f.

tambourine n tambourin m.

tame adj apprivoisé, domestiqué; * vt apprivoiser, domestiquer.

tamper vi tripoter.

tampon n tampon m.

tan vt vi bronzer; * n bronzage m.

tang n saveur forte f.

tangent n tangente f.

tangerine n mandarine f.

tangle vt enchevêtrer, embrouiller.

tank n réservoir m; citerne f.

tanker n pétrolier m; camion-citerne m.

tantalising adj tentant.

tantrum n accès de colère m.

tap vt taper doucement; exploiter; inciser; * n petite tape f; robinet m.

tape n ruban m; * vt enregistrer.

tape measure n mètre à ruban m.

taper n cierge m.

tape recorder n magnétophone m.

tapestry n tapisserie f.

tar n goudron m.

target n cible f.

tariff n tarif m.

tarmac n piste f (d'aéroport).

tarnish vt ternir.

tarpaulin n bâche (goudronnée) f.

tarragon n (bot) estragon m.

tart adj acidulé; * n tarte, tartelette f.

tartar n tartre m.

task n tâche f.

tassel n gland m (décoration).

taste n goût m; saveur f; pincée f; penchant m; * vt sentir le goût de; goûter à; déguster; savourer; * vi avoir du goût.

tasteful adj de bon goût.

tasteless adj insipide, sans goût.

tasty adj savoureux.

tattoo n tatouage m.

taunt vt railler; accabler de sarcasmes; * n raillerie f, sarcasme m.

taut adj tendu.

tax n impôt m; contribution f; * vt imposer; mettre à l'épreuve.

taxation n imposition f.

taxi n taxi m; * vi rouler sur la piste.

tax payer n contribuable mf.

tea n thé m.

teach vt enseigner, apprendre; * vi enseigner.

teacher n professeur m; instituteur m - trice f.

teaching n enseignement m.

teacup n tasse à thé f.

team n équipe f.

teamwork n travail d'équipe m.

teapot n théière f.

tear vt déchirer.

tear n larme f.

tearful adj larmoyant.

tear gas n gaz lacrymogène m.

tease vt taquiner.

tea-service, tea-set n service à thé m.

teaspoon n petite cuiller f.

teat n tétine f, mamelon m.

technical adj technique.

technician n technicien m -ne f.

technique n technique f.

technology n technologie f.

teddy (bear) n ours en peluche m.

tedious adj ennuyeux, fastidieux.

tedium n ennui, manque d'intérêt m.

teem vi grouiller (de).

teenage adj adolescent; ~r adolescent(e) m(f).

teens npl adolescence (de 13 à 20 ans) f.

teeth npl de **tooth**.

teethe vi faire ses premières dents.

teetotal adj antialcoolique, qui ne boit jamais d'alcool.

telegram n télégramme m.

telepathy n télépathie f.

telephone n téléphone m.

telephone call n appel téléphonique m.

telephone directory n annuaire m.

telephone number n numéro de téléphone m.

telescope n télescope m.

telescopic adj télescopique.

televise vt téléviser.

television n télévision f.

television set n téléviseur, poste de télévision m.

telex n télex m; vt envoyer par télex.

tell vt dire; raconter.

teller n (banque) caissier m -ière f.

telling adj révélateur.

telltale adj dénonciateur.

temper vt tempérer, modérer; * n colère f.

temperament n tempérament m.

temperance n tempérance, modération f.

temperature n température f.

tempestuous adj de tempête.

temple n temple m; tempe f.

temporary adj temporaire.

tempt vt tenter.

temptation n tentation f.

ten adj n dix m.

tenacious *adj* tenace.

tenacity *n* ténacité *f*.

tenant *n* locataire *mf*.

tend *vt* garder, surveiller; * *vi* avoir tendance (à).

tendency *n* tendance *f*.

tender *adj* tendre, délicat; sensible.

tendon *n* tendon *m*.

tenement *n* appartement *m*.

tenet *n* doctrine *f*; principe *m*.

tennis court *n* court *ou* terrain de tennis *m*.

tennis racket *n* raquette de tennis *f*.

tenor *n* (*mus*) ténor *m*; sens *m*; substance *f*.

tense *adj* tendu; * *n* (*gr*) temps *m*.

tension *n* tension *f*.

tent *n* tente *f*.

tentacle *n* tentacule *m*.

tentative *adj* timide, hésitant.

tenth *adj n* dixième *mf*.

tenuous *adj* ténu.

tepid *adj* tiède.

term *n* terme *m*; trimestre *m*; mot *m*; condition, clause *f*; * *vt* appeler, nommer.

terminal *adj* terminal; * *n* aérogare *f*; terminal *m*.

terminate *vt* terminer.

termination *n* fin, conclusion *f*.

terrace *n* terrace *f*.

terrain *n* (*mil*) terrain *m*.

terrestrial *adj* terrestre.

terrible *adj* terrible.

terrier *n* terrier *m* (chien).

terrific *adj* terrifiant; fantastique.

terrify *vt* terrifier, épouvanter.

territorial *adj* territorial.

territory *n* territoire *m*.

terror *n* terreur *f*.

terrorise *vt* terroriser.

terrorist *n* terroriste *mf*.

terse *adj* concis, net.

test *n* essai *m*; épreuve *f*; * *vt* essayer; examiner.

testament *n* testament *m*.

testicles *npl* testicules *mpl*.

testify *vt* témoigner, déclarer sous serment.

testimonial *n* certificat *m*.

testimony *n* témoignage *m*.

test tube *n* éprouvette *f*.

testy *adj* irritable.

text *n* texte *m*.

textbook *n* manuel *m*.

textiles *npl* textile *m*.

textual *adj* textuel.

texture *n* texture *f*; (*med*) tissu *m*.

than *adv* que; de.

thank *vt* remercier, dire merci à.

thankful *adj* reconnaissant.

thankless *adj* ingrat.

thanks *npl* remerciement(s) *m(pl)*.

that *pn* cela, ça, ce; qui, que; celui-là; * *conj* que; afin que; **so ~** pour que.

thatch *n* chaume *m*; * *vt* couvrir de chaume.

thaw *n* dégel *m*; * *vi* fondre, dégeler.

the *art* le, la, l', les.

theatre *n* théâtre *m*.

theatrical *adj* théâtral.

theft *n* vol *m*.

their *pn* leur(s); **~s** le leur; la leur; les leurs; à elles; à eux.

them *pn* les; leur.

theme *n* thème *m*.

themselves *pn pl* eux-mêmes *mpl*, elles-mêmes *fpl*; se.

then *adv* alors, à cette époque-là; ensuite; en ce cas; * *conj* donc; en ce cas; *

adj d'alors; **now and** ~ de temps en temps.

theology n théologie f.

theorem n théorème m.

theoretical adj ~**ly** adv théorique(ment).

theorise vt théoriser.

theory n théorie f.

therapist n thérapeute mf.

therapy n thérapie f.

there adv y, là.

therefore adv donc, par conséquent.

thermal adj thermal.

thermometer n thermomètre m.

thermostat n thermostat m.

these pn pl ceux-ci, celles-ci.

thesis n thèse f.

they pn pl ils, elles.

thick adj épais, gros; dense; obtus.

thicken vi (s')épaissir, grossir.

thicket n fourré m.

thickset adj trapu; râblé.

thick-skinned adj endurci, blindé.

thief n voleur m -euse f.

thigh n cuisse f.

thimble n dé (à coudre) m.

thin adj mince, fin, maigre; clair; * vt amincir; délayer; éclaircir.

thing n chose f; objet m; truc m.

think vi penser, réfléchir, imaginer; * vt penser, croire, juger.

third adj troisième; * n troisième mf; tiers m.

thirst n soif f.

thirsty adj assoiffé.

thirteen adj n treize m.

thirteenth adj n treizième mf.

thirtieth adj n trentième mf.

thirty adj n trente m.

this adj ce, cet, cette, ces; * pn ceci, ce.

thistle n chardon m.

thorn n épine f; aubépine f.

thorough adj consciencieux, approfondi; ~**ly** adv minutieusement, à fond.

thoroughbred adj pur-sang, de race.

thoroughfare n rue, artère f.

those pn pl ceux-là, celles-la; * adj ces, ces... là.

though conj bien que, malgré le fait que; * adv pourtant.

thought n pensée, réflexion f; opinion f; intention f.

thoughtful adj pensif.

thoughtless adj étourdi; irréfléchi.

thousand adj n mille m.

thrash vt battre; rouer de coups.

thread n fil m; filetage m; * vt enfiler.

threadbare adj râpé, élimé.

threat n menace f.

threaten vt menacer.

three adj n trois m.

three-dimensional adj à trois dimensions, tridimensionnel.

threshold n seuil m.

thrifty adj économe.

thrill vt faire frissonner; * n frisson m.

thriller n film ou roman à suspense m.

throat n gorge f.

throb vi palpiter; vibrer; lanciner.

throne n trône m.

throttle n accélérateur m; * vt étrangler.

through prep à travers; pendant; par, grâce à.

throughout prep partout dans; * adv partout.

throw vt jeter, lancer, projeter; * n jet m; lancement m; ~ **away** vt jeter; ~ **out** vt jeter dehors; ~ **up** vt vi vomir.

thrush *n* grive *f*.

thrust *vt* pousser violemment; enfoncer; * *n* poussée *f*.

thud *n* bruit sourd *m*.

thug *n* voyou *m*.

thumb *n* pouce *m*.

thump *n* coup de poing *m*; * *vi* frapper, cogner; * *vt* cogner à.

thunder *n* tonnerre *m*; * *vi* tonner.

thunderstorm *n* orage *m*.

Thursday *n* jeudi *m*.

thus *adv* ainsi, de cette manière.

thwart *vt* contrecarrer.

thyme *n* (*bot*) thym *m*.

thyroid *n* thyroïde *f*.

tiara *n* tiare *f*.

tic *n* tic *m*.

tick *n* tic-tac *m*; instant *m*; * *vt* cocher.

ticket *n* billet, ticket *m*; étiquette *f*, carte *f*.

tickle *vt* chatouiller.

tidal *adj* (*mar*) de la marée.

tide *n* marée *f*, (*fig*) afflux *m*, cours *m*.

tidy *adj* rangé, en ordre; ordonné; soigné.

tie *vt* attacher, nouer; * *vi* se nouer; ~ **up** *vt* ficeler; attacher; amarrer; conclure; * *n* attache *f*; lacet *m*; égalité *f*.

tier *n* gradin *m*; étage *m*.

tiger *n* tigre *m*.

tight *adj* raide, tendu; serré; hermétique; * *adv* très fort.

tighten *vt* (re)serrer, tendre.

tightfisted *adj* avare.

tightrope *n* corde raide *f*.

tigress *n* tigresse *f*.

tile *n* tuile *f*; carreau *m*; * *vt* couvrir de tuiles.

tiled *adj* en tuiles, carrelé.

till *n* caisse *f*; * *vt* labourer, cultiver.

tiller *n* barre du gouvernail *f*.

tilt *vt* pencher; * *vi* s'incliner.

timber *n* bois de construction *m*; arbres *mpl*.

time *n* temps *m*; période *f*; heure *f*; moment *m*; (*mus*) mesure *f*; **in** ~ à temps; **from** ~ **to** ~ de temps en temps; * *vt* fixer; chronométrer.

timely *adj* opportun.

time off *n* temps libre *m*.

time scale *n* durée *f*.

time zone *n* fuseau horaire *m*.

timid *adj* timide, timoré.

timing *n* chronométrage *m*.

tin *n* étain *m*; boîte (de conserve) *f*.

tinfoil *n* papier d'aluminium *m*.

tinge *n* teinte *f*.

tingle *vi* picoter; vibrer, frissonner.

tinkle *vi* tinter.

tinsel *n* guirlande *f*.

tint *n* teinte *f*; * *vt* teinter.

tiny *adj* minuscule, tout petit.

tip *n* pointe *f*, bout *m*; pourboire *m*; conseil, tuyau *m*; * *vt* donner un pourboire à; pencher; effleurer.

tip-off *n* avertissement *m*.

tipsy *adj* gai, éméché.

tirade *n* diatribe *f*.

tire *vt* fatiguer; * *vi* se fatiguer; se lasser.

tireless *adj* infatigable.

tiresome *adj* ennuyeux, fatigant.

tiring *adj* fatigant.

tissue *n* (US) tissu *m* (*bot*); mouchoir *m* en papier.

tissue paper *n* papier *m* de soie.

titbit *n* friandise *f*; bon morceau *m*.

titillate *vt* titiller.

title *n* titre *m*.

titter *vi* rire sottement; * *n* petit rire sot *m*.

to *prep* à; vers; en; chez; moins; de.

toad *n* crapaud *m*.

toadstool *n* (*bot*) champignon véné-neux *m*.

toast *vt* (faire) griller; porter un toast à la santé de; * *n* toast *m*.

toaster *n* grille-pain *m invar*.

tobacco *n* tabac *m*.

tobacconist *n* marchand(e) de tabac *m(f)*.

today *adv* aujourd'hui.

toddler *n* enfant qui commence à marcher *m*.

toe *n* orteil *m*; pointe *f*.

together *adv* ensemble; en même temps.

toil *vi* travailler dur, peiner; se donner du mal.

toilet *n* toilette *f*; toilettes *fpl*.

toilet bag *n* trousse de toilette *f*.

toilet paper *n* papier hygiénique *m*.

toiletries *npl* articles de toilette *mpl*.

token *n* signe *m*; marque *f*; souvenir *m*; bon *m*; jeton *m*.

tolerance *n* tolérance *f*.

tolerant *adj* tolérant.

tolerate *vt* tolérer.

toll *n* péage *m*; nombre de victimes *m*.

tomato *n* tomate *f*.

tomb *n* tombeau *m*; tombe *f*.

tomboy *n* garçon manqué *m*.

tomorrow *adv*, *n* demain *m*.

ton *n* tonne *f*.

tone *n* ton *m*; tonalité *f*; * *vi* s'harmo-niser; **~ down** *vt* adoucir.

tone-deaf *adj* qui n'a pas l'oreille musicale.

tongs *npl* pinces *fpl*.

tongue *n* langue *f*.

tonic *n* (*med*) tonique *m*.

tonight *adv*, *n* ce soir (*m*).

tonsil *n* amygdale *f*.

too *adv* aussi; trop.

tool *n* outil *m*; ustensile *m*.

tool box *n* caisse à outils *f*.

tooth *n* dent *f*.

toothache *n* rage de dents *f*.

toothbrush *n* brosse à dents *f*.

toothpaste *n* dentifrice *m*.

top *n* sommet *m*, cime *f*; haut *m*; tête *f*; dessus *m*; couvercle *m*; étage supérieur *m*; * *adj* du haut; premier.

topaz *n* topaze *f*.

top floor *n* dernier étage *m*.

top-heavy *adj* instable, déséquilibré.

topic *n* sujet *m*; **~al** *adj* d'actualité.

topless *adj* torse nu, aux seins nus.

top-level *adj* au plus haut niveau.

topmost *adj* le plus haut.

topple *vt* renverser; * *vi* basculer.

top-secret *adj* ultra-secret.

topsy-turvy *adv* sens dessus dessous.

torch *n* torche *f*.

torment *vt* tourmenter; * *n* tourment *m*.

tornado *n* tornade *f*.

torrent *n* torrent *m*.

tortoise *n* tortue *f*.

tortoiseshell *adj* en écaille de tortue.

tortuous *adj* tortueux, sinueux.

torture *n* torture *f*; * *vt* torturer.

toss *vt* lancer, jeter; agiter, secouer.

total *adj* total, global.

totalitarian *adj* totalitaire.

totter *vi* chanceler.

touch *vt* toucher; **~ on** effleurer; **~ up** retoucher; * *n* toucher *m*; contact *m*; touche *f*.

touchdown *n* atterrissage *m*; but *m*.

touched *adj* touché; timbré.

touching *adj* touchant, attendrissant.

touchy *adj* susceptible.

tough *adj* dur; pénible; résistant; fort; * *n* dur *m*.

toughen *vt* durcir.

toupee *n* postiche *m*.

tour *n* voyage *m*; visite *f*; * *vt* visiter.

tourism *n* tourisme *m*.

tourist *n* touriste *mf*.

tournament *n* tournoi *m*.

tow *n* remorquage *m*; * *vt* remorquer.

toward(s) *prep* vers, dans la direction de; envers, à l'égard de.

towel *n* serviette *f*.

towelling *n* tissu éponge *m*.

tower *n* tour *f*.

towering *adj* imposant.

town *n* ville *f*.

toy *n* jouet *m*.

trace *n* trace, piste *f*; * *vt* tracer, esquisser; retrouver.

track *n* trace *f*; empreinte *f*; chemin *m*; voie *f*, piste *f*; * *vt* suivre à la trace.

tracksuit *n* survêtement *m*.

tract *n* étendue *f*, région *f*; brochure *f*.

traction *n* traction *f*.

trade *n* commerce *m*, affaires *fpl*; échange *m*; métier *m*; * *vi* faire le commerce (de), commercer.

trademark *n* marque de fabrique *f*.

trader *n* négociant *m* -e *f*.

tradesman *n* fournisseur, commerçant *m*.

trade union *n* syndicat *m*.

trading *n* commerce *m*; * *adj* commercial.

tradition *n* tradition *f*

traditional *adj* traditionnel.

traffic *n* circulation *f*; négoce *m*; * *vi* faire le commerce (de).

traffic jam *n* embouteillage *m*.

traffic lights *npl* feux de signalisation *mpl*.

tragedy *n* tragédie *f*.

tragic *adj* ~ally *adv* tragi-que(ment).

trail *vt* suivre la piste de; traîner; *vi* traîner; * *n* traînée *f*; trace *f*; queue *f*.

train *vt* entraîner; former; * *n* train *m*; traîne *f*; file *f*.

trainee *n* stagiaire *mf*.

training *n* formation *f*, entraînement *m*.

trait *n* trait *m*.

traitor *n* traître *m*.

tramp *n* clochard *m* -e *f*; (*sl*) putain *f*; * *vi* marcher d'un pas lourd; * *vt* piétiner.

trample *vt* piétiner.

trampoline *n* trampoline *m*.

trance *n* transe *f*; extase *f*.

tranquil *adj* tranquille.

tranquilliser *n* tranquillisant *m*.

transaction *n* transaction *f*; opération *f*.

transatlantic *adj* transatlantique.

transcend *vt* transcender, dépasser; surpasser.

transcription *n* transcription *f*; copie *f*.

transfer *vt* transférer, déplacer; * *n* transfert *m*; mutation *f*, décalcomanie *f*.

transformation *n* transformation *f*.

transfusion *n* transfusion *f*.

transit *n* transit *m*.

transition *n* transition *f*; passage *m*.

translate *vt* traduire.

translation *n* traduction *f*.

translator *n* traducteur *m* -trice *f*.

transmission *n* transmision *f*.

transmit *vt* transmettre.

transmitter *n* transmetteur *m*; émetteur *m*.

transparency *n* transparence *f*; diapositive *f*.

transparent *adj* transparent.

transplant *vt* transplanter; * *n* transplantation *f*.

transport *vt* transporter; * *n* transport *m*.

transportation *n* moyen de transport *m*.

trap *n* piège *m*; * *vt* prendre au piège; bloquer.

trapeze *n* trapèze *m*.

travel *vi* voyager; * *vt* parcourir; * *n* voyage *m*.

travel agency *n* agence de voyages *f*.

travel agent *n* agent de voyages *m*.

traveller *n* voyageur *m* -euse *f*.

traveller's cheque *n* chèque de voyage *m*.

travel sickness *n* mal de mer/de l'air *m*.

travesty *n* parodie *f*.

trawler *n* chalutier *m*.

tray *n* plateau *m*; tiroir *m*.

treacherous *adj* traître, perfide.

treachery *n* traîtrise *f*.

tread *vi* marcher; écraser; * *n* pas *m*; bruit de pas *m*; bande de roulement *f*.

treason *n* trahison *f*.

treasure *n* trésor *m*; * *vt* conserver précieusement.

treasurer *n* trésorier *m* -ière *f*.

treat *vt* traiter; offrir; * *n* cadeau *m*; plaisir *m*.

treatment *n* traitement *m*.

treaty *n* traité *m*.

treble *adj* triple; * *vt vi* tripler; * *n* (*mus*) soprano *m*.

tree *n* arbre *m*.

trellis *n* treillis *m*.

tremble *vi* trembler.

tremendous *adj* terrible; énorme; formidable.

tremor *n* tremblement *m*.

trend *n* tendance *f*, direction *f*, mode *f*.

trendy *adj* dernier cri.

trespass *vt* transgresser, violer.

tress *n* boucle de cheveu *f*; ~es chevelure *f*.

trial *n* procès *m*; épreuve *f*; essai *m*; peine *f*.

triangle *n* triangle *m*.

triangular *adj* triangulaire.

tribal *adj* tribal.

tribe *n* tribu *f*.

tribunal *n* tribunal *m*.

tributary *adj n* tributaire *m*.

tribute *n* tribut *m*.

trick *n* ruse, astuce *f*, tour *m*; blague *f*; pli *m*; * *vt* attraper.

trickery *n* supercherie *f*.

trickle *vi* couler goutte à goutte; * *n* filet *m*.

tricky *adj* délicat; difficile.

trifle *vi* jouer; badiner.

trifling *adj* futile, insignifiant.

trigger *n* gâchette *f*, ~ off *vt* déclencher.

trim *adj* net, soigné; bien tenu; en parfait état; * *vt* arranger; tailler; orner.

trimmings *npl* ornements *mpl*.

trinket *n* bibelot *m*, babiole *f*, colifichet *m*.

trio *n* (*mus*) trio *m*.

trip *vt* faire trébucher; * *vi* trébucher; faire un faux pas; ~ up *vi* trébucher; *vt* faire trébucher; * *n* faux pas *m*; voyage *m*.

triple *adj* triple; * *vt vi* tripler.

triplets *npl* triplés *mpl*.

triplicate *n* copie en trois exemplaires *f*.

tripod *n* trépied *m*.

trite *adj* banal; usé.

triumph *n* triomphe *m*; * *vi* triompher.

triumphant *adj* triomphant; victorieux;.

trivia npl futilités fpl.

trivial adj insignifiant, sans importance.

trolley n chariot m.

trombone n trombone m.

troop n bande f; ~s npl troupes fpl.

trophy n trophée m.

tropical adj tropical.

trot n trot m; * vi trotter.

trouble vt affliger; tourmenter; * n problème m; ennui m; difficulté f; affliction, peine f.

troublemaker n agitateur m, -trice f.

troublesome adj pénible.

trousers npl pantalon m.

trout n truite f.

trowel n truelle f.

truce n trêve f.

truculent adj brutal, agressif.

trudge vi marcher lourdement.

true adj vrai, véritable; sincère; exact.

trumpet n trompette f.

trunk n malle f, coffre m; trompe f.

trust n confiance f; trust m; fidéicommis m; * vt avoir confiance en; confier à.

trustee n fidéicommissaire m, curateur m -trice f.

trusting adj confiant.

trustworthy adj digne de confiance.

truth n vérité f.

truthful adj véridique; qui dit la vérité.

try vt essayer, tâcher, chercher à; expérimenter; mettre à l'épreuve; tenter; juger; * vi essayer; ~ on vt essayer; ~ out vt essayer; * n tentative f, essai m.

trying adj pénible; fatigant.

tub n cuve f, bac m; baignoire f.

tuba n tuba m.

tube n tube m; métro m.

tuck n pli m; * vt mettre.

Tuesday n mardi m.

tuft n touffe f; houppe f.

tug vt remorquer; * n remorqueur m.

tuition n cours, enseignement m.

tulip n tulipe f.

tumble vi tomber, faire une chute; se jeter; * vt renverser; culbuter; * n chute f; culbute f.

tumbledown adj délabré.

tumbler n verre m.

tummy n ventre m.

tumour n tumeur f.

tumultuous adj tumultueux.

tuna n thon m.

tune n air m; accord m; harmonie f; * vt accorder; syntoniser.

tuneful adj mélodieux, harmonieux.

tunic n tunique f.

tunnel n tunnel m; * vt creuser un tunnel dans.

turban n turban m.

turbulence n turbulence, agitation f.

turbulent adj turbulent, agité.

turf n gazon m; * vt gazonner.

turkey n dinde f.

turmoil n agitation f; trouble m.

turn vi (se) tourner; devenir; changer; se retourner; se changer, se transformer; ~ **back** revenir; ~ **down** vt rejeter; rabattre; ~ **in** aller se coucher; ~ **off** vi tourner; vt éteindre; fermer; ~ **on** vt allumer; ouvrir; ~ **out** s'avérer; ~ **up** vi arriver; se présenter; vt monter; * n tour m; tournure f; virage m; tendance f.

turning n embranchement m.

turnip n navet m.

turn-off n sortie (d'autoroute) f; embranchement m.

turnover n chiffre d'affaires m.

turnstile n tourniquet m.

turntable n platine f.

turpentine n (essence de) térébenthine f.

turret n tourelle f.

turtle n tortue marine f.

tusk n défense f.

tutor n professeur particulier m; directeur d'études m; * vt enseigner, donner des cours particuliers à.

tweezers npl pince à épiler f.

twelfth adj n douzième mf.

twelve adj n douze m.

twentieth adj n vingtième mf.

twenty adj n vingt m.

twice adv deux fois.

twig n brindille f; * vi piger.

twilight n crépuscule m.

twin n jumeau m -elle f.

twine vi s'enrouler; serpenter; * n ficelle f.

twinge vt élancer; * n élancement m; remords m.

twinkle vi scintiller; clignoter.

twirl vt faire tournoyer; * vi tournoyer; * n tournoiement m.

twist vt tordre, tortiller; entortiller; * vi serpenter; * n torsion f; tournant m; rouleau m.

twitch vi avoir un mouvement nerveux; * n tic m.

two adj n deux m.

two-faced adj hypocrite.

tycoon n magnat m.

type n type m; caractère m; exemple m; * vi taper à la machine.

typecast adj enfermé dans un rôle.

typescript n texte dactylographié m.

typewriter n machine à écrire f.

typical adj typique.

tyrant n tyran m.

tyre n pneu m.

U

ubiquitous adj doué d'ubiquité.

udder n pis m.

ugly adj laid; inquiétant.

ulcer n ulcère m.

ulterior adj ultérieur.

ultimate adj final; ~ly adv finalement; à la fin.

ultimatum n ultimatum m.

ultrasound n ultrason m.

umbilical cord n cordon ombilical m.

umbrella n parapluie m.

umpire n arbitre m.

umpteen adj un très grand nombre de, beaucoup de.

unable adj incapable.

unaccompanied adj non accompagné, seul.

unaccountably adv inexplicablement.

unaccustomed adj inaccoutumé, inhabituel.

unadorned adj sans ornement.

unadulterated adj pur; sans mélange.

unaffected adj sincère; non affecté.

unaided adj sans aide.

unambitious adj sans ambition.

unanimity n unanimité f.

unanimous adj ~**ly** adv unanime(ment).

unapproachable adj inaccessible.

unassuming adj sans prétention, modeste.

unattended adj sans surveillance.

unauthorised adj sans autorisation.

unavoidably adv inévitablement.

unawares adv à l'improviste; par mégarde.

unbalanced adj déséquilibré; non soldé.

unbearable adj insupportable.

unbecoming adj malséant, déplacé, peu seyant.

unbelievable adj incroyable.

unbiased adj impartial.

unblemished adj sans tache, sans défaut.

unbreakable adj incassable.

unbroken adj non brisé; intact; ininterrompu; indompté.

unbutton vt déboutonner.

uncalled-for adj injustifié.

uncanny adj mystérieux.

uncertain adj incertain, douteux.

uncertainty n incertitude f.

unchanging adj invariable, immuable.

uncharitable adj peu charitable.

uncivilised adj barbare, non civilisé.

uncle n oncle m.

uncomfortable adj inconfortable; incommode; désagréable.

uncomfortably adv inconfortablement; mal; désagréablement.

uncommon adj rare, extraordinaire.

unconditional adj inconditionnel, absolu.

unconnected adj sans rapport.

unconscious adj inconscient; ~**ly** adv inconsciemment, sans s'en rendre compte.

uncontrollable adj irrésistible; qui ne peut être maîtrisé.

unconventional adj peu conventionnel.

unconvincing adj peu convaincant.

uncouth adj grossier.

uncover vt découvrir.

undecided adj indécis.

undeniable adj indéniable, incontestable; ~**bly** adv incontestablement.

under prep sous; dessous; moins de; selon; * adv au-dessous, en -dessous.

under-age adj mineur.

undercharge vt ne pas faire payer assez.

underclothing n sous-vêtements mpl.

undercoat n première couche f.

undercover adj secret, clandestin.

undercurrent n courant sous-marin m.

underdeveloped adj sous-développé, insuffisamment déve-loppé.

underdog n opprimé m -e f.

underdone adj pas assez cuit.

underestimate vt sous-estimer.

undergo vt subir; supporter.

undergraduate n étudiant(e) en licence m(f).

underground n mouvement clandestin m.

undergrowth n broussailles fpl, sous-bois m.

underhand adv en cachette; * adj secret, clandestin.

underline vt souligner.

undermine vt saper.

underneath adv (en) dessous; * prep sous, au-dessous de.

underprivileged adj défavorisé.

underrate vt sous-estimer.

underside n dessous m.

understand vt comprendre.

understandable *adj* compréhensible.

understanding *n* compréhension *f*; intelligence *f*; entendement *m*; accord *m*; * *adj* compréhensif.

understatement *n* affirmation en dessous de la vérité *f*.

undertake *vt* entreprendre.

undertaking *n* entreprise *f*; engagement *m*.

undervalue *vt* sous-estimer.

underwater *adj* sous-marin; * *adv* sous l'eau.

underwear *n* sous-vêtements *mpl*, dessous *mpl*.

underworld *n* pègre *f*.

underwriter *n* assureur *m*.

undeserving *adj* peu méritant.

undesirable *adj* peu souhaitable.

undisputed *adj* incontesté.

undivided *adj* indivisé, entier.

undo *vt* défaire; détruire.

undoing *n* ruine *f*.

undoubted *adj* ~**ly** *adv* indubitable(ment).

undress *vi* se déshabiller.

undue *adj* excessif; injuste.

undulating *adj* ondulant.

unduly *adv* trop, excessivement.

undying *adj* éternel.

unearth *vt* déterrer.

unearthly *adj* surnaturel.

uneasy *adj* inquiet; troublé, gêné.

uneducated *adj* sans instruction.

unemployed *adj* au chômage.

unemployment *n* chômage *m*.

unending *adj* interminable.

unenviable *adj* peu enviable.

uneven *adj* inégal; impair.

unexpected *adj* inattendu; inopiné.

unfailing *adj* infaillible, certain.

unfair *adj* injuste; inéquitable.

unfaithful *adj* infidèle.

unfamiliar *adj* peu familier, peu connu.

unfashionable *adj* démodé.

unfasten *vt* détacher, défaire.

unfathomable *adj* insondable, impénétrable.

unfavourable *adj* défavorable.

unfeeling *adj* insensible, impitoyable.

unfinished *adj* inachevé, incomplet.

unfit *adj* inapte; impropre.

unfold *vt* déplier; révéler; * *vi* s'ouvrir.

unforeseen *adj* imprévu.

unforgettable *adj* inoubliable.

unforgivable *adj* impardonnable.

unforgiving *adj* implacable.

unfortunate *adj* malheureux, malchanceux; ~**ly** *adv* malheureusement, par malheur.

unfounded *adj* sans fondement.

unfriendly *adj* inamical.

unfurnished *adj* non meublé.

ungainly *adj* gauche.

ungentlemanly *adj* peu galant.

ungrateful *adj* ingrat; peu reconnaissant.

unhappiness *n* tristesse *f*.

unhappy *adj* malheureux.

unhealthy *adj* malsain; maladif.

unheard-of *adj* inédit, sans précédent.

unhoped(-for) *adj* inespéré.

unhurt *adj* indemne.

unicorn *n* licorne *f*.

uniform *adj* uniforme; * *n* uniforme *m*.

uniformity *n* uniformité *f*.

unify *vt* unifier.

unimaginable *adj* inimaginable.

unimpaired *adj* non diminué, intact.

unimportant *adj* sans importance.

uninformed *adj* mal informé.

uninhabitable *adj* inhabitable.

uninhabited *adj* inhabité, désert.

unintelligible *adj* inintelligible.

unintentional *adj* involontaire.

uninterested *adj* indifférent.

uninteresting *adj* inintéressant.

uninterrupted *adj* ininterrompu, continu.

uninvited *adj* sans être invité.

union *n* union *f*; syndicat *m*.

unionist *n* syndicaliste *mf*.

unique *adj* unique, exceptionnel.

unison *n* unisson *m*.

unit *n* unité *f*.

unite *vt* unir; * *vi* s'unir.

unity *n* unité, harmonie *f*, accord *m*.

universal *adj* ~**ly** *adv* universel(lement).

universe *n* univers *m*.

university *n* université *f*.

unjust *adj* ~**ly** *adv* injuste(ment).

unkempt *adj* négligé; débraillé.

unkind *adj* peu aimable; méchant.

unknowingly *adv* inconsciemment.

unknown *adj* inconnu.

unlawful *adj* illégal, illicite.

unleash *vt* lâcher, déchaîner.

unless *conj* à moins que/de, sauf.

unlicensed *adj* illicite.

unlike *adj* différent, dissemblable.

unlikelihood *n* improbabilité *f*.

unlikely *adj* improbable; invraisemblable; *adv* improbablement.

unlimited *adj* illimité.

unload *vt* décharger.

unlock *vt* ouvrir, déverrouiller.

unluckily *adv* malheureusement.

unlucky *adj* malchanceux.

unmanageable *adj* difficile, peu maniable; impossible.

unmannerly *adj* rustre.

unmarried *adj* célibataire, qui n'est pas marié.

unmask *vt* démasquer.

unmentionable *adj* qu'il ne faut pas mentionner.

unmerited *adj* immérité.

unmistakable *adj* indubitable.

unmitigated *adj* absolu.

unmoved *adj* insensible, impassible.

unnatural *adj* non naturel; pervers; affecté.

unnecessary *adj* inutile, superflu.

unnoticed *adj* inaperçu.

unobserved *adj* inaperçu.

unobtainable *adj* impossible à obtenir; introuvable.

unobtrusive *adj* discret.

unoccupied *adj* inoccupé.

unoffending *adj* inoffensif, innocent.

unofficial *adj* non officiel.

unorthodox *adj* hétérodoxe; peu orthodoxe.

unpack *vt* défaire; déballer.

unpaid *adj* non payé.

unpalatable *adj* désagréable au goût.

unparalleled *adj* incomparable; sans pareil.

unpleasant *adj* ~**ly** *adv* désagréable(ment).

unplug *vt* débrancher.

unpolished *adj* non ciré; fruste, rude.

unpopular *adj* impopulaire.

unpractised *adj* inexpérimenté, inexercé.

unprecedented *adj* sans précédent.

unpredictable *adj* imprévisible.

unprejudiced *adj* impartial.

unprepared *adj* qui n'est pas préparé.

unprofitable *adj* inutile; peu rentable.

unprotected *adj* sans protection; exposé.

unpublished *adj* inédit.

unqualified *adj* non qualifié; inconditionnel.

unquestionable *adj* incontestable, indiscutable.

unravel *vt* débrouiller.

unread *adj* qui n'a pas été lu; inculte.

unreal *adj* irréel.

unrealistic *adj* irréaliste.

unreasonable *adj* déraisonnable.

unrelated *adj* sans rapport; sans lien de parenté.

unrelenting *adj* implacable.

unreliable *adj* peu fiable.

unremitting *adj* inlassable, constant.

unrepentant *adj* impénitent.

unreserved *adj* sans réserve; franc.

unrest *n* agitation *f*; troubles *mpl*.

unrestrained *adj* non contenu; non réprimé.

unripe *adj* vert, pas mûr.

unrivalled *adj* sans égal, sans pareil.

unroll *vt* dérouler.

unruly *adj* indiscipliné.

unsafe *adj* dangereux, peu sûr.

unsatisfactory *adj* peu satisfaisant.

unsavoury *adj* désagréable, insipide.

unscathed *adj* indemne.

unscrew *vt* dévisser.

unscrupulous *adj* sans scrupules.

unseemly *adj* inconvenant.

unseen *adj* invisible; inaperçu.

unselfish *adj* généreux.

unsettled *adj* perturbé; instable; variable.

unshaken *adj* inébranlable, ferme.

unshaven *adj* non rasé.

unsightly *adj* disgracieux, laid.

unskilled *adj* inexpérimenté.

unsociable *adj* insociable, sauvage.

unspeakable *adj* ineffable, indicible.

unstable *adj* instable.

unsteady *adj* instable.

unsuccessful *adj* infructueux, vain.

unsuitable *adj* peu approprié; inopportun.

unsure *adj* peu sûr.

unsympathetic *adj* peu compatissant.

untamed *adj* sauvage.

untapped *adj* non exploité.

unthinkable *adj* inconcevable.

unthinking *adj* irréfléchi, étourdi.

untidy *adj* en désordre; peu soigné.

untie *vt* dénouer, défaire.

until *prep* jusqu'à; * *conj* jusqu'à ce que.

untimely *adj* intempestif.

untiring *adj* infatigable.

untold *adj* jamais révélé; indicible; incalculable.

untouched *adj* intact.

untoward *adj* fâcheux; inconvenant.

untried *adj* qui n'a pas été essayé *ou* mis à l'épreuve.

untroubled *adj* tranquille, paisible.

untrue *adj* faux.

untrustworthy *adj* indigne de confiance.

untruth *n* mensonge *m*, fausseté *f*.

unused *adj* neuf, inutilisé.

unusual *adj* inhabituel, exceptionnel; **~ly** *adv* exceptionnellement, rarement.

unveil *vt* dévoiler.

unwavering *adj* inébranlable.

unwelcome *adj* importun.

unwell *adj* indisposé, souffrant.

unwieldy *adj* peu maniable.

unwilling *adj* peu disposé; **~ly** *adv* de mauvaise grâce.

unwind *vt* dérouler; * *vi* se détendre.

unwise *adj* imprudent.

unwitting *adj* involontaire.

unworkable *adj* impraticable.

unworthy *adj* indigne.

unwrap *vt* défaire.

unwritten *adj* non écrit.

up *adv* en haut, en l'air; levé; * *prep* au haut de; plus loin.

upbringing *n* éducation *f*.

update *vt* mettre à jour.

upheaval *n* bouleversement *m*.

uphill *adj* difficile, pénible; * *adv* en montant.

uphold *vt* soutenir.

upholstery *n* tapisserie *f*.

upkeep *n* entretien *m*.

uplift *vt* élever.

upon *prep* sur.

upper *adj* supérieur; (plus) élevé.

upper-class *adj* aristocratique.

upper-hand *n* (*fig*) dessus *m*.

uppermost *adj* le plus haut, le plus élevé.

upright *adj* droit, vertical; droit, honnête.

uprising *n* soulèvement *m*.

uproar *n* tumulte, vacarme *m*.

uproot *vt* déraciner.

upset *vt* renverser; déranger, bouleverser; * *n* désordre *m*; bouleversement *m*; * *adj* vexé; bouleversé.

upshot *n* résultat *m*; aboutissement *m*; conclusion *f*.

upside-down *adv* sens dessus dessous.

upstairs *adv* en haut (d'un escalier).

upstart *n* parvenu *m* -e *f*.

uptight *adj* très tendu.

up-to-date *adj* à jour.

upward *adj* ascendant; **~s** *adv* vers le haut; en montant.

urban *adj* urbain.

urbane *adj* courtois.

urchin *n* gamin *m*; **sea ~** oursin *m*.

urge *vt* pousser; * *n* impulsion *f*; désir ardent *m*.

urgency *n* urgence *f*.

urgent *adj* urgent.

urinal *n* urinoir *m*.

urinate *vi* uriner.

urine *n* urine *f*.

urn *n* urne *f*.

us *pn* nous.

usage *n* utilisation *f*; usage *m*.

use *n* usage *m*; utilisation *f*, emploi *m*; * *vt* se servir de, utiliser.

useful *adj* **~ly** *adv* utile(ment).

useless *adj* **~ly** *adv* inutile(ment).

user-friendly *adj* facile à utiliser.

usher *n* huissier *m*; placeur *m*.

usherette *n* ouvreuse *f*.

usual *adj* habituel, courant.

usurp *vt* usurper.

utensil *n* ustensile *m*.

uterus *n* utérus *m*.

utilise *vt* utiliser.

utility *n* utilité *f*.

utmost *adj* extrême, le plus grand; dernier.

utter *adj* complet; absolu; total; * *vt* prononcer; proférer; émettre.

utterance *n* expression *f*.

utterly *adv* complètement, tout à fait.

V

vacancy *n* chambre libre *f.*

vacant *adj* vacant; inoccupé; libre.

vacate *vt* quitter; démissionner.

vaccinate *vt* vacciner.

vaccination *n* vaccination *f.*

vaccine *n* vaccin *f.*

vacuous *adj* vide.

vacuum *n* vide *m.*

vagina *n* vagin *m.*

vagrant *n* vagabond *m* -e *f.*

vague *adj* ~**ly** *adv* vague(ment).

vain *adj* vain, inutile; vaniteux.

valet *n* valet de chambre *m.*

valiant *adj* courageux, brave.

valid *adj* valide, valable.

valley *n* vallée *f.*

valour *n* courage *m*, bravoure *f.*

valuable *adj* précieux, de valeur; ~**s** *npl* objets de valeur *mpl.*

valuation *n* évaluation, estimation *f.*

value *n* valeur *f*; * *vt* évaluer; tenir à, apprécier.

valued *adj* précieux, estimé.

valve *n* soupape *f.*

vampire *n* vampire *m.*

van *n* camionnette *f.*

vandal *n* vandale *mf.*

vandalise *vt* saccager.

vandalism *n* vandalisme *m.*

vanguard *n* avant-garde *f.*

vanilla *n* vanille *f.*

vanish *vi* disparaître, se dissiper.

vanity *n* vanité *f.*

vantage point *n* position avantageuse *f.*

vapour *n* vapeur *f.*

variable *adj* variable; changeant.

variance *n* désaccord, différend *m.*

variation *n* variation *f.*

varicose vein *n* varice *f.*

varied *adj* varié.

variety *n* variété *f.*

various *adj* divers, différent.

varnish *n* vernis *m*; * *vt* vernir.

vary *vt vi* varier; *vi* changer.

vase *n* vase *m.*

vast *adj* vaste; immense.

vat *n* cuve *f.*

vault *n* voûte *f*; cave *f*, caveau *m*; saut *m*; * *vi* sauter.

veal *n* veau *m.*

veer *vi* (*mar*) virer.

vegetable *adj* végétal; * *n* végétal *m*; ~**s** *pl* légumes *mpl.*

vegetarian *n* végétarien *m* -ne *f.*

vegetate *vi* végéter.

vegetation *n* végétation *f.*

vehemence *n* véhémence, fougue *f.*

vehement *adj* véhément, violent.

vehicle *n* véhicule *m.*

veil *n* voile *m*; * *vt* voiler, dissimuler.

vein *n* veine *f*; nervure *f*; disposition *f.*

velocity *n* vitesse *f.*

velvet *n* velours *m.*

vending machine *n* distributeur automatique *m.*

veneer *n* placage *m*; vernis *m.*

venereal *adj* vénérien.

vengeance *n* vengeance *f.*

venison *n* venaison *f.*

venom *n* venin *m.*

venomous *adj* vénéneux.

vent *n* orifice *m*; conduit *m*; * *vt* (*fig*) décharger.

ventilation *n* ventilation, aération *f*.

ventilator *n* ventilateur *m*.

ventriloquist *n* ventriloque *mf*.

venture *n* entreprise *f*; * *vi* s'aventurer; * *vt* risquer, hasarder.

venue *n* lieu *m* (de réunion).

veranda(h) *n* véranda *f*.

verb *n* (*gr*) verbe *m*.

verbal *adj* verbal, oral.

verbatim *adv* textuellement, mot pour mot.

verbose *adj* verbeux.

verdict *n* (*law*) verdict *m*; jugement *m*.

verification *n* vérification *f*.

verify *vt* vérifier.

veritable *adj* véritable.

vermin *n* vermine *f*.

versatile *adj* doué de talents multiples; versatile.

verse *n* vers *m*; verset *m*.

version *n* version *f*.

versus *prep* contre.

vertical *adj* ~**ly** *adv* vertical(ement).

very *adj* vrai, véritable; exactement, même; * *adv* très, fort, bien.

vessel *n* récipient *m*; vase *m*; navire *m*.

vest *n* gilet *m*.

vestibule *n* vestibule *m*.

vestige *n* vestige *m*.

vestry *n* sacristie *f*.

vet *n* vétérinaire *mf*.

veteran *adj n* vétéran *m*.

veterinary *adj* vétérinaire.

veto *n* véto *m*; * *vt* opposer son véto à.

vex *vt* contrarier.

via *prep* via, par.

viaduct *n* viaduc *m*.

vial *n* fiole, ampoule *f*.

vibrate *vi* vibrer.

vibration *n* vibration *f*.

vice *n* vice *m*; défaut *m*; étau *m*.

vice versa *adv* vice versa.

vicinity *n* voisinage *m*, proximité *f*.

vicious *adj* méchant.

victim *n* victime *f*.

victimise *vt* prendre pour victime.

victor *n* vainqueur *m*.

victorious *adj* victorieux.

victory *n* victoire *f*.

video *n* vidéo *f*; vidéocassette *f*; magnétoscope *m*.

video tape *n* bande vidéo *f*.

viewer *n* téléspectateur *m* -trice *f*.

vie *vi* rivaliser.

view *n* vue *f*, perspective *f*; opinion *f*; panorama *m*; * *vt* voir; examiner.

viewpoint *n* point de vue *m*.

vigil *n* veille *f*; vigile *f*.

vigilant *adj* vigilant, attentif.

vigorous *adj* vigoureux.

vigour *n* vigueur *f*; énergie *f*.

vile *adj* vil, infâme; exécrable.

villa *n* pavillon *m*; maison de campagne *f*.

village *n* village *m*.

villager *n* villageois *m* -e *f*.

villain *n* scélérat *m*.

vindicate *vt* venger, défendre.

vindication *n* défense *f*; justification *f*.

vindictive *adj* vindicatif.

vine *n* vigne *f*.

vinegar *n* vinaigre *m*.

vineyard *n* vignoble *m*.

vintage *n* millésime *m*; époque *f*.

vinyl *n* vinyle *m*.

violate *vt* violer.

violation *n* violation *f*.

violence *n* violence *f.*

violent *adj* violent.

violet *n* (*bot*) violette *f.*

violin *n* (*mus*) violon *m.*

viper *n* vipère *f.*

virgin *n, adj* vierge *f.*

virginity *n* virginité *f.*

virile *adj* viril.

virility *n* virilité *f.*

virtual *adj* virtuel; quasiment; **~ly** *adv* de fait, pratiquement.

virtue *n* vertu *f.*

virtuous *adj* virtueux.

virus *n* virus *m.*

vis-à-vis *prep* vis-à-vis.

viscous *adj* visqueux, gluant.

visibility *n* visibilité *f.*

visible *adj* visible.

vision *n* vision *f.*; vue *f.*

visit *vt* visiter; * *n* visite *f.*

visitor *n* visiteur *m* -euse *f*; touriste *mf.*

visor *n* visière *f.*

vista *n* vue, perspective *f.*

visual *adj* visuel.

visualise *vt* s'imaginer.

vital *adj* vital; essentiel; indispensable; **~s** *npl* organes vitaux *mpl.*

vitality *n* vitalité *f.*

vital statistics *npl* statistiques démographiques *fpl.*

vitamin *n* vitamine *f.*

vivacious *adj* vif.

vivid *adj* vif; vivant; frappant.

vocabulary *n* vocabulaire *m.*

vocal *adj* vocal.

vocation *n* vocation *f*; profession *f*, métier *m*; **~al** *adj* professionnel.

vogue *n* vogue *f*; mode *f.*

voice *n* voix *f*; * *vt* exprimer.

void *adj* vide; * *n* vide *m.*

volatile *adj* volatile; versatile.

volcanic *adj* volcanique.

volcano *n* volcan *m.*

volition *n* volonté *f.*

volley *n* volée *f*; salve *f*; grêle *f.*

volleyball *n* volley-ball *m.*

voltage *n* voltage *m.*

volume *n* volume *m.*

voluntary *adj* volontaire.

volunteer *n* volontaire *mf*; * *vi* se porter volontaire.

voluptuous *adj* voluptueux.

vomit *vt vi* vomir; * *n* vomissement *m.*

vote *n* vote, suffrage *m*; voix *f*; * *vt* voter.

voter *n* électeur *m* -trice *f.*

voting *n* vote *m.*

voucher *n* bon *m.*

vow *n* vœu *m*; * *vt* jurer.

vowel *n* voyelle *f.*

voyage *n* voyage par mer *m*; traversée *f.*

vulgar *adj* vulgaire; grossier.

vulgarity *n* grossièreté *f*; vulgarité *m.*

vulnerable *adj* vulnérable.

vulture *n* vautour *m.*

W

wad *n* tampon *m*; bouchon *m*, liasse *f.*

waddle *vi* se dandiner.

wade *vi* patauger.

wafer *n* gaufrette *f*; plaque *f.*

waffle n gaufre f.

waft vt porter, apporter; * vi flotter.

wag vt vi remuer.

wage n salaire m.

wager n pari m; * vt parier.

wages npl salaire m.

waggle vt remuer.

wail n gémissement m, plainte f; * vi gémir.

waist n taille f.

waistline n taille f.

wait vi attendre; * n attente f; arrêt m.

waiter n serveur m.

waiting list n liste d'attente f.

waiting room n salle d'attente f.

waive vt renoncer à.

wake vi se réveiller; * vt réveiller; * n veillée f; (mar) sillage m.

waken vt réveiller; * vi se réveiller.

walk vi marcher, aller à pied; * vt parcourir; * n promenade f; marche f.

walking stick n canne f.

wall n mur m; muraille f; paroi f.

wallet n portefeuille m.

wallflower n (bot) giroflée f.

wallow vi se vautrer.

wallpaper n papier peint m.

walnut n noix f; noyer m.

walrus n morse m.

waltz n valse f.

wan adj pâle.

wand n baguette (magique) f.

wander vi errer; aller sans but.

wane vi décroître.

want vt vouloir; demander; * vi manquer; * n besoin m; manque m.

war n guerre f.

ward n salle f; pupille mf.

wardrobe n garde-robe f, penderie f.

warehouse n entrepôt m.

warfare n guerre f.

warm adj chaud; chaleureux; * vt réchauffer; ~ **up** vi se réchauffer; s'échauffer; s'animer; vt réchauffer.

warm-hearted adj affectueux.

warmth n chaleur f.

warn vt prévenir; avertir.

warning n avertissement m.

warp vi se voiler; * vt voiler; fausser.

warrant n garantie f; mandat m.

warranty n garantie f.

warren n terrier m.

warrior n guerrier m -ière f.

warship n navire de guerre m.

wart n verrue f.

wary adj prudent, circonspect.

wash vt laver; * vi se laver; * n lavage m; lessive f.

washing n linge à laver m; lessive f.

washing machine n machine à laver f.

washing-up n vaisselle f.

wash-out n (sl) fiasco m.

wasp n guêpe f.

wastage n gaspillage m; perte f.

waste vt gaspiller; dévaster, saccager; perdre; * vi se perdre; * n gaspillage m; détérioration f; terre inculte f; déchets mpl.

wasteful adj gaspilleur; prodigue.

waste paper n vieux papiers mpl.

waste pipe n tuyau d'échappement m.

watch n montre f; surveillance f; garde f; * vt regarder; observer; surveiller; faire attention à; * vi regarder; monter la garde.

watchdog n chien de garde m.

watchful adj vigilant.

water n eau f; * vt arroser, mouiller; * vi pleurer, larmoyer.

watercolour n aquarelle f.

waterfall n cascade f.

watering-can n arrosoir m.

water level n niveau de l'eau m.

waterlogged adj imprégné d'eau.

watermelon n pastèque f.

watershed n (fig) moment m critique.

watertight adj étanche.

waterworks npl usine hydraulique f.

watery adj aqueux; détrempé; délavé.

wave n vague f; lame f; onde f; * vi faire signe de la main; onduler; * vt agiter.

wavelength n longueur d'ondes f.

waver vi vaciller, osciller.

wavering adj hésitant.

wavy adj ondulé.

wax n cire f.

waxworks n musée de cire m.

way n chemin m; voie f; route f; manière f; direction f; **to give ~** céder.

waylay vt attaquer, arrêter au passage.

wayward adj capricieux.

we pn nous.

weak adj **~ly** adv faible(ment).

weaken vt affaiblir.

weakling n personne faible f.

weakness n faiblesse f; point faible m.

wealth n richesse f; abondance f.

wealthy adj riche.

wean vt sevrer.

weapon n arme f.

wear vt porter; user; * vi s'user; **~ away** vt s'user; vi s'user; **~ down** vt user; épuiser; **~ off** vi s'effacer; **~ out** vi s'user; s'épuiser; vt user; * n usage m; usure f.

weary adj las, fatigué; ennuyeux.

weasel n belette f.

weather n temps m; * vt surmonter.

weather-beaten adj ayant souffert des intempéries.

weather forecast n prévisions météorologiques fpl.

weave vt tisser; entrelacer.

web n tissu m; toile f d'araignée; palmure f.

wed vt épouser; * vi se marier.

wedding n mariage m; noces fpl.

wedding ring n alliance f.

wedge n cale f; * vt caler; enfoncer.

Wednesday n mercredi m.

wee adj petit.

weed n mauvaise herbe f; * vt désherber.

weedkiller n désherbant m.

week n semaine f.

weekday n jour de semaine, jour ouvrable m.

weekend n week-end m, fin de semaine f.

weekly adj de la semaine, hebdomadaire; * adv chaque semaine, par semaine.

weep vt vi pleurer.

weigh vt vi peser.

weight n poids m.

weightlifter n haltérophile m.

weighty adj lourd; important.

welcome adj opportun; **~!** bienvenue !; * n accueil m; * vt accueillir.

weld vt souder; * n soudure f.

welfare n bien-être m; assistance sociale f.

welfare state n État-providence m.

well n source f; fontaine f; puits m; * adj bien, bon; * adv bien; **as ~ as** aussi bien que, en plus de, comme.

wellbeing n bien-être m.

well-bred adj bien élevé.

well-built adj bien bâti, solide.

well-dressed adj bien habillé.

well-known adj connu, célèbre.

well-mannered *adj* poli, bien élevé.

well-meaning *adj* bien intentionné.

well-off *adj* aisé, dans l'aisance.

well-to-do *adj* aisé, riche.

well-wisher *n* admirateur *m* -trice *f*.

west *n* ouest, Occident *m*; * *adj* ouest, de/à l'ouest; * *adv* vers/à l'ouest.

westerly, western *adj* (d')ouest.

wet *adj* mouillé, humide; * *n* humidité *f*; * *vt* mouiller.

wet suit *n* combinaison de plongée *f*.

whack *vt* donner un grand coup à; * *n* grand coup *m*.

whale *n* baleine *f*.

wharf *n* quai *m*.

what *pn* qu'est-ce qui,(qu'est-ce) que, quoi; que, qui; ce qui, ce que; quel(le), que; * *adj* quel(s), quelle(s); * *excl* quoi! comment!.

whatever *pn* quoi que; tout; n'importe quoi.

wheat *n* blé *m*.

wheedle *vt* cajoler, câliner.

wheel *n* roue *f*; volant *m*; gouvernail *m*; * *vt* tourner; pousser, rouler; * *vi* tourner en rond, tournoyer.

wheelbarrow *n* brouette *f*.

wheelchair *n* fauteuil roulant *m*.

wheelclamp *n* sabot *m*.

wheeze *vi* respirer bruyamment.

when *adv, conj* quand.

whenever *adv* quand; chaque fois que.

where *adv* où; * *conj* où; **any~** n'importe où; **every~** partout.

wherever *adv* où que.

whet *vt* aiguiser.

whether *conj* si.

which *pn* lequel, laquelle; celui/ celle(s)/ceux que, celui/celle(s)/ceux qui; ce qui, ce que; quoi, ce dont * *adj* quel(s), quelle(s).

whiff *n* bouffée, odeur *f*.

while *n* moment *m*; **a ~** quelque temps; * *conj* pendant que; alors que; quoique.

whim *n* caprice *m*.

whimper *vi* gémir, pleurnicher.

whimsical *adj* capricieux, fantasque.

whine *vi* gémir, se plaindre; * *n* gémissement *m*, plainte *f*.

whip *n* fouet *m*; cravache *f*; * *vt* fouetter; battre.

whipped cream *n* crème fouettée *f*.

whirl *vi* tourbillonner, tournoyer; aller à toute allure; * *vt* faire tourbillonner, faire tournoyer.

whirlpool *n* tourbillon *m*.

whirlwind *n* tornade *f*.

whisper *vi* chuchoter; murmurer.

whistle *vi* siffler; * *n* sifflement *m*.

white *adj* blanc; pâle.

whitewash *n* blanc de chaux *m*; * *vt* blanchir à la chaux; disculper.

whiting *n* merlan *m*.

whitish *adj* blanchâtre.

who *pn* qui.

whoever *pn* quiconque, qui que ce soit, quel(le) que soit.

whole *adj* tout, entier; intact, complet; sain; * *n* tout *m*; ensemble *m*.

wholehearted *adj* sincère.

wholemeal *adj* complet.

wholesale *n* vente en gros *f*.

wholesome *adj* sain, salubre.

wholly *adv* complètement.

whom *pn* qui; que.

whooping cough *n* coqueluche *f*.

whore *n* putain *f*.

why *n* pourquoi *m*; * *conj* pourquoi; * *excl* eh bien!, tiens!

wick *n* mèche *f*.

wicked *adj* méchant, mauvais.

wicker *n* osier *m*; * *adj* en osier.

wide *adj* large, ample; grand; **~ly** *adv* partout; **far and ~** de tous côtés.

wide-awake *adj* bien réveillé.

widen *vt* élargir, agrandir.

wide open *adj* grand ouvert.

widespread *adj* très répandu.

widow *n* veuve *f*.

widower *n* veuf *m*.

width *n* largeur *f*.

wield *vt* manier, brandir.

wife *n* femme *f*; épouse *f*.

wig *n* perruque *f*.

wiggle *vt* agiter; * *vi* s'agiter.

wild *adj* sauvage, féroce; désert; fou; furieux.

wilderness *n* étendue déserte *f*.

wild life *n* faune *f*.

will *n* volonté *f*, testament *m*; * *vt* vouloir.

willing *adj* prêt, disposé; **~ly** *adv* volontiers, de bon cœur.

willingness *n* bonne volonté *f*, empressement *m*.

willow *n* saule *m*.

willpower *n* volonté *f*.

wilt *vi* se faner.

wily *adj* astucieux.

win *vt* gagner, conquérir; remporter.

wince *vi* tressaillir.

wind *n* vent *m*; souffle *m*; gaz *mpl*.

wind *vt* enrouler; envelopper; donner un tour de; * *vi* serpenter.

windfall *n* fruit abattu par le vent *m*; (*fig*) aubaine *f*.

winding *adj* tortueux.

windmill *n* moulin à vent *m*.

window *n* fenêtre *f*.

window box *n* jardinière *f*.

window cleaner *n* laveur(-euse) *m(f)* de carreaux.

window pane *n* carreau *m*.

windpipe *n* trachée *f* artère.

windscreen *n* pare-brise *m invar*.

windscreen washer *n* lave-glace *m invar*.

windy *adj* venteux.

wine *n* vin *m*.

wing *n* aile *f*.

winger *n* ailier *m*.

wink *vi* faire un clin d'œil; * *n* clin d'œil *m*; clignement *m*.

winner *n* gagnant *m* -e *f*; vainqueur *m*.

winter *n* hiver *m*; * *vi* hiverner.

wintry *adj* d'hiver, hivernal.

wipe *vt* essuyer; effacer.

wire *n* fil *m*; télégramme *m*; * *vt* installer des fils électriques à; télégraphier.

wiring *n* installation électrique *f*.

wiry *adj* effilé et nerveux.

wisdom *n* sagesse, prudence *f*.

wisdom teeth *npl* dents de sagesse *fpl*.

wise *adj* sage, avisé, judicieux, prudent.

wisecrack *n* bon mot *m*, plaisanterie *f*.

wish *vt* souhaiter, désirer; * *n* souhait, désir *m*.

wisp *n* brin *m*; mince volute *f*.

wistful *adj* nostalgique, rêveur.

wit *n* esprit *m*, intelligence *f*.

witch *n* sorcière *f*.

witchcraft *n* sorcellerie *f*.

with *prep* avec; à; de; contre.

withdraw *vt* retirer; rappeler; annuler; * *vi* se retirer.

withdrawal *n* retrait *m*.

withdrawn *adj* réservé.

wither *vi* se flétrir, se faner.

withhold *vt* détenir, retenir, empêcher.

within *prep* à l'intérieur de; * *adv* dedans; à l'intérieur.

without *prep* sans.

withstand *vt* résister à.

witless *adj* sot, stupide.

witness *n* témoin *m*; témoignage *m*; * *vt* être témoin de; attester.

witticism *n* mot d'esprit *m*.

witty *adj* spirituel, plein d'esprit.

wizard *n* sorcier, magicien *m*.

wobble *vi* trembler.

woe *n* malheur *m*; affliction *f*.

woeful *adj* triste, malheureux.

wolf *n* loup *m*.

woman *n* femme *f*.

womb *n* utérus *m*.

wonder *n* merveille *f*; miracle *m*; émerveillement *m*; * *vi* s'émerveiller.

wonderful *adj* merveilleux.

won't *abrev de* **will not**.

woo *vt* faire la cour à.

wood *n* bois *m*.

wooden *adj* de bois, en bois.

woodland *n* région boisée *f*.

woodpecker *n* pic *m*.

woodwind *n* (*mus*) bois *mpl*.

woodwork *n* menuiserie *f*.

woodworm *n* ver du bois *m*.

wool *n* laine *f*.

woollen *adj* de laine.

woollens *npl* lainages *mpl*.

woolly *adj* laineux, de laine.

word *n* mot *m*; parole *f*; * *vt* exprimer; rédiger.

wording *n* formulation *f*.

word processor *n* machine *f* à traitement de texte.

wordy *adj* verbeux.

work *vi* travailler; opérer; fonctionner; fermenter; * *vt* (faire) travailler, faire fonctionner; façonner; * ~ **out** *vi* marcher; * *vt* résoudre; * *n* travail *m*; œuvre *f*; ouvrage *m*; emploi *m*.

workaholic *n* drogué du travail *m*.

worker *n* travailleur *m* -euse *f*; ouvrier *m* -ère *f*.

workforce *n* main-d'œuvre *f*.

working-class *adj* ouvrier.

workman *n* ouvrier, artisan *m*.

workshop *n* atelier *m*.

world *n* monde *m*; * *adj* du monde; mondial.

worldly *adj* mondain; terrestre.

worldwide *adj* mondial.

worm *n* ver *m*.

worn-out *adj* épuisé; usé.

worried *adj* inquiet.

worry *vt* inquiéter; *n* souci *m*.

worrying *adj* inquiétant.

worse *adj adv* pire; * *n* le pire.

worship *n* culte *m*; adoration *f*; * *vt* adorer, vénérer.

worst *adj* le pire; * *adv* le plus mal; * *n* le pire *m*.

worth *n* valeur *f*, prix *m*; mérite *m*.

worthless *adj* sans valeur; inutile.

worthwhile *adj* qui vaut la peine; louable.

worthy *adj* digne; louable.

would-be *adj* soi-disant.

wound *n* blessure *f*; * *vt* blesser.

wrangle *vi* se disputer; * *n* dispute *f*.

wrap *vt* envelopper.

wrath *n* colère *f*.

wreath *n* couronne, guirlande *f*.

wreck *n* naufrage *m*; ruines *fpl*; destruction *f*; épave *f*; * *vt* causer le naufrage de; démolir.

wreckage *n* naufrage *m*; épave *f*, débris *mpl*.

wren *n* roitelet *m*.

wrench *vt* tordre; forcer; tourner violemment; * *n* clé *f*, torsion violente *f*.

wrestle *vi* lutter.

wrestling *n* lutte *f*.

wretched *adj* malheureux, misérable.

wriggle *vi* remuer, se tortiller.

wring *vt* tordre; essorer; arracher.

wrinkle *n* ride *f*; * *vt* rider; * *vi* se rider.

wrist *n* poignet *m*.

wristwatch *n* montre-bracelet *f*.

writ *n* écriture *f*; assignation *f*; acte judiciaire *m*.

write *vt* écrire; composer; ~ **off** annuler; réduire.

write-off *n* perte *f*.

writer *n* écrivain *m*; auteur *m*.

writhe *vi* se tordre.

writing *n* écriture *f*; œuvres *fpl*; écrit *m*.

writing paper *n* papier à lettres *m*.

wrong *n* mal *m*; injustice *f*; tort *m*; injure *f*; * *adj* mauvais, mal; injuste; inopportun; faux, erroné; * *adv* mal, inexactement; * *vt* faire du tort à, léser.

wrongful *adj* injuste.

wrongly *adv* injustement.

wry *adj* ironique, narquois.

XYZ

Xmas *abbr* Noël *m*.

X-ray *n* rayon X *m*.

xylophone *n* xylophone *m*.

yacht *n* yacht *m*.

yard *n* yard (0.914 m) *m*; cour *f*.

yarn *n* longue histoire *f*; fil *m*.

yawn *vi* bâiller; * *n* bâillement *m*.

yawning *adj* béant.

yeah *adv* oui, ouais (*fam*).

year *n* année *f*.

yearbook *n* annuaire *m*.

yearling *n* animal âgé d'un an *m*.

yearly *adj adv* annuel(lement).

yearn *vi* languir.

yearning *n* désir ardent *m*.

yeast *n* levure *f*.

yell *vi* hurler; * *n* hurlement *m*.

yellow *adj n* jaune *m*.

yelp *vi* japper, glapir; * *n* jappement *m*.

yes *adv*, *n* oui *m*.

yesterday *adv*, *n* hier (*m*).

yet *conj* pourtant; cependant; * *adv* encore.

yew *n* if *m*.

yield *vt* donner, produire; rapporter; * *vi* se rendre; céder; * *n* production *f*; récolte *f*; rendement *m*.

yoga *n* yoga *m*.

yog(h)urt *n* yaourt *m*.

yoke *n* joug *m*.

yolk *n* jaune d'œuf *m*.

yonder *adv* là-bas.

you *pn* vous; tu; te; toi.

young *adj* jeune.

youngster *n* jeune *mf*.

your(s) *pn* ton, ta, tes; votre, vos; le tien, la tienne, les tiens, les tiennes; le/ la vôtre, les vôtres.

yourself *pn* toi-même; vous-même(s).

youth *n* jeunesse, adolescence *f*; jeune homme *m*.

youthful *adj* jeune.

yuppie (*adj*) *n* (de) jeune cadre dynamique *m*.

zany *adj* farfelu.

zap *vt* flinguer.

zeal *n* zèle *m*; ardeur *f*.

zealous *adj* zélé.

zebra *n* zèbre *m*.

zero *n* zéro *m*.

zest *n* enthousiasme *m*.

zigzag *n* zigzag *m*.

zinc *n* zinc *m*.

zip *n* fermeture éclair *f*.

zodiac *n* zodiaque *m*.

zone *n* zone *f*; secteur *m*.

zoo *n* zoo *m*.

zoology *n* zoologie *f*.

zoom *vi* vrombir.

zoom lens *n* zoom *m*.

Verbes Irréguliers en Anglais

	Prétérit	*Participe passé*		*Prétérit*	*Participe passé*
arise	arose	arisen	dream	dreamed,	dreamed,
awake	awoke	awaked,		dreamt	dreamt
		awoke	drink	drank	drunk
be [I am, you/we/they are, he/she/			drive	drove	driven
it is, *gérondif* being]			dwell	dwelt,	dwelt,
	was, were	been		dwelled	dwelled
bear	bore	borne	eat	ate	eaten
beat	beat	beaten	fall	fell	fallen
become	became	become	feed	fed	fed
begin	began	begun	feel	felt	felt
behold	beheld	beheld	fight	fought	fought
bend	bent	bent	find	found	found
beseech	besought,	besought,	flee	fled	fled
	beseeched	beseeched	fling	flung	flung
beset	beset	beset	fly [he/she/it flies]		
bet	bet, betted	bet, betted		flew	flown
bid	bade, bid	bid, bidden	forbid	forbade	forbidden
bite	bit	bitten	forecast	forecast	forecast
bleed	bled	bled	forget	forgot	forgotten
bless	blessed,	blessed,	forgive	forgave	forgiven
	blest	blest	forsake	forsook	forsaken
blow	blew	blown	forsee	foresaw	foreseen
break	broke	broken	freeze	froze	frozen
breed	bred	bred	get	got	got,
bring	brought	brought			gotten (US)
build	built	built	give	gave	given
burn	burnt,	burnt,	go [he/she/it goes]		
	burned	burned		went	gone
burst	burst	burst	grind	ground	ground
buy	bought	bought	grow	grew	grown
can	could	(been able)	hang	hung,	hung,
cast	cast	cast		hanged	hanged
catch	caught	caught	have [I/you/we/they have,		he/she/it has,
choose	chose	chosen	*gérondif* having]		
cling	clung	clung		had	had
come	came	come	hear	heard	heard
cost	cost	cost	hhide	hid	hidden
creep	crept	crept	hit	hit	hit
cut	cut	cut	hold	held	held
deal	dealt	dealt	hurt	hurt	hurt
dig	dug	dug	keep	kept	kept
do [he/she/it does]			kneel	knelt	knelt
	did	done	know	knew	known
draw	drew	drawn	lay	laid	laid

369

	Prétérit	Participe passé		Prétérit	Participe passé
lead	led	led			shorn
lean	leant, leaned	leant, leaned	shed	shed	shed
			shine	shone	shone
leap	leapt, leaped	leapt, leaped	shoot	shot	shot
			show	showed	shown, showed
learn	learnt, learned	learnt, learned			
			shrink	shrank	shrunk
leave	left	left	shut	shut	shut
lend	lent	lent	sing	sang	sung
let	let	let	sink	sank	sunk
lie [gérondif lying]			sit	sat	sat
	lay	lain	slay	slew	slain
light	lighted, lit	lighted, lit	sleep	slept	slept
			slide	slid	slid
lose	lost	lost	sling	slung	slung
make	made	made	smell	smelt, smelled	smelt, smelled
may	might	-			
mean	meant	meant	sow	sowed	sown, sowed
meet	met	met			
mistake	mistook	mistaken	speak	spoke	spoken
mow	mowed	mowed, mown	speed	sped, speeded	sped, speeded
must	(had to)	(had to)	spell	spelt, spelled	spelt, spelled
overcome	overcame	overcome			
pay	paid	paid	spend	spent	spent
put	put	put	spill	spilt, spilled	spilt, spilled
quit	quit, quitted	quit, quitted			
read	read	read	spin	spun	spun
rid	rid	rid	spit	spat	spat
ride	rode	ridden	split	split	split
ring	rang	rung	spoil	spoilt	spoilt
rise	rose	risen	spread	spread	spread
run	ran	run	spring	sprang	sprung
saw	sawed	sawn, sawed	stand	stood	stood
			steal	stole	stolen
			stick	stuck	stuck
say	said	said	sting	stung	stung
see	saw	seen	stink	stank	stunk
seek	sought	sought	stride	strode	stridden
sell	sold	sold	strike	struck	struck
send	sent	sent	strive	strove	striven
set	set	set	swear	swore	sworn
sew	sewed	sewn, sewed	sweep	swept	swept
			swell	swelled	swelled, swollen
shake	shook	shaken			
shall	should	-	swim	swam	swum
shear	sheared	sheared,	swing	swung	swung

	Prétérit	Participe passé		Prétérit	Participe passé
take	took	taken	weave	wove,	wove, woven
teach	taught	taught	wed	wedded	wed,
tear	tore	torn			wedded
tell	told	told	weep	wept	wept
think	thought	thought	win	won	won
throw	threw	thrown	wind	wound	wound
thrust	thrust	thrust	withdraw	withdrew	withdrawn
tread	trod	trodden,	withhold	withheld	withheld
		trod	withstand	withstood	withstood
understand	understood	understood	wring	wrung	wrung
upset	upset	upset	write	wrote	written
wake	woke	woken			
wear	wore	worn			

French Verbs

Regular Verbs

infinitive	donn**er**	fin**ir**	vend**re**
	to give	*to finish*	*to sell*
present participle	donn**ant**	fin**issant**	vend**ant**
past participle	donn**é**	fin**i**	vend**u**
present	je donn**e**	je fin**is**	je vend**s**
	tu donn**es**	tu fin**is**	tu vend**s**
	il donn**e**	il fin**it**	il vend
	nous donn**ons**	nous fin**issons**	nous vend**ons**
	vous donn**ez**	vous fin**issez**	vous vend**ez**
	ils donn**ent**	ils fin**issent**	ils vend**ent**
imperfect	donn**ais**	fin**issais**	vend**ais**
	donn**ais**	fin**issais**	vend**ais**
	donn**ait**	fin**issait**	vend**ait**
	donn**ions**	fin**issions**	vend**ions**
	donn**iez**	fin**issiez**	vend**iez**
	donn**aient**	fin**issaient**	vend**aient**
future	donn**erai**	fin**irai**	vend**rai**
	donn**eras**	fin**iras**	vend**ras**
	donn**era**	fin**ira**	vend**ra**
	donn**erons**	fin**irons**	vend**rons**
	donn**erez**	fin**irez**	vend**rez**
	donn**eront**	fin**iront**	vend**ront**
conditional	donn**erais**	fin**irais**	vend**rais**
	donn**erais**	fin**irais**	vend**rais**
	donn**erait**	fin**irait**	vend**rait**
	donn**erions**	fin**irions**	vend**rions**
	donn**eriez**	fin**iriez**	vend**riez**
	donn**eraient**	fin**iraient**	vend**raient**
past historic	donn**ai**	fin**is**	vend**is**
	donn**as**	fin**is**	vend**is**

		finit	vendit
	donna	finîmes	vendîmes
	donnâmes	finîtes	vendîtes
	donnâtes	finirent	vendirent
	donnèrent		
present	donne	finisse	vende
subjunctive	donnes	finisses	vendes
	donne	finisse	vende
	donnions	finissions	vendions
	donniez	finissiez	vendiez
	donnent	finissent	vendent
imperfect	donnasse	finisse	vendisse
subjunctive	donnasses	finisses	vendisses
	donnât	finît	vendît
	donnassions	finissions	vendissions
	donnassiez	finissiez	vendissiez
	donnassent	finissent	vendissent

Auxiliary verbs

infinitive		*conditional*	
être	**avoir**	serais	aurais
to be	*to have*	serais	aurais
present participle		serait	aurait
étant	ayant	serions	aurions
past participle		seriez	auriez
été	eu	seraient	auraient
present	*past historic*		
je suis	j'ai	fus	eus
tu es	tu as	fus	eus
il est	il a	fut	eut
nous sommes	nous avons	fûmes	eûmes
vous êtes	vous avez	fûtes	eûtes
ils sont	ils ont	furent	eurent
imperfect		*present subjunctive*	
étais	avais	sois	aie
étais	avais	sois	aies
était	avait	soit	ait
étions	avions	soyons	ayons
étiez	aviez	soyez	ayez
étaient	avaient	soient	aient
future		*imperfect subjunctive*	
serai	aurai	fusse	eusse
seras	auras	fusses	eusses
sera	aura	fût	eût
serons	aurons	fussions	eussions
serez	aurez	fussiez	eussiez
seront	auront	fussent	eussent

Irregular Verbs

acheter	acquérir	aller	appeler
to buy	*to acquire*	*to go*	*to call*
present			
achète	acquiers	vais	appelle
achètes	acquiers	vas	appelles
achète	acquiert	va	appelle
achetons	acquérons	allons	appelons
achetez	acquérez	allez	appelez
achètent	acquièrent	vont	appellent
imperfect			
achetais	acquérais	allais	appelais
achetais	acquérais	allais	appelais
achetait	acquérait	allait	appelait
achetions	acquérions	allions	appelions
achetiez	acquériez	alliez	appeliez
achetaient	acquéraient	allaient	appelaient
future			
achèterai	acquerrai	irai	appellerai
achèteras	acquerras	iras	appelleras
achètera	acquerra	ira	appellera
achèterons	acquerrons	irons	appellerons
achèterez	acquerrez	irez	appellerez
achèteront	acquerront	iront	appelleront
conditional			
achèterais	acquerrais	irais	appellerais
achèterais	acquerrais	irais	appellerais
achèterait	acquerrait	irait	appellerait
achèterions	acquerrions	irions	appellerions
achèteriez	acquerriez	iriez	appelleriez
achèteraient	acquerraient	iraient	appelleraient
past historic			
achetai	acquis	allai	appelai
achetas	acquis	allas	appelas
acheta	acquit	alla	appela
achetâmes	acquîmes	allâmes	appelâmes
achetâtes	acquîtes	allâtes	appelâtes
achetèrent	acquirent	allèrent	appelèrent
present subjunctive			
achète	acquière	aille	appelle
achètes	acquières	ailles	appelles
achète	acquière	aille	appelle
achetions	acquérions	allions	appelions
achetiez	acquériez	alliez	appeliez
achètent	acquièrent	aillent	appellent
imperfect subjunctive			
achetasse	acquisse	allasse	appelasse
achetasses	acquisses	allasses	appelasses

373

achetât	acquît	allât	appelât
achetassions	acquissions	allassions	appelassions
achetassiez	acquissiez	allassiez	appelassiez
achetassent	acquissent	allassent	appelassent

appuyer	**s'asseoir**	**battre**	**boire**
to lean	*to sit down*	*to hit*	*to drink*

present

appuie	m'assieds	bats	bois
appuies	t'assieds	bats	bois
appuie	s'assied	bat	boit
appuyons	nous asseyons	battons	buvons
appuyez	vous asseyez	battez	buvez
appuient	s'asseyent	battent	boivent

imperfect

appuyais	m'asseyais	battais	buvais
appuyais	t'asseyais	battais	buvais
appuyait	s'asseyait	battait	buvait
appuyions	nous asseyions	battions	buvions
appuyiez	vous asseyiez	battiez	buviez
appuyaient	s'asseyaient	battaient	buvaient

future

appuierai	m'assiérai	battrai	boirai
appuieras	t'assiéras	battras	boiras
appuiera	s'assiéra	battra	boira
appuierons	nous assiérons	battrons	boirons
appuierez	vous assiérez	battrez	boirez
appuieront	s'assiéront	battront	boiront

conditional

appuierais	m'assiérais	battrais	boirais
appuierais	t'assiérais	battrais	boirais
appuierait	s'assiérait	battrait	boirait
appuierions	nous assiérions	battrions	boirions
appuieriez	vous assiériez	battriez	boiriez
appuieraient	s'assiéraient	battraient	boiraient

past historic

appuyai	m'assis	battis	bus
appuyas	t'assis	battis	bus
appuya	s'assit	battit	but
appuyâmes	nous assîmes	battîmes	bûmes
appuyâtes	vous assîtes	battîtes	bûtes
appuyèrent	s'assirent	battirent	burent

present subjunctive

appuie	m'asseye	batte	boive
appuies	t'asseyes	battes	boives
appuie	s'asseye	batte	boive
appuyions	nous asseyions	battions	buvions
appuyiez	vous asseyiez	battiez	buviez
appuient	s'asseyent	battent	boivent

imperfect subjunctive

appuyasse	m'assisse	battisse	busse
appuyasses	t'assisses	battisses	busses
appuyât	s'assît	battît	bût
appuyassions	nous assissions	battissions	bussions
appuyassiez	vous assissiez	battissiez	bussiez
appuyassent	s'assissent	battissent	bussent

commencer	**conduire**	**connaître**	**courir**
to begin	*to drive*	*to know*	*to run*

present

commence	conduis	connais	cours
commences	conduis	connais	cours
commence	conduit	connaît	court
commençons	conduisons	connaissons	courons
commencez	conduisez	connaissez	courez
commencent	conduisent	connaissent	courent

imperfect

commençais	conduisais	connaissais	courais
commençais	conduisais	connaissais	courais
commençait	conduisait	connaissait	courait
commencions	conduisions	connaissions	courions
commenciez	conduisiez	connaissiez	couriez
commençaient	conduisaient	connaissaient	couraient

future

commencerai	conduirai	connaîtrai	courrai
commenceras	conduiras	connaîtras	courras
commencera	conduira	connaîtra	courra
commencerons	conduirons	connaîtrons	courrons
commencerez	conduirez	connaîtrez	courrez
commenceront	conduiront	connaîtront	courront

conditional

commencerais	conduirais	connaîtrais	courrais
commencerais	conduirais	connaîtrais	courrais
commencerait	conduirait	connaîtrait	courrait
commencerions	conduirions	connaîtrions	courrions
commenceriez	conduiriez	connaîtriez	courriez
commenceraient	conduiraient	connaîtraient	courraient

past historic

commençai	conduisis	connus	courus
commenças	conduisis	connus	courus
commença	conduisit	connut	couru
commençâmes	conduisîmes	connûmes	courûmes
commençâtes	conduisîtes	connûtes	courûtes
commencèrent	conduisirent	connurent	coururent

present subjunctive

commence	conduise	connaisse	coure
commences	conduises	connaisses	coures
commence	conduise	connaisse	coure

commencions	conduisions	connaissions	courions
commenciez	conduisiez	connaissiez	couriez
commencent	conduisent	connaissent	courent

imperfect subjunctive

commençasse	conduisisse	connusse	courusse
commençasses	conduisisses	connusses	courusses
commençât	conduisît	connût	courût
commençassions	conduisissions	connussions	courussions
commençassiez	conduisissiez	connussiez	courussiez
commençassent	conduisissent	connussent	courussent

couvrir	**craindre**	**croire**	**devoir**
to cover	*to fear*	*to believe*	*to owe, to have to*

present

couvre	crains	crois	dois
couvres	crains	crois	dois
couvre	craint	croit	doit
couvrons	craignons	croyons	devons
couvrez	craignez	croyez	devez
couvrent	craignent	croient	doivent

imperfect

couvrais	craignais	croyais	devais
couvrais	craignais	croyais	devais
couvrait	craignait	croyait	devait
couvrions	craignions	croyions	devions
couvriez	craigniez	croyiez	deviez
couvraient	craignaient	croyaient	devaient

future

couvrirai	craindrai	croirai	devrai
couvriras	craindras	croiras	devras
couvrira	craindra	croira	devra
couvrirons	craindrons	croirons	devrons
couvrirez	craindrez	croirez	devrez
couvriront	craindront	croiront	devront

conditional

couvrirais	craindrais	croirais	devrais
couvrirais	craindrais	croirais	devrais
couvrirait	craindrait	croirait	devrait
couvririons	craindrions	croirions	devrions
couvririez	craindriez	croiriez	devriez
couvriraient	craindraient	croiraient	devraient

past historic

couvris	craignis	crus	dus
couvris	craignis	crus	dus
couvrit	craignit	crut	dut
couvrîmes	craignîmes	crûmes	dûmes
couvrîtes	craignîtes	crûtes	dûtes
couvrirent	craignirent	crurent	durent

present subjunctive

couvre	craigne	croie	doive
couvres	craignes	croies	doives
couvre	craigne	croie	doive
couvrions	craignions	croyions	devions
couvriez	craigniez	croyiez	deviez
couvrent	craignent	croient	doivent

imperfect subjunctive

couvrisse	craignisse	crusse	dusse
couvrisses	craignisses	crusses	dusses
couvrît	craignît	crût	dût
couvrissions	craignissions	crussions	dussions
couvrissiez	craignissiez	crussiez	dussiez
couvrissent	craignissent	crussent	dussent

dire	**écrire**	**envoyer**	**faire**
to say	*to write*	*to send*	*to do; to make*

present

dis	écris	envoie	fais
dis	écris	envoies	fais
dit	écrit	envoie	fait
disons	écrivons	envoyons	faisons
dites	écrivez	envoyez	faites
disent	écrivent	envoient	font

imperfect

disais	écrivais	envoyais	faisais
disais	écrivais	envoyais	faisais
disait	écrivait	envoyait	faisait
disions	écrivions	envoyions	faisions
disiez	écriviez	envoyiez	faisiez
disaient	écrivaient	envoyaient	faisaient

future

dirai	écrirai	enverrai	ferai
diras	écriras	enverras	feras
dira	écrira	enverra	sera
dirons	écrirons	enverrons	ferons
direz	écrirez	enverrez	ferez
diront	écriront	enverront	feront

conditional

dirais	écrirais	enverrais	ferais
dirais	écrirais	enverrais	ferais
dirait	écrirait	enverrait	ferait
dirions	écririons	enverrions	ferions
diriez	écririez	enverriez	feriez
diraient	écriraient	enverraient	feraient

past historic

dis	écrivis	envoyai	fis
dis	écrivis	envoyas	fis

dit	écrivit	envoya	fit
dîmes	écrivîmes	envoyâmes	fîmes
dîtes	écrivîtes	envoyâtes	fîtes
dirent	écrivirent	envoyèrent	firent

present subjunctive

dise	écrive	envoie	fasse
dises	écrives	envoies	fasses
dise	écrive	envoie	fasse
disions	écrivions	envoyions	fassions
disiez	écriviez	envoyiez	fassiez
disent	écrivent	envoient	fassent

imperfect subjunctive

disse	écrivisse	envoyasse	fisse
disses	écrivisses	envoyasses	fisses
dît	écrivît	envoyât	fît
dissions	écrivissions	envoyassions	fissions
dissiez	écrivissiez	envoyassiez	fissiez
dissent	écrivissent	envoyassent	fissent

fuir	**haïr**	**jeter**	**lire**
to flee	*to hate*	*to throw*	*to read*

present

fuis	hais	jette	lis
fuis	hais	jettes	lis
fuit	hait	jette	lit
fuyons	haïssons	jetons	lisons
fuyez	haïssez	jetez	lisez
fuient	haïssent	jettent	lisent

imperfect

fuyais	haïssais	jetais	lisais
fuyais	haïssais	jetais	lisais
fuyait	haïssait	jetait	lisait
fuyions	haïssions	jetions	lisions
fuyiez	haïssiez	jetiez	lisiez
fuiront	haïssaient	jetaient	lisaient

future

fuirai	haïrai	jetterai	lirai
fuiras	haïras	jetteras	liras
fuira	haïra	jettera	lira
fuirons	haïrons	jetterons	lirons
fuirez	haïrez	jetterez	lirez
fuiront	haïront	jetteront	liront

conditional

fuirais	haïrais	jetterais	lirais
fuirais	haïrais	jetterais	lirais
fuirait	haïrait	jetterait	lirait
fuirions	haïrions	jetterions	lirions
fuiriez	haïriez	jetteriez	liriez

fuiraient	haïraient	jetteraient	liraient

past historic

fuis	haïs	jetai	lus
fuis	haïs	jetas	lus
fuit	haït	jeta	lut
fuîmes	haïmes	jetâmes	lûmes
fuîtes	haïtes	jetâtes	lûtes
fuirent	haïrent	jetèrent	lurent

present subjunctive

fuie	haïsse	jette	lise
fuies	haïsses	jettes	lises
fuie	haïsse	jette	lise
fuyions	haïssions	jetions	lisions
fuyiez	haïssiez	jetiez	lisiez
fuient	haïssent	jettent	lisent

imperfect subjunctive

fuisse	haïsse	jetasse	lusse
fuisses	haïsses	jetasses	lusses
fuît	haït	jetât	lût
fuissions	haïssions	jetassions	lussions
fuissiez	haïssiez	jetassiez	lussiez
fuissent	haïssent	jetassent	lussent

manger	**mettre**	**mourir**	**mouvoir**
to eat	*to put*	*to die*	*to drive, to move*

present

mange	mets	meurs	meus
manges	mets	meurs	meus
mange	met	meurt	meut
mangeons	mettons	mourons	mouvons
mangez	mettez	mourez	mouvez
mangent	mettent	meurent	meuvent

imperfect

mangeais	mettais	mourais	mouvais
mangeais	mettais	mourais	mouvais
mangeait	mettait	mourait	mouvait
mangions	mettions	mourions	mouvions
mangiez	mettiez	mouriez	mouviez
mangeaient	mettaient	mouraient	mouvaient

future

mangerai	mettrai	mourrai	mouvrai
mangeras	mettras	mourras	mouvras
mangera	mettra	mourra	mouvra
mangerons	mettrons	mourrons	mouvrons
mangerez	mettrez	mourrez	mouvrez
mangeront	mettront	mourront	mouvront

conditional

mangerais	mettrais	mourrais	mouvrais

mangerais	mettrais	mourrais	mouvrais
mangerait	mettrait	mourrait	mouvrait
mangerions	mettrions	mourrions	mouvrions
mangeriez	mettriez	mourriez	mouvriez
mangeraient	mettraient	mourraient	mouvraient

past historic

mangeai	mis	mourus	mus
mangeas	mis	mourus	mus
mangea	mit	mourut	mut
mangeâmes	mîmes	mourûmes	mûmes
mangeâtes	mîtes	mourûtes	mûtes
mangèrent	mirent	moururent	murent

present subjunctive

mange	mette	meure	meuve
manges	mettes	meures	meuves
mange	mette	meure	meuve
mangions	mettions	mourions	mouvions
mangiez	mettiez	mouriez	mouviez
mangent	mettent	meurent	meuvent

imperfect subjunctive

mangeasse	misse	mourusse	musse
mangeasses	misses	mourusses	musses
mangeât	mît	mourût	mût
mangeassions	missions	mourussions	mussions
mangeassiez	missiez	mourussiez	mussiez
mangeassent	missent	mourussent	mussent

naître	**partir**	**plaire**	**pouvoir**
to be born	*to leave*	*to please*	*to be able; can*

present

nais	pars	plais	peux
nais	pars	plais	peux
naît	part	plaît	peut
naissons	partons	plaisons	pouvons
naissez	partez	plaisez	pouvez
naissent	partent	plaisent	peuvent

imperfect

naissais	partais	plaisais	pouvais
naissais	partais	plaisais	pouvais
naissait	partait	plaisait	pouvait
naissions	partions	plaisions	pouvions
naissiez	partiez	plaisiez	pouviez
naissaient	partaient	plaisaient	pouvaient

future

naîtrai	partirai	plairai	pourrai
naîtras	partiras	plairas	pourras
naîtra	partira	plaira	pourra
naîtrons	partirons	plairons	pourrons
naîtrez	partirez	plairez	pourrez

| naîtront | partiront | plairont | pourront |

conditional

naîtrais	partirais	plairais	pourrais
naîtrais	partirais	plairais	pourrais
naîtrait	partirait	plairait	pourrait
naîtrions	partirions	plairions	pourrions
naîtriez	partiriez	plairiez	pourriez
naîtraient	partiraient	plairaient	pourraient

past historic

naquis	partis	plus	pus
naquis	partis	plus	pus
naquit	partit	plut	put
naquîmes	partîmes	plûmes	pûmes
naquîtes	partîtes	plûtes	pûtes
naquirent	partirent	plurent	purent

present subjunctive

naisse	parte	plaise	puisse
naisses	partes	plaises	puisses
naisse	parte	plaise	puisse
naissions	partions	plaisions	puissions
naissiez	partiez	plaisiez	puissiez
naissent	partent	plaisent	puissent

imperfect subjunctive

naquisse	partisse	plusse	pusse
naquisses	partisses	plusses	pusses
naquît	partît	plût	pût
naquissions	partissions	plussions	pussions
naquissiez	partissiez	plussiez	pussiez
naquissent	partissent	plussent	pussent

| **préférer** | **prendre** | **recevoir** | **rire** |
| *to prefer* | *to take* | *to receive* | *to laugh* |

present

préfère	prends	reçois	ris
préfères	prends	reçois	ris
préfère	prend	reçoit	rit
préférons	prenons	recevons	rions
préférez	prenez	recevez	riez
préfèrent	prennent	reçoivent	rient

imperfect

préférais	prenais	recevais	riais
préférais	prenais	recevais	riais
préférait	prenait	recevait	riait
préférions	prenions	recevions	riions
préfériez	preniez	receviez	riiez
préféraient	prenaient	recevaient	riaient

future

| préférerai | prendrai | recevrai | rirai |
| préféreras | prendras | recevras | riras |

préférera	prendra	recevra	rira
préférerons	prendrons	recevrons	rirons
préférerez	prendrez	recevrez	rirez
préféreront	prendront	recevront	riront

conditional

préférerais	prendrais	recevrais	rirais
préférerais	prendrais	recevrais	rirais
préférerait	prendrait	recevrait	rirait
préférerions	prendrions	recevrions	ririons
préféreriez	prendriez	recevriez	ririez
préféreraient	prendraient	recevraient	riraient

past historic

préférai	pris	reçus	ris
préféras	pris	reçus	ris
préféra	prit	reçut	rit
préférâmes	prîmes	reçûmes	rîmes
préférâtes	prîtes	reçûtes	rîtes
préférèrent	prirent	reçurent	rirent

present subjunctive

préfère	prenne	reçoive	rie
préfères	prennes	reçoives	ries
préfère	prenne	reçoive	rie
préférions	prenions	recevions	riions
préfériez	preniez	receviez	riiez
préfèrent	prennent	reçoivent	rient

imperfect subjunctive

préférasse	prisse	reçusse	risse
préférasses	prisses	reçusses	risses
préférât	prît	reçût	rît
préférassions	prissions	reçussions	rissions
préférassiez	prissiez	reçussiez	rissiez
préférassent	prissent	reçussent	rissent

savoir	**suffire**	**suivre**	**tenir**
to know	*to be enough*	*to follow*	*to hold*

present

sais	suffis	suis	tiens
sais	suffis	suis	tiens
sait	suffit	suit	tient
savons	suffisons	suivons	tenons
savez	suffisez	suivez	tenez
savent	suffisent	suivent	tiennent

imperfect

savais	suffisais	suivais	tenais
savais	suffisais	suivais	tenais
savait	suffisait	suivait	tenait
savions	suffisions	suivions	tenions
saviez	suffisiez	suiviez	teniez

savaient	suffisaient	suivaient	tenaient
future			
saurai	suffirai	suivrai	tiendrai
sauras	suffiras	suivras	tiendras
saura	suffira	suivra	tiendra
saurons	suffirons	suivrons	tiendrons
saurez	suffirez	suivrez	tiendrez
sauront	suffiront	suivront	tiendront
conditional			
saurais	suffirais	suivrais	tiendrais
saurais	suffirais	suivrais	tiendrais
saurait	suffirait	suivrait	tiendrait
saurions	suffirions	suivrions	tiendrions
sauriez	suffiriez	suivriez	tiendriez
sauraient	suffiraient	suivraient	tiendraient
past historic			
sus	suffis	suivis	tins
sus	suffis	suivis	tins
sut	suffit	suivit	tint
sûmes	suffîmes	suivîmes	tînmes
sûtes	suffîtes	suivîtes	tîntes
surent	suffirent	suivirent	tinrent
present subjunctive			
sache	suffise	suive	tienne
saches	suffises	suives	tiennes
sache	suffise	suive	tienne
sachions	suffisions	suivions	tenions
sachiez	suffisiez	suiviez	teniez
sachent	suffisent	suivent	tiennent
imperfect subjunctive			
susse	suffisse	suivisse	tinsse
susses	suffisses	suivisses	tinsses
sût	suffît	suivît	tînt
sussions	suffissions	suivissions	tinssions
sussiez	suffissiez	suivissiez	tinssiez
sussent	suffissent	suivissent	tinssent

valoir	**venir**	**vivre**	**voir**
to be worth	*to come*	*to live*	*to see*
present			
vaux	viens	vis	vois
vaux	viens	vis	vois
vaut	vient	vit	voit
valons	venons	vivons	voyons
valez	venez	vivez	voyez
valent	viennent	vivent	voient
imperfect			
valais	venais	vivais	voyais

valais	venais	vivais	voyais
valait	venait	vivait	voyait
valions	venions	vivions	voyions
valiez	veniez	viviez	voyiez
valaient	venaient	vivaient	voyaient

future

vaudrai	viendrai	vivrai	verrai
vaudras	viendras	vivras	verras
vaudra	viendra	vivra	verra
vaudrons	viendrons	vivrons	verrons
vaudrez	viendrez	vivrez	verrez
vaudront	viendront	vivront	verront

conditional

vaudrais	viendrais	vivrais	verrais
vaudrais	viendrais	vivrais	verrais
vaudrait	viendrait	vivrait	verrait
vaudrions	viendrions	vivrions	verrions
vaudriez	viendriez	vivriez	verriez
vaudraient	viendraient	vivraient	verraient

past historic

valus	vins	vécus	vis
valus	vins	vécus	vis
valut	vint	vécut	vit
valûmes	vînmes	vécûmes	vîmes
valûtes	vîntes	vécûtes	vîtes
valurent	vinrent	vécurent	virent

present subjunctive

vaille	vienne	vive	voie
vailles	viennes	vives	voies
vaille	vienne	vive	voie
valions	venions	vivions	voyions
valiez	veniez	viviez	voyiez
vaillent	viennent	vivent	voient

imperfect subjunctive

valusse	vinsse	vécusse	visse
valusses	vinsses	vécusses	visses
valût	vînt	vécût	vît
valussions	vinssions	vécussions	vissions
valussiez	vinssiez	vécussiez	vissiez
valussent	vinssent	vécussent	vissent